T0396171

The History of the Book in the West: 1455–1700

The History of the Book in the West: A Library of Critical Essays
Series Editor: Alexis Weedon

Titles in the Series:

The History of the Book in the West: 400AD–1455
Volume I
Jane Roberts and Pamela Robinson

The History of the Book in the West: 1455–1700
Volume II
Ian Gadd

The History of the Book in the West: 1700–1800
Volume III
Eleanor F. Shevlin

The History of the Book in the West: 1800–1914
Volume IV
Stephen Colclough and Alexis Weedon

The History of the Book in the West: 1914–2000
Volume V
Alexis Weedon

The History of the Book in the West: 1455–1700

Volume II

Edited by

Ian Gadd

Bath Spa University, UK

ASHGATE

Wherever possible, these reprints are made from a copy of the original printing, but these can themselves be of very variable quality. Whilst the publisher has made every effort to ensure the quality of the reprint, some variability may inevitably remain.

Published by
Ashgate Publishing Limited
Wey Court East
Union Road
Farnham, Surrey
GU9 7PT
England

Ashgate Publishing Company
110 Cherry Street
Suite 3-1
Burlington, VT 05401-3818
USA

Ashgate website: http://www.ashgate.com

British Library Cataloguing in Publication Data
The history of the book in the West.
    Volume 2, 1455-1700.
    1. Books–History–1450-1600. 2. Books–History–17th
    century. 3. Books–Western countries–History.
    I. Gadd, Ian.
    002'.091821-dc22

Library of Congress Control Number 2009921962

ISBN: 978 0 7546 2771 5

Reprinted 2013

Printed and bound in Great Britain by
the MPG Books Group, UK

Contents

Acknowledgements

The editor and publishers wish to thank the following for permission to use copyright material.

The Bibliographical Society for the essay: John Barnard (1999), 'Bibliographical Note: The Survival and Loss Rates of Psalms, ABCs, Psalters and Primers from the Stationers' Stock, 1660–1700', *The Library,* 6th ser., **21**, pp. 148–50.

The Bibliographical Society of the University of Virginia for the essay: D.F. McKenzie (1969), 'Printers of the Mind: Some Notes on Bibliographical Theories and Printing-House Practices', *Studies in Bibliography*, **22**, pp. 1–75. Copyright © 1969 by the Bibliographical Society of the University of Virginia.

Cambridge University Press for the essay: Andrew Pettegree and Matthew Hall (2004), 'The Reformation and the Book: A Reconsideration', *Historical Journal*, **47**, pp. 785–808. Copyright © 2004 Cambridge University Press.

Journal of Interdisciplinary History for the essay: Anthony T. Grafton (1980), 'Review: The Importance of Being Printed', *Journal of Interdisciplinary History*, **11**, pp. 265–86. Reprinted from *The Journal of Interdisciplinary History*, XI (1980), 26–286, with the permission of the editors of *The Journal of Interdisciplinary History* and The MIT Press, Cambridge, Massachusetts. Copyright © 1980 by the Massachusetts Institute of Technology and The Journal of Interdisciplinary History, Inc.

Ian Maclean for the essay: Ian Maclean (1991), 'The Market for Scholarly Books and Conceptions of Genre in Northern Europe, 1570–1630', in Georg Kauffmann (ed.), *Die Renaissance im Blick der Nationen Europas*, Wiesbaden: Harrassowitz, pp. 17–31.

Oak Knoll Press for the essays: Nicolas Barker (1994), 'The Aldine Italic', in Robin Myers and Michael Harris (eds), *A Millennium of the Book*, Winchester: St Paul's Bibliographies, pp. 45–59; Roger Chartier (2000), 'Orality Lost: Text and Voice in the Sixteenth and Seventeenth Centuries', in Bill Bell, Philip Bennett and Jonquil Bevan (eds), *Across Boundaries: The Book in Culture and Commerce*, Winchester: St Paul's Bibliographies, pp. 1–28; John L. Flood (2007), '"Omnium totius orbis emporiorum compendium": The Frankfurt Fair in the Early Modern Period', in Robin Myers, Michael Harris and Giles Mandelbrote (eds), *Fairs, Markets, and the Itinerant Book Trade*, New Castle, DE: Oak Knoll Press, pp. 1–42.

Oxford University Press for the essay: Lisa Jardine and Anthony Grafton (1990), '"Studied for Action": How Gabriel Harvey Read His Livy', *Past and Present*, **129**, pp. 30–78.

The University of Chicago Press for the essays: Elizabeth L. Eisenstein (1968), 'Some Conjectures about the Impact of Printing on Western Society and Thought: A Preliminary

Report', *Journal of Modern History*, **40**, pp. 1–56; Paul F. Grendler (1975), 'The Roman Inquisition and the Venetian Press 1540–1605', *Journal of Modern History*, **47**, pp. 48–65.

University of Texas Press for the essay: David Cressy (1986), 'Books as Totems in Seventeenth-Century England and New England', *Journal of Library History*, **21**, pp. 92–106.

Wiley-Blackwell for the essay: Natalie Zemon Davis (1966), 'A Trade Union in Sixteenth-Century France', *Economic History Review*, 2nd ser., **19**, pp. 48–69.

Every effort has been made to trace all the copyright holders, but if any have been inadvertently overlooked the publishers will be pleased to make the necessary arrangement at the first opportunity.

Series Preface

Book history focuses on empirical research into the production and dissemination of the printed word, characterised by studies of the materiality of the book. Yet within these boundaries a variety of approaches has been taken as researchers seek to answer different questions. Key discussions are represented within the series such as the role of Gutenberg's invention of the printing press in the socio-political changes of the Renaissance; the attempts to secure national and international distribution networks in the seventeenth and eighteenth centuries; and the reasons behind the exponential growth in printed output as it became the first mass media in the nineteenth century, a position which was then challenged by electronic media in the twentieth century. These debates within the discipline are reflected within Ashgate's History of the Book in the West.

The five volumes of the series present a selection of the very best scholarship on the history of the book in this internationally-vibrant research field. It represents the wide range of research approaches taken within book history which owes its origins to the fields of bibliography, history, and literary production. The burgeoning of scholarship in recent decades has been fuelled by the increasing number of online resources. Trade periodicals, historical newspaper databases, and the books themselves can, in many cases, be interrogated over the Internet and digitisation has enabled archivists to make available items from their collections to individual scholars electronically. Researchers have sought to utilise the range of archival material by adapting quantitative and qualitative methods to analyse book production. With this information the current generation of scholars have critiqued the theoretical interpretations of cultural production, specifically those of Pierre Bourdieu.

The first volume covers the history of the book in the west from late Antiquity to the publication of the Gutenberg Bible (AD 400 to 1455). As Jane Roberts and Pamela Robinson say, 'The millennium saw many developments in the book's history, including the most fundamental of all: the consolidation of the codex's position as the standard form for a book.' Great claims are made for the advent of printing by movable type, which did have an enormous impact. However, the codex format with its list of contents, illustration, pagination, punctuation, and indexes which we recognise today as the printed book, did not suddenly appear in the mid-fifteenth century, it was a progressive development of many centuries.

Ian Gadd's selection of essays reflect the direction scholarship has taken in the history of the book from the mid-fifteenth century through to the end of the seventeenth. The essays, he says 'are not intended to represent the full historical range of studies into aspects of the making, selling, and consumption of books but rather are a deliberate and considered reflection of how the 'history of the book' has manifested itself in the English language since the publication of what many consider to be the subject's foundational work, Lucien Febvre and Henri-Jean Martin's *L'Apparition du Livre* in 1958.'

Influenced by Enlightenment principles and commercial transformations, the history of the book in the eighteenth century witnessed not only the final decades of the hand-press era but also debates and developments that pointed to its future: 'the foundations of modern copyright; a rapid growth in the publication, circulation, and reading of periodicals; the promotion of niche marketing; alterations to distribution networks; and the emergence of the publisher as a central figure in the book trade, to name a few.' The pace and extent of these changes varied greatly within the different sociopolitical contexts across the western world. Eleanor Shevlin's selection of essays highlights the range of developments and the intricacies of debates while simultaneously pointing to potential directions for scholarship.

Stephen Colclough and Alexis Weedon are the editors of the fourth volume and their own interests in publishing economics, distribution and reading practices are represented. The collection 'reflects Anglo-American book history of this period which is characterised by detailed analyses of the publication of an individual book or the reading of a particular person'. Arranged to reflect the publishing cycle from author to reader, this volume examines the impact of the second printing revolution through the nineteenth century and to the outbreak of the first world war.

Finally, in the last volume of the series, Alexis Weedon frames the history of the book within the globalisation of the media industries and the challenge to the cultural status of the book from electronic media in the twentieth century. The invention of photomechanical typesetting and the application of computer technology profoundly changed the technology and processes of production, distribution, sales and consumption of the book. These effects continue in the twenty-first century and have led to the development of 'The Long Tail' niche book publishing strategies.

The editors of each volume have written an informative introduction which sets the context of book history within their period, providing a critical analysis of the selected essays within their volumes. It is not an easy task to select and order essays from the enormous number published by scholars in the field, many of which are worthy of inclusion on different grounds. The essays are drawn from scholarly print journals inaccessible online, papers published in subscription journals and chapters from monographs. I thank the editors for their diligence and hard work in consistently applying their professional scholarly judgement to making difficult choices. They have done an excellent job.

ALEXIS WEEDON
Series Editor
Research Institute for Media, Art and Design
University of Bedfordshire

Introduction

Selecting a group of essays that together adequately represent the 'History of the Book in the West' from the mid-fifteenth century through to the end of the seventeenth is a Sisyphean task – not merely because of the diversity of subjects to be covered, but also because of the sheer volume of books, articles, essays, and notes from which to choose.[1] The latter may seem a slightly unexpected claim to make given that the field of the 'history of the book' appears, in the English-speaking world, to be a phenomenon only a few decades old, but European scholarly interest in topics such as the invention of printing, censorship, the production and sale of books and editorial practice dates back well into the sixteenth century, while antiquarians, bibliographers, librarians and book collectors have been paying close attention to the physical features of books for almost as long. In one sense, therefore, the 'history of books' is nothing new; but what *has* changed in recent decades is the nature of that history. Bibliographical scholarship – that is, the description and analysis of the physical features of books – continues to remain a lively field (indeed, a number of the essays in this volume are unapologetically bibliographical in character) but over the last half century, a new kind of interest in the book as an object of study has emerged – one that is more concerned with the book *in* history, the book as cultural artefact, the book as social phenomenon. And with it has come a concomitant proliferation of publications, conferences and even organizations devoted to this new kind of history of the book.[2]

It is not the purpose of this Introduction to provide a detailed account of the rise of the history of the book (or *l'histoire du livre* from which the rather unsatisfactory English phrase derives),[3] but it is this that has directly informed the selection for this volume. The essays presented here are *not* intended to represent the full historical range of studies into aspects of the making, selling and consumption of books, but are instead a deliberate and considered reflection of how the 'history of the book' has manifested itself in the English language since the publication of what many consider to be the subject's foundational work, Lucien Febvre and Henri-Jean Martin's *L'Apparition du Livre* in 1958.[4] The most visible effect of this approach is that none of the essays here dates from before 1966. However, no fewer than eight

---

[1]   In my selection, I am particularly grateful for the advice of Professor Ian Maclean, Dr Paul Arblaster and Dr Cathy Shrank.

[2]   For example, the most recent printed volume of the *Annual Bibliography of the History of the Printed Book and Libraries*, listing relevant publications from the year 2000, contains no fewer than 5660 entries (this has now been superseded by *Book History Online* http://www.kb.nl/bho/) while the latest edition of G. Thomas Tanselle's *Introduction to Bibliography: Seminar Syllabus* (2002) runs to over 360 pages. For a brief overview of the rise of the 'history of the book', see Finkelstein and McCleery (2005, pp. 7–27).

[3]   Robert Darnton's oft-cited 1982 essay 'What is the History of Books?' (reprinted in Finkelstein and McCleery (2002, pp. 9–26)) appears to have been the first work to popularize the term in English.

[4]   Translated as *The Coming of the Book: The Impact of Printing 1450–1800* (Febvre and Martin, 1976; repr. 1990).

are over 25 years old and, although their findings or conclusions may have been challenged or superseded, the significance and legacy of their scholarship means that they remain key essays in the field.

It is important, too, to recognize that the disciplinary heterogeneity of the scholars collected here (librarians, bibliographers, literary scholars, historians) reflects the fundamental *inter*disciplinarity of the history of the book.[5] Not every contributor included here would consider themselves to be a 'book historian', while almost half of the essays were first published in journals or books not primarily bibliographical or book-historical in focus. Consequently, there are often striking and stimulating differences in tone, approach and level of detail between the essays, with a number assuming a fair degree of prior bibliographical knowledge (some of which this Introduction will aim to supply). Some differences stem directly from the dates of publication, as a comparison of Eisenstein's essay with that of Pettegree and Hall, or of Davis's essay with Griffin's makes clear. Nonetheless, each essay was shaped by, and has helped shape, the development of the history of the book in the early modern period (a term I have stretched only slightly to apply to this volume's chronological span); collectively, they show how and why the history of the book is the way it is now.

There were some important limits to the selection process. This volume, as with its companion volumes, was conceived primarily as an Anglophone collection, which means that those few foreign scholars included appear either writing in their second language or through translation; consequently this volume cannot pretend to represent *l'histoire du livre* or *geschichte des buchwesens* as it has developed in other countries. I have tried, as much as is possible, to be international in coverage and have resisted the temptation to pack the selection with English-focused pieces, although I recognize that the inclusion of even five such essays still overrepresents England's significance for European printing during this period. Chronologically, the volume covers the first two and a half centuries of the printed word in Europe (taking the 'West' to mean primarily Western Christendom), from Johann Gutenberg onwards: 1455 marking the date not of the first surviving example of printing by Gutenberg using 'moveable type' (see below), but his publication of the first printed bible (known by scholars as the '42-line bible' to distinguish it from a later edition of 36 lines per page).[6] Because of the debate surrounding printing's arrival and impact in Europe, I have included a number of essays specifically on this; of the remaining essays, disproportionally more focus on the sixteenth century rather than the seventeenth century – a reflection of both printing's impact on the political, religious and cultural landscape of early sixteenth-century Europe and the particular interest of recent scholars.[7] In addition, the volume has

---

[5] Darnton characterized the history of the book as 'interdisciplinarity run riot' (2002, p. 10). For more recent considerations of its interdisciplinarity, see: Clegg (2001a); Bell (2002); McDonald (2004); Howsam (2006); Gillespie (2007). Darnton has produced a sequel to his earlier essay: '"What is the History of Books?" Revisited' (2007).

[6] The earliest of Gutenberg's printed items date from about 1450. The 42-line bible was in production from 1452 and sample quires were available from 1454; whether this meant that the whole edition had been printed by late 1454 rather than 1455 is unclear.

[7] There are relatively few supranational histories of the book in early modern England: Febvre and Martin's book; the work of Elizabeth Eisenstein (cited below); Clair, *A History of European Printing* (1976); Steinberg, *Five Hundred Years of Printing* (1996). (For a recent historical overview, see van Vliet, 2007.) There have, however, been a number of national histories, such as: Kapp and

been shaped by two types of exclusion: the first pragmatically, but reluctantly, omits essays
that are not primarily focused on the period at hand (which means, for example, that Walter
Ong's important work on orality (1982) has not been included), while the second recognizes
that monographs do not take kindly to the excerpting that a collection such as this requires, so
seminal books – Febvre's and Martin's *L'Apparition*, Elizabeth L. Eisenstein's *The Printing
Press as an Agent of Change* and so on – appear only in passing or in the footnotes.

Within these parameters, I have attempted to ensure a spread of topics (from orality, to
type design, to reading practices), approaches (bibliographical, literary, historical) and
regions (France, Spain, Italy, the Germanic region, Britain), and have limited the number
of long essays, but space has meant that there are inevitable omissions in terms of subjects
and countries – nothing specifically on Scandinavia,[8] on women (as producers, sellers or
readers),[9] on libraries,[10] or on the spread of news,[11] for example. However, with all this taken
into consideration, the 17 essays selected represent what I feel to be among the very best
history of the book scholarship of the last five decades.

'A suitable remedy'

On 4 May 1515, the Fifth Lateran Council of the church at Rome issued a decree concerning
printing, *Super impressione librorum,* in the name of Pope Leo X. Despite being the first – and
one of the very few – truly international attempts to regulate the trade in printed books, the
decree is very rarely cited, let alone quoted, in English studies of the European book trade; I
reproduce it at length:

> Among the anxieties resting on our shoulders, we come back with constant thought to how we can
> bring back to the path of truth those going astray, and gain them for God (by his grace working in us).
> This is what we truly seek after with eagerness; to this we unremittingly direct our mind's desires; and
> over this we watch with anxious earnestness.
>
> It is certainly possible to obtain without difficulty some learning by reading books. The skill of
> book-printing has been invented, or rather improved and perfected, with God's assistance, particularly
> in our time. Without doubt it has brought many benefits to men and women since, at small expense, it
> is possible to possess a great number of books. These permit minds to devote themselves very readily
> to scholarly studies. Thus there can easily result, particularly among Catholics, men competent in
> all kinds of languages; and we desire to see in the Roman church, in good supply, men of this type
> who are capable of instructing even unbelievers in the holy commandments, and of gathering them

Goldfriedrich,(1886–1913); Martin and Chartier (1982–86; 2nd edn, 1989–91); the *Geschichte des
Buchhandels* series, published by Harrassowitz-Verlag, which has so far covered the Soviet Union,
Czechoslovakia, Austria, Italy and elsewhere; van Delft and de Wolf (2003); *The Cambridge History of
the Book in Britain* (1997–); *The Oxford History of the Irish Book* (2006–); and *The Edinburgh History
of the Book in Scotland* (2007–).

   [8]   See, for example, the essays by Anne Riising and Rémi Kick in Gilmont (1998).

   [9]   On women in the book trade, see Lenkey (1975); Parker (1996); and Bell (1996).

   [10]   On libraries, see Harris (1995); Chartier (1994); and *The Cambridge History of Libraries in
Britain and Ireland* (2006).

   [11]   Newsbooks were a particular phenomenon of seventeenth-century print culture: see Dooley and
Baron (2001) and Raymond (2006).

for their salvation into the body of the faithful by the teaching of the christian faith. Complaints from many persons, however, have reached our ears and those of the apostolic see. In fact, some printers have the boldness to print and sell to the public, in different parts of the world, books – some translated into Latin from Greek, Hebrew, Arabic and Chaldean as well as some issued directly in Latin or a vernacular language – containing errors opposed to the faith as well as pernicious views contrary to the christian religion and to the reputation of prominent persons of rank. The readers are not edified. Indeed, they lapse into very great errors not only in the realm of faith but also in that of life and morals. This has often given rise to various scandals, as experience has taught, and there is daily the fear that even greater scandals are developing.

That is why, to prevent what has been a healthy discovery for the glory of God, the advance of the faith, and the propagation of good skills, from being misused for the opposite purposes and becoming an obstacle to the salvation of Christians, we have judged that our care must be exercised over the printing of books, precisely so that thorns do not grow up with the good seed or poisons become mixed with medicines. It is our desire to provide a suitable remedy for this danger, with the approval of this sacred council, so that the business of book-printing may go ahead with greater satisfaction the more that there is employed in the future, with greater zeal and prudence, a more attentive supervision. We therefore establish and ordain that henceforth, for all future time, no one may dare to print or have printed any book or other writing of whatever kind in Rome or in any other cities or dioceses, without the book or writings having first been closely examined, at Rome by our vicar and the master of the sacred palace, in other cities and dioceses by the bishop or some other person who knows about the printing of books and writings of this kind and who has been delegated to this office by the bishop in question, and also by the inquisitor of heresy for the city or diocese where the said printing is to take place, and unless the books or writings have been approved by a warrant signed in their own hand, which must be given, under pain of excommunication, freely and without delay.

In addition to the printed books being seized and publicly burnt, payment of a hundred ducats to the fabric of the basilica of the prince of the apostles in Rome, without hope of relief, and suspension for a whole year from the possibility of engaging in printing, there is to be imposed upon anyone presuming to act otherwise the sentence of excommunication. Finally, if the offender's contumacy increases, he is to be punished with all the sanctions of the law, by his bishop or by our vicar, in such a way that others will have no incentive to try to follow his example. (*Decrees*, 1990, vol. 1, pp. 632–33)[12]

The decree is a remarkable document, not least because it seems so removed from the conventional view of sixteenth-century Rome's attitude to printing. Here, the Church acknowledges, and seeks to address, the potential misuse of this relatively new technology but seems otherwise unexpectedly sanguine about its broader impact: printing is 'a healthy discovery for the glory of God, the advance of the faith, and the propagation of good skills'. Given that the crisis of the Reformation was to break only a few years later, it is tempting to dismiss the decree as naive and short-sighted but for two features. First, the regulatory system it imposed – the ecclesiastical approval of all books prior to printing, known in England as licensing – was as pragmatic as it was hard-nosed, and it would remain a standard (but not the only) mechanism for state press regulation across Europe for decades to come, a point recognized by John Milton in *Areopagitica*. Second, with remarkable prescience, the Lateran Council managed to highlight some of the key characteristics of printing that would enable it to have such a dramatic effect on European society.

---

[12]   See also Hirsch (1973). Milton alludes to the decree in *Areopagitica* (1644).

It is important not to overstate the novelty of printed books for fifteenth-century Europe. As Paul Saenger provocatively remarks in Chapter 15 of this volume, the 'proper context' for understanding early printing is 'the history of the late medieval book' (p. 385) and that, in effect, is what the papal decree implies by its observation that '[i]t is certainly possible to obtain without difficulty some learning by reading books'.[13] Writing, paper, ink, books – none was new: there were already authors, scribes, bookbinders, booksellers and readers. This, of course, should not be that surprising: the advantages in economies of scale that printing had over existing manuscript practices would only be worth exploiting if there was already an established market for books. Moreover, because those same economies of scale actively militated against producing very small numbers of copies of any one text and because one had to meet the costs for the printing of *all* the copies before a single one could be sold, successful printing (or, more correctly, publishing) depended on a sophisticated (or, at least, fortuitous) sense of the market.[14] The technology of printing *did* stimulate the market in crucial ways, helping it to develop and expand with remarkable speed, but it did not *create* the market in the first place. This, although obvious, reminds us of two key things: that the earliest printers sought to be conservative in terms of what their printed books looked like and what they were about; and that manuscript production itself did not suddenly fall and cease. There was no sudden and irrevocable break with the scribal past.[15]

'The skill of book-printing has been invented ... with God's assistance'

The technology of printing owed much to existing knowledge and practice. The basic principle of transferring an impression from a raised die on to a surface had been put to a variety of uses, such as coining, for centuries, while a more refined version that left an inked mark on the surface rather than a physical impression was used for printing on cloth and, in the fifteenth century, for block-books, in which pages were printed from carved wood-blocks. Oil- and wine-making relied on screw-presses that allowed considerable pressure to be exerted evenly and carefully; more recently, the traditional writing surface, vellum, had been challenged by the cheaper and more pliable paper.[16] Moreover, when Thomas More and Francis Bacon later wrote about the technology of printing, it seemed that printing techniques were readily understood. More's Utopians, admittedly an intellectually astute audience, 'immediately

---

[13]   Gillespie, in an essay that deserves much wider attention among those who work on the history of the printed book, goes further: 'the history of the book might be written in newly illuminating ways if written about books (fixed, endlessly mobile), rather than about printing. This would reveal more about "print culture" than any print-centric history could' (2007, p. 266).

[14]   It is important to distinguish between printers (who ran printing houses), publishers (who paid for a work to be printed), and booksellers (who sold printed and/or manuscript books, either wholesale or retail). Although these were separate roles, they were frequently combined, especially in the first century or so of printing. In early modern England, the distinction between these roles was blurred by the terminology: 'printer' could mean both printer and publisher, 'bookseller' could also mean 'publisher', while 'publisher' was, apart from a very specific and narrow meaning, not used.

[15]   On the shifting and complex relationship between manuscript and print, see McKitterick (2003); Gillespie (2007); and the discussion of Saenger, below.

[16]   These points are explored in more detail in Febvre and Martin (1976, pp. 29–76). On paper, see Barker (1992) and Bidwell (1998).

grasped the basic principles [of paper-making and printing]...[t]heir first attempts were not altogether successful, but with practice they soon mastered both arts' (More, 1995, p. 79; Bacon was more direct: 'there is surely nothing in the craft of printing that is not open and almost obvious' (Bacon, 1994, p. 114). If the raw materials and relevant skills were already present, and the principles were self-evident, what was new or difficult about printing?

Printing's apparent simplicity belied complex realities. The transfer of ink from printed type to page seems straightforward in principle but in practice relied on a long series of specialized steps: composition, justification, imposition, making ready, preparing the ink, dampening the paper, beating, pulling, proofing, registering, perfecting, drying, folding, stitching. Even once the press was ready, the type inked and the paper in place, printing required a combination of three distinct movements of the press machinery: folding the frisket and tympan over the locked forme; rolling the bed of the press under the platen; pulling the platen on to the press.[17] Nor should we overemphasize the continuities with existing practice and knowledge: a printing press differed significantly from other screw presses; scribal ink was useless for printing purposes; and even paper had to be prepared differently for printing than for manuscript writing. Finally, of the steps cited above, all but folding and stitching were specific to the craft of printing. In other words, the arrival of printing in the mid-fifteenth century necessitated the development of new techniques and skills.

The most crucial and innovative of all these new skills is the one about which we know least: the making of printing type. To a seventeenth-century printer like Joseph Moxon (whose *Mechanick Exercises* of 1683–84 provides the first full account, in any European language, of printing),[18] making type began with the engraving of a single steel punch for each character ('sort') in a particular typeface. With this punch, the base of a mould (or 'matrix') could be struck, from which, using a specially constructed hand-held mould, individual iterations of that particular sort could be cast. A full fount of cast type, consisting of different-sized groupings of all the sorts needed, could then be arranged into a sequence to produce a particular work and, once the work had been printed, that sequence could be broken up and the process could start again to 'set' and print a different work.[19] This was the key to printing's technological success: moveable type, individual pieces that could be rearranged at will. When Moxon was writing, the use and production of moveable type had been craft-orthodoxy time out of mind, and it would remain the standard way of producing type until the industrial period.

For centuries, the scholarly consensus was that it was *this* technological breakthrough – the process of manufacturing moveable type – that was Gutenberg's real achievement.[20] Yet, as the first essay in this volume, by Blaise Agüera y Arcas, contends, it does not seem to fit with the bibliographical facts.[21] Sophisticated computer analysis suggests that there was much more variation in the individual sorts than one might expect. The sheer number of versions of 'i', for example, in Gutenberg's 1456 *Bulla Thurcorum* would fit awkwardly

---

[17]   For an explanation of all these processes, see Gaskell (1972). These last two movements were repeated as the platen was only large enough to cover half a full-size forme.

[18]   See Moxon (1962). The following account is drawn from Moxon, via Gaskell.

[19]   Or, in many cases, part of the same work.

[20]   On Gutenberg, see Kapr (1987, English edition 1996); and Boghardt and Schneider (1990). Hellinga (2007) provides a summary overview.

[21]   The essay is a summary of research that Paul Needham and Agüera y Arcas first announced in 2001.

with the conventional one-punch-per-sort model: why would a punch-cutter painstakingly produce different versions of a single letter when the punch-matrix-mould process would have made it much easier and quicker to cast as many identical copies as necessary?[22] This suggests that, for this work at least, Gutenberg was using some other kind of method to produce and cast the type: Agüera y Arcas posits 'elemental punches' (that is, punches for different elements of a letter's shape) made from a less durable (but more readily carved) material such as wood.[23]

The technically detailed nature of Agüera y Arcas's essay may make it seem an arcane choice for this volume, particularly as the opening essay. However, it does raise some points of relevance to the volume as a whole. The first is that, to some, this essay might not be considered an example of the 'history of the book' at all, as its aims and methodology are firmly bibliographical. Even a cursory comparison between this essay and those in Part II demonstrates that there is a distinct difference in style and approach, but nonetheless I feel that this essay (along with others in the volume) is an important reminder that books are *made objects*. The essay also powerfully demonstrates the limits of the surviving evidence not only for the mid-fifteenth century, but also for much of the next 250 years. No records explaining Gutenberg's processes nor any of his equipment survive; all that remains are the books themselves. Bibliographical analysis can at times be highly sophisticated but, more often than not, its claims can only rely on the physical evidence of the products themselves.[24] Finally, Agüera y Arcas's essay also shows that there is still no consensus over what exactly Gutenberg's technical legacy was. There are surviving examples of punches, matrices, hand-moulds, type and presses from the sixteenth century (most notably at Plantin-Moretus Museum in Antwerp) that bear out Moxon's description from the late seventeenth century, but at what point did this process of type-casting establish itself? Gutenberg presumably experimented with different type-making and type-setting methods (there has also been considerable debate about the type-setting for the Mainz *Catholicon*), but the nature of such experiments and how they might have led to the 'standard' process is still unclear (Mosley, 2007). Half a millennium after the first type-printed books appeared in Europe, we still do not know quite how they were made.

One characteristic of early type that we *can* analyse is its design.[25] The earliest printed books sought, deliberately, to imitate manuscript books: a printed bible looked like a manuscript one. Early printers incorporated scribal initials and rubrication to 'finish' the page; they retained many of the same abbreviated forms of words that scribes used even though it considerably complicated the process of making type; and the visual design of the typeface itself followed contemporary scribal conventions. The dominant typeface of the very earliest books, such as Gutenberg's bibles, was what we have come to call 'black letter' ('textura' is more accurate), derived from ecclesiastical scribal styles. Within a decade or two, however, roman typefaces,

---

[22]   Stephen Pratt (2003), however, has argued that such variation is merely a consequence of the contingencies of type-making itself.

[23]   The principle of elemental punches would also fit with Gutenberg's own training as a goldsmith; metalworkers frequently used different punches to chase decorative features.

[24]   McKenzie's essay (Chapter 11) highlights the serious problems that this kind of analysis can create.

[25]   On type design, Johnson (1966) is still a standard source; see also Carter (1969). For a useful overview, see Greetham (1994, pp. 225–53).

themselves imitative of the newer humanistic scripts, began to be used for classical works. Nicolas Barker's essay (Chapter 2) considers a further development in the history of early humanist typography and its relationship to manuscript: the appearance of italic.

Aldus Manutius (or, to give his Italian name, Theobaldo Manucci) was a Venetian printer and publisher, active from 1490 (see Davies, 1995). He carved a distinct niche for himself as a publisher of classical works, so much so that his 'logo' of a dolphin entwined about an anchor became an internationally recognized mark of scholarly distinction. The focus of Barker's essay[26] is the Aldine edition of Virgil's works in 1501, for which Aldus had commissioned Francesco Griffo to design a typeface that was both compact and legible: the result, a face based on a cursive humanistic script, was what we recognize as italic. Barker notes that the fount included an unusually large number of 'letter combinations' or 'ligatures' – almost a hundred cases of different multiple letters cast as a single piece of type (either for technical reasons, such as the overhanging 'f' alongside an 'l', 't' or 'i', or aesthetic ones, such as 'ct', some of which are still with us) – suggesting that italic was self-consciously explicit in its scribal antecedents. Each of this italic's purely aesthetic ligatures can be found in Aldus's own handwriting but, as Barker points out, it would be wrong to assume that the typeface was a 'slavish' reflection of his own scribal style or of other famous humanist figures such as Pomponio Leto or Bartolomeo Sanvito. Instead, the face was designed to suit the book in which it appeared,[27] as Aldus was also innovative in his introduction of a new 'long and narrow' pocket-sized format. Yet for all such novelty, Aldus's design strategy was deliberately nostalgic: as Barker states, '[the letter and format] conformed to an older set of conventions, now so deeply ingrained that their acceptance was automatic, even unconscious' (p. 29).

'[Books] permit minds to devote themselves very readily to scholarly studies'

In 1958, *L'Apparition du Livre* was published by Éditions Albin Michel in Paris. Its authorship was shared between the great French *Annales* historian Lucien Febvre and a more junior figure, Henri-Jean Martin, a curator at the Bibliothèque Nationale. Febvre had died during the preparation of the book and, while Martin acknowledged that he was 'more or less solely responsible for the work as it stands', it was Febvre who was responsible for the book's 'conception and reception' (Febvre and Martin, 1976, p. 7). The nature of that conception is clear from Febvre's own preface:

> ... we hope to establish how and why the printed book was something more than a triumph of technical ingenuity, but was also one of the most potent agents at the disposal of western civilisation in bringing together the scattered ideas of representative thinkers ... The book created new habits of thought not only within the small circle of the learned, but far beyond, in the intellectual life of all who used their minds. In short we are hoping to prove that the printed book was one of the most effective means of mastery over the whole world. (pp. 10–11)

---

[26]   As Barker notes, the essay is a summary of his own book-length study of Aldus's types (Barker, 1985a).

[27]   Barker remarks on the face's 'pleasing lack of uniformity', echoing, perhaps, the variation that Agüera y Arcas had detected in Gutenberg's printing of 45 years earlier.

This study of 'The Book in the Service of History' – to quote Febvre's suggested alternative title (p. 9) – aimed 'to examine the influence and practical significance of the printed book during the first 300 years of its existence' (p. 11). As Febvre noted, although there were many histories of printing, this approach represented something new: the book was 'a journey in which no previous guide, so far as we know, has ever pointed out the hazards or come up with the results we are looking for' (p. 13). And with it, the 'history of the book' (a term Febvre used in the second paragraph of the preface) was born.

Febvre and Martin's wide-ranging geographical and chronological coverage, combined with the grand questions they were posing, could not be further removed from the focused and detailed approach of bibliography of Agüera y Arcas, Barker and others. Here, the printed book was not a subject in its own right but rather a means for recovering 'the history of the use of the intellect', to use Stanley Morison's potent phrase (1972, p. 1). However, as Febvre and Martin's book was not translated into English until 1976, the history of the book in the English language required other pioneers, the most notable of whom was Elizabeth Eisenstein.

Eisenstein's 1968 essay (Chapter 3) is one of a number about printing that she published in major English-language history journals during the late 1960s and very early 1970s (see Eisenstein, 1966, 1969, 1970). In these essays, Eisenstein developed a thesis that identified the printing press as fundamental in transforming Renaissance culture and thought, most notably in religion and science: 'a communications revolution' (this volume, p. 36). As she wrote towards the end of the essay included here:

> The appearance of a Protestant ethic, a spirit of capitalism, a middle-class ethos, new concepts of the family and the child, educational reforms, and a bureaucratic officialdom all owed much to multiple, complex interactions introduced by typography. (p. 79)

As the title of her essay indicates, she was initially cautious about her claims – 'a work … still in progress', 'some tentative hypotheses', '[s]peculations that are possibly unfounded and certainly still shaky' – but this did not prevent her from recognizing, with remarkable prescience, that here was a subject that 'calls for the pooling of many talents and the writing of many books' (pp. 35–36).

For all its provisionality and lack of detailed primary evidence, Eisenstein's essay was ground-breaking, seasoned with some bracing turns of phrase: 'the printer's workshop became the most advanced laboratory of erudition of the sixteenth century' (p. 47); 'permanence … introduced progressive change. The preservation of the old, in brief, launched a tradition of the new' (p. 59). The issues it raised – the 'shift' from manuscript to print, the economics of the printed book trade, print as a tool of 'standardization' (where multiple 'identical' copies could be distributed all across Europe), print saving classical texts (particularly Greek) from scholarly oblivion, print shaping the nascent nation-state itself, print as an engine for social action – were ones Eisenstein would return to in subsequent essays and formed the framework for *The Printing Press as an Agent of Change*, published in 1979.[28]

---

[28]   It was issued in a single abridged, illustrated volume as *The Printing Revolution in Early Modern Europe* (1983). Eisenstein also published a summary of her book as 'On the Printing Press as an Agent of Change' in Olson, Torrance and Hildyard (1985, pp. 19–33). I have used the 1994 one-

Eisenstein's work did not go unchallenged. Theodore K. Rabb responded to her 1969 essay 'The Advent of Printing and the Problem of the Renaissance' with a published 'comment' that admits the force of her claims while remaining singularly unconvinced:

> Professor Eisenstein's plea for printing will doubtless share the fate of all the other 'causes of intellectual change' so beloved of the textbooks ... The overburdened historian will simply acknowledge that more must be said about printing, and it will either be added to his list of 'features of the Renaissance' or it will be given higher billing. (Rabb, 1971, p. 139)[29]

Much more recently, Eisenstein's work on the standardization (or 'fixity') of print met with a sustained challenge from Adrian Johns, both in his *The Nature of the Book* (1998) and in a debate between the two scholars published in the *American Historical Review* (Grafton, Eisenstein and Johns, 2002) . However, it is an extended review of Eisenstein's 1979 book by Anthony T. Grafton (Chapter 4) that most effectively identifies the strengths and weaknesses of her work.

Grafton begins with generous praise – 'No historian of early modern Europe will be able to avoid a confrontation with the problems she has raised; for that alone we owe her a great debt' (p. 93) – but, in a curious echo of Rabb's criticism, he admits that 'a certain uneasiness' remains (p. 95),[30] principally about the type of evidence she uses (little direct use of primary sources) and the ways in which it is deployed (not 'entirely judicious' (p. 98)). The strength of her work is undermined by two major flaws: 'inadequate foundation in research and exaggerated claims of explanatory power' (p. 111). '[A]s a piece of intellectual history', Eisenstein's book 'not only brings rewards but inspires misgivings' (p. 107). Although it may seem invidious to include a hostile review of a book that itself is represented here only by way of a self-confessed conjectural essay written a full decade before that book's publication, Grafton (among the most learned of Eisenstein's critics) demonstrates that Eisenstein's legacy is less to do with the details of her scholarship (which, in many cases, has been superseded) but rather with how she established a wholly new way of thinking about the Renaissance itself and provided the terms in which to debate the impact of printing upon it.

'books ... containing errors opposed to the faith ... so that thorns do not grow up with good seed'

The spread of printing across Europe in the immediate decades after Gutenberg's achievements in Mainz in the 1450s was remarkably rapid.[31] A map in Febvre and Martin (1976, pp. 178–9) shows how, in a single decade (1471–80), presses had been established not only throughout many parts of the Holy Roman Empire, but also as far west as Salamanca (Seville's press had been established even earlier), as far east as Budapest and Krakow, and from southern

---

volume paperback edition of *Printing Press* for citations. Baron, Lindquist and Shevlin (2007) re-assess Eisenstein's legacy.

[29]   Eisenstein's reply appears immediately afterwards (Eisenstein, 1971).

[30]   Compare Rabb: 'And yet an uneasiness remains' (1971, p. 135).

[31]   Books printed in Europe up to and including 1500 are known as incunabula or, in a more anglicized form, incunables. It is a convenient but arbitrary term: European printing did not suddenly change its character in 1501.

Italy to London, Oxford and St Albans in England. In the final two decades of the fifteenth century, presses continued to proliferate across Europe, with printing operations established in Portugal and Sweden (pp. 184–5). Many of these printing and publishing houses proved ill-fated – printing and publishing were precarious ventures from the outset – but, for a large number of European early modern towns and cities, printing houses became a familiar feature of the urban economy. Moreover, the geographical spread of printing continued, albeit not quite as dramatically, throughout the next two centuries: Scotland in 1508, Mexico in 1539, Moscow by 1555, Peru in 1584, New England in 1638. In England, printing's spread beyond London and the universities was effectively stifled by the craft monopoly granted to the London Stationers' Company from the mid-sixteenth century onwards; only with the lapsing of this monopoly in 1695 did presses begin to appear in English provincial towns and cities.

In Chapter 6 Jean-François Gilmont provides a useful overview of how printing itself developed in Europe in the century after Gutenberg.[32] His essay is not an entirely free-standing one; it comes from a book that explores the role of the printed book in the Reformation from a variety of angles. Consequently, his essay (essentially an introduction to later essays in his own volume) touches on a variety of issues of importance without exploring them in particular detail. These include: the sporadic spread of the craft of printing across Europe and the clear relationship between printing workshops and major urban centres and trading routes; the practical economics of the printing house (the unit of production being the sheet rather than the page or even the book, the tremendous expense of paper, the probable average print run); the significance of literacy and reading habits.[33] Nonetheless, his essay provides us with an instructive context within which to consider a pair of essays that focus on the relationship between the European Reformation and the book trade.

Print played an undeniably powerful role in both the spread and response to the Reformation in Europe in the sixteenth century, but the conventional view that the reformers understood and exploited the power of print far more effectively than their opponents needs to be nuanced.[34] Paul Grendler's essay (Chapter 5) – later to form part of his *Roman Inquisition and the Venetian Press* (1977) – explores the realities of censorship, and specifically the enforcement of the *Index Librorum Prohibitorum* (*Index of Prohibited Books*) in Venice in the late sixteenth century. Censorship, with its associations of banned books, smuggling, *auto-da-fés* and executions of authors, printers and publishers, is one of the more emotive aspects of the early modern book trade, and, in consequence, scholarly attention to it has sometimes been too much led by ideological perspectives, whether Whiggish or Marxist.[35] It has also,

---

[32] Gilmont has published widely (in French): see, for example, Gilmont (2003) and Gilmont (2005)

[33] The economics of the printing house will be touched upon in McKenzie (Chapter 11), while reading habits will be discussed by Chartier (Chapter 8), Saenger (Chapter 15) and Jardine and Grafton (Chapter 16). Literacy, a vexed subject for early modern scholarship, has been the subject of several studies: see, for example: Baumann (1986); Mignolo (1995); and Crain (2007).

[34] For the 'standard' view, see Eisenstein (1994, pp. 303–450).

[35] The former argues for a declining effectiveness of censorship as society progressed inexorably from monarchy to democracy; the latter identifies censorship as a key part of the state's ideological apparatus. For English examples, compare Siebert (1965) with Patterson (1984) and Hill (1985–86). Cyndia Susan Clegg's recent trilogy – *Press Censorship in Elizabethan England* (1997), *Press*

perhaps unfairly, been considered to be a particular speciality of the Roman Catholic Church, as evidenced by its creation of the system of pre-print licensing in 1515 and the establishment of the *Index* in the mid-sixteenth century: these may, in fact, be better considered a reflection of the Church's own administrative capacity rather than a symptom of an innate Catholic antagonism to print.[36] Protestant England, for example, also relied on licensing as the primary means of controlling the output of the printed word throughout the sixteenth and seventeenth centuries and was not averse to maintaining lists of forbidden works, burning those books, or violently punishing those associated with their production.[37] Indeed, the London book trade's plea to parliament in 1643 for firmer regulation openly cited the Catholic model not least, it seems, because of its potential benefits to the trade itself:

> We must in this give Papists their due; for as well where the Inquisition predominates, as not, regulation is more strict by far, then [*sic*] it is amongst Protestants; we are not so wise in our Generation, nor take so much care to preserve the true Religion as they do the false from alteration: and for that cause not onely their Church is the more fortified, but the Art of Printing thrives, and the Artists grow rich also beyond any examples amongst us. (*To the High Court*, sig. A1v.)

Seeking to censor sixteenth-century Venice was, in Grendler's words, a 'formidable task'. The city was one of Europe's greatest printing centres: 'about 500 publishers appeared on the title pages of Venetian books during the sixteenth century' (p. 114); in addition, its market for books, as for many of the other commodities it traded in, was emphatically international.[38] However, despite such exceptionalism, the Venetian book trade's relationship with those that sought to regulate its output was shaped by two, often overlooked, factors common to attempts to censor across Europe: local politics and the economics of the trade. As Grendler argues, the efficacy of the Roman Inquisition depended partly on the Venetian government's own view of Rome and partly on the lobbying of the book trade itself, most clearly seen in the booksellers' successful attempt to challenge the proposed 1555 *Index*. Censorship did not, of course, necessarily depend on local political or trade consent and could be coercive but, as Venice shows (and as the 1643 view of the London book trade quoted above supports), control was always more effective when political expediency and economic interest coincided with regulatory effort. To understand the realities of interventions by the state or Church (of whatever

---

Censorship in Jacobean England (2001) and *Press Censorship in Caroline England* (2008) – offers a nuanced and balanced overview.

[36] Surprisingly, there are few international explorations of early modern censorship: Duke and Tamse (1987); Grendler (1988); and there is a very brief overview in van Vliet (2007).

[37] See Siebert (1965) – although he takes an excessively secular view of English censorship – and Clegg (1997, 2001a, 2008).

[38] However, Grendler's estimated annual output of editions seems improbably low compared with the equivalent figures for London over the same period as cited in Volume IV of *The Cambridge History of the Book in Britain* (Barnard, McKenzie and Bell (2002), pp. 779–84). Grendler does acknowledge that his figure does not include 'pamphlets that did not receive imprimaturs' (this volume, p. 114) but, even so, it would seem astonishing that sixteenth-century Venice, which even at its lowest ebb claimed to have 40 active presses, was only capable of 85 per cent of the output of London's two dozen printers. Much more likely is that the Venetian statistics Grendler cites are substantially incomplete. For more on the problems of using book production data, see below.

stripe) into the early modern European book trade, it is not enough merely to read proclamations, decrees or statutes.

Just as Grendler's essay cautions us against a reductive reading of the Catholic Church's approach to censorship, so the essay by Andrew Pettegree and Matthew Hall (Chapter 7) seeks to reconsider the apparent close relationship between the printed word and the success of the early Protestant reformers. Specifically, it argues that the extraordinary success of print in galvanizing and driving the evangelical movement in Germany (which led, for example, to the transformation of Wittenberg 'from a small outpost of the publishing world to one of the pillars of the German print industry' within a single decade (p. 146)) cannot be applied to other countries. As with censorship, the effective spread of Reformation ideas through books depended crucially on local conditions and so, as 'the dynamics of the book industry varied very markedly from country to country' (p. 145), so too did the impact of the Reformation.

Through a series of analyses of a sample of 10,000 consecutive entries from the *Index Aureliensis* (1965–), an as yet incomplete catalogue of sixteenth-century European printed books, the authors show that 'the German paradigm' differs distinctly from much of the rest of Europe: few other countries could match the diversity and number of different printing centres. As Table 5 in the essay most strikingly shows, only Spain came close to Germany in the devolved and dispersed nature of its publishing industry (p. 152). Pettegree and Hall also remind us not to overlook the extensive international market for Latin works throughout the century as, in promoting an alternative vernacular tradition, Protestants 'were arguing very much against the grain of sixteenth-century culture' (p. 158).[39] Finally, particular attention is paid to France whose distinctive trade structure and political context provided radically different conditions for a print-driven evangelical movement. While the authors are hesitant to conclude a broad survey essay with definitive claims, they are right to conclude that when studying 'the print culture of the sixteenth-century [*sic*], business questions – questions of distribution and the organizing of the market – are as important as the location of publication' (p. 166).

The statistical (or 'bibliometric') nature of both these essays not only reflects an increasingly important strand in studies of the history of early modern European print culture, but also highlights the problems in compiling and analysing such data. Books are not uniform commodities: a single-sheet indulgence printed by Gutenberg and his 42-line bible may each take up just one entry in a library or bibliographical catalogue but they represent vastly different objects in terms of raw materials, labour, time and cost. Printers and booksellers of the period understood this, which is why the printed sheet (which might, depending on the format of the book, contain anything from one printed page to 32 or more) was a unit of both production and exchange across Europe.[40] Even when the number of sheets in a particular book can be calculated, however, the general absence of reliable information about a work's print-run means that the margin for error when estimating the economics of even a single work is considerable.[41] In addition, survival rates (that is, the likelihood of a work

---

[39] For the importance of this import trade for the English book trade, see, for example, Bland (1999). See also Maclean (Chapter 13).

[40] Books were more highly differentiated than many other early modern commodities and so *Tauschhandel* enabled publishers to exchange different kinds of books with one another on a sheet-by-sheet basis.

[41] The most common estimates for pre-1700 print-runs, based on what little evidence does survive, range from 750 to 1,000, but lower or higher print runs were entirely possible, of course, and, in many

having survived to the present day) are often unquantifiable (as we most likely do not know the original print-run), with survival itself depending on a variety of factors including size, format, ownership, subject matter and luck (see Barnard, Chapter 14, this volume). Finally, the source of the statistical data itself – the hand, eye and judgment of a person examining a particular surviving copy – also varies considerably, not merely in terms of the level of detail or accuracy but also in the confidence with which different editions (let alone, to use the bibliographical terms, different 'states', 'impressions' and 'issues') can be distinguished from one another.[42] These 'known unknowns' mean that, frustratingly, the broader the data sample, the more likely that the data is in some way flawed. It is only in recent years that the history of the book has begun to establish a reliable methodology of handling its bibliometric data, but it remains a discipline in urgent need of serious statistical rigour.[43]

Towards the end of their essay, Pettegree and Grendler argue that 'in order for the [French Protestantism] movement to broaden its appeal beyond the unlettered it must have continued to rely on oral dissemination: primarily the spoken word, and song' (p. 165). Oral culture (or orality) has been the subject of several recent studies, but its evidentiary absence – in contrast with the written word's archival or bibliographical presence – has meant that analysis has had to rely on the occasional and problematic moments where the oral is 'captured' by the written record, whether through legal records, 'oral' genres such as ballads, or literary portrayal.[44] Even then, however, orality's difference from the written word requires different scholarly methodologies, and it is not surprising that Roger Chartier's essay on the topic (at Chapter 8) is distinctively literary in its style, its references (Borges, Shakespeare, Cervantes, ballads) and its acute sensitivity to the 'effects of *meaning* produced by forms (whether they be written, printed, or oral)' (p. 191, my emphasis). Mindful of its difference from the other essays in this volume, I feel it deserves more explication than most.

Chartier's essay does engage directly with reading practices (that is, how people read, what they read, where they read, why they read and so on) and, as such, could have been placed alongside the essays by Saenger, Jardine and Grafton, and Cressy in Part V of this volume, but by placing it in Part II I intend to counter not only the positivistic nature of the essays that precede it, but also some of those essays' underlying assumptions about how readers read. In particular, Chartier warns against universalizing our own reading practices, predicated as they are on our experience of the written word:

> This [essay's] point of departure is an attempt to break with the uncritical posture which assumes that all texts, all works, all genres must reasonably be read, identified, and received according to criteria which characterise our own relation to the written word. It is thus a question of historicising criteria

---

cases, likely. The statistical confidence with which a work's individual sheet-count (how many sheets were used in a single edition of any particular work) can be extrapolated is, consequently, low.

[42]   See, for example, Blayney (1994). These caveats have intensified with the move from printed catalogues to electronic ones, where compiling statistical data is much easier.

[43]   Useful statistical methodologies are evaluated in: Suarez (2003–4, esp. pp. 164ff); Weedon (2007); and Suarez (2009).

[44]   Early modern orality, unlike literacy and reading with which it is often paired, is little explored: in addition to Ong (1982), see Fox (2002) and Fox and Woolf (2002). On English ballads, see Watt (1991).

of classification between genres, ways of reading, and representations of the structure of address and the addressee of texts as they have been bequeathed to us by the 'literary institution'. (p. 167)

As readers, Chartier argues, we approach any text – literary or otherwise – in the belief that it must exhibit three defining characteristics: it is fixed and stable (it can be accurately and repeatedly written down);[45] it is addressed to a silent, solitary reader (a phenomenon of relatively recent history – see Saenger, 1997 and Chartier, 1989, pp. 124–27); and that, in reading, we seek the text's 'meaning' in and of itself. However, this is to consider the text as a 'monument' – something that endures, conforms, repeats – when oral texts should be understood as performed, meaningful 'events': '[i]rreducibly singular, the [oral] text can be neither written down nor repeated' (p. 172). The text-as-monument, rather than the text-as-event, has remained our dominant literary paradigm since post-Homeric Greece, thus effacing the differences 'between the oral, communal and ritual performance of texts, that obeys its own laws, and a reading of these same texts as practised by a reader who is in the position of a *lector* in search of meaning' (p. 185).

To explore the complexities of the text-as-event, Chartier considers the early modern English ballad – both printed ballads and 'popular' oral ballads, knowledge of whose existence depends solely on their citation in contemporary defamation suits. He observes the 'inseparable duality of adhesion and distance' (p. 179) inherent in the ballads' ability to be simultaneously credible and fictive (which Chartier links to theatrical performance more generally), but also notes that the oral ballads differed markedly from their written counterparts in the 'irregularity of forms, local circulation, [and] the particularising of the text' (p. 182). Chartier's other case-study concerns the shifting relationship between orality and print in the case of sixteenth- and seventeenth-century Castilian poetic *romances*: 'the same genre could, in diverse forms, be addressed to completely different publics serving a variety of uses' (p. 184). Yet, how can we recover the text-as-event in early modern European oral culture? Chartier argues that we should adopt a method similar to that he employed in analysing the ballads ('to decipher in literary representations the practices of orality: recitation, song, reading aloud, etc' (p. 185)) and to pay close attention to a written text's own 'indicators of orality … implicit or explicit devices that destine texts to addresses who read aloud or listen to a text being read' (p. 186), ranging from the simplification of plots to punctuation itself.

'Some printers have the boldness to print and sell to the public'

As Roger Stoddard has wisely observed:

> Whatever they may do, authors do *not* write books. Books are not written at all. They are manufactured by scribes and other artisans, by mechanics and other engineers, and by printing presses and other machines. (Stoddard, 1987, p. 4)

---

[45]   The post-structural implications of Chartier's argument here are beyond the scope of this Introduction.

The history of the book has the capacity to recover 'the human presence in any recorded text' (McKenzie, 1999, p. 29),[46] but it is important not to replace one individual, the author, with another, whether printer or publisher: in nearly all cases, the production and distribution of books was a collaborative process. Moreover, as the making of books was a craft and the selling of books a trade, early modern printing workers, booksellers, bookbinders and others sought to group themselves into homogeneous or heterogeneous artisanal organizations just like any other early modern craft or trade. The most ubiquitous such organization of early modern Europe was the guild (known variously *Amt, gilde,* corporation, *laug, skrå* and, to further confuse matters, company) which, despite the extraordinary number of different shapes, structures, sizes and strengths in which it came, usually offered certain constant characteristics: regulation of training and labour, quality standardization, arbitration, welfare and conviviality.[47] A large proportion of the printers, booksellers and other ancillary craftsmen and tradesmen across Europe would have been members of guilds – ranging from the four separate Venetian guilds for printers and publishers, stationers, compositors, and type-founders to the general book-trade guilds of London (the Stationers' Company) and Antwerp, from the printing confraternities dedicated to St John in Barcelona, Madrid, Salamanca and Seville to the haphazard portmanteau 'companies' of English provincial towns where the epithet 'Stationers' might appear alongside up to ten different trades in a single organization (Gadd, 1999, pp. 113–16, 208–13).[48] However, apart from studies of the Stationers' Company, very few essays have considered the associational tendencies of the European book trade.

Aside from the bible, Natalie Zemon Davis's essay (Chapter 9) does not mention a single printed book by name or indeed consider at any length the actual books produced by the Lyonnaise printing journeymen who form its subject – and, as such, may seem out of place in a volume such as this. In fact, the distinctive nature of Davis's work is signalled by the essay's place of publication, title and opening paragraph, but such features reveal something more significant about the historiography of the history of the book since Febvre and Martin. With only a few exceptions, most English-speaking history-of-the-book essays have found their home either in bibliographical journals or collections, or in mainstream historical journals (here represented by *The Journal of Modern History, Past and Present, Historical Journal* and so on). English-speaking *economic* historians, by contrast, have not been particularly interested in the book trade despite (or perhaps even because of) the plethora of published data – notable exceptions being St Clair (2004) and Raven (2007). Consequently, Davis's work is rather different to the majority of history of the book scholarship in the English-speaking world.[49]

---

[46]   McKenzie here uses the term 'bibliography' (a term that, in his book, he redefines as 'the sociology of texts') rather than 'history of the book'. There are important definitional distinctions between these three terms but, for my immediate purpose here, 'history of the book' is adequate.

[47]   Early modern guild historiography is extensive, although only very rarely has it considered the book trade. For two recent contributions, see Gadd and Wallis (2006) and Epstein and Prak (2008).

[48]   The Stationers' Company excepted, guilds do not seem to feature at all in the standard English-language accounts of the European book trade beyond a brief discussion in Febvre and Martin (1976, pp. 140–41; see also p. 191) and, more honourably, several entries in *Bibliopolis* (van Delft and de Wolf, 2003).

[49]   It should be said that, for all its economic history trappings, this is not really an economic history essay: Davis's later work took her into cultural history and this essay is much more interested in cultural

However, that does not make it marginal or inconsequential; indeed, recovering the lives and careers of the men and women who made and sold books is a vital first step to understanding how printed books circulated and the impact that they had.[50] In this essay, Davis focuses on a craft organization, the Company of the Griffarins, formed by the journeymen printers of Lyon during the sixteenth century. Lyon was a large printing city: with over a hundred presses by the 1570s, it dwarfed the entire printing trade of England, for example. However, as elsewhere in sixteenth-century Europe, the Lyon book trade was becoming increasingly economically and occupationally stratified, with wealthy merchant-publishers sitting on the city's consulate while most of the city's printers were running 'modest establishments' (p. 199) with only a handful of employees. The emergence and success of the journeymen printers' company was driven not only by real economic grievances (principally wages and the 'food salary') but also by a strong sense of craft identity grounded in the tacit knowledge and skills peculiar to printing. Their rhetoric, as quoted by Davis, sought both to elevate the craft of printing ('"an excellent and noble calling"') and to distinguish it from other crafts and trades ('"we can't be compared to other artisans who work independently as they choose"' (p. 201)); the argument that making books was different and hence the book trade should receive special economic treatment was one that would be repeated across Europe in different forms throughout the next 500 years.

Davis's essay reminds us of the cooperative, collective and corporate (in its true sense) nature of the early modern book trade. Although guilds were a dominant organization model for early modern Europe, their role and power varied considerably. Lyon was one city where membership of a guild was not a requirement of anyone seeking to work or sell in, and this allowed the Company of Griffarins to meet the desire for a collective voice among the city's printing workforce and take advantage of the lack of a craft-specific guild overseeing the workforce's activity. The former is reflected in the Company's sophisticated and complex rituals and hierarchies which Davis describes in some detail, the latter helps explain the Company's cunning reappropriation of existing civic groups and bodies in order to mask its real activities, and both underwrote its evident success – through strikes and organized violence – in representing the city's printer journeymen during the sixteenth century.

Davis concludes her essay by contrasting the Lyonnaise experience with that of sixteenth-century London and suggesting that, while part of the difference lay with the strength of the Stationers' Company, it was through the London printers' incorporation of similar kinds of rituals from the Netherlands into the so-called 'printing chapel' (to which all the employees of a single printing-house belonged) that the trade managed to contain and hence defuse any similar impulses for labour agitation (see further Turner, 1957; Voet, 1961; Materné, 1994). This is an ingenious suggestion which may well have some truth in it but there are instructive difficulties about making such a comparison in the first place. London's printing workforce was much smaller than that of Lyon and the craft carried much less political and economic significance within the capital. There were also crucial structural differences: guilds were a fundamental part of London's economic, social and political life whereas, unlike much of

---

practice and identities than in the precise economics of the book trade.

[50]   Robert Darnton has done more than most to recover the lives and careers of printers and publishers as his essays 'What is the History of Books?' (2002) and '"What is the History of Books?" Revisited' (2007) make clear. For a critical view of this tendency as represented by both Darnton and D.F. McKenzie, see Sutherland (1988).

mainland Europe, early modern England never had a tradition of journeymen organizations (or indeed of 'wandering' journeymen such as we shall see in the next essay). Finally, London's printers *were* increasingly seeking to develop their own craft identity, a desire which almost succeeded in establishing a wholly separate printing organization in the 1660s (Gadd, 1999, pp. 190–97) . If nothing else, the significance of these differences underlines the perils of making any kind of international comparisons about the European book trade.

In 1582 or 1583, during one such moment of printer-related agitation in London, the printer John Wolfe declared defiantly: 'Luther was but one man, and reformed all [the] world for religion, and I am that one man, [who] must and will reforme the government in this trade' (*Transcript*, 1875–94, vol. II, p. 782). The conflation of book-trade activity with the religious revolution of the sixteenth century is hardly surprising given, as we have already seen, the important role printing played in the impact of the Reformation across Europe. However, it reminds us that the religion and printing overlapped not just in the form of books, but also in terms of the men (and women) who made and sold them.

In Chapter 10 Clive Griffin explores the hitherto little-considered Spanish and Portuguese Inquisitional records in search of members of the book trade: not to uncover their religious allegiances (interesting though they are) but to reconstruct their careers from the evidence they submitted as part of their defence.[51] His focus is a young French journeyman printer, Antonio de La Bastida, whose careless scepticism about the apparently miraculous recovery of Prince Carlos of Spain led to his arrest and interrogation by the Spanish Inquisition. La Bastida's career to date seems to have been remarkably itinerant, as he has been contracted to 17 presses in 13 different Spanish towns, but it was not particularly unusual: many French-born and French-trained printers spent the first part of their careers on the move from city to city (many of them finding work in Spain), while the spread of printing itself in the first half-century after Gutenberg was entirely due to such craft migration.[52] Griffin argues that '[t]he similarity of working practices in the printing industry throughout Europe meant that itinerant craftsmen found no difficulty in fitting in with the operation of any press' (p. 239), an intriguing observation that contrasts the broadly similar techniques of printing (compositorial practice aside)[53] with other manufacturing trades that often relied on localized and closely guarded knowledge about quality standards or technical practices (for example, in metal or cloth trades). Also, Spain proved an attractive option for young French craftsmen: there was a demand for labour, wages were relatively high and, unlike in France, there was no formal requirement of a completed apprenticeship. Griffin's research also reveals the strong craft solidarity so evident in sixteenth-century Lyon. Printing required close cooperation with other members of the printing house: La Bastida was a 'puller' – he had learnt 'the art of pulling the bar' (p. 228) – which meant he would have worked alongside the 'beater' whose job it was to re-ink the type between La Bastida's pulls of the press. Such literally close relationships,

---

[51]   Griffin's essay anticipated a monograph on the subject: *Journeymen-printers, heresy, and the inquisition in sixteenth-century Spain* (2005).

[52]   Journeymen in much of Europe were also traditionally forbidden from marrying until their journeymen 'stage' had been formally completed which, in its way, discouraged craftsmen from settling down until later in their careers.

[53]   As the layout (or 'lay') of the type cases (especially the lower case) depended on the frequency of letters used, these varied from language to language: see Gaskell (1969). There were also national idiosyncrasies: see Sayce (1979).

combined with peripatetic careers, created a cohesive and yet diffuse community: '[t]hese printing-workers all knew each other, news and gossip travelling rapidly among them from mouth to mouth or, on occasion, through the letters they sent each other' (p. 239). The only disruptions, as La Bastida discovered to his cost, came from 'quarrels over women, cards, or religion' (p. 237) – although only the last tends to provide the necessary documentary evidence that book historians seek.

D.F. McKenzie (Chapter 11) is also concerned with the realities of a printer's life, but his subject is practice rather than malpractice. This essay is one of the most important bibliographical essays to be published on the early modern English book trade but, to a reader unfamiliar with the debates and arguments to which McKenzie is responding, its ground-breaking, not to say iconoclastic, nature is not immediately apparent. Moreover, some of the specific points of discussion (for example, skeleton formes, press figures) along with the several pages of tabulated data may seem daunting to the non-specialist. Nonetheless, one does not need to follow the detail of McKenzie's argument in order to appreciate the wide-reaching nature of his conclusions.

In short, McKenzie is arguing (not for the only time in his career) for a reorientation of bibliographical method.[54] Very little is known about the actualities of early modern English printing house practice: there is only one detailed printing manual from the period (Moxon's *Mechanick Exercises*, already mentioned) and very few account books of printing houses survive (indeed, none for London prior to the eighteenth century); consequently, much bibliographical analysis depends solely on the evidence of the printed objects themselves. The problem is how general hypotheses about printing-house practice are thus constructed from this kind of evidence; the inductive method, McKenzie argues, is not a suitable approach for bibliography. Instead, bibliography should '[recognise] the present situation of multiple "probabilities" [that is, different suggestions of what may have happened in the printing house in any one case] as the desirable one and [regard] them as hypotheses to be tested *de*ductively' (p. 247); this both 'welcomes conjectures in the positive knowledge that such productive conditions [in the printing house] were extraordinarily complex and unpredictable' and 'insists that such conjectures be scrutinized with the greatest rigour and, if refuted, rejected' (p. 248). It may seem strange that an essay so focused on practice should begin with a meditation on 'scientific method' but, given the essay's ambitions, such a preamble is vital.

Central to McKenzie's argument is his challenge of a core bibliographical belief that there were 'normal' working patterns for early modern printing house. This belief means that, for example, if one has evidence for a particular rate of printing (so many sheets produced in an hour), this can then be used to calculate how long any particular work took to be printed. However, such a supposition is not supported by documentary evidence. Painstaking analysis of the archives of Cambridge University Press for the late seventeenth and eighteenth century and those of the eighteenth-century London printing house of William Bowyer reveals 'patterns ... of such an unpredictable complexity ... that no amount of inference from what we think of as bibliographical evidence could ever have led to their reconstruction' (p. 249) (see also McKenzie, 1966; *Bowyer Ledgers*, 1991). Little wonder, then, that McKenzie notes (almost in passing): 'I doubt that "normality", in any serious and extended sense, is a meaningful concept' (p. 246). With matters as fundamental to early modern English

---

[54] Most notably in *Bibliography and the Sociology of Texts* (1999).

bibliographical scholarship as rates of production (how many pieces of type could be set in an hour, how many sheets could be printed), the order and pattern of printing any single book (whether books were printed successively, one edition at a time, or concurrently; the order in which individual sheets were printed; the reliability of using 'skeleton formes' as a way of identifying particular workmen or presses and so on), McKenzie repeatedly sets the received bibliographical wisdom (mischievously characterized in his title as 'printers of the mind') against the 'supreme importance of primary evidence' (p. 302) and finds the former wanting every time.[55] McKenzie's tone may be measured, modest and even downbeat ('Bright lights will cast deep shadows ... Bibliography will simply have to prove itself adequate to conditions of far greater complexity than it has hitherto entertained' (p. 302)), but the implications of his argument for bibliography or history of the book, both of which regularly extrapolate from the printed object, are as profound as they are challenging.[56]

'at small expense ... in different parts of the world'

In terms of their physical features, books reveal much more about the process of their manufacture than their sale: apart from the often misinterpreted imprint (Shaaber, 1944; Blayney, 1997) and, occasionally, details of price (either printed or handwritten),[57] information about a book's sale usually has to be inferred either from provenance evidence (see Pearson, 1994) or, more implicitly, from the book's own design and form (large books, for example, cost more than smaller ones). Moreover, while early modern printing equipment and, in certain cases, entire printing houses have been preserved,[58] the same is not true of bookshops; in fact, relatively few detailed descriptions of early modern bookshops survive.[59] Booksellers' accounts (as distinct from publishers'), too, are few and far between.

The book trade has always been an international activity, and books (whether manuscript or print) crossed national borders, licitly or illicitly, on a regular basis throughout the early modern period. In some places, like Venice, there was a thriving export trade in books; for others, like London, the import of foreign books was a defining characteristic of the trade's activity (see Pollard and Ehrman, 1965; Barker, 1985b). As with all commodities able to bought and sold internationally, a crucial component of the international book trade was the trade fair, with Frankfurt being the most famous of all the early modern fairs that dealt in

---

[55]   McKenzie's contribution to recovering the primary evidence of relevance to the early modern English book trade is second to none: see his three separate volumes on the Stationers' Company apprentices (McKenzie, 1961, 1974, 1978) and McKenzie and Bell (2005), a comprehensive chronology of documents relating to the London book trade.

[56]   This is not to say that bibliographical scholarship must always be underwritten by archival evidence; McKenzie (2002) shows that one can 'read' a work's bibliographical 'codes' with remarkable results.

[57]   On retail prices of early modern English books, see Bennett (1950) and Johnson (1950).

[58]   The Plantin-Moretus Museum in Antwerp is the best example of a surviving early modern printing house; records and equipment also survive from the university presses of Oxford and Cambridge. See Voet (1969–72); Carter (1975); McKenzie (1966); and McKitterick (1992–2004).

[59]   Johns (1998, pp. 108–26), discusses bookshops (drawing on some mainland European portrayals). The layout and dimensions of London bookshops are described in Blayney (1990, 2000).

books. However, as John L. Flood notes in Chapter 12, Frankfurt was a latecomer to the world of printing (the first established printing house dates from 1530), and its spectacular rise to become the pre-eminent German publishing centre was relatively short-lived.[60] As a small but geographically, politically and commercially strategic city, Frankfurt had held an autumn fair from at least the thirteenth century; a spring or 'Lenten fair' also dated back into the medieval period. The fair always dealt in far more than just books, but from the mid-fifteenth century onwards books increasingly featured: in 1454, samples of Gutenberg's bible were on display. The French printer and publisher Henri Estienne II described the autumn fair in 1574 as "'the sum of all the fairs of the whole world'" (p. 328); however, by then, there was already 'second' fair devoted just to the book trade.

Books were (and remain) heavy and awkward objects to transport and, when shipped for commercial purposes, attracted tolls and fees. Nonetheless, attending international fairs was evidently crucial to becoming a successful international publisher or bookseller: the fair was a place to promote and sell one's latest publications (mostly, it seems, directly to booksellers), to stock up one's own holdings and to settle up accounts with other members of the trade. Large publishers maintained warehouses in the city, and many publishers and booksellers would attend in person.[61] However, one distinctive feature of the Frankfurt fair was the catalogues of books for sale, first issued privately and later through official channels.[62] There were many contemporary advantages to such listings: Georg Willer (who first produced catalogues based on stock available at the fair) used them to inform his own customers what he could purchase on their behalf, while in the early seventeenth century the Bodleian Library relied on them to guide future library acquisitions. For later scholars, these catalogues (although they list only about 20–25 per cent of books available at the fair and, for sound commercial reasons, focused primarily on books with a potential international market) are the nearest thing to an early modern *Books in Print*.

It is through the contraction of its international character that we can trace the decline of the Frankfurt book fair from the early seventeenth century onwards. The Thirty Years' War (1618–48) brought inevitable disruption to the German book trade and to international trade more generally; Frankfurt was itself besieged by the Swedish army in 1631 and never recovered its former position thereafter. Instead, Leipzig overtook it as the main German book fair, thriving well into the eighteenth century, although it never managed to achieve the same international profile as Frankfurt in its heyday.[63]

Frankfurt's changing fortunes underline the vicissitudes of being a European printer or publisher, but they also point to more fundamental changes in the nature of the European book trade. Ian Maclean's essay (Chapter 13) provides a fascinating companion piece to Flood's account by focusing specifically on one section of the international book market, the scholarly

---

[60]   The standard history is Dietz (1921).

[61]   John Norton, one of the wealthiest booksellers in England in the late sixteenth and early seventeenth century, regularly sent an employee, John Bill, to Frankfurt. See Barnard (2005, pp. 35–40).

[62]   Such catalogues could then be adapted for local markets: John Bill produced English versions between 1617 and 1628.

[63]   For an international perspective of these two fairs, Laeven (1992).

book, during a period that not only marked a 'crisis' in intellectual thought, but also saw a corresponding decline in the scholarly book market.[64]

Maclean's essay is, in many ways, a model history of the book account, in that it explicitly relates the intellectual to the material realities of the book trade: it investigates 'the economic conditions which may have contributed to intellectual decline' in order to show that

> ... the material and legal conditions governing publication promoted certain trends in the marketing and consumption of books which influenced conceptions of genre and contributed to the collapse ... of the boom in scholarly books in the 1620s. (p. 364)

Maclean begins with the apparent threefold increase in the output of scholarly books between the 1570s and the first three decades of the seventeenth century (based on the Frankfurt catalogues): does this indicate a change in readership, in taste, or merely in the size of print runs?[65] The economics of the trade reveal not only the interdependence between printers, publishers and booksellers as a means of spreading financial risks and maintaining lines of credit in a trade notorious for its slow returns, but also the genuine fear of piracy (that is, the reprinting of another publisher's work without permission, deliberately to undercut their price) which led many publishers to secure the official protection of imperial or royal privileges or licences.[66] These licences could be applied to whole genres of books produced by specific publishers but, crucially, were only applicable to new or improved editions; moreover, their cost meant that they only made commercial sense if the work was profitable.[67] Securing the financial success of these works was vital and, by analysing the catalogues issued by the Wechel press between 1579 and 1618 (see also Evans, 1975), Maclean identifies 'a number of academic preferences and objectives ... [although] it is difficult to separate such objectives from notions of profit' (pp. 370–71). He continues:

> As well as subscribing to the view that the truths of scholarship are eternal, publishers are obliged, by the system of licences and the nature of the market in which they operate – a market which requires that new and better editions are forever pressed on the potential purchasers of scholarly books – to accede to the view that there is continual improvement and expansion in the world of letters, and thereby to commit themselves both to an ideology of progress and, practically, to the view that publishing is an expanding economy. (p. 371)

Here, however, lay two irreconcilable desires: the humanist ideal of the 'perfect' library composed of definitively accurate works that were organized upon rational and intellectual

---

[64]   This essay has been reprinted, along with others, in Maclean (2009).

[65]   The last point has misled many an unwary historian. One large book with a substantial print-run can constitute the same proportion of a city's overall book production as dozens of very short works in small print-runs. It is this, for example, which helps explain the spectacular rise in editions in England in the early 1640s even though the productive capacity of the London book trade as a whole had not increased by anything like as much.

[66]   Book trade privileges were a Europe-wide phenomenon, although they developed and adapted according to local conditions. See Armstrong (1990, pp. 1–20), which provides a survey of European practice. However, for an important corrective to previous accounts of English privileges (with implications for the rest of Europe), see Grant Ferguson (2004).

[67]   As Maclean notes, the rhetoric of these licences strikingly juxtaposes the intellectual value of the book with the commercial cost of its production.

principles ran counter to the realities of successful publishing, where the achievement of a 'perfect' edition would undermine the commercial imperative of producing new editions to receive privileges and where books were classified primarily according to commercial pragmatism.[68]

'Survival rate' (or, more lugubriously, 'loss rate') has already been mentioned in this Introduction: the proportion of printed items that have now been 'lost' (a catch-all euphemism that, in most cases, means either deliberate or accidental destruction or disposal).[69] The word 'rate' is misleading in that it implies the possibility of identifying a standard rate of loss for early modern books, whereas the survival of any single copy of a book depends in practice on a unique combination of contingencies, only some of which are linked to the book's content (as nowadays, certain works are much more disposable) and form (larger books, generally speaking, survive better than smaller ones). Moreover, the paucity of reliable information about print-runs for any single edition or, indeed, the number of surviving copies makes determining any precise rate difficult. However, by cross-referencing the detailed records of the Stationers' Company (see also Myers, 1990) with the relevant entries in Donald Wing's *Short-title catalogue...1641–1700* (1982–98), John Barnard (Chapter 14) demonstrates for certain popular genres of works, published by the Company in very large numbers, just how few copies survive.[70] The fact that of 84,000 copies of primers printed in London in the financial year 1676–77 only one copy is known to survive serves as a salutary reminder not only that scholars are only able to examine a small fraction of the printed material that was produced in the period but also that, in many cases, the printed materials most familiar to early modern society are those that are least likely to have survived to the present day.[71]

'it is possible to possess a great number of books'

Print and manuscript, both as processes and as products, coexisted throughout the early modern period (McKitterick, 2004; also Love, 1993 and Beal, 1998 on scribal culture in England). Early printed books looked, deliberately and meticulously, like manuscripts and, as we have seen earlier, even print's innovation may in fact be a reappropriation of earlier forms. Libraries did not distinguish between print and manuscript books until the sixteenth century but, even then, they were not catalogued separately until the eighteenth century. Moreover, there was considerable slippage between print and manuscript: not only, as we shall see, did readers annotate books, but an important part of many printers' output were printed items – forms, indentures, bills, tickets and so on – that required scribal intervention (see, for example, Slavin, 1982; Stallybrass *et al.*, 2004).

---

[68] On the implications of library organization, see Chartier (1994).

[69] On the multipurpose nature of books, see Donaldson (1998). The Reformation, too, wrought its own bibliographical destruction – see, for example, Ramsay (2004).

[70] For explorations of the 'popular' press, see Chartier and Lüsebrink (1996); Capp (1979); and Watt (1991).

[71] This is even more applicable to 'jobbing' printing – the printing of notices, proclamations, posters and so on for specific customers – which made up a substantial part of many printers' work. As nowadays, it is extremely rare for such ephemera to have survived: see Andrews (2007). For a case-study of the varied work that an early modern printing house took on, see Bellettini (1993).

Paul Saenger's essay (Chapter 15) provides further evidence for why we should be wary of overprivileging the arrival of print in Europe. For readers of printed texts, the impact of the new technology was 'specific but limited' (p. 390) in comparison with other earlier transformations such as the differentiation of upper and lower cases, the introduction of word spacing (which allowed for silent reading), and changes in punctuation (Saenger, 1997; Parkes, 1992, Cavallo and Chartier, 1999). Nonetheless, as Saenger demonstrates, printing *did* make a difference to the reading experience. First, it rationalized – and so limited – the plurality of ligatures and abbreviations which in manuscript production saved time and space but in printing militated against the efficacy of using only individual sorts; the simplification and standardization of abbreviations also broadened a work's potential readership. Second, while print did not mark an advance in legibility *per se*, its normalizing imperative meant that 'ordinary books' that, in manuscript, would be copied in a much lower-quality hand were now as legible as more elevated manuscript books. Third, it enhanced what Saenger terms 'metalinguistic consciousness' (p. 397), mostly visibly in the development of new print-specific punctuation, including the reappropriation of existing forms such as parentheses, and in the standardization of foliation and, from the late fifteenth century, pagination. The significance of this last point should not be underestimated: leaf numbering, combined with a table of contents, meant that a reader 'did not require a prolonged apprenticeship in the arcane and often highly complex principles of textual division peculiar to each of scholasticism's varied genres of text' (p. 404). Taken together, all these developments meant that one did not need to be an 'expert' reader in order to read printed books.

Moreover, it was now possible to navigate printed books in different, easier ways. Erasmus, for example, cited page numbers in his correspondence about books as well in the alphabetical tables, indices and errata of the printed books he wrote, allowing for a increasingly sophisticated means of cross-referencing between texts. The numbering of biblical verses first appears in a printed book of 1496, a convention that would later be criticized by John Locke as having 'chop'd and minc'd' the biblical text into 'loose Sentences' in such a way that reading itself was transformed: 'Scripture crumbled into Verses, which quickly turn into independent Aphorisms' (quoted in McKenzie, 1999, p. 56; see also Stallybrass, 2002). This reorientation of the textual world took on more material manifestations. 'Finding tabs' – physical attachments to leaves to allow the quick identification of a specific section – proliferated while the increasing demand for readier and easier consultation of individual volumes led to a simple but dramatic shift in institutional library practice: the shelving of books vertically rather than horizontally.

Reading, especially silent reading, is an immaterial act; it leaves no trace upon the object read.[72] Consequently, while, as Saenger demonstrates, it is possible to recover the parameters of a reading experience through sensitive analysis of the material book, an individual's actual reading experience is much more elusive. On occasion, however, the combination of annotations within books and archival evidence outside them can reveal the experiences of a real early modern reader, as Lisa Jardine and Anthony Grafton (Chapter 16) discover.[73] The reader was the English writer Gabriel Harvey, but the aim of Jardine and Grafton's essay is

---

[72]   For early modern views on the physiology of reading, see Johns (1998).

[73]   The book cited in footnote 1 of this essay is as yet unpublished. For other single-reader case-studies, see Sherman (1995) and Sharpe (2000).

not so much to recover Harvey's specific reading habits, but to demonstrate that his reading was *active*:

… not just the energy which must be acknowledged as accompanying the intervention of the scholar/reader with his text, nor the cerebral effort involved in making the text the reader's own, but reading as intended to *give rise to something else* … It was conducted under conditions of strenuous attentiveness; it employed job-related equipment (both machinery and techniques) designed for efficient absorption and processing of the matter read; it was normally carried out in the company of a colleague or student; and was a public performance, rather than a private meditation, in its aims and character. (pp. 451–52)

The 'public' nature of such reading in particular may seem strange to us who are used to solitary, silent and affective reading but, as Jardine and Grafton show, active reading could not only serve important political purposes, but also shape one's own personal reading: 'critical reading, skilful annotation and active appropriation emerge as the central skills…of the intellectual *tout court*' (p. 497).

The work in question was Livy's history of Rome, published in Basle in 1555. Harvey's own copy of this work[74] contains dense annotations covering a period of at least 20 years of reading, and from this it is clear that Harvey acted as a 'facilitator' (p. 456) of the work for the courtier Philip Sidney, using the text as a source of political advice, and also reread sections with other influential individuals as well as on his own. In each case, the reading was for a specific purpose, whether pragmatic, moral, political, philosophical or personal. Jardine and Grafton trace, in considerable detail, Harvey's complex and shifting position in relation to the work, but tease out his own personal preferences for stylish and aphoristic writing: 'Harvey read not simply to reflect, boil down and imitate, but also to savour, speculate and admire' (p. 490).

Books, however, could serve other purposes beyond mere reading, as the volume's final essay (by David Cressy) illuminates. While books have a material versatility that tends towards their own destruction, given the manifold savoury and unsavoury uses to which paper and bindings could be put, certain kinds of books, principally bibles, took on talismanic qualities in the early modern period (Donaldson, 1998). Oaths were sworn upon bibles, family births were inscribed within them, and they might be carried, brandished, kissed or, in the case of the *Book of Common Prayer* in an Edinburgh service of 1638, thrown (and so help precipitate civil war). Bibles were used to heal the sick (fanning pages on to faces or placing volumes under pillows) or, for the desperate, to offer spiritual guidance through the chance selection of a passage (bibliomancy or *sortes Virgilianae*). Books had meanings far beyond the words on pages (see further Watson, 2007).

'Hitherto, the Author has had it all his own way'

These bold words of the nineteenth-century scholar and bibliographer, Edward Arber, highlight the one obvious lacunae of this volume, this Introduction, and, strikingly, the 1515 papal decree: the author (*Transcript*, 1875–94, vol. I, p. xiii). There were, of course, authors

---

[74]   The copy was on deposit at Princeton University Library at the time of the essay's writing; the library subsequently purchased it from the estate of the previous owner.

in early modern Europe, even in the Foucauldian sense of the 'author-function' (Foucault, 1984), and many of them developed close and effective working relationships with individual printers and publishers. Some became national or even international 'print-celebrities', capable of selling books solely by their name on the title page.[75] Conceptions of authorial responsibility (intellectually or legally), ownership (the right of a creator of a work to control its dissemination by print) and remuneration (earning directly from the sale of one's work) were being articulated and explored in the sixteenth and seventeenth centuries but, for all this, the systematic legal and economic professionalization of the author belongs more to the Enlightenment than the early modern period.[76] While authors do obviously play a role in the history of early modern Europe, they were just one part of a complex series of processes and transactions along with scribes, compositors, printers, publishers, booksellers and readers:

> The book becomes ... an object to be preserved and catalogued for itself, thus making the fact of publication culturally significant no matter through what means or in whose interest it first came about. The book becomes also an object to be collected as a potentially valuable possession, as a token of social or intellectual prestige, as an item of exchange, and not just the physical manifestation of a message to be consumed by an intellect. (Maclean, this volume, p. 377)

References

Andrews, Martin (2007), 'The Importance of Ephemera', in Simon Eliot and Jonathan Rose (eds), *A Companion to the History of the Book*, Oxford: Blackwell, pp. 434–50.

Armstrong, Elizabeth (1990), *Before Copyright: The French Book-Privilege System 1498–1526* (Cambridge: Cambridge University Press.

Bacon, Francis (1994), *Novum Organon*, trans. and ed. Peter Urbach and John Gibson (Chicago: University of Chicago Press.

Barker, Nicolas (1985a), *Aldus Manutius and the Development of Greek Script and Type in the Fifteenth Century*, Sandy Hook, CT: Chiswick. Second edn, Bronx, NY: Fordham University Press, 1992.

Barker, Nicolas (1985b), 'The Importation of Books into England 1460–1526', in Herbert G. Göpfert *et al.* (eds), *Beiträge zur Geschichte des Buchwesens im konfeßionellen Zeitalter*, Wiesbaden: Kommission bei O. Harrassowitz, pp. 251–66.

Barker, Nicolas (1992), 'The Trade and Manufacture of Paper before 1800', in Simonetta Cavaciocchi (ed.), *Produzione e commercio della carta e del libro secc. XIII–XVIII*, Firenze: Le Monnier, pp. 213–20.

Barnard, John (2005),'The Financing of the Authorised Version 1610–1612: Robert Barker and "Combining" and "Sleeping" Stationers', *Publishing History*, **57**, pp. 5–52.

Barnard, John, McKenzie, D.F. and Bell, Maureen (eds) (2002), *The Cambridge History of the Book in Britain. Volume IV: 1557–1695*, Cambridge: Cambridge University Press.

Baron, Sabrina Alcorn, Lindquist, Eric N. and Shevlin, Eleanor F. (eds) (2007), *Agent of Change: Print Culture Studies after Elizabeth L. Eisenstein*, Amherst and Boston: University of Massachusetts Press.

Baumann, Gerd (1986), *The Written Word: Literacy in Transition* (Oxford: Clarendon Press.

[75] Erasmus being probably the best example. For ways in which print could reanimate authors from previous generations, see Gillespie (2006).

[76] The principal case in point being authorial copyright: see, for example, Loewenstein (2002) and Rose (1993).

Beal, Peter (1998), *In Praise of Scribes: Manuscripts and their Makers in Seventeenth-century England*, Oxford: Clarendon Press.

Bell, Bill (2002), 'English Studies and the History of the Book', *European English Messenger*, **11**, pp. 27–33.

Bell, Maureen (1996), 'Women in the English Book Trades 1557–1700', *Leipziger Jahrbuch zur Buchgeschichte*, **6**, pp. 13–45.

Bellettini, Pierangelo (1993), 'Publishing in the Provinces: Printing Houses in Romagna in the 17th Century', in Denis V. Reidy (ed.), *The Italian Book 1465–1800*, London: The British Library, pp. 291–322.

Bennett, H.S.(1950), 'Notes on English Retail Book-prices, 1480–1560', *The Library*, 5th ser., **5**, pp. 172–78.

Bidwell, John (1998), 'The Study of Paper as Evidence, Artefact and Commodity', in Peter Davison (ed.), *The Book Encompassed: Studies in Twentieth-century Bibliography*, New Castle, DE and Winchester: Oak Knoll Press, pp. 69–82.

Bland, Mark (1999), 'The London Book-Trade in 1600', in David Scott Kastan (ed.), *A Companion to Shakespeare*, Oxford: Blackwell, pp. 450–63.

Blayney, Peter W.M. (1990), *The Bookshops in Paul's Cross Churchyard*, London: The Bibliographical Society.

Blayney, Peter W.M. (1994), 'The Numbers Game: Appraising the Revised *STC*', *Papers of the Bibliographical Society of America*, **88**, pp. 353–407.

Blayney, Peter W.M. (1997),'The Publication of Playbooks', in John D. Cox and David Scott Kastan (eds), *A New History of Early English Drama*, New York: Columbia University Press, pp. 383–422.

Blayney, Peter W.M. (2000), 'John Day and the Bookshop That Never Was', in Lena Cowen Orlin (ed.), *Material London, ca. 1600*, Philadelphia: University of Pennsylvania Press, pp. 322–43.

Boghardt, Martin and Schneider, Cornelia (1990), 'Gutenberg – die Technick und der Erfinder', in Paul Raabe (ed.), *Gutenberg: 550 Jahre Buchdruck in Europa*, Weinheim: VCH Acta Humanoria, pp. 24–52.

The Bowyer Ledgers (1991), ed. Keith Maslen and John Lancaster, London and New York: The Bibliographical Society.

The Cambridge History of Libraries in Britain and Ireland (2006), ed. Peter Hoare *et al.*, 3 vols, Cambridge: Cambridge University Press.

The Cambridge History of the Book in Britain (1997–), Cambridge: Cambridge University Press.

Capp, B.S. (1979), *Astrology and the Popular Press: English Almanacs, 1500–1800*, London: Faber & Faber.

Carter, Harry (1969), *A View of Early Typography up to about 1600*, Oxford: Oxford University Press.

Carter, Harry (1975), *A History of the Oxford University Press. Volume I: To the Year 1780*, Oxford: Oxford University Press.

Cavallo, Guglielmo and Chartier, Roger (eds) (1999), *A History of Reading in the West*, trans. Lydia Cochrane, Amherst: University of Massachusetts Press.

Chartier, Roger (ed.) (1989), 'The Practical Impact of Writing', in *A History of Private Life: III: Passions of the Renaissance*, trans. Arthur Goldhammer, Cambridge, MA: Harvard University Press, pp. 111–59.

Chartier, Roger (1994), *The Order of Books: Readers, Authors, and Libraries in Europe between the Fourteenth and Eighteenth Centuries*, trans. Lydia G. Cochrane, Cambridge : Cambridge University Press.

Chartier, Roger and Lüsebrink, Hans- Jürgen (eds) (1996), *Colportage et lecture populaire: imprimés de large circulation en Europe: XVIe–XIXe siècles*, Paris: IMEC Ed.

Clair, Colin (1976), *A History of European Printing*, London and New York: Academic Press.

Clegg, Cyndia Susan (1997), *Press Censorship in Elizabethan England*, Cambridge: Cambridge University Press.

Clegg, Cyndia Susan (2001a), 'Review Essay: History of the Book: An Undisciplined Discipline?' *Renaissance Quarterly*, **54**, pp. 221–45.

Clegg, Cyndia Susan (2001b), *Press Censorship in Jacobean England*, Cambridge: Cambridge University Press.

Clegg, Cyndia Susan (2008), *Press Censorship in Caroline England*, Cambridge: Cambridge University Press.

Crain, Patricia (2007), 'New Histories of Literacy', in Simon Eliot and Jonathan Rose (eds), *A Companion to the History of the Book*, Oxford: Blackwell, pp. 467–79.

Darnton, Robert (2002), 'What is the History of Books?', in David Finkelstein and Alistair McCleery (eds), *The Book History Reader*, London: Routledge, pp. 9–26. First published in 1982.

Darnton, Robert (2007), '"What is the History of Books?" Revisited', *Modern Intellectual History*, **4**(3), pp. 495–508.

Davies, Martin *Aldus Manutius: printer and publisher of Renaissance Venice* (London, 1995).

Decrees of the Ecumenical Councils (1990), ed. Norman P. Tanner, 2 vols, London and Georgetown, WA: Georgetown University Press.

Dietz, Alexander (1921), *Zur Geschichte der Frankfurter Büchermesse 1462–1792*, Frankfurt-am-Main.

Donaldson, Ian (1998), 'The Destruction of the Book', *Book History*, **1**, pp. 1–10.

Dooley, Brendan and Baron, Sabrina (eds) (2001), *Politics of Information in Early Modern Europe*, London: Routledge.

Duke, A.C. and Tamse, C.A. (eds) (1987), *Too Mighty To be Free: Censorship and the Press in Britain and the Netherlands*, Zutphen: De Walburg Pers.

The Edinburgh History of the Book in Scotland (2007), Edinburgh: Edinburgh University Press.

Eisenstein, Elizabeth (1966), 'Clio and Chronos: An Essay on the Making and Breaking of History-book Time', *History and Theory*, **6**, pp. 36–64.

Eisenstein, Elizabeth (1969), 'The Advent of Printing and the Problem of the Renaissance', *Past and Present*, **45**, pp. 19–89.

Eisenstein, Elizabeth (1970), 'The Advent of Printing in Current Historical Literature: Notes and Comments on an Elusive Transformation', *American Historical Review*, **75**(3), pp. 727–43.

Eisenstein, Elizabeth (1971), 'A Reply', *Past and Present*, **52**, pp. 140–44.

Eisenstein, Elizabeth (1994), *The Printing Press as an Agent of Change*, Cambridge: Cambridge University Press. First published in 2 vols in 1979.

Eisenstein, Elizabeth (1983), *The Printing Revolution in Early Modern Europe*, Cambridge: Cambridge University Press.

Eisenstein, Elizabeth (1985), 'On the Printing Press as an Agent of Change', in David R. Olson, Nancy Torrance and Angela Hildyard (eds), *Literacy, Language, and Learning*, Cambridge: Cambridge University Press, pp. 19–33.

Epstein, S.R. and Prak, Maarten (eds) (2008), *Guilds, Innovation and the European Economy, 1400–1800*, Cambridge: Cambridge University Press.

Evans, J.W. (1975), 'The Wechel Presses: Humanism and Calvinism in Central Europe 1572–1627', *Past & Present*, Supplement 2, pp. 1–74.

Febvre, Lucien and Martin, Henri-Jean (1976), *The Coming of the Book: The Impact of Printing 1450–1800*, ed. Geoffrey Nowell-Smith and David Wootton, trans. David Gerard More, London: Verso. Reprinted in paperback 1990. First published in 1958 as *L'apparition du livre*, Paris: Les Editions Albin Miche.

Finkelstein, David and Alistair McCleery (2002), *The Book History Reader*, London: Routledge.

Finkelstein, David and McCleery, Alistair (2005), *An Introduction to Book History*, London: Routledge.

Foucault, Michel (1984), 'What Is an Author?', in *The Foucault Reader*, ed. Paul Rabinow, New York: Pantheon, pp. 101–20.

Fox, Adam (2002), *Oral and Literate Culture in England, 1500–1700*, Oxford: Oxford University Press.

Fox, Adam and Woolf. D.R. (eds) (2002), *The Spoken Word: Oral Culture in Britain, 1500–1850*, Manchester: Manchester University Press.

Gadd, Ian Anders (1999),'"Being like a Field": Corporate Identity in the Stationers' Company 1557–1684', unpublished D.Phil., University of Oxford.

Gadd, Ian A. and Wallis, Patrick (eds) (2006), *Guilds and Association in Europe, 900–1900*, London: Centre for Metropolitan History, University of London.

Gaskell, Philip (1969), 'The Lay of the Case', *Studies in Bibliography*, **22**, pp. 125–42.

Gaskell, Philip (1972), *A New Introduction to Bibliography*, Oxford: Oxford University Press.

Gillespie, Alexandra (2006), *Print Culture and the Medieval Author: Chaucer, Lydgate, and their Nooks 1473–1557*, Oxford: Oxford University Press.

Gillespie, Alexandra (2007), 'The History of the Book', *New Medieval Literatures*, **9**, pp. 245–86.

Gilmont, Jean-François (ed.) (1998), *The Reformation and the Book*, trans. Karin Maag, Aldershot: Ashgate.

Gilmont, Jean-François (2003), *Le livre et ses secrets*, Geneva and Louvain: Librairie Droz.

Gilmont, Jean-François (2005), *Le livre réformé au XVIe siècle*, Paris: Bibliothèque Nationale de France.

Grafton, Anthony, Eisenstein, Elizabeth L and Johns, Adrian (2002), 'AHR Forum: How Revolutionary was the Print Revolution?', *American Historical Review*, **107**(1), pp. 84–128.

Grant Ferguson, Meraud (2004), '"In Recompense of his Labours and Inuencyon": Early Sixteenth-century Book Trade Privileges and the Birth of Literary Property in England', *Transactions of the Cambridge Bibliographical Society*, **13**, pp. 14–32.

Greetham, D.C. (1994), *Textual Scholarship: An Introduction*, New York and London: Routledge.

Grendler, Paul F. (1977), *The Roman Inquisition and the Venetian Press, 1540–1605*, Princeton, NJ: Princeton University Press.

Grendler, Paul F. (1988), 'Printing and Censorship', in Quentin Skinner and Eckhard Kessler (eds), *The Cambridge History of Renaissance Philosophy*, Cambridge: Cambridge University Press, pp. 25–53.

Griffin, Clive (2005), *Journeymen-printers, Heresy, and the Inquisition in Sixteenth-century Spain*, Oxford: Oxford University Press.

Harris, Michael H. (1995), *History of Libraries in the Western World* (4th edn), Metuchen, NJ and London: Scarecrow Press.

Hellinga, Lotte (2007), 'The Gutenberg Revolution', in Simon Eliot and Jonathan Rose (eds), *A Companion to the History of the Book*, Oxford: Blackwell, pp. 207–19.

Hill, Christopher (1985–86), 'Censorship and English Literature', in *The Collected Essays of Christopher Hill*, Brighton: Harvester Press, pp. 32–71.

Hirsch, Rudolph (1973), 'Bulla Super Impressione Librorum, 1515', *Gutenberg Jahrbuch*, pp. 248–51.

Howsam, Leslie (2006), *Old Books and New Histories: An Orientation to Studies in Book and Print Culture*, Toronto: University of Toronto Press.

Index Aureliensis: catalogus librorum sedecimo saeculo impressorum (1965–), Baden Baden: Aureliae Aquensis.

Johns, Adrian (1998), *The Nature of the Book: Print and Knowledge in the Making*, Chicago and London: University of Chicago Press.

Johnson, A.F. (1966), *Type Designs: Their History and Development*, London: Andre Deutsch.

Johnson, Francis R (1950), 'Notes on English Retail Book-prices 1550–1640', *The Library*, 5th ser., **5**, pp. 83–112.

Kapp, Friedrich and Goldfriedrich, Johann (1886–1913), *Geschichte des deutschen Buchhandels*, 4 vols, Leipzig.

Kapr, Albert (1987), *Johannes Gutenberg: Persönlichkeit und Leistung*, München: C.H. Beck.

Kapr, Albert (1996), *Johann Gutenberg: The Man and his Invention*, trans. Douglas Martin, Aldershot: Ashgate.

Laeven, A.H. (1992), 'The Frankfurt and Leipzig Book Fairs and the History of the Dutch Book Trade in the Seventeenth and Eighteenth Centuries', in C. Berkvens-Stevelinck *et al.* (eds), *Le magasin de l'univers: The Dutch Republic as the Centre of the European Book Trade*, Leiden: E.J. Brill, pp. 185–97.

Lenkey, Susan V. (1975), 'Printers' Wives in the Age of Humanism', *Gutenberg Jahrbuch*, pp. 331–37.

Loewenstein, Joseph (2002), *The Author's Due: Printing and the Prehistory of Copyright*, Chicago: University of Chicago Press.

Love, Harold (1993), *Scribal Publication in Seventeenth-century England*, Oxford: Clarendon Press.

McDonald, Peter D. (2004), 'Discipline Envy and Book History', *European English Messenger*, **13**, pp. 51–56.

McKenzie, D.F. (1961), *Stationers' Company Apprentices 1605–40*, Charlottesville: Bibliographical Society of the University of Virginia.

McKenzie, D.F. (1966), *The Cambridge University Press, 1696–1712: A Bibliographical Study*, Cambridge: Cambridge University Press.

McKenzie, D.F. (1974), *Stationers' Company Apprentices 1641–1700*, Oxford: Oxford Bibliographical Society.

McKenzie, D.F. (1978), *Stationers' Company Apprentices 1701–1800*, Oxford: Oxford Bibliographical Society.

McKenzie, D.F. (1999), *Bibliography and the Sociology of Texts*, Cambridge: Cambridge University Press.

McKenzie, D.F. (2002), 'Typography and Meaning: The Case of William Congreve', in Peter D. McDonald and Michael F. Suarez SJ (eds), *Making Meaning: 'Printers of the Mind' and Other Essays*, Amherst: University of Massachusetts Press, pp. 198–236.

McKenzie, D.F. and Bell, Maureen (2005), *A Chronology and Calendar of Documents Relating to the London Book Trade 1641–1700*, 3 vols, Oxford: Oxford University Press.

McKitterick David (1992–2004), *A History of Cambridge University Press*, 3 vols, Cambridge: Cambridge University Press.

McKitterick, David (2003), *Print, Manuscript and the Search for Order: The Uses of Script and Print, 1300–1700*, Cambridge: Cambridge University Press.

Maclean, Ian (2009), *Learning and the Market Place: Essays in the History of the Early Modern Book*, Leiden: Brill Academic Publishers.

Martin, Henri-Jean and Chartier, Roger (eds) (1982–86), *Histoire de l'édition française*, Paris: Promodis. Second edn, Paris : Fayard, 1989–91.

Materné, Jan (1994), 'Chapel members in the Workplace: Tension and Teamwork in the Printing Trades in the Seventeenth and Eighteenth Centuries', *International Review of Social History*, **39**, Supplement 2, pp. 53–82.

Mignolo, Walter D. (1995), *The Darker Side of the Renaissance: Literacy, Territoriality, and Colonization*, Ann Arbor: University of Michigan Press.

Milton, John (1644), *Aeropagitica*, London.

More, Thomas (1995), *Utopia*, ed. George M. Logan and Robert M. Adams, Cambridge: Cambridge University Press.

Morison, Stanley (1972), *Politics and Script*, ed. Nicolas Barker, Oxford: Clarendon Press.

Mosley, James (2007), 'Fallen and Threaded Types', *Typefoundry: Documents for the History of Type and Letterforms*, at: http://typefoundry.blogspot.com/2007_06_01_archive.html (accessed 11 July 2008).

Moxon, Joseph (1962), *Mechanick Exercises on the Whole Art of Printing* (2nd edn), ed. Herbert Davis and Harry Carter, Oxford: Oxford University Press.

Myers, Robin (1990), *The Stationers' Company Archive 1554–1984*, Winchester: St Paul's Bibliographies.

Olson, David R., Torrance, Nancy and Hildyard, Angela (eds) (1985), *Literacy, Language, and Learning*, Cambridge: Cambridge University Press.

Ong, Walter J. (1982), *Orality and Literacy: The Technologizing of the Word*, London: Methuen Press.

The Oxford History of the Irish Book (2006–), Oxford: Oxford University Press.

Parker, Deborah (1996), 'Women in the Book Trade in Italy, 1475–1620', *Renaissance Quarterly*, **49**(3), pp. 509–41.

Parkes, M.B. (1992), *Pause and Effect: An Introduction to the History of Punctuation in the West*, Aldershot: Ashgate.

Patterson, Annabel (1984), *Censorship and Interpretation: The Conditions of Writing and Reading in Early Modern England*, Madison: University of Wisconsin Press.

Pearson, David (1994), *Provenance Research in Book History: A Handbook*, London: The British Library.

Pollard, Graham and Ehrman, Albert (1965), *The Distribution of Books by Catalogue from the Invention of Printing to A.D. 1800 Based on Material in the Broxbourne Library*, Cambridge: Roxburghe Club.

Pratt, Stephen (2003), 'The Myth of Identical Types: A Study of Printing Variations from Handcast Gutenberg Type', *Journal of the Printing Historical Society,* new ser., **6**, pp. 7–17.

Rabb, 'Theodore K. (1971), 'The Advent of Printing and the Problem of the Renaissance: A Comment', *Past and Present*, **52**, pp. 135–40.

Ramsay, Nigel (2004), '"The Manuscripts flew about like Butterflies": The Break-Up of English Libraries in the Sixteenth Century', in James Raven (ed.), *Lost Libraries: The Destruction of Great Book Collections since Antiquity*, Basingstoke: Palgrave Macmillan, pp. 125–44.

Raven, James (2007), *The Business of Books: Booksellers and the English Book Trade*, New Haven, CT and London: Yale University Press.

Raymond, Joad (ed.) (2006), *News Networks in Seventeenth-century Britain and Europe*, London: Routledge.

Rose, Mark (1993), *Authors and Owners: The Invention of Copyright*, Cambridge, MA: Harvard University Press.

Saenger, Paul (1997), *Space Between Words: The Origins of Silent Reading*, Stanford, CA: Stanford University Press.

St Clair, William (2004), *The Reading Nation in the Romantic Period*, Cambridge: Cambridge University Press.

Sayce, R.A. (1979), *Compositorial Practices and the Localization of Printed Books, 1530–1800*, Oxford: Oxford Bibliographical Society.

Shaaber, M.A. (1944), 'The Meaning of the Imprint in Early Printed Books', *The Library*, 4th ser., **24**, pp. 120–41.

Sharpe, Kevin (2000), *Reading Revolutions: The Politics of Reading in Early Modern England*, New Haven, CT and London: Yale University Press.

Sherman, William H. (1995), *John Dee: The Politics of Reading and Writing in the English Renaissance*, Amherst: University of Massachusetts Press.

Siebert, Frederick Seaton (1965), *Freedom of the Press in England 1476–1776: The Rise and Decline of Government Control*, Urbana: University of Illinois Press.

Slavin, Arthur J. (1982), 'The Tudor Revolution and the Devil's Art: Bishop Bonner's Printed Forms', in Delloyd J. Guth and John W. McKenna (eds), *Tudor Rule and Revolution: Essays for G.R. Elton from his American Friends*, Cambridge: Cambridge University Press, pp. 3–23.

Stallybrass, Peter (2002), 'Books and Scrolls: Navigating the Bible', in Jennifer Andersen and Elizabeth Sauer (eds), *Books and Readers in Early Modern England*, Philadelphia: University of Pennsylvania Press, pp. 42–79.

Stallybrass Peter *et al.* (2004), 'Hamlet's Tables and the Technologies of Writing in Renaissance England' *Shakespeare Quarterly*, **55**(4), pp. 379–419.

Steinberg, S.H. (1996), *Five Hundred Years of Printing* (rev. edn), London: Oak Knoll Press.

Stoddard, Roger E. (1987), 'Morphology and the Book from an American Perspective', *Printing History*, **17**, pp. 2–14.

Suarez SJ, Michael F. (2003–04), 'Historiographical Problems and Possibilities in Book History and National Histories of the Book', *Studies in Bibliography*, **56**, pp. 141–70.

Suarez SJ, Michael F. (2009), 'Towards a Bibliometric Analysis of the Surviving Record, 1701–1800', in Michael F. Suarez SJ and Michael L. Turner (eds), *The Cambridge History of the Book in Britain. Volume V: 1695–1830*,Cambridge: Cambridge University Press, pp. 39–65.

Sutherland, John (1988), 'Publishing History: A Hole at the Centre of Literary Sociology', *Critical Inquiry*, **14**, pp. 574–89.

Tanselle, G. Thomas (2002), *Introduction to Bibliography: Seminar Syllabus* Charlottesville, VA: Book Arts Press.

To the High Court of Parliament: The Humble Remonstrance of the Company of Stationers (London, 1643).

A Transcript of the Registers of the Company of Stationers 1554–1640 AD (1875–94), ed. Edward Arber, 5 vols, London and Birmingham.

Turner, Philip J. (1957), 'The Origins of the Printer's Chapel', *Gutenberg Jahrbuch*, pp. 350–54.

van Delft, Marieke and de Wolf, Clemens (eds) (2003), *Bibliopolis: History of the Printed Book in the Netherlands*, Zwolle: Koninklijke Bibliotheek.

van Vliet, Rietje (2007), 'Print and Public in Europe 1600–1800', in Simon Eliot and Jonathan Rose (eds), *A Companion to the History of the Book*, Oxford: Blackwell, pp. 247–58.

Voet, Léon (1961), 'The Printers' Chapel in the Plantinian House', *The Library,* 5th ser., **15**, pp. 1–14.

Voet, Léon (1969–72), *The Golden Compasses: A History and Evaluation of the Printing and Publishing Activities of the Officina Plantiniana at Antwerp*, 2 vols, Amsterdam: Van Gendt.

Watson, Rowan (2007), 'Some Non-textual Uses of Books', in Simon Eliot and Jonathan Rose (eds), *A Companion to the History of the Book*, Oxford: Blackwell, pp. 480–92.

Watt, Tessa (1991), *Cheap Print and Popular Piety, 1550–1640*, Cambridge: Cambridge University Press.

Weedon, Alexis (2007), 'The Uses of Quantification', in Simon Eliot and Jonathan Rose (eds), *A Companion to the History of the Book*, Oxford: Blackwell, pp. 33–49.

Part I
Typography

[1]

TEMPORARY MATRICES AND ELEMENTAL PUNCHES IN GUTENBERG'S DK TYPE[1]

BLAISE AGÜERA Y ARCAS

INTRODUCTION

THE 'STANDARD MODEL' for Western typographic printing comprises two different processes, one for making movable types, and another for printing from them. Type-making begins with the carving of a steel punch for each sort, which is then punched into a copper matrix; the matrices are then used to cast a large supply, or fount, of interchangeable pieces of lead-alloy type in an adjustable mould. To produce a printed page, types are composed in lines, locked into a forme, inked, and pressed against paper or vellum. Inking and pressing are repeated. After the desired number of copies has been printed, the type is cleaned and re-distributed into the typecase, ready to be composed into another page.

Gutenberg's position as the first European typographic printer is difficult to contest on the basis of the surviving evidence. Yet historians of printing, from the eighteenth century through the first half of the twentieth century, have consistently encountered difficulty in defining Gutenberg's intellectual contribution to the history of technology. This entails knowing precisely *what* Gutenberg invented. It has often been assumed that he invented the 'standard model', as first described in detail by Joseph Moxon in 1683 – a technology that would persist with only incremental improvements until the late nineteenth century. Perhaps in an attempt to isolate the elements of the standard model which distinguish it from earlier Chinese and Korean printing, the punch, matrix, and adjustable mould have been singled out as the essence of Gutenberg's invention, and indeed as the foundation of the typographic arts. The adjustable mould allows the creation of characters with non-uniform widths; and the casting method, because it uses a durable matrix struck from a unique punch, enables the mass-production of any number of virtually identical types of each sort.

But is there any evidence that Gutenberg in fact used these tools and methods to manufacture his type? Harry Carter, in his 1969 survey *A View of Early Typography up to about 1600*,[2] wrote only, 'I can find nothing in the documents on early printing or in the printing itself to negative the use from the first of punches, matrices, and moulds' (pp. 13-14). This surprisingly noncommittal statement summed up the state of the field in 1969, and indeed in 1999. There has never been any direct evidence that Gutenberg used the type-making and printing processes described by the standard model.

Documentation of the workings of printshops in the incunabula period is extremely

BLAISE AGÜERA Y ARCAS

scarce. Our first direct view inside the shop is not until the famous *Danse macabre*[3] woodcut of 1499, printed by Mathias Huss in Lyons. Yet the essential first step, type-making, is not addressed in this image, nor is it discussed technically in any surviving fifteenth century source. We are afforded a certain amount of indirect documentation about typemaking in lawsuits, inventories, and wills that mention punches and matrices, but the earliest of these references, to our knowledge, date to the late 1470s.[4] In sum, for the first quarter-century of printing, the only evidence that can give us insight into the underlying technological process comes from the printed survivals themselves. We can never prove that any particular technology was used to create these; but we can *disprove* the use of particular technologies by showing that their use is inconsistent with the printed result, which we can see, touch, and analyse at first hand.

In our research, we have used digital imaging and computational methods to study several early incunabula, focusing on survivals from Gutenberg's press, and we have found that the earliest printing exhibits irregularities inconsistent with the usual punch/matrix system for type manufacture. In the sections that follow, we will first discuss our methods, and then present our findings. Finally, we will advance a hypothetical type-making method consistent with our observations.

METHODS

The main subject of our analysis is the unique Scheide Library copy of the 1456 *Bulla Thurcorum*, a 20-page papal Bull of Calixtus III printed in Gutenberg's DK (*Donatus-Kalender*) fount (Fig. 1). Sample quires of the 42-line Bible, printed in the smaller B42 fount, had been completed as early as 1454. However, the earliest known European printing – the *Sibyllenbuch* and the 27-line *Donatus* fragments of circa 1450 – are all in DK, so to the best of our knowledge DK is Gutenberg's first fount. These earliest works are highly irregular in appearance and lack kerned sorts. The *Bulla* is more regular, and the fount is in a later state, though the overall effect is still less polished than the 42-line Bible.

To digitize the *Bulla* we have used a high-resolution scanning camera.[5] After scanning each page, we convert the resulting data from colour into an estimate of ink density at every point, or, to a good approximation, 'blackness'. In areas where the blackness falls below a threshold, it is assumed to be zero. The threshold is set to filter out most of the image features that are irrelevant to our analysis, including paper grain, stains, marginalia in brown ink, and rubrication in red ink. The result is similar to a high-contrast photocopy (Fig. 2). There are occasional imperfections – for example, the red stripes through the title and through the capitals that mark the beginnings of sentences may partially obliterate the ink underneath – but on the whole, the 'ink image' is an accurate reflection of the printing surface, though slightly thickened by ink spread.

The original printing surface would have consisted of many movable types locked into a forme; hence the next step in a complete typographic analysis would be to identify the boundaries between these types. Though trivial for a modern fount, this presents special challenges in Gutenberg's typography, due to the complexity of the textura character set and its profusion of contractions and ligatures. It is often unclear, for example, whether pairs of ligatured letters constitute a single type (as is likely for

Temporary Matrices and Elemental Punches in Gutenberg's DK type

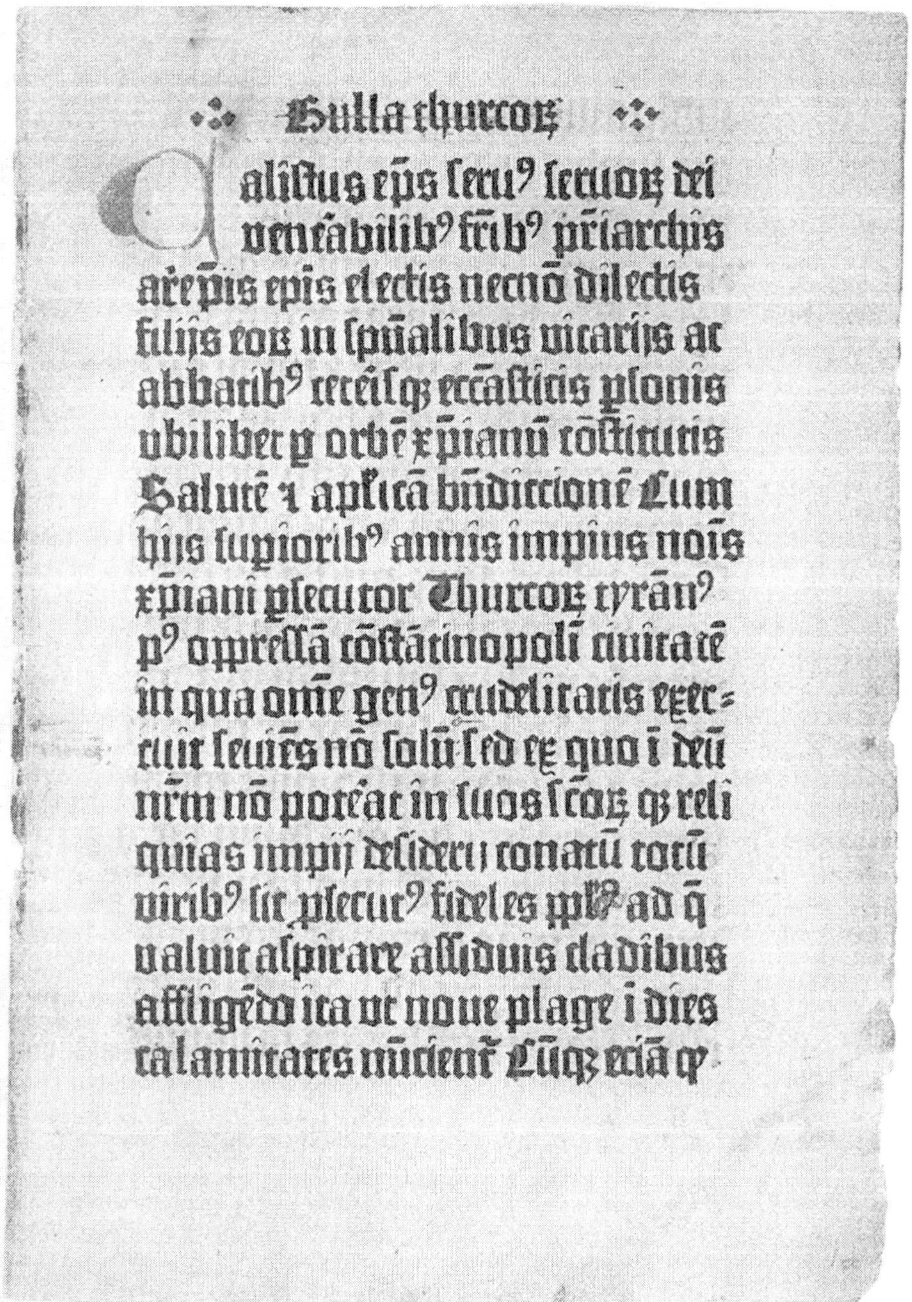

Bulla thurcoꝝ
Calistus ep̄s seru⁹ seruoꝝ dei
venerabilib⁹ frib⁹ p̄riarchis
arep̄is ep̄is electis necnō dilectis
filijs eoꝝ in sp̄ualibus vicarijs ac
abbatib⁹ ceterisq₃ ecclāsticis p̄sonis
vbilibet p̄ orbē xp̄ianū cōstitutis
Salutē ⁊ aplicā bn̄dictionē Cum
hijs supiorib⁹ annis impius nois
xp̄iani p̄secutor Thurcoꝝ tyrān⁹
p⁹ oppressā cōstātinopoli ciuitatē
in qua oīe gen⁹ crudelitatis exer-
cuit seuiēs nō solū sed ex quo i deū
nr̄m nō poterat in suos scoꝝ q₃ reli
quias impij desiderij conatū totū
virib⁹ sic p̄secut⁹ fideles xp̄i ad q̄
valuit aspirare assiduis cladibus
affligēdo ita vt noue plage i dies
calamitates nūciēt Cumq₃ etiā q̄

Fig. 1. The Scheide Library *Bulla Thurcorum*, Mainz 1456.

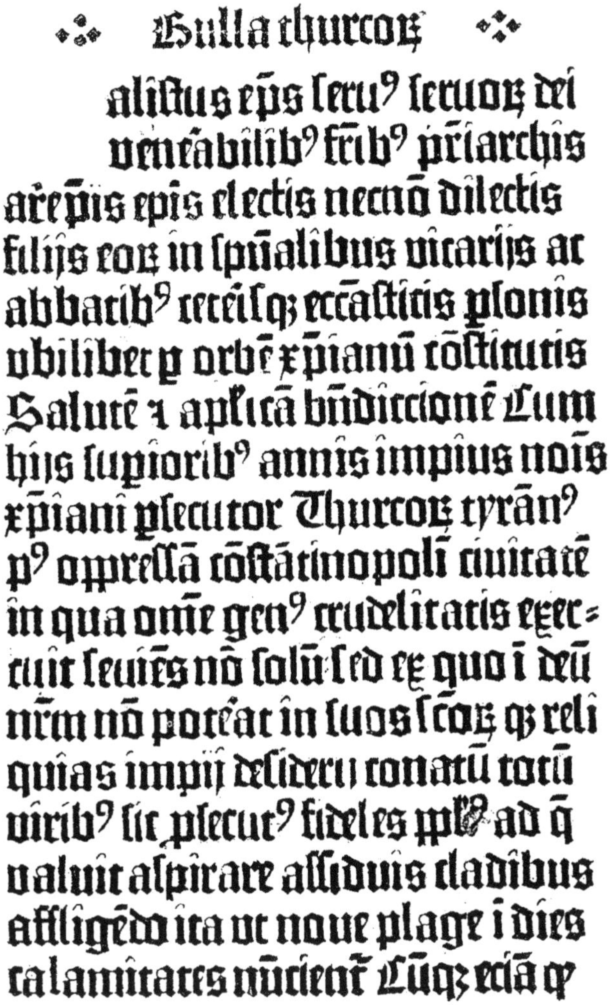

BLAISE AGÜERA Y ARCAS

❖ Bulla thurcoꝛ ❖

aliftus eps lecu⁹ lecuoꝛ dei
venrabilib⁹ frib⁹ priarchis
arepis epis electis necnõ dilectis
filijs eoꝛ in spualibus vicarijs ac
abbatib⁹ rereilqꝫ eccalticis plonis
ubilibet p orbé xpianũ coltitutis
Salute ꝫ aplica bñdiccionẽ Cum
hijs lupiorib⁹ annis impius noīs
xpiani plecutor Thurcoꝛ tyrãn⁹
p⁹ opprella coltatinopoli ciuitatẽ
in qua onīe gen⁹ crudelitatis exec-
tuit leuiẽs nõ folũ led eꝫ quo ī deũ
nrm nõ poreat in luos lcoꝛ qꝫ reli
quias impij deliderii conatũ totũ
virib⁹ lic plecut⁹ fideles ppłℓ ad q̃
valuit alpirare allibuis cladibus
affligẽdo ita ut noue plage ī dies
calamitates nũcient Cũqꝫ etiã qꝫ

Fig. 2. 'Ink image' corresponding to fig. 1.

st) or two specially designed and closely set types (as is the case for *de*). Rather than addressing the complete problem here, we will restrict our analysis to a single representative letter: the lower-case *i*.

Collation of *i*s alone would be of limited interest for a modern fount, because there is normally only one *i* sort – though such a collation could identify individual damaged *i*s, in the spirit of Charlton Hinman's typographic analysis of Shakespeare's *First Folio*.[6] In DK, however, an *i* may be abutting or non-abutting, it may be decorated with a bow, an overbar, or a tilde, or it may take the '*j*-form' if it is the second *i* in a pair. An *i* following an overhanging letter, like *f*, will be undotted, to allow tighter kerning. Hence

Temporary Matrices and Elemental Punches in Gutenberg's DK type

all three *i*s in the word *filii* would be typeset with different sorts in the DK fount (Fig. 3a). Because each sort presumably corresponds to a different punch, making a synopsis of *i*s alone presents, in miniature, all the challenges of making a complete DK synopsis.

The *i* is especially well suited to computational collation for several reasons: first, because it is the narrowest letter, it is usually well separated from the adjacent letters. The *i* body, or minim stroke, thus tends to form an isolated 'ink island'. The bows, tildes or overbars form a second 'ink island'. It is easily verified that these accents, as we will call them, are on the same piece of type as their corresponding *i* bodies; as, for example, when an *i* is mistakenly set upside-down (Fig. 3b). We can therefore test the accuracy of our computational collation methods by verifying that independent collations of the *i* bodies and accents match up. In principle, this test could fail also if the matrices for types like the *i* are struck using a separate accent punch; then, for example, identical bows might occur above a variety of *i* body forms.

The principal technique we have used for collation is *pairwise clustering*. This method assumes that pairs of objects – ink islands, in this case – can be compared to yield a quantitative measure of difference, or dissimilarity. Schematically, we calculate dissimilarity between a pair of ink islands by overlaying them in the position and orientation such that their shapes overlap as much as possible, and summing their area of non-overlap. Identical ink islands would overlap precisely, yielding a dissimilarity of zero. Any alteration in one (but not both) of the ink islands will then necessarily increase the non-overlapping area.

The clustering algorithm itself breaks a large set of heterogeneous objects into smaller, homogenous groups, or clusters.[7] Similar objects will be classified as belonging to the same cluster, while dissimilar objects will be separated into different clusters. The number of desired clusters must be set externally; the algorithm may then produce either a few clusters containing many objects each, or many clusters with only a few objects each. One of the limitations of most clustering techniques is that they are unable to determine the 'correct' number of clusters automatically. For example, if there are only 20 meaningful categories for a set of objects, then attempting to cluster them into 21 clusters will usually split one of the meaningful clusters in half arbitrarily. Conversely, requesting only 19 clusters will usually yield one cluster containing two categories. It is often difficult to determine the best choice of cluster count.

It must also be kept in mind that, in our data, two ink islands never have precisely zero dissimilarity, even if they were printed from the same piece of type. Random variations, generically called *noise*, inevitably arise from slight differences in paper and printing conditions. Sometimes these random variations are large enough that they confound the clustering, and the algorithm fails to assign a particularly irregular or smeared impression to the appropriate cluster. This uncertainty in the collation process contrasts with most bibliographic analyses. For example, in analysing paper stock, there is seldom any doubt about whether the shape of a watermark is a bull's head or a bunch of grapes: no intermediate states exist. The same cannot be said of the analysis of single types. As Janet Ing Freeman writes in *Johann Gutenberg and His Bible* when discussing a synopsis of the 42-line Bible, 'Because one bibliographer's "alternate sort" may be another's "defective type", not even the exact number of sorts in the B42 fount can be stated with confidence'.[8] In the language of clustering, one might say that a

BLAISE AGÜERA Y ARCAS

Fig. 3. filii and upside-down *i*. (a) Three variants of *i* used to print *filii* (Scheide *Bulla Thurcorum*, fol. 1ʳ line 5).

Fig. 3. (b) *singulis* with upside-down *i* (*Bulla Thurcorum*, fol. 7ᵛ line 10).

Temporary Matrices and Elemental Punches in Gutenberg's DK type

systematically deviant type may belong in its own cluster, or it may be merely an outlier in a larger cluster.

EVIDENCE

In their unpublished 1988 synopsis of DK type as represented in the *Bulla Thurcorum*, Janet Ing Freeman and Paul Needham identified twelve differently-shaped *i* variants, shown in Fig. 4. Several of these variants are typographically identical, that is, both used interchangeably and lacking salient differences in design. These 'supererogatory types', as they were termed, are nonetheless distinctive enough in shape that they could not have been manufactured from a common punch. Forty-eight of the 204 sorts identified in the 1988 synopsis were similarly supererogatory, including examples of almost every lower-case letter. In general only rare characters, such as the upper-case initials, were *not* found to have supererogatory forms; because in most of these cases there were only one or two occurrences of the character in the *Bulla*, it is likely that a larger text would have revealed many more variants in a similar analysis.

Our automated clustering of *i* bodies and accents not only confirms this surprising variability, but also shows that the 1988 synopsis identifies only a fraction of the redundant *i* forms in the *Bulla*. Fig. 5a shows a sample of the several hundred *i* accent clusters discovered. Each line, consisting of a black accent followed by between two and eight grey accents, represents a cluster. The grey accents are individual cluster members, as extracted from the *Bulla* ink images. The black accent is the cluster average, constructed by superimposing all cluster members, as if they were transparencies. Fig. 5b shows an independent clustering of *i* bodies, which yielded very similar results. Fewer clusters are shown, due to space constraints.

We do not claim that our cluster count is definitive, or even accurate; it is in fact likely that the true number is higher, as we have attempted to be conservative and we have been limited by the size of the document. Neither can cluster assignment ever be error-free, due to the unavoidable random variations arising from the printing process itself. We can assert, however, that the clustering is meaningful, based upon several lines of evidence. First, we note that certain of the *i* bodies have nicks, or other obvious distinctive features. In each such case, the clustering algorithm successfully identifies the damage, and groups together all *i* body impressions with the same damage in the document. In an independent visual search for damaged *i* bodies, we could find no errors of misclassification or omission in the automated clustering of these 'easy' cases. At a minimum, this suggests that our methods can perform damaged type collation in the spirit of Hinman's *First folio* analysis. It also suggests that the clusters of figure 5 can be interpreted as identified single type pieces, with each cluster member representing a re-use of the type piece. Type pieces typically recur approximately every four pages; this gives some impression of the printing and composing environment, as well as the size of the type-case.

A majority of the clusters lack any obvious damage, and would be extremely difficult to collate by hand; yet most of the accent clusters correspond well to a single body cluster, and vice versa. This observation holds for both damaged and undamaged examples. Because accent and body clustering are carried out independently and without any contextual knowledge, this is strong statistical proof that both accent and body

BLAISE AGÜERA Y ARCAS

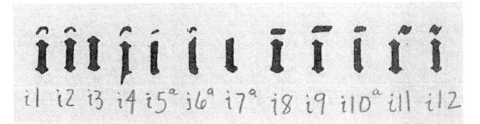

Fig. 4. Twelve *i* variants identified by Janet Ing Freeman and Paul Needham in their 1988 synopsis of the DK type as represented in the *Bulla Thurcorum* (unpublished).

clusterings are meaningful. Put differently, if *i*s were clustered solely on the basis of their accents, the resulting cluster assignment would be very similar to that of a clustering based solely on their bodies.

Thus our visual impression of Fig. 5 is confirmed: namely, that both accents and bodies differ sufficiently to clearly distinguish one cluster from another – hence, one piece of type from another. The high variability observed in the type impressions therefore does not arise primarily from the printing process itself, for within a cluster impressions are quite similar. The variability is in the printing surfaces of the type pieces. Although most letterpress printing is sprinkled with damaged type impressions, this degree of variability in undamaged types is not found in later printing. We have verified this using a variety of control cases, including the Aldine *Saint Catherine of Siena* of 1500,[9] Plantin's *Biblia polyglotta* of 1568-72,[10] and even the Ashendene Press *Inferno* of Dante, printed in 1902.[11]

Other aspects of DK typography exhibit a similar lack of repeatability. For example, it has been suggested that the suspension stroke might have been struck with a separate punch; this would certainly have improved efficiency, as strokes occur above *a*, *c*, *e*, *g*, *i*, *m*, *n*, *o*, *p*, *q*, *r*, *s*, *t*, and *u*. Tildes and other accents are used above many letters as well. Such situations could even have been addressed by making an entirely separate piece of type for the accent, though this would have complicated typesetting and made it harder to lock up the types in the forme. The near-perfect correspondence between a sub-population of *i* body clusters and their matching suspension stroke clusters, however, rules out this possibility in DK. Not only do particular *i* bodies always co-occur with particular suspension strokes, but if these *i*s with strokes are overlaid, there is no discernible jitter between the body and the stroke within a particular cluster. As with bows, suspension strokes are clearly on the same piece of type as their companion letters.

More surprisingly, however, suspension strokes are unique: particular versions of the stroke correspond to particular versions of the *i* body. Moving between clusters instead of within a cluster, we find both substantial jitter between the body and the stroke, and widely varying stroke lengths and shapes. *i8* and *i9* in the 1988 synopsis (Fig. 4) illustrate this effect; the clustering algorithm finds more than twelve different versions of this character (non-abutting *i* with overbar) in the *Bulla*. All the suspension strokes in the *Bulla* have also been clustered out of context, with similar results. There are again many distinct and well-defined clusters, although only a small fraction of these show

Temporary Matrices and Elemental Punches in Gutenberg's DK type

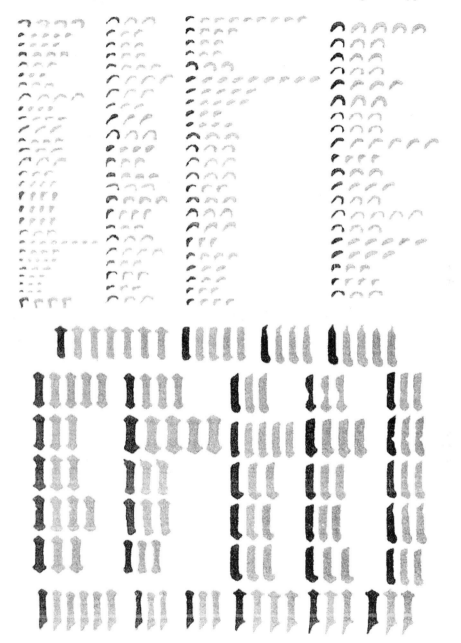

Fig. 5. A selection of *i* accent (*top*) and body (*lower*) clusters from independent clusterings of accents and bodies. Black images are cluster centroids, and the grey images to their right are the individual cluster members (lightened ink images from the document).

9

BLAISE AGÜERA Y ARCAS

Fig. 6. B36 hyphens: 14 hyphens, chosen at random, from a 10-page sample of the 36-line Bible.

any discernible damage. Most of the clusters correspond to strokes that occur above only one of the fourteen possible companion letters. At least for the *is*, we know that this correspondence goes much further, with most particular stroke clusters matching particular letter body clusters.

Careful study of the suspension strokes confirms, then, that not only are they on the same piece of type as their companion letters, but that there is no common, separate suspension stroke punch. Suspension strokes appear to have been manufactured along with the rest of the type piece, and their shapes show the same distinctiveness as the shapes of the type bodies.

The nature of this variability between types cannot in general be explained by differential wear or damage, beginning with a common original shape. Many of the type impressions appear perfectly sharp and well-formed, but have overbars of different lengths, or with different shapes. Movement of the entire overbar up or down relative to the letter is particularly difficult to explain as an effect of damage, given that the overbar is clearly on the same piece of type as the letter.

The irregularity of DK printing can be demonstrated in yet another way using the 36-line Bible (B36). This final appearance of the much-used DK fount does not come from Gutenberg's shop, but was printed in Bamberg in 1461. Hyphens, which hardly appear in the *Bulla*, are used liberally in the two-column B36. Fig. 6 reproduces a random selection of these hyphens, based on digital photography of ten leaves. Great variability between hyphens is evident: the lengths of the two strokes vary substantially, as do their angles, and the spacing between them. While differing stroke lengths might be explained by partial obliteration of some of the types or imperfect casting, such defects cannot account for variable spacing between the strokes.

CONCLUSIONS

The high degree of variability between pieces of DK type presents problems for the standard hypothesis of type manufacture, involving the use of steel punches, copper matrices, and a hand mould to produce a fount of lead-alloy types. Even the one or two duplicate forms per character evident in the 1988 synopsis posed a minor mystery in light of this standard model. A steel punch is time-consuming and difficult to carve, even today requiring a full day of work by a skilled craftsman. Why would Gutenberg have chosen to repeat this exercise several times per sort? An examination of the type variants across DK states does not consistently suggest an aesthetic evolution to explain this effort.

With new evidence not only confirming duplicate type forms, but raising their number from one or two per sort to – conservatively – dozens, the hypothesis that DK type was manufactured using the standard method becomes untenable. The most

Temporary Matrices and Elemental Punches in Gutenberg's DK type

obvious conclusion consistent with our evidence is that each physical piece of type was manufactured individually, and was not the outcome of a mass-reproduction process at all.

While a discussion of the historical precedent for the argument is beyond the scope of this paper, we note that this position has been taken before. It is possible to print from wooden type, and such types must be individually carved. The suggestion that Gutenberg's DK type was wooden is problematic, however. The effort involved in carving an entire such fount by hand would have been immense. Ensuring square, proportional wooden type bodies would have presented further challenges. Finally, wood is not particularly durable, and would have suffered much from high turnover and heavy use. It is one thing to use wood for a large, infrequently used decorative initial, and quite another to use it for a minuscule *i*, which is re-used every few words for every kind of publication, ranging from bibles to grammar books to indulgences, the latter of which might have been printed in very large runs. While wooden DK type cannot be absolutely ruled out on the strength of the evidence presented here, this possibility seems unlikely from a practical point of view.

If the DK types were made of metal, then it is a near-certainty that they were made by casting. The only alternative is individual engraving from blanks – a process that Gerard Meerman proposed in the eighteenth century as part of his 'rational' schema for the invention of printing in small steps.[12] Although this would also produce the variability we observe, the amount of work involved in engraving an entire fount would have been still greater than the effort of carving it in wood. Once again, individually engraved blanks are unlikely, especially as we know that Gutenberg was familiar with casting. Aside from his father's oft-cited connection with a mint, he may have used sandcasting to mass-produce pilgrim mirrors during his Strasbourg period. He certainly used casting of some sort to make the two-line slugs with which he printed the Mainz *Catholicon* and several smaller works.[13]

If types were cast, yet differ greatly in their final shape, then they could not have been cast from a common matrix. Either many matrices were used in parallel, or equivalently, the matrix was temporary and needed to be re-formed between castings – or both. Lead and sand matrices are temporary, but there are other possibilities as well, such as clay, plaster, and papier mâché. All of these have been used, at one time or another, to make secondary castings during the era of hand printing.

Whether many matrices existed in parallel or were re-formed sequentially, it is also clear that the matrices for a single sort could not have been formed by a common whole-letter punch or pattern. If they had been, then while we might observe higher variability between types than expected due to imperfectly formed matrices, the nature of this variability would be different. In particular, overbars would not move relative to their companion letters, and the strokes of the hyphen would not move relative to each other. A handful of patterns per sort still do not suffice to explain our observation; if whole-letter patterns were used, it would appear that the number of such patterns would need to be of the same order as the number of single types.

It is possible to reconcile a casting process with the apparent absence of reused whole-letter patterns by considering systems in which temporary matrices are made by striking or impressing not a single punch, but a series of smaller, 'elemental' punches. A matrix would then be the product not only of the shapes of the constituent elements,

BLAISE AGÜERA Y ARCAS

but of their overall configuration, which would inevitably vary every time the matrix is re-formed.

This suggestion, too, is not entirely unprecedented. Separate accent punches, as discussed in *Evidence*, present a simple case of matrices formed by combinations of two punches. More interestingly, typefounders have occasionally produced ligatured types, such as Œ, from a combination of the O and E punches, struck in an overlapping configuration, which saves the work of making a separate Œ punch. Eighteenth century matrices struck in this fashion by Rosart survive in the Enschedé collection.[14] Were this technique used in combination with temporary matrices, the effect would be a set of Œ types with variable overlap between the letters, resulting in a variety of shapes.

Preliminary observations suggest that DK types may have been constructed in a similar way, though from more elemental components corresponding roughly to single scribal strokes rather than entire letters such as O and E. Hence the hyphen would have been made from two such elements, but even simple letters might have been formed from between four and seven elements. If we take overbars to be representative of single elements, then the non-uniformity of overbar lengths across multiple sorts – or even across different variants of the same sort – suggests that, if these 'elemental punches' existed, they did not have the permanence or uniqueness of true whole-letter punches. This is unsurprising, as their shapes are very simple, and if temporary matrices were used, they could easily have been carved from wood.

In summary, our observations appear to be inconsistent with the assumption that permanent matrices were used in casting DK type. They are also inconsistent with the idea of static whole-letter punches for each sort. A consistent picture emerges if we hypothesize the use of temporary matrices, in combination with 'elemental punches' which would have allowed the typemaker to form these matrices from multiple overlapping strokes. Preliminary results suggest that this rather counter-intuitive type-making method was not merely an early experiment of Gutenberg's, but may have been common to a number of early typefoundries.

NOTES

TEMPORARY MATRICES AND ELEMENTAL PUNCHES
IN GUTENBERG'S DK TYPE

1 This work was done in collaboration with Paul Needham, Scheide Librarian, with the generous support of William H. Scheide and Princeton University.

2 Harry Graham Carter, *A View of Early Typography up to about 1600* (Oxford, 1969).

3 *Danse macabre* [Lyons: Mathias Huss], 18 Feb. 1499 [/1500?]. GW 7954.

4 Among the earliest unambiguous surviving references to punches is Nicolaus Jenson's will of September 1480 (Carlo Castellani, *La stampa in Venezia* (Venice, 1889 [1973 reprint]), pp. 85 et seq.) mentioning among Jenson's bequests '... ponzoni cum quibus stampantur matrices, cum quibus matribus fiunt littere ...'.

5 The camera back is a 4 × 5" Phase One PowerPhase, with a 6000 × 8400 pixel scan area and 12-bit internal colour depth (www.phaseone.com). The printed area of the *Bulla Thurcorum* measures 10 × 16.5 cm, yielding a scan resolution of ~500 pixels/cm (or ~1200 dpi). We have used a ReproGraphic copystand, view camera, and tungsten lighting from Tarsia Technical Industries (www.ttind.com). All analysis software is our own, written in C++ and Matlab™ (www.mathworks.com).

6 Charlton Hinman, *The Printing and Proof-Reading of the First Folio of Shakespeare* (Oxford, 1963).

7 For an overview, see Kenneth Rose, 'Deterministic Annealing for Clustering, Compression, Classification, Regression, and Related Optimisation Problems', *The Proceedings of the IEEE*, 86(11) (1988), 2210-39.

8 Janet Ing, *Johann Gutenberg and His Bible* (New York, 1988), p. 78.

9 Catharina Senensis, *Epistole*. Venice: Aldus Manutius, Romantus, '15' [i.e. not before 19] Sept. 1500. GW 6222.

10 *Biblia sacra, Hebraice, Chaldaice, Græce, & Latine*. Antverpiæ: Christoph. Plantinus: 1569 [1571]-73.

11 *Lo Inferno di Dante Alighieri fiorentino* [Chelsea: Nella stamperia di Ashendene, 1902].

12 Gerard Meerman, *Origines typographicae* (The Hague, 1765), I, 26.

13 Paul Needham, 'Johann Gutenberg and the Catholicon Press', *Papers of the Bibliographical Society of America*, 76 (1982), 395-456.

14 Stanley Nelson, Smithsonian Institution, personal communication.

[2]

The Aldine Italic

NICOLAS BARKER

THE ORIGIN OF the Aldine italic type has been much discussed, and attributed, with varying degrees of conviction, to various hands, among them Pomponio Leto and Bartolomeo di Sanvito.[1] The connection of both these, and others, has been more based on the similarity of the Latin texts, particularly of verse, as written by them to the new Aldine octavo format for such texts than on the resemblance of individual letter-forms. It may be that no such resemblance exists and that the sloped humanistic cursive, by now the familiar and indeed appropriate script for the sort of book that Aldus intended to publish, was sufficiently current for Griffo to make his own version, without any 'model' such as may have been necessary for the creation of new Greek types.

It is as well to maintain this caution, but there are resemblances between the development of italic and Greek script.[2] The analysis of individual letter-forms, then, which has produced interesting results when applied to Greek, may at least be worth attempting for the Aldine italic. There is another reason for pursuing this. The octavo classics were clearly intended to be a series from the outset, a series that was to contain not only Latin and vernacular but also Greek texts. The italic was to be matched by the Aldine Greek Type 4, with which it shares a largely common fount of small capitals, originally cut for Type 3. Type 4 was closely based on Aldus's own Greek script; does this offer a parallel for the source of the italic?

There is, so far as I know, no example of formal script by Aldus comparable with the autograph fair copy of the Greek grammar in the Biblioteca Ambrosiana.[3] Samples of his ordinary script in different contexts exist: the text of his translation of the Musaeus *Hero et Leander*, which probably served as printer's copy for the expanded bilingual edition *c.*1498 (Sélestat, MS 336); the contract for the *Epistole* of St Catharine, printed in 1500 (Venice, Biblioteca Marciana, MS Ital. XI. 207); and letters. These cover a fair span of time, but none is early; they include both Latin and Italian texts, written on different occasions.

46   A MILLENNIUM OF THE BOOK

Fig.1. The hand of Pomponio Leto. BL King's MS 32, f.2.

None of them offers a parallel as exact as the Greek grammar, but together they contain some characteristic if not individual forms that may be compared with those of the italic type itself.

The type was by no means as economical in the number of individual characters as the Greek Type 4. There are a number of possible reasons for this: unlike the Greek, it was the first of its kind; the evidence suggests that it preceded Type 4, and the new small size may have created problems resolved before Griffo embarked on the latter. At any rate there are (or may be, for there are some uncertainties) almost a hundred combinations in addition to the basic 22 letters of the lower-case alphabet. For a fount of type of the Roman alphabet this is, by 1500, an exceptionally large number. The reasons why the early printers employed founts of type with a large or small range of characters is difficult to fathom today. We are (or used to be) familiar with a standard lay of the case that had been standardized (if with some local variation) for over 300 years. The only extended study of the variations found in the range of characters available to early printers is Wytze and Lotte Hellinga's *The Fifteenth-Century Printing Types of the Low Countries* (1966). The examples given there show that, despite the demands made by different languages (Latin and Dutch, and also French and English), the range of different founts can extend from as few as 60 to over 150 characters. One of the largest was used consistently for printing in Latin by the press of the Brothers of the Common Life at Brussels. Generally speaking, however, there is an observable progression from large towards smaller ranges of characters. The types that Johannes de Westfalia, already a professional printer, brought to the Low Countries from Venice and used with remarkable consistency for a long period have a typically small range.[4] The same progression is to be seen in the evolution of the Aldine Greeks.

In general, however, the rule (rather assumed than stated earlier) that the nearer a type is to the manuscript hand on which it was based, the larger the range of characters it will exhibit, appears to be true. The exhaustive pains taken by Gutenberg or the engraver or engravers working under his direction to achieve an absolute evenness of minim and space to match the rigidly disciplined *textura* as practised by 15th-century Mainz scribes resulted in the B42 type with over 300 characters.[5] Many of these variations and combinations were maintained by printers reproducing the same or analogous hands. The Burgundian *lettre batarde*, combining the regularity of *textura* with the flexibility of cursive,

48   A MILLENNIUM OF THE BOOK

was clearly felt by Caxton and Colard Mansion (and their engraver or engravers) to require a range of ligatures almost as great as that of the B42 type.

A wide range of characters, as exhibited in these two instances, may represent the size of the initial investment available. The same factor may be responsible for the same phenomenon in the type of the press of the Brothers of the Common Life. It may also explain the even greater range of characters required in the first Aldine Greek, a range extended by an evolutionary process not easy to trace or record in tabular form. But this factor, whose substance cannot be determined, can at least be set in perspective by the patent need for a very much greater investment in paper. The Gutenberg Bible, the Bartholomaeus Anglicus printed at Cologne in 1471, probably at Caxton's instance, were big books that demanded an exceptional quantity of paper. The Brothers of the Common Life introduced their large-fount type in 1476 for a very big book, the *Gnotosolitos* of Arnoldus de Gheilhoven. The Aldine Aristotle, a very common book today, was outstanding both in size and in quantity.

The decrease in the range of characters used is, however, not an index of any reduction in the scale of enterprise, but rather of change of circumstance: 'wandering printers' who worked in more than one place had an obvious need to simplify equipment; equally, entrepreneurs such as Koberger and Amerbach, or those working in a highly competitive market, such as Johannes de Westfalia, owed their success to a new measure of industrial efficiency, in which the simplification of the lay of the case (if such existed now) would have had a part.

If we apply these hypotheses to the typographic development of the Aldine Press, we can see that the extended range of characters in both the first roman and the first Greek types was due to a desire to achieve a right graphic image, where the extra cost of a wide range of characters was dwarfed by a much greater investment in paper. The risk involved in this required that every care should be taken to make the print look worth its cost. It is evident that the same principles applied to the development of the third Aldine innovation, something, as noted, more novel than any of its predecessors: there had been many roman types and other Greek types before *De Aetna* and Lascaris *Erotemata*, but the few letters on the title page of St Catharine's *Epistole* were the world's first sight of the italic type intended for the series of pocket classics of which the Virgil, in April 1501, was the first proper exemplar. It is worth

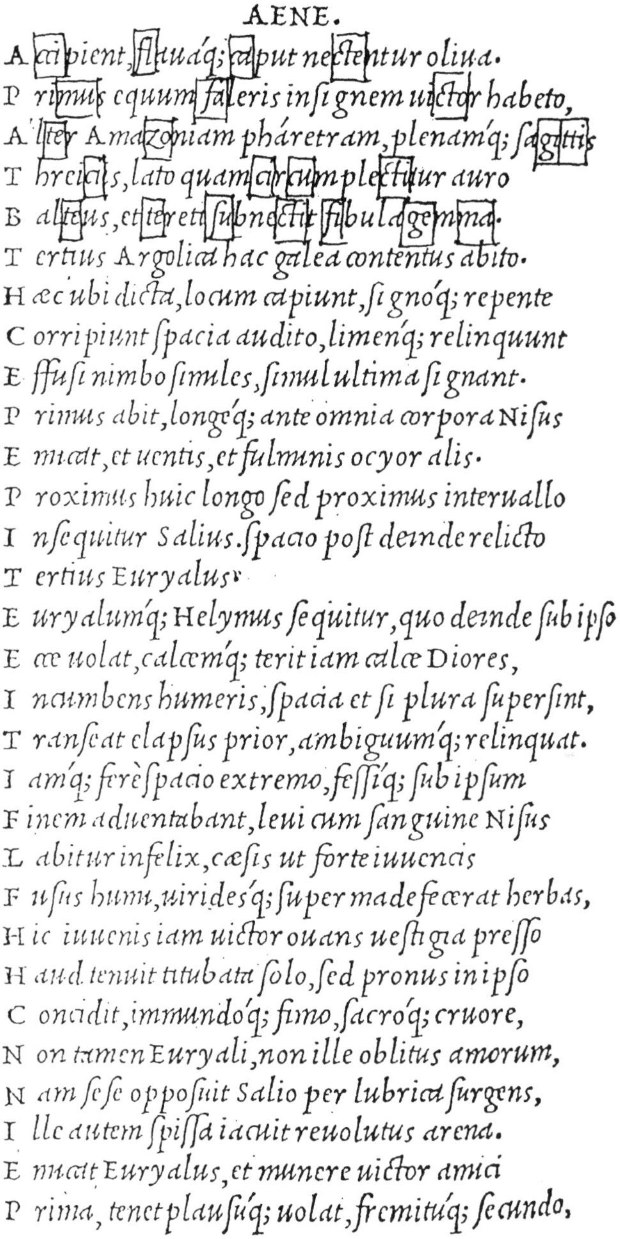

AENE.

A *cipient, fluuáq; caput nectentur oliua.*
P *rimus equum faleris insignem uictor habeto,*
A *lter Amazoniam pháretram, plenámq; sagittis*
T *hreicijs, lato quam circum plectitur auro*
B *alteus, et tereti subnectit fibula gemma.*
T *ertius Argolica hac galea contentus abito.*
H *æc ubi dicta, locum capiunt, signóq; repente*
C *orripiunt spacia audito, limenq; relinquunt*
E *ffusi nimbo similes, simul ultima signant.*
P *rimus abit, longéq; ante omnia corpora Nisus*
E *micat, et uentis, et fulminis ocyor alis.*
P *roximus huic longo sed proximus interuallo*
I *nsequitur Salius. spacio post deinde relicto*
T *ertius Euryalusᵛ*
E *uryalúmq; Helymus sequitur, quo deinde sub ipso*
E *cce uolat, calcémq; terit iam calce Diores,*
I *ncumbens humeris, spacia et si plura supersint,*
T *ranseat elapsus prior, ambiguúmq; relinquat.*
I *amq; ferè spacio extremo, feßíq; sub ipsum*
F *inem aduentabant, leui cum sanguine Nisus*
L *abitur infelix, cæsis ut forte iuuencis*
F *usus humi, uiridésq; super madefecerat herbas,*
H *ic iuuenis iam uictor ouans uestigia presso*
H *aud tenuit titubata solo, sed pronus in ipso*
C *oncidit, immundóq; fimo, sacróq; cruore,*
N *on tamen Euryali, non ille oblitus amorum,*
N *am sese opposuit Salio per lubrica surgens,*
I *lle autem spißa iacuit reuolutus arena.*
E *micat Euryalus, et munere uictor amici*
P *rima, tenet plausúq; uolat, fremitúq; secundo,*

Fig.2. A page from the Aldine Virgil, 1501, enlarged and with the ligatures marked.

noting that the innovation was a double one: a new format, as well as a new type. This aspect of the revolution has been admirably treated by Armando Petrucci.[6] We shall return to it, after some further investigation of the new type.

A few general observations can be made about the nature, as well as the quantity, of the special characters. First, very few are required for abbreviations: five with the suspension mark for *m* or *n*, plus two standard *q* abbreviations, no more. Secondly, although the majority are required for ligatures, they are by no means what may be called a standard or normal assortment. Although a large number are required for *s* and *f*, as was customary, there are none for *b*, and *d*, or *p* (normally, like *q*, rich in abbreviations), few for *e*, and only the standard *ae* and *oe* diphthongs for *a* and *o*. By contrast, there are a long range of ligatures for *c* and *t*, for all the vowels following *g*, and a surprising number for *m*, *n* and *u*, where frequency (in Latin) induces running together in script so that similarity can cause confusion. The two forms of *z* presuppose the ligatures that occur with it, and their frequency in Italian. The existence of two forms of medial *s*, of *i* with high, low or no dot, are puzzling signs, perhaps of a need for variety, or of trial and error, rather like the multiple *e* forms in the *De Aetna*.

Where do these characteristics, reproduced with such care, come from? The answer is simple, indeed predictable: from the hand of Aldus himself – not uniformly or slavishly or invariably, but with a sufficient number of peculiar forms and – more important – with similarity of *ductus* that make the identification certain, or at least as certain as any of those offered for the Greek types discussed earlier. The most striking resemblance is to be seen in the most obvious combinations, those of *s*, *f*, *m*, *n* and *y*. Oddly enough, it is these multi-literal combinations that give the Aldine italic its irregularity, a pleasing lack of uniformity of size and strike, not to say alignment. The combinations of *m*, *n* and *u* are different in size from each other, and most are slightly larger than the single letters. The very frequency with which they recur prevents them from standing out; they are a pervasive part of the overall pattern of the letter. The ligature *ei*, *eis*, by contrast, is conspicuous not only by its size but its relative rarity (the use of this ancient form of long *i* is discussed in the appendix to the 1501 Virgil).

The reason for the use of all these ligatures is mechanical: that is, it derives either from the structure of script (*m*, *n*, *u*) or the structure of printing type (the *f* and *s* forms avoid the risk of breakage due to a multiplicity of kerning sorts). Why then the combinations of *c*, *g* and *t*? The interesting common feature of all three is that the *trait d'union* is at the top, necessary in *t* but not in the others. All three, however, are to be found in the autograph script of Aldus. Three examples of this are available in reproduction: the Latin translation of Musaeus, which may have served as printer's copy for the enlarged edition of *c.* 1498; the 1499 contract with Antonio Condelmer for the edition of the letters of St Catharine of Siena; and a letter to Paolo Bombasio, dated 20 April 1511.[7] The first is a fair copy; the next a copy, if more hastily written; the last is Aldus's natural compositional hand. In all three these ligatures are to be found, regularly if not uniformly.

These, and other characteristics of the italic, are not peculiar to the hand of Aldus, which has, moreover, several forms not to be found in the type. Some of the printed forms may have been dictated by an already established typographic convention, although the most obvious, the *f* and *s* ligatures, correspond closely with Aldus's more formal usage. The differences in the hand include Greek *alpha* and *epsilon* used as majuscule *a* and *e*, *r*, for which Aldus invariably used the old 'u' shape, and — apparently — *g and* e, where Aldus used the single-stroke single-eye-and-tail and the two stroke or semi-epsilon form, respectively. I say 'apparently' because close examination shows that Aldus, even at his hastiest, always made *g* with two strokes, flattening the side of the upper eye and converting the lower eye into a loop more often than not (although, again, not invariably); equally, the typographic form of *e*, particularly in the ligatures, shows that two-stroke *e* is intended, the eye or counter pointed not looped. Other characteristics are *a* with the downstroke protruding sharply above the counter, *h* with the right foot firmly bent back, and the ascenders tending to the left, the tendency accentuated by the serif. Oddly, Aldus's habit of joining terminal *us* and *is* was not originally reproduced.

Something further can be learned from what can be seen of the development of the type. The two *i* forms, with high and low dot, were used from the outset and continuously; *ij* and *is* were only introduced in the prelims (*a* 1v) of Lucan in April 1502, the sixth book in italic. The double *ll* was apparently only introduced in the Petrarch (July 1501). The two forms of long *s*, with and without a loop at the foot, apparent in the ligatures, do not seem to have been given separate typographic form; appearances to the contrary are probably due to defective sorts. The *sp* ligature was not introduced until the latter part of the *Aeneid*;

the form with looped *p* there used was dropped in favour of straight *p* with a seriffed foot, introduced in quire *q* of Horace (May 1501). Most if not all of the *z* ligatures were only introduced in the Petrarch. No *sfi* ligature was cut; sometimes single *s* was used with *fi* (Petrarch, a 5); elsewhere, *ffi* was used with the stroke across the first letter cut away (Lucan, o 4).

The punctuation marks are less interesting. The full point is invariably high, and the comma low; the colon is narrow, the semi-colon wide. There is a single parenthesis. Various accents, acute (long and short), grave and circumflex, the diaeresis and apostrophe, and the curious sign for the aspirate used in the appendix to Virgil, are taken over from the Greeks, and seen to have been inserted as separate sorts, excepting the diaeresis. Two forms of query were used, the later (and uglier) form being more inclined; the original form continued in use after the later was introduced. The most interesting form is the ampersand. The *et* form with the *t* made by an extension of the tail of the *e*, crossed at the end with a curved stroke, was never used by Aldus; he invariably used the & form, made like a reversed 8; one can only speculate on the reasons for this change, and the source of the form.

Why, finally, did Aldus have such strong views about the correct shape of italic, so strong that they required an extra hundred punches to be cut? It cannot, in a man of notorious personal humility, be put down to pride in his own hand. What was the source of his own writing, and why did he feel that its forms were so canonically right? The answer to these questions is simple: there was a canon, and it was established by Pomponio Leto. Alfred Fairbank, his eye unclouded by speculation as to any relationship that may have subsisted between Aldus and Pomponio, saw this when he pointed out the resemblance of the hand of BL King's MS 32 to the Aldine italic. This is not to say, however, that it was modelled deliberately, or even unconsciously, on that hand. There were many others in the circle round the Accademia Romana who wrote a very similar hand: 'They all wrote beautifully and they all wrote alike'.[8] It has been lately suggested that Aldus was not part of this circle and that he rejected the influence of Pomponio, Domizio Calderini and the Roman school.[9] The formation of the italic contradicts this: Aldus did not leave the Lazio of his birth until he was past 20 years old; his handwriting must have been formed then, within the ambit of Rome, and so, evidently, were his ideas of what 'italic' script should look like.

To what extent can this be attributed to the example of Pomponio himself? That Pomponio's manuscripts had a special importance to his followers is attested by Fulvio Orsini's pioneering inventory of 1602.[10] Others have since added to and amended this list,[11] but a full study of the manuscripts written, or written in, by Pomponio, or written by his students or under his direction, remains to be made. The most recent analysis of his hand has been made by Giovanni Muzzioli,[12] and the characteristics there identified have a bearing on our problem. He draws particular attention to the 'peculiar form of the *et* ligature like a sloped 8 with, on the right, an oblique stroke slightly curved downwards, which forms a trial element no less evident in the *g*'.[13] He also draws attention to the downstroke of the *a*, 'as if detached from the curve', the capital *N* 'made all at once' (but with two strokes, not a single one), the *f* 'with the eyelet closed' (that is, with the upper curve closed to the stem), the *s* leaning to the right and joined to the next letter, the majuscule form of *s* used only at the end of words, the rare use of uncial *d*, the stroke of *b* leaning slightly to the left (and he could have added the other ascenders), and other characteristics, many familiar in Aldus's hand or his italic type.

These details, in particular the irregularity in the *g* form, resemble the Aldine equivalents. The manuscripts illustrated by Muzzioli vary in formality, but MS Vat. Ottob. lat. 1956 shows the same forms of *c*, *f*, *g*, *s* and *t* ligatures. The 7-shaped *r* is occasionally used, and these characteristics can also be seen (the ligatures less frequent) in Pomponio's more formal script (for example MS Vat. lat. 3302 or Biblioteca Casanatense, cod. 15). Aldus occasionally made *f* with the upper loop closed as Pomponio did, a feature not repeated in the italic. He did not imitate Pomponio's distinctive preference for uncial *g* in his formal script, which Muzzioli suggests that he may have adopted from the 5th-century Medicean Vergil, which he certainly used.

The last apart, it is salutary to remember that all the characteristics hitherto noted, the *c*, *f*, *g*, *f*, *s* and *t* ligatures, as well as those for the linked minims, even the same terminal forms for *is* and *us*, the pointed *a* and bent back *h*, though not the 7-shaped *r*, can be found in the hand of Niccolo Niccoli, the founder of the sloped italic script. The individual shapes vary and develop; *ct* with its striking loop can be made with two, three or even four strokes; *g*, in particular, changes in a Protean way. Indeed, this, the most difficult and fascinating of all letters for the calligrapher, exercised its usual fascination on all three—Niccoli, Pomponio and Aldus.

It remains, however, to be seen whether Pomponio had a distinctive style, and whether Aldus's hand was influenced by it in any other than a general way. One of the most fascinating manuscripts discussed by Muzzioli is the Cicero (MS Vat. lat. 3233) in which Pomponio can be seen experimenting with some unique forms, in which Muzzioli sees clear signs of Greek influence (Pomponio learned Greek from Theodore Gaza from 1469), and, behind it, of ancient Latin script.[14] The use of Greek *mu* for *m*, the hesitancies about the linkage of ascenders noted earlier, and the extraordinary use of the *epsilon upsilon* ligature for *e* and a sort of *xi* for *s*, are the most striking examples. None of these lasted except the novel one-stroke form for *sp*, taken over from the *rho* combinations, which were so common a feature of contemporary Greek script, and were reproduced by Aldus in type. Aldus did not use this in his own hand, but some uncertainty about the ideal form of *sp* may underlie the change from the looped to the seriffed form in the italic type. Pomponio's one-stroke form is, however, a prominent feature of Bartolomeo Sanvito's script. There is one final link between Greek and Latin in Aldus's script and the types based on it: the only letters in which he did not preserve the form that he wrote in type are the same: *r* and *rho*.

This is, perhaps, a somewhat negative note on which to end this analysis of the sources of the italic type. But the real proof of the link with Aldus's hand and its Roman origins cannot be described: it lies in a resemblance of *ductus*, the unconscious similarity that defies verbal description, for which Fairbank is the best witness. Again, negative evidence may help: the italic type does not look like Sanvito's hand; despite similarities of individual forms, due (no doubt) to common Roman influence, there is no overall visual resemblance. Yet it is an undeniable fact that Sanvito may have had a link with the Aldine press: he worked for Bernardo Bembo, and Aldus recorded, in the dedicatory letter to Pietro Bembo in the 1514 Virgil, that he 'took the small size, the pocket book format, from your library, or rather from that of your most kind father', who was still lending Aldus books, aged 81 at the same time as he wrote. In recording these details, Fletcher rightly draws attention to the importance of these facts, which have, however, confused two essentially different innovations: the type and the format.[15] It is time now to turn our attention to the second of these.

In a sense, the format of the 'libri portatiles', as Aldus called them in the 1503 catalogue, was dictated by the size of the standard paper used by Aldus.[16] The normal measurements of ordinary paper, the size called 'chancery', 42–45 × 30–33cm, would produce an untrimmed octavo of about 160 × 110mm. Although bound (and therefore trimmed) copies exist scarcely smaller than this, most copies in contemporary bindings are considerably narrower, the trimmed width being about 95mm, while the height is undiminished.

There are two possible explanations: either the paper was made squarer than usual, or the binder varied the amount of trim ploughed off. Of the two, the former seems to be the case.[17] But the explanation is less important that the fact: why was it that a long narrow format was thought preferable for the *libri portatiles*?

The long narrow format had long been used for unglossed verse manuscripts. The Latin hexameter, and still more the shorter lines of the lyric metres and hendecasyllables, as well as the metres of vernacular verse, produced a shorter line than was customary in prose. The lines of vernacular verse were often so short that a two-column format on a larger page was preferable. Whichever layout was adopted, the treatment of the first letter of each line was given special prominence. The history of this practice is still to be written: it may date back to a time when written texts were still a mnemonic device, subordinate to recitation, in which the distinction and isolation of first letters form a series of signposts to the text. The importance of this practice was emphasized in the medieval manuscripts by single or even double vertical rules separating initial from subsequent text. The convention was still considered sufficiently important to be preserved by Aldus, the distinction further emphasized by the contrast between upright capital and the sloped italic or Greek minuscule that followed it.

All these conventions applied to verse. In prose, the proportions of the page were variable, but conformed to a familiar oblong, once squarer (a proportion derived from the papyrus roll) but becoming narrower to between 4:3 and 3:2.[18] Books for the pocket were smaller and narrower: a copy of the Statutes and Register of Writs written in England in 1342 (Bodleian, Rawlinson c. 454) measures only 118 × 78mm. A still narrower proportion for verse can be traced back to the 13th century. A striking early example is not classical but contemporary Latin verse, the *Carolinus* of Gilles de Paris, written *c.*1200 (Paris, Bibliothèque de l'Arsenal, MS 686), which measures 226 × 128mm. A smaller Petrus Riga *Aurora*, dated 1199, measures 190 × 118mm (Bodleian, Rawlinson c. 819). The *Anticlaudianus* of Alan de Insulis (BL Arundel MS 244), written at Esslingen in 1316, is 210 × 117mm. Other examples of classical texts of the same period could be added.

It may be no coincidence that an increasing number of narrow codices of the classics were produced in Italy towards the end of the 14th century, some large, such as the North Italian Homer in Leontio Pilato's translation, *c.*1370, 327 × 195mm (B.N. lat 7880), others smaller, e.g. the Horace, Persius and Juvenal dated 1391 (BL Add. MS 11964), 230 × 110mm, or the Seneca written at San Gimignano in 1387 (BL Burney MS 250), 220 × 145mm. None of these is glossed; the preference for a plain text was a mark of the new humanism. It is significant that two of Petrarch's autograph copies of his own works are not only small but narrow. His copy of his own *De sui ipsius et multorum ignorantia*, now at Berlin (Staatsbibliothek, Hamilton 493) measures 160 × 110mm, and the even more famous *Bucolicum carmen* (Biblioteca Apostolica Vaticana, cod. lat. 3558) is almost the same, 158 × 112mm. These dimensions correspond closely to those of the Aldine octavo, at least in its untrimmed state.

Petrarch's example was no doubt influential, but, equally, there were other sources. There is a marked increase in the number of classical texts produced in Italy in pocketable proportions which dates back to at least the beginning of the 15th century. An early example of the pocket-sized classical text is the Ovid (BL Add. MS 17408), certainly written in Italy, perhaps at Florence, and dated 1411, which measures 185 × 90mm. This and its predecessors are mostly plain texts, but the taste for the small narrow format moved up to luxurious copies, elegantly decorated for princes and potentates, secular and ecclesiastic. This fashion may have begun in Florence:[19] the Gallican Psalter without gloss (an interesting text) written and decorated for Lorenzo de' Medici, perhaps on the occasion of his marriage to Clarice Orsini in 1469, is an early example (formerly Abbey MS 3217). The same narrow format was already familiar in Rome, used by Pomponio Leto and others, and it was now given extensive and much more luxurious form by Bartolomeo Sanvito.[20] The vogue spread to North Italy and Naples before the century was out.

Armando Petrucci has shown how the 'modern book' evolved from the combination of the university text, the humanistic revival of the classics, and the popular 'vernacular' book, meant to be carried in a satchel, and how the invention of printing repeated, at much accelerated speed, the same progress.[21] By 1500 the market for printed books was ready for a format made popular in manuscript form a century earlier. The nature of the type for these books also dictated itself. The fashioning of the italic type not only answered to contemporary fashion; it also conformed to a convention at least 40 years old. The style of letter and the format had a resonance of still greater antiquity. In short, the pains that Aldus gave to the design of the italic type are another example of Harry Carter's notion of the 'backward look'.[22] The size and layout of the page were dictated by the same impulse. The creation of Greek Type 4 on exactly the same lines as the italic must be evidence that the experiment was held to have been a success.

As with the Greek types, then, the italic must be considered not as slavishly modelled on any particular hand or model, although, just as with Type 4, the evidence is clear that Aldus used his own hand to exemplify what he wanted. But the real model cannot be separated from the page on which it appeared or the decoration with which it was (or was intended) to be accompanied. The pages that struck the book-buyer in 1501 as so novel were not only welcome on that account, but because they conformed to an older set of conventions, now so deeply ingrained that their acceptance was automatic, even unconscious.

References

Note. The text above is slightly adapted from the writer's *Aldus Manutius and the Development of Greek Script and Type* (Sandy Hook, 1985; 2nd edition, New York, 1992).

1. The sources of these, and of the earlier attribution to Petrarch (based on a misunderstanding of the preface to the Aldine edition of 1501), are summarized in A. S. Osley, 'The Origins of Italic Type', *Calligraphy and Palaeography: Essays Presented to Alfred Fairbank on his 70th Birthday* (London, 1975), pp.107-11. See also James Wardrop, *The Script of Humanism: some Aspects of Humanistic Script 1460-1560* (Oxford, 1963), p.35; Alfred Fairbank, 'Three Renaissance Scripts', *Journal of the Society for Italic Handwriting*, no.32 (1962), pp.9-11; and A. F. Johnson, *Type Designs: their History and Development*, 2nd edition (London, 1959), pp.92-6. A more general view is provided in L. Balsamo and A. Tinto, *Origini del Corsivo nella Tipografia italiana del Cinquecento* (Milan, 1967), pp.1, 13-21, 25-41. The typographical evidence is most thoroughly analysed in G. Mardersteig, 'Aldo Manuzio e i Caratteri di Francesco Griffo da Bologna', *Studi di Bibliografia in Onore de Tammaro de Marinis* (Verona, 1964), III.105-47, especially pp.139-43. The latest

58   A MILLENNIUM OF THE BOOK

account, with some original observations, is by H. G. Fletcher, in *New Aldine Studies* (San Francisco, 1988), pp.77-87.

2.   N. Barker, *Aldus Manutius and the Development of Greek Script and Type*, 2nd ed. (New York, 1992), p.22.

3.   Ibid., p.60.

4.   W. and L. Hellinga, *The Fifteenth-Century Types of the Low Countries* (Amsterdam, 1966), I, tables 1-128, and pp.4-9, 14-17, 25-8 and 59-62.

5.   George Painter, 'Gutenberg and the B-36 Group: a Re-consideration'. *Essays in Honour of Victor Scholderer* (Mainz, 1970), pp.292-322.

6.   A. Petrucci, 'Alle origini del libro moderno: libri da banco, libri da bisaccia, libretti da mano', *Italia Medioevale e Umanistica* 12 (1969), pp.295-313, especially pp.306-11.

7.   Reproduced in *Griechische Handschriften und Aldinen*, ed. D. Harlfinger and M. Sicherl (Wolfenbüttel, 1978), pl.47; C. Castellani, *L'arte della stampa nel Rinascimento italiano* (Venice, 1894), pl. facing p.15; and *Aus der Handschriften-Abteilung der Preussischen Stattsbibliothek: Abhandlungen und Nachbildungen von Autographen Ludwig Darmstaedter zum 76 Geburtstage dergebracht von H. Degering, K. Christ & J. Schuster* (Berlin, 1922), pp.116-19 (rep. p.119).

8.   Wardrop, p.22.

9.   M. Lowry, *The World of Aldus Manutius* (Oxford, 1979), pp.48-51, 183, 193.

10. Vat. lat. 7205, ff.1-52. Cf. P. Nolhac, *La bibliothèque de Fulvio Orsini* (Paris, 1887), pp.116-21 and 334-96.

11. Nolhac, op. cit., and V. Zabughin, *Giulio Pomponio Leto: saggio critico* (Grottaferrata, 1909-12).

12. 'Due nuovi codici autografi di Pomponio Leto', originally published in 1948, and reprinted with corrections in *Italia medioevale e umanistica* 2 (1959), pp.337-51.

13. Muzzioli, p.343.

14. Ibid., p.350.

15. Fletcher, pp.78-9.

16. See *A Catalogue of the Ahmanson –Murphy Aldine Collection at U.C.L.A.*, Fasc. I (Los Angeles, 1989), pp.xxi-xxx.

17. I owe this observation to Paul Needham, who suggested that it may be responsible for the perceptible alteration (taller folios and octavos, squarer quartos) observable in the late 16th and 17th centuries. Either way, it is unlikely to be connected with the complaints of Urceus Codrus in 1498 about the expense and unnecessarily large margins of Aldine books (see Lowry, p.168, n.21).

18. A 9th-century formulary for layout indicates a proportion for the page of 5:4 (Paris, B.N. lat. 11884). See E. K. Rand and L. W. Jones, *Studies in the Script of Tours* (Cambridge, Mass., 1934), II.88. There is, as far as I know, no other documentary evidence about the relative proportion of the page in the middle ages, apart from the diagram in the Villard de Honnecourt model book. It may, however, be not without significance that the narrow Aldine format follows the Golden Rule or Section (1:1.618). See J. Tschichold, 'Non-Arbitrary Proportions of Page and Type Area', *Calligraphy and Palaeography: Essays Presented to Alfred Fairbank on his 70th Birthday*, ed. A. S. Osley (London, 1965), pp.179-91.

19. See Petrucci, loc. cit., p.302, for the special significance of the 'libro popolare' (not necessarily, however, in narrow format) at Florence.

THE ALDINE ITALIC   59

20. The handful of humanistic classical texts acquired by Joseph Smith (BL King's MSS 24-29), including the Virgil written by Sanvito and Pomponio Leto's Martial, all conform to the narrow proportion, and most are in the small format.
21. Petrucci, loc. cit.
22. H. Carter, *A View of Early Typography* (Oxford, 1979), p.31.

Part II
The Impact of Print

[3]

Some Conjectures about the Impact of Printing on Western Society and Thought: A Preliminary Report

Elizabeth L. Eisenstein
American University

We should note the force, effect, and consequences of inventions which are nowhere more conspicuous than in those three which were unknown to the ancients, namely, printing, gunpowder, and the compass. For these three have changed the appearance and state of the whole world.—FRANCIS BACON, *Novum organum,* Aphorism 129

This paper presents portions of a work that is still in progress. It deals with "the force, effect, and consequences" of the first invention singled out by Bacon. Much has been written about how the way was paved for Gutenberg's invention and about the problem of defining just what he did invent. There are few studies, however, of the consequences that ensued once the new process had been launched.[1] Explicit theories as to what these consequences were have not yet been framed, let alone tested or contested. To develop such theories is much easier said than done. Still, I think the effort should be made. Consequences entailed by a major transformation have to be reckoned with whether we pay attention to them or not. In one guise or another they will enter into our accounts and can best be dealt with when they do not slip in unobserved.

To dwell on the reasons why Bacon's advice ought to be followed by others is probably less helpful than trying to follow it oneself. This

---

[1] The scarcity of historical treatments of this topic came to my attention when reading Marshall McLuhan's *The Gutenberg Galaxy: The Making of Typographical Man* (Toronto, 1962). The author has deliberately jumbled his data and is unconcerned about historical context. Despite the vast literature on printing, an adequate context has not yet been supplied. A good recent selective bibliography is in W. T. Berry and H. E. Poole, *Annals of Printing A Chronological Encyclopædia from Earliest Times to 1950* (London, 1966), pp. 287–94. More recent works include two particularly pertinent titles, i.e., J. Carter and P. Muir (eds.), *Printing and the Mind of Man: The Impact of Print on the Evolution of Western Civilization during Five Centuries* (Cambridge, 1967)—an enlarged descriptive catalogue offering four hundred-odd entries on "great books" displayed at a 1963 London exhibition—and Rudolph Hirsch, *Printing, Selling, Reading 1450–1550* (Wiesbaden, 1967)—an uneven study whose defects and merits are summarized in the *Times Literary Supplement* (Sept. 21, 1967), p. 848. There is a large monographic literature on early printers, the book trade, censorship, journalism, and other special aspects. Different portions of it have been synthesized by Lucien Febvre and H. J. Martin, *L'Apparition du livre* (*L'Évolution de l'humanité,* Vol. XLIX [Paris, 1958]), and by S. H. Steinberg, *Five Hundred Years of Printing* (rev. ed.; Bristol, 1961). It has not been assimilated into other historical treatments. When sections are devoted to printing in general works, the topic is segregated from related developments.

2   *Elizabeth L. Eisenstein*

task clearly outstrips the competence of any single individual. It calls for the pooling of many talents and the writing of many books. Collaboration is difficult to obtain as long as the relevance of the topic to different fields of study remains obscure. Before aid can be enlisted, it seems necessary to develop some tentative hypotheses and to suggest how they relate to particular historical problems. This is the purpose of my work in progress, some samples of which I am offering here. Speculations that are possibly unfounded and certainly still shaky will be presented to stimulate thought and encourage further study.

I. Defining the Initial Change of Phase: An Invisible Revolution in the Late Fifteenth Century

As you may have noted, I have already reformulated Bacon's advice by taking it to pertain, not to a single invention that is coupled with others, but rather to the launching of a new process and to a major transformation. Indecision about what is meant by the advent of printing has, I think, helped to muffle concern about its possible consequences and made them more difficult to track down. It is difficult to find out what happened in a particular Mainz workshop in the 1450's. When pursuing other inquiries, it seems almost prudent to bypass so problematic an event. This does not apply to the appearance of new occupational groups, workshops, techniques, trade networks, and products unknown anywhere in Europe before the mid-fifteenth century and found in every regional center by the early sixteenth century. To pass by all that when dealing with other problems would seem to be incautious. For this reason, among others, I am skipping over the perfection of a new process for printing with movable types and will take as my point of departure, instead, the large-scale utilization of this process.

By the advent of printing, then, I mean the establishment of presses in major urban centers throughout Europe during an interval that coincides, roughly, with the era of incunabula.[2] So few studies have been devoted to this point of departure that no conventional label has yet been attached to it. One might talk about a basic change in a mode of production, or a communications revolution, or (most explicitly) a shift from scribal to typographical culture. Whatever label is used, it should be understood to cover a large cluster of relatively simultaneous, closely interrelated changes, each of which needs closer study and more explicit treatment—as the following quick sketch may suggest.

---

[2] That the era of incunabula should be extended to encompass the first few decades of the sixteenth century is persuasively argued by Steinberg. By subdividing the first century of printing into successive phases, Steinberg brings out the initial transformation more clearly than do the other authorities cited above.

The Impact of Printing on Western Society and Thought **3**

First of all, the marked increase in the output of books and the more drastic reduction in the number of man-hours required to turn them out deserve stronger emphasis. At present there is a tendency to think of a steady increase in book production during the last century of scribal culture followed by a steady increase during the first century of printing. An evolutionary model of change is applied to a situation that seems to call for a revolutionary one. A hard-working copyist turned out two books in little less than a year. An average edition of an early printed book ranged from two hundred to one thousand copies. Chaucer's clerk longed for twenty books to fill his shelf; ten copyists had to be recruited to serve each such clerk down to the 1450's, whereas one printer was serving twenty before 1500.[3] The point is that references to "enormous numbers" of scribal books are deceptive.[4] With regard to quantitative output, an abrupt change, not a gradual one, probably occurred.

Similarly, qualitative changes affecting the nature of the book itself—its format, arrangement of contents, page layouts, and illustrations—need to be underlined. That late manuscripts resembled early incunabula, that scribes and printers copied each others' products for several decades,[5] should not distract attention from changes that occurred when the single text was replaced by a first edition and the manuscript became "copy" that was edited and processed before duplication. Even before 1500 such changes were being registered. Title pages and running heads

---

[3] I have simplified figures offered by D. McMurtrie, *The Book* (Oxford, 1943), p. 214, as to 268 printers in Venice who turned out two million volumes between 1481–1501 and those given by M. Plant, *The English Book Trade* (London, 1939), p. 22, concerning the ten thousand copyists at work in regions near Paris and Orleans during the fifteenth century in order to contrast very roughly the probable output of a major center of scribal book production with that of a main early printing center.

[4] See, e.g., remarks by P. O. Kristeller, *Renaissance Thought,* Vol. I: *The Classic, Scholastic and Humanist Strains* (New York, 1961), pp. 14–15. The establishment of paper mills probably did *not* produce an effect "similar" to that of the printing press. Paper could quicken the pace of private, official, and commercial correspondence and enable more men-of-letters to be their own scribes. But, since it still took almost a year for a professional scribe to turn out two books, a relatively sluggish increase in the output of books probably occurred.

[5] Curt F. Bühler, *The Fifteenth Century Book The Scribes The Printers The Decorators* (Philadelphia, 1960), describes the late fifteenth century as a "no-man's-land" between written and printed books (p. 16) and proves that most late manuscripts are copies of printed books. This temporary physical resemblance makes it more difficult to see how incunabula differed from late manuscripts and more important to emphasize that two fundamentally disparate products were involved. A detailed, vivid account of this disparity is given by E. P. Goldschmidt, *Medieval Texts and Their First Appearance in Print* (Bibliographical Society Publication [London, 1943]), pp. 89 ff.

4   *Elizabeth L. Eisenstein*

were becoming common, and texts were being illustrated by "exactly repeatable pictorial statements" designed by woodcarvers and engravers.[6] Not only were products from artisan workshops introduced into scholarly texts, but the new mode of book production itself brought metalworkers and merchants into contact with schoolmen. A most interesting study might be devoted to a comparison of the talents and skills mobilized within printers' workshops with those previously employed in scriptoria.

Other changes associated with the shift from a retail trade to a wholesale industry also need to be explored. Early crises of overproduction and drives to tap new markets could be contrasted with the incapacity of manuscript dealers and copyists to supply existing demands. The movement of centers of book production from university towns and patrician villas to commercial centers, the organization of new trade networks and fairs, competition over lucrative privileges and monopolies, and restraints imposed by new official controls have all been covered in special accounts.[7] But the implications of such changes need to be spelled out. If it is true that the main bulk of book production was taken out of the hands of churchmen, who ran most large scriptoria, and was lodged in those of early capitalists, who established printing plants, this is surely worth spelling out. If such a statement will not hold up or merely needs to be qualified, then this too is something we need to be told.

We also need to hear more about the job printing that accompanied book-printing.[8] It lent itself to commercial advertising, official propaganda, seditious agitation, and bureaucratic red tape as no scribal procedure ever had. A new form of silent publicity enabled printers not only to advertise their own wares but also to contribute to, and profit from, the expansion of other commercial enterprises. What effects did the appearance of new advertising techniques have on commerce and industry? Possibly some answers to this question are known. Probably others can still be found. Many other aspects of job printing and the changes it entailed clearly need further study. The calendars and indulgences issued from the Mainz workshops of Gutenberg and Fust, for example, warrant at least as much attention as the more celebrated Bibles. Indeed the mass production of indulgences[9] illustrates very

[6] See William Ivins, *Prints and Visual Communication* (Cambridge, Mass., 1953). Ivins persuasively describes the revolutionary effects produced by woodcuts and engravings but underestimates (in my view) those produced by typography. His study is nonetheless invaluable.

[7] Much of this is covered in detail by Febvre and Martin. See chap. vi.

[8] Although Steinberg, p. 22, stresses this aspect of Gutenberg's invention as the most far reaching, it is underplayed in most accounts.

[9] *Ibid.,* p. 139. On an interesting connection between the fall of Constantinople

The Impact of Printing on Western Society and Thought   5

neatly the sort of change that often goes overlooked so that its consequences are more difficult to reckon with than perhaps they need be.

In contrast to the changes sketched above, those that were associated
with the consumption of new printed products are more intangible, indirect, and difficult to handle. A large margin for uncertainty must be
left when dealing with such changes. Many of them—those associated
with the spread of literacy, for example—also have to be left for later
discussion, since prolonged transformations were entailed. Yet relatively
abrupt changes belonging to my original cluster *were* experienced by
already literate sectors. More thought might be given to the social composition of these sectors. Although rigorous analysis is impossible on the
basis of scribal records, useful guesses could be made. Did printing at
first serve an urban patriciate as a "divine art" or more humble folk as
a "poor man's friend"? Since it was described in both ways by contemporaries, possibly it served in both ways. If we think about Roman
slaves or later parish priests, lay clerks, and notaries, it seems that literacy was by no means congruent with elite social status. The new presses,
therefore, probably did not *gradually* make available to low-born men
what had previously been restricted to the high born. Instead, changes in
mental habits and attitudes entailed by access to printed materials affected a wide social spectrum from the outset. In fifteenth-century England, for example, mercers and scriveners engaged in a manuscript book
trade were already catering to the needs of lowly bakers and merchants
as well as to those of lawyers, aldermen, and knights.[10] The new mode
of book production also left many unlettered nobles and squires untouched for some time.

While postponing until later conjectures about social and psychological transformations, certain points should be noted here. One must
distinguish, as Altick suggests, between literacy and habitual book-
reading. Even down to the present, by no means all who master the
written word become members of a book-reading public.[11] Learning
to read is different, moreover, from learning *by reading*. Reliance on
apprenticeship training, oral communication, and special mnemonic

---

and Gutenberg's indulgences (the first dated printed products), see McMurtrie,
p. 149. The first known piece of printing in England was also an indulgence,
issued by Caxton for an abbot in 1476.

[10] E. F. Jacob, *The Fifteenth Century 1399–1485 (Oxford History of England*
[Oxford, 1961]), pp. 663–67. See also J. W. Adamson, "The Extent of Literacy
in England in the Fifteenth and Sixteenth Centuries: Notes and Conjectures,"
Library, X (Sept. 1929), 163–93; H. S. Bennett, *English Books and Readers
1475–1557* (Cambridge, 1952), p. 20. Continental developments are noted by
Hirsch, pp. 147–53.

[11] R. Altick, *The English Common Reader. A Social History of the Mass
Reading Public, 1800–1900* (Chicago, 1963), p. 31.

6   *Elizabeth L. Eisenstein*

devices had gone together with mastering letters in the age of scribes. After the advent of printing, however, learning by doing became more sharply distinguished from learning by reading, while the role played by hearsay and memory arts diminished. Since they affected the transmission of all forms of knowledge, such changes seem relevant to historical inquiries of every kind. Issues pertaining to shifts in book-reading habits go far beyond the special concerns of literary historians. They have a direct bearing on economic, legal, technological, and political developments as well. Last but not least, the most important members of the new book-reading public in the age of incunabula are most often overlooked. They belonged to the new occupational groups created by the new mode of production. Those who processed texts or presided over the new presses were the first to read the products that came off them. In particular, early scholar-printers themselves registered most forcefully the consequences of access to printed materials. It is possibly because of this kind of "feedback" that the infant industry was so rapidly modernized. As early as the 1480's, "modern" workshops had already displaced "medieval" ones, and several "large capitalist firms" had already been launched.[12]

II. RELATING THE TYPOGRAPHICAL REVOLUTION TO OTHER DEVELOPMENTS

Granted that some sort of revolution did occur during the late fifteenth century. How did this affect other historical developments? Since the consequences of printing have not been thoroughly explored, guidance is hard to come by. Most conventional surveys stop short after a few remarks about the wider dissemination of humanist tomes or Protestant tracts. Several helpful suggestions—about the effects of standardization on scholarship and science, for example—are offered in works devoted to the era of the Renaissance or the history of science. By and large, the effects of the new process are vaguely implied rather than explicitly defined and are also drastically minimized. One example may illustrate this point. During the first centuries of printing, old texts were duplicated more rapidly than new ones. On this basis we are told that "printing did not speed up the adoption of new theories."[13] But where did these new theories come from? Must we invoke some spirit of the times, or is it possible that an increase in the output of old texts contributed to the formulation of new theories? Maybe other features that distinguished the new mode of book production from the old one also contributed to such theories. We need to take stock of these features before we can relate the advent of printing to other historical developments.

[12] Febvre and Martin, p. 193.
[13] *Ibid.*, pp. 420–21.

The Impact of Printing on Western Society and Thought   7

I have found it useful, in any case, to start taking stock by following up clues contained in special studies on printing. After singling out certain features that seemed peculiar to typography, I held them in mind while passing in review various historical developments. Relationships emerged that had not occurred to me before, and some possible solutions to old puzzles were suggested. Conjectures based on this approach may be sampled below under headings that indicate my main lines of inquiry.

A. *A Closer Look at Wide Dissemination: Various Effects Produced by Increased Output*

Most references to wide dissemination are too fleeting to make clear the specific effects of an increased supply of texts directed at different markets. In particular they fail to make clear how patterns of consumption were affected by increased production. Here the term "dissemination" is sufficiently inappropriate to be distracting. Some mention of cross-fertilization or cross-cultural interchange should be included in surveys or summaries. More copies of one given text, for instance, *were* "spread, dispersed, or scattered" by the issue of a printed edition.[14] For the individual book-reader, however, different texts, which were previously dispersed and scattered, were also brought closer together. In some regions, printers produced more scholarly texts than they could sell and flooded local markets.[15] In all regions, a given purchaser could buy more books at lower cost and bring them into his study or library. In this way, the printer provided the clerk with a richer, more varied literary diet than had been provided by the scribe. To consult different books it was no longer so essential to be a wandering scholar. Successive generations of sedentary scholars were less apt to be engrossed by a single text and to expend their energies in elaborating on it. The era of the glossator and commentator came to an end, and a new "era of intense cross referencing between one book and another"[16] began. More abundantly stocked bookshelves increased opportunities to consult and compare different texts and, thus, also made more probable the formation of new intellectual combinations and permutations. Viewed in this

[14] Since this enabled scattered readers to consult the same book, it may be regarded as an aspect of standardization which is discussed in the next section.

[15] Early crises of overproduction of humanist works are noted by Denys Hay, "Literature, the Printed Book," in G. R. Elton (ed.), *The New Cambridge Modern History* (Cambridge, 1958), II, 365. The failure of printers to assess their markets shrewdly, which accounts for some of these crises, is noted by Bühler, pp. 59–61. Inadequate distribution networks at first were largely responsible. Zainer's firm, e.g., turned out 36,000 books when the population of Augsburg was half that number (Bühler, p. 56).

[16] Hay, p. 366. By the mid-sixteenth century, "even obscure scholars could possess a relatively large collection of books on a single topic," according to A. R. Hall, "Science," in Elton (ed.), II, 389.

8   *Elizabeth L. Eisenstein*

light, cross-cultural interchanges fostered by printing seem relevant to Sarton's observation: "The Renaissance was a transmutation of values, a 'new deal,' a reshuffling of cards, but most of the cards were old; the scientific Renaissance was a 'new deal,' but many of the cards were new."[17] Combinatory intellectual activity, as Koestler has recently suggested, inspires many creative acts. Once old texts came together within the same study, diverse systems of ideas and special disciplines could be combined. Increased output directed at relatively stable markets, in short, created conditions that favored, first, new combinations of old ideas and, then, the creation of entirely new systems of thought.

Merely by making more scrambled data available, by increasing the output of second-century Ptolemaic maps and twelfth-century *mappae mundi,* for instance, printers encouraged efforts to unscramble these data. Hand-drafted portolans had long been more accurate, but few eyes had seen them.[18] Much as maps from different regions and epochs were brought into contact, so too were diverse textual traditions previously preserved by specially trained groups of schoolmen and scribes. It should be noted that cross-cultural interchange was not solely a consequence of augmented output. For example, texts were provided with new illustrations drawn from artisan workshops instead of scriptoria. Here again, different traditions were brought into contact. In this case, words drawn from one milieu and pictures from another were placed beside each other within the same books.[19] When considering new views of the "book of nature" or the linking of bookish theories with observations and craft skills, it may be useful to look at the ateliers of Renaissance artists. But one must also go on to visit early printers' workshops, for it is there above all that we "can observe the formation of groups . . . conducive to cross-fertilization"[20] of all kinds.

[17] George Sarton, "The Quest for Truth: Scientific Progress during the Renaissance," in W. K. Ferguson *et al., The Renaissance: Six Essays* (Metropolitan Museum of Art Symposium, 1953 [New York, 1962]), p. 57.

[18] These maps are compared and the superiority of manuscript charts to early printed maps is noted by Boies Penrose, *Travel and Discovery in the Renaissance 1420–1620* (New York, 1962), chap. xvi. The logical conclusion—that intelligent, literate sixteenth-century printers did not know what cartographers and mariners in coastal regions did—is, however, not drawn.

[19] See R. J. Forbes and E. J. Dijksterhuis, *A History of Science and Technology* (London, 1963), Vol. II, chap. xvi, on how "technology went to press" in the sixteenth century. A. R. Hall, *The Scientific Revolution 1500–1800: The Formation of the Modern Scientific Attitude* (Boston, 1957), p. 43, states: "Vesalius' cuts are sometimes less traditional and more accurate than his text." The cuts were made, however, by a wood-carver, Stephan of Calcar. (See n. 20 below.)

[20] Erwin Panofsky, "Artist, Scientist, Genius: Notes on the Renaissance-Dämmerung," in Ferguson *et al.,* p. 160. This whole essay (which passes over

The Impact of Printing on Western Society and Thought   9

Cross-cultural interchange stimulated mental activities in contradictory ways. The first century of printing was marked above all by intellectual ferment and by a "somewhat wide-angled, unfocused scholarship."[21] Certain confusing cross-currents may be explained by noting that new links between disciplines were being forged before old ones had been severed. In the age of scribes, for instance, magical arts were closely associated with mechanical crafts. Trade skills were passed down by closed circles of initiates. Unwritten recipes used by the alchemist were not clearly distinguished from those used by the apothecary or surgeon, the goldsmith or engraver. When "technology went to press," so too did a vast backlog of occult lore, and few readers could discriminate between the two.

The divine art or "mystery" of printing unleashed a "churning turbid flood of Hermetic, cabbalistic, Gnostic, theurgic, Sabaean, Pythagorean, and generally mystic notions."[22] Historians are still puzzled by certain strange deposits left by this flood. They might find it helpful to consider how records derived from ancient Near Eastern cultures had been transmitted in the age of scribes. Some of these records had dwindled into tantalizing fragments pertaining to systems of reckoning, medicine, agriculture, mythic cults, and so forth. Others had evaporated into unfathomable glyphs. All were thought to come from one body of pure knowledge originally set down by an Egyptian scribal god and carefully preserved by ancient sages and seers before becoming corrupted and confused. A collection of writings containing ancient lore was received from Macedonia by Cosimo de' Medici, translated by Ficino in 1463, and printed in fifteen editions before 1500. It seemed to come from this body of knowledge—and was accordingly attributed to "Hermes Trismegistus." The hermetic corpus ran through many more editions during the next century before it was shown to have been compiled in the third century A.D. On this basis we are told that Renaissance scholars had made a radical error in dating.[23] But to assign definite dates to scribal compilations, which were probably derived from earlier sources, may be an error as well.

The transformation of occult and esoteric scribal lore after the advent

---

the role of printing) is relevant to the above discussion. Stephan of Calcar's role in Vesalius' work is noted on p. 162, n. 36.

[21] E. Harris Harbison, *The Christian Scholar in the Age of the Reformation* (New York, 1956), p. 54.

[22] G. de Santillana, review of F. Yates's *Giordano Bruno and the Hermetic Tradition*, *American Historical Review*, LXX (Jan. 1965), 455.

[23] See Frances Yates, *Giordano Bruno and the Hermetic Tradition* (London, 1964), *passim*. That ancient Egyptian ingredients *were* present in the third-century compilation is suggested on pp. 2–3, n. 4, and p. 431.

10   *Elizabeth L. Eisenstein*

of printing also needs more study. Some arcane writings, in Greek, Hebrew or Syriac, for example, became less mysterious. Others became more so. Thus hieroglyphs were set in type more than three centuries before their decipherment. These sacred carved letters were loaded with significant meaning by readers who could not read them.[24] They were also used simply as ornamental motifs by architects and engravers. Given baroque decoration on one hand and complicated interpretations by scholars, Rosicrucians, and Freemasons on the other, the duplication of Egyptian picture writing throughout the Age of Reason presents modern scholars with puzzles that can never be solved. In brief, when considering the effects produced by printing on scholarship, it is a mistake to think only about new forms of enlightenment. New forms of mystification were entailed as well.

It is also a mistake to think only about scholarly markets when considering the effects of increased output. Dissemination as defined in the dictionary does seem appropriate to the duplication of primers and *ABC* books, almanacs, and picture Bibles. An increased output of devotional literature was not necessarily conducive to cross-cultural interchange. Catechisms, religious tracts, and Bibles would fill some bookshelves to the exclusion of all other reading matter. A new wide-angled, unfocused scholarship had to compete with a new single-minded, narrowly focused piety. At the same time, guidebooks and manuals also became more abundant, making it easier to lay plans for getting ahead in this world—possibly diverting attention from uncertain futures in the next one. It is doubtful whether "the effect of the new invention on scholarship" was more important than these other effects "at the beginning of the sixteenth century."[25] What does need emphasis is that many dissimilar effects, all of great consequence, came relatively simultaneously. If this could be spelled out more clearly, seemingly contradictory developments might be confronted with more equanimity. The intensifi-

[24] On the "Hieroglyphics of Horapollo" (first printed by Aldus in Greek, 1505, in Latin, 1515) and later developments, see Erik Iversen, *The Myth of Egypt and Its Hieroglyphs in European Tradition* (Copenhagen, 1961), *passim.* Additional data is given by E. P. Goldschmidt, *The Printed Book of the Renaissance: Three Lectures on Type, Illustration, Ornament* (Cambridge, 1950), pp. 84–85, and Mario Praz, *Studies in Seventeenth Century Imagery* (Rome, 1964), chap. i. Yates implies that baroque argumentation about *hermetica* ended with Isaac Casaubon's early seventeenth-century proof that Ficino had translated works dating from the third century A.D. But Greek scholarship alone could not unlock the secrets of the pyramids. Interest in arcana associated with Thoth and "Horapollo" continued until Champollion. By then the cluster of mysteries that had thickened with each successive "unveiling of Isis" was so opaque that even the decipherment of the Rosetta stone could not dispel them.

[25] Myron Gilmore, *The World of Humanism 1453–1517* (*Rise of Modern Europe* [New York, 1952]), p. 189.

The Impact of Printing on Western Society and Thought   11

cation of both religiosity and secularism could be better understood. Some debates about periodization also could be bypassed. Medieval world pictures, for example, were duplicated more rapidly during the first century of printing than they had been during the so-called Middle Ages. They did not merely *survive* among the Elizabethans. They became *more available* to poets and playwrights of the sixteenth century than they had been to minstrels and mummers of the thirteenth century.

In view of such considerations, I cannot agree with Sarton's comment: "It is hardly necessary to indicate what the art of printing meant for the diffusion of culture but one should not lay too much stress on diffusion and should speak more of standardization."[26] How printing changed patterns of cultural diffusion deserves much more study than it has yet received. Moreover, individual access to diverse texts is a different matter than bringing many minds to bear on a single text. The former issue is apt to be neglected by too exclusive an emphasis on "standardization."

B. *Considering Some Effects Produced by Standardization*

Although it has to be considered in conjunction with many other issues, standardization certainly does deserve closer study. One specialist has argued that it is currently overplayed.[27] Yet it may well be still under-stressed. Perhaps early printing methods made it impossible to issue the kind of "standard" editions with which modern scholars are familiar. Certainly press variants did multiply, and countless errata were issued. The fact remains that Erasmus or Bellarmine could issue errata; Jerome or Alcuin could not. The very act of publishing errata demonstrated a new capacity to locate textual errors with precision and to transmit this information simultaneously to scattered readers. It thus illustrates, rather neatly, some of the effects of standardization. However fourteenth-century copyists were supervised, scribes were incapable of committing the sort of "standardized" error that led printers to be fined for the "wicked Bible" of 1631.[28] If a single compositor's error could be circulated in a great many copies, so too could a single scholar's emendation.[29] However, when I suggest that we may still underestimate the implications of standardization, I am not thinking primarily about

[26] Sarton, p. 66.

[27] On what follows, see remarks by M. H. Black, "The Printed Bible," in S. L. Greenslade (ed.), *The Cambridge History of the Bible* (Cambridge, 1963), pp. 408–14.

[28] The word "not" had been omitted from the seventh commandment (*ibid.,* p. 412).

[29] How important this was is stressed both by Gilmore, p. 189, and Sarton, p. 66.

12   *Elizabeth L. Eisenstein*

textual emendations or errors. I am thinking instead about the new output of exactly repeatable pictorial statements, such as maps, charts, diagrams, and other visual aids;[30] of more uniform reference guides, such as calendars, thesauruses, dictionaries; of increasingly regular systems of notation, whether musical, mathematical, or grammatical. How different fields of study and aesthetic styles were affected by such developments remains to be explored. It does seem worth suggesting that both our so-called two cultures were affected. Humanist scholarship, belles lettres, and fine arts must be considered along with celestial mechanics, anatomy, and cartography.[31]

Too many important variations were, indeed, played on the theme of standardization for all of them to be listed here. This theme entered into every operation associated with typography, from the replica casting of precisely measured pieces of type[32] to the subliminal impact upon scattered readers of repeated encounters with identical type styles, printers' devices, and title-page ornamentation.[33] Calligraphy itself was affected. Sixteenth-century specimen books stripped diverse scribal "hands" of personal idiosyncracies. They did for handwriting what style books did for typography itself; what pattern books did for dressmaking, furniture, architectural motifs, and ground plans. In short the setting of standards —used for innumerable purposes, from cutting cloth to city-planning— accompanied the output of more standardized products.

Here, as elsewhere, we need to recall that early printers were responsible not only for issuing new standard reference guides but also for compiling many of them.[34] A subsequent division of labor tends to

[30] The historical importance of new standardized images is spelled out most clearly by Ivins. K. Boulding, *The Image* (Ann Arbor, Mich., 1961), pp. 64–68, incorrectly assigns to the invention of writing the capacity to produce uniform spatiotemporal images. His remarks about the "disassociated transcript" do not seem applicable to scribal culture.

[31] Ernst Curtius, *European Literature and the Latin Middle Ages,* trans. W. Trask (New York, 1963; 1st ed., 1948), exemplifies erudite humanistic scholarship at its best. Yet his remarks on scribal book production are remarkably fanciful, on changes wrought by printing entirely vacuous (p. 238). His failure to consider how all the issues he deals with were affected by the new technology is shared by most literary scholars and historians of ideas.

[32] See Steinberg, p. 25.

[33] The probable effect of title-page ornamentation on sixteenth-century fine arts and the necessity of taking printing into account when dealing with new aesthetic styles is noted by André Chastel, "What is Mannerism?" *Art News,* LXIV (Dec. 1965), 53.

[34] This applies particularly to the publisher-printer (or printer-bookseller) as described, e.g., by Elizabeth Armstrong, *Robert Estienne Royal Printer: An Historical Study of the Elder Stephanus* (Cambridge, 1954), pp. 18, 68. It is also applicable to many independent master printers, to some merchant-publishers (who, literally defined, were not printers at all and yet closely supervised the processing of texts—even editing and compiling some themselves), and finally to

The Impact of Printing on Western Society and Thought 13

divert attention from the large repertoire of roles performed by those who presided over the new presses. A scholar-printer himself might serve as indexer-abridger-lexicographer-chronicler. Whatever roles he performed, decisions about standards to be adopted when processing texts for publication could not be avoided. A suitable type style had to be selected or designed and house conventions determined. Textual variants and the desirability of illustration and translation also had to be confronted. Accordingly, the printer's workshop became the most advanced laboratory of erudition of the sixteenth century.

Many early capitalist industries required efficient planning, methodical attention to detail, and rational calculation. The decisions made by early printers, however, directly affected both toolmaking and symbolmaking. Their products reshaped powers to manipulate objects, to perceive and think about varied phenomena. Scholars concerned with "modernization" or "rationalization" might profitably think more about the new kind of brainwork fostered by the silent scanning of maps, tables, charts, diagrams, dictionaries, and grammars. They also need to look more closely at the daily routines pursued by those who compiled and produced such reference guides. These routines were conducive to a new *esprit de système*. "It's much easier to find things when they are each disposed in place and not scattered haphazardly," remarked a sixteenth-century publisher.[35] He was justifying the way he had reorganized a text he had edited. He might equally well have been complaining to a clerk who had mislaid some account papers pertaining to the large commercial enterprise he ran.

C. *Some Effects Produced by Editing and Reorganizing Texts: Codifying, Clarifying, and Cataloguing Data*

Editorial decisions made by early printers with regard to layout and presentation probably helped to reorganize the thinking of readers. McLuhan's suggestion that scanning lines of print affected thought processes is at first glance somewhat mystifying. But further reflection suggests that

some skilled journeymen (who served as correctors or were charged with throwing together, from antiquated stock, cheap reprints for mass markets). The divergent social and economic positions occupied by these groups are discussed by Natalie Z. Davis in "Strikes and Salvation at Lyons," *Archiv für Reformationsgeschichte,* LXV (1965), 48, and in "Publisher Guillaume Rouillé, Businessman and Humanist," in R. J. Schoeck (ed.), *Editing Sixteenth Century Texts* (Toronto, 1966), pp. 73–76. Within workshops down through the eighteenth century, divisions of labor varied so widely and were blurred so frequently that they must be left out of account for the purpose of developing my conjectures. Accordingly I use the term "printer" very loosely to cover all these groups throughout this paper.

[35] Cited by Davis, "Guillaume Rouillé," p. 100.

14   *Elizabeth L. Eisenstein*

the thoughts of readers are guided by the way the contents of books are arranged and presented. Basic changes in book format might well lead to changes in thought patterns. Such changes began to appear in the era of incunabula. They made texts more lucid and intelligible. They involved the use "of graduated types, running heads . . . footnotes . . . tables of contents . . . superior figures, cross references . . . and other devices available to the compositor"—all registering "the victory of the punch cutter over the scribe."[36] Concern with surface appearance necessarily governed the handwork of the scribe. He was fully preoccupied trying to shape evenly spaced uniform letters in a pleasing symmetrical design. An altogether different procedure was required to give directions to compositors. To do this, one had to mark up a manuscript while scrutinizing its contents. Every scribal text that came into the printer's hands, thus, had to be reviewed in a new way. Within a generation the results of this review were being aimed in a new direction—away from fidelity to scribal conventions and toward serving the convenience of the reader. The competitive and commercial character of the new mode of book production encouraged the relatively rapid adoption of any innovation that commended a given edition to purchasers. In short, providing built-in aids to the reader became for the first time both feasible and desirable.

The introduction and adoption of such built-in aids, from the 1480's on, has been traced and discussed in special works on printing but has been insufficiently noted in other accounts. We are repeatedly told about "dissemination," occasionally about standardization, almost never at all about the codification and clarification that were entailed in editing copy.[37] Yet changes affecting book format probably contributed much to the so-called rationalization of diverse institutions. After all, they

[36] Steinberg, p. 28. A detailed account of the effects of printing on punctuation is given by Hirsch, pp. 136–37.

[37] The "diagrammatic tidiness" imparted by print to "the world of ideas" *is* discussed by Walter J. Ong, S.J., *Ramus: Method and the Decay of Dialogue from the Art of Discourse to the Art of Reason* (Cambridge, Mass., 1958), p. 311. See also his "System, Space and Intellect in Renaissance Symbolism," *Bibliothèque d'humanisme et Renaissance—travaux et documents,* XVIII, No. 2 (1956), 222–40; and his "From Allegory to Diagram in the Renaissance Mind," *Journal of Aesthetics and Art Criticism,* XVII (June 1959), 4. Father Ong's somewhat abstruse discussion has recently been substantiated and supplemented by a straightforward study of changes registered on repeated editions of a popular sixteenth-century reference work, which provides detailed confirmation of the above discussion. See Gerald Straus, "A Sixteenth Century Encyclopedia: Sebastian Münster's *Cosmography* and Its Editions," in C. H. Carter (ed.), *From the Renaissance to the Counter Reformation: Essays in Honor of Garret Mattingly* (New York, 1965), pp. 145–63. See also the discussion of Robert Estienne's pioneering work in lexicography (in Armstrong, chap. iv), and Davis, "Guillaume Rouillé," pp. 100–101.

The Impact of Printing on Western Society and Thought   **15**

affected texts used for the study and practice of law—and consequently had an impact on most organs of the body politic as well.[38] This has been demonstrated by a pioneering study of the "englishing and printing" of the "Great Boke of Statutes 1530–1533."[39] I cannot pause here over the many repercussions, ranging from statecraft to literature, that came in the wake of Tudor law-printing according to this study. To suggest why we need to look at new built-in aids, I will simply point to the introductory "Tabula" to the "Great Boke"; "a chronological register by chapters of the statutes 1327–1523." Here was a table of contents that also served as a "conspectus of parliamentary history"[40]—the first many readers had seen.

This sort of spectacular innovation, while deserving close study, should not divert attention from much less conspicuous but more ubiquitous changes. Increasing familiarity with regularly numbered pages, punctuation marks, section breaks, running heads, indexes, and so forth helped to reorder the thought of *all* readers, whatever their profession or craft. Hence countless activities were subjected to a new *esprit de système*. The use of arabic numbers for pagination suggests how the most inconspicuous innovation could have weighty consequences —in this case, more accurate indexing, annotation, and cross-referencing resulted.[41] Most studies of printing have quite rightly singled out the provision of title pages as the most important of all ubiquitous print-made innovations.[42] How the title page contributed to the cataloguing of books and the bibliographer's craft scarcely needs to be spelled out. How it contributed to a new habit of placing and dating in general does, I think, call for further thought.

On the whole, as I have tried to suggest throughout this discussion, topics now allocated to bibliophiles and specialists on printing are of general concern to historians at large—or, at least, to specialists in

[38] The interplay between the printing of existing laws and laws pertaining to (or necessitated by) printing is an instance of complex interaction that deserves special study.

[39] H. J. Graham, " 'Our Tongue Maternall Marvellously Amendyd and Augmentyd': The First Englishing and Printing of the Medieval Statutes at Large, 1530–1533," *U.C.L.A. Law Bulletin*, XIII (Nov. 1965), 58–98.

[40] *Ibid.,* p. 66.

[41] G. Sarton, "Incunabula Wrongly Dated," in D. Stimson (ed.), *Sarton on the History of Science* (Cambridge, Mass., 1962), pp. 322–23. Arabic numerals appear for the first time on each page of the Scriptures in Froben's first edition of Erasmus' New Testament of 1516, which also "set the style" for the well-differentiated book and chapter headings employed by other Bible-printers (Black, p. 419). See also Francis J. Witty, "Early Indexing Techniques: A Study of Several Book Indexes of the Fourteenth, Fifteenth, and Early Sixteenth Centuries," *Library Quarterly*, XXXV (July 1965), 141–48.

[42] Steinberg, pp. 145–53.

16 *Elizabeth L. Eisenstein*

many different fields. The way these fields are laid out could be better understood, indeed, if we opened up the one assigned to printing. "Until half a century after Copernicus' death, no potentially revolutionary changes occurred in the data available to astronomers."[43] But Copernicus' life (1473–1543) spanned the very decades when a great many changes, now barely visible to modern eyes, were transforming "the data available" to all book-readers. A closer study of these changes could help to explain why systems of charting the planets, mapping the earth, synchronizing chronologies, and compiling bibliographies were all revolutionized before the end of the sixteenth century.[44] In each instance, one notes, ancient Alexandrian achievements were first reduplicated and then, in a remarkably short time, surpassed. In each instance also, the new schemes once published remained available for correction, development, and refinement. Successive generations of scholars could build on the work of their sixteenth-century predecessors instead of trying to retrieve scattered fragments of it.

The varied intellectual revolutions of early modern times owed much to the features that have already been outlined.[45] But the great tomes, charts, and maps that are now seen as "milestones" might have proved

[43] Thomas Kuhn, *The Copernican Revolution* (Cambridge, Mass., 1957), p. 131.

[44] Ortelius' "epoch-making" *Theatrum orbis terrarum* was published in Antwerp in 1570. (Although Mercator's "milestone" was published in 1569, his new projection remained little known until 1599, when Edmund Wright published a set of rules for its construction.) See Penrose, pp. 324–27. Febvre and Martin, p. 418, point to the fact that Copernicus' *De revolutionibus orbium cælestium* (1543) was not republished in a second edition until 1566 to support the view that printing did not speed up the acceptance of new ideas. In 1551, however, Erasmus Reinhold issued a "complete new set of astronomical tables," based on the *De revolutionibus*. These so-called Prutenic Tables were widely used. See Kuhn, pp. 125, 187–88. The duplication of Napier's logarithms and their use by Kepler in constructing his Rudolphine Tables also seem to me to argue against Febvre and Martin's thesis. See Arthur Koestler, *The Sleepwalkers* (London, 1959), pp. 410–11. J. J. Scaliger's *De emendatione temporum,* which "revolutionized all received ideas of chronology," was published in 1583; R. C. Christie and J. E. Sandys, "Joseph Justus Scaliger (1540–1609)," *Encyclopædia Britannica* (11th ed.; New York, 1911), XXIV, 284. Theodore Besterman, *The Beginnings of Systematic Bibliography* (Oxford, 1936), pp. 7–8, 15–21, 33, argues that Conrad Gesner's *Bibliotheca universalis* (1545), a 1,300-page tome listing 12,000 Latin, Greek, and Hebrew works, does not warrant calling Gesner the "father of bibliography," since Johannes Tritheim's much smaller and restricted *Liber de scriptoribus ecclesiasticus* (1494) preceded it. The "foundations of systematic bibliography were well and truly laid" at any rate before 1600.

[45] The issues dealt with by studies such as F. Smith Fussner's *The Historical Revolution: English Historical Writing and Thought 1580–1640* (London, 1962) and Wylie Sypher's "Similarities between the Scientific and Historical Revolutions at the End of the Renaissance," *Journal of the History of Ideas,* XXV (July–Sept. 1965), 353–68, need particularly to be reviewed in the light of the above discussion.

The Impact of Printing on Western Society and Thought   **17**

insubstantial had not the preservative powers of print also been called into play. Typographical fixity is a basic prerequisite for the rapid advancement of learning. It helps to explain much else that seems to distinguish the history of the past five centuries from that of all prior eras— as I hope the following remarks will suggest.

D. *Considering the Preservative Powers of Print: How Fixity and Accumulation Altered Patterns of Cultural and Institutional Change*[46]

Of all the new features introduced by the duplicative powers of print, preservation is possibly the most important. To appreciate its importance, we need to recall the conditions that prevailed before texts could be set in type. No manuscript, however useful as a reference guide, could be preserved for long without undergoing corruption by copyists, and even this sort of "preservation" rested precariously on the shifting demands of local elites and a fluctuating incidence of trained scribal labor. Insofar as records were seen and used, they were vulnerable to wear and tear. Stored documents were vulnerable to moisture and vermin, theft and fire. However they might be collected or guarded within some great message center, their ultimate dispersal and loss was inevitable. To be transmitted by writing from one generation to the next, information had to be conveyed by drifting texts and vanishing manuscripts.

When considering developments in astronomy (or geography or chronology) during the age of scribes, it is not the slow rate of cognitive advance that calls for explanation. Rather, one might wonder about how the customary process of erosion, corruption, and loss was temporarily arrested. When viewed in this light, the "1,800 years" that elapsed between Hipparchus and Copernicus[47] seem less remarkable than the advances that were made in planetary astronomy during the 600 years that elapsed between Aristotle and Ptolemy. With regard to all computations based on large-scale data collection, whatever had once been clearly seen and carefully articulated grew dimmed and blurred with the passage of time. More than a millennium also elapsed between Eratosthenes and Scaliger, Ptolemy and Mercator. The progress made over the course of centuries within the confines of the Alexandrian

---

[46] For the most part I have omitted from this section issues relating to historical consciousness and historiography, since I have discussed them elsewhere; Elizabeth L. Eisenstein, "Clio and Chronos: An Essay on the Making and Breaking of History-Book Time," *History and the Concept of Time* (*History and Theory*, Suppl. 6 [1966]), pp. 42–64. Certain portions of this essay seemed too pertinent to be excluded, however. They have, therefore, been repeated in a slightly altered form and reworked along with fresh material into a different context here.

[47] Kuhn, p. 73, remarks on this "incredibly long time."

18   *Elizabeth L. Eisenstein*

Museum seems, in short, to have been most exceptional.[48] To be sure, there were intermittent localized "revivals of learning" thereafter, as well as a prolonged accumulation of records within certain message centers. Ground lost by corruption could never be regained, but migrating manuscripts could lead to abrupt recovery as well as to sudden loss. Yet a marked increase in the output of certain kinds of texts resulted generally in a decreased output of other kinds. Similarly, a "revival" in one region often signified a dearth of texts in another.

The incapacity of scribal culture to sustain a simultaneous advance on many fronts in different regions may be relevant to the "problem of the Renaissance." Italian humanist book-hunters, patrons, and dealers tried to replenish a diminished supply of those ancient texts that were being neglected by scribes serving medieval university faculties. Their efforts have been heralded as bringing about a "permanent recovery" of ancient learning and letters.[49] If one accepts the criteria of "totality and permanence" to distinguish prior "revivals" from the Renaissance,[50] then probably the advent of the scholar-printer should be heralded instead. He arrived to cast his Greek types and turn out grammars, translations, and standard editions in the nick of time—almost on the eve of the Valois invasions.[51]

[48] The strategic position occupied by this unique ancient message center (which apparently swallowed up the contents of its only rival in Pergamum in the first century B.C. to make up for losses suffered in the famous fire) has only recently become apparent to me. Possibly it is well known to specialists in ancient history, but it still needs to be spelled out in more general accounts. According to Edward A. Parsons, *The Alexandrian Library* (Amsterdam, 1952), p. xi, the actual use of the museum by scholars over the course of seven (maybe nine) centuries "is still a virgin field of inquiry."

[49] Like almost all other Renaissance scholars, Kristeller, p. 17, while noting that a selection of the "classics" circulated in medieval times, singles out as the special contribution of Renaissance humanism that "it extended its knowledge almost to the entire range of . . . extant remains." This boils down to the fact that most of what was recovered in the trecento and early quattrocento was not again lost. But it came very close to being lost. The manuscript of *De rerum natura* found by Poggio Bracciolini in 1417 *has* disappeared. The future of the copy that was made remained uncertain until 1473, when a printed edition was issued. Thirty more followed before 1600. A school of pagan philosophy intermittently revived and repeatedly snuffed out was thus permanently secured. See Danton B. Sailor, "Moses and Atomism," *Journal of the History of Ideas*, XXV (Jan.–Mar. 1964), 3–16. Other findings from palimpsests and papyri would come later, as Kristeller notes. They came too late to be inserted into a curriculum of classical studies that was "fixed" (by typography) in the sixteenth century. Hence they are regarded as being somewhat peripheral to the central corpus of classical works.

[50] These same criteria, employed implicitly by Kristeller, are more explicitly and forcefully set forth by Erwin Panofsky, *Renaissance and Renascences in Western Art* (Stockholm, 1960), pp. 108, 113. The capacity to view antiquity from a "fixed distance" is, in my view, placed much too early in this study.

[51] Burckhardt notes as a "singular piece of good fortune" that "Northerners

The Impact of Printing on Western Society and Thought   19

Once Greek type fonts had been cut, neither the disruption of civil order in Italy, the conquest of Greek lands by Islam, nor even the translation into Latin of all major Greek texts saw knowledge of Greek wither again in the West. Instead it was the familiar scribal phrase *Graeca sunt ergo non legenda* that disappeared from Western texts. Constantinople fell, Rome was sacked. Yet a cumulative process of textual purification and continuous recovery had been launched. The implications of typographical fixity are scarcely exhausted by thinking about early landmarks in classical scholarship and its auxiliary sciences: paleography, philology, archeology, numismatics, etc. Nor are they exhausted by reckoning the number of languages that have been retrieved after being lost to all men for thousands of years. They involve the whole modern "knowledge industry" itself, with its mushrooming bibliographies and overflowing card files.

They also involve issues that are less academic and more geopolitical. The linguistic map of Europe was "fixed" by the same process and at the same time as Greek letters were. The importance of the fixing of literary vernaculars is often stressed. The strategic role played by printing is, however, often overlooked.[52] How strategic it was is suggested by the following paraphrased summary of Steinberg's account:

> Printing "preserved and codified, sometimes even created" certain vernaculars. Its absence during the sixteenth century among small linguistic groups "demonstrably led" to the disappearance or exclusion of their vernaculars from the realm of literature. Its presence among similar groups in the same century ensured the possibility of intermittent revivals or continued expansion. Having fortified language walls between one group and another, printers homogenized what was within them, breaking down minor differences, standardizing idioms for millions of writers and readers, assigning a new peripheral role to provincial dialects. The preservation of a given literary language often depended on whether or not a few vernacular primers,

---

like Agricola, Reuchlin, Erasmus, the Stephani and Budaeus" had mastered Greek when it was dying out—with the "last colony" of Byzantine exiles—in the 1520's in Italy; Jacob Burckhardt, *The Civilization of the Renaissance in Italy,* trans. S. G. C. Middlemore (New York, 1958), I, 205. The Aldine Press (among others) had already insured its perpetuation, however. All these "northerners," one notes, were close allies of scholar-printers or (as with the "Stephani," i.e., Estiennes) famous printers themselves.

[52] Compare abundance of relevant data in Febvre and Martin, chap. viii, with what is missing in H. Stuart Hughes, *History as Art and as Science* (New York, 1964), pp. 38–40, where the relation between linguistic fixity and nationalism, individualism, capitalism, and the nation-state is discussed. Hughes urges historians to make use of linguistic studies, but linguists, while careful to discriminate between "spoken" and "written" languages, say little about scribal versus printed ones. Judging by my own experience, books on linguistics are most difficult to master and seem to lead far afield. I found the reverse to be true when consulting literature on printing.

20   Elizabeth L. Eisenstein

catechisms or Bibles happened to get printed (under foreign as well as domestic auspices) in the sixteenth century. When this was the case, the subsequent expansion of a separate "national" literary culture ensued. When this did not happen, a prerequisite for budding "national" consciousness disappeared; a spoken provincial dialect was left instead.[53]

Studies of dynastic consolidation and/or of nationalism might well devote more space to the advent of printing. Typography arrested linguistic drift, enriched as well as standardized vernaculars, and paved the way for the more deliberate purification and codification of all major European languages. Randomly patterned sixteenth-century type-casting largely determined the subsequent elaboration of national myth-ologies on the part of certain separate groups within multilingual dynastic states. The duplication of vernacular primers and translations con-tributed in other ways to nationalism. A "mother's tongue" learned "naturally" at home would be reinforced by inculcation of a homogen-ized print-made language mastered while still young, when learning to read. During the most impressionable years of childhood, the eye would first see a more standardized version of what the ear had first heard. Particularly after grammar schools gave primary instruction in reading by using vernacular instead of Latin readers, linguistic "roots" and root-edness in one's homeland would be entangled.

Printing helped in other ways to permanently atomize Western Christendom. Erastian policies long pursued by diverse rulers could, for example, be more fully implemented. Thus, the duplication of documents pertaining to ritual, liturgy, or canon law, handled under clerical auspices in the age of the scribe, was undertaken by enterprising laymen, subject to dynastic authority, in the age of the printer. Local firms, lying outside the control of the papal curia, were granted lucrative privileges by Habsburg, Valois, or Tudor kings to service the needs of national cler-gies.[54] The varied ways in which printers contributed to loosening or severing links with Rome, or to nationalist sentiment, or to dynastic

[53] Steinberg, pp. 120–26. Cases pertaining to Cornish, Cymric, Gaelic, Latvian, Estonian, Lithuanian, Finnish, Pomeranian, Courlander, Czech, Basque, etc., are cited. Of course, other factors may have been at work in other instances than those cited, but the number of instances where sixteenth-century typecasting seems to have been critical is noteworthy.

[54] R. M. Kingdon, "Patronage, Piety, and Printing in Sixteenth-Century Europe," in D. H. Pinkney and T. Ropp (eds.), *A Festschrift for Frederick B. Artz* (Durham, N.C., 1964), pp. 32–33, offers a detailed view of how Plantin's Antwerp firm implemented the Erastian policy of Philip II in order to evade payments to a rival firm (none other than Manutius) that had been granted the concession to print Catholic breviaries by Rome. Graham, pp. 71–72, also shows how closely allied Thomas Cromwell was with a circle of law-printers led by Thomas More's brother-in-law, John Rastell—an independent crusader for "Englishing" all law, French or Latin, canon or civil.

The Impact of Printing on Western Society and Thought 21

consolidation cannot be explored here. But they surely do call for further study.[55]

Other consequences of typographical fixity also need to be explored. Religious divisions and legal precedents were affected. In fact, all the lines that were drawn in the sixteenth century (or thereafter), the condemnation of a heresy, the excommunication of a schismatic king, the settling of disputes between warring dynasts, schisms within the body politic—lines that prior generations had repeatedly traced, erased, re-traced—would now leave a more indelible imprint. It was no longer possible to take for granted that one was following "immemorial custom" when granting an immunity or signing a decree. Edicts became more visible and irrevocable. The Magna Carta, for example, was ostensibly "published" (i.e., proclaimed) twice a year in every shire. By 1237 there was already confusion as to which "charter" was involved.[56] In 1533, however, Englishmen glancing over the "Tabula" of the "Great Boke" could see how often it had been repeatedly confirmed in successive royal statutes.[57] In France also the "mechanism by which the will of the sovereign" was incorporated into the "published" body of law by "registration" was probably altered by typographical fixity.[58] Much as M. Jourdain learned that he was speaking prose, monarchs learned from political theorists that they were "making" laws. But members of parliaments and assemblies also learned from jurists and printers about ancient rights wrongfully usurped. Struggles over the right to establish precedents probably became more intense as each precedent became more permanent and hence more difficult to break.

On the other hand, in many fields of activity, fixity led to new departures from precedent marked by more explicit recognition of individual innovation and by the staking of claims to inventions, discoveries, and creations. By 1500, legal fictions were already being devised to accommodate the patenting of inventions and the assignment of literary properties.[59] Upon these foundations, a burgeoning bureaucracy would

[55] By pursuing this line of inquiry, one could usefully supplement the theoretical views developed by Karl Deutsch (*Nationalism and Social Communication: An Inquiry into the Foundations of Nationality* [Cambridge, Mass., 1953] with a more empirical, historically grounded approach.

[56] J. C. Holt, *Magna Carta* (Cambridge, 1965), pp. 288–90.

[57] Graham, p. 93.

[58] Franklin Ford, *Robe and Sword* (*Harvard Historical Studies,* Vol. LXIV), (Cambridge, Mass., 1953), p. 80, describes this mechanism—not, however, how it was altered. See also his remarks about the "great advance in publicity techniques" and how major parlement remonstrances were being "published" by 1732 in printed form (p. 101).

[59] A landmark in the history of literary property rights came in 1469, when a Venetian printer obtained a privilege to print and sell a given book for a given interval of time. See C. Blagden, *The Stationers Company, A History 1403–1959*

22   *Elizabeth L. Eisenstein*

build a vast and complex legal structure. Laws pertaining to licensing and privileges have been extensively studied. But they have yet to be examined as by-products of typographical fixity. Both the dissolution of guild controls and conflicts over mercantilist policies might be clarified if this were done. Once the rights of an inventor could be legally fixed and the problem of preserving unwritten recipes intact was no longer posed, profits could be achieved by open publicity, provided new re-straints were not imposed. Individual initiative was released from re-liance on guild protection, but at the same time new powers were lodged in the hands of a bureaucratic officialdom. Competition over the right to publish a given text also introduced controversy over new issues involving monopoly and piracy. Printing forced legal definition of what belonged in the public domain and clear articulation of how one sort of literary product differed from another.[60] When discussing the emer-gence of a new kind of individualism, it might be useful to recall that the eponymous inventor and personal authorship appeared at the same time and as a consequence of the same process.

The emergence of uniquely distinguished, personally famous artists and authors out of the ranks of more anonymous artisans and minstrels was also related to typographical fixity. Cheaper writing materials en-couraged the separate recording of private lives and correspondence. Not paper mills but printing presses, however, made it possible to pre-serve personal ephemera intact. As an expanding manuscript culture found its way into print, formal compositions were accompanied by inti-mate anecdotes about the lives and loves of their flesh-and-blood authors. Was it the "inclination" to "publish gossip" that was new in the Renaissance,[61] or was it, rather, the possibility of doing so? The characteristic individuality of Renaissance masterpieces surely owes much to the new possibility of preserving the life-histories of those who produced them. As art historians have shown, the hands of medieval illuminators or stone-carvers were, in fact, no less distinctive. Their

(London, 1960), p. 32. According to Forbes and Dijksterhuis, I, 147, although occasional privileges had been granted previously, the state of Venice was also the first to provide legal protection for inventors in 1474.

[60] Raymond Birn, "Journal des savants sous l'Ancien Regime," *Journal des savants* (1965), pp. 29, 33, shows how diverse fields of learning (and a division between "serious" and "frivolous" literature) were clearly defined by the terms of the official privilege granted this journal to cover a wide variety of different topics of serious concern. Both this article and Fredrick S. Siebert's *Freedom of the Press in England 1476–1776, The Rise and Decline of Government Control* (Urbana, Ill., 1952), *passim,* suggest how laws regulating printing raised new issues pertaining to privilege and monopoly, which became an acute source of conflict down through the eighteenth century.

[61] P. O. Kristeller, *Renaissance Thought,* Vol. II: *Papers on Humanism and the Arts* (New York, 1965), p. 11.

The Impact of Printing on Western Society and Thought 23

personalities remain unknown. Vestiges of their local celebrity have vanished. They must therefore be portrayed as faceless master guildsmen in terms of the garb they wore or the life-style they shared with colleagues. What applies to personality may also apply to versatility. Alberti probably was not the first architect who was also an athlete, orator, scholar, and artist. But he *was* the first whose after-dinner speeches, boasts about boyhood feats, and "serious and witty sayings" were collected and transmitted to posterity along with the buildings he designed and formal treatises he composed. He may be displayed at home and in public, as an athletic youth and elderly sage, moving through all the ages of man, personifying earlier archetypes and collective roles. Possibly this is why he appears to Burckhardt in the guise of a new ideal type, *homo universalis.*[62]

Similar considerations are also worth applying to authors. The personal hand and signature of the scribe was replaced by the more impersonal type style and colophon of the printer. Yet, by the same token, the personal, private, idiosyncratic views of the author could be extended through time and space. Articulating new concepts of selfhood, wrestling with the problem of speaking privately for publication, new authors (beginning, perhaps, with Montaigne) would redefine individualism in terms of deviation from the norm and divergence from the type. The "drive for fame" itself may have been affected by print-made immortality. The urge to scribble was manifested in Juvenal's day as it was in Petrarch's. But the *insanabile scribendi cacoethes* may have been reoriented once it became an "itch to publish."[63] The wish to see one's work in print (fixed forever with one's name, in card files and anthologies) is different from the urge to pen lines that could never get fixed in a permanent form, might be lost forever, altered by copying, or—if truly memorable—carried by oral transmission and assigned ultimately to "anon." When dealing with priority disputes among scientists or debates about plagiarism among scholars, the advent of print-made immortality has to be taken into account. Until it became possible to distinguish between composing a poem and reciting one or between writing a book and copying one, until books could be classified by something other than incipits, how could modern games of books and authors be played?

Many problems about assigning proper credit to scribal "authors" may result from misguided efforts to apply print-made concepts where they do not pertain. The so-called forged book of Hermes is a good case

[62] Burckhardt, I, 149–50.
[63] See a witty discussion of these terms by Robert K. Merton, *On The Shoulders of Giants: A Shandean Postscript* (New York, 1965), pp. 83–85.

24   *Elizabeth L. Eisenstein*

in point. But countless other scribal works are too. Who *wrote* Socrates'
lines, Aristotle's works, Sappho's poems, any portion of the Scriptures?
Troublesome questions about biblical composition, in particular, suggest
how new forms of personal authorship helped to subvert old concepts
of collective authority.[64] Veneration for the wisdom of the ages was
probably modified as ancient sages were retrospectively cast in the role
of individual authors—prone to human error and possibly plagiarists
as well.[65] Treatment of battles of books between "ancients and moderns" might profit from more discussion of such issues. Since early
printers were primarily responsible for forcing definition of literary property rights, for shaping new concepts of authorship, for exploiting best
sellers and trying to tap new markets, their role in this celebrated quarrel
should not be overlooked. By the early sixteenth century, for example,
staffs of translators were employed to turn out vernacular versions of
the more popular works by ancient Romans and contemporary Latin-
writing humanists.[66] This might be taken into account when discussing
debates between Latinists and the advocates of new vulgar tongues.[67]

It is also worth considering that different meanings may have been
assigned terms such as "ancient" and "modern," "discovery" and "recovery," "invention" and "imitation" before important departures from
precedent could be permanently recorded. "Throughout the patristic
and medieval periods, the quest for truth is thought of as the *recovery*
of what is embedded in tradition . . . rather than the *dis*covery of what
is new."[68] Most scholars concur with this view. It must have been
difficult to distinguish discovering something new from recovering it in
the age of scribes. To "find a new art" was easily confused with retrieving a lost one, for superior techniques and systems of knowledge
were frequently discovered by being recovered.[69] Probably Moses,

[64] The issue of authorship versus authority is discussed by McLuhan, pp.
130–37. The nature of medieval scribal authorship is brilliantly illuminated by
Goldschmidt, *Medieval Texts,* Part III.

[65] See the citation from Glanvill's *Essays* of 1676 cited by Merton, p. 68 n.
Ramus, in the 1530's, had already stated: "All that Aristotle has said is forged,"
according to H. Baker, *The Wars of Truth* (Cambridge, Mass., 1952), p. 93.

[66] Febvre and Martin, p. 410. Additional data on the production of vernacular
as opposed to Latin works during the first century of printing is supplied by
Hirsch, pp. 132–34.

[67] Hans Baron's "The Querelle of the Ancients and Moderns as a Problem
for Renaissance Scholarship," *Journal of the History of Ideas,* XX (Jan. 1959),
3–22, like many other treatments of this battle of books, passes over the possible
role played by printers. Curtius, pp. 251–56, covers the scribal use of terms such
as "ancients" and "moderns" but fails to note how they were altered after printing. All of Merton's (tongue in cheek) treatment of the giant and dwarf aphorism
is also relevant and points to a vast literature on the topic.

[68] Harbison, p. 5.

[69] E. Rosen, "The Invention of Eyeglasses," *Journal of the History of Medicine and Allied Sciences,* XI (1956), 34, n. 99, regards an early fourteenth-

The Impact of Printing on Western Society and Thought   25

Zoroaster, or Thoth had not "invented" all the arts that were to be found.[70] But many were retrieved from ancient giants whose works reentered the West by circuitous routes. The origins of such works were shrouded in mystery. Their contents revealed a remarkable technical expertise. Some pagan seers were believed to have been granted fore-knowledge of the Incarnation. Possibly they had also been granted a special secret key to all knowledge by the same divine dispensation. Veneration for the wisdom of the ancients was not incompatible with the advancement of learning, nor was imitation incompatible with in-spiration. Efforts to think and do as the ancients did might well reflect the hope of experiencing a sudden illumination or of coming closer to the original source of a pure, clear, and certain knowledge that a long Gothic night had obscured.

When unprecedented innovations did occur, moreover, there was no sure way of recognizing them before the advent of printing. Who could ascertain precisely what was known—either to prior generations within a given region or to contemporary inhabitants of far-off lands? "Steady advance," as Sarton says, "implies exact determination of every previous step." In his view, printing made this determination "incomparably easier."[71] He may have understated the case. *Exact* determination must have been impossible before printing. Given drifting texts, migrating manuscripts, localized chronologies, multiform maps, there could be no systematic forward movement, no accumulation of stepping stones en-abling a new generation to begin where the prior one had left off. Progressive refinement of certain arts and skills could and did occur. But no sophisticated technique could be securely established, per-manently recorded, and stored for subsequent retrieval. Before trying to account for an "idea" of progress, we might look more closely at the duplicating process that made possible a continuous accumulation of fixed records. For it seems to have been permanence that introduced progressive change. The preservation of the old, in brief, launched a tradition of the new.

---

century preacher as inconsistent when he is recorded as saying in one sermon, "Nothing remains to be said . . . today a new book could not be made nor a new art" and in a preceding one as referring to "all the arts that have been found by man and new ones yet to be found." *Finding* a new art was not, how-ever, necessarily equivalent to *making* one.

[70] The Italian word for "invention" has been located only once in fourteenth-century literature—a reference by Petrarch to Zoroaster as the *inventore* of the magic arts (*ibid.,* p. 192). Thoth (or "Hermes Trismegistus") was responsible for inventing writing and numbering or measurement. Adam had, of course, named all things and (in a prelapsarian state) may have also known all things. A full inventory would include countless other (often overlapping) ancient claimants to the role of originators.

[71] Sarton, "The Quest for Truth," p. 66.

26   *Elizabeth L. Eisenstein*

The advancement of learning had taken the form of a search for lost wisdom in the age of scribes. This search was rapidly propelled after printing. Ancient maps, charts, and texts once arranged and dated, however, turned out to be dated in more ways than one. Ordinary craftsmen and mariners appeared to know more things about the heavens and earth than were dreamt of by ancient sages. More schools of ancient philosophy than had previously been known were also uncovered. Scattered attacks on one authority by those who favored another provided ammunition for a wholesale assault on all received opinion. Incompatible portions of inherited traditions were sloughed off, partly because the task of preservation had become less urgent. Copying, memorizing, and transmitting absorbed fewer energies. Some were released to explore what still might be learned. Studying variant versions of God's words gave way to contemplating the uniformity of His works. Investigation of the "book of nature" was no longer undertaken by studying old glyphs and ciphers. Magic and science were divorced. So too were poetry and history. Useful reference books were no longer blotted out or blurred with the passage of time. Cadence and rhyme, images and symbols ceased to fulfil their traditional function of preserving the collective memory. The aesthetic experience became increasingly autonomous, and the function of works of art had to be redefined. Technical information could be conveyed more directly by plain expository prose and accurate illustration. Although books on the memory arts multiplied after printing, practical reliance on these arts decreased. Scribal schemes eventually petrified, to be ultimately reassembled, like fossil remains, by modern research. The special formulas that had preserved recipes and techniques among closed circles of initiates also disappeared. Residues of mnemonic devices were transmuted into mysterious images, rites and incantations.[72]

Nevertheless, scribal veneration for ancient learning lingered on, long after the conditions that had fostered it had gone. Among Rosicrucians and Freemasons, for example, the belief persisted that the "new philosophy" was in fact very old. Descartes and Newton had merely retrieved the same magical key to nature's secrets that had once been known to ancient pyramid-builders but was later withheld from the laity or deliberately obscured by a deceitful priesthood. In fact, the

---

[72] The most recent study is Frances Yates' *The Art of Memory* (London, 1966), which centers on use made of "memory theaters." According to J. Finegan, *Handbook of Biblical Chronology* (Princeton, N.J., 1964), p. 57, the term "Amen" encapsulated in the three Hebrew letters aleph, mem, and nun (to which different numbers were assigned) a scheme for remembering four ninety-one-day seasons of the solar year. When consulting works on this topic, I find it difficult to decide whether the ingenuity of modern scholars or that of ancient ones is being displayed.

The Impact of Printing on Western Society and Thought   27

Index came only after printing and the preservation of pagan learning owed much to monks and friars. Enlightened freethinkers, however, assigned Counter-Reformation institutions to the Gothic Dark Ages and turned Zoroaster into a Copernican. Similarly, once imitation was detached from inspiration and copying from composing, the classical revival became increasingly arid and academic. The search for primary sources was assigned to dry-as-dust pedants. But the reputation of ancient seers, bards, and prophets was not, by the same token, diminished. Claims to have inherited their magic mantle were put forth by new romanticists who reoriented the meaning of the term "original" and tried to resurrect scribal arts in the age of print. Even the "decay of nature" theme, once intimately associated with the erosion and corruption of scribal writings, would be reworked and reoriented by gloomy modern prophets who felt that regress, not progress, characterized their age.

E. *Amplification and Reinforcement: Accounting for Persistent Stereotypes and Increasing Cultural Differentiation*

Many other themes imbedded in scribal writings, detached from the living cultures that had shaped them, were propelled as "typologies" on printed pages. Over the course of time, archetypes were converted into stereotypes, the language of giants, as Merton puts it, into the clichés of dwarfs. Both "stereotype" and "cliché" are terms deriving from a typographical process developed three and a half centuries after Gutenberg. They point, however, to certain other features of typographical culture in general that deserve closer consideration. During the past five centuries, broadcasting new messages has also entailed amplifying and reinforcing old ones. I hope my use of the terms "amplify" and "reinforce" will not distract attention from the effects they are meant to designate. I am using them simply because I have found no others that serve as well. Some such terms are needed to cover the effects produced by an ever-more-frequent repetition of identical chapters and verses, anecdotes and aphorisms drawn from very limited scribal sources. This repetition is not produced by the constant republication of classical, biblical, or early vernacular works, although it undoubtedly sustains markets for such works. It is produced by an unwitting collaboration between countless authors of new books or articles. For five hundred years, authors have jointly transmitted certain old messages with augmented frequency even while separately reporting on new events or spinning out new ideas. Thus, if they happen to contain only one passing reference to the heroic stand at Thermopylae, a hundred reports on different military campaigns will impress with a hundredfold-impact Herodotus' description on the mind of the reader who scans

28　*Elizabeth L. Eisenstein*

such reports. Every dissimilar report of other campaigns will be received only once. As printed materials proliferate, this effect becomes more pronounced. (I have encountered several references to Thermopylae in the daily newspaper during the past year.) The same is true of numerous other messages previously inscribed on scarce and scattered manuscripts. The more wide ranging the reader at present, the more frequent will be the encounter with the identical version and the deeper the impression it will leave. Since book-writing authors are particularly prone to wide-ranging reading, a multiplying "feedback" effect results. When it comes to coining familiar quotations, describing familiar episodes, originating symbols or stereotypes, the ancients will generally outstrip the moderns. How many times has Tacitus' description of freedom-loving Teutons been repeated since a single manuscript of *Germania* was discovered in a fifteenth-century monastery? And in how many varying contexts—Anglo-Saxon, Frankish, as well as German —has this particular description appeared?

The frequency with which all messages were transmitted was primarily channeled by the fixing of literary linguistic frontiers. A particular kind of reinforcement was involved in relearning mother tongues when learning to read. It went together with the progressive amplification of diversely oriented national "memories." Not all the same portions of an inherited Latin culture were translated into different vernaculars at the same time.[73] More important, entirely dissimilar dynastic, municipal, and ecclesiastical chronicles, along with other local lore, both oral and scribal, were also set in type and more permanently fixed. The meshing of provincial medieval *res gestæ* with diverse classical and scriptural sources had, by the early seventeenth century, imbedded distinctively different stereotypes within each separate vernacular literature.[74] At the same time, to be sure, a more cosmopolitan *Respublica litterarum* was also expanding, and messages were broadcast across linguistic frontiers, first via Latin, then French, to an international audience. But messages received from abroad were not amplified over the course of several centuries in the same way. They only occasionally reinforced what was learned in familiar tongues at home.[75]

[73] Bennett, p. 158, notes a "striking difference" between the large number of pagan classics translated into French in the sixteenth century and the greater number of "edifying" devotional works translated into English.

[74] How this was done in sixteenth-century England is traced with remarkable clarity by William Haller, *The Elect Nation: The Meaning and Relevance of Foxe's Book of Martyrs* (New York, 1963), *passim*—an exceptional work that integrates printing with other historical developments. Children's books about Elizabeth I are still being written from bits and pieces drawn from Foxe's massive *apologia*.

[75] The most important exceptions are France and Geneva, where by the

The Impact of Printing on Western Society and Thought   29

On the other hand, the fixing of religious frontiers that cut across linguistic ones in the sixteenth century had a powerful effect on the frequency with which certain messages were transmitted. Passages drawn from vernacular translations of the Bible, for example, would be much more thinly and weakly distributed throughout the literary cultures of Catholic regions than of Protestant ones.[76] The abandonment of church Latin in Protestant regions made it possible to mesh ecclesiastical and dynastic traditions more closely within Protestant realms than in Catholic ones—a point worth noting when considering how church-state conflicts were resolved in different lands. Finally, the unevenly phased social penetration of literacy, the somewhat more random patterning of book-reading habits, and the uneven distribution of costly new books and cheap reprints of old ones among different social sectors also affected the frequency with which diverse messages were received within each linguistic group.

III. Considering the Rise of the Reading Public: Unevenly Phased Social and Psychological Transformations during Early Modern Times

These last remarks are relevant to most of the issues that have been

mid-seventeenth century two differently oriented native literary cultures coincided with a single cosmopolitan one. A sounding board was thus provided for Rousseau, Mme de Staël, Sismondi, and other Genevans who might otherwise have been as obscure as their German, Swiss, or Dutch counterparts. The reasons for the conquest of the Gallic tongue (which paradoxically linked the most populous and powerful consolidated dynastic Catholic state with the tiny canton that had served as the protestant Rome and with the cosmopolitan culture of civilized Europe) deserve further study. Louis Réau, *L'Europe française au Siècle des Lumières* (*L'Evolution de l'humanité,* Vol. LXX [Paris, 1938]), although devoted to this important topic, slides over issues that need more rigorous analysis. David Pottinger, *The French Book Trade in the Ancien Regime 1500–1791* (Cambridge, Mass., 1958), offers some useful statistics, pp. 19–23, as does Steinberg, p. 118. Some further consequences of the spread of French are touched on below. See pp. 51–52. One might note that the reaction to French armies and the rejection of French influence, among Germans and eastern Europeans in the early nineteenth century, necessarily involved disowning the cosmopolitan culture of the Enlightenment as well.

[76] R. A. Sayce, "French Continental Versions to c. 1600," in Greenslade (ed.), p. 114, contrasts the deep penetration of vernacular scriptural versions into the literary culture of German and English-speaking peoples with the shallow effect of French Bible translations. From Pascal to Gide, he notes, Latin citations from the Vulgate appear most frequently when biblical references are evoked. The immense repercussions of the decision taken by the Council of Trent to proscribe vernacular translations and uphold the "authenticity" of the Vulgate are difficult to locate throughout this massive collaborative volume. A clear view of how, when, and where the decision itself was taken is not offered. F. J. Crehan, S.J., "The Bible in the Roman Catholic Church from Trent to the Present Day," pp. 199–237, ostensibly covers this issue but actually obfuscates it.

30   *Elizabeth L. Eisenstein*

raised by McLuhan in connection with the "making of typographical man." By making us more aware that both mind and society were affected by printing, McLuhan has performed, in my view at least, a most valuable service. But he has also glossed over multiple interactions that occurred under widely varying circumstances in a way that may discourage rather than encourage further study. "The print-made split between heart and head is the trauma that affects Europe from Machiavelli to the present."[77] Since this sort of statement cannot be tested, it provides little incentive for further research. Granted that the replacement of discourse by silent scanning, of face-to-face contacts by more impersonal interactions probably did have important consequences. It follows that we need to think less metaphorically and abstractly and more historically and concretely about the sort of effects that were entailed and how different groups were affected. Even at first glance both issues appear to be very complex.

In many cases, for example, spoken words would be conveyed by printed messages without being replaced by them. While often transposed into print, sermons and public orations thus continued to be delivered orally. These traditional forms of discourse were nonetheless altered by the new possibility of silent publication. The printing of parliamentary debates probably affected exchanges between members of parliament. The printing of poems, plays, and songs altered the way "lines" were recited, sung, and composed. Academic dialogues were conducted along different lines after the advent of closet philosophers. On one hand, some "dying speeches" were fabricated for printing and never did get delivered; on the other, printed publicity enabled evangelists and demagogues to practice traditional arts outdoors before large hearing publics. A literary culture created by typography was conveyed to the ear, not the eye, by classroom lectures, repertory companies, and poetry-readings. No simple formula will cover the changes these new activities reflect.

The same is true of how different groups were affected. Most rural villagers, for example, probably belonged to an exclusively hearing public down to the nineteenth century. Yet what they heard had, in many instances, been transformed by printing two centuries earlier.

---

[77] McLuhan, p. 170. This formulation owes much to Lewis Mumford, *Technics and Civilization* (New York, 1934), pp. 136–37. An excellent introduction to problems associated with the shift from a hearing public to a reading one is H. J. Chaytor's *From Script to Print* (Cambridge, 1945). This study of medieval literature, which has already been exploited by McLuhan, needs to be exploited by historians as well. It should be noted, however, that a very limited area of scribal culture is covered by Chaytor. Near the bookshops of Augustan Rome or in the libraries of Alexandria, for example, the conditions he describes may not be pertinent at all.

The Impact of Printing on Western Society and Thought　31

In the seventeenth century the storyteller was being replaced by the exceptional literate villager who read out loud from a stack of cheap books and ballad sheets turned out anonymously for distribution by peddlers.[78] A fairly sleazy "popular" culture, based on the mass production of antiquated vernacular medieval romances, was thus produced well before the steam press and mass literacy movements of the nineteenth century. Yet the bulk of this output was consumed by a medieval hearing public, separated by a vast psychological gulf from their contemporaries who belonged to an early modern reading one.[79]

The disjunction between the new mode of production and older modes of consumption is only one of many complications that need further study. Members of the same reading public, who confronted the same innovation in the same region at the same time, were nonetheless affected by it in markedly different ways. One cannot, for example, talk about the effect of Bible-printing on "typographical man" in general or even on sixteenth-century Protestants in particular. Instead, one must consider a disjunction between producers and consumers, that is, between printers and purchasers.[80] To be enabled to read the holy words of God in one's own tongue was probably an awesome experience for a devout sixteenth-century reader. It seems quite likely that new forms of sect-type Christianity and literal fundamentalism resulted from an increased consumption of vernacular Bibles. A great many Protestant printers were also devout, and some were even martyred for their faith. They were persuaded, however, that God's words could be spread further by printing than by preaching.[81] For this purpose, markets had to be gauged, financing secured, privileges sought, Catholic officials evaded, compositors supervised, distribution organized. What appeared to the devout consumer in a quasi-miraculous guise involved an exercise

---

[78] Robert Mandrou, *De la culture populaire aux 17ᵉ et 18ᵉ siècles: La Bibliothèque bleue de Troyes* (Paris, 1964), *passim*, illustrates this topic in detail for France. Altick, *passim*, touches on it, in scattered passages, for England.

[79] This gulf may be found even within some printers' workshops during the sixteenth century and separates some journeymen typographers from master printers. See Natalie Z. Davis, "The Protestant Printing Workshops of Lyons in 1551," in Henri Moylan (ed.), *Aspects de la propagande religieuse* (*Travaux d'humanisme et Renaissance*, Vol. XXVIII, [Geneva, 1957]), pp. 252–57. The illiterate journeymen, however, sang songs composed by Marot and Beza which were circulated in printed form.

[80] On my use of the term "printer," see n. 34.

[81] Pottinger, p. 81, describes French martyrs to the faith who were hanged, burned, or broken on the wheel during the wars of religion. Various essays in *Aspects de la propagande religieuse* cover the activities of Protestant printers in Lyons, Paris, and Geneva. The group of zealous Puritans associated with John Day who turned to printing as the most formidable weapon in their campaign against the papal Antichrist is studied in detail by Haller, *passim* (see Foxe's remark about every press as a "block house," cited on p. 110).

32   *Elizabeth L. Eisenstein*

in processing texts, shrewd politicking, and practical problem-solving for the equally devout producer.[82] Mammon as well as Caesar necessarily entered into the latter's calculations. So, too, did variant readings of the same sacred words.

Moreover, printers themselves did not share a "common mind" and hence were diversely affected by involvement in a new mode of production. Some were fiery apostles wholly committed to serving one true church and one "elect nation." But others were not and tried to serve many. Genevan printers surreptitiously turned out books for populous Catholic markets in France. The same Antwerp firm won a privileged position from Catholic Spain under Philip II but served Calvinist Holland and Jewish communities as well.[83] Paradoxically enough, the printing press helped fan the flames of religious controversy even while creating a new vested interest in ecumenical concord and toleration. Similarly, religious, dynastic, and linguistic frontiers were fixed more permanently by the same wholesale industry that operated most profitably by tapping cosmopolitan markets. Even as Henri IV felt that Paris was worth a mass or Cardinal Richelieu that *raison d'état* dictated alliance with infidel Turks, so too did a Manutius, an Estienne, or a Plantin keep family firms solvent and presses in operation by alliances with Protestants, Catholics, Jews, Spaniards, Dutchmen, and all shades of Frenchmen alike. The formation of syndicats of heterodox businessmen and printers, linked to far-flung distribution networks, indicates how the new industry encouraged informal social groupings that cut across dynastic or religious and linguistic frontiers. Circles associated with Aldus Manutius' "Academy" and Plantin's "House of Love" suggest how a syncretist faith was in some ways more compatible than a Protestant one with the new wholesale book trade.[84] Such syndicats and networks

---

[82] The vocational shift from cleric, preacher, or teacher to printer, journalist, or author during the sixteenth and seventeenth centuries (noted by Haller, p. 112) might, incidentally, make an interesting study. Birn mentions a few instances of French Jesuits who became professional lay journalists and publicists in seventeenth-century France. R. Colie, *Light and Enlightenment: A Study of the Cambridge Platonists and the Dutch Arminians* (Cambridge, 1957), pp. 29–33, 75, offers some Dutch examples during the same era. Here, as elsewhere, the gradual displacement of the pulpit by the periodical press also deserves more attention.

[83] Febvre and Martin, pp. 293, 405; Kingdon, p. 29. A seventeenth-century English printer, Henry Hill, served all comers: army, Anabaptists, Cromwell, James II, etc. See Steinberg, p. 109.

[84] On Plantin's "House of Love" and suggestion *re* the "Banque Protestante" myth, see R. M. Kingdon, "Christopher Plantin and His Backers 1575–1590, A Study in the Problems of Financing Business during War," *Mélanges d'histoire economique et sociale* (Geneva, 1963), pp. 303–16. Additional information on the sect (customarily called the "Family of Love" and founded by Hendric Niclaes) to which Plantin belonged—along with other printers—is given by J. A. Van Dorsten, *Thomas Basson 1555–1613: English Printer at Leiden* (Leiden, 1961). The "Familists" overlapped with Arminian and Remonstrant circles in England

The Impact of Printing on Western Society and Thought   33

should be closely studied as a possible source of later conspiratorial legends pertaining to the Banque Protestante or Freemasons. (Protestants and foreigners did subsidize the output of French men of letters in the eighteenth century. Behind debates about Masonic involvement in the *Grande encyclopèdie* lies the somewhat shadowy figure of the printer who initiated, financed, and pushed through its publication.[85])

A more cosmopolitan and ecumenical outlook on the part of many printers should not, however, be regarded as a mere "rationalization" of their financial interests. Sacred and devotional works *did* look different to those who saw copy through all the stages of publication than they did to those who procured the finished product. Belief in the Sacred Scriptures as an ultimate source of truth has been correctly singled out, by Kingdon, as a most important element in the rise of early printing industries. (Overnight, Wittenberg was transformed into an important printing center.) Unlike other sacred books, however, that of Western Christendom happened to be composed in many tongues. It thus fed a demand for Greek, Aramaic, Syriac, and Hebrew grammars and dictionaries, bringing arcane letters into printers' workshops[86] and sometimes even heterodox foreigners into printers' households.[87]

---

and the Netherlands and were centered first in Antwerp, then in Leiden. Possibly they also included members of the Elzevir firm who were linked with Plantin. See David W. Davies, *The World of the Elseviers 1580–1712* (The Hague, 1954), pp. 2–3. Much as Plantin rode out the "Spanish fury," Aldus Manutius had earlier kept his firm going during the Italian time of troubles that hit Venice in 1504. Not only as the greatest scholar-printer of his day, but also as Pico della Mirandola's protégé, who later numbered Erasmus and Linacre among members of his "Academy," both Aldus and his circle also deserve a modern book-length appraisal.

[85] See below, pp. 51–52, on the collaboration between French authors and foreign printers. For the debate on the role of Freemasons in the publication of the *Encyclopèdie,* see A. Wilson, *Diderot: The Testing Years* (New York, 1957), pp. 74–81 and references cited pp. 358–59. Wilson's interpretation seems to underrate the role played by the printer André-François Le Breton and to overrate that of Diderot, a salaried editor brought in after the project was under way. Evidence of Le Breton's close supervision of a costly project for which he employed fifty workers and of how he rewrote several articles to protect his investment is given by Frank Kafker, "The Effect of Censorship on Diderot's Enclopedia," *Library Chronicle* (University of Pennsylvania), XXX (Winter 1964), 42. To assess the printer's role correctly is more feasible and important, in my view, than to decide whether he was or was not the Le Breton who is listed as a master mason.

[86] Plantin, linked via Hebrew type and Jewish financing to Jewish communities, produced a polyglot Bible under Philip II's patronage (Kingdon, "Patronage, Piety, and Printing," p. 23). Aldus had planned one in 1497–98 and cut types for a specimen page before abandoning it. (Steinberg, p. 76). Robert Estienne's stock of type fonts included Hebrew letters (Armstrong, pp. 54–55). For data pertaining to struggles to get Aramaic and Syriac as well as Hebrew studies launched, see Basil Hall, "Biblical Scholarship: Editions and Commentaries," in Greenslade (ed.), pp. 44–45, 74–75.

[87] Thus Robert Estienne had "correctors" representing ten disparate national-

34 *Elizabeth L. Eisenstein*

Such considerations may help to explain how new semisecret brother-
hoods espousing syncretic and irenic creeds came to be formed during
the era when religious zeal was at its height and the claims of orthodox
faith seemed most compelling. For printers like the Estiennes and
Plantin, solvency required a steady output of devotional literature
during the first century of printing.[88] But processing and marketing
texts also engendered attitudes that were more conducive to modernism
than to fundamentalism, to practicality than to otherworldliness. And
this in turn might be registered on other staple products that were compiled by printers themselves.[89] By looking more closely at their daily
routines and then looking again at the incidental information contained
in seventeenth-century English almanacs, for example, a few elusive
spirits might be trapped. "No book in the english language had as large
a circulation as the annual Almanack."[90] Like many other practical
manuals and household guides, such almanacs registered the views of
men who knew, well before Ben Franklin and *Poor Richard,* that time
was money, that profits went with piety, and that bookkeeping went
with book-reading.

The Protestant ethic and the spirit of capitalism may indeed be
linked in ways most discussions have bypassed. "Printing," said Luther,
"was God's highest act of grace." He also castigated printers who
garbled passages of the Gospel and marketed hasty reprints for quick
profit.[91] His insistence on scriptural revelation nonetheless entangled
spiritual illumination with a commercial enterprise. Moreover, even
before Luther had appeared with his "apple of discord," the printer's
devil had already been at work, turning out playing cards and holy
images, vernacular Bibles and indulgences—all on a scale hitherto
unknown. Because the fifteenth-century revolution is still invisible, most

---

ities in his household at one time, according to his son's account, cited by Armstrong, p. 15. The necessity of housing foreign translators and proofreaders may
have contributed even more than financial exigencies did to the notion of families
or houses of love.

[88] How profits derived from religious works subsidized humanist publications
is noted by Kingdon, "Patronage, Piety, and Printing," pp. 35–36. The case of the
publisher who relied on legal and scientific texts instead of devotional works to
supply a steady source of income is discussed by Davis, "Guillaume Rouillé,"
pp. 88–89. She shows, however, how Rouillé also hedged his bets by diversifying
his products.

[89] Thus a practical handbook compiled by Charles Estienne, *Guide des chemins
de France* (1553), guided merchants along routes followed by those who were
engaged in the book trade and reflected the experience of the compiler's own
family (Armstrong, p. 34).

[90] Eustace F. Bosanquet, "English 17th Century Almanacks," *Library,* 4th
ser., X (Mar. 1930), 361. (These almanacs contained tables for computing costs
of goods or payment of wages, distances between main towns, lists of weights
and measures, even dentifrice ads.)

[91] Relevant citations are in Black, p. 432.

The Impact of Printing on Western Society and Thought   35

studies of the Reformation place first things last. Only after various socioeconomic and political developments, theological issues, ecclesiastical abuses, and charismatic leaders have been discussed and only after controversies over causation have been explored does the printing press appear in conventional accounts—in conjunction with a wide dissemination of Luther's sermons and other Protestant broadsides. A more fruitful debate about causes and consequences might result if first things were placed first. After all, Gutenberg had preceded Luther. Similarly, dissension among churchmen over new issues posed by printing preceded the division of Western Christendom.

The necessity of making new decisions helped to polarize opinions about "one true church." These decisions involved justifying producing indulgences on a mass scale, advertising relics, and commercializing iconography. They involved determining how glad tidings should be spread, who should be allowed to perform the apostolic function of the clergy, whether grammarians, philologists, and lay scholars should pass judgment on God's words. Earlier heretics, such as Wycliffe or Huss, might aspire to place the vernacular Scriptures in the hands of every layman;[92] and new semi-lay orders such as the "Brethren of the Common Life" might try to bring literacy and prayer books to the "people."[93] Only after Gutenberg, however, could such programs be fully implemented. Thereafter, collaboration with existing teaching or preaching orders and the winning of papal approval for the creation of new ones was no longer required by Christian reformers. Programs could be implemented, instead, by winning the favor of Erastian princes and by close collaboration with the book-trade network in that "golden age" between printing "and its antidote, the Index."[94] Collaboration with printers, however, meant contact with men who, by the very nature of their trade, shared a common contempt for monkish learning and ungrammatical theologians. Pacific Christian humanists and zealous Protestant reformers did, one should note, both collaborate with printers and share this contempt.

It was not only the learning of monks and friars that came under

[92] Medieval heresies based on efforts to get the Bible into the vernacular and to the people are well described by Margaret Deansley, *The Lollard Bible* (Cambridge, 1920). The Waldensians used oral transmission and instructed initiates in how to learn the Scriptures by heart (p. 28).

[93] The chief purpose of the new orders founded by Gerhard Groote are often blurred by the catchall term "pietist." The Windesheim Congregation was set up to provide centers of scholarly studies and supervised scriptoria; the Brethren of the Common Life, to teach reading and circulate devotional books among the "people" (McMurtrie, p. 126). They *did* implement their program with the new presses (Bühler, p. 28).

[94] H. Trevor Roper, "Desiderius Erasmus," *Men and Events* (New York, 1957), p. 39.

36   *Elizabeth L. Eisenstein*

attack when new laboratories of erudition had been established. The regular orders of the clergy also were more vulnerable to the charge of being social parasites. The socially useful functions they had performed—such as preserving and copying old texts (for which village tithes had been collected by abbeys)[95] or providing books for university faculties (which the mendicant orders had supplied)[96]—were transferred to urban entrepreneurs. With this transfer the balance between organs within the body politic was subtly altered in a way that subverted traditional hierarchies. For many functions traditionally assigned to churchmen belonging to the first estate were silently assumed by lay commoners belonging to the third. Although the full consequences of this shift took centuries to spin out, divergent responses to its initial effects shaped the course of later developments. In Protestant regions, these effects were swiftly implemented. Regular orders were dissolved, and the printer was assigned the apostolic mission of spreading glad tidings in different tongues. Within frontiers held by the Counter-Reformation church, measures were taken to curtail and counteract these effects. New orders, such as the Jesuits or the congregation of the Propaganda, were created; teaching and preaching from other quarters were checked by Index and imprimatur. That the fortunes of printers waned in regions where prospects had previously seemed bright and waxed in smaller, less populous states where the reformed religion took root may be connected with these divergent responses.

Before lines were drawn in the sixteenth century, men in Catholic regions appear to have been just as eager to read the Bible in their own tongues as were men in what subsequently became Protestant regions. Similarly, Catholic printers combined humanist scholarship with piety and profit-seeking. They were just as enterprising and industrious as Protestant printers. They also served the most populous, powerful, and culturally influential realms of sixteenth-century Europe: Portugal and Spain (with their far-flung empires), Austria, France, southern German principalities, and Italian city-states. But they do appear to

[95] See the reference to the allotment to the priory of Evesham in 1206 of village tithes for parchment and copyists' wages and of other funds for ink and illuminating and binding materials in C. H. Haskins, *The Renaissance of the Twelfth Century* (Cambridge, Mass., 1939), p. 75. Bühler, pp. 25–27, notes that monastic scriptoria flourished after Gutenberg—down to 1500. However, the missals and choir books they turned out became lucrative privileges granted to printers by monarchs and popes thereafter.

[96] K. W. Humphreys, *The Book Provisions of the Medieval Friars 1215–1400* (Amsterdam, 1964), *passim,* suggests how organizational energies were channeled by this task. I have not found a study of scribal book provisions for lay faculties of law and medicine or how the scriptoria serving them were supervised. What happened to clerical control of university book production after the advent of printing in various Catholic and Protestant regions also needs to be explored.

The Impact of Printing on Western Society and Thought   37

have been less successful in expanding their markets and in extending and diversifying their operations during the sixteenth and seventeenth centuries.[97] Needless to say, like those of other early capitalist enterprises, the fortunes of printing industries hinged on an exceedingly complex network of multiple interactions. Venetian printers, for example, were affected by a commercial decline that can scarcely be explained by singling out Protestant-Catholic divisions. If we want to understand how these divisions *did* affect an important early capitalist enterprise, however, this can be done better by looking at printing than at metallurgy, mining, textiles, ship-building, or other such enterprises.

Here the contrast registered on the title-page illustration of Foxe's *Actes and Monuments*—showing devout Protestants with books on their laps and Catholics with prayer beads in their hands[98]—seems to me highly significant. After the Council of Trent, vernacular Bibles that had been turned out previously in all regions were forbidden to Catholics and made almost compulsory for Protestants. An incentive to learn to read was, thus, eliminated among the former and reinforced among the latter. Book markets were apt to expand at different rates thereafter. Since Bible-printing was a special privilege, its extinction in Catholic centers directly affected only a small group of printers.[99] The entire industry, however, suffered a glancing blow from the suppression of the large potential market represented by a Catholic lay Bible-reading public. Furthermore, vernacular Bibles were by no means the only best sellers that were barred to Catholic readers after the Council of Trent. Erasmus had made a fortune for his printers before Luther outstripped him. Both, along with many other popular authors, were placed on the

[97] See Steinberg's remarks (p. 194) about the movement of printing industries from southern to northern Germany after the mid-sixteenth century. "Type-founding, printing, publishing, book-selling" became "almost Protestant preserves," in his words. That this oversimplifies and exaggerates a more subtle shift is suggested by Hirsch, pp. 109–10, and by Febvre and Martin's most useful chapter on the "geography of the book," chap. vi.

[98] Haller, p. 118, and see illustration facing p. 25.

[99] The relocation of continental Bible printing centers following its extinction in Venice is described by Black, pp. 440–51. H. S. Bennett. *English Books and Readers, 1558 to 1603* (Cambridge, 1965), p. 141, notes how the pace of Bible-printing accelerated under Edward VI and came "almost to a standstill" under Mary Tudor. Thomas Cromwell's order to place a Bible in every parish church was, incidentally, granted at the bequest of the privileged printer who stood to profit from the order (Plant, p. 50). That certain Catholic privileged printers could and did profit from Tridentine decrees by supplying new breviaries and missals to priests is noted by Kingdon, "Patronage, Piety, and Printing," pp. 31–35. The promising French market for vernacular psalters that was closed by Catholic victories at the end of the sixteenth century, is, however, also evident in same article (pp. 28–30). The crippling effect of French censorship on printers, who could not afford long delays entailed by Sorbonnist debates, is described by Pottinger, chap. iv.

38   *Elizabeth L. Eisenstein*

Index. Being listed as forbidden served as a form of publicity and may have spurred sales. It was, however, more hazardous for Catholic printers than for Protestant ones to profit thereby.[100] To be sure, pastors and printers were often at odds in regions governed by new consistories.[101] But the "Protestant Rome," despite the spread of Calvinism, was not served by an international clergy controlled from one center, could not block a free trade in ideas outside its narrow confines, and above all could not "fix" church policy in a permanent mold in the mid-sixteenth century. Nor did it discourage (quite to the contrary!) the expansion of a vernacular book-reading laity. Cautious Anglicans might temporarily (in 1543) forbid Bible-reading among "women, apprentices, husbandmen."[102] Fiery Puritans would never thus abandon the most vital principle of their creed. "The essential, imperative exercise of religious life, the one thing not to be omitted was for everyone the reading of the Bible. This was what the reformers put in place of the Mass as the decisive high point of spiritual experience—instead of participation in the sacrament of the real presence on one's knees in church, they put encounter with the Holy Spirit in the familiar language of men on the printed page of the sacred text."[103]

That Protestantism was above all a "book religion" has certainly been noted repeatedly.[104] But this could be more fully exploited in comparative studies if it were related to other unevenly phased changes set in motion by printing. Given a clearly defined incentive to learn to read that was present among Protestants *qua* Protestants and not among Catholics *qua* Catholics, for example, one might expect to find a deeper social penetration of literacy among the former than among the latter during the second century of printing. Earlier lines dividing literate from unlettered social strata—magistrates, merchants, and masters from journeymen artisans and yeomen—might grow fainter in Protestant regions and more indelible in Catholic ones between the 1550's and 1650's. This, in turn, would affect the timing of "revolutions of rising expectations" and help to account for different patterns of social agitation and mobility, political cleavage and cohesion. We know that the mechanization of

[100] Being listed as forbidden *on the Index,* that is. After the advent of printing, censorship and book-banning were practiced in most principalities. Different lists were drawn up by magistrates and princes in accordance with varying policies. Only in Catholic areas, however, was guidance provided by the Index superimposed on these policies.

[101] Examples of conflict are given by Davis, "Strikes and Salvation at Lyons," pp. 58–64, and by Kingdon, "The Business Activities of Printers, Henri and François Estienne," in Meylan (ed.), p. 265.

[102] Cited by Bennett, *English Books and Readers 1475–1557,* p. 27.

[103] Haller, p. 52.

[104] Altick, pp. 24–25.

The Impact of Printing on Western Society and Thought **39**

most modes of production came much more gradually in France than in England. The effects of the steam press, however, probably came more explosively. Certainly religion had not acted on Bible-reading German Anabaptists or English regicides as an opiate. Many low-born Londoners were already steeped in book-learning, were turning out tracts and proclaiming themselves "free born," well before Parisian journeymen had mastered letters.[105] One might compare the silent war of words in seventeenth-century England with the efflorescence of chansons and festivals in eighteenth-century France. With regard to morals, the Jacobins were "puritan"; with regard to oral and visual propaganda, they were not. In brief, literacy rates among revolutionary crowds on both sides of the Channel are worth further thought.

Possibly the most fundamental divergence between Catholic and Protestant cultures may be found closest to home. The absence or presence of family prayers and family Bibles is a matter of some consequence to all social historians. Where functions previously assigned only to priests in the church were also entrusted to parents at home, a patriarchical ethic was probably reinforced. Concepts of the family were probably also transformed where the Holy Spirit was domesticated. Of course, family life was sanctified among Protestants by clerical marriage. But boundaries between priesthood and laity, altar and hearthside, were most effectively blurred, I think, by bringing Bibles and prayer books within reach of every God-fearing householder. It might be noted that where Bibles did displace confessors in upper-class Catholic homes, in French Jansenist circles, for example,[106] domestic codes set by Counter-Reformation moralists were also rigorously followed and a so-called bourgeois life-style was manifested, even among nobles of the robe.

Going by the book seems to be somehow related to the formation of a distinctive "middle class" or "secularized Puritan" ethos. To understand this relationship it may be useful to look more closely at what some kinds of early book-learning involved. In particular, we need to think about domestic manuals and household guides while recalling, once again, new features introduced by typography. Like cookbooks and herbals, domestic books were written in the age of scribes. But they

---

[105] Much useful data on the shaping of an indigenous working-class tradition in seventeenth-century England is given by E. P. Thompson, *The Making of the English Working Class* (New York, 1966), Part I. In her biography of John Lilburne, Pauline Gregg, *Free-born John* (London, 1961), brings out clearly how much Lilburne's career owed to the printing press. Is there any seventeenth-century French equivalent of "free-born John"?

[106] Crehan, p. 222, notes Jansenist insistence on Bible-reading as a layman's duty.

40   *Elizabeth L. Eisenstein*

were not duplicated uniformly in repeated editions. Reliance on unwritten recipes, here as elsewhere, prevailed. Elizabethans who purchased domestic guides and marriage manuals learned in a new way how
family life should be conducted in a well-regulated household.[107] A
more limited and standardized repertoire of roles was extended to them
than had been extended to householders before. Instead of a cross-fire
of gossip conveying random impressions about what was expected or
haphazard interpretations of what a sermon meant, books came that
set forth (with all the *i*'s dotted and all the *t*'s crossed) precise codes
for behavior that godly householders should observe. These codes were
known to others—to relatives and neighbors—as well as to oneself.
Insofar as they were internalized by silent and solitary readers, the voice
of individual conscience was strengthened. But insofar as they were
duplicated in a standardized format, conveyed by an impersonal medium
to a "lonely crowd" of many readers, a collective morality was also
simultaneously created. Typecasting in printers' workshops thus contributed to role-playing at home.

     In dealing with altered concepts of the family and the roles per-
formed within it, we need then to consider the sort of cultural differentiation that came in the wake of the printing press. Early book-
learning among Protestants was more homely, perhaps, and less courtly
than among Catholics. But we also might note that primers and grammars, arithmetic books and writing manuals became more abundant at
the same time in all regions. Both domestic and educational institutions
were transformed in a manner that affected well-nurtured youths of all
faiths. The sort of changes that affected family life between the fifteenth
and eighteenth century have been brilliantly illuminated by Ariès' pioneering study of French society.[108] Studies based on other regions are
needed to supplement his findings. But new theories are also needed if
we wish to understand how and why the changes he describes occurred
when they did. "The family ceased to be simply an institution for the
transmission of a name and an estate," it assumed moral and spiritual
functions, it "moulded bodies and souls." How and why this happened
remains to be explored. In setting out to do this, a revival "of an interest
in education" seems to me the wrong place to begin. Why not consider,
first of all, how child-rearing and schooling were affected by the printed
book?

     [107] Louis B. Wright, *Middle Class Culture in Elizabethan England* (Chapel
Hill, N.C., 1935), pp. 106–10, 206, 211, contains many relevant titles and references. See also p. 203 for the contrast between English domestic books and more
aristocratic foreign imports.
     [108] Philippe Ariès, *Centuries of Childhood, A Social History of Family Life,*
trans. R. Baldick (New York, 1962).

The Impact of Printing on Western Society and Thought   41

Possibly no social revolution in European history is as fundamental as that which saw book-learning (previously assigned to old men and monks) gradually become the focus of daily life during childhood, adolescence, and early manhood. Ariès has described the early phases of this vast transformation: "The solicitude of family, Church, moralists and administrators deprived the child of the freedom he had hitherto enjoyed among adults." The school "was utterly transformed" into "an instrument of strict discipline."[109] I would argue that such changes are probably related to the shift from "learning by doing" to "learning by reading." Surely some sort of new discipline was required to keep healthy youngsters at their desks during daylight hours. Some sort of new profession—that of tutor, schoolmaster, or governess—was required to keep them there. And some sort of new attitude on the part of parents was probably also apt to result. A new "concept of childhood" indeed might owe much to the widened gap between literate and oral cultures. The more adult activities were governed by conscious deliberation and going by the book, the more striking the contrast offered by the spontaneous and impulsive behavior of young offspring[110] and the more strenuous the effort required to remould young "bodies and souls."

The appearance of a stricter domestic discipline, together with new forms of child-rearing, schooling, and worship, was probably linked to the inculcation of book-reading habits. But new forms of scurrilous gossip, erotic fantasy, idle pleasure-seeking, and freethinking were also linked to such habits. Like piety, pornography assumed new forms. Book-reading did not stop short with guides to godly living or practical manuals and texts any more than printers stopped short with producing them. The same silence, solitude, and contemplative attitudes associated formerly with pure spiritual devotion also accompanied the perusal of scandal sheets, "lewd Ballads," "merry bookes of Italie," and other "corrupted tales in Inke and Paper."[111] Not a desire to withdraw from a worldly society or the city of man but a gregarious curiosity about them could by the eighteenth century be satisfied by silent perusal of journals, gazettes, or newsletters. Increasingly the well-informed man of affairs had to spend part of each day in temporary isolation from his fellowmen.

As communion with the Sunday paper has replaced churchgoing, there is a tendency to forget that sermons had at one time been coupled with news about local and foreign affairs, real estate transactions, and

[109] *Ibid.*, pp. 412–13.

[110] This sort of analysis seems relevant also to the problems considered by Michael Foucault, *Madness and Civilization: A History of Insanity in the Age of Reason*, trans. R. Howard (New York, 1965). A redefinition of *la folie* went together with that of *l'enfant*.

[111] Cited by Wright, pp. 232–33.

42   *Elizabeth L. Eisenstein*

other mundane matters. After printing, however, news-gathering and circulation were more efficiently handled under exclusively lay auspices. Such considerations might be noted when thinking about the "secularization" or "desacralization" of Western Christendom. For in all regions (to go beyond the eighteenth century for a moment) the pulpit was ultimately displaced by the periodical press and the dictum "nothing sacred" came to characterize a new career. Pitted against "the furious itch of novelty" and the "general thirst after news,"[112] efforts by Catholic moralists and Protestant evangelicals, even Sunday schools and other Sabbatarian measures,[113] proved of little avail. The monthly gazette was succeeded by the weekly and finally by the daily paper. Provincial newspapers were founded. By the last century, gossiping churchgoers could often learn more about local affairs by scanning columns of newsprint in silence at home.

In the meantime, however, communal solidarity among parishioners had been dissolved and vicarious participation in more distant events had been enhanced. Indeed, a sharper division between private and public zones of life accompanied the advent of printed publicity. The family, itself, "advanced in proportion as sociability . . . retreated. . . . It was a movement which was sometimes retarded by geographical or social isolation. It would be quicker in Paris than in other towns, quicker in the middle classes than in the lower classes. Everywhere it reinforced private life at the expense of neighborly relationships, friendships and traditional contacts."[114]

But even while social bonds linking parishioners were loosened, the claims of larger collective units also became more compelling. Printed materials encouraged silent adherence to causes whose advocates could not be located in any one parish and who addressed an invisible public from afar. As Ariès himself notes, the "concept of class and perhaps . . . the concept of race"[115] appeared alongside a new privacy assigned to family life within the home. Like national consciousness, class consciousness reflected a new form of group identity that displaced an older, more localized nexus of loyalties. Similarly, the amorphous overlapping categories that were assigned different "ages of man" would later give way to chronologically numbered and segmented age grades. Newly

---

[112] Citations from the *British Mercury* of 1712 and Addison in Preserved Smith, *The Enlightenment 1687–1776* (New York, 1934), p. 284.

[113] See Altick, p. 128.

[114] Ariès, p. 406.

[115] *Ibid.*, p. 415. The increasing remoteness and impersonality of political theorizing in the seventeenth century, discussed by Lionel Rothkrug, *Opposition to Louis XIV. The Political and Social Origins of the French Enlightenment* (Princeton, N.J., 1965), pp. 458–59, seems relevant to the above analysis.

The Impact of Printing on Western Society and Thought   43

segregated at schools and receiving special printed materials geared to distinct stages of learning, separate "peer groups" ultimately emerged; a distinctive "youth culture" that was somewhat incongrous with the "family" came into being. Such developments, however, did not really crystallize until the last century, after both typography and schooling underwent new transformations.

Public life was nonetheless profoundly transformed from the sixteenth to the eighteenth centuries, as many historical studies suggest. They say little about the advent of printing. It must have affected traditional governing groups in many ways. The printing of emblems of heraldry and orders of chivalry, for example, probably encouraged class consciousness among hereditary nobles and helped to codify notions about rank, priority, and degree.[116] One may learn from Curtis how "drastic changes introduced by printing" affected undergraduate studies at Oxford and Cambridge and how "well-born successors to medieval clerks" profited from these changes.[117] Unfortunately, Curtis' approach seems to be exceptional. The effects produced by printing on higher education and academic institutions usually have to be inferred from occasional casual remarks. The same is true of treatments of other pertinant topics. How access to printed materials affected attitudes toward estates of the realm, the cultivation of landed estates, the collection of seigneurial dues, the conduct of courtiers, the strategies of councilors, military and fiscal policies, even the aspirations of would-be gentlemen—all could be usefully explored. Recently some historians have begun to abandon, as fruitless, older debates about the "rise" of a new class to political power in early modern times. They seek to focus attention instead on the re-education and regroupment of older governing elites—and have, thereby, precipitated new debates. Both lines of inquiry might be reconciled and fruitfully pursued if the consequences of printing received more attention.

According to Hexter, for example, "a revaluation of our whole conception of social ideas, social structure and social function in Europe in the Age of the Renaissance is long overdue." We must start "by thinking in terms not of the decline of the aristocracy but of its reconstruction." This reconstruction, moreover, was marked by a "new and radical"

---

[116] See the reference to Caxton's *Ordeyne de chevalrie* and other early books on heraldry in Jacob, p. 665. On the very different form taken by the art of heraldry before printing, see N. Denholm-Young, *History and Heraldry 1254–1310* (Oxford, 1965). The hardening of the concept of "degree" is treated by Altick, p. 31. The printing of the *Almanach de Gotha* from the eighteenth century on has helped to perpetuate the existence of a hereditary aristocracy despite its political abolition in some regions.

[117] Mark Curtis, *Oxford and Cambridge in Transition 1558–1642* (Oxford, 1959), pp. 89–111.

44   *Elizabeth L. Eisenstein*

suggestion that "bookish learning" was not "supererogatory" but in-dispensable to ruling a commonwealth and by "a stampede to bookish education" which "edged the clergy" out of some schools.[118] If Hexter is right, it is also time to start thinking about changes that affected the nature of bookish learning itself. Hereditary nobles were probably forced by these changes to choose between old ways and new ways of training their sons. "In my day, gentlemen studied only to go into the Church and even then were content with Latin and their prayer book. Those who were trained for court or army service went, as was fitting, to the academy. They learned to ride, to dance, to handle weapons, to play the lute . . . a bit of mathematics and that was all. . . . Montmorency, the late Constable, knew how to hold his own in the provinces and his place at court without knowing how to read."[119]

Once military command required mastering a "copious flow of books" on weaponry and strategy[120] and royal councilors were called upon "to think clearly, analyze a situation, draft a minute, know law's technicalities, speak a foreign language,"[121] it must have become more difficult to hold one's place in court without knowing how to read. Fail-ure to adopt new ways in some instances probably paved the way for the ascension of new men. Whether we describe it as a "rise" or "re-grouping" the increasing pre-eminence assigned robe nobles in France, for example, might be examined with this in mind.[122] Officials and magistrates who acquired landed estates and adopted a noble life-style from the sixteenth century on apparently abandoned many of "their bourgeois ways."[123] Yet they did not relinquish them all. From the early sixteenth century on, robe nobles were acquiring private libraries that outstripped those of the clergy by the end of the sixteenth century and left those of the *noblesse d'épée* far behind.[124] Was it not largely because

[118] J. T. Hexter, *Reappraisals in History* (Evanston, Ill., 1961), chap. iv. See also Lawrence Stone, "The Educational Revolution in England, 1560–1640," *Past and Present,* No. 28 (July 1964), pp. 41–80.

[119] Remarks of a seventeenth-century French nobleman, reported by Saint-Evremond and cited by John Lough, *An Introduction to Seventeenth Century France* (London, 1960; 1st ed., 1954), p. 203. See also the exchange between Richard Pace and a Tudor gentleman in 1514 relating to the same issue, cited by Curtis, p. 58.

[120] John Hale, "War and Public Opinion in the 15th and 16th Centuries," *Past and Present,* No. 22 (July 1962), pp. 20–22. This whole article contains much relevant material on the effect of printing on military affairs.

[121] Lawrence Stone, *The Crisis of the Aristocracy 1558–1641* (Oxford, 1965), p. 673. See also W. T. MacCaffrey, "Elizabethan Politics: The First Decade," *Past and Present,* No. 24 (April 1963), pp. 32–33.

[122] See Ford, pp. 246–52.

[123] J. Russel Major, "Crown and Aristocracy in Renaissance France," *American Historical Review,* LXIX (Apr. 1964), 631–45.

[124] Febvre and Martin, pp. 398–99.

The Impact of Printing on Western Society and Thought   45

learning by reading was becoming as important as learning by doing that the robe took its place alongside the sword? New powers were lodged in the hands of a legal bureaucracy which defined and interpreted rules pertaining to privileges, patents and office-holding while seeking privileges, profits, and places itself. Some of these new powers redounded to the benefit of the crown and to the royal officials who served it. But the provincial parliament commanding its own press also became the focal point of resistance to the extension of royal prerogatives; it often played a leading role in the formation of new learned societies and turned out propaganda that mobilized regional loyalties. The issue of literacy is already beginning to appear in discussions of the modernization of privileged status groups, which went hand in hand with the modernization of the royal court.[125] To discuss this issue, however, one must also take cognizance of the activities of printers and booksellers and of how their markets and sources of supply were diversely patterned in different regions. A comparative study of the effects of law-printing in England and in France, for example, might illuminate many issues.

Similarly, when discussing the "quiet" rise of modern science amid the "noisy" clash of rival Christian faiths, one must also consider the unevenly phased changes that came in the wake of the printing press. In this regard, it seems unwarranted to single out science from all "other European movements of the sixteenth and seventeenth centuries." In comparison with the worldwide revolution introduced by Western science, the Reformation may be viewed as "a domestic affair of the European races."[126] Nonetheless, the noisy domestic affair profoundly affected the more silent worldwide process. The appearance of a Protestant ethic, a spirit of capitalism, a middle-class ethos, new concepts of the family and the child, educational reforms, and a bureaucratic officialdom all owed much to multiple, complex interactions introduced by typography. That this applies most particularly to the "rise of modern science" is suggested by previous comments. On this basis, I would argue that medieval schoolmen should not be chided for relying too much on oral disputation.[127] Renaissance artisans did not turn *"from books* to nature" for instruction.[128] Aphorisms about the "book of na-

[125] See the contrast between education of robe nobles vis-à-vis those of the sword (Ford, pp. 217–21).

[126] A. N. Whitehead, *Science and the Modern World* (London, 1933), pp. 11–12.

[127] E. J. Dijksterhuis, *The Mechanization of the World Picture*, trans. C. Dikshoorn (Oxford, 1961), pp. 167–68.

[128] L. M. Marsak, "Introduction," in L. M. Marsak (ed.), *The Rise of Science in Relation to Society* (*Main Themes in European History*, ed. B. Mazlish [New York, 1964]), p. 1; italics mine.

46   *Elizabeth L. Eisenstein*

ture" may be traced to scribal writings, but their meaning was probably altered when the nature of the book was changed.[129] If Leonardo's notebooks "contributed nothing" to the "organization of anatomy as a discipline," this was probably not because he lacked "talent for classification and arrangement"[130] but because his notebooks were not processed by sixteenth-century printers. His curious position as a scientific genius who contributed almost nothing to sixteenth-century science serves to underline connections between a "scientific contribution" and the act of publication. Debates over contributions made by medieval schoolmen and Renaissance humanists,[131] Aristotelians and neo-Platonists, later Catholics and Protestants, or Puritans and Anglicans[132] all might become more fruitful if printing occasionally entered into the discussion.

To illustrate this last remark, let us look at a recent summary of efforts to explain "why the acceleration of scientific advance took place between 1540 and 1700." A seemingly interminable argument is in progress. Should one stress the role played by individual genius, the internal evolution of a speculative tradition, a new alliance between intellectuals and artisans, or a host of concurrent socioeconomic or religious changes affecting the "environment against which these discoveries took place"?[133] To say that this sort of argument is pointless because *all* these "factors" were at work still leaves open the question of how and why they became operative when they did. Unless some new strategy is devised to handle this question, the old argument will break out once again. Since it perpetually revolves about the same issues, diminishing returns soon set in. One advantage of bringing printing into the discussion is that it enables us to tackle the open question directly without prolonging the same controversy ad infinitum. As previous remarks suggest, the effects produced by printing do seem relevant to

---

[129] Curtius, pp. 316–26.

[130] Hall, *The Scientific Revolution 1500–1800*, p. 42.

[131] See, e.g., J. H. Randall, *The Making of the Modern Mind* (Cambridge, Mass., 1926), p. 212; Dana B. Durand, "Tradition and Innovation in Fifteenth Century Italy," *Journal of the History of Ideas*, IV (Jan. 1943), 1–20; Edward Rosen, "Renaissance Science as Seen by Burckhardt and His Successors," in T. Helton (ed.), *The Renaissance: A Reconsideration of the Theories and Interpretations of the Age* (Madison, Wis., 1964), pp. 77–105.

[132] To sample this controversy, see references cited by S. F. Mason, "Science and Religion in 17th Century England," *Past and Present*, No. 3 (Feb. 1953), pp. 28–43; H. F. Kearney, "Puritanism, Capitalism, and the Scientific Revolution," *Past and Present*, No. 28 (July 1964), pp. 81–101; contributions by C. Hill *et al.* to debates on "Science, Religion, and Society in the Sixteenth and Seventeenth Centuries," *Past and Present*, No. 31 (July 1965), pp. 97–126; and Leo F. Solt, "Puritanism, Capitalism, Democracy, and Science," *American Historical Review*, LXXIII (Oct. 1967), 18–29.

[133] Kearney, p. 81.

The Impact of Printing on Western Society and Thought 47

cognitive advance, creative acts, and indeed to each of the contested factors in the dispute. Problems pertaining to the "environment against which these discoveries took place" might also be more squarely confronted if we took into account studies pertaining to the "geography of the book."

Clearly the outcome of dynastic and religious wars affected the conditions under which printers and booksellers operated. Forms of piety and patronage, licensing and censorship, literacy and book-reading habits varied from region to region in accordance with this outcome. Since the distribution of printing industries can be determined with a fair degree of accuracy, the "geography of the book" can be mapped out. The movement of printing centers can be correlated with the fixing of new frontiers.

The printer can be readily identified before the scientist began to emerge. The distribution of talents contributing to "scientific" advances in the early modern era is, therefore, much more difficult to ascertain. A wide variety of activities (mathematical descriptions, instrument-making, data collection, and so forth) and occupational groups have to be considered. The question of where and how to apply the term "scientist" to men who did not regard themselves as such is open to dispute. Furthermore, from the 1540's to the 1640's, investigations now regarded as scientific were still largely unco-ordinated. Scattered "centers" containing very small clusters of talents—an observatory on a Danish island, a university in Padua, a group of lens-grinders in Amsterdam, a court in Prague—dot the map somewhat randomly. Given two Italian academies and Abbé Mersenne's letter box to go by (and they do not appear till the end of the interval), the location of the most energetic centers of activity is also a matter for dispute. Those who argue that the rise of modern science was a cosmopolitan movement, unaffected by political and religious divisions, or that Catholic Italy, with its universities and academies, played a preponderant role during its formative phases base their views on an interval where activities can only be co-ordinated in retrospect. They take for granted that co-ordination would be forthcoming and hence overlook the conditions that made it possible. They also assume that a free flow of information was secured during an interval when it was, instead, most vulnerable to every turn of fortune's wheel.[134]

It is not until the second half of the seventeenth century that a clearly localized center of fruitful collaboration can be found. To reach

[134] "By 1640, with the work of Galileo, Harvey, and Descartes virtually complete, one can safely say that science had risen"; T. Rabb, "Religion and the Rise of Modern Science," *Past and Present,* No. 3 (July 1965), p. 112.

48   *Elizabeth L. Eisenstein*

it one must travel north toward the English Channel. The formation of this center has been noted by many authorities. They try to account for it in various ways. The prior relocation of printing industries is left out of their accounts. Thus Butterfield aptly describes a cross-channel "humming activity" entailing "the publication in Holland of journals written in French, communicating English ideas."[135] Following Hazard, he glides over the role played by Dutch presses in order to point instead to the Huguenot printers who manned some of these presses. The Huguenots, however, were latecomers to the world of the Elzevirs. The wars of Dutch independence had ushered in a golden age of printing in Holland (and had established at Leiden a great Protestant university) before the Edict of Nantes had even been proclaimed. The works of Descartes and Galileo (and of Bacon, Comenius, Hobbes, Grotius, Gassendi, *et al.*) were being turned off Dutch presses before this edict had been revoked. The humming activity that propelled scientific advances toward the end of the seventeenth century hinged on defeats suffered by the Spaniards a century earlier—minor scuffles on a corner of the globe, to be sure, but with worldwide repercussions nonetheless.

"In the story of the rise of modern science, religion is of peripheral concern."[136] I think this statement can be made only because the full story has not been told. The makers of early popular almanacs in England "generally adopted the Copernican system of the world."[137] In French popular almanacs down through the eighteenth century one will find "not the slightest trace . . . of the Copernican astronomy."[138] This particular contrast, based on two secondary accounts, may not stand up on closer examination. I offer it merely to suggest that the divergent routes taken by science in Catholic and Protestant lands have not all been traveled. What Jesuit presses turned out in Peking is, I think, really "of peripheral concern."[139] In Europe, propagation of the new philosophy, from the time of Newton's birth on, did not come from

---

[135] Herbert Butterfield, *The Origins of Modern Science 1300–1800* (New York, 1951), p. 140.

[136] Rabb, p. 126.

[137] Cited from Marjorie Nicolson, by Mason, p. 41. Nicolson's article, which shows how the Copernican system triumphed first over the Ptolemaic and then the Tychonic in the course of the seventeenth century, is worth consulting in full. See "English Almanachs and the 'New Astronomy,' " *Annals of Science,* IV (Jan. 15, 1939), 1–33.

[138] Mandrou, p. 157.

[139] Rabb, p. 117, and Koestler, p. 495 n., both suggest that Jesuit propagation of the Copernican theory in China in the late seventeenth century is somehow applicable to the question of how religious divisions affected scientific developments on the Continent. Yet we know, on other issues, that what the Jesuits taught in China brought them into disrepute at home. See Paul Hazard, *La crise de la conscience européenne (1680–1715)* (Paris, 1935), I, 29.

The Impact of Printing on Western Society and Thought   49

Rome, Madrid, Vienna, or Paris. The completion of the Copernican revolution drew on books that seldom received an imprimatur and often turned up on the Index. I have already suggested that conditions which favored the expansion of book markets and a literate artisanate were linked to scientific advance. The fact that unauthorized vernacular versions of the book of nature could be duplicated and circulated more freely among Protestants than among Catholics also must be taken into account.

Seventeenth-century Protestant printers ran afoul of authorities with political or theological tracts. But they could serve virtuosos in relative peace. In noting this fact, it has been suggested that Protestant convictions had simply lost their force and should not be dragged into the discussion. Early Protestant divines had after all condemned the new astronomy. The point is, however, that their faith did not entail preserving the old astronomy. There was nothing in the Bible about crystalline spheres or epicycles. Insofar as pagans, scholastics, and papists had contributed to the old astronomy, it was also viewed with some suspicion by Protestant divines. The Bible was of no use at all to the professional astronomer. Yet no society could dispense with his services. Reliance on the Scriptures and not a watered down faith probably forced a divorce between Protestant theology and mathematical astronomy. The professional astronomer was left alone to get on with his reckonings. Given a free hand and the new flow of information, he did get on, moving ahead by astonishing leaps and bounds. "In the year 1500 Europe knew less than Archimedes . . . in the year 1700 Newton's *Principia* had been written"[140]—not merely written, published as well.

If the connection between the act of publication and a scientific contribution could be drawn more firmly, reasons for the turmoil over Galileo's "crime" might be better understood. What has been uncovered by recent historians was scarcely perceptible to printers and virtuosos two centuries ago. Nor were they aware that Bruno had been burned because of his theological rather than his astronomical views. The consequences of the "mild reproof" of Galileo were, at all events, not nearly as trifling as some accounts suggest.[141] Copernican views were

[140] Whitehead, p. 16.

[141] On this point, Koestler leads his readers astray by diverting attention from the effect of Galileo's trial to that of the condemnation of Copernicus' *De revolutionibus*. Koestler argues (p. 458) that the book remained on the Index only four years while "trifling" corrections were made, that any Catholic publisher could reprint it thereafter but that no one (Catholic or Protestant) bothered to, since it was outdated already, and that hence the "temporary suspension had no ill effects on the progress of science." Even here, his interpretation seems to me wide of the mark. As Kuhn notes (p. 199), "Not until 1822 did the Church permit the printing of books that treated the earth's motion as physically real." Freedom

50   *Elizabeth L. Eisenstein*

thereafter linked to the antipapist cause. On patriotic and religious grounds, their adoption was sanctioned among Protestants. The contrary occurred among Catholics, for whom they were tainted with sedition. Proselytizing had to be conducted cautiously and often surreptitiously. It is notable that Anglicans and Puritans, bitterly divided over God's words in the seventeenth century, were brought together by the study of His "works." According to Bishop Sprat, the Royal Society served as a refuge from political and religious controversy. Across the Channel, as Voltaire noted, things were ordered differently. There, programs associated with the advancement of learning, the spread of book-reading, data collection, and the popularization of the new cosmology were not peaceful at all. To appreciate the difference, one need only compare the quiet reception of Chambers' *Cyclopædia* in England with what happened to the project to translate it in France.

Possibly because all transformations introduced by printing are "quiet," increasing tensions that accompanied the subterranean expansion of the Republic of Letters in Catholic lands are often overlooked. Since these tensions were explosive and of major historical consequence, the contours of this invisible republic need to be brought into clearer focus. This is difficult because one must deal with a realm that had no tangible existence as an institutional organization—not even a shadowy existence as a legal fiction.

It is clear enough that Bayle's *Nouvelles de la République des Lettres* came from Rotterdam. It is also evident that the language of its inhabitants had shifted in the course of the seventeenth century from Latin to French. Its central city in the eighteenth century was, according to one authority, Amsterdam.[142] But a margin for uncertainty has to be left when trying to pinpoint its headquarters or designate its frontiers on real maps. It remained, from the beginning a fanciful domain, issuing products from "Cosmopolis" or "Utopia,"[143] conveying by the same

to print speculations about what is physically real is not, in my view, a "trifling" matter and does have a bearing on the progress of science. Galileo's *Dialogue* remained on the Index for 192 years. As for his later *Discourses,* Koestler suggests he might have had them printed in Vienna rather than Leiden. On why this must have seemed inadvisable, see G. de Santillana, *The Crime of Galileo* (Chicago, 1955), p. 326.

[142] Febvre and Martin, p. 298.

[143] See invented accommodation addresses mentioned by Steinberg, pp. 264–65. Bennett, *English Books and Readers 1475–1557,* p. 210, provides an amusing early English example: "Printed in Jerico in the land of Promes by Thome Truth" (London, 1542). During the first centuries after Gutenberg, a considerable amount of illicit literature, both pornographic and political) was circulated in manuscript form (Bühler, pp. 30–31). This tradition persisted in eighteenth-century France. See Ira O. Wade, *The Clandestine Organization and Diffusion of Philosophic Ideas in France from 1700 to 1750* (Princeton, N.J., 1938), *passim.*

The Impact of Printing on Western Society and Thought   51

clandestine channels strangely assorted forbidden works by austere philosophers, libertines, pornographers, political-party hacks, visionary
fanatics, scientists, and romancers. Yet those who took advantage of the
new career opened to the talents of skilful writers were not disembodied
spirits who must be materialized to be believed. They were, rather, real
men. Those who provided the foundries, workshops, and officials scattered throughout this imaginary realm made real profits by tapping the
talents that gravitated to it. By the eighteenth century, most of these
printers were located in northern Protestant regions—Holland, Switzerland, England, Denmark,[144] and smaller buffer states on the fringes of
France[145]—and were seeking populous markets for an expanding industry. Most of the authors were Frenchmen whose way had been paved
by the conquests of the French language. Their command of their native
tongue made them indispensable when translation was required and still
sought after when it could be bypassed. "For a century, from 1690 to
1790, the works of the most famous French writers were read throughout Europe in editions published outside France."[146]

New career opportunities were thus opened for ambitious and industrious young men of obscure parentage who happened to be born in
French-speaking regions and who were gifted with their pens. The lure
of international celebrity channeled aspirations toward achievement in a
new direction. To older dreams of purchasing land or titles and offices
was added another, possibly more glamorous pursuit—one that has
proved particularly attractive to able young Frenchmen down to the
present. Young men from varied backgrounds who set out on a "perilous
voyage to prosperous distinction"[147] in the seventeenth century won their
way to acceptance at Parisian salons and foreign courts (as well as to
prison and penury) in the next century by wielding their pens for

---

But the circulation of hand-copied political lampoons or scatological verse seems
to me socially inconsequential compared to the organized underground trade in
printed books.

[144] Pottinger, p. 76, notes the large proportion of French works that came
from these regions.

[145] A most useful, detailed case study of a French playwright turned foreign
publisher and propagandist for the Encyclopedists is given by Raymond Birn,
Pierre Rousseau and the Philosophes of Bouillon (*Studies on Voltaire and the
Eighteenth Century,* ed. T. Besterman, Vol. XXIX [Geneva, 1964]). Birn offers
much relevant data on the role played by buffer states and also on the clandestine
book trade between 1760–1789. A. Bachman, *Censorship in France from 1715 to
1750* (New York, 1934), *passim,* describes difficulties with parliaments, bureau-
crats, and censors experienced by French publishers. Members of the *librairie*
were hit harder than authors, who could and did turn to foreign printers in
neighboring regions.

[146] Febvre and Martin, p. 278.

[147] Pottinger, p. 11.

52   *Elizabeth L. Eisenstein*

printers everywhere. Some were treated as lackeys by unenlightened aristocrats, some served other nobles as hired hands, while a number of the most celebrated Enlightenment authors—Condorcet, Condillac, Mably, Helvétius, *et al.*—were of noble birth themselves. Still, in no other eighteenth-century region would the hope of obtaining an independent eminence and international prestige be similarly encouraged by aid forthcoming from foreign workshops.

Drawn from diverse strata and detached from local loyalties, the new careerists would appear to posterity either as ghost-writers for others or as free-floating intellectuals. No group, however, had a stronger vested interest in the inculcation of book-reading habits or as close a connection with the book-trade network than did the French philosophes. Their cosmopolitan outlook, their values and attitudes reflected conditions that were peculiar to their new occupation. Particular pecuniary interests and personal vanity (often a most important element in the outlook of authors) have to be considered when accounting for their views. But book-writing authors were also wide-ranging readers. Even as an ecumenical faith came naturally to continental printers, so too did the notion of a timeless consensus among all reasonable men from all eras and places come naturally to men who were more at home in the world of books than in their own home towns.

It was, I think, as spokesmen for their own particular pressure group—as a new class of men of letters rather than as spokesmen for the robe nobility, the *tiers état,* or the royal power—that the philosophes urged men to trust their own understanding, assailed the church, attacked privileges and monopolies, fought for a free trade in ideas, and hoped to wean enlightened monarchs away from collaboration with the Index and the presses of the Propaganda. Their political attitudes and the pressures they exerted were distinctive and need to be considered as such. They should not be classed among traditional parvenus seeking offices closed by the so-called feudal reaction. Did not the fall of the Bastille in 1789 signify something of particular importance to men of letters in comparison with all other social groups? Over eight hundred authors, printers, booksellers, and print-dealers had been incarcerated there between 1600 and 1756.[148] The crowds who stormed the fortress seeking gunpowder may have seen cannon trained on crowded *quartiers* or thought about toll barriers and bread prices. To the journalists who hailed its fall, it probably appeared as a symbol of the fate of a somewhat different sort of tyranny. Certainly printers, authors, and "publicists" began at once (and have continued to the present) to amplify the meaning of its capture.

[148] *Ibid.,* p. 79.

The Impact of Printing on Western Society and Thought   53

The sort of influence that was exerted by this new class of men of letters has been the topic of an unending argument.[149] General theories about the relationship between ideas and social action are frequently invoked. Seldom, if ever, do the specific effects of the advent of printing enter into the discussion. Yet both the thrust of Enlightenment propaganda and the invisible meeting of minds that came with its diffusion can scarcely be understood without taking these effects into account. It was after all printing that made possible vicarious encounters with famous philosophers who turned out to be kindred spirits. They boldly spelled out the repressed content of interior dialogues. They argued at length with persuasive power about matters one could not discuss in front of one's servants, parents, or neighbors. Few visible traces, save thumbprints on well-worn volumes or a chance remark about a youthful enthusiasm for a favorite author, would be left by such encounters. Yet fear of disapproval, a sense of isolation, the force of local community sanctions, the habit of respectful submission to traditional authority— all might be weakened among many obscure provincial book-readers by recognition that their innermost convictions were shared by fashionable and famous men of letters. Moreover, print is a singularly impersonal medium. Lay preachers and teachers who addressed congregations from afar often seemed to speak with a more authoritative voice than those who could be heard and seen within a given community. The publication in numerous editions of thoughts hitherto unthinkable involved a new form of social action that was indirect and at a distance. "The revolutionary spirit was surely not formed in silence and solitude. One might write revolutionary works, but they would remain pure and inoffensive speculations if their ideas had not fermented in the heat of conversation, discussion, and battles of words. In order for such ideas to become *idées forces,* they required a public."[150] A most important consequence of the printing press, however, was that it did create a new kind of public for *idées forces.*[151] The reading public was not necessarily vocal, nor

[149] For a brief review, see Henri Peyre, "The Influence of Eighteenth Century Ideas on the French Revolution," in Franklin L. Baumer (ed.), *Intellectual Movements in Modern European History (Main Themes in European History,* ed. B. Mazlish [New York, 1965]), pp. 63–85.

[150] Daniel Mornet, *Les origines intellectuelles de la Révolution française (1715–1787)* (Paris, 1947; 1st ed., 1933), p. 281.

[151] This view conflicts not only with Mornet's work but also with more recent French studies of the eighteenth-century bookish world—currently the topic of intensive investigation. Much as Febvre and Martin hold that printing retarded the adoption of new ideas by duplicating old ones in the sixteenth century, so Dupront argues that, far from contributing to revolutionary dynamics, eighteenth-century book production reinforced tradition and acted as a brake: "le livre retarde"; Alphonse Dupront, "Livre et culture dans la société française au XVIII° siècle (Réflexions sur une Enquete)," *Annales économies—soiiétés—civilisations*

54   *Elizabeth L. Eisenstein*

did its members necessarily frequent cafés, clubs, and salons of known political complexion. It was instead composed of silent and solitary individuals who were often unknown to each other and who were linked only by access to bookshops, lending libraries, or *chambres de lecture* and, here and there, also by membership in "corresponding societies."[152]

There is no way of knowing, with certainty, what really went on in the minds of silent, solitary readers who have long since gone to their graves. Authors are often surprised by what gets read into their works. A wide margin for uncertainty must be left whenever one tries to read the minds of other readers. It is precisely because it shows where this margin lies and why it cannot be eliminated that speculation on this matter may be useful. Interactions that cannot be determined with certainty in retrospect could not be foreseen or controlled in prospect. Failure to speculate about the indirect effects exerted by the philosophes on their public prolongs the search for some alien invisible hand that set Frenchmen in motion by 1789. The law-abiding subjects of Bourbon France did behave in a manner that astounded contemporaries. If we sidestep the problem in social psychology their unexpected behavior poses, the myth-makers are apt to step in, and debates will center on thickly documented solutions that leave no margin for uncertainty at all.

The conspiratorial myths that have been woven around Masonic lodges, reading societies, and the French Revolution could themselves be better understood if various effects produced by printing were taken into account. New forms of secrecy, publicity, duplicity, and censorship underlie all modern myths of this genre. Examination of these issues cannot be undertaken here. Let me just note in passing that conspiratorial hypotheses in general are more often propelled than dispelled by efforts that stop short with disproving them. Bibliographies grow thicker, the atmosphere more charged, as skeptics and true believers fail alike to convince each other.[153] The possibility that multiple invisible interactions

---

(1965), pp. 895–97. This article was recently republished in an important collaborative volume sponsored by the Sixième Section of the Ecole Pratique des Hautes Etudes: *Livre et sociéte dans la France du XVIII*° (*Civilisations et sociétés*, Vol. I [The Hague, 1967]).

[152] On *chambres de lecture*, see Augustin Cochin, *Les sociétés de pensée et la révolution en Bretagne 1788–1789* (Paris, 1925), I, 20. On corresponding societies that circulated hundreds of thousands of copies of Paine's *Age of Reason* between 1791 and 1793 in the British Isles, see Altick, p. 70, and Thompson, chap. v.

[153] A cogent example is Norman Cohn's *Warrant for Genocide: The Myth of the Jewish World Conspiracy and the Protocols of the Elders of Zion* (New York, 1966). The author concludes with useful insights. But by reproducing lurid tales and vicious cartoons, the bulk of his work helps to keep the same virus in circulation and even revives some old strains. It was, incidentally, a satire on Napoleon III's regime as "journalism incarnate" that provided a model for the

The Impact of Printing on Western Society and Thought   55

were introduced by a silent communications system is a point that both parties tend to ignore and that the skeptics, at least, should be persuaded to explore. Most of them agree that pens can poison the atmosphere when they are used to accuse Protestants or papists, Masons or Jacobins, Jesuits, Jews, or Bolsheviks of sinister plots. If this is true, then climates of opinion can be affected by pens, including those wielded by enlightened philosophes. A clearer understanding of social "action at a distance" might at least help to explain how earlier views of conspiracy—pertaining to assassination plots or rabble-rousers hired by seditious factions—gave way to the more awesome image of a vast network, controlled from secret headquarters, that set men to do its bidding from afar.[154]

Many other developments could be clarified by exploring the new complex interplay between different groups of writers and readers. Vicarious experiences with newly created fictional worlds, for example, affected human hearts as well as heads. Empathy induced by novel-reading probably helped to sustain humanitarian movements of various kinds. Powers of calculation and abstraction were sharpened by access to printed materials. New imaginative and sympathetic faculties were also brought into play. Were all the senses save sight partly atrophied? McLuhan's suggestion that a heightened visual stress served to dull other senses is debatable. Since authors became more skilled in simulating the noisy, colorful, odorous, rich-textured stuff of life, it seems likely that readers also became more keenly sensitive to varied tactile and sensory stimuli. It should be noted that printers served not only pedants and scientists but composers and painters, gourmets and gardeners, connoisseurs and aesthetes as well.

Unfortunately, space does not permit setting down further conjectures here. Although I have tried to touch on varied fields of study, the full range of problems that might be reviewed by those who are concerned with early modern Europe has by no means been displayed. As for the more recent past, I have had to stop well short of the interval when the power of the press was harnessed to steam and hence have said nothing about issues that seem to be particularly relevant to present concerns. The arbitrary nature of this stopping point should be underlined. When

---

protocols. See David Kulstein, "Government Propaganda and the Press during the Second Empire," *Gazette: International Journal for Mass Communication Studies,* X (1964), 125–44.

[154] The effect of printing on collective psychopathology urgently needs further study. Recent analyses by Richard Hofstader on "the paranoid style in politics" and by Hugh Trevor Roper on the "witch craze" and a spate of studies on differences between medieval and modern anti-Semitism might be reconsidered in this light.

56   *Elizabeth L. Eisenstein*

dealing with the effects of printing, it is a mistake, in my view, to think in terms of periods that open and close. These effects were exerted always unevenly, always continuously and cumulatively from the late fifteenth century on. I can find no point at which they ceased to be exerted or even began to diminish. I find much to suggest that they have persisted, with ever augmented force, right down to the present. Scribal culture did come to an end. Despite the advent of new audiovisual media, one cannot say the same about typographical culture. At least I do not think one can say this. Recent obituaries on the Age of Gutenberg show that others disagree.[155] As yet, however, so few historians have been heard from that final verdicts seem unacceptable and, in more ways than one, premature.

The deliberately inconclusive nature of this stopping point also must be underlined. These conjectures have been based on very uneven acquaintance with relevant data, much of it drawn from unreliable general accounts, all of it pertinent to very few regions. Numerous gaps have been filled in by logical inference—at best a poor substitute for empirical findings. No conclusions are in order at this point. Let me simply recapitulate: A new method for duplicating handwriting— an *ars artificialiter scribendi*—was developed and first utilized five centuries ago. Recent historians still concur with Bacon's opinion that this changed "the appearance and state of the whole world." "It brought about the most radical transformation in the conditions of intellectual life in the history of western civilization . . . its effects were sooner or later felt in every department of human life."[156] At present we must reckon with effects "felt in every department of human life" without knowing which came sooner, which later, and, indeed, without any clear notions as to what these effects were. Explicit theories, in short, are now overdue. To make a start at providing them, I have cut across fields properly cultivated by specialists and made sweeping assertions that have not been substantiated. This rash course has been pursued with a more prudent goal in mind. Collaboration is required to achieve it. If my conjectures have alerted some readers to how much remains to be done and aroused some concern about doing it, then they have fulfilled their purpose.

---

[155] The obsolescence of print technology and its supercession by electric media is repeatedly asserted by McLuhan, not only in *The Gutenberg Galaxy* but also in *Understanding Media, The Extensions of Man* (New York, 1965). See also George Steiner, "The Retreat from the Word," *Kenyon Review* (Spring 1961), pp. 187–216, and Kenneth Winetrout, "The New Age of the Visible. A Call to Study," *A. V. Communication Review*, XII (Spring 1964), 46–52.

[156] Gilmore, p. 186.

[4]

The Importance of Being Printed

Anthony T. Grafton

Anyone who wishes to know what an early printing-house was like should begin with the *Orthotypographia* of Jerome Hornschuch. The engraving by Moses Thym that precedes Hornschuch's text shows a printer's staff hard at work. In one small room a compositor sets type, a corrector reads copy, a warehouseman sorts paper, a printer and an inker work a handpress, and a workman lifts wet sheets to dry on a ceiling-level rack. In the background, a girl comes through the door, clutching a jug of beer, the pressman's traditional perquisite; in a corner, an author speaks excitedly to an unidentified companion. In the foreground, dominating the scene, stands the master-printer—a majestic, Prospero-like figure, who seems to be counting on his fingers.[1]

The picture alone reveals some of the complexities and the fascination of early printing and, above all, its unprecedented employment under one roof of intellectuals and craftsmen, scholars and entrepreneurs. Hornschuch's text tells us even more. It was written by and for correctors, the new class of educated printing workers. It demanded that they master a range of skills no earlier job would have required. They had to grasp the mechanics of printing and the intellectual principles of consistent spelling, punctuation, and proofreading. It asked the author as

[1] Philip Gaskell and Patricia Bradford (eds. and trans.), *Hornschuch's Orthotypographia, 1608* (Cambridge, 1972). I follow the excellent analysis in Percy Simpson, *Proof-Reading in the Sixteenth, Seventeenth and Eighteenth Centuries* (London, 1935), 126–130.

266 | ANTHONY T. GRAFTON

well as the printer to stretch himself. He was required to appreciate the possibilities printing offered for exact and attractive reproduction of his work, to learn to give his printers clean copy, to help them choose an appropriate type-face, and to leave them alone to get on with printing and proofreading his work. Publication as we know it, that drawn-out struggle among author, businessmen, and craftsmen, had come into being.

Early modern historians have long been interested in this strange little world of the printing-house. Eisenstein challenges them to do more. The burden of her book is that the printing-house was more than an important locus of cultural and social

Fig. 1   A Renaissance Printing House.

SOURCE: From Jerome Hornschuch, *Orthotypographia* (Leipzig, 1608), courtesy of the Joseph Regenstein Library, University of Chicago.

change; it was the crucible in which modern culture was formed. But since cultural historians have persistently ignored its pervasive influence, they have given a distorted account of the Renaissance, the Reformation, and the Scientific Revolution.

Eisenstein began to work this thesis out more than a decade ago. She developed it in a series of brilliant polemical articles, all of them distinguished by absolute independence from received ideas, an extraordinary range of interests, and a considerable breadth of knowledge. Now she has stated it in the powerful form of a two-volume study teeming with ideas and information. No historian of early modern Europe will be able to avoid a confrontation with the problems she has raised; for that alone we owe her a great debt.[2]

To be sure, Eisenstein is far too learned and too subtle a scholar to claim that printing by itself brought about the Renaissance, the Reformation, and the Scientific Revolution. Nor does she claim that it affected every area of culture in the same way. Indeed, one of the great strengths of her book is its insistence on the enormous variety and frequent contradictoriness of the developments linked with printing. Yet it is still clear that she sees printing as far more than one among many "factors in modern history." It changed the directions of existing cultural movements as suddenly and completely as a prism bends and transforms a beam of light. If printing did not create the Renaissance, for example, it nonetheless made it undergo a sea change. Printing made an Italian movement of limited scope and goals into a European one. It preserved in unprecedented quantities and disseminated at an unprecedented speed the classical discoveries of humanists, thus preventing their classical revival from being as limited and transitory as those of the Carolingian period and the twelfth century. And it made enough sources of information about the past available to all readers so that men came for the first time to see the ancient world as something clearly different from their own. Without printing, the characteristic Renaissance sense of history and sensitivity to anachronism could never have widely established themselves.

2 Eisenstein, "Clio and Chronos," *History and Theory*, Beiheft VI (1966), 36–64; *idem*, "The Advent of Printing and the Problem of the Renaissance," *Past & Present*, 45 (1969), 19–89; *idem*, "L'Avènement de l'Imprimerie et la Réforme," *Annales*, XXVI (1971), 1355–1382.

In the field of religion, printing had rather different effects. It spread Luther's message with amazing speed and so preserved it from the suppression that had been the fate of medieval heresies. But that, after all, has long been a commonplace of Reformation historiography. For Eisenstein, the role of printing in preparing the way for the Reformation holds more interest than its role in spreading it. She argues persuasively that the printing press did much to undermine the authority of the Church simply by making available to a wide public Biblical texts, with all of their apparent contradictions, as well as by spreading new forms of devotional literature and changing old ones.

For science, finally, printing served still other ends. By making available complete and newly accurate texts of the great ancient works, above all those of Ptolemy and Galen, it created a new foundation of theories, methods, and data on which practitioners of the classical sciences could build more systematically than would ever have been possible in the age of scribes. By making possible the accurate reproduction and systematic improvement of illustrations, it literally revolutionized the collection and checking of data about the natural world. The wide diffusion of classical and modern texts enabled scientists to educate themselves and to become aware of contradictions that had not bothered the less well-informed readers of medieval times. And it did more than any other force to create the disciplinary communities and standards that characterize modern science, with its emphasis on collaboration and competition.

The protagonist in each of these movements is the master-printer, a pioneer both as businessman and as intellectual. It was in his shop that artisans came together with intellectuals to create the greatest works of the new science; it was his opposition to authority, something almost inherent in the nature of his calling, that turned networks of printing-shops into the relays along which ran messages of change.

These are only some of Eisenstein's main arguments. No summary can do justice to so rich a book. Every reader will have his favorite pages; my own, perhaps, are those in which she treats the divergence between popular and learned traditions in religious literature after the Reformation and those in which she speculates strikingly about the effects of manuals of "civility" on the relations between parents and children. Every reader will also profit

ON PRINTING | **269**

from the many epigrammatic obiter dicta that enrich the book. Eisenstein is often more perceptive than professional students of the fields she treats. She is absolutely right to point out that the Renaissance recovery of classical scientific works was not a retreat to blind worship of authority but the indispensable foundation for the Vesalian and Copernican revolutions—a point on which many historians of science still go wrong. More generally, she is right to hold that historians of ideas, especially in the English-speaking world, have paid far too little attention to the social, economic, and material realities that affected past intellectuals, and to point out in particular that the conditions of publication deserve a more prominent place among those realities than even the broadest-minded intellectual historians have accorded them.

For all of the excitement it inspires, however, Eisenstein's book also leaves the reader with a certain uneasiness. It is not surprising that in 700 pages of vigorous argument she has some-times missed her aim, or that at times she seems to be tilting at windmills rather than real opponents. What is more surprising, and causes more concern, is that many of her errors and exaggerations seem to stem directly from the goals at which she aims and the methods she has chosen.

Eisenstein has decided to do her research not in primary but in secondary sources. She herself describes the book as "based on monographic literature not archival research" (xvi). What she does not explain is why she has abstained so rigorously from studying the thousands of published primary sources on the effects of printing that are available in any major scholarly library. Anthologies of early prefaces and other documents can help to initiate a reader into the field. The colophons of incunabula give us a chance to watch dozens of editors and printers at work, and thousands of such texts are accurately reproduced in the modern catalogs of early printed books. The letters of many of the most influential editors can be read in well-annotated modern editions. And, of course, the early printed books that fill the shelves of the Folger Library, where Eisenstein did much of her reading, are their own best witnesses.[3]

---

3 The best place to begin is Hans Widmann, Horst Kliemann, and Bernhard Wendt (eds.), *Der deutsche Buchhandel in Urkunden und Quellen* (Hamburg, 1965), 2v., which provides samples of almost every relevant sort of document. For prefaces, see, e.g., Beriah Botfield (ed.), *Prefaces to the First Editions of the Greek and Roman Classics and of the Sacred*

One need not do "archival research" to master these materials; but though Eisenstein has consulted some of them, they have not left much of a precipitate in her book. What a pity, one feels, that she has filled her pages with ungainly chunks of quotation from modern textbooks and articles, with other scholars' summaries and descriptions. Such passages block the lively flow of her prose. It seems a shame that she did not replace them with direct readings of the sources and with well-chosen plates (she uses no illustrations at all). What a pity, for example, that she did not enrich her discussion of the spread of Luther's writings with a quotation from Johann Froben's splendid letter to the reformer:

> The Leipzig book dealer Blasius Salomon gave me a selection of your writings at the last Frankfurt Fair. Since they received much applause from scholars I reprinted them at once. We have sent 600 copies to France and Spain. They were bought up in Paris, and were read and praised by the scholars at the Sorbonne, so our friends have reported to us . . . Calvo too, the Pavian book dealer, a well-educated man and a friend of the Muses, took a considerable number of your writings to Italy in order to retail them in every city. In doing so he is concerned not to make money but to serve the new devotion as best he can. He promised that he would send epigrams applauding you by all the scholars in Italy . . . Moreover we have sent your works to Brabant and England.[4]

Here we see a printer taking on just the sort of innovative role as both entrepreneur and intellectual that Eisenstein's thesis calls for.

Scriptures (Cambridge, 1861); Eugene F. Rice, Jr. (ed.), *The Prefatory Epistles of Jacques Lefèvre d'Etaples and Related Texts* (New York, 1972); Giovanni Orlandi (ed.), *Aldo Manuzio Editore: dediche, prefazioni, note ai testi* (Milan, 1975), 2v. (the rich introduction by Carlo Dionisotti is by far the best study in existence of Aldo). The richest single source for colophons is the *Catalogue of Books Printed in the XVth Century Now in the British Museum* (London, 1963–1971; rev. ed.), 12v. The serious student will also consult older works, above all Ludwig Hain, *Repertorium Bibliographicum* (Stuttgart, 1826–1838), 2 v.; the supplements by D. Reichling (1905–1914) and W. A. Copinger (1895–1902). He will go when possible to the greatest of all such lists, the *Gesamtkatalog der Wiegendrucke,* which is now being continued after a hiatus of many years and is up to the letter F. For editors' letters see, for example, P. S. Allen, H. M. Allen, and H. W. Garrod (eds.), *Opus Epistolarum Des. Erasmi Roterodami* (Oxford, 1906–1958), 12v.; A. Hartmann (ed.), *Die Amerbachkorrespondenz* (Basel, 1942–1974), 8v. Naturally, many sixteenth-, seventeenth-, and eighteenth-century editions remain indispensable—for example, Pieter Burman (ed.), *Sylloge Epistolarum a viris illustribus scriptarum* (Leiden, 1727), 5v.
4   Widmann et al., *Der deutsche Buchhandel,* I, 345.

ON PRINTING | **271**

A rather limited amount of reading—certainly less than a year's work, and she worked for ten—would have enabled her to turn up many passages as revealing as this one and to excise many unnecessary dead patches from every chapter. As the book stands, Eisenstein's few excursions into the documents tantalize the reader without satisfying him. Again and again, the book comes alive as an early intellectual is quoted or an early book or print is discussed; but all too soon we are back in a world of textbook-style generalities.[5]

In some ways, too, the general plan of Eisenstein's structure is as troubling as its foundations are disappointing. She has not told a story but carried on a series of arguments about the importance of printing in a great many fields over two centuries. As a result, she has tended to pull from her sources those facts and statements that seemed to meet her immediate polemical needs, both positive and negative. Sometimes the statements that she quotes are torn so far from their original context that they take on a meaning that their author could not have intended, or are denounced for failing to meet standards that their author could not possibly have reached. Eisenstein criticizes textbooks as if they had been meant to meet the same rigorous standards as monographs. She dissects incidental remarks as if they had been meant to describe complex events and situations in a complete and final way. And she tends, especially in her chapter on the Renaissance, to criticize modern historians in the light of her own interests and knowledge rather than in that of their intellectual contexts. Thus, she does not try to understand *why* Jacob Burckhardt saw the Renaissance as a piercing of a veil that had long hung between men and the natural world; instead, she suggests that his views should be "reformulated" to take into account the role of printing and the continuities between medieval and Renaissance culture that historians have discovered since Burckhardt's time (226). Surely it would be more sensible to try to understand Burckhardt's methods and standards than to criticize him for not living up to ours. These tactics infuse into parts of Eisenstein's book an unpleasant, and certainly unintentional, tone of hectoring.

5 For example, Eisenstein's excellent discussion of Andrew Maunsell, though suggestive, breaks off all too soon (106-107).

272 | ANTHONY T. GRAFTON

Yet these attacks on other scholars, however unnecessary, cause less unease than the ways in which Eisenstein sometimes deploys the evidence that they have given her. Facts as well as obiter dicta tend to be pulled out of shape by the force with which she sets upon them. At one point, for example, she argues that the systematic historical study of the ancient world could not come into being until printing had made it possible to have "adequate equipment" for "systematically reconstructing a past civilization" (187). In support of this claim she quotes some lines from a well-known essay by Momigliano, describing the great antiquarians of the sixteenth century. What she does not quote is his description, in the same passage, of the work of earlier antiquarians—in particular, that of Flavio Biondo, whose systematic survey of Roman civilization, *Roma Triumphans,* was completed in the 1450s, well before the existence of printing could have had any impact on the author. "It required at least a century of printing," says Eisenstein, "however before a 'systematic collection' of relics . . . could occur" (187). But what of Biondo's amazingly complete and accurate description of the material relics of ancient Rome, *Roma Instaurata?* That was completed in the 1440s. And it is fully described in another work that Eisenstein knows—Weiss, *The Renaissance Discovery of Classical Antiquity.* I do not think that anyone who has read the works on which Eisenstein relies would agree that her account of them is entirely judicious. And the case of the antiquarians is, unfortunately, not exceptional. It is hard to see how anything but the desire to prove a point could have led Eisenstein to repeat the old canard that the humanists knew almost nothing about the Middle Ages (190-191). The great humanist histories—Leonardo Bruni, *History of the Florentine People* and Biondo, *Decades*—were precisely histories of medieval Italy, based on wide reading in medieval chronicles and an impressive amount of digging in the archives. These facts are clearly presented in the standard works of Ullman, Baron, and Hay.[6]

---

6 Arnaldo Momigliano, "Ancient History and the Antiquarian," *Studies in Historiography* (London, 1966), 5-6; Roberto Weiss, *The Renaissance Discovery of Classical Antiquity* (Oxford, 1969), 68-70; B. L. Ullman, "Leonardo Bruni and Humanistic Historiography," *Studies in the Italian Renaissance* (Rome, 1955), 321-344; Hans Baron, "Das Erwachen des historischen Denkens im Humanismus des Quattrocento," *Historische Zeitschrift,* CXLVII (1932-33), 5-20; Denys Hay, "Flavio Biondo and the Middle Ages," *Proceedings of the British Academy,* XLV (1959), 97-128.

These problems of method and approach affect more than isolated points of detail. No craftsman is better than his tools, and at times the defects of Eisenstein's equipment have injured the very substance and structure of her book. Both her lively survey of the change from script to print and her suggestive speculations about its intellectual consequences suffer seriously from her one-sided presentation of the evidence.

Eisenstein wishes to emphasize how radical the break was between the age of scribes and that of printers. To do so she minimizes the extent to which any text could circulate in stable form before mechanical means of reproduction became available. She suggests that almost no reader in any age of manuscripts could have access to a large number of texts. She both argues and implies that the scribal book trade was a casual and ill-organized affair; she clearly holds that no single scribe could produce any large number of books. She relies heavily on De la Mare's pioneering demonstration that Vespasiano da Bisticci, the most famous Florentine manuscript dealer, operated on a far smaller scale than traditional accounts suggest. And she tends to downplay evidence that lay literacy was increasing rapidly even before printing was invented.[7]

I cannot feel that Eisenstein has done justice to the available evidence. She talks a great deal about Vespasiano's backwardness, but not at all about that well-organized and productive scribe Diebold Lauber, who was innovative enough to issue written broadsides listing and advertising his wares. She says very little about the effects of the new educational institutions that popped up like mushrooms in many parts of Europe during the period 1350 to 1500, which must have had a sizeable impact on the level of literacy among members of the lay elite: for example, the ten German universities, all with law faculties, that were founded between 1365 and 1472. And though she criticizes Kristeller for suggesting that a work preserved in three copies "attained a certain diffusion" (211), she says nothing at all about the well-known studies by Soudek and Schucan, both inspired by Kristeller. These two scholars have proved that some of Bruni's translations from

7 Albinia De la Mare, "Vespasiano da Bisticci, Historian and Bookseller," unpub. Ph.D. diss. (University of London, 1965). This rich work, which Eisenstein uses in a highly selective way, provides much further evidence both for and against her thesis.

274 | ANTHONY T. GRAFTON

the Greek were literally best sellers before printing. Of one of the works studied, more than 200 manuscript copies survive; of the other, more than 300. Many more must have perished. The extant copies belonged to an extraordinary cross-section of the literate, one that included merchants as well as clerics, teachers as well as lawyers and notaries. Such cases make a rather formidable exception to the norms Eisenstein describes.[8]

Nor does Eisenstein say much about the evidence that a private scholar could assemble quite a large and varied library of manuscripts. Niccoli and Salutati had some 800 manuscripts each, which they catalogued carefully and made available freely to other scholars. And even a much poorer man like Poggio, while still a secretary in the Papal Curia, could assemble an astonishingly diverse collection of Latin and Greek texts of every kind. When such men could simply buy manuscripts, they did so. More often they borrowed texts and paid a scribe to copy them. This process had its difficulties—Poggio referred to the scribes who worked for him as "the excrement of the universe"—and collectors were not uncommonly forced to make their own transcripts. Yet the results were libraries far more diverse and rich than one would expect from Eisenstein's account.[9]

Facts like these suggest that the Renaissance might not have been another transitory revival even if printing had not been invented. They suggest that the experience of collectors and readers changed rather less sharply than one might expect with the advent of printed books. And they suggest that earlier scholars may well have been right to hold that it was new forms of

8   For the text of Lauber's broadside, see Widmann et al., *Der deutsche Buchhandel*, I, 15–16. For a discussion of the document, see Widmann, *Geschichte des Buchhandels vom Altertum bis zur Gegenwart* (Wiesbaden, 1975), I, 37; Eisenstein mentions Lauber once in passing (13, n. 28). On universities, see Karl Heinz Burmeister, *Das Studium der Rechte im Zeitalter des Humanismus im deutschen Rechtsbereich* (Wiesbaden, 1974), 40–51. On Bruni's translations, see Josef Soudek, "Leonardo Bruni and his Public: A Statistical and Interpretative Study of his Annotated Latin Version of the (Pseudo-) Aristotelian Economics," *Studies in Medieval and Renaissance History*, V (1968), 49–136; Luzi Schucan, *Das Nachleben von Basilius Magnus 'ad adolescentes.' Ein Beitrag zur Geschichte des christlichen Humanismus* (Geneva, 1973).

9   B. L. Ullman, *The Humanism of Coluccio Salutati* (Padua, 1963), chs. 9–11; *idem* and Philip A. Stadter, *The Public Library of Renaissance Florence: Niccolò Niccoli, Cosimo de' Medici and the Library of San Marco* (Padua, 1972), ch. 2. Ernst Walser, *Poggius Florentinus: Leben und Werke* (Leipzig, 1914), 104–110. For further information on the contents of libraries before the invention of printing, see Pearl Kibre, "The Intellectual Interests Reflected in Libraries of the Fourteenth and Fifteenth Centuries," *Journal of the History of Ideas*, VII (1946), 257–297.

education and changes in the nature of governments, rather than the invention of printing, which created the new lay reading public of the Renaissance. At all events, one must regret that Eisenstein's decision to write in so polemical a vein led her to neglect them.

Eisenstein's picture of the printing-house is as bright as that of the scribe's study is dim. These "new centers of erudition," ruled by laymen, became Europe's most active centers of cultural change. We should think in terms of "many print shops located in numerous towns, each serving as an intellectual cross-roads, as a miniature 'international house'—as a meeting place, message center, and sanctuary all in one . . ." (448). In these new circumstances, "the printer's workshop attracted the most learned and disputatious scholars of the day." "Learned laymen . . . were less likely to gather on the church steps than in urban workshops where town and gown met to exchange gossip and news, peer over editors' shoulders, check copy and read proof" (309). Indeed, "Most inhabitants of the sixteenth-century Republic of Letters spent more time in printers' workshops than in 'secluded studies' " (154).

This description certainly fits a few of the great Renaissance print-shops at certain periods: those of Aldo Manuzio in the time of his Academy, Froben in the 1520s, and Christopher Plantin in the 1560s. But I fear that it has little to do with the printing shops that most citizens of the Republic of Letters knew best. Some shops, to be sure, like that of Anton Koberger in Nuremberg, were orderly and well-disciplined operations where the workers arrived and departed at fixed times, while work followed a remarkably regular schedule. But most plants, as McKenzie and others have shown, were typical pre-industrial places of work. Filled with the noise of machinery and the curses of workers when the presses were in operation, noisy with quarrels and dirty, the printing-house was not the sort of place that a gentleman wanted to frequent.[10] And we must not let our prejudices prevent

---

10   On Koberger, see J. C. Zeltner, *C. D. Correctorum in typographiis eruditorum centuria* (Nuremberg, 1716), 15–16. This work remains the richest collection of information on the activities of correctors in the first two centuries of printing; like many other products of eighteenth-century erudition, it is unjustly ignored by modern scholars, whose own works are rarely as rewarding. D. F. McKenzie, "Printers of the Mind: Some Notes on Bibliographical Theories and Printing-House Practices," *Studies in Bibliography,* XXII (1969), 1–75; Philip Gaskell, *A New Introduction to Bibliography* (Oxford, 1972), 48–49.

us from seeing that most early modern intellectuals saw themselves as gentlemen. They constantly complained that, as Professor Martinus Crusius of Tübingen put it, "the printers' journeymen hate to set Greek but want plenty of tips; [they're] an ill-
behaved, ignorant rabble."[11] Even scholars whose close friends
and relations were printers sometimes indignantly denied that
they themselves had ever worked for pay in a printing-shop.[12]

The presence of workmen was not all that made many print-
shops unattractive. There was also the absence of scholars. Naturally there were shops, especially the famous ones, where master,
correctors, or both were learned and original intellectuals. Paolo
Manuzio, for example, bargained with his authors in the perfect
Ciceronian Latin that befitted the scholar whose commentaries on
Cicero were standard works until the nineteenth century. When
Commelin printed a school text of the Greek poet Theognis "to
keep his workmen busy," he could add interesting text-critical
and exegetical notes of his own. Such masters naturally attracted
the interest of scholars. But I fear that Eisenstein has extended
this model of a printing-shop rather too far. Estienne tells us—
admittedly, in a polemical context—that most of his colleagues
were ignoramuses who printed whatever works academic conmen offered them, scrimped by refusing to buy good base texts
to print from, and hired hacks to write Greek and Latin prefaces
under their names, which most of them could not even read. As
to the correctors, even Hornschuch admitted that if they were
really learned men, "most of them would be off like a shot from
this sweat-shop, to earn their living by their intelligence and
learning, not by their hands."[13]

Ample evidence suggests that most Renaissance print-shops

11 Widmann et al., *Der deutsche Buchhandel*, II, 28: "Die Truckergesellen setzen ungern
Graeca: hetten aber gern vil Trinckgaelts. Ein loses ungelehrts Gesindlin." Cf. also Angelo
Poliziano, *Epistolarum libri XII* (Amsterdam, 1642), 410: ". . . semidocti illi qui librorum
excusoribus operam navant" ("those ignoramuses who work for printers").
12 Allen et al., *Opus Epistolarum Erasmi*, IX, 398 (Ep. 2581); Isaac Casaubon, *De rebus
sacris et ecclesiasticis exercitationes XVI* (Geneva, 1655), 38b–39a; also cited by Zeltner,
Correctorum centuria, 108–109.
13 See the interesting series of letters to Marcantonio Natta in *Epistolarum Pauli Manutii
libri XII* (Leipzig, 1603), III, 155–172. Jerome Commelin (ed.), *Theognidis, Phocylidis,
Pythagorae, Solonis et aliorum poemata gnomica* (Utrecht, 1659), ep. ded., sig. A 2ʳ: ". . . ne
operae, dum majora paramus, cessarent." Henri Estienne, *Epistola de statu suae typographiae*,
in *idem* (ed. F. G. Roloffius), *Pseudo-Cicero* (Halle, 1737), ccclxii–ccclxiv. Gaskell and
Bradford, *Hornschuch's Orthotypographia*, 27.

were much less sophisticated places than Eisenstein would have us believe. Her account conveys little of the variety, fragility, and tiny scale of the majority of printing shops. One thinks of the English printers of the sixteenth century, almost all of whom were small-scale operators of no great skill. One thinks, too, of the starving *petits imprimeurs* of the faubourgs Saint Jacques and Saint Marcel, described so well by Parent, clinging together to survive in companies that grew and disintegrated with amazing speed, like primitive organisms seen through a microscope.[14]

The intellectual level of many printing shops was as low as their finances were unsound. Consider Estienne's gloomy story about a corrector he had met:

> I met one of these fellows who was doing the job of a corrector with such savagery that he ruined every passage where he found the word *procos* (suitors) by putting *porcos* (pigs) in its place . . . "I know," he said, "that *porcos* is the name of a real animal; but I don't think that *procos* refers to animals or anything else in Latin."[15]

Anyone experienced in working with early books knows that many of them were, if not untouched by human hands, at least uninspected by human brains in the course of printing. Take the strange case of Paul the Silentiary's epigram from the Greek Anthology. Since this poem was written in extremely short verses, Aldo printed it in two columns to save space, with the verses in the following order:

1   2

3   4

5   6.

When the Giunti reprinted Aldo's edition of the Anthology, however, they did not bother to read the epigram and reprinted it with column 2 following rather than flanking column 1. The poem thus became incoherent. The proudest editors and printers in Europe—Badius, Gelenius, Estienne, and Wechel—one after

---

14 Ronald B. McKerrow, *An Introduction to Bibliography for Literary Students* (Oxford, 1960; orig. pub. 1928), 281; James Binns, "STC Latin Books: Evidence for Printing-House Practice," *The Library*, XXXII (1977), 1–27. Annie Parent, *Les métiers du livre à Paris au XVIᵉ siècle (1535–1560)* (Geneva, 1974), 133–135.

15 Henri Estienne, *Artis Typographicae querimonia*, in *idem, Pseudo-Cicero*, ccclxxvi–ccclxxvii.

278 | ANTHONY T. GRAFTON

another proceeded to reprint the poem in the same unintelligible form, thus providing striking proof that not one of them employed a corrector who knew Greek. Worse printers made even worse blunders. No wonder, then, that some texts deteriorated so far in the course of several editions as to become unintelligible.[16]

After all, printers were businessmen. They had to make money. When, as often happened, this need or the practical difficulties it imposed interfered with scholars' plans, the scholars tended to fly off the handle. Often they were blind to the printer's point of view. Martin Luther, enraged at the bad state of some proofs he had been sent, refused to send any more copy "until I'm convinced that these *Schmutzfinken* and *Geldmacher* are less interested in their own profit than in the books' utility for readers." True, he later changed his mind and sent the proofs. But he never ceased to berate the printers who not only reprinted his works without permission but also made such a bad job of them "that at many points I didn't recognize my own work."[17] Similarly, Nicolaas Heinsius saw the Elzeviers' insistence on printing his works in their favorite small format as the result not of commercial necessity but of an incomprehensible stinginess: "Our printers have been irremediably infected by that wretched custom. They think their books are worthless unless they can be carried around handily by someone who is out for a walk."[18] Given these clashing values and interests, it is not surprising that so many scholars felt that the association with commerce had ruined what could have been the liberal art of printing.[19]

I would not deny that Eisenstein's brilliant picture conveys something of the feel of a great house like Plantin's. It is certainly

16 A. A. Renouard, *Annales de l'Imprimerie des Alde, ou Histoire des trois Manuce et de leurs éditions* (Paris, 1834; 3d ed.), 43. Aldo, too, sometimes made use of incompetent correctors, as well-informed contemporaries complained. See Allen et al., *Opus Epistolarum Erasmi*, XI, 288–289 (Ep. 3100); Daniel Wyttenbach, *Opuscula* (Leiden, 1821), I, 360–361. On the deterioration of some other classical texts, see the evidence collected by Estienne, *Epistola de statu suae typographiae*, cccxxxviii–cccli.

17 Widmann et al., *Der deutsche Buchhandel*, II, 16, 327.

18 Hans Bots (ed.), *Correspondance de Jacques Dupuy et de Nicolas Heinsius (1646–1656)* (The Hague, 1971), 78. On Heinsius's relations with the Elzeviers, see the exemplary study by F. F. Blok, *Nicolaas Heinsius in dienst van Christina van Zweden* (Delft, 1949), 92–99.

19 See the evidence collected by Zeltner, *Correctorum centuria*, 18–20; Orlandi, *Aldo Manuzio Editore*, I, 170. Luther quoted in Widmann et al., *Der deutsche Buchhandel*, II, 327–328.

true that bookshops—which, however, were not always printing-shops as well, especially in the seventeenth century—and the great Frankfurt bookfair were gathering places for intellectuals. It is also true that many of the most original products of early modern scholarship and science—Abraham Ortelius, *Theatrum Orbis Terrarum* (Antwerp, 1570) and Andreas Vesalius, *De Humani Corporis Fabrica* (Basel, 1543)—were the result of unusually close collaboration between innovative scholars and responsive printers. But I do think that she paints a pastel-colored picture of the printing house and of the connections that it fostered between town and gown. I wonder if, even in those presses that became the meeting-places of learned men, it was not the attraction of the master-printer's scholarship, rather than the nature of his activity, that drew others to him. In that sense, was the attraction of Plantin's printing-house so very different from that of Cujas' study? We ought to remember that when Lipsius and Plantin held their most serious conversations about religion, they left the work-place and went for a long walk in the country.[20]

The exaggerations in Eisenstein's account of the shift from script to print inevitably affect her account of the shift's ramifications for intellectuals. She holds that the writer in an age of scribes had a fundamentally different relation to his public than the writer of a printed book. The scribal author could not hope that his work would be distributed in anything like a stable form, or even under his name. He could not bring out his private idiosyncrasies for public inspection as Montaigne could in his printed *Essays*. Nor could he hope to win lasting fame from works that were so unlikely to be preserved. "The conditions of scribal culture," as Eisenstein remarks in another context, "thus held narcissism in check" (233). Indeed, it is probably wrong even to speak of "publication before printing," as scholars sometimes do.

Here, too, I fear, there is a measure of exaggeration. Surely an author like Petrach deserves more part in the development of the modern notion of authorship than Eisenstein accords him. He

---

20 Certainly some great printers took enormous pride in the excellent work that their craftsmen did and made no bones about working right alongside their men in the shop; Paolo Manuzio added a legend to each of the three volumes of his 1554 edition of Demosthenes, stating that he himself had served as corrector (Zeltner, *Correctorum centuria*, 334). But I would still hold that Eisenstein overstates her case. On Lipsius and Plantin, see B. Rekers, *Benito Arias Montano (1527–1598)* (London, 1972), 102, 156–157—a stimulating book, but one to be used with caution. See Basil Hall, "A Sixteenth-Century Miscellany," *Journal of Ecclesiastical History*, XXVI (1975), 318–320.

took the greatest care to edit and polish his works before he allowed them to be seen. He cut up and rearranged his letters, not so much to portray himself in a better light as to give what he felt would be a clearer picture of his spiritual development. He even concluded one of the collections of his letters with a formal "Letter to Posterity," in which he speaks to the future reader very much as man to man. True, he feared that some of his works might not survive to find readers, and Eisenstein helps us to grasp the pathos of that fear. Yet he clearly did not find in scribal culture the fearful constraint on self-expression that Eisenstein describes.[21]

In fact, I am not entirely convinced that the process of publication itself changed so radically as Eisenstein holds, especially from the author's point of view. Kristeller showed long ago that publication followed the same course for a fifteenth-century author whether the book in question was to be copied or printed. The author either made or had made a fair copy of his work, called the *archetypum*. This he gave either to a scribe to copy or to a printer to print. The book was said to be "published" (*editus*) "on the day on which the author first allowed the completed *archetypum* to be reproduced by others." In either case, the author's part of the activity of publication remained scribal in character.[22]

21   Aldo S. Bernardo, "Letter-Splitting in Petrarch's *Familiares*," *Speculum*, XXXIII (1958), 236–241. For the Latin text of "Letter to Posterity" see Petrarch (ed. Giovanni Ponte), *Opere* (Milan, 1968), 886–900; English translation in David Thompson (ed.), *Petrarch: A Humanist Among Princes* (New York, 1971), 1–13. Petrarch expresses the suspicion that future readers will "have heard the bare titles" of his works: Petrarch, *Opere*, 886; Thompson (ed.), *Petrarch,* 1. In fact the *Epistula posteritati* remained incomplete and was therefore not included among Petrarch, *Seniles*. But the majority of Petrarch's works did circulate in a very carefully finished form; see Hans Baron, *From Petrarch to Leonardo Bruni* (Chicago, 1968), 7–101. In braving the difficulties of publishing his works— and in believing that they would win him eternal fame—Petrarch was, of course, following a path that the Roman authors he knew best had laid out. See esp. Horace, *Odes* III.30 and *Epistles,* I.20; Ovid, *Tristia,* IV.10. He thus had more reason than Eisenstein suggests to believe that his works would survive pretty much intact. In general, Eisenstein's account fits the histories of technical texts—lexica, grammars, commentaries, and handbooks—and vernacular literary texts far better than it does that of classical or late medieval literary texts, in Greek and Latin, which were valued for the exact form of their wording.

22   Paul Kristeller, "De traditione operum Marsilii Ficini," *Supplementum Ficinianum* (Florence, 1937), I, clxviii–clxxxi, esp. clxix–clxx, clxxiii. Kristeller's analysis has now been supplemented and slightly revised in its details by Silvia Rizzo, *Il lessico filologico degli umanisti* (Rome, 1973), 303–323; but his general arguments remain valid. Rizzo's work is essential reading for anyone who hopes to understand the relations among intellectuals,

If we combine these facts with the findings of students of sixteenth-century printing—with the fact that few authors actually wrote in printing-houses, and the fact that few even came to the printing house to correct proofs—we may see a less radical shift in the life-experience of writers than Eisenstein suggests. If we take into account the vast amount of time that any early modern writer spent in copying—in taking notes, copying unpublished or rare books, and writing his own works—we may be even more inclined to feel that the pace of change has been exaggerated. Scholars remained scribes for a long time. Some of us still are.[23]

In the end, however, it is less the process of publication than its intellectual consequences which Eisenstein seeks to illuminate. Her book must be tested as a piece of intellectual history. In this regard, too, it not only brings rewards but inspires misgivings.

Eisenstein tries to show that it was printing, not internal developments in Italian culture, that did the most to create the Renaissance sense of history. To prove this point she must refute a number of influential modern interpretations. She must argue, for example, that Panofsky was wrong to suggest that the Renaissance came to see the ancient world "from a fixed distance" and thus to gain a "total and rationalized view" of it. In Eisenstein's words, "That a 'total rationalized' view of any past civilization could be developed before the output of uniform reference guides and gazeteers seems implausible to me" (186). She admits that such "scribal scholars" as Lorenzo Valla had "a growing sensitivity to anachronism." But they lacked a "fixed spatial-temporal reference frame" (187). They had little sense of the chronological order in which ancient texts had been composed or of the great disagreements that had sometimes separated their authors. And to reproach early scholars for making historical or

scribes, and printers during the fifteenth century. See also the excellent case study by Helene Harth, "Niccolò Niccoli als literarischer Zensor. Untersuchungen zur Textgeschichte von Poggios 'De Avaritia,'" *Rinascimento*, VII (1967), 29–53.

23   On authors' participation in proof-correction, which took every form from standing over the printers while they worked to complete neglect, see the evidence collected by Simpson, *Proof-Reading*; Widmann, "'Die Lektüre unendlicher Korrekturen,'" *Archiv für Geschichte des Buchwesens*, V (1963–64), 777–826; Binns, "STC Latin Books." See also Gaskell, *A New Introduction to Bibliography*, 111. For evidence of the "scribal" efforts of scholars long after the invention of printing, see, for example, *Bibliotheca Universitatis Leidensis, Codices Manuscripti*, II: *Codices Scaligerani (praeter Orientales)* (Leiden, 1910); *ibid.*, IV: *Codices Perizoniani* (Leiden, 1946).

philological errors, as Seznec and others have done, is to forget
the inevitably narrow limits of what they could know.[24]

Here, too, I fear, Eisenstein's eagerness to prove her thesis
has led her to play down a large amount of contrary evidence.
Why Renaissance men developed a new historical sense I cannot
say. But I do know that they began to do so earlier and had far
more success at the enterprise than Eisenstein believes.

One finds a new interest in historical and philological questions among Italian intellectuals from the very beginning of the
fourteenth century. Take the case of Giovanni of Verona and the
two Plinys. Both the *Natural History* of the elder Pliny and the
letters of his nephew, Pliny the Younger, which vividly described
the uncle's life and death, were widely read in the Middle Ages.
Vincent of Beauvais, for example, quoted hugely from both
works. Yet both he and other medieval readers attributed both
works to the same man, even though the letters made clear that
this view was impossible. For some reason, Giovanni read the
two Plinys in a new way. He realized that the elder Pliny could
not have written a letter about his own death. And he found this
discovery so exciting that he wrote a little treatise about it, which
began "It is known that there were two Plinys." The treatise, in
turn, found some diffusion in Renaissance manuscripts of the
Natural History—a fact that suggests that Giovanni's interests and
viewpoint were shared by others.[25]

Discoveries of this kind multiplied throughout the fourteenth
century. Petrarch, in particular, made his life into a joyous expedition across the *mare magnum* of classical literature. Modern
scholars, especially Nolhac and Billanovich, have taught us to
follow the stages of his journey in the margins of his many books.
And they have proved that he amassed a systematic enough
knowledge of the ancient world to solve many technical problems
in a way that can still be accepted. He emended corrupt passages
in Livy with impressive dexterity. And he did a better job than
a whole team of twentieth-century classicists at identifying some

---

24   For the fullest statement of his views, see Erwin Panofsky, *Renaissance and Renascences
in Western Art* (New York, 1969). Jean Seznec (trans. Barbara F. Sessions), *The Survival
of the Pagan Gods* (New York, 1953).
25   Elmer Truesdell Merrill, "On the Eight-Book Tradition of Pliny's *Letters* in Verona,"
Classical Philology, V (1910), 175-188. Giovanni de Matociis, *Brevis adnotatio de duobus
Pliniis Veronensibus, ibid.*, 186: "Plinii duo fuisse noscuntur, eodem nomine et praenomin-
ibus appellati . . ."

of the sources from which the ancient scholar Servius drew his enormous commentary on Virgil.[26]

Later generations were even more sophisticated and knowledgeable. Salutati and Valla discovered and exposed clear chronological errors in the ancient accounts of Roman history. Bruni wrote a perceptive and well-documented life of Aristotle that set the philosopher's life into a general chronological system (that of the Greek Olympiads) and carefully distinguished his ideas from those of his teacher Plato. Polenton compiled a comprehensive and critical history of Latin literature. He assimilated many of the discoveries of earlier scholars; his section on the Plinys, for example, begins: "Lest anyone be deceived by their identical names, I think I should begin by pointing out that there were two Plinys, uncle and nephew." And he added new ones of his own. He showed that Cicero could not have praised Virgil's sixth Eclogue even if ancient scholars claimed that he had: "Chronology shows that Cicero, who died before the battle of Philippi, could not possibly have praised what Virgil wrote after it." Biondo and Cyriac of Ancona assembled with painstaking care the material relics of the ancient world.[27] Biondo also rightly argued that the ancient Romans must have spoken Latin, not Italian—thus showing a considerable ability to imagine a civilization different from his own.[28] By the end of the fifteenth century such scholars as

26   Pierre de Nolhac, *Pétrarque et l'humanisme* (Paris, 1907; 2d ed.), 2v.; Giuseppe Billanovich, "Petrarch and the Textual Tradition of Livy," *Journal of the Warburg and Courtauld Institutes*, XIV (1951), 137–208; *idem, Un nuovo esempio delle scoperte e delle letture del Petrarca. L'"Eusebio-Girolamo-PseudoProspero"* (Krefeld, 1954). I cite only two of Billanovich's most important works. The serious student will find many more studies by him and his students in the journal *Italia Medioevale e Umanistica*. For a particularly revealing case study, see Lucia A. Ciapponi, "Il 'De Architectura' di Vitruvio nel primo Umanesimo," *Italia Medioevale e Umanistica*, III (1960), 59–99. On Petrarch and Servius, see Eduard Fraenkel, *Kleine Beiträge zur klassischen Philologie* (Rome, 1964), II, 372–373.

27   Ullman, *The Humanism of Coluccio Salutati*, 98–99; H. J. Erasmus, *The Origins of Rome in Historiography from Petrarch to Perizonius* (Assen, 1962), 28–29 (though excellent as an analysis of Valla's argument, this work somewhat overstates Valla's superiority to his contemporaries); Bruni, *Aristotilis vita*, in Ingemar Düring, *Aristotle in the Ancient Biographical Tradition* (Göteborg, 1957), 168–178; Sicco Polenton (ed. B. L. Ullman), *Scriptorum illustrium Latinae linguae libri XVIII* (Rome, 1928), 227, 82. In addition to Weiss, *The Renaissance Discovery of Classical Antiquity*, see Riccardo Fubini, "Biondo, Flavio," *Dizionario biografico degli Italiani* (Rome, 1968), X, 536–559; Bernard Ashmole, "Cyriac of Ancona," *Proceedings of the British Academy*, XLV (1959), 25–41; for a contrasting case, see Charles Mitchell, "Felice Feliciano *Antiquarius*," *ibid.*, XLVII (1961), 197–221.

28   John Rowe, "The Renaissance Foundations of Anthropology," *American Anthropologist*, LXVII (1965), 1–20, reprinted in Regna Darnell (ed.), *Readings in the History of Anthropology* (New York, 1974), 72.

Angelo Poliziano had arrived at an extraordinarily sophisticated historical understanding of both Latin and Greek culture and had formulated most of the technical methods which modern scholars still use in editing and explicating ancient sources.[29]

Eisenstein is right to say, as others have before her, that printing dramatically affected the nature of scholarship—that it broadened the range of available sources, made it much easier to learn Greek, and made cross-checking and collation of texts far more practicable.[30] But she certainly exaggerates the historical ignorance and ineptness of those whom she demeaningly calls "scribal scholars." By trying to prevent scholars from modernizing the Renaissance unduly, Eisenstein has made the Renaissance less modern than it really was.

Eisenstein's account of the Reformation seems to me altogether more rewarding. She is right to point out that the relationship between printing and the Reformation did not begin with the publication of Luther's first broadside. Printing did offer new careers and a newly widespread power to the reforming literati of Erasmus's generation. It did offer new opportunities to peddlers of indulgences. I suspect that she is also on the right track when she suggests that printing by its very nature worked against clerical authority.

Yet here, too, exaggeration and unimaginative research sometimes harm her arguments. One would not suspect from her account that there was a rather successful Catholic translation of the Bible into German—much less that it appeared in print before Luther's complete Bible and went through some 100 editions, seventeen of them during the sixteenth century.[31] And her account of Simon's contributions to biblical exegesis is less history than travesty. More engagement with the sources, then, could have enriched this already fascinating chapter and made possible a more subtle approach to the problems it raises.[32]

29 See now Grafton, "On the Scholarship of Politian and Its Context," *Journal of the Warburg and Courtauld Institutes,* XL (1977), 150–188, with extensive references to older studies.

30 As Eisenstein says, this point had been made before, above all by P. S. Allen, *Erasmus: Lectures and Wayfaring Sketches* (Oxford, 1934), 30–40.

31 Widmann, *Geschichte des Buchhandels,* I, 69.

32 Cf. Eisenstein, 321, with Richard Simon, *Histoire critique du Vieux Testament (Suivant la Copie, imprimée à* Paris, 1680), I, 16–23, 49–50. Whatever Simon was doing—and that is a complex question—he was not "casting in the role of an archivist the prophet who was once believed to have received the Ten Commandments from God on Sinai . . ."

About the Scientific Revolution, finally, Eisenstein makes some of her best points. Her whole second volume is allotted to science. It makes fresher reading than the earlier chapters, perhaps because it is based on more recent research. It rests on a compelling, though incomplete, account of the historiography of science. Many of its arguments carry conviction. In particular, it does seem that the revival and transformation of such descriptive sciences as anatomy, botany, and zoology clearly stemmed, although in different ways, from the new possibilities offered by printing for the checking and correction of data. And her suggestion that the connection between Protestantism and science may have resulted from the relative lack of censorship in Protestant Europe seems plausible.

But even Eisenstein's volume on science suffers from a tendency to exaggeration. She overestimates the instability of manuscript texts and the difficulties involved in gaining access to them. She underestimates the effectiveness of the communications networks that bound intellectuals together across Europe long before 1450—above all, the networks that linked monastic houses and universities. She plays down evidence that does not fit her thesis—for example, Regiomontanus's mastery, derived entirely from manuscript sources, of precisely those problems in astronomy that most exercised Copernicus.[33]

These remarks have been intended only to begin a debate that will probably be long and lively. But they do suggest that Eisenstein's enterprise suffers from two flaws at its heart: inadequate foundation in research and exaggerated claims of explanatory power. Even the most suggestive pages of the book contain too much that is misleading.

Eisenstein considered it more "urgent" to amalgamate her ideas in this form than to do further reading, but I confess that I am not certain why she felt this way. Her views have received extended expression in some of the most influential historical journals in the Western world. Since she began to work in this field, moreover, intellectual historians have begun to show far

---

33 See, e.g., M. L. W. Laistner, *Thought and Letters in Western Europe, a.d. 500 to 900* (London, 1957; 2d ed.), 229; L. D. Reynolds and N. G. Wilson, *Scribes and Scholars: A Guide to the Transmission of Greek and Latin Literature* (Oxford, 1974; 2d ed.), 82–105. Eisenstein's account quite rightly stresses Regiomontanus's pioneering activity as a publisher (584–588); she lays much less stress on the great originality of his work as an astronomer.

286 │ ANTHONY T. GRAFTON

more interest in the phenomenon and the effects of printing. The best recent American survey of Renaissance and Reformation culture—Eugene F. Rice, Jr., *The Foundations of Early Modern Europe, 1460-1559* (New York, 1970)—begins with a long discussion of printing and its effects. Historians of science have also begun to show more interest in the effects of printing on the formation of scientific disciplines. And a vastly productive and influential group of historians of printing, including both French and American scholars, has done much to give the subject wide publicity and to win younger scholars to its study. In these circumstances, Eisenstein might well have taken the time to carry out case studies using primary sources.[34]

"Books do furnish a room"; whether they do anything else depends on those who read them far more than on those who copy or print them. The story of early modern intellectuals must in the end be a history of ideas, however unfashionable that enterprise has come to be. Like all good histories of ideas, it will have to be based on the primary sources. The role of scribes and printers will certainly form part of that history, and we will owe that in some part to Eisenstein's work. But the story of the medium cannot be substituted for the story of the message.

34 For Eisenstein's earlier publications, see n. 2 above. For the history of science, see, for example, Robert S. Westman, "Three Responses to the Copernican Theory: Johannes Praetorius, Tycho Brahe, and Michael Maestlin," in *idem* (ed.), *The Copernican Achievement* (Los Angeles, 1975), 285-345. For recent work on the history of printing and the book, see Eisenstein, 29, n. 71; 30, n. 72.

[5]

The Roman Inquisition and the Venetian Press, 1540–1605

Paul F. Grendler
University of Toronto

The external history of the Index of Prohibited Books, that is, its list of authors and rules, is generally known, but the internal history is not. How effective in practice were the Index and its enforcing agent, the Roman Inquisition? When, and to what extent, were the decrees and prohibitions enforced? Why, or why not, were they enforced? By and large, answers to these questions are lacking for sixteenth-century Italy. In any attempt to answer these questions, a study of Venice is essential, because it was the largest Italian center for printing, producing perhaps half or more of all Cinquecento Italian books. Equally important, the Inquisition records in Venice are accessible to scholars and are reasonably complete.

The development in Venice of the Inquisition activity against heretical literature is the focus of this brief paper on a large subject.[1] In the 1540s the machinery for censorship was set up, but the level

---

[1] This is a revised version of a paper read at the 1972 meeting of the American Historical Association in a session jointly sponsored by the American Society for Reformation Research and the American Catholic Historical Association. Because it is a précis of a monograph in preparation, the documentation has been abbreviated. The two fundamental works on Venetian censorship are Horatio F. Brown, *The Venetian Printing Press, 1469–1800: An Historical Study Based upon Documents for the Most Part Hitherto Unpublished* (London, 1891; reprint Amsterdam, 1969); and Giovanni Sforza, "Riflessi della Controriforma nella Repubblica di Venezia," *Archivio storico italiano* 93, pt. 1 (1935): 5–34, 189–216; 93, pt. 2 (1935): 25–52, 173–86. Not concerned with Venice but of great interest are the documents printed by Antonio Rotondò, "Nuovi documenti per la storia dell'*Indice dei libri proibiti* (1572–1638)," *Rinascimento*, ser. 2, 3 (1963): 145–211; and John Tedeschi, "Florentine Documents for a History of the *Index of Prohibited Books*," in *Renaissance Studies in Honor of Hans Baron*, ed. Anthony Molho and John Tedeschi (Florence and DeKalb, Ill., 1971), pp. 577–605. Also see the recent survey of Rotondò, "La censura ecclesiastica e la cultura," in *Storia d'Italia*, vol. 5, *I documenti* (Turin: Einaudi, 1973), pp. 1397–1492. All sixteenth-century Indices are printed in Franz Heinrich Reusch, ed., *Die Indices Librorum Prohibitorum des sechzehnten Jahrhunderts* (Tübingen, 1886; reprint Nieuwkoop, 1961). Reusch analyzed the Indices in *Der Index der verbotenen Bücher: Ein Beitrag zur Kirchen- und literaturgeschichte*, 2 vols. in 3 pts. (Bonn, 1883–85; reprint Darmstadt, 1967). Unless otherwise indicated, all documents cited are to be found in the Archivio di Stato, Venice, including the Holy Office (Santo Uffizio) records. The following abbreviations are used: SU, Santo Uffizio; ASVa, Archivio Segreto Vaticano, Rome; Bu., Busta; F., Filza; R., Registro.

of prosecution was low. In the 1550s the Venetians started to become inquisitors, although they still resisted jurisdictional initiatives from the papacy. In the 1560s, climaxing in 1569–71, the Venetians prosecuted heretical books with as much zeal as even Pope Pius V could want. Over the next twenty years enforcement continued, but the fervor gradually waned, until the papacy and the Republic quarreled over books in 1596, as they disputed other matters in that decade.

Whoever sought to censor the Venetian press faced a formidable task, for the Adriatic city harbored one of the great concentrations of printers in the sixteenth century. To make a conservative estimate, Venetian bookmen[2] printed more than 8 million books (i.e., 8 million individual volumes) in the second half of the sixteenth century. This total was the result of about 8,150 editions, new and reprints, an average of 163 annually. These figures do not include pamphlets that did not receive imprimaturs. In any given year, fifty or more publishers produced at least one title, and about 500 publishers appeared on the title pages of Venetian books during the sixteenth century.[3] A Venetian pressrun varied according to the anticipated demand and whether the publishing firm was large or small. The

[2] Rather than attempt to distinguish among publisher, printer, and bookseller (an artificial distinction in any case, because one man or firm frequently did all three), the general term "bookman" is preferred. In the documents, *stampatore, libraio,* and *bibliopola* are used interchangeably and indiscriminately.

[3] The figures are arrived at in the following way. A new title or a substantially revised edition had to receive a governmental imprimatur (permission to print). These, for 1550–99, are recorded in Capi del Consiglio dei Dieci, Notatorio, R. 14–31 and F. 1–14. The average yearly total was seventy-one, giving an estimate of the number of new titles per year. Then, for every new title there were one or more reprints; Gabriel Giolito, for example, published 1.09 reprints for every original title (Salvatore Bongi, *Annali di Gabriel Giolito de' Ferrari da Trino di Monferrato, stampatore in Venezia,* 2 vols. [Rome, 1890–97; reprint Rome, n.d.], supplemented by Paolo Camerini, "Notizia sugli Annali Giolitini di Salvatore Bongi," *Atti e memorie della R. Accademia di scienze, lettere ed arte in Padova,* n.s., 51 [1934–35]: 103–238). If one multiplies 71 × 2.09 for the average yearly production of 148, and then × 50 for the half-century, one arrives at 7,400 editions, a conservative estimate, because publishers did not obtain an imprimatur for every title, especially in the 1550s and early 1560s. Possibly for every ten titles for which an imprimatur was granted, one title was published in first edition and subsequent reprint without an imprimatur. If the total number of editions for the half-century is increased by 10 percent in order to add the works published without imprimaturs, then the total for the half-century is approximately 8,150 editions (148 plus 15 × 50). Then, if the average press run was approximately 1,000 copies (see n. 4 below), over 8 million books were printed in the half-century. The count of *privilegi* (copyrights) by Brown, pp. 236–40, is inaccurate, and the count of editions by Ester Pastorello, *Tipografi, editori, librai a Venezia nel secolo xvi* (Florence, 1924), is underestimated by approximately 50 percent.

50   *Paul F. Grendler*

normal, average pressrun of a title of ordinary sales potential was about 1,000 copies; a major publisher with a title of assured high demand printed pressruns of 2,000 or 3,000.[4] Then reprints followed. Sixteenth-century Venice, a city of 125,000–190,000 people, produced an enormous number of books for an international market.

Neither church nor state in the Renaissance—or perhaps at any other time—believed in complete freedom of the press. The church was interested in doctrinal censorship, the state in political censorship, and both in moral censorship, that is, protecting public morality. The Riformatori dello Studio di Padova were charged by the government with press censorship, but in practice the Venetian press had a minimum of censorship until the 1540s. Then the Venetians made an important administrative move. For several years the papacy had pressured the Venetians to do something about heretics and heretical books within the Venetian dominion. The Venetians resisted the papacy until political miscalculation put them in an awkward position necessitating some gesture toward Rome. Throughout 1546 the Venetians looked benignly on the Schmalkalden League and England, although they stopped short of active support. The Republic's policy awakened openly voiced hopes among Italian philo-Protestants that the Republic would take an active role in the reform of the church. But Henry VIII and Francis I died in early 1547, and Charles V defeated the Schmalkalden League in April 1547, decisively changing the European political balance. As if to erase the memory of their sympathy for the Protestant cause, and to assure pope and emperor of their orthodoxy, the Venetians in the spring of 1547 established a new magistracy with particular competence in heresy, the Tre savi sopra eresia. Their task was to assist the Venetian Inquisition in every aspect of its activity.[5]

---

[4] There is no study of this aspect of the press, but a number of references support these figures: Ant. Aug. Renouard, *Annales de l'Imprimerie des Alde, ou Histoire des Trois Manuce et de leurs éditions* (Paris, 1834), pp. 270–76; Alberto Tinto, *Annali tipografici dei Tramezzino* (Venice and Rome, 1968), pp. 117–19; Paul F. Grendler, *Critics of the Italian World, 1530–1560: Anton Francesco Doni, Nicolò Franco, and Ortensio Lando* (Madison, Wisc., Milwaukee, Wisc., and London, 1969), p. 179; Lorenzo Campana, "Monsignor Giovanni della Casa e i suoi tempi," *Studi storici* 18 (1909): 465 (letter of July 28, 1548); SU, Bu. 159, "Acta S. Officij Venetiarum 1554–1555," pt. 5, fol. 27ʳ (August 23, 1555), pt. 2, fol. 24ʳ (January 10, 1555).

[5] Aldo Stella, "Utopie e velleità insurrezionali dei filoprotestanti italiani (1545–1547)," *Bibliothèque d'Humanisme et Renaissance* 27 (1965): 133–82; Sforza, pt. 1, pp. 194–96.

From that point the Venetian Inquisition consisted of six members, three clerical and three lay. The inquisitor, the patriarch (or his vicar), and the papal nuncio (or his representative) constituted the ecclesiastical component, the three Venetian nobles the civil component. It met every Tuesday, Thursday, and Saturday, month after month, year after year, with very few missed days. All six could be present at a trial, and at least one of the Tre savi had to be present for the proceedings to be valid, but only the three clergymen handed down the sentence. Then the three laymen authorized the execution of the sentence.

But there can be little doubt that the laymen regulated the tribunal's activity. If the clerical members were unaware of their sentiments, the tribunal could not function. The Inquisition could not issue a warrant for arrest without the concurrence of the three lay assistants, and it depended on the nobles for liaison with the government. If an inquisitor disregarded the views of the lay deputies, the government could press Rome for his removal, as it did, successfully, in the case of Fra Felice Peretti da Montalto (the future Sixtus V) in 1560. Indeed, the Tre savi were the government. They were selected from the most important members of the patriciate, men who were frequently Procurators of St. Mark and often were members of the Consiglio dei Dieci and Collegio. On the whole, however, those nobles who were more sympathetic toward Rome tended to be named to the Inquisition, while notorious antipapalists like Nicolò Da Ponte and Leonardo Donà were seldom selected.[6]

The Roman Inquisition, which Paul III viewed as a tribunal independent of local secular and ecclesiastical control but assisted

---

[6] The names of the Tre savi do not appear in the records of the Segretario delle voci (the magistracy which recorded officeholders), because they were not elected by the Senate or Maggior Consiglio but were appointed by the doge in consultation with the Collegio (his cabinet). But neither do the Tre savi appear in Collegio, Notatorio, the series which usually records Collegio appointments. Then in 1595 selection passed to the Senate, and from that date the Segretario delle voci, Elezioni del Senato documents contain the names. For the period 1547–95, a nearly complete list has been compiled from the SU trials themselves, as the Tre savi were normally mentioned. A comparison with the lists of those who held the highest offices (the Consiglio dei Dieci, the Savii Grandi, Savii di Terraferma, and the Procuratori di San Marco) shows how important those nobles who served as Tre savi were. Indeed, two patricians who acted as lay deputies to the Inquisition later became doge: Alvise Mocenigo (1570–77) and Nicolò Da Ponte (1578–85). Contemporary observers agreed that the lay deputies were "senatori principalissimi."

52   *Paul F. Grendler*

by the state, was a contradiction in terms unless church and state were in substantial agreement. In Venice, the level of inquisitorial activity, whether it prosecuted vigorously or half-heartedly, reflected the majority opinion of the ruling nobility.

From a slow start in the 1540s, when the nobility were little concerned with heresy and heretical books, Inquisition prosecution grew as the patriciate became Counter-Reformation minded. In the late 1540s, the Inquisition confiscated and burned books in fair quantity. In July 1548, for example, probably about 1,400 volumes were burned publicly.[7] (They were ordinarily burned in Piazza San Marco or near the Rialto Bridge.) The trials of this period, however, show a limited scope of prosecution. The Inquisition normally investigated only upon receipt of a denunciation; then it burned the books and fined the owner but did not investigate the religious opinions of the accused, even if he had Protestant books and was accused of Protestant ideas and associations.[8]

If book censorship is to be effective, some kind of list or index of banned titles is necessary. In January 1549 the Consiglio dei Dieci ordered the Inquisition to draw up such a list. The list or catalog was to include "all the heretical books," "other suspect books," and books "containing things against good morals." The list was completed and printed in May. But no sooner was it printed than the Venetians drew back. Nicolò Da Ponte led the opposition with the argument that in Rome itself no such index existed and every sort of book was sold publicly. The lay deputies were asking Venice to take stronger measures against heresy than the pope was taking in Rome, he argued. Another important senator opposed it because the catalog contained a work composed by a friend of his. By the end of June 1549 the battle was lost and the catalog was suppressed.[9]

Yet, in the next decade, the patriciate showed that it was no friend of the press and not immune from Counter-Reformation sentiment when it came down heavily on the large and important Hebrew printing industry of Venice. As early as 1548, zealots in Rome were concerned with the danger to the faith of Hebrew books, despite earlier papal encouragement of Jewish learning. Then

[7] Campana, "Giovanni della Casa," *Studi storici* 17 (1908): 267. Also see the comments of the Father Inquisitor for the years 1544–50 in SU, Bu. 12, Processo Padre Marin da Venezia, fol. 3ᵛ (August 9, 1555).

[8] Two examples are SU, Bu. 13, Processo Antonio Brucioli (1548); SU, Bu. 7, Processo Francesco Stella (1549).

[9] Consiglio dei Dieci, Comune, R. 18, fols. 194ᵛ–195ʳ (January 16, 1549); Campana, "Giovanni della Casa," pp. 272–74.

in September 1553 the Inquisition in Rome ordered the burning of the Talmud all over Italy. The Venetian government promptly followed suit. On October 20 the Consiglio dei ʾDieci ordered everyone—Jews, Christians, and bookmen—to give up all Talmuds. The secular government, not the Inquisition, enforced the order, with the result that, in the nuncio's words, "a good fire" burned in Piazza San Marco.[10] The Venetians burned the Talmud in October, before all parts of the papal state complied. In papal Urbino they were burned only in December, and nothing yet had been done in papal Ancona.[11] In 1554 the papacy modified the regulations to permit the holding of Hebrew books after corrections, but in Venice Jewish publishing stopped completely for ten years. The Venetians paid little or no attention to the economic losses to the city, as they joined other Italian clerical and lay rulers in persecuting Hebrew publishing.

The 1550s witnessed a prolonged effort by the papacy to get an Index adopted by the Venetians, while the bookmen fought tenaciously with the limited weapons at their disposal to stop them. In March 1555 Rome sent a new Index to the Venetian Inquisition. The bookmen were given three months to comment on it before it would go into effect. They availed themselves of the opportunity by presenting three protest memorials, in which they made several points: (1) Many authors had their *opera omnia* banned despite the fact that most of their books had nothing to do with religious matters. (2) The bookmen pointed out the financial losses that the book industry would suffer. (3) They argued that the church had tolerated the works of such pagan authors as Lucian for 1,400 years; such titles were of great importance to humanistic studies and should not be banned. (4) They again used the argument of 1549 that the Inquisition wanted to subject the bookmen of Venice to an Index not in effect in Rome. Rome heeded the protests, as it modified and then suspended entirely the 1555 Index.[12]

[10] Consiglio dei Dieci, Comune, R. 21, fols. 58^v–59^r (October 20, 1553); letters of Nuncio Ludovico Beccadelli of August 19, 26, September 23, October 14, 21, 1553, Venice, in *Nunziature di Venezia*, vol. 6, Istituto storico italiano per l'età moderna e contemporanea, Fonti per la storia d'Italia, no. 86, ed. Franco Gaeta (Rome, 1967), pp. 255, 258, 267, 274–75, 277.

[11] See the letter of Girolamo Muzio to Fra Michele Ghislieri of December 16, 1553, Pesaro, in *Lettere catholiche del Mutio Iustinopolitano* (Venice, 1571), pp. 185–86.

[12] SU, Bu. 156, "Librai e libri proibiti, 1545–1571," fols. [55^r–55^v, 60^r–62^v, 64^r–66^v], and Bu. 159, "Acta S. Officij Venetiarum 1554–1555," pt. 2, fol. 48^v, pt. 3, fol. 42^v, pt. 5, fol. 5^r–5^v.

54   *Paul F. Grendler*

Paul IV issued the next Index in early 1559. From January through March, the Venetian bookmen refused to obey. If they were to give up sóme of their books to be burned, they demanded financial compensation from the papacy. Nevertheless, the papacy discovered a weapon to enforce compliance. All the major Venetian publishers owned bookstores outside the Venetian state, usually all over Italy, including the papal dominion. The papacy threatened to seize the stores and their contents within the papal state. In the face of this threat, the bookmen began to comply. From April though August they made their submissions, offering inventories and some books to be burned. However, it appears that they did not give up all their prohibited books. From the inventories, it appears that they yielded the northern Protestant books but did not yet give up such Italian authors as Machiavelli and Aretino.[13] Also, at this point the Inquisition began to check at the customs house books imported from abroad.[14]

By 1560 the intellectual atmosphere had changed greatly. A generation of free, mocking, anticlerical authors had died or had found the climate uncongenial to their writing and had gone into retirement. Machiavelli's name was disappearing from books, and writers were noticeably more cautious. At the same time, a genuine religious revival under the leadership of a reformed papacy occurred.

The bookmen were businessmen attuned to the intellectual atmosphere. They clearly saw what was happening and reacted like good merchants: they began to publish more religious books and fewer titles of secular vernacular literature. (By secular vernacular literature is meant poetry, drama, collections of letters, dialogues on various topics, courtesy books, vernacular grammars, and vernacular classics like Dante, Petrarch, Boccaccio, and Ariosto. Into this group fall most of the works of the most popular and prolific sixteenth-century authors, like Pietro Aretino, Anton Francesco Doni, et al.) An analysis of the imprimaturs, that is, the government's permissions to publish new books, from 1550 through 1606, shows the changeover (see table 1).

[13] Letters of Cardinal Michele Ghislieri to the Venetian inquisitor Fra Felice Peretti of December 31, 1558, January 19, 25, 28, February 4, 11, 18, 25, March 4, 11, 1559, Rome, in SU, Bu. 160, "Dispacci ai Capi del Consiglio dei Dieci, 1500–1560," no pagination, organized chronologically; SU, Bu. 14, Processi Vincenzo Valgrisi et al., testimony of Valgrisi and other bookmen of August 9, 11, 14, 17, 19, 1559, September 1, 1570, no pagination. Some inventories are found in SU, Bu. 156, "Librai e libri proibiti, 1545–1571," fols. [72^r–72^v, 86^r–86^v, 88^r, 89^r–90^v]. Part of the Valgrisi testimony is printed in Sforza, pt. 2, pp. 175–77.

[14] For the Inquisition decree, see Brown, pp. 127, 213 (text), 364.

TABLE 1
IMPRIMATURS ISSUED FOR NEW TITLES, 1550–1606

| | SUBJECT MATTER (%) | | |
	Religious	Secular Vernacular Literature	Average Number of Imprimaturs per Year*
1550–54	13.1	32.7	55.2
1555–59	14.8	23.0	78.0
1560–64	23.2	22.2	87.0
1565–69	23.2	20.6	92.4
1570–74	22.7	18.0	88.6
1575–79	31.6	11.7	45.2†
1580–84	30.5	28.3	45.25‡
1585–89	33.3	21.3	81.4
1590–94	35.5	16.7	63.6§
1595–99	27.5	18.3	73.7**
1600–1604	30.0	20.0	79.2
1605–6	35.3	22.2	113.0

SOURCE.—Capi del Consiglio dei Dieci, Notatorio, R. 14–33 and F. 1–14.
* The average yearly total of imprimaturs, 1550–1606, was seventy-one.
† Great Plague of 1575–77.
‡ 1584 data missing.
§ Famine, 1590–91.
** 1595 and 1596 data missing.

From 1550 through 1559, secular vernacular literature accounted for approximately 27 percent of the new titles published, while religious titles accounted for approximately 14 percent. During the 1560s the figures altered as vernacular literature dropped and the number of religious books rose. Then from 1570 through 1606 the figures reversed: secular vernacular literature accounted for approximately 20 percent of the total and religious titles approximately 30 percent. In short, Italians were more interested in religious matters, and the bookmen supplied them the books. The majority of these religious titles were devotional works rather than theological or doctrinal, that is, inspirational treatises, meditations, books of sermons, hagiography, and the like, and the majority were in the vernacular. These were books for the average devout person, cleric and layman, rather than for professional theologians. The publishers simply switched from supplying a secular market to a comparable devotional one. There is no evidence that they lost money or that their presses were idled by the changeover.

The political climate changed as much as the intellectual atmosphere. For the Venetians, the major threat was from the Turks, and, to meet this threat, the Republic had need of papal assistance.

56   *Paul F. Grendler*

Indeed, because of the Turks, the Venetians were on friendlier terms with the papacy than at any other time in the century.

Both the growth of religiosity and the political situation inclined the Venetians toward a more militant Counter-Reformation posture. But probably the clinching reason was the discovery that Protestantism had made inroads among the younger members of the nobility. Between 1565 and 1569, eight nobles abjured heretical views.[15] Most of them fitted a pattern: they were young, acquainted with each other, and had developed heretical views under the tutelage of Protestant humanists and schoolmasters. These young nobles read Calvin's *Catechism* and *Institutes* and titles of Bernardino Ochino, Peter Martyr Vermigli, and Pier Paolo Vergerio.

The presence of a few Protestants among the younger nobility did not mean that there was any possibility of the city moving into the Protestant orbit, then or later. Not only was it too late politically for such a move, but more important, Venetian loyalties were fundamentally and traditionally Catholic. Nevertheless, the discovery of Protestantism among the nobility must have been disconcerting, for the Venetian elders always worried greatly about the moral and political training of their successors. In addition, like most princes and nobles of the century, the Venetians believed that religious division inevitably led to sedition; how much worse might the situation be if some of the dissenters were nobles? In the 1560s the Venetians fervently proclaimed their orthodoxy to the world[16] and

[15] SU, Bu. 20, Antonio Loredano and Alvise Malipiero, contains the abjurations of these two and Giacomo Malipiero, all in 1565; Bu. 20, Michele De Basili, Carlo Corner, and Venturino Dalle Modonette, has Corner's abjuration of 1565; Bu. 22, Francesco Emo, has his abjuration of 1567; Bu. 23, Silvestro, Cipriano, and Stefano Semprini, Andrea Dandolo, Marc'Antonio Canale, et al., contains the abjurations of Andrea Dandolo (1568), Marc'Antonio Canale (1568), and Alvise Mocenigo (1569). In addition, other nobles were accused but not questioned. The only study of these patrician heretics is Edouard Pommier, "La société vénitienne et la Réforme protestante au XVIᵉ siècle," *Bollettino dell'Istituto di storia della Società e dello Stato Veneziano* 1 (1959): 7–14. Pommier sees these heretical nobles as moved by "une sorte de dilettantisme religieux" (p. 10). Perhaps he underestimates the seriousness of their quest, for they developed their beliefs over several years of clandestine activity. Some of them considered following Andrea Da Ponte, brother of future doge Nicolò, to Geneva. And the anguish revealed in the testimony of Marc'Antonio Canale appears to be deeper than what one would expect from a dilettante.

[16] In 1562, for example, the government reacted angrily to French court gossip which reported that Protestant preachers enjoyed large audiences in Venice. The Consiglio dei Dieci dispatched an indignant letter denying the allegations and affirming that the city was *cattolicissima* (Consiglio dei Dieci, Secrete, R. 7, fol. 88ʳ–88ᵛ, August 7, 1562). Nevertheless, at that time Venetian nobles and commoners gathered at the Fondaco dei tedeschi and elsewhere to be taught by Protestants.

took the necessary steps to make the reality conform to the image. While the new censorship decrees of the 1560s did not present the discovery of local heresy as their justification (such an admission would have been acutely embarrassing), it is hard to escape the conclusion that the two were linked.

In the 1560s, church and state cooperated to enact new censorship legislation. A number of decrees erected various tedious legal hurdles before an author or publisher could obtain the necessary license to publish a book. These regulations were not new, but they were more extensive and better enforced. The government tightened the inspection of imported books at the customs house, giving the Inquisition power to have a man on the spot to inspect the books. All this was summarized in an omnibus law of the Consiglio dei Dieci of June 28, 1569.[17]

For its part, the Tridentine Council issued a new authoritative Index of Prohibited Books with extensive rules for authors and publishers. The Venetian government accepted this Index along with all the other Tridentine decrees without a murmur in 1564, but the bookmen ignored it. Then with the passage of the law of June 28, 1569, the Inquisition began to enforce the Tridentine Index. The tribunal demanded inventories and the consignment of prohibited titles. The inquisitor's men began making personal visits to the shops and storehouses of the bookmen. These visits were new; in the past the Inquisition had no such authority. From 1569 through 1571, the inquisitor's men systematically visited the Venetian bookstores. Catching some of the bookmen unprepared, they found and confiscated a large number of prohibited volumes, this time Italian books of Machiavelli and Aretino as well as nonreligious titles of northern Protestants. The Holy Office burned the books and warned or fined twenty-two bookmen, assessing fines of from a few ducats to fifty, depending on their guilt or ability to pay.[18]

In addition, all through the 1560s and early 1570s there were a number of trials in which individual bookmen or others were denounced for having prohibited titles. The Inquisition in this way caught and punished—almost always with fines—a number of people.

The parallel civil court, the Esecutori contro la bestemmia, also burned books in the late 1560s. Like the Inquisition, in March 1568

---

[17] Consiglio dei Dieci, Comune, R. 29, fols. 30^r–31^r.

[18] SU, Bu. 156, "Librai e libri proibiti, 1545–1571," fols. 6^r–9^v, 15^v–34^r (August 9, 18, 23, 25, 28, 30, September 6, 13, 18, 20, 27, October 2, 5, 8, 11, 15, 24, 1571).

58   *Paul F. Grendler*

it appointed an official, a former printer, to visit bookstores and to spy on bookmen, and he cooperated with the Holy Office.[19] The Esecutori also fell on the Jews again. Hebrew publishing had resumed in 1563, although the Talmud was still banned, under the condition of prepublication censorship. But in 1568 the Esecutori arrested a number of Jews and several of their Christian printers for publishing volumes lacking the proper corrections. The Esecutori confiscated well over 15,000 volumes and imposed fines of over 2,200 ducats, to be paid to the Arsenal. Venetian Jews who had commissioned the books had to pay most of the fines, up to 500 ducats per individual. The civil tribunal assessed much heavier fines than did the Inquisition.[20]

Yet there were limits to the Venetian acceptance of the war against heresy. The Venetian government demonstrated very little sympathy for the bookmen and the Jews, but it did protect the German Protestant scholars at Padua. Of a total of 1,000–1,500 students in any given year, the Germans, by far the largest group of foreigners, numbered from 100 to 300. Most were Protestants, and a good number of the French scholars there were Huguenots. As scholars and students, these foreign Protestants brought prohibited books into the Venetian territory and were customers for the prohibited titles of Erasmus, Melanchthon, and others. The papacy wanted to keep Protestant scholars and their books out of Padua, but the Venetians turned a deaf ear for reasons of politics, economics, and prestige: (1) They hesitated to offend German princes by turning away German students. (2) They did not wish to lose the 25,000–30,000 ducats that the Germans spent annually on food, accommodation, clothing, books, and other expenses. (3) The Venetians believed that the greater the number of scholars, especially foreign ones, the greater the reputation of the university.[21] The papacy tried to answer these arguments, and the Venetian government agreed that every scholar had to make a profession of

[19] Esecutori contro la bestemmia, Bu. 56, Notatorio Terminazioni, R. 1561–1582, fol. 38ᵛ (March 7, 1568); SU, Bu. 25, Processo Girolamo Calepin, testimony of Alvise Zio, the Esecutori official, of March 20(?), 1568, no pagination.

[20] Esecutori contro la bestemmia, Bu. 56, Notatorio Terminazioni, R. 1561–1582, fols. 41bisʳ–47ᵛ (September 22, 24, 27, October 29, 1568).

[21] Biagio Brugi, *Gli scolari dello Studio di Padova nel Cinquecento, con un'appendice sugli studenti tedeschi e la S. Inquisizione a Padova nella seconda metà del secolo XVI*, 2d ed. rev. (Padua and Verona, 1905), esp. pp. 71–100; letter and memorial of Nuncio Giovanni Antonio Facchinetti of September 14, 1566, Venice, *Nunziature di Venezia*, vol. 8, ed. Aldo Stella (Rome, 1963), pp. 105–9.

faith before receiving his degree. But the law was not enforced, and Rome knew it.

The first, small sign that the high-water mark of book burning had been reached and that potential for disagreement existed occurred in the early 1570s over what at first glance might be considered an insignificant issue: exclusive papal permission to print canonical and liturgical works. In its concluding decrees of 1563, the Council of Trent authorized the papacy to revise and promulgate Catholicism's two most important devotional manuals, the Roman Breviary and the Missal, as well as the Tridentine Catechism and the Index. As the revised editions were completed, the papacy promulgated them, forbidding the use of many older ones. In order to ensure accuracy, the papacy authorized exclusive printing rights to the press of Paolo Manuzio in Rome for all of Catholic Christendom. Manuzio printed the first editions of these texts and then sold rights to other printers across Europe.

These exclusive privileges provoked intense, prolonged disputes which heralded future conflict. The reason is obvious: the market was enormous. Every priest or religious had to have a breviary; a Missal was necessary for the celebration of every single mass. In addition, pious laymen and women used breviaries or simplified offices. In short, while humanist texts earned prestige, the Roman Breviary and the Missal paid the bills. Publishers in Protestant lands were similarly dependent on the Psalter.[22]

The controversy over the exclusive privilege for the reformed Little Office of Our Lady (Officium Beatae Mariae Virginis nuper reformatum) illustrates the nature and results of these disputes.[23] As

---

[22] See the important articles of Robert M. Kingdon, "Patronage, Piety, and Printing in Sixteenth-Century Europe," in *A Festschrift for Frederick B. Artz,* ed. David H. Pinckney and Theodore Ropp (Durham, N.C., 1964), pp. 19–36, and "The Plantin Breviaries: A Case Study in the Sixteenth-Century Business Operations of a Publishing House," *Bibliothèque d'Humanisme et Renaissance* 22 (1960): 133–50.

[23] SU, Bu. 156, "Librai e libri proibiti, 1545–1571," fols. 9ᵛ–10ᵛ, 12ʳ–15ᵛ, 19ʳ–20ʳ, 37ᵛ–47ʳ (testimony of various bookmen of August 18, 21, 23, 25, 28, 30, 1571, January 3, 31, July 26, 29, 31; August 9, October 30, 1572); letters of Nuncio Facchinetti of July 26, August 2, 9, 23, October 25, November 15, 29, 1572, Venice, in ASVa, Segretario di Stato, Venezia, F. 12, fols. 40ᵛ–41ʳ, 43ʳ–43ᵛ, 46ʳ–47ʳ, 56ʳ, 98ʳ–98ᵛ, 119ᵛ–120ʳ, 129ᵛ–130ʳ; letter of Venetian Patriarch Giovanni Trevisan of November 1, 1572, Venice, in ibid., fol. 100ʳ. For final resolution of the conflict, see the papal letter of January 27, 1573, authorizing Luc'Antonio Giunti to print the Little Office notwithstanding the previous exclusive privilege granted to Paolo Manuzio (see the letter in the following copy of the Little Office: Biblioteca Apostolica Vaticana, Barb. C. I. 24, *Officium Beatae Mariae Virginis nuper reformatum Pij V. Pont. Max. iussu editum,* Venetiis Apud Iunctam, Permittente Sede Apostolica, MDLXXXI, Sigs. +iᵛ–+iiʳ).

60   *Paul F. Grendler*

the title suggests, it is a smaller office consisting of psalms, hymns, and prayers, for the most part in honor of Mary. It was used not only by many monks and nuns, but also by laymen and laywomen and even children. The Aldine press of Venice won the exclusive Venetian privilege, and it was sanctioned by the Venetian Senate. The Aldine press quickly began to capitalize on the privilege by printing 20,000 copies in seven or eight months in 1572. The other bookmen were acutely unhappy and began to contravene the exclusive privilege. This provoked a controversy which lasted for two years; it was finally resolved by personal negotiation between the Venetian ambassador and the pope.

Rome defended the exclusive privilege by arguing that only in that way could she ensure accuracy, and the Venetian printers were not above carelessness or adding unauthorized material. Rome also argued that since the original printers had had heavy expenses in preparing the new editions, they deserved to be rewarded. The Venetian bookmen saw the issue as acutely financial. Some smaller printers pleaded that the printing and sale of the Little Office and similar books meant the difference between success and starvation.

At first unsympathetic and unconcerned for the bookmen, the government eventually responded when the dispute would not go away. At first a few nobles, like the anticlerical Nicolò Da Ponte, supported the bookmen, and eventually the majority did. When the nobility eventually supported them, they justified their stance on economic and jurisdictional grounds. These motives should not be overemphasized, because it took a long time for the government to bestir itself. Moreover, the government came to the defense of the bookmen only when it was apparent to everyone, including the papal nuncio, that profit, not piety, was at the bottom of the dispute. The disputes over the Breviary, Little Office, Missal, and Catechism ended in 1573 with the victory of the bookmen. The papacy sanctioned the violation of the exclusive privilege, a minor defeat in comparison with the successful enforcement of the Index of Prohibited Books.

The disputes demonstrated that papal regulation of the Venetian press had reached a plateau. From 1573 until the early 1590s, the Index was strongly enforced on the surface. Certainly very few prohibited books were published. But there are many signs that there was a great deal of violation in the sale and importation of prohibited titles. Certain kinds of heretical and prohibited books could be found without difficulty if one knew where to look.

Humanistic works by northern Protestant authors like Melanchthon, Protestant editions of the Bible like that of Antonio Brucioli, the works of Erasmus, Italian titles like the works of Aretino and Machiavelli, titles of Ochino, Calvin's *Catechism*, and a few works by Luther could be purchased at Venetian bookstores if the customer knew where to look. Some bookstores, like the firms of Francesco and Giordano Ziletti, made a practice of selling these books under the counter.[24]

Scholars in the humanities particularly resented and disobeyed the regulations of the Index and Inquisition. Northern humanists, many of them Protestants, wrote a great deal and very well in these disciplines. Italian humanists who obeyed the Index had little or no access to much northern scholarship. Since it was practically impossible to obtain from the Inquisition permission to hold these titles, many disobeyed the laws and tried to be discreet about it. They seldom fell into the hands of the Holy Office unless they were flagrant violators. To cite a case of 1580, one monk was not denounced for heretical books and opinions until he had been in the monastery for six years, had tried repeatedly to persuade his fellow monks to accept heretical views, and showed himself to be an irascible and tactless man.[25] It is a reasonable assumption that others, less outspoken and contentious, held heterodox religious books without being disturbed.

Throughout the 1570s and 1580s Venetian bookmen continued to smuggle prohibited books from Germany and Switzerland into Venice. On their regular journeys from the Frankfurt bookfairs, they acquired prohibited works, especially in Basel, and brought them into Venetian territory. Then the bookmen found a way of eluding the Inquisition check at the customs house.[26] One can only speculate on how they did it. Bribery, of either the customs officials or the Inquisition agents, is a possibility, although the dedication of the latter appears to have put them beyond bribery. False title pages were a common device. Most likely, the sheer cumbersomeness of the process, involving several people and minute lists of titles,

---

[24] For examples, see the following trials: SU, Bu. 25, Girolamo Calepin (1573); Bu. 37, Giovanni Battista Sanudo (1574); Bu. 37, Bartolomeo de Sabio (1574); Bu. 38, Fra Leonardo (1574); Bu. 50, Guidone Simottini (1583); Bu. 59, Gioachino Brugnoli (1587).

[25] SU, Bu. 47, Fra Clemente Valvassore (1580–82).

[26] See the following trials: SU, Bu. 49, Francesco Ziletti and Felice Valgrisi (1582), Bu. 50, Bonifacio Ciera, Luc'Antonio Giunti, Melchiorre Scoto, and Antonio Bragia (1583).

62   *Paul F. Grendler*

generated shortcuts and carelessness that defeated the inspection. Noting or copying the titles of hundreds of books is a tiresome process. Probably the habit developed of not looking at all the books; perhaps the Inquisition agent only examined those at the top of the bale. The written lists were possibly not done carefully, or the Inquisition agent accepted a list already prepared by the bookman, who falsified it if necessary. Once the bookmen were through customs, the Inquisition found it practically impossible to trace the books.

But focusing solely on the known violations gives a one-sided view of these two decades. In 1559, and again in 1569–71, the Inquisition found and destroyed large quantities of prohibited titles, thus asserting its will on the book industry and driving commerce in prohibited titles underground. In the 1570s and 1580s, the tribunal's task was to hold traffic to a low level. The Inquisition used customs checks, bookstore visitations, and denunciations to do this. Once it learned of a violation, the tribunal questioned witnesses and made arrests; sometimes it located the guilty party and contraband titles, and other times it did not. Given the size and scope of the book trade and the limited Holy Office resources, total enforcement was not possible, nor was it necessary. The Holy Office realized that it did not need to catch each violator or to destroy every prohibited title to be effective. Rather, it aimed at keeping prohibited titles out of the hands of the vast majority of the reading public by maintaining enough pressure to hold the traffic down to an acceptable level. The evidence of the trials suggests that the Holy Office achieved this goal, for while a range of prohibited titles appeared in these trials, they were discovered in single copies rather than in quantity. As long as banned titles could not be printed in Venice, and the clandestine traffic was kept within bounds, the tribunal with the aid of time gradually diminished the stock of prohibited titles.

As the century waned, the Venetians argued that the press was in economic decline. In 1588 the government told the nuncio that the number of Venetian presses had declined from 120 to seventy, and in 1596 the bookmen lamented that the number had fallen to forty.[27] Significantly, the Venetians attributed the decline of the local press to the growth of the Vatican and other Roman presses.

[27] The documents do not state at what date there were 120 presses (letter of Nuncio Girolamo Matteucci of April 2, 1588, Venice, in ASVa, Segretario di Stato, F. 26, fol. 181ᵛ; petition of the bookmen of May 3, 1596 to the Venetian government and forwarded to Rome in ASVa, Fondo Borghese IV, 224, fol. 117ʳ).

The available documentation does not support the Venetian view. The number of presses in operation at a given moment is unknown, but reliable statistics on the number of imprimaturs issued for new or substantially revised titles are available. Using the period 1550–74 as the base, during the plague of 1575–77 the number of imprimaturs dropped to 50 percent of the previous figures and remained at this low level through 1584. Then, for the period 1585–1605, the number of imprimaturs rose to 95 percent of the base period.[28] These figures do not include the unchanged reprints for which an imprimatur was not needed, but it is unlikely that the reprint figure was different. Thus, despite the Index and the gradual demise of such publishing giants as the Aldine press and Giolito, Venetian publishing quantitatively declined, but only modestly. Nevertheless, the Venetians constantly stressed the economic decline of the press in their disputes with Rome.

What had changed was the Venetian attitude toward the jurisdictional prerogatives of church and state.[29] To put it succinctly, the Venetian government was now determined to enlarge its control over the religious, moral, and social lives of its citizens, and this could only occur at the expense of the papacy. The battle over the 1596 Index illustrated this new sensibility.

The Venetians in 1596 did not object to the papacy's right to censor books, nor did they object to the titles listed in the Index. They did object very strenuously to the new rules which were appended.[30] One of these gave local ecclesiastical authorities the power to prohibit other titles not on the Index which they judged to be heretical or immoral. Another rule decreed that the bookmen had

---

[28] See table 1.

[29] Gaetano Cozzi, *Il doge Nicolò Contarini: Ricerche sul patriziato veneziano agli inizi del Seicento* (Venice and Rome, 1958); Aldo Stella, *Chiesa e stato nelle relazioni dei nunzi pontifici a Venezia: Ricerche sul giurisdizionalismo veneziano dal XVI al XVIII secolo,* Studi e testi, no. 239 (Vatican City, 1964); William J. Bouwsma, *Venice and the Defense of Republican Liberty: Renaissance Values in the Age of the Counter Reformation* (Berkeley and Los Angeles, 1968); also see Martin J. C. Lowry, "The Church and Venetian Political Change in the Later Cinquecento" (Ph.D. diss., University of Warwick, 1970–71).

[30] The rules and the concluding concordat are summarized by Brown, pp. 144–52. The struggle over the Index is discussed by Mario Brunetti, "Schermaglie veneto-pontificie prima dell'Interdetto: Leonardo Donà avanti il Dogado," in *Paolo Sarpi e i suoi tempi: Studi storici* (Città di Castello, 1923), pp. 124–33. However, there is more information available than what Brown and Brunetti uncovered. The chief sources are Collegio, Esposizioni Roma, R. 6, fols. 112^r–170^v, passim; Senato, Deliberazioni Roma, R. 11, fols. 67^v–113^r, passim; Senato, Dispacci da Roma, F. 37, fols. 202^r–409^v, passim, and F. 38, fols. 32^r–33^v, for the ambassador's letters; ASVa, Segretario di Stato, Venezia, F. 32, fols. 293^r–351^r, passim, for the nuncio's letters.

64   *Paul F. Grendler*

to swear an oath before the bishop and inquisitor that they would obey the new Index and would not knowingly admit into the guild anyone suspected of heresy. The Venetians, led by Leonardo Donà and Giacomo Foscarini, objected above all to the oath as encroaching on civil jurisdiction.

The dispute was heated, but in the end the papacy agreed to the Venetian conditions. A concordat was signed and issued with the new Index. The oath was revoked and other rules modified. The concordat of 1596 was a clear victory for the bookmen and the Venetians. While it did not touch the list of prohibited titles or the guidelines for expurgation, it substantially restricted in practical ways papal and inquisitorial control of the book trade. Moreover, the concordat provided the jurisdictional platform from which Paolo Sarpi and the Senate might expand state control of censorship in the future. The fight over the Index and the resultant concordat were the logical result of a slow growth of Venetian solicitude for the press and the Republic's growing insistence that she, rather than the papacy, should rule the moral and, to a growing extent, the spiritual lives of her citizens. Finally, the Index dispute contributed to the strained relations between the two which led to the Interdict conflict of 1606–7.

Probably more prohibited materials entered Venice in the period 1590–1605 than in any previous decade since the implementation of the Tridentine Index in 1569. Gone were the days of surprise inspections of bookstores. The outbreak of the Interdict conflict provided little or nothing new in such areas as clandestine book importation but accentuated or increased the tendencies already evident by providing greater public support, even approbation, for violations and violators. The clandestine traffic became for all intents and purposes open, and the Inquisition could do little or nothing about it. This state of affairs continued for a few years after the Interdict until Venetian-papal relations regained their former equilibrium.

This study suggests several conclusions. The Index and Inquisition became effective when the Venetian patriciate decided to support them. This took a number of years and the joining together of political and religious motives. But once the ruling class made its decision, neither economic and jurisdictional reasons nor the pleas of the bookmen moved it. Once supported by the Venetian government, the censorship was very effective. Prepublication censorship ensured that very few banned titles were printed in Venice. Halting the clandestine importation of prohibited titles and the resale of older banned volumes was more difficult, but again the Inquisition had notable success. For the vast majority of the reading population, the banned books were unavailable. But for the determined few, enough loopholes existed so that any title could be found if the reader was willing to bear the necessary difficulty, risk, and cost. Weighing the exact impact of the Index and Inquisition on Italian intellectual life is beyond the scope of this study, but a precise understanding of the availability of prohibited titles would be part of this assessment. With the passage of time, state support for the Index waned. Just as a combination of circumstances generated this support earlier, so jurisdictional, political, and, to a lesser extent, economic motives eroded it in the 1590s. Banned titles still could not be printed in Venice, but it became easier to acquire those printed abroad. Eventually, in the seventeenth century, the fervor of the Counter-Reformation cooled to the point that even some prohibited titles of the previous century were reprinted in Venice.[31]

[31] Between 1628 and 1633, Marco Ginammi published Machiavelli's *Discourses,* which he attributed to "Amadio Niecollucci," and six of Aretino's religious titles, attributed to "Partenio Etiro."

[6]

Printing at the dawn of the sixteenth century

Jean-François Gilmont

What was the situation of printed books when the Reformation began? Printing technology and the religious movement centred on Luther met at the precise moment when after decades of fine tuning, the new

1.1 Discussion during a Protestant sermon. Cicero, *De Officiis* (Augsburg: Heinrich Steiner, 1530)

PRINTING AT THE DAWN OF THE SIXTEENTH CENTURY   **11**

invention gained its independence from manuscripts. Thus the first paragraphs of this chapter describe the early stages of printing. But the history of the book is also tied to that of reading, and therefore the development of reading practices at the dawn of the Reformation constitutes another major theme of this analysis. The final sections of this chapter examine the actual technical constraints imposed on the book, on publishing and on printing.

The first tentative steps: incunabula

When Luther first appeared at the forefront of the European stage, printing was a relatively recent phenomenon, less than 70 years old, and beginning to leave its cradle. This image is reinforced by the name given to fifteenth-century imprints. However, the end-date of incunabula, traditionally set around 1500, is unfortunate, since the real transition period for printing occured between 1520 and 1540.[1]

At the beginning, the *ars artificialiter scribendi* was firmly based on the manuscript. As time went on, printers discovered the possibilities inherent in the new technology, giving imprints their own identity. The timing of this new mastery of printing techniques coincided approximately with Luther's attack on the preaching of Indulgences.

Due to daily contact with manuscripts from the early Middle Ages and incunabula, the first decades of printing showed more signs of continuity than of change. The external appearance of books remained the same. Pagination, division into sections, and the set-up of the entire work copied the format of manuscripts. Signalling and reference devices were based on manuscript practices, in terms of the organization of sections through signatures and announcements, to help in reading (foliation, pagination, illuminated initials, marginalia) or in reference work (alphabetical indices, concordances). Slowly, over the course of 80 years, printers discovered that the repeated reproduction of a text led to new commercial constraints, particularly as regards the external aspect of the book. A mass-produced book needed individual features, to distinguish it from the other works on the market. Little by little, printers realized the need for a title-page specifying the contents of the book and its place of origin, by indicating the name of the author and title of the book, and the name of the publisher, together with the date and place of publication. The use of printers' marks provided an added decorative feature.

---

[1] In his exemplary study of Aldus Manutius, M. Lowry showed clearly how this humanist printer carved a path for himself in a world in rapid transition: *The World of Aldus Manutius* (Oxford, 1979).

12   THE REFORMATION AND THE BOOK

At the same time, typesetters moved away from the models provided by manuscript calligraphy. Around 1540, making print characters became an independent and specialized industry.[2] The first fifteenth-century fonts contained multiple ligatures, which were easily drawn by hand, but which needlessly complicated typesetters' work. In the first decades of the sixteenth century, fonts were simplified, and the number of characters with ligatures was considerably reduced.[3]

Slowly, the choice of texts to be published also evolved. Understandably enough, the first printers chose their works from the *scriptoria*. Only as time went on did they realize that a more widespread distribution of texts changed the patterns of reading, that the growing numbers of readers meant that new works were needed, that medieval best sellers needed to be replaced by other works and that contemporary writers' works also had a place in the books to be published.[4]

The geographical map of European printing needed, therefore, more than 50 years before achieving a measure of stability. The first spread of printing was due to travelling printers guided more by chance than by any assessment of profitable centres in which to establish themselves. Starting from the German lands, they migrated first into Italy and then across Europe. This ceaseless anarchic development continued for a number of decades. Estimates of the number of cities which housed printing presses at the dawn of the sixteenth century vary between 240 and 270 cities.[5] A slow filtering process enabled a few printing centres to emerge as leaders in the following centuries. A classification of cities based on the earliest evidence of printing occuring there does not, therefore, match the list of cities which later controlled the book trade. In France, Paris and Lyon held a monopoly on new inventions, while in Italy, more than half of all books produced came from Venice alone, and in The Netherlands, Antwerp became the centre of printing *par excellence*. There were no such clear winners in the cities of the German Empire. More peripheral lands took longer to gain their independence in terms of printing, as in the case of England, still reliant on foreign imports at the beginning of the sixteenth century.

---

[2] Lowry, *The World*, p. 11.

[3] W. J. Ong, 'Oral residue in Tudor prose style', *PMLA (Proceedings of the Modern Language Association)*, 80 (1965), 146. Indeed, this is the reason for criticism of the Greek characters used by Aldus Manutius: as they imitate manuscript writing, they use a large number of ligatures and decorative flourishes (see Lowry, *The World*, pp. 129–35).

[4] Several contributions underline this. See pp. 66–8 and 285. For France, see H.-J. Martin and J.-M. Dureau, 'Années de transition, 1500–1530', *HÉF*, 217–25; H.-J. Martin, 'Classements et conjonctures', *HÉF*, 429–57.

[5] See Febvre/Martin, pp. 275–81; J. M. Lenhart, *Pre-Reformation Printed Books* (New York, 1935).

Indeed the map of printing centres does not match that of the most densely populated European cities.[6] Although printing was indeed a primarily urban activity, every large European city did not automatically house a flourishing printing industry. In southern Europe several cities of more than 100 000 inhabitants by 1500, such as Milan or Naples, were not major typographical centres. Other cities containing populations of 60 000 to 100 000 like Seville, Cordova, Granada, Florence and Genoa played only modest roles in the printing world. In contrast, more northern cities with between 40 000 and 60 000 inhabitants like Lyon, Antwerp, Augsburg and Cologne had flourishing printing presses. Even cities of 10 000 inhabitants, like Basle, played a major role in the international book trade.

The establishment of printing in specific cities was tied to the development of trade routes. While small-scale printers provided books for local consumption, large printing firms looked to wider markets. From the fifteenth century onwards, booksellers built links with colleagues in other cities to sell their stock. The fairs, with roots in the early Middle Ages, were the ideal location to exchange printed works, to announce new publications, to purchase typographical material, to hire workers, and to settle bills. From the first years of the sixteenth century, all the features of the international book trade were in place. Besides the Lyon and Leipzig fairs, those of Frankfurt am Main drew the leading European publishers.

Varied reading practices

In *The Printing Press as an Agent of Change*, E. Eisenstein attempts to prove that the introduction of printing led to deep divisions in the history of western culture. This viewpoint is not shared by all. Other scholars argue the opposite; that Gutenberg's invention, in the course of the long history of the book, was much less revolutionary than it might seem at first. Changes like the move from the *rotulus* to the *codex* or the more scientific approach to learning in medieval universities made a much greater impact on reading and the book. This view is upheld by R. Hirsch and R. Chartier, to name but two scholars.[7] This perspective

---

[6] For the publishing centres, see *HÉF*, 442. For the size of cities, see R. Mols, 'Population in Europe 1500–1700', in C. M. Cipolla (ed.), *The Fontana Economic History of Europe: The Sixteenth and Seventeenth Centuries* (London, 1974), p. 41.

[7] R. Hirsch, *Printing, Selling and Reading, 1450–1550* (Wiesbaden, 1967), p. 2; R. Chartier, 'De l'histoire du livre à l'histoire de la lecture: les trajectoires françaises', *Archives et Bibliothèques de Belgique*, 60 (1989), 161–89.

14   THE REFORMATION AND THE BOOK

does not see the Reformation bursting on the scene at a key point in the history of reading practices. The large-scale changes which brought Europe from an oral society to a literate one began in the Middle Ages, and their final impact only became clear in the eighteenth and nineteenth centuries.

Several ways of reading have coexisted since ancient times. Silent reading to oneself may have occurred, but was uncommon, and rare during the high Middle Ages. Reading softly to oneself, by murmuring or ruminating, or by speaking out loud were the norm.[8] Until the development of the first universities in the twelfth and thirteenth centuries, to read a book meant to enter into a text slowly and to explore it from start to finish. The growth of canon law and scholasticism led to a new use of the written word, namely as a reference tool. Reading practices moved from gaining knowledge of the whole work to rapid searching for quotations as 'authorities'. This new approach led to the creation of techniques for easier access to texts, namely indices and concordances, and redeveloped the format characteristics of the book.

The university textbook in the thirteenth and fourteenth centuries with its compact pages and overuse of abbreviations was not yet a model of clarity. Furthermore it is possible that at the time sight reading was a specialist task, as individuals were only able to read fluently in their heads in the limited areas of their own studies.[9] Armando Petrucci highlighted the revolutionary changes brought about in the world of the book and of reading by 'a band of arrogant young Florentines' in the late fourteenth and early fifteenth centuries. Following Niccolò Niccoli's lead, they fundamentally reshaped the book, abandoning traditional Gothic script in favour of a new font borrowed from Carolingian models. They transcribed texts into small-sized books, eliminating many abbreviations, and making the text less cluttered by refusing to include invasive commentaries, preferring to be in direct contact with the text itself. A. Petrucci refers to these transformations as the introduction of bourgeois reading. Thanks to the innovations of Italian humanists, printed texts which were created in the German Empire following the model of university manuscripts found a new format in Italy. Aldus

---

[8] P. Saenger's chronology may be too rigid and systematic ('Silent reading: its impact on late medieval script and society', *Viator: Medieval and Renaissance Studies*, 13 (1982), 367–414; Saenger, 'Manières de lire médiévales', *HÉF*, 131–41). A. Petrucci takes a more nuanced approach ('Lire au moyen âge', *Mélanges de l'École française de Rome. Moyen âge et temps modernes*, 96 (1984), 603–16). For manuscript books, see J. Glénisson (ed.), *Le livre au moyen âge* (Paris, 1988), a very thorough book which unfortunately makes little mention of reading practices.

[9] This is a perceptive suggestion of H.-J. Martin, *Histoire et pouvoirs de l'écrit* (Paris, 1988), p. 152.

Manutius is the symbol of this rebirth of the printed book. In the long run, these changes favoured silent reading thanks to a better balance between print and blank space on the page.[10]

Preceding the development of printing, the *Devotio Moderna* based itself firmly on silent sight reading. The importance given to individual contact with the text led to a policy encouraging the transcription of manuscripts and the development of education.[11] The Brethren of the Common Life adopted the *ars artificialiter scribendi* without difficulty, opening several printing shops from the end of the fifteenth century onwards. Evidence of the mastery of silent reading before Gutenberg can easily be gathered from elsewhere in Europe in the late Middle Ages.

Furthermore, the sudden appearance of reading in the context of piety opens up a secondary debate on the nature of prayer. Was prayer a collective ritual act, often described as a magical practice by its opponents, or was it meant to be a private, interior dialogue? This debate first surfaced in the fifteenth century. 'The contrast [between the partisans of each of these two views] appeared first and foremost between those who can be broadly categorized as the representatives of book culture and those who followed the practices of oral culture'.[12]

The study of reading practices is essential, for the progressive transition from an oral to a written society involves changes which are both far-reaching and profound. One of the main consequences of silent reading is certainly the increasing privacy of actions and thoughts. Was the Reformation, through its systematic encouragement of reading, really responsible for this evolution?

However, this central question runs into numerous unknown factors, particularly as regards the nearly insoluble question of the number of literate people in sixteenth-century Europe. R. Chartier believes that due to the lack of information, one can only measure this rate at the very end of the sixteenth century.[13] The situation is even more unclear if one wishes to examine the levels of literacy. The main historical evi-

---

[10] See Petrucci, 'Lire' pp. 613–14; Petrucci, 'Typologie du livre et de la lecture dans l'Italie de la Renaissance: de Pétrarque à Politien', in *From Script to Book: A Symposium* (Odense, 1986), pp. 127–39; M. Lowry, *The World*, pp. 135–44.

[11] There are some very significant quotations in Saenger, 'Manières', pp. 136–7. On the printing done by the Brethren of the Common Life, see R. R. Post, *The Modern Devotion: Confrontation with Reformation and Humanism* (Leiden, 1968), pp. 346–9. See also Saenger, 'Silent reading', pp. 396–8.

[12] A. Prosperi, 'Les commentaires du Pater Noster entre XVe et XVIe siècles', in P. Colin et al. (eds), *Aux origines du catéchisme en France* (Paris, 1989), pp. 89–90.

[13] R. Chartier, 'Les pratiques de l'écrit', in Ph. Ariès and G. Duby (eds), *Histoire de la vie privée*, vol. 3: *De la Renaissance aux Lumières* (Paris, 1986), p. 122.

16   THE REFORMATION AND THE BOOK

dence is provided by the ability to sign one's name. But on the one
hand, the link between signing and writing is not a constant, and on the
other, the connection between writing and reading is not straightforward.[14]

Therefore, one must gather together all the clues about the contacts
between the people of the Reformation period and the printed book. All
external facets of the life of the book deserve analysis, whether from
above or from below. In the context of the use of printed books, the
study of book collections has now been given a role in its own right.
Lists of books owned by specific individuals provide fascinating insights
as to the readership of specific works, but it would be wrong to assume
that book owners read all the books on their shelves, and furthermore,
'that the readers necessarily agreed with the ideas expressed in the
books they read'.[15] As the repeated rereading of a book in the end
leaves traces in the most literal sense, examining the copies which have
survived can also provide certain information.

At the same time, one must go back to the conception of the book,
and examine the intentions of its creators. The external features of the
book – format, set-up of the pages, illustration, etc. – provide crucial
evidence as to the kind of reading which the publisher suggested. A.
Petrucci expresses this aptly in his distinction between *libri da banco,
libri da bisaccia, libretti da mano*, books to go on bookrests, books to
go in bags, and booklets to be carried by hand.[16] The relative weight of
the book automatically specified the type of reading which would be
done. The folio size needs a bookrest, while as Jean Crespin said at the
beginning of an edition of the *Iliad*, and in sexto-decimo 'can be carried
around at home, is not cumbersome outside, and still allows one to
stroll through the countryside without encumbrance'.[17]

However, one must not be taken in entirely by the preoccupations of
publishers. As N. Z. Davis points out, one must make a clear distinction

---

[14] See R. S. Schofield, 'The measurement of literacy in pre-industrial England', in J.
Goody (ed.), *Literacy in Traditional Societies* (Cambridge, 1975), pp. 311–25; M. de
Certeau, *L'invention du quotidien*, vol. 1: *Arts de faire* (Paris, 1980), pp. 283–5; R.
Chartier, 'Du livre au lire', in R. Chartier (ed.), *Pratiques de la lecture* (Paris, 1985), pp.
61–88. Precise information regarding the distinct learning processes of reading and
writing are available for the seventeenth century in D. Julia, 'La leçon de catéchisme
dans l'*Escole paroissiale* (1654)', in Colin et al. (eds), *Aux origines*, pp. 164, 166.

[15] N. Z. Davis, 'Printing and the people', in N. Z. Davis, *Society and Culture in Early
Modern France* (Stanford, 1975), p. 191.

[16] A. Petrucci, 'Alle origini del libro moderno: libri da banco, libri da bisaccia, libretti
da mano', *Italia medioevale e umanistica*, 12 (1969), 295–313.

[17] Homer, *The Iliad*, Geneva, J. Crespin, 1559, fol. a ii[r]. See J.-Fr. Gilmont, *Bibliographie
des éditions de Jean Crespin* (Verviers, 1981), vol. 1, p. 117.

'between the readership of books, those who actually read them – and their audience – those to whom authors and publishers direct their works'.[18] One must therefore distinguish clearly between indications of the authors' and publishers' intentions, and evidence of actual reactions from readers. Both are linked, since a publisher cannot bring out books for long if he has absolutely no interest in his readership.

Technical problems in manual typography

Across sixteenth-century Europe, the daily use of typography was a constant feature.[19] The first point to bear in mind is that the printed text is made up of independent sheets. To make the book into a unit, sheets are assembled in order, having been printed recto–verso and then folded and bound. In discussions of price and length of production, one must base oneself on a measure of the book in terms of its number of sheets. This measuring system goes back to former practices, as specified in contracts between publishers and printers,[20] and in the inventories of booksellers' stocks.[21] Although it may seem odd today, the

---

[18] Davis, 'Printing', pp. 192–3.

[19] The best general survey of these problems is that of Ph. Gaskell, *A New Introduction to Bibliography* (Oxford, 1972). J. Veyrin-Forrer offers a good synthesis in 'Fabriquer un livre au XVIe siècle', in *HÉF*, 279–301. The information gathered from the Plantin archives is priceless, even though one should always bear in mind that Plantin exemplified exceptional success in the field. (L. Voet, *The Golden Compasses: A History and Evaluation of the Printing and Publishing Activities of the Officina Plantiniana at Antwerp*, vol. 2: *The Management of a Printing and Publishing House in Renaissance and Baroque* (Amsterdam, 1972)). Crucial data taken from notary records in particular in A. Parent, *Les métiers du livre à Paris au XVIe siècle (1535–1560)* (Geneva, Paris, 1974); and H.-J. Bremme, *Buchhändler zur Zeit der Glaubenskämpfe: Studien zur Genfer Druckgeschichte, 1565–1580* (Geneva, 1969). These studies enabled me to establish Crespin's working conditions (J.-Fr. Gilmont, *Jean Crespin, un éditeur réformé du XVIe siècle* (Geneva, 1981), ch. II). Conditions were generally similar in Spain (Cl. Griffin, *The Crombergers of Seville: the History of a Printing and Merchant Dynasty* (Oxford, 1988) especially ch. V).

[20] For example, see Parent *Les métiers du livre*, especially the table inserted between pp. 136 and 137. This was also Lazarus Spengler's calculation method when deciding the price of the *Kirchenordnung* of Brandenburg–Nuremberg: 1 denier per ordinary sheet, 1.5 deniers for sheets printed in red and black. (H.-O. Keunecke, 'Die Drucklegung der Brandenburg–Nürnbergischen Kirchenordnung' *AGB*, 21 (1980), col. 786–7; see also pp. 49–50.

[21] This was the case for the posthumous inventory of the Genevan bookseller Laurent de Normandie (Bremme, *Buchhändler*, pp. 42–3, 31). I am now less certain about this measuring system following my analysis of the inventory of Laurent de Normandie: 'L'imprimerie réformée à Genève au temps de Laurent de Normandie (1570)', *Bulletin du bibliophile* (1995) no. 2, 262–78.

18   THE REFORMATION AND THE BOOK

production cost of four in folio pages printed in large type was approximately the same as that of 32 pages in sexto-decimo in small type. The notion of the sheet, printed on the basis of two forms, is a direct consequence of the work of the printing press. There was very little difference in terms of book format in the eyes of the printing workers, as the same effort was required each time in applying the pressure of the plate on to the forme. The historian analysing the rhythm of book production must counterbalance the data provided by the number of book titles by calculating the number of formes needed.[22]

From this starting-point one should also emphasize certain economic constraints; first, the economic links between the printer who made the books and the bookseller who financed their production. Setting up a printing press did not require vast sums of money. The major expense lay in the purchase of fonts. By the 1550s, while one needed 20 to 40 *livres tournois* to buy a printing press and associated material, purchasing a font cost between 250 and 600 *livres*. In this light, the investment needed to bring out a book was very large: in the same period, an in-octavo of 800 pages with a print-run of 1 400 copies cost at least 450 *livres tournois*, for a book containing only 50 sheets.[23] In other words the costs of producing a book of this format for a bookseller were about the same as the expense of setting up a press.

An analysis of the average cost of a printed sheet is equally revealing of work practices in the period. The greatest expense was that of paper. As an approximate generalization, the minimum cost of paper was between 40 and 50 per cent of the production costs, and this percentage varied enormously depending on the quality of the paper.[24] The printing costs themselves, including the salaries of the typesetters and the press-men as well as the profit of the master printer came to approximately 50 per cent of the total. A maximum of 10 per cent remained, covering any additional production or administrative expenses.[25] This very rough estimate shows that large print-runs held little benefit. There were no savings in terms of paper costs, nor in terms of the workers' salaries.

---

[22] See the contributions of M. U. Chrisman, Al. Kawecka-Gryczowa and R. Kick, pp. 216, 411 and 452.

[23] Gilmont, *J. Crespin* pp. 49–50; 53–4.

[24] L. Voet's calculations based on Plantin's accounts put the price of paper at between 60 and 65 per cent, or even 75 per cent of the production cost. However, unlike the pattern described above, Plantin was not a publisher dealing with a printer, and having to take the latter's profit margins into account. Instead, Plantin's internal accounting only mentions the cost of paper, the workers' salaries and potential reproduction costs (paying the author, translation costs, etc.); see Voet, *The Golden Compasses*, vol. 2, pp. 379–86.

[25] Gilmont, *J. Crespin*, p. 54.

Both the costs of paper and wages were directly linked to the size of the print-run. Any profit was measured against the composition costs, around 15 to 20 per cent of the total outlay. This minimal profit was also put at risk by the danger of unsold copies, immobilizing printed paper with its associated high cost.[26]

The retail sales price of books was obviously affected by other expenses, principally the bookseller's profit and transportation costs. A book could easily be sold for twice the cost-price paid by the bookseller.[27] Transportation costs, including the risks of losses, explain why works which could easily be sold were re-edited. Works attracting a broad readership were best printed near their sale locations, rather than being brought there from afar.

Therefore it is understandable that print-runs remained small until the nineteenth century. The size of print-runs is a much researched topic. Several scholars have attempted estimates of the number of works for sale at various times. In fact, the only certainty is the link between the print-run and the production capacity of a printing press in a day.[28] Depending on the area, this meant a daily print-run of 1 300 to 1 500 sheets printed on both sides. This norm, set out by the ancient printing ordinances, forms the basis of debates on the printing profession, although the norm may not always have been respected. An analysis of the actual print-runs in Paris or at Plantin's in Antwerp highlights large variations, going from 250 to 2 600 copies in Paris and from 100 to 5 000 copies at Plantin's presses. Furthermore these variations are not arbitrary, as they correspond to workdays based on certain simple formulas: 1, 1.5, 2, 3, or 4 formes were printed daily. The Parisian average for 33 books is 940 copies of each, while Plantin and his son-in-law Moretus produced an average of 1 300 to 1 550 copies of more than 400 works. A reasonable estimate of the average print-run in the sixteenth century is between 1 000 and 1 350 copies.

Too often, certain basic consequences of the set-up of printed texts for the transmission of books are ignored. The major expense of print fonts, and perhaps also printers' lack of imagination meant that in most cases sixteenth-century print shops operated continuously. A team of workers, often two typesetters and two pressworkers were given a 'task'. As the formes were typeset, pages were printed, and once the printing work was done, the formes were returned to the typesetter in

---

[26] In establishing this data, one must avoid any confusion between the number of sheets and the number of formes needed to produce a book, which would otherwise double the figures.

[27] Bremme, *Buchhändler*, pp. 42–3.

[28] J.-Fr. Gilmont, 'Printers by the rules', *The Library*, 6th series, 2 (1980) 143–8.

20   THE REFORMATION AND THE BOOK

order to reuse the fonts. Correcting proofs was both a rushed and a slow task. The rush was caused by the fact that the typesetter often only had half a day to correct a forme. The slow-down was due to the fact that corrections were done gradually, forme by forme. In the case of large folio volumes, this could take months if not an entire year.[29] Present-day correction of proofs is very different.

---

[29] Gilmont, 'Printers', pp. 129–55.

[7]

THE REFORMATION AND THE BOOK: A RECONSIDERATION

ANDREW PETTEGREE AND MATTHEW HALL

University of St Andrews

ABSTRACT. *Perceptions of the role of the book in the Reformation are shaped by our knowledge of the German print world during the first decades of Protestant expansion. All indications point to evangelical domination of the press in the years when Luther first became a public figure, when the printed book undoubtedly played a crucial role in the dissemination of the evangelical message, and printing enjoyed a period of exuberant growth. But it is by no means certain that assumptions derived from this German model hold good for other parts of Europe. This article re-examines the German paradigm of book and Reformation in the light of two recent bibliographical projects. The first, a trial survey of publishing outputs throughout Europe, demonstrates that the different regional print cultures that made up the European book world were organized in radically contrasting ways. These structural differences were highly significant from the point of view of assisting or impeding the output of controversial literature. The lessons from this survey are then applied to an individual case study, France, which, it emerges, deviated from the German model in almost every particular. Together these two sets of data force us to call into question the natural affinity between print and Protestantism suggested by the German paradigm.*

There can be little doubt that the book was one of the great forces for change in sixteenth-century Europe. And at the centre of this lay the Reformation. The connection between the book and the Reformation seems so obvious that it needs little extra comment. The powerful impetus given to the spread of the new doctrines by the medium of print was widely recognized in its own day – indeed, part of Luther's great genius as a reformer was his speedy recognition of the power of the printed word to carry on his fight with the papacy and articulate his theological precepts. Early critics within the church were first scandalized and then alarmed by Luther's blatant courting of a broad public through printed tracts and sermons. The connection between the book and the Reformation – in their eyes a malign one – was immediately obvious. And it has continued to be a cornerstone of historical interpretation from that day to this.[1]

It is not our intention in this reconsideration of these issues to offer any analysis that would deny this relationship – that is simply not possible. The evidence for the impact of the book on the Reformation (and perhaps less obviously, the

---

[1] As an introduction to this enormous literature, Mark J. Edwards, *Printing, propaganda and Martin Luther* (Berkeley, 1994); Jean-François Gilmont, ed., *The Reformation and the book*, trans. Karin Maag (Aldershot, 1998).

impact of the Reformation on the book) is too overwhelming. But it is certainly possible to suggest that our broadest assumptions regarding the natural affinity between the evangelical movement and the medium of print are susceptible of some refinement. Here, based on a survey of the print world that extends beyond the immediate context of Luther's challenge to embrace the broader print culture of sixteenth-century Europe, we hope to offer some observations that will at least place the relationship between the book and the Reformation in a slightly different context.[2]

This is important, because when we approach the question of the role of the book in the Reformation our assumptions regarding that relationship are based almost exclusively on analysis of the first decade, when Luther's message became a movement, and when the output of religious pamphlets in Germany was at its height. When we turn to other countries that experienced a successful or less successful Reformation we tend to carry these assumptions with us: that the book necessarily functioned as an agent of change and on the side of the critics of the old church. Our knowledge of the pamphlet wars of the 1520s also indelibly shapes our assumption of what was necessary, in printing terms, for a successful mass movement. We know that Luther's arguments quickly touched a nerve with a broad German public; and that printers in a large number of German cities easily seized on the opportunities presented by the resulting controversies to enter the market for vernacular *Flugschriften*. Yet it is by no means certain that assumptions developed through analysis of the first German decade can hold true for the Reformation elsewhere. Different parts of the European book market operated in quite different ways. Some lacked the industrial infrastructure either to service or to inspire a broad public debate – even if that had been their wish.

These are important issues, if not always fully acknowledged in discussions of the play of ideas during the Renaissance and Reformation period. In our admiration for the genius of Luther, our recognition of the eloquent skills of those who took up his teachings, and those who (often with considerable courage) took up their pens to refute him, we sometimes forget that a text is not an autonomous object that simply finds its own readers. In the craft world of medieval Europe, from which the book industry had so recently emerged, nothing, in fact, could be farther from the truth. The manufacture, distribution, and marketing of the printed word was as much an industrial as an intellectual process. Behind every Erasmus, or Luther, lay a small army of brawny artisans, who did hard, demanding work to turn an idea into an artefact. In the printing shops there were typesetters, pressmen, and proofreaders, and behind them lay the typefounders in their foundry, not to mention the papermakers in their mills. And that was just to produce the sheets that made up the finished book. Between Luther and his

---

[2] The responsibility of the two authors can be further specified as follows. The raw data and the initial analysis of the study from the *Index Aureliensis* in section II of this paper are the responsibility of Matthew Hall. The two other sections and the overall interpretative framework are the work of Andrew Pettegree.

THE REFORMATION AND THE BOOK   787

readers lay another small army of merchants, booksellers, and bookbinders – and as the trade spread through Europe, another small army of boatmen, hauliers, and travelling salesmen came into play, to spread the message to its new readers.

Here I want to apply some of the insights that flow from the study of the book as an industrial product rather than simply as an intellectual process. This is a relatively new aspect of the discipline but in our view an urgent necessity, particularly in an age like our own when we simply assume the dominance of text-based information systems. If, at the same time, we broaden the scope of our investigation from Luther's Germany to other parts of the European world of print, we will see that the conditions for the successful conduct of such a business were not equally available in different parts of Europe – in fact, the dynamics of the book industry varied very markedly from country to country. This had the most profound implications for the likely success of a Reformation movement in different parts of the western Christian world.

I

First, however, let us turn our attention back to the Reformation heartland – the German lands of the Holy Roman Empire – and review briefly the dynamic of publishing in the first crucial years of Luther's movement. Here we see that the role of the printed book, particularly in the relatively new form of the pamphlet, was absolutely paramount in first creating public interest in the controversies surrounding Luther, then in moulding a coherent movement that looked to the Wittenberg reformer for inspiration and leadership. Contemporaries were well aware that in harnessing the previously rather formal, stolid world of the book to serve these ends evangelical critics of the church had achieved something fundamentally new. A new form of book, the *Flugschriften*, came rapidly to dominate the output of German print shops.[3] Demand for books expanded very rapidly after 1517, as religious debate engaged the interest of a new, largely non-clerical audience. An exceptionally high proportion of these books addressed the new controversies: and in Luther, a writer of genius and extraordinary facility, Germany's publishers had found their ideal partner. Luther could write with phenomenal speed and quickly developed an extraordinary range, from the homiletic sermon, through excoriating satire, to careful, systematic exposition of complex theological issues.[4]

For a man in middle age, already twenty years into a successful and conventional career as preacher and theologian, this discovery of a popular voice was a quite extraordinary event; and one that truly shaped the Reformation. It also made fortunes for many in the book world. Those who were fortunate enough to be running the modest print shops of Wittenberg and Leipzig before 1517 were

[3] Hans-Joachim Köhler, ed., *Fluschriften als Massenmedium des Reformationszeit* (Stuttgart, 1981).
[4] The statistically dominant role of Luther in these years is demonstrated in the statistical analysis in Edwards, *Printing, propaganda*, pp. 14–40.

among the first to benefit; but they soon had to defend their profits against other eager entrepreneurs for whom the evidence of the phenomenal public interest in Luther spelt obvious opportunity. In ten years Wittenberg was transformed from a small outpost of the publishing world to one of the pillars of the German print industry: the lure of Luther's Gospel preaching brought not only students and intellectual disciples to the small Saxon town, but merchant entrepreneurs eager to share in the profits of bringing Luther's words to a wider public. They in turn recruited experienced artisans to man the new and expanding print shops; the wily Lucas Cranach was on hand to supply the woodcuts that provided the Wittenberg *Flugschriften* with their distinctive decorated title-pages.[5] From the point of view of a new entrepreneurial industry, the *Flugschriften* were the ideal product: generally short, they were quick and simple to produce. Because of the high demand (and many of Luther's own writings went through multiple editions in the years immediately after their publication) they turned a far more rapid profit than was usual in the slow-moving world of the book, where classical and patristic editions might take some years to sell out. The profits flowing back to the Wittenberg print shops (though not to Luther) allowed the grateful publishers to embark on more ambitious projects, such as Luther's new Bible translation. Here, the level of investment required to turn out a long, complex book in the traditional folio format was very considerable: a book of this scale might be several months in the press, and required considerable investment capital to purchase paper and pay wages before there was any prospect of return. But even here the courageous entrepreneurs were well rewarded, as the Luther Bible became one of the publishing sensations of the century.[6] The experience of Wittenberg, where fortunes were made, was replicated on a smaller scale in other parts of the German Empire where more established print industries adapted their output to share in the profits of Luther's popularity: in Strasbourg, for instance, and in Basle.[7]

The tremendous energy of the German print industry in the 1520s is now rather taken for granted, though at the time it required a shift of orientation in the rather conservative world of German urban craft industry that was really rather remarkable: a plausible analogy might be the expansion of armaments production in the mid-twentieth century as the industrial powers of Europe shifted to a war footing. Within a few years those involved in the German publishing trades found the capital, cast the new type, milled and supplied the paper, commandeered warehouse space and bookshops, and developed the distribution network to service an entirely new readership. Their success in this extraordinary business operation made possible the exposition of Luther's teachings to a hugely enlarged public: in the process it completely reshaped the world of the book, in Germany at least.

---

[5] *Cranach im Detail: Buchschmuck Lucas Cranachs des Älteren und seiner Werkstatt* (Wittenberg, 1994).

[6] Heimo Reinitzer, ed., *Biblia deutsch: Luthers Bibelübersetzung und ihre Tradition* (Wolfenbüttel, 1983).

[7] Miriam Usher Chrisman, *Bibliography of Strasbourg imprints, 1480–1599* (Yale, 1982); idem, *Conflicting visions of reform: German lay propaganda pamphlets, 1519–1530* (Boston, MA, 1996).

THE REFORMATION AND THE BOOK   789

The experience of the German book world in the 1520s would not in fact prove to be archetypal for Europe as a whole: this burst of intellectual energy and business creativity would not be widely replicated in other parts of Europe, for all that the religious stirs in Germany excited both curiosity and controversy. But the experience of Germany in the first years after Luther's defiant exposition of a radical theology of dissent has inevitably been the subject of a great deal of scholarly analysis, with the role of print well to the fore. This analysis, conducted not least on the basis of a thorough enumeration and analysis of the *Flugschriften*, has repeatedly highlighted several aspects of the Reformation print controversies, and this complex of issues had in effect become the paradigm for our understanding of the relationship between print and Reformation. The principal features of this understanding, what we may call the German paradigm, are as follows:

- evangelical dominance of print
- rapid spread of print to multiple printing centres; popular texts spread by local reprints
- difficulty of control assisting spread of dissident ideas
- victory of vernacular over Latin
- importance of illustration in spreading message to the non-literate.

All of these features of the movement are clearly a part of the German Reformation experience, particularly in the ten crucial years that followed Luther's first articulation of his theses on indulgences. In recent years a great deal of detailed work has refined our understanding of the conflict of print in these early years. It is now widely recognized that Catholic authors were not unaware of the need to challenge Luther – and did so, on occasions, with wit and style.[8] But there was still an enormous imbalance between evangelicals and defenders of the old church in their access to print.[9] This was partly because of undoubted misgivings among supporters of the old church about the appropriateness of wide public debate on theological issues, but mostly because of market demand. All statistical analysis undertaken demonstrates the extent to which Luther and his allies dominated – one might almost say swamped – the book market in Germany between 1520 and 1526. The demand for Luther's writings was apparently inexhaustible, and swiftly came also to embrace those who took up their pens to support the Wittenberg reformer. This body of writings is impressive both for its sheer extent, and for its variety: sermons, satirical tracts, dialogues, and manifestos for reform all vied for the interest of the discerning purchaser.

The same can be said of other aspects of the paradigm set out above. The Wittenberg printers enjoyed the priceless privilege of having first access to

---

[8] David V. N. Bagchi, *Luther's earliest opponents: Catholic controversialists, 1518–1525* (Minneapolis, 1991); Frank Aurich, *Die Anfänge des Buchdrucks in Dresden: Die Emserpresse, 1524–1526* (Dresden, 2000).
[9] Mark U. Edwards, 'Catholic controversial literature, 1518–1555: some statistics', *Archiv für Reformationsgeschichte*, 79 (1888), pp. 189–205.

Luther's new writings, but they could not control reprints in other parts of the extended network of the German cities where interest in the Reformation proved so intense. With small texts for which there was very heavy demand, market factors spoke strongly for quick, local reprints, rather than transporting large quantities of copies from a single production centre – and this is what occurred. The complexity of political jurisdiction in the patchwork of secular and ecclesiastical territories and Imperial Free cities would in any case have made the enforcement of copyright a forlorn hope; equally it rendered hopeless the attempt by Charles V and others to restrict expressions of support for the Reformation. The print trade had, until this point, been as well controlled as many other new or experimental technologies in the European craft world, not least to protect the interests of investors. It is in this respect a fallacy to regard censorship as a force imposed by government on an unwilling industry – most demand for control came from within the industry itself. But in the era of the Reformation, the print world of the Empire escaped this apparatus of control. The combination of market forces and Germany's particular political make-up made effective control of output impossible.

The Reformation also witnessed a significant development in the emergence of new sorts of vernacular print. Books in the vernacular were of course a familiar feature of the first age of print (1470–1520), and many lay people possessed some books. But the Reformation was the first real challenge to the dominance of Latin in several critical genres: theology, Biblical and critical scholarship, and history. When contemporaries remarked – often with regret and alarm – on the new phenomenon of books that mixed satire, invective, and teaching in a powerful (or poisonous) cocktail in the common tongue of the laity, they were, as so often, correct to identify a fundamental change in the terms of religious debate. The disadvantage Luther's opponents were under was reinforced by their reluctance to be seen to endorse this change by trading arguments and insults in the common tongue. Soon though, satire moved beyond words to scabrous illustrations and broadsheets that mixed text and picture; meanwhile Luther's image was promoted in multiple woodcuts that emphasized the dignity and simplicity of the learned monk.[10] Whether these images played a real role in spreading the ideas of the Reformation to parts of the population that did not read is less certain – though it is frequently asserted that woodcuts did act as the crucial link in the chain that spread the Reformation message across a broad mass of the population.[11]

So our understanding of the relationship between the book and the Reformation is based on solid foundations. The difficulty emerges when we treat this analysis of the impact of print in the particular context of Germany in the 1520s as normative for the experience of Reformation in other European lands.

[10] Martin Warnke, *Cranachs Luther: Entwürfe für ein Image* (Frankfurt, 1984).

[11] Robert W. Scribner, *For the sake of simple folk: popular propaganda for the German Reformation* (Cambridge, 1981).

THE REFORMATION AND THE BOOK   791

II

We propose to develop this argument by introducing material derived from a general survey of European print culture based on an analysis of some 10,000 consecutive entries from the *Index Aureliensis*. The *Index Aureliensis* was a project initiated in the 1960s as an attempt at a global survey of sixteenth-century printed books. It lists all books known to the editors, wherever printed, ordered alphabetically by author. The project made slow progress, and in forty years has advanced only as far as the letter G. The list seems to have been compiled through a process of conflating largely familiar library catalogues, such as the printed catalogue of the British Library and the Bibliothèque Nationale in Paris. The records do not seem to have been refined by examination of copies to distinguish different editions or states; nor has the list been enhanced by incorporation of records from manuscript catalogues. It is in consequence very incomplete and has to some extent been superseded by more recent, systematic projects such as the *VD16* for Germany and the *Typographia Batava* and *Belgica Typographia* for the Low countries.

The *Index Aureliensis* is manifestly a bibliographical project of a different, pre-digital age; in the third section of this article we will introduce some more refined data from a more modern national bibliographical project (for France) which does make extensive use of more modern on-line resources. But for all its faults the *Index Aureliensis* remains the only project that attempts a global survey of all European print; for that reason it remains useful for precisely the sort of sampling that has been attempted here.

Some years ago one of the authors, Matthew Hall, entered into a rudimentary database a sequence of 10,000 entries from the *Index Aureliensis*. He then analysed this data according to a variety of criteria: language, format, date, and place of publication.[12] The patterns that emerge paint a fascinating picture of a global world of print that was remarkable for the contrasting ways in which the industry was organized in different parts of Europe.

Tables 1 and 2 show the basic data for place and language of publication. There are few surprises here. We see that the print world of the sixteenth century continued to be dominated by the three great powerhouses that had emerged in the first age of print: the Empire, particularly the southern German cities; Italy; and France. Here lay most of Europe's most prestigious universities, and the major concentrations of great cities: together these two comprised both the major providers and consumers of books. The emergence of Antwerp as an economic and cultural force in the sixteenth century cements the place of the Netherlands in the second rank of European print culture alongside Spain and England; other peripheral cultures lag far behind.

Thus far our survey reveals much what one might expect: that books over the length of the sixteenth century were published conveniently close to their main

---

[12] Matthew Hall, 'European print culture in the sixteenth century: a sample from the *Index Aureliensis*' (M.Litt. dissertation, St Andrews, 2001).

Table 1   *Place of publication: percentage of total recorded editions by country*

Germany	32·0
France	21·4
Italy	18·4
Low Countries	7·2
England	5·5
Swiss Confederation	5·4
Spain	3·1
Poland	1·9
Bohemia	1·6
Others[a]	1·7

[a] Denmark, Hungary, Ireland, Portugal, Scotland, Sweden.
Source: Analysis of 10,000 consecutive items taken from the *Index Aureliensis*.

Table 2   *Language of books published (number of items)*

Latin	5,474
German	1,347
Italian	1,046
French	961
English	521
Spanish	275
Dutch	211
Danish	60
Polish	40
Hungarian	19
Czech	17
Portuguese	8
Swedish	4
Welsh	6

Source: Analysis of 10,000 consecutive items taken from the *Index Aureliensis*.

markets, and that these lay in the complex of European conurbations north and south of the Alps, and east and west of the Rhine. But what these initial figures do not reveal is that behind all of these emerging national print cultures lay a rather separate dynamic. This is true even of the three dominant markets of Italy, France, and Germany.

We see this clearly when we turn to table 3, which lists the number of printing centres in each national market. This figure is very high for Germany, where an exceptionally large number of cities at some stage during the sixteenth century

Table 3　*Number of printing centres by country*

Germany	92
Italy	60
France	53
Low Countries	27
Spain	20
Poland	13
Swiss Confederation	10
Hungary	9
Bohemia	8
England	6
Denmark	5
Portugal	3
Sweden	3
Scotland	2
Ireland	1

Source: Analysis of 10,000 consecutive items taken from the *Index Aureliensis*.

boasted a printing press. The number is high also for Italy and France; England, on the other hand provides evidence of a printing press in only a handful of different towns (and few of these in fact operated continuously throughout the sixteenth century). This contrast is even starker if we confine our attention only to places that turn up a significant number of books in our sample (table 4 – here we have listed only places which are named as place of publication in more than thirty books). Here the Empire is revealed as being in a category all of its own: no other print world relied on so diverse a range of significant printing centres. In England, the starkest contrast, only one place (London) is revealed as significant in the terms of our sample; and even France, where books are at some point printed in a huge number of different places during the course of the century, reveals a very high measure of concentration. This finding is confirmed by our more refined ongoing survey of the world of French print, which forms the basis of the analysis in the last part of this paper.

The true extent of the contrasting organization of different national print cultures emerges most starkly if we turn to table 5, which deals with the relationship between the dominant print centre in each part of Europe and other satellite publishing towns. To probe the relationship between the centre and periphery, we calculated the proportion of the books printed in each print zone that emanated from the largest centre of printing. This calculation reveals the full extent of the variation in organizational models. One may in effect identify three different experiences. First we have print cultures in which the centre is totally dominant. This is true of England, and some of the very small peripheral print

Table 4   *Significant centres of European printing*

Germany	22	
Italy	8	
France	5	(Paris/Lyon 75 per cent)
Low Countries	3	(Antwerp 56 per cent)
Spain	3	
Swiss Confederation	2	(Basle/Geneva 73 per cent)
Bohemia	1	
England	1	(London 97 per cent)
Denmark	1	
Poland	1	

Source: Analysis of 10,000 consecutive items taken from the *Index Aureliensis*.

Table 5   *Centre and periphery: proportion of the total number of books printed in each country published in the largest printing centre*

		%
England	London	97
Denmark	Copenhagen	88
Poland	Cracow	75
Bohemia	Prague	70
Italy	Venice	56
Low Countries	Antwerp	56
France	Paris	53
Swiss Confederation	Basle	51
Spain	Salamanca	23
Germany	Cologne	13

Source: Analysis of 10,000 consecutive items taken from the *Index Aureliensis*.

cultures. Then there are a number of examples characterized by what one might call the partially dominant centre. There is one predominant centre of print, but also other significant printing centres which carve out either an independent existence, at a rather more modest level that the main centre (this characterizes the relationship between Paris and Lyon in France) or a significant niche market. Aside from France, the Low Countries, Italy, and the Swiss Confederation – all important centres of print culture – all conform to this partially dispersed model.

The fully dispersed model is most clearly represented by the experience of Germany, where there is no one main centre of print: here, indeed, the output of the largest centre of print in the Empire comprises no more than 13 per cent of the total, as against 53 per cent for Paris in France and 97 per cent for London in England. The totally dispersed model characteristic of the Empire in fact finds an echo only in Spain, a secondary, though still important centre of print. In this respect, then, Germany, far from being normative for the sixteenth-century book world, was in fact highly exceptional.

It is only in the last few years that the value of this sort of bibliometric research has really begun to be appreciated by students of the intellectual culture of the Renaissance. Even now, it may not be immediately obvious why it was so important where, within a particular nation or language market, books were published. The critical importance of these different organizational models only becomes clear if one recognizes that each model created its own dynamic for the local book world.

England, for instance, was both a comparatively small market, and one wholly dominated by the centre. The English were not major producers of books for a number of reasons. England was a largely rural society, it had only two universities, and its population was relatively modest: around 3 million in 1500, against the 15 million of France. Intellectually as well as geographically it lay on the periphery of the main cultural and intellectual streams of European society, at the beginning of the sixteenth century at least. In consequence it played little part in the wider book culture of the continent: the relatively small number of books published in England were overwhelmingly for home consumption. This was a small book industry, where everybody would have been known to everybody else, and where the amount of work available to individual printers was heavily dominated by official commissions. This was not a difficult industry to control, partly because the printers all lived and worked cheek by jowl in one city, but also because none wanted to risk compromising their chance of official patronage. If that were not enough, England had no indigenous paper production; all the paper used by English printers had to be imported through the well-regulated ports.[13] All of these factors made clandestine printing very difficult. It was partly for these practical reasons that dissident publications – in the early Reformation Protestant, later in the century Catholic – were by and large published abroad and then smuggled back into the country. In fact there was very little unauthorized printing in England at any point during the sixteenth century; the sort of explosion of popular demand that Germany witnessed in the 1520s would simply not have been possible.[14]

In France, the largest market, Paris, was very closely regulated, but other alternative centres of French print did exist – not least Lyon, always happy to steal a march on its larger rival. The Netherlandish book market was very large,

---

[13] John Bidwell, 'French paper in English books', in John Barnard and D. F. McKenzie, eds., *The Cambridge history of the book in Britain*, IV: *1557–1695* (Cambridge, 2002), pp. 583–601.

[14] Andrew Pettegree, 'Printing and the Reformation: the English exception', in Peter Marshall and Alec Ryrie, eds., *The beginnings of English Protestantism* (Cambridge, 2002), pp. 157–79.

proportional to the size of the population, but also rigorously controlled. The Netherlandish regime of Charles V introduced some of the most draconian legislation for book censorship anywhere in Europe. The impact of this was somewhat ameliorated by Antwerp's position as a major international trading metropolis – the sheer scale of trade made the movement of books more difficult to control.

These different print cultures evince considerable variation in their mode of organization, but all of these descriptions tend to confirm the exceptionalism of the German market. Here a large number of significant centres of printing, all relatively close to one another, rendered control of output and distribution exceptionally difficult. The nearest equivalent is found in a later age – the Dutch Republic in the seventeenth century – where the ruling authorities faced similar difficulties in establishing any real control over the expression of opinion in print. In sixteenth-century Germany this problem is compounded by the existence of a multiplicity of ruling powers.

But the rather lax regulation of print in Germany evident in the early sixteenth century is very much the exception. Elsewhere, strong pressures for regulation of print came both from the government, wishing to control the expression of dissident opinion, and from within the industry itself. It is in this respect inaccurate to talk of censorship, because most curbs on freedom of production were entered into willingly by printers and publishers, who had no wish to see unauthorized editions spoil their market. These pressures were far less acute in Germany in the 1520s when the market itself was both large and growing rapidly.

All of these observations have proceeded from an assumption of markets driven by a large public interest in vernacular print. This is certainly the assumption underlying our analysis of the polemical battles of the German Reformation: that Luther's protest unlocked a new market for religious and political debate among the laity, and that this was pursued essentially through the local vernacular (or, if we think of Low German as a separate tongue, vernaculars). But the world of the Latin book should not be ignored. It may not be immediately clear why we should offer more than a cursory glance at Latin books, since our paradigm of the book and the Reformation assumes the easy dominance of the vernacular. But a consideration of the statistics gathered from our trial survey of European print culture suggests that the importance of Latin publishing can scarcely be ignored.

For, if we consider merely the raw figures presented in table 2, over half the books published during the century were in Latin, rather than one of Europe's vernacular languages. The startling significance of this must be emphasized: taking the Reformation century as a whole, works published in Latin still outnumbered books published in all other languages put together. In the first half of the century, despite the undoubted impact of the German *Flugschriften*, Latin retained an easy dominance of the European world of print; indeed, if we are to believe our more detailed analysis, it is only towards the very end of the century that vernacular publishing began first to match and then to overtake publishing in Latin.

It is worth pausing a moment to consider why this should be so. There is no doubt that Latin publishing continued to dominate the market for books in Europe's universities and other branches of learned and scientific culture. Even in markets where, and with revolutionary impact, the Reformation was beginning to engage a new audience, Latin still remained the language of debate among trained theologians. It goes without saying that Luther could not have hoped to gain converts among his intellectual peers had he not also been a skilled Latin author. The growth of counter-churches also stimulated a vast controversial and exegetical literature in the learned languages. Beyond this, there were vast areas of the book world where the vernacular made comparatively little impact. Scientific, legal, and medical texts remained predominantly in Latin. Interest in the classical authors remained high throughout the century, and this ensured another strong market for Latin print. Interestingly, Latin also played a predominant role in many areas where the book made the greatest strides during the sixteenth century: one thinks here of the relatively new genres of books, such as technical books, books on architecture, astrology and cosmography, or the natural sciences. These were genres that relied heavily on the illustrative potential of the woodcut, but they were not for that reason more popular genres. On the contrary, the claim to respectability on the part of the new sciences relied heavily on use of the learned language: these relatively innovative printing projects were therefore published predominantly in Latin. One is forced to conclude that in the book world as a whole, the importance of Latin was not much diminished by popular religious controversy. Latin remained the badge of honour that distinguished the man of culture.

An inevitable consequence is that while the vernacular texts of Reformation polemic are those which have caught the eye, Latin publishing continued to loom large in the financial considerations of anyone concerned with the business of books. Crucially for our investigations, the publication of books in Latin was structured in a totally different way from the output of vernacular books (see table 6). There were major centres of Latin print in most of the significant centres of printing in continental Europe: in France, the Netherlands, Germany, and the Swiss Confederation. There were surprisingly few Latin books published in Italy and Spain. Meanwhile, English consumers of Latin books, as we can see from the miniscule numbers published in London, relied almost wholly on imports (as they had, indeed, in the manuscript era).[15]

If we now look behind these broad national markets to a closer investigation of the publication of Latin books, we can see that the European market for learned print was organized in a very particular way, and one that contrasts markedly with the production of vernacular texts. In general terms, a very high proportion of Latin books were published in a small number of Europe's largest centres of

[15] Margaret Lane Ford, 'Importation of printed books into England and Scotland', in Lotte Hellinga and J. B. Trapp, eds., *The Cambridge history of the book in Britain*, III: *1400–1557* (Cambridge, 1999), pp. 179–201.

798   ANDREW PETTEGREE AND MATTHEW HALL

Table 6   *Latin and vernacular (percentage of total for each country)*

	Latin	Vernacular
Germany	61	39
Italy	45	55
France	61	39
England	11	89
Low Countries	67	33
Spain	28	72
Swiss Confederation	77	23
Bohemia	80	20
Denmark	11	89
Hungary	66	34

Source: Analysis of 10,000 consecutive items taken from the *Index Aureliensis*.

print. Places like Basle in the Swiss Confederation, Lyon and Paris in France, and Antwerp in the Low Countries became renowned centres of Latin print. The reasons for this heavy degree of market concentration were both economic and aesthetic. Many of these Latin books were large, complex, and therefore expensive projects. Editions of the classics might use many different fonts of type to distinguish text, textual variations, side-notes, and footnotes. The Renaissance concern for textual accuracy imposed a heavy burden of expectation: the books themselves were usually published in large formats and in a pleasing italic type. The new genres of book that enjoyed a growing vogue in the sixteenth century, such as architectural texts or books on botany, also often required considerable specialist expertise, not least in crafting the illustrative woodcuts that were fundamental to their success.

These were difficult, expensive projects, that could only as a rule be taken on by experienced printers, and in well-capitalized publishing houses. These tended to be found in the largest and best-financed centres of European printing. Further, if the initial expense tended to militate against the involvement of smaller printing shops, the same economic considerations militated against local reprints. The market for Latin books in Europe was clearly very large, but it was also very dispersed. It therefore inevitably worked to somewhat different rules from the more concentrated national print markets. Books tended to be moved over longer distances to their purchasers. Because the projects were larger, and involved heavier initiation costs, publishers tended to print larger editions, and expect to stockpile copies for longer before an edition was exhausted. All of this played into the hands of the industry's most established figures. There was much less room for alert, speculative players intent on a quick profit by exploiting a sudden rise in demand – the classic model of the German Reformation.

THE REFORMATION AND THE BOOK   799

Before moving to draw further conclusions from this sketch of Latin print, a word of caution should perhaps be entered. It might well be argued that the bare figures presented here might misrepresent the whole world of print culture in this one, important respect: for it is very obvious that big books survive much better than small books. It is almost certainly the case that these differential survival rates weigh the odds heavily in favour of Latin, the learned language. We are likely to have at least one surviving copy of almost all the books published in Latin during the sixteenth century; one can certainly not say the same of all books, pamphlets and broadsheets published in the vernacular.

The evidence for this simple statement is overwhelming. Latin books were by and large published to be studied, and to be preserved; many items published in the vernacular, whether these be broadsheets, pamphlets, or small handbooks, were not. The fact that a very high proportion of all vernacular pamphlets published in the sixteenth century survive in only one, two, or three copies suggests that a large number must have been published which do not survive at all. If we regard any book published, whether it be a single sheet broadsheet or a large folio of 400 leaves, as a single bibliographical item, the raw figures from the *Index Aureliensis* must greatly understate the quantity of vernacular publishing.

To balance this, one should note that Latin books are on the whole much larger. This is true in all respects. A high proportion of Latin books are in the larger formats (folio or quarto); Latin books are on the whole much longer. On the other side an overwhelming proportion of printed items of two sheets or less (that is, broadsheets or pamphlets of thirty-two pages or less in octavo) were in the vernacular. From the point of view of printer and publisher this was an absolutely crucial distinction. A broadsheet proclamation was a valuable commission for a printer (since it was often produced for a single official purchaser, and therefore helped cash flow) but it was only one day's work. A major Latin edition might employ the press – and often more than one press – for months at a time.

Thus to understand the real impact of Latin publishing on the European world of print, one has to look not only at the raw data of numbers of editions, but at the length of books, and thus at the amount of time they would have occupied the presses. Paris, for instance, was a major centre of Latin print. Judging from an analysis of the books listed by Bridget Moreau in her bibliography of books published in Paris 1500–35, Latin books commanded the market throughout the period: about 75 per cent of all books published in Paris during this time were in Latin.[16] Furthermore, and despite the upsurge of popular religious controversy that followed the Reformation, the proportion of books published in Latin in Paris was in no way diminished towards the end of this period. Given that many of these projects were very substantial and ambitious books, intended for an international as much as a local market, it is very likely that the average Paris print shop would have been dominated by the demand for Latin print. It is more

---

[16] Brigitte Moreau, *Inventaire chronologique des editions parisiennes du XVIe siècle, 1501–1535* (4 vols., Paris, 1972–92).

than likely that during this whole period Paris's presses spent on average less than 15 per cent of their time – one day in a six day week – printing works in French.

This has many important implications for our study of the Reformation. It certainly should warn us that when Protestants, for their own purposes, began to promote the idea of the greater dignity and nobility of the vernacular, they were arguing very much against the grain of sixteenth-century culture. And while the rise of the *Flugschriften* created and developed other new markets for books in Europe, it did little to dent the appeal of the existing market for Latin books – in fact, the two markets seem to have grown together as the century wore on. For Europe's printers and publishers, in particular, the Reformation was not a life-line; indeed, for many in the most established print centres, away from the immediate turmoil of Luther's movement, it represented a considerable complicating factor. We can see this clearly if we turn to an investigation of one particular market, France, where the impact of the Reformation on a sophisticated and complex book world was very different from that in Luther's own homeland.

III

With France we turn to a particular focus of our recent scholarly interest, and to research undertaken partly to test the wider applicability of the German paradigm of book and Reformation set out above. France was a country with a mature, robust printing industry. It also experienced a genuine, popular Reformation, albeit a generation later than Germany: in the early 1560s, when the rapid growth of the Huguenot movement was a major contributing factor to the extended political and religious crisis we know as the French Wars of Religion. What, it is fair to ask, was the contribution of printing to this complex of events? How far did France's experience of print and the Reformation parallel that of Luther's homeland?

To address this issue we are able here to draw on a major new research project that will, in due course, shed a great deal of new light on French print culture in the sixteenth century. During the last seven years a group of graduate students and researchers at the University of St Andrews have been engaged in creating a new database of books printed in French during the sixteenth century. With the help of a programme of visits to libraries throughout France and elsewhere in Europe, this work has now gathered information on about 50,000 editions.[17] What is presented here is based on a preliminary analysis of this data.

In the first days of the stirs raised by Luther, news of the controversies did not take long to reach France. The enterprising Swiss publisher Froben reported brisk sales in Paris for his early (Latin) edition of Luther's collected writings in 1519, and

---

[17] For up-to-date information on the St Andrews project, the working method, database, and libraries incorporated into the project files, visit the project website at http://www.st-andrews.ac.uk/~www_rsi/book/book.htm

the distinguished university in Paris became a critical early test case for the wider appeal of Luther's teachings.[18] Throughout the 1520s, in fact, one can gather plentiful evidence of interest both in the issue of church reform, and in German events. But for all that the movement in France did not achieve the same coherence and potency as was the case in its German homeland.

There were several reasons why this proved to be the case. First, the French authorities took swift action to contain publication and distribution of evangelical print. Paris, as we have seen, was one of the largest centres of Europe's publishing industry, but it was also one of the best organized and most tightly controlled. Parisian printers were not free to engage in the speculative publication of translated reprints of the German *Flugscriften*, even had they wished to – and there is little reason to believe that established members of the Paris book world would have turned from the lucrative, mainly Latin works that were the mainstay of their business without the assurance of either official encouragement or overwhelming public demand. Neither, in fact, was forthcoming. For in France, Luther's struggle was not a national, patriotic issue: a crucial element in the early drama of public support for Luther in Germany was missing. In fact, in the particular context of France, national, patriotic factors tended to militate against Luther's movement, since the identification of the crown with a Catholic, Gallican church was a crucial source of strength for the established order. French evangelicals had hopes that they could manoeuvre through these shoals, by converting the king's undoubted interest in Renaissance scholarship into a genuine interest in church reform, but this called for a subtle process of lobbying in private and at court. The raising of popular passions would only damage this cause.

Thus in France the political context was entirely different from that in Luther's own homeland; but so too was the degree of resonance that the Reformation found, both among churchmen, and the public at large. Striking in our analysis of the output of French books in the 1520s is the swift and effective Catholic response to the evangelical criticism emanating from Germany. This, of course, provides an instructive contrast with Germany, which is further reinforced when we delve a little more deeply into the type of works published against Luther in France – and in French – in the years immediately after the Reformation controversies. The campaign against Luther was led from the beginning by doctors of the Sorbonne who, like Luther on the other side, quickly found an effective popular voice. These authors also swiftly identified themes important to French Catholics that had to be defended, foremost among them the Catholic Mass. Both these factors are epitomized in the career of Pierre Doré, Dominican and Doctor of Theology, and a man now little known outside the narrow world of scholarly specialists. But in his day he was one of the most popular religious writers in France: his fifty-six known editions of twenty-four different works place him

---

[18] For the early history of Luther's reception in France see Francis Higman, *Censorship and the Sorbonne* (Geneva, 1979).

ahead of Luther in the popularity of religious writers who published in French.[19] In purely statistical terms only Calvin would surpass his impact on the world of French vernacular religious publishing in the first half of the sixteenth century. Luther, of course, laboured under a considerable handicap, in that his works were officially outlawed. All the works of Luther that appeared in French were printed with greater or lesser degree of subterfuge, and Luther was never named on the title-page.[20] Pierre Doré, in contrast, enjoyed the support of major Parisian printing houses.

We have then to recognize that the overwhelming superiority evangelicals enjoyed in the polemical battle in Germany simply did not carry over into other European print cultures. From the earliest days of the Reformation controversies, in France Catholic authors at least matched the church's critics in their output of popular theological works, and this continued to be the case for all but a short period in mid-century when the Huguenot surge was as its most intense. There were many reasons for this, not least the early ban on Lutheran publications in France, and the reluctance of Parisian printers to involve themselves in risky disapproved projects. But the extent of popular demand for books defending familiar, popular beliefs can also not be doubted.[21]

Nevertheless, it is certainly the case that in their eagerness to defend the church from foreign heresies, the French authorities took one decision that ultimately was to prove very damaging. In 1526, spurred by evidence that the call for the pure Gospel, *rein Evangelium*, had become a powerful polemical tool in Germany, the Parisian authorities ordered a ban on publication of vernacular scripture in France.[22] One can only imagine the frustration of Parisian printers. Already, not least in the popularity of the New Testament of Lefèvre, there was plentiful evidence that editions of the Bible in French would constitute a major market. And Parisian printers had the equipment, technical skill, and resources to produce large, illustrated books, of the sort that would be required for the most lavish Bible editions. But the printers fell reluctantly into line. Too many had too much to lose by defying the king – and Bibles were not the sort of books that could be produced in a clandestine way. So the production of vernacular Bibles took place away from Paris – first in Antwerp, then in Lyon, and finally in Geneva.[23] In Geneva, the publication of multiple editions of the Bible in French

[19] On Doré see Francis Higman, *Piety and the people: religious printing in French, 1511–1551* (Aldershot, 1996), pp. 5, 177–90.

[20] Bernd Moeller, 'Luther in Europe: his works in translation, 1517–1546', in E. I. Kouri and Tom Scott, eds., *Politics and society in Reformation Europe* (Basingstoke, 1987), pp. 235–51. Francis Higman, 'Les traductions françaises de Luther, 1524–1550', in his *Lire et découvrir: la circulation des idées au temps de la Réforme* (Geneva, 1998), pp. 201–32.

[21] Issues effectively explored in Christopher Elwood, *The body broken: the Calvinist doctrine of the Eucharist and the symbolization of power in sixteenth-century France* (Oxford, 1999).

[22] Higman, *Censorship and the Sorbonne*, pp. 26–7.

[23] B. T. Chambers, *Bibliography of French Bibles: fifteenth- and sixteenth-century French-language editions of the Scriptures* (Geneva, 1983).

THE REFORMATION AND THE BOOK   803

became one of two cornerstones of the Genevan book market – the other being the works of Calvin.

Calvin began to make himself felt in the French publishing world from the early 1540s.[24] Like Luther, the Genevan reformer showed an acute awareness of the need to nurture relationships with printers. In the 1540s, the first decade after he was permanently established in Geneva, Calvin published many short, popular works. The success of these sharp, pungent polemical tracts helped to finance other major projects, such as editions of his Biblical commentaries and the *Institutes*. As Geneva became known as a centre of Protestant print, the new industry attracted a number of members of major Parisian printing dynasties. They brought with them capital, skill, and expertise in handling large projects. Soon, the Genevan publishing industry was one of the most dynamic industries in a fast-growing town. Here the comparison with Wittenberg is very close. The education industry – that is, publishing and the university (in the Genevan case, the Academy) – was a cornerstone of economic growth. It is not always acknowledged the extent to which fortunes were made through the Reformation (though one only has to go and stand outside Lucas Cranach's house in Wittenberg for the point to be abundantly clear). So it was in Geneva. Calvin was one of the most talented preachers and authors of the day. But he was also very good for business.

Back in France, the debate inspired by the Reformation continued to rage. Evangelicals had high hopes of the king, and particularly of the king's sister. But after 1535 the commitment of the crown to suppress heresy never really wavered. Protestantism became an underground movement. For all that, by the 1550s it had become increasingly clear that the policy of repression had failed. Prosecutions and executions had not prevented the steady growth of evangelical communities, inspired and strongly supported from Geneva. In 1559 the then king, Henry II, made peace with Spain, intending to devote his attention to the final suppression of heresy. But his death in a freak accident plunged France into political crisis, and evangelicals, together with their sympathizers at court, seized the moment.

The result was that France experienced in the next six years (1560–5) a genuine popular Reformation. The explosive growth of the Calvinist movement during these years stands comparison with Germany during the first years when Luther's message found a mass audience (1520–5). Churches grew from small underground cells to large congregations, a mass movement that enjoyed the support of 50 per cent of the French nobility and 25 per cent of the urban population. Most important of all for the gathering political crisis was the rate of growth, and the obvious self-confidence of the movement. As in Germany in the 1520s, no one knew where it would end. The potential seemed boundless.

As in Germany, this new popular Protestantism was accompanied by a surge of printing. As part of our wider survey of French print culture, the St Andrews project has made a special study of Protestant printing in the French language,

---

[24] Jean-François Gilmont, *Jean Calvin et le livre imprimé* (Geneva, 1997).

charting growth from the first tentative evangelical works in French in 1520, through to the end of the century and the end of the religious wars. This has, for the first time, created the secure statistical base with which we can compare the French experience of evangelical print with that of Germany. There are important points of comparison, but also of difference.

First, this statistical work brings home the importance of this extraordinary burst of energy and excitement in the early 1560s. Over 30 per cent of all Protestant works published in French during the sixteenth century appeared during the years 1560–5. This was the only point in the century at which French Protestants outpublished their Catholic opponents. This surge in demand also demanded rapid reorganization of the means of production. With events moving so fast, Geneva was too far away from the major markets within France to meet demand for small political and religious tracts, editions of the Bible, and psalms. New centres of Protestant publication grew up in Caen, Orléans, and Lyon.[25]

For all that, French Catholics marshalled a robust defence of their church, and of traditional beliefs. In France, Protestants never wholly dominated the world of print. By 1562, after the initial shock of adapting to the new political climate, Catholic authors had found their voice, pouring out a flood of tracts which both offered a lucid and eloquent defence of the essentials of the Catholic faith and poured scorn on Calvin.[26] The printing houses of Paris gave themselves very willingly to this polemical effort, for the Catholic hold on Paris was never shaken. This may well have been crucial to the survival of French Catholicism. When the royal government, led by Catherine of Medici, felt itself so weakened that concessions to the Huguenots seemed inevitable, it was the Catholic populations of Paris and other cities that made it clear that this was unacceptable.[27] Spurred by their preachers, inspired by the scabrous sermons and religious literature, they rallied to those who identified with the cause of resistance, notably the house of Guise. Ultimately war broke out in 1562 because French Catholics would not accept crown concessions to Protestants. Catholicism in France was a popular cause.

Once war broke out, Catholics soon gained the upper hand, both in military terms, and in the polemical battle. The momentum of Protestant growth was decisively arrested by the events of the first war (1562–3), and Protestantism was in decline even before the St Bartholomew's Day massacre of 1572. By the second decade of the war, the polemical battle was less one between the faiths – the

---

[25] Louis Desgraves, *Elie Gibier imprimeur à Orléans (1536–1588)* (Geneva, 1966); Andrew Pettegree, 'Protestantism, publication and the French Wars of Religion: the case of Caen', in Robert J. Bast and Andrew C. Gow, eds., *Continuity and change: the harvest of late-mediaeval and Reformation history* (Leiden, 2000); idem, 'Protestant printing during the French Wars of Religion: the Lyon press of Jean Saugrain', in Tom Brady and James Tracy, eds., *Essays presented to Heiko Oberman on his seventieth birthday* (Brill, 2003).

[26] Luc Racaut, *Hatred in print: Catholic propaganda and Protestant identity during the French Wars of Religion* (Aldershot, 2002).

[27] Barbara Diefendorf, *Beneath the cross: Catholics and Huguenots in sixteenth-century Paris* (New York, 1991).

THE REFORMATION AND THE BOOK 805

Huguenots had conceded that the conversion of France was beyond them – and more one within Catholicism: between those who prepared to offer some toleration to the increasingly embattled Huguenot movement, and those who favoured a policy of extermination.

French Protestantism, then, ultimately failed, and for reasons which had much to do with the local culture of religion. Despite its failure – indeed, perhaps because of the contrast it provides in this respect with Germany – it still provides material for an important case study. Looking primarily at the brief period of hectic evangelical growth between 1559 and 1565, what can we say of the relationship revealed between print culture and belief in the particular French context?

We can see that, as in Germany, the opportunity of sudden widespread popular interest brought a rapid restructuring of the French print world. As demand for Protestant books increased exponentially in the years after 1559, new printing centres swiftly emerged to cater to the demand: often in French towns that had until this point played only a modest role in French print culture. The content and tone of these books also bears closer examination, for in these years when the churches expanded most rapidly the movement was far less closely controlled from Geneva. The Genevan reformers were too geographically distant to react to the speed of change in political events, or the raging religious debate. Genevan publications were noticeably more measured in tone than the more polemical works published in France during these years. In the new print centres within France, we notice that each different place has its own distinctive style. There is a high degree of specialism between different publishing centres.

Nevertheless, it is clear that, in France at least, a local print industry is not essential to the rapid growth of an evangelical movement. The Huguenot movement made some of its most rapid and enduring progress away from Paris, in the far south, where towns like Nîmes, Montpellier, and Montauban swiftly became important strongholds of the new movement. None of these towns ever developed a substantial indigenous printing industry.[28] In these cases, it seemed, the supply lines from Geneva and Lyon were adequate to supply the books required by these new congregations.

These observations direct our attention to other important aspects of the relationship between the book and the Reformation that have proved most elusive to scholarly investigation. What can we say about the reasons why people adhered to the new churches? Obviously here a whole range of stimuli played a part: charismatic preaching, peer pressure, the example of a family member or social superior. But in the realm of the book, it is particularly clear that in the French example, verse and song played a crucial role in creating a popular movement. We see this at work at two levels. Contemporary observers were

---

[28] Philip Conner, *Huguenot heartland: Montauban and southern French Calvinism during the French Wars of Religion* (Aldershot, 2002); idem, 'A provincial perspective: Protestant print culture in southern France', in Andrew Pettegree, Paul Nelles, and Philip Conner, eds., *The sixteenth century French religious book* (Aldershot, 2001), pp. 286–302.

certainly aware of the particular role of the psalms in creating Huguenot group solidarity. The metrical Psalter was an original, inspired creation of Calvinism. The product of twenty years of development in the Genevan church, the full translation of the psalms was finally completed in 1562: just in time to play its part in the largest movement of church forming. The metrical Psalter proved to be a marvellously adaptable, as well as distinctive, tool of church building. The psalms were suitable both for communal worship and for use outside the church. There were psalms for all moods and occasions. Since the psalms were set to an unusually wide repertoire of tunes, the association of tune and words was very close. Since they were rapidly memorized, not least through repeated use in the churches, they formed a crucial bridge in building the movement from a literate core to the wider population.[29] Alongside the psalms the Huguenots popularized a range of political and satirical songs often put to the tunes of well-known psalms. These songs ridiculed the Catholic clergy and Catholic political leadership, while praising Protestant champions like Condé and Coligny. Others were penned to celebrate Protestant victories on the field of battle, or the takeover of French cities. These too helped create popular momentum at moments of maximum excitement.

It is important to dwell on this point, not least because historians of the Reformation have consistently undervalued the importance of song in sixteenth-century culture, and paid scant attention to its role as a tool of the Reformation. In France it was clearly crucial: the illustrative woodcut, on the other hand, played no role whatsoever. Much has been written about the use of visual material to bridge the gap between the literate and the unlettered. It has become a common assumption, as those of us who teach undergraduates know, that the evangelical message crossed the barrier between the literate and illiterate with the help of visual culture. To our very visual age this seems a natural assumption; and perhaps for that reason it has not been sufficiently tested.

With respect to France, however, one can with some confidence assert the following. The quantity of illustration in religious print certainly *declined* after the Reformation. Illustrations were much used in traditional, pre-Reformation works such as books of hours. These were popular books, but promoted images and core beliefs of which the reformers could scarcely approve. After the Reformation, the market for books of hours gradually declined, yet woodcuts continued to appear mostly in expensive books (and, indeed, are one of the most expensive features of these books). In France, most illustrations appeared in books with no polemical intent: technical, scientific, or medical. They are also used in books of astrology; where they find their way into cheap print, it is mostly in newsbooks or calendars.

French Protestants very largely spurned illustration, or the illustrated broadsheet, as a polemical weapon. In the French Wars of Religion illustration plays a role in cheap print only in the period 1589–90, in the conflict between the Guise

---

[29] Andrew Pettegree, *Huguenot voices: the book and the communication process during the Protestant Reformation* (Brewster Lecture Series, Greenville, 2000).

THE REFORMATION AND THE BOOK   807

and the crown. This is a conflict within Catholicism. Only a handful of the more than 1,000 Protestant works published between 1560 and 1565 make any use of illustration.

How then does French Protestantism become a popular movement? The overwhelming conclusion is that in order for the movement to broaden its appeal beyond the unlettered it must have continued to rely on oral dissemination: primarily the spoken word, and song. The full extent of this culture of song is only now emerging as the St Andrews French book project continues its survey of French libraries: these are small tracts, which often only survive in one solitary copy. But they played a vital and distinctive role in building a French Protestant church.

IV

We are now perhaps in a position to draw some conclusions from this survey of contrasting examples: the global survey of European book culture, and a closer look at the particular example of France. The evidence we have laid out here suggests, most obviously, that the German paradigm of the relationship between print and Reformation has no general applicability: that all Reformation movements have their own character. The nature of this local character is shaped partly by social and political structures, but partly also by the organization of the local publishing industry. In this respect the German experience was not normative, or typical, but very much the exception.

It is certainly possible to create a popular evangelical movement without the particular structural circumstances of the German movement. Other countries, France as we have seen, but also the Netherlands, have their popular moment. A well-developed print culture plays an important role in this. The role of the charismatic leader is also important – in Germany, Luther, in France, Calvin. The charismatic leader extends the range of influence beyond those that can meet or hear them personally. But he is also important because the charismatic leader becomes a major economic force – a key local wealth generator. This helps consolidate their authority with a local elite, whose political instincts are likely otherwise to be more conservative. For Wittenberg to have given Luther up after 1520 would have been like killing the goose that laid the golden eggs. In Geneva, Calvin's writings were a cornerstone of the local economy, just as his sermons were a major tourist attraction.[30] Frequently during the 1540s and early 1550s Calvin and his colleagues found themselves in dispute with the city council, but his role in the local economy was a source of extraordinary strength and power – if not one upon which he dwells in his correspondence.[31] The laws of supply and demand, it must be emphasized, operate even in the realm of ideas.

---

[30] As outstanding example of preacher tourism is related by the Catholic author Florimond de Raemond. See Alastair Duke, Gillian Lewis, and Andrew Pettegree, eds., *Calvinism in Europe, 1540–1610: a collection of documents* (Manchester, 1992), pp. 37–8.
[31] William G. Naphy, *Calvin and the consolidation of the Genevan Reformation* (Manchester, 1994).

Most of all, the evidence presented in the last part of this article suggests that it may be necessary to rethink our sense of the process by which Reformation becomes popular. In particular we suggest that it is time to subject the role of visual culture to more sceptical re-examination: and this for Germany, as much as for the French example we have studied. Here too we need to investigate more systematically the role of song.[32]

Finally, it is necessary to recognize that print will not always operate to the advantage of those arguing for change – print was not necessarily, in terms of twentieth-century debate, a progressive force.[33] If we consider the whole realm of print in French, the balance is fairly even. Print played an important role in the growth of science, but also disseminated much nonsense, particular in the realm of medicine and astronomy. Print can disseminate error, as well as truth. In the realm of religious ideas, in France print was used every bit as effectively by defenders of old ways as by promoters of new.

So where does this leave the complex print and Reformation? Can one envisage a genuine mass movement without print? Perhaps this calls for a more systematic investigation of the process of evangelical growth in a country like Scotland, which experienced a Protestant revolution with little or no indigenous print. Certainly it reminds us that, for those who study the print culture of the sixteenth-century, business questions – questions of distribution and the organizing of the market – are as important as the location of publication.

---

[32] Rebecca Wagner Oettinger, *Music as propaganda in the German Reformation* (Aldershot, 2001).

[33] As in the classic formulation of Elizabeth Eisenstein, *The printing press as an agent of change* (Cambridge, 1982).

[8]

ORALITY LOST: TEXT AND VOICE IN THE SIXTEENTH AND SEVENTEENTH CENTURIES

ROGER CHARTIER

THIS PAPER IS devoted to the nexus of relations formed during the sixteenth and seventeenth centuries between the forms of transmission of texts or, to put it another way, the different modalities of their 'performance', and their possible reception by different audiences. Our inquiry has two objectives: on the one hand, to identify the modes of circulation and appropriation of works and genres whose original status, function, and usages were not those exclusively implied either by printed inscription or by silent, individual reading habits; and on the other hand, to study the relationships which two accepted versions of the category of genre entertain: the one discursive and literary, the other material and editorial.

I would like to show that the contemporary relationship to works and to genres cannot be considered either invariable or universal. Against the temptations of an 'ethnocentrism of reading', it is necessary to recall how numerous are the ancient texts which in no way implied, as addressee, a solitary and silent reader, in search of meaning. Composed to be spoken or to be read out loud and shared before a listening audience, invested with a ritual function, thought of as machines designated to produce certain effects, they obey the laws proper to 'performance' or to oral and communal transmission. I will situate this question within my own field of interest, one which strives to link the study of texts, whether they be canonical or ordinary, 'literary' or not, the analysis of their material forms and their modes of circulation, and their interpretations, usages, and appropriations by their different reading and listening audiences.

This point of departure is an attempt to break with the uncritical posture which assumes that all texts, all works, all genres must reasonably be read, identified, and received according to criteria which characterise our own relation to the written word. It is thus a question of historicising criteria of classification between genres, ways of reading, and representations of the structure of address and the addressee of texts as they have been bequeathed to us by the 'literary institution'. Confronted with works dating from the sixteenth and

Roger Chartier

seventeenth centuries (and *a fortiori* from earlier periods or from non-Western cultures), categories which we have used unreflectingly begin to lose their assumed self-evidence and universality.

Let us consider, to illustrate the above, the reading of a 'tale' – a *'cuento'* as its author Borges writes. It is a 'fiction' entitled *El espejo y la máscara* (*The Mirror and the Mask*), published in the collection *El libro de arena* (*The Book of Sand*) (Borges, 1975a). In it, Borges tells a story about a king and a bard. After having conquered his Norwegian enemy, the High King of Ireland asks the poet Ollan to write an ode that will celebrate his triumph and establish his glory for all eternity. 'Las proezas más claras pierden su lustre si no se las amoneda en palabras [. . .] Yo seré Eneas; tu serás mi Virgilio.' ('The greatest deeds lose their lustre if they are not coined in words. [. . .] I will be Aeneas; you will be my Virgil.') Three times, at one-year intervals, the bard returns to the king with a different poem. And, each time, the poetic writing, the aesthetic which governs it, the form of publication of the text, and the figure of its addressee find themselves modified.

The bard composed his first ode according to the rules of his art, mobilising all the knowledge which is his: a knowledge of words, images, verse, examples, genres, tradition. The poem is declaimed by its author 'con lenta seguridad, sin una ojeada al manuscrito' ('slowly, confidently, without a glance at the manuscripts') before the king, the court, the 'School of Bards' and crowds of those who 'agolpados en las puertas, no descifraban una palabra' ('thronging at the doorways, were unable to make out a single word'). This first panegyric is a 'monument': it respects rules and conventions, it summarises all of Ireland's literature, it is set down in writing. Inscribed within the order of representation, it leads one to believe in the exploits of the sovereign. It should thus be conserved and disseminated: the king commands 30 scribes to copy it twelve times each. The bard has been a good artisan who has faithfully reproduced the teachings of the ancients: 'has attribuido a cada vocablo su genuina acepción y a cada nombre sustantivo el epíteto que le dieron los primeros poetas. No hay en toda la loa una sola imagen que no hayan los clásicos. [. . .] Has manejado con destreza la rima, la aliteración, la asonancia, las cantidades, los artificios de la docta retórica, la sabia alteración de los metros.' ('You have given each word its true meaning, and each substantive the epithet given it by the poets of old. In your whole panegyric there is not a single image unknown to the classics. [. . .] You have skilfully handled rhyme, alliteration, assonance, quantities, the artifices of learned rhetoric, the wise variations of metres.') In recompense, the bard is given a mirror, the work of an artisan like himself which, like the ode of praise, reflects what is already there.

The king, however, remains dissatisfied. Although it is perfect, the poem remains lifeless. It does not produce effect either on the soul or on the body:

Orality Lost

'Todo está bien y sin embargo nada ha pasado. En los pulsos no corre más a prisa la sangre. Las manos no han buscado los arcos. Nadie ha palidecido. Nadie profirió un grito de batalla, nadie opuso el pecho a los vikings.' ('All is well and yet nothing has happened. In our veins the blood runs no faster. Our hands have not sought the bow. No one has turned pale. No one uttered a battle cry or set his breast against the Vikings.') The bard deserves a reward, but in order to qualify he must compose another work: 'Dentro del término de un año aplaudiremos otra loa, poeta' ('Before the year is out, poet, we shall applaud another ode').

One year later, the poet is back before the king. His new poem is quite different from the preceding one. On the one hand, it breaks all existing rules, whether they be grammatical ('Un sustantivo singular podía regir un verbo plural. Las preposiciones eran ajenas a las normas communes' – 'A singular noun could govern a plural verb. The prepositions were alien to common usage'), poetic ('La aspereza alternaba con la dulzura' – 'Harshness alternated with sweetness'), or rhetorical ('Las metáforas eran arbirarias o así lo parecían' – 'Metaphors were arbitrary or so they seemed'). The work in no way conforms to the conventions of literary art; it is no longer imitation but invention.

As the poet reads his work, he no longer recites it with the mastery which was demonstrated one year earlier. He reads with uneasiness, hesitation, uncertainty – 'lo leyó con visible inseguridad, omitiendo ciertos pasajes, como si él mismo no los entendiera del todo o no quisiera profanarlos'. ('He read with a visible lack of self-confidence, omitting certain passages, as if he did not completely understand them himself or did not wish to profane them.') This reading again takes place before the king and the circle of men of letters, but this time the public has disappeared. This new text, strange, surprising, no longer belongs to the order of representation but, through its invention, to that of illusion. It does not lead one to believe in the exploits of the king. It *is* these exploits, shown to the listening audience. 'No era una descripción de la batalla, era la batalla.' ('It was not a description of the battle, it was the battle.') The poem gives rise to the event itself, in its original force. *Ekphrasis* has been substituted for representation.

The poem captures and captivates its audience: 'Suspende, maravilla y deslumbra' ('It astounds, it dazzles, it causes wonderment.') It exerts an effect which the first ode failed to accomplish in spite of its formal perfection. Borges goes back, in order to characterise these effects, to the very vocabulary of the Spanish 'Golden Age' literature: 'embelesar', 'maravillar', 'encantar', a time when fiction was thought of and described as a dangerous enchantment that annuls the gap between the world of the text and the world of the reader (Ife, 1985). The poet's second ode is to be preserved, though not destined for the illiterate but, rather, only for a small company of the learned: 'Un cofre de

ROGER CHARTIER

marfil será la custodia del único ejemplar' ('An ivory casket will be the resting place of its single copy'). In return for his creation, which has the force of theatrical illusion, the poet receives a theatrical object, a golden mask, a sign of his inventiveness. Yet the king requires a work still more sublime.

Upon his return one year later, the bard brings with him an ode which is no longer written, consisting only of a single line. The bard and the king are alone. The bard utters the ode a first time, after which 'el poeta y su Rey la paladearon, como si fuera una plegaria o una blasfemia' ('the poet and his king savoured it as if it were a secret prayer or a blasphemy'). Turning everything upside down, the poem is inscribed within the order of the sacred, a prayer or a blasphemy, inhabiting the poet like an inspired word. The poet has not respected the rules; nor has he transgressed them but has been overwhelmed like the Homeric bard or the lyric poet by an inspired word: 'En el alba, me recordé diciendo unas palabras que al principio no comprendí. Esas palabras son un poema.' ('In the dawn I woke up speaking words I did not at first understand. Those words were a poem.') Thus inhabited by a language other than his own, the poet becomes other. 'Casi era otro. Algo, que no era el tiempo, había surcado y transformado sus rasgos. Los ojos parecían mirar muy lejos o haber quedado ciegos.' ('He was like another man. Something other than time had furrowed and transformed his features. His eyes seemed to stare into the distance or to be blind.')

Ollan is thus inscribed in the line of blind poets, dear to Borges. In a lecture given in 1977, *La ceguera (Blindness)*, he reminds us that it was at the very moment when he was named Director of the National Library in Buenos Aires, in 1955, that he became aware that he had lost his sight (Borges, 1980). The *Poema de los dones* (the *Poem of gifts*) begins as follows: 'Nadie rebaje a lágrimas / Esta declaración de la maestría / De Dios que con magnífica ironía / Me dio a la vez los libros y la noche' ('Let no one debase with pity or reprove / This declaration of God's mastery, / Who with magnificent irony/Gave me at once books and the night.') A librarian and blind, Borges is doubly heir: of the blind librarians who preceded him in his position at the National Library, Paul Groussac and José Marmól, and of the blind poets, inspired in their dark night – Homer, Milton, Joyce.

Murmured, the third ode is an event and not a monument. It was not written; it will not be repeated. It constitutes a unique experience, and no reading of it is possible. Its mystery leads those who utter it to forbidden contemplation. 'Sentí que había cometido un pecado, quizá el que no perdona el Espíritu'. ('I felt I had committed a sin, perhaps one the Holy Ghost does not forgive') says the poet. And the king replies: 'El que ahora compartimos los dos. El de haber conocido la Belleza, que es un don vedado a los hombres. Ahora nos toca expiarlo.' ('The one we two now share. The sin of having known Beauty, which is a gift forbidden to men. Now it behoves us to

4

Orality Lost

expiate it.') The king's third gift is thus an instrument of death: a dagger with which the poet commits suicide. The king's expiation takes another form, one appropriate for the 'great theatre of the world' where roles are ephemeral and interchangeable: 'es un mendigo que recorre los caminos de Irlanda, que fue su reino, y no ha repetido nunca el poema' ('he is a beggar wandering the length and breadth of Ireland – which was once his kingdom and he has never repeated the poem').

Borges's fable takes us from the monument to the event, from inscription to 'performance'. It designates, with the acuteness of a Cervantes, the different registers of opposition that span written culture. These have to do with aesthetic norms (imitation, invention, inspiration), modes of transmission of the text (recitation, reading aloud, saying it to oneself), the nature of the addressee (the public at large, the learned, the prince or, finally, the poet himself), and the relationship between words and things (inscribed within the order of representation, that of illusion, or that of mystery). The 'tale' of the mirror and the mask, of the poet and the king, thus provides points of reference which allow the historian to enter into the analysis of forms of production, circulation and appropriation of texts, considering as essential their variations across time, place, and community. The lesson does not fully account for the poetic optimism of Borges's text but it is perhaps faithful to what Borges wrote in a preface to *Macbeth*: 'Art happens (El arte ocurre) declaró Whistler, pero la conciencia de que no acabaremos nunca de descifrar el misterio estético no se opone al examen de los hechos que lo hicieron posible.' ('*Art happens* declared Whistler, but the idea that we will never have done with deciphering the aesthetic mystery does not stand in the way of our examination of the facts which made it possible.') (Borges, 1975b).

The opposition I made between the text 'monument' and the text 'event' was proposed by a historian of classical literature, Florence Dupont, in a book entitled *The Invention of literature. From Greek intoxication to the Latin book* (Dupont, 1994). Dupont's book serves to underscore the insufficiency of categories traditionally associated with the idea of literature as a means of accounting for the production and circulation of texts in Antiquity. What are, in fact, the fundamental notions which constitute the 'literary institution'? First of all, the identification of the text with a writing that is fixed, stabilised, and manipulable owing to its permanence. Second, the idea that the work is produced for a reader – and a reader who reads in silence, for himself and alone, even where he happens to be in a public space. Finally, the characterisation of reading as a quest for meaning, a work of interpretation, a search for signification. The fundamental genres of Greek or Roman literature show that we must distance ourselves from these three suppositions in order to

ROGER CHARTIER

understand the reasons for their production, the modalities of their performance, and the forms of their appropriation.

The ode, for example, should not be thought of as a 'literary' genre, but as
a ritual speech act which takes place in a form of religious sociability that is
essential to ancient Greece, the *symposión*, or banquet of Dionysiac drunkenness. The ode is a song addressed to the gods of the banquet, and above all to
Dionysius, as well as a song inspired by the Muses, of which the singer is but
the instrument. Far from being the result of an individual creation, the product
of a poetic art, the banquet song manifests the overpowering of the speaker by
sacred inspiration. The meaning of the text depends entirely on its ritual effectiveness. It cannot be separated from the circumstances in which the poetry is
sung since, by invoking the gods, it requires their participation in the banquet.
Irreducibly singular, the text can be neither written down nor repeated. It is a
moment of surging forth, it is mystery, it is event.

It is in Greek antiquity itself that this poetic, ritual, and singular word was
progressively transformed into 'literature'. During the festivals and competi-
tions accompanying the cults of the city-states or the great panhellenic sanc-
tuaries (such as Delphi or Epidaurus), the song inspired by the Muses
becomes a genre which has its rules and whose productions can be classified
and hierarchised.

This transformation of a ritual event into a poetic monument has considerable consequences. The most fundamental is the gap introduced between the
circumstances of actual enunciation – namely, the poetic competition which
seeks to crown literary excellence – and the fictional scene of enunciation in
the poem itself which refers back to an already vanished situation – that of the
banquet where the ode was sung for its ritual function. The primeval enunciation has become a literary fiction. The banquet which it evokes is no longer a
Dionysiac *symposión* but an imagined feast. A second effect of the transformation from ritual word into literary monument is the necessity to assign it to
an author. For this mythical authors were required and each genre became
associated with one author considered as its founder: Homer for the epic,
Anacreon for lyric poetry. The primordial author becomes as it were the guar-
antor for the genre in which new creations are inscribed. A third consequence
is the possibility (or the necessity) of elaborating a poetics that codifies the
rules. The inspired word that overwhelms the poet who conveys it, is substituted by the idea of the work as creation and as labour. That is why it is only
with lyrical poetry, Pindar or Baccylides, that the poem can for the first time
be compared to a woven textile, and art to a craft. Never in the *Iliad* or the
Odyssey is the metaphor of verbal weaving, which is used to designate con-
tests in eloquence, ever applied to the song of the poet which, after all, is not
his but the Muses' (Scheid and Svenbro, 1994).

When the production of the text is no longer attributed to the wild and

6

Orality Lost

spontaneous irruption of the sacred word, it comes to depend on the correct application and imitation of rules. This is why, according to Aristotle's *Poetics*, or at least his commentators, a tragedy ought to be judged, not on the basis of its theatrical performance, but through a reading which measures its conformity to the norm. The opposition between rules and performance as the fundamental criterion for the evaluation of works (as established in the classical *ars poetica*) provides the foundation for polemical arguments mobilised during the literary *querelles* of the seventeenth century, for example those concerning plays by Corneille (Merlin, 1994) or Lope de Vega (Lope de Vega, 1609). They oppose, in fact, the learned, who judge plays on the basis of rules and reading, and those (not least the authors themselves) who consider the effects produced on the audience during the theatrical representation to be of prime importance. Recalling in 1609 in his *Arte nuevo de hacer comedias en este tiempo*, addressed to an Academy of Men of Letters assembled in Madrid by the count of Saldaña, that he is the author of 483 'comedies', Lope de Vega adds: 'Fuera de seis, las demás todas / pecaron contra el arte gravamente. / Sustento, en fin, lo que escribí, y conozco / que, aunque fueran mejor de otra manera, / no tuvieran el gusto que han obtenido / porque a veces lo que es contra lo justo / por la misma razón deleita al gusto.' ('Except for six in fact, all without exception / have gravely sinned against the laws of the art. / No matter, I uphold what I have written and I know / that, if done otherwise, they would have been better, / but they would not have enjoyed such favour / for sometimes that which runs counter to what is right, for that very reason is what pleases the most.')

From these three features (the disjunction between the actual circumstances of the enunciation and the fictive enunciation inscribed in the text; the invention of founding authors; the formulation of an *ars poetica* stating what the rules ought to be) there follows another: the written inscription of texts which thus constitutes, by this very fact, a scholarly canon, an object of apprenticeship, and a repertoire from which to draw citations, examples, and models necessary for composing new texts. The trajectory of the Greek world thus takes us from a poetry fundamentally linked to its performance, one governed by the forms of sociability and religious rituals in which it is sung, to a poetry that is governed by the rules of the 'literary institution'. The endpoint of such a trajectory occurs during the Hellenistic period, with the constitution of the Library and the Museum of Alexandria in the third century A.D. It is at that time that the fundamental categories which structure the order of modern literary discourse, as characterised by Foucault in two famous texts, *Qu'est-ce qu'un auteur?* (*What is an Author?*) and *L'ordre du discours* (*The Order of Discourse*) (Foucault, 1969 and 1970, Chartier, 1992), were crystallised in the concept of work, with its criteria of unity, coherence, fixity; the category of author which assigns the work to a proper name; finally the commentary,

ROGER CHARTIER

identified with the work of interpretation, which brings meaning to light. The three fundamental disciplines of the 'literary institution' (philology, literary history, hermeneutics) are thus set in place at the close of a trajectory leading from 'event' to 'monument' and they find their formulation in the dream of a universal library.

Dupont offers two other examples from the Roman world. First of all, the poetic and erotic games linked to another form of banquet, not the sacred banquet which convokes the presence of the gods, but the banquet of conversations and cultivated pleasures: the *commissatio*. The evolution of poems recited during these feasts is similar to that of the lyric ode. It transforms into literature a form of entertainment whose meaning was fully linked to its circumstances. The ephemeral nature of the poetic event is substituted by written inscription, by the constitution of a repertoire, by the development of commentaries, by the reuse of citations.

The second example is to be found in the novel: *The Golden Ass* of Apuleius or *The Satyricon* by Petronius. In both cases, the question is the same: why were these collections of loosely structured stories composed for recitation fixed in writing? There is in every form of oral transmission of tales or stories a certain mobility of the text which comes from the singularity of each of its performances. The gap thus appears irreducible between written inscription which, by definition, sets things down in a fixed form and the practice of recitation which is invention, variation, movement. These features, which are valid for all Latin 'tales', are also valid for those of the modern age. Take, for example, chapter XX of the First Part of *Don Quixote* in which Sancho recounts a tale to Don Quixote (Cervantes 1605). The description shows with extraordinary acuteness, which one might define as 'ethno-sociological', the gap that separates Sancho's way of telling a story and the expectations of the reader which are those of Don Quixote's. Sancho tells his story by multiplying the repetitions, the relative clauses, the broken clauses. He constantly interrupts his story with references to the situation in which he finds himself with Don Quixote. Don Quixote, however, expects a linear narrative, without repetition, without digression. Cervantes thus stages the absolute gap which differentiates between ways of speaking and manners of reading (or of listening to a reading). Sancho tells his story the way one tells a story (*consejas*) in his village. But Don Quixote becomes impatient upon hearing this manner of telling so foreign to a reader accustomed to a text that is written, stable, fixed, linear (Moner, 1989).

The resulting tale does not belong to the canonical repertoire of literature, its cultural disqualification militating against its becoming a 'monument' like the lyric ode or the poetry of the banquets. Why then its written inscription? The question leads one to reflect on the type of reading involved and the use that can be made of collections of stories and tales. It seems that, in the case

Orality Lost

of *The Golden Ass* or *The Satyricon*, the hypothesis of individual acts of reading is implausible in relation to a genre linked so explicitly to sociability, public occasions, and the sharing of texts, as is the hypothesis of reading aloud for an audience of listeners. In Antiquity, reading out loud serves, basically, two purposes. On the one hand, a pedagogical function: demonstrating that one is a good reader by reading out loud constitutes an obligatory rite of passage for young men who thus display their mastery of rhetoric and public speaking. On the other hand, a literary purpose: to read aloud is, for an author, to put a work into circulation, to 'publish' it. This form of publication, incidentally, will survive well into the modern period, insofar as it will function, between the sixteenth and eighteenth centuries, as a primary form of circulation, before the appearance of the printed edition.

The reading of the stories from *The Golden Ass* or *The Satyricon* does not belong to either of these two categories. Stories are not part of the academic repertoire and are not considered legitimate texts. It may thus be thought that they constitute above all collections of models and *exempla* destined to produce other stories, good for the telling. To read them is to understand the rules and recipes which allow one to invent new narratives. By recording some of the stories circulating in the oral tradition, novels constitute the matrix of a new orality which is based on a series of examples which they gather together. They are like machines for producing discourses whose reading serves for the mobilisation of resources which they make available to makers of tales and stories.

This detour through Antiquity suggests several fundamental principles which might also be seen to apply to early modern times. The first defines the 'literary institution' starting with the objectification of literary expressions separated from their ritual functions and made available for pedagogy, citation, commentary. The second cautions against all forms of anachronism, that is to say, all forms of projecting as universal what are individual experiences, localised in time and space – not least, our own. Readers of Antiquity did not read an ode by Anacreon, a poem by Catullus, or the *Satyricon* as we read them. Their relationship to texts was governed by the ritual or practical efficacy of works read or heard. They were not necessarily silent or solitary readers, characterised by a hermeneutic position. Their reading remained strictly linked to orality and to ritual. Whence the importance of a history of reading devoted to recording the historicity of fundamental morphological differences: for example, between reading in silence and reading aloud, reading in solitude and reading in public, reading for oneself and reading for others, etc. (Cavallo and Chartier, 1995). The third principle reveals a trajectory from the inspired word to controlled imitation, from the singularity of the speech act to its inscription in writing, from the ephemeral of the poetic performance to the repetitiveness of reading. These displacements which

9

ROGER CHARTIER

characterise ancient literature are not without parallel in modernity. By going through the same itinerary in reverse, Ollan, Borges's Irish poet, attests to the lasting nostalgia for an orality lost.

Let us consider two major poetic genres of the sixteenth and seventeenth centuries studied from the perspective of the same question: how should one understand the relationship between their oral performance and their written inscription, whether written by hand or printed? The ballads will take us to Elizabethan England; the *romances* to the Castille of the Golden Age.

Ballads are a basic poetic and editorial genre in England from the mid-sixteenth to the mid-seventeenth century, the number of titles in circulation having been estimated at about three thousand. They are texts with a very wide diffusion owing to a low price which put them within reach of the most modest of buyers. Ballads were generally printed on a single side of a sheet, according to a regular disposition with, from top to bottom of the sheet, the title, directions for the tune to which the ballad ought to be sung, a woodcut, and the text set in two columns. These broadside ballads (the term *broadside* designating a sheet of paper printed on one side) could be pasted on a wall, in the interior of the house or in a public place, and could also circulate from hand to hand (Watt, 1991).

Broadside ballads constituted a large market, progressively won by specialised publishers, which established a quasi-monopoly on the genre. From 1624 onward, in fact, five publishers of the Stationers' Company, the *ballad partners*, take over the large-scale diffusion of printed ballads. It is during the course of the very history of the genre that its characteristics were established: the image, in the form of woodcuts, became more frequent after 1600 (we find it in five ballads out of six); the lay-out of the text also found its canonical form in the 'two-part folio sheet' in which directions for the tune to which the text is to be sung are present more often than not. On the other hand, between the mid-sixteenth and the mid-seventeenth century, a preference arises for secular at the expense of religious ballads, as if the songs found themselves progressively excluded from a legitimate religious culture, tending toward other poetic forms: psalms, for example, chanted at home or in church. Linked to a more popular and more communal culture, the ballad is excluded from the religious domain and becomes, thereby, a fundamentally secular genre.

One must begin with the very materiality of the broadside ballads in order to attempt to reconstitute how they were 'read' in the England of the sixteenth and seventeenth centuries. It is clear that the object itself provides an indication of something other than solitary and silent reading. It suggests, first of all, a reading that is done in common – posted on a wall, the ballad can be read aloud by those who, better educated, can serve as reading mediators

Orality Lost

for the less learned. The directions for the melody which figure on many of these broadsides also indicate that the text is written in order to be sung, with or without instrumental accompaniment.

According to Tessa Watt, oral performances of the ballads, when they were executed by 'professionals', might be seen to have applied within different contexts. The first was that of the professional musicians, minstrels or waits, who are often accompanied by an instrument (violin, lute, harp) and played during fairs, at markets, in taverns, on the occasion of urban festivals or in aristocratic houses. A second more theatricalised form, was provided by companies of actors, more or less professional, who inscribed the songs in 'interludes' (dramas, morality plays or histories) at country fairs and markets or in the houses of the nobility. Finally, a third mode of the oral circulation of ballads was provided by the peddlers who not only sold them, but sung them as well. Such peddlers were not professional singers but merchants who, in order to attract a clientele, sang either the text of the ballads they were peddling, or the list of goods they were selling.

In *The Winter's Tale*, Shakespeare creates a vending and ballad-singing peddler – Autolycus – who intervenes on numerous occasions during the fourth and fifth acts of the play (Shakespeare, 1611). Several features characterise him, not least his name which is that of the son of Hermes (Mercury for the Romans), a rakish and deceitful god. And, in fact, Autolycus is not simply a vendor and singer of ballads. He is also a sheet thief ('My traffic is sheets') and a pickpocket ('My revenue is the silly cheat'). In scene III of the fourth Act, he works with wiliness to steal the Clown's purse by feigning the man of property who was himself robbed by a 'rogue', about whom he sketches a funny biography – which is supposedly his own: 'he hath been since an ape-bearer, then a process-server, then he compassed a motion of the Prodigal Son, and married a tinker's wife: Some call him Autolycus'. A crafty thief, expert in the ruses of the intellect, Autolycus is also a cunning peddler whose figure Shakespeare construes out of different features which characterise the craft in Elizabethan England.

The first of these features makes of Autolycus a character of the performance, one who not only sings the ballads he sells because, as he says, 'I can bear my part; you must know 'tis my occupation' but one who also sings out the inventory of his pack as found in the two songs *Lawn as while* and *Will you buy*. The fiction here works through reference to the peddler's songs, present in other contemporary plays and later collected by folklorists. Announced by the Servant as one who peddles ballads ('he sings several tunes, faster than you'll tell money; he utters them as he had eaten ballads') and merchandise ('he sings 'em over as they were gods or goddesses'), Autolycus is a close relative of all the itinerant merchants who, like the blind peddlers of printed materials in Castille or *colporteurs* of pamphlets in Paris (those whom

ROGER CHARTIER

Pierre de L'Estoile calls *porte-paniers* or *contre-porteux*) cry out, utter, or sing the titles and the texts they proffer.

A second feature that characterises Autolycus's trade is the link between songs and haberdashery. If all that he sells as far as printed texts go are ballads, he tries to sell to the imaginary Bohemian peasants of the last two acts of *The Winter's Tale* all the objects which are to be found in the packs of the English peddlers of the seventeenth century: woven fabrics, everything necessary for sewing and embroidery, vestimentary ornaments, pieces of jewelry, perfume, as well as writing notebooks (the 'table books') (Spufford, 1984). A relation is thus established, in the plots that are knotted around Autolycus, between the ballads, which for the most part are songs of love, and all the objects which are so many presents offered by young men to young maidens in order to seduce them. The link between the ballads which speak of love and the objects which are love-tokens is at the heart of the dispute between the Clown and the peasant girl Mopsa to whom he has promised perfumed gloves and a silk ribbon ('a tawdry-lace and a pair of sweet gloves').

Autolycus 'hath songs for man or woman, of all sizes' and, among them, 'the prettiest love-songs for maids' whose proclaimed innocence is ironically given the lie by the words of the Servant, words which allude to their double meaning, rendering them licentious and ribald. Of the 'ballads in print' sold by Autolycus, Shakespeare indicates three titles, which comically play upon the genre's repertoire. The first, 'to a very doleful tune', recounts 'how a usurer's wife was brought to bed of twenty money-bags at a burden, and how she longed to eat adder's heads and toads carbonated'. The second tells the fantastic story about a young girl transformed into a fish because she refused the advances of her lover. The third is a 'merry ballad', a love song which 'goes to the tune of "Two maids wooing a man"' and in which two maidens pay court to the same young man – which, in the play, finds a parallel in the situation of the Clown who is coveted by Mopsa and Dorcas, who, in addition, sing the ballad along with Autolycus. The titles of the staged ballads are in the case of the first two at least parodic inventions, but inventions that are based on the repertoire of ballads produced at the time by London publishers, exploiting, like their French counterparts, the register of monstrous births, fantastic creatures, terrifying and exemplary punishments.

The Shakespearean text ironically dismantles the strategies employed in the ballads in order to guarantee the truth of the extraordinary narratives put forth in the songs. Autolycus multiplies, in fact, the details which lead the audience to take as true the hard-to-believe facts they narrate. The monstrous birth is attested to in writing by the midwife ('Here's the midwife's name to 't') and 'five or six honest wives that were present'. The story of the maiden transformed into a fish has 'five justices' hands at it, and witnesses more than my pack will hold'. The attraction of the genre thus appears to lie in the

Orality Lost

reader's belief in the narratives that he or she sings or hears. On a number of occasions, Mopsa and Dorcas interrogate Autolycus in order to be reassured about the truth of the stories that he is selling: 'Is it true, think you?', 'Is it true too, think you?'. The pleasure experienced during the reading or the hearing supposes that the ballads can be taken as true. But, at the same time, this desire for authenticity, just like the marks of authentification, are always parodically contradicted. The midwife who is supposed to have delivered the wife of the usurer is named 'Mistress Taleporter'. The date of the metamorphosis into a 'cold fish' of the frigid maiden is 'Wednesday the forescore of April'.

How are we to interpret this tension between the expectation of truth on the part of the buyers of ballads and the parody (which is not only Shakespearean but is also present in contemporary texts produced by London publishers) serving to situate the narratives within the order of the unbelievable? Does this tension point out the credulity of the fictional peasants on the stage who take as truth the implausible (something the clever and forewarned learned spectator refuses to do)? Or does it describe a 'popular' relation (in the sense of shared or common) to literary fiction; a relation which, at one and the same time, persuades and dissuades, makes one believe and not believe, linking together adhesion and distance?

This model of intelligibility, both subtle and complex, is one that Richard Hoggart proposes in *The Uses of Literacy* (Hoggart, 1957) in which he describes, based on his own experience, the relations working-class readers and listeners entertain in the England of the 1950s with mass circulation newspapers, magazines, horoscopes, serials, love songs. He characterises this relation by the ambiguity of attitudes, as if the necessity and the pleasure of believing shared common ground with the greatest lucidity concerning the falseness of what is believed. Logically contradictory categories are thus paradoxically associated, as if belief experienced moments of eclipse, as if the 'suspension of disbelief' did not efface clairvoyance. A similar perspective is brought into play in Paul Veyne's *Did the Greeks Believe in their Myths?*: 'Among the learned, critical credulity, so to speak, alternated with a global skepticism and it rubbed elbows with the rash credulity of the less learned – these three attitudes tolerated one another and popular credulity was not culturally devalorised. This peaceful coexistence of contradictory beliefs had an effect that was sociologically curious: each individual would interiorise the contradiction and would think concerning the myths irreconcilable things, 'irreconcilable' according to a logician at least: the particular individual, however, did not suffer from these contradictions, quite on the contrary: they each served different purposes' (Veyne, 1983). Before Hoggart, before Veyne, Shakespeare staged – with his shepherds and shepherdesses of Polixenes's Bohemia – the inseparable duality of adhesion and distance.

13

ROGER CHARTIER

There is perhaps here, as well, a way of characterising the relationship between the spectators and the play. What it recounts, in fact, is a 'winter's tale' as the title says, restated on several occasions throughout the text. Take for example the first scene of the second Act, when Hermione asks her son Mamilius to tell her a story. He replies that 'a sad tale's best for winter' and begins the narrative of the story about a man who used to live close to a ceme- tery – which will be the fate of Leontes after the death of Hermione, unjustly accused of adultery. Another example occurs in scene II of the last Act, when the marvellous story about the child who was lost and found again and about the dead queen who came back to life is compared, at one and the same time, to 'an old tale' whose truth is suspect and to a series of prodigies such that 'ballad-makers cannot be able to express it'. The play, just as implausible as the tales or the songs, is nevertheless, just like them, supposed to captivate the listener, to persuade him of its plausibility, to make him or her believe in the unbelievable. With paramount skilfulness, *The Winter's Tale* explicitly desig- nates, by assimilating the plot to an old tale, the ambivalence that any reader or spectator feels when confronted with a work of fiction: he knows about the imposture and, yet, he believes in it, for the duration of a ballad or a theatrical play. The relation of Mopsa and Dorcas to the songs by Autolycus ('Is it true, think you?') is thus transformed into a metaphor for the central theme of a play that deals with the tension between nature and art, between truth and artifice (or, better, the truth of artifice) and that also deals with the *jouissance* of those who give way to the pleasure of believing without however being duped by their belief.

The literary text can thus allow us, on condition that its 'literariness' be respected, to reconstruct something of the oral circulation of printed genres and to comprehend the relationship with texts that this particular form of communication and reception of works implies. In the case of the ballads, a supplementary step is possible, which is much rarer, to move no longer from the printed text to its oral performance, but from the editorial genre to its popular production. A large number of ballads, in fact, were not written in order to be printed, if indeed they were written; and they were composed, not by professional authors working for the publishers of the Stationers' Company, but within the confined world of the rural community (Fox, 1994). An examination of them has been possible thanks to the archives of the Star Chamber which was charged with judging all defamation lawsuits. Plaintiffs brought their cases to the tribunal if they felt that they had been slandered or insulted. In the case where an insult had taken the form of a song, the plain- tiffs had either to provide evidence in the law courts of the manuscript ballad as it had been posted on walls, or produce a *verbatim* copy of the text that had been sung or recited.

Adam Fox has worked on these 'popular' ballads, defined as 'libellous',

Orality Lost

'scandalous', 'infamous', or 'lascivious'. He has thus been able to compare, for the same genre, printed forms with spontaneous forms, either written by hand or simply oral, which are their contemporaries. We have here a fascinating piece of work which has very few equivalents owing to the fact that such popular forms (which is not to imply unlearned) have left few written traces, having been collected quite late. Consider, for example, the fairy tales whose printed versions used to circulate during the seventeenth and eighteenth centuries in the *colportage* repertoire, but whose oral versions were not knowable until after a point in time when folklorists undertook to collect them. What is unique about the case of the English ballads is the contemporaneity which exists between the printed ballads and those, simply written by hand or sung, which are conserved in the archives of the Star Chamber. The only comparable body of documents (though in a genre not codified in the same way as the ballad) is furnished by manuscript placards such as those conserved by the Archives of the *Tribunale del Governatore* (Antonucci, 1989), posted in Rome on doors as a means of ridicule or insult. As in the case of the later ballads, we encounter here the expression of a popular literature of denunciation. And, in both cases, the preoccupation of justice is to identify the authors of the defamatory texts – presupposing, in the Roman case, an expertise allowing one to trace from the written text the hand that wrote it.

Popular and spontaneous ballads were born in tavern culture. Their written inscription often required the intervention of someone who knew how to write. In their own defence, a number of the accused pointed out that they were incapable of writing, often more explicitly declaring that they were incapable of reading or writing 'the written hand'. This notation in the form of an excuse points out the difference, fundamental in the societies of the *Ancien Régime*, between the capacity to read and perhaps to form characters of printed writing (since the acquisition of reading is done with printed texts) and a more complete mastery of writing, which allows one to read handwriting and to write by hand. This dichotomy opposes, in the French language of the seventeenth century, the '*lettre moulée*' that is to say typographical characters, and 'writing' (*l'écriture*) which is handwriting. Since the school curriculum of children from the working classes often terminated with the acquisition of reading, one can suppose that the majority of them were incapable of writing and reading hand-written script. The opposition between reading and writing does not simply distinguish between two competencies; it also distinguishes between what is possible (or impossible) to read when one only knows how to read. The defence of the accused before the Star Chamber is thus not simply a skilful attempt to have the indictment dismissed. It implies a recourse to those who know how to write for the transcription of ballads that have been collectively composed – for example,

15

ROGER CHARTIER

itinerant merchants, schoolmasters, students returning to their villages, clerics – that is, intermediary 'learned men' who write for others. The delegation of writing here occurs, not within the confines of a single social rank, as is the case in contemporary Rome (Petrucci, 1989), but within a network of social practices that reunites the members of a village community.

The ballads born of tavern culture knew several forms of 'publication'. Some are linked to the oral tradition (texts are declaimed, sung by their authors or sung by professional musicians hired for this purpose); others to the placarding tradition (on the doors of churches, the walls of inns, on crosses, the pillory, etc.). Just as there was mediation in writing, so there was in reading: some people read for the others assembled around a placarded text. In both cases, the oral performance is essential for the dissemination process.

Between the accusers and the accused, the social difference is striking. The accusers belong to the world of authority and the élite: they are officers of the Crown, tax collectors, landowners, pastors, millers, tradesmen, etc. Among the accused, about half come from the lower or middle strata of English society. Consequently, the ballads give vent to a popular mode of protest which takes a poetic form and which is neither revolt nor submission to order. The ballads are inscribed within another register, that of 'local poetic mockery', as Adam Fox puts it, which points to the private existence of those who are 'balladed' and ridiculed for the unfaithfulness of their wives, their illegitimate children, or their sexual misconduct, as well as to the 'local knowledge' which is necessary to appreciate such mockery. 'Popular' ballads are thus entirely caught up within the network of tensions and conflicts characterising the communities in which they are placarded and sung.

They nevertheless also entertain relationships with the editorial genre of ballads printed for the marketplace. These relations have a double face. On the one hand, as rarely happened, London publishers had manuscript ballads retouched by a professional prior to publication. On the other hand, and in reverse manner, some manuscript ballads can be seen to adopt aspects of the printed version (thus, the layout of the text in two columns or the inclusion of directions for the tune to be played) or else adapt the text of a broadside ballad to local circumstances. But, in spite of these few borrowings, emphasis ought rather to be placed on the heterogeneity of the two repertoires – printed and spontaneous – and on the autonomy of popular poetic protest with respect to printed production. The irregularity of forms, local circulation, the particularising of the text strongly differentiate oral and manuscript ballads from the mass of texts produced by London publishers. A similar difference is to be found in the case of tales in the French tradition where significant gaps separate the oral versions, such as have been collected by folklorists, and the

Orality Lost

printed versions which, even in the repertoire of *colportage*, come out of the learned tradition (Velay-Vallantin, 1992).

The second example that I would like to propose is that of the Castillian *romances*, which also provided a highly codified poetic genre. *Romances* are poems composed in octosyllabic verse, whose even-numbered lines are assonanced, and whose origin is linked either to medieval epic poetry, that is to say, to the *chansons de geste* (of which they are fragments which had later become autonomous) or to traditional lyric poetry. Composed in order to be sung, like all epico-lyric poetry, set down in writing and then in print, the *romances* were destined to have a double circulation in the Hispanic world of the sixteenth and seventeenth centuries. Their oral circulation is attested to, at one and the same time, by their transcription both in the song-books and in music books, and by their presence in the modern tradition. Collected, then recorded by folklorists, *romances* are sung with or without accompaniment, by one singer or by several, sometimes alternating between singer and chorus, and, most frequently, using feminine voices (Romancero, 1994).

Starting from the beginning of the sixteenth century, *romances* circulated also in print, but in two very different forms. The first of these was in anthologies, collections, compilations which take the form of *cancioneros* (or collections of songs) and which comprise several scores or even hundreds of *romances*. One can say that these collections, whose series began with the *Cancionero general* of Hernando del Castillo in 1511 and which rather often carried the title of *Silva de romances*, are addressed to well-to-do readers, who belong to the world of the literate. A second form of circulation was made possible by the *pliegos sueltos*. A *pliego* is a sheet of paper, folded twice, resulting in a printed object in an in-quarto format, composed of four leaves, in eight pages. The oldest conserved *pliego* carrying a *romance* dates from 1510 and was printed in Saragosa by Jorge Coci. The *pliego* is thus a very inexpensive form of printed material, lending itself to a very wide diffusion. In the *pliego* we thus find associated a concise poetic genre and an editorial genre wholly adapted to the possibilities of Spanish printing in the sixteenth and seventeenth centuries, characterised by small workshops with a capacity for limited production but which can, with a single printing press, print between 1,250 and 1,500 copies of a sheet in one day (Cátedra and Infantes, 1983; Infantes, 1986). The success of the formula is attested to by the number of titles published in the sixteenth century (of which at least one copy of each survives): about 1,250 titles have been counted (Rodríguez Moñino, 1970).

If, in its first stage, the printed formula adjusted itself to the poetic form, one finds subsequently a reverse movement. The first repertoire of printed *romances*, that of the *romances viejos*, resulted from the choice made by publishers during the first half of the sixteenth century within the corpus of

ROGER CHARTIER

the oral and manuscript tradition in which a certain number of texts were fixed and reproduced without wide variation from one edition to another. The *romances nuevos*, which were then composed by lettered poets (Góngora, Lope de Vega) for learned readers, reused the traditional metrics of the *romancero viejo*, playing with archaisms of the language and conforming to the dimensions of the *pliego*. A similar observation can be made regarding the seventeenth century *romances de ciego*, or *de cordel*, composed for a popular public by specialised and anonymous authors, presented by those responsible for their itinerant sale – namely, blind peddlers of print (García de Enterría, 1973, Marco, 1977).

The relationship between these two generic definitions (poetic and material) is often forgotten by a literary criticism which rarely turns its attention to those forms and objects, which are the very vehicles of texts. The printed form of the *pliego* gained authority because of its correspondence to the poetic format of the *romances* drawn from medieval tradition. This form was subsequently responsible for certain constraints on the *romances nuevos* and the *romances de ciego*. With the blind *colporteurs* one once again encounters Hispanic culture's obsession with blindness. A Castillian Autolycus would surely have been blind since it was a fraternity of blindmen who held in Castile the monopoly on the sale of 'papeles públicos' defined by a late royal decree of 1739 as 'Gacetas, Almanaques, Coplas y otros papeles de devoción y diversión que no excedan de cuatro hojas' ('Gazettes, almanacs, songs and other books of devotion or diversion which do not exceed four leaves') – 'cuatro hojas', that is to say the very definition of the *pliego* in the in-quarto format (Botrel, 1993).

The social usages with which the *romances* were invested were wide-ranging, deeply penetrating the culture of the everyday thanks to their printed circulation in the form of the *pliego*. Recited or sung, they accompanied work, dances, festivals. Read, they served as manuals for the acquisition of reading. Learned by heart, they provided a repertoire of formulas and clichés that could be deployed in ordinary oral tradition. The circulation of poetic *pliegos* (caught between oral transmission, printed inscription, and a return to orality) illustrates how the same genre could, in diverse forms, be addressed to completely different publics serving a variety of uses.

Singling out the effects specific to the different modes of representation, transmission, and reception of texts allows for the anthropological, sociological, and historical understanding of works. Here it is necessary to follow the programme traced out by Pierre Bourdieu: 'S'interroger sur les conditions de possibilité de la lecture, c'est s'interroger sur les conditions sociales de possibilité des situations dans lesquelles on lit [. . .] et aussi sur les conditions sociales de production des *lectores*. Une des illusions du *lector* est celle qui

Orality Lost

consiste à oublier ses propres conditions sociales de production, à universaliser inconsciemment les conditions de possibilité de sa lecture.' (Bourdieu, 1987) ('Inquiring into the conditions of possibility of reading means inquiring into the social conditions which make possible the situations in which one reads [. . .] and inquiring also into the social conditions of production of *lectores*. One of the illusions of the *lector* is that which consists in forgetting one's own social conditions of production, and unconsciously universalising the conditions of possibility of one's own reading.') The fundamental aim of this remark consists in opposing the logic of practice – that of the performance of myths or rites – to the logic of the interpretation, and commentary, which is a logic of the order of discourse. Imposing a textual logic on rite or myth is submitting it to categories that are foreign to them. On a smaller scale and one more compatible with my own research, this remark leads one to distinguish between the oral, communal and ritual performance of texts, that obeys its own laws, and a reading of these same texts as practised by a reader who is in the position of a *lector* in search of meaning. Here we have a pertinent warning against any temptation to project our own relationship with classical texts onto that of the ancients – which would be an error similar to the one that projects 'into practices what is the function of practices for someone who studies them as something to be deciphered' (Bourdieu, 1987).

Whence, for the historian, a problem of method: how to reconstruct situations proper to the *oral* appropriation of ancient texts when these are for us, by definition, mute forms of orality? There are, it seems to me, several strategies which allow us to confront this difficulty. The first seeks to decipher in literary representations the practices of orality: recitation, song, reading aloud, etc. It is therefore a question of constituting the corpus of these silent forms of orality which certain texts represent through the fiction of writing. This is the case with the tale told by Sancho or the ballads sung by Autolycus. It is also the case with other texts – for example, in chapter V of the *Rustical Sayings* (*Propos rustiques*) of Noël du Fail that stage the way in which a rich peasant, Robin Chevet, recounts some old folk tales before his assembled household (Du Fail, 1548). The features that Du Fail retains in order to characterise this recitation are the very ones that Cervantes uses in order to qualify the manner with which Sancho tells his *consejas* – thus the appeals to the audience, the digressions, the parenthetical remarks, the repetitions, etc. This first path of inquiry is in no way to be understood as reducing the text to a documentary status, but it does take into account the fact that the literary representations of the practices of orality designate (while displacing them onto the register of fiction) the specific procedures that govern them (Chartier, 1980).

The second mode of inquiry seeks to collect in the works themselves the 'indicators of orality' such as they have been defined by Paul Zumthor: 'By

ROGER CHARTIER

indicator of orality, I mean anything that, within the text, informs us about the intervention of the human voice in its *publication*, I mean in the mutations through which the text passed, once or many times, from a virtual state to its current form and henceforth existed in the mind and the memory of a certain number of individuals' (Zumthor, 1987). These indicators of orality, deposited within texts, are not representations of oral practices, but implicit or explicit devices that destine texts to addressees who read aloud or listen to a text being read. They may be indisputable, just as when a musical notation indicates that a text is to be sung. They may be simply probable, as in the case of texts that are addressed to a double audience: those who will read and those who will listen to the text being read to them. In all European languages, a couple of verb pairs mark this double reception: *to read* and *to hear*, *ver* and *oír* or *leer* and *escuchar*, *voir* and *écouter*. Prologues, notices to the reader, and chapter titles very frequently indicate this double nature of address and double circulation of the text (Frenk, 1981).

Other indicators, inscribed within the formal structure of works, may equally suggest the oral destination of texts. A number of works, starting with the greatest, such as *Don Quixote*, are organised in short chapters, perfectly adapted to the necessities of 'oral performance', assuming a limited time of delivery in order not to tire the audience and to account for the audience's inability to memorise an overly complex plot. Brief chapters, which are so many textual units, can be considered units of reading, closed in upon themselves and separate. William Nelson has thus demonstrated how the rewriting of certain works (the *Amadigi* by Bernardo Tasso or the *Arcadia* by Spenser) can be understood as the adjustment of the work to the constraints of reading aloud at a time when this practice was a major form of lettered sociability (Nelson, 1976/77). The division of the text into shorter units, the multiplication of autonomous episodes, and the simplification of the plot are all indicators of the adaptation of the work to a modality essential to its transmission. This is doubtless the case for a number of older verse or prose works – in particular, the collections of short stories where a staged fictive enunciation (which imagines the reunion of several storytellers within an enclosed space) possibly coincides with the real conditions of its circulation (through reading out loud).

A last line of inquiry is more technical and more specific. It is devoted to the transformations of punctuation beginning with the hypothesis of the passage from a punctuation of oralisation to a grammatical punctuation or, as William Nelson writes, from mutation (which according to him dates from the end of 'the late seventeenth century') such that elocutionary punctuation indicative of pauses and pitches was then largely supplanted by syntactic punctuation. Verifying such a hypothesis poses a preliminary difficulty: to whom should one attribute the orthographic and graphic forms of ancient editions? According to diverse traditions of study, the answer varies widely.

20

Orality Lost

In the context of analytical bibliography, graphic and orthographic choices are the doing of compositors. The compositors of ancient printing workshops did not share a consensus in matters of spelling and punctuation. Whence the regular recurrence of the same forms in the various quires of a book, according to preferences of orthography, punctuation, or layout of the compositor who set the pages of the different formes. It is the reason why 'spelling analysis' and 'compositor studies' which allows one to attribute the composition of such and such a sheet or a forme to such and such a compositor constitutes, with the analysis of damaged types and ornaments, one of the surest means to reconstruct the very process of the making of a book, by formes or *seriatim* (McKenzie, 1959, Hinman, 1963, Flores, 1975, Tanselle, 1981, Veyrin-Forrer, 1989). In this line of inquiry, based on the study of the materiality of printed works, punctuation is considered, in the manner of graphic or orthographic variations, as the result, not of the will of the author who wrote the text, but of the habits of the compositors who composed the printed book.

From another perspective, that of the philological history of language, the essential role is played out elsewhere: in the preparation of the manuscript for composition as practiced by the '*corrector*', that is to say the copy editor who adds capitals, accents, and punctuation marks and who thus standardises the spelling and establishes graphic conventions. If they remain the result of a work linked with the printing house, choices relative to punctuation are no longer here assigned to the compositors, but to the humanists (clerics, university graduates, schoolmasters, etc.) employed by publishers and printers in order to assure the greatest possible correctness of their editions. Paolo Trovato has reminded us how important it was, for the advertising of a new book in *cinquecento* Italy to emphasise the exactitude of its 'correctness' (Trovato, 1991). Whence the decisive role of the copy editors whose interventions are spread out over several stages of the publishing process: the preparation of the manuscript, the stop-press corrections made during the printing process, the proofreading, the compilation of *errata* in their diverse forms (corrections made in ink on each printed copy, loose leaves which encourage the reader to make the corrections himself on his own copy, or pages of *errata* added at the end of the book).

The role of copy editors and proofreaders in the graphic and orthographic fixation of the vernacular tongues was far more decisive than the propositions for the reform of orthography advanced by those writers who wanted to impose an 'oral writing', entirely governed by pronunciation (Catach, 1968). There is, for example, a wide gap between the moderation of the solutions chosen for the printed editions and the boldness of the 'reforms' suggested by the authors of the Pléiade. Ronsard, for example, in his *Short History of French Poetic Art (Abrégé de l'Art poétique françois)*, proposes doing away

ROGER CHARTIER

with 'all superfluous orthography' (that is to say, all the letters that are not pronounced), transforming the written appearance of words so that they would be closer to the manner in which they are spoken (as is the case with '*roze*', '*kalité*', '*Franse*', '*langaje*' etc. – thus rendering the q and the c useless), and introducing letters in imitation of the Spanish like ll or ñ so as to correctly pronounce 'orgueilleux' or 'Monseigneur' (Ronsard, 1565). In the advice that he addresses to the reader as a preface to the first four books of the *Franciade*, Ronsard directly links punctuation marks and reading: 'Je te supliray seulement d'une chose, Lecteur: de vouloir bien prononcer mes vers et accomoder ta voix à leur passion, et non comme quelques uns les lisent, plutost à la façon d'une missive, ou de quelques lettres Royaux, que d'un Poëme bien prononcé; et te suplie encore derechef, où tu verras cette marque *!* vouloir un peu eslever ta voix pour donner grace à ce que tu liras' ('I will ask of you but one thing, Reader: to pronounce carefully my poetry and to accommodate your voice to its passion, and not as some read them, more in the manner of a letter or some Royal missive than of a well-read poem- and I also ask you once again that where you see this mark ! to raise your voice a little so as to give grace to what you are reading') (Ronsard, 1572).

Far from such radical propositions, the practice of publishers and printers, if they preserve some link with oralisation, tends to limit innovation in regard to the determination of the length of pauses. Here, the fundamental text is that of the printer (and author) Etienne Dolet, entitled *La Punctuation de la langue françoise* (reproduced in Catach, 1968). He defines in 1540 the new typographical conventions which were to distinguish, according to the length of the interruption or its position in the sentence, the '*point à queue* or comma', the 'comma' (or semi-colon), 'which is placed in a suspended sentence and not at all at the endpoint', and the 'round point' (or period) which 'is always placed at the end of the sentence'. Language dictionaries at the end of the seventeenth century record both the efficiency of the system proposed by Dolet (enriched by the colon which indicates a pause of intermediate duration between that of the comma and the semi-colon) and the distance established between the reader's voice and punctuation, considered heretofore, according to the terminology of Furetière's dictionary, to be a 'grammatical observation' marking the logical divisions of discourse. Exemplary passages from the same dictionary by Furetière, published in 1690, include: 'Ce Correcteur d'Imprimerie entend fort bien la ponctuation' ('This copy editor understands punctuation perfectly well') and 'L'exactitude de cet Auteur va jusques là qu'il prend soin des points et des virgules' ('This author is exact to the point of paying attention to periods and commas'). If the first example normally assigns punctuation to the technical skills proper to the copy editors and proofreaders employed by the printers, the second example implicitly refers back to a common lack of interest on the part of authors concerning punctuation.

Orality Lost

Furetière points out, nevertheless, that there are authors who are attentive to the punctuation of their texts. Is it possible to find traces of this *'exactitude'* in the printed editions of their works? Let us take the case of Molière. It would be very risky to attribute to him in too direct a manner the punctuation choices such as are to be found in the original editions of his plays, since, as has been shown for the 1660 edition of *Les Précieuses Ridicules*, punctuation varies from sheet to sheet, even from forme to forme, according to the preferences of different compositors (Veyrin-Ferrer, 1987). And yet, the different usages of punctuation that exist between the first editions of the plays, published shortly after their first Parisian productions, and the later editions allow one to reconstruct, if not the author's 'intention', at least the circumstances of the implied destination of the printed text.

Molière's reticence concerning the printed publication of his plays is well-known (Zanger, 1988). Before *Les Précieuses Ridicules* and the necessity of acquiring an advance on the publication of the text by Somaize and Ribou, a text made from a pirated copy and under cover of a privilege obtained by surprise, never had Molière sent any of his plays to the printers. There were financial reasons for this fact since, once published, a play could be staged by any theatrical troupe; but there were aesthetic reasons also. For Molière, in fact, the theatrical effects of the play depend entirely on the 'action', that is to say on performance. The address to the reader which opens the edition of *L'Amour médecin*, produced at Versailles, then at the Theatre of the Palais Royal in 1665, and published the following year, underscores the gap that exists between the spectacle and the reading: 'Il n'est pas nécessaire de vous avertir qu'il y a beaucoup de choses qui dépendent de l'action: on sait bien que les comédies ne sont faites que pour être jouées; et je ne conseille de lire celle-ci qu'aux personnes qui ont des yeux pour découvrir dans la lecture tout le jeu du théâtre'. ('There's no need to tell you that there are several Things in it which depend upon the Action. 'Tis generally known that Comedies are only writ to be Acted; and I won't have no Body read this but such as have Eyes to discover the Acting in the Reading of it.') (Molière, 1666). Punctuation is one of the possible devices (along with the image and stage directions) that allow for the restoration of something of the *'action'* to the printed text and its reading.

Systematically compared to the punctuation adopted in the later editions (not only in the nineteenth century but also as early as the eighteenth and late seventeenth centuries), the punctuation of the first editions of Molière's plays clearly attests to its link with orality, either insofar as it destines the printed text for reading aloud or for recitation, or in that it permits the readers who will read it in silence to reconstruct, for themselves, the timing and the pauses in the play of the actors. The passage from one form of punctuation to another has more than a little effect on the very meaning of the works (Hall, 1983). On the one hand, the original punctuation marks, always more numerous,

Roger Chartier

portray the characters in different ways – thus the comma, present in the 1669 edition yet suppressed thereafter, following the first word ('Fat') in this line of verse from *Tartuffe*: 'Gros, et gras, le teint frais, et la bouche vermeille' ('Stout, and fat, with blooming cheeks and ruddy lips') (Act I, scene 4, line 233), or the accumulation of commas and capitals in order to distinguish the Master of Philosophy's way of speaking from that of the Master of Danse in *Le Bourgeois Gentilhomme* (Act II, scene 3). On the other hand, the punctuation marks of the original editions give the reader the time needed for reconstituting or imagining the play of the actors. For example, in the scene of the portraits from *Le Misanthrope* (Act II, scene 4, lines 586–594), the 1667 edition contains six commas more than modern editions, which allows Célimène to emphasise some words, to introduce pauses, and to elaborate upon the mimicry. Finally, these original punctuation marks throw into relief those words which are charged with a particular signification. While the last two verses of *Tartuffe* do not contain any comma in the modern editions, this is not so in the edition of 1669: 'Et par un doux hymen, couronner en Valère, / La flamme d'un Amant généreux, & sincère' ('And, with my daughter's hand, reward Valère / For this, a love both generous, and sincere'). The last word of the play, 'sincere', is thus clearly designated as the antonym of the word who figures in the title, *Le Tartuffe, ou l'Imposteur* (The Impostor). These abundant punctuation marks, which point out certain pauses that are more numerous and, generally, longer than those retained in later editions, inform readers how they should say (or read) the lines of verse and give emphasis to a certain number of words, endowed with capital printed letters which have generally been suppressed with the commas in the later printed editions.

The inquiry which I have sketched here raises several problems of a general nature. The first is that of dating the passage from rhetorical punctuation to grammatical punctuation. Is this passage organised around a single chronological trajectory wherein a decisive moment would be constituted by the end of the seventeenth century? Does it obey different rhythms depending on the genre? Or even, according to the hypothesis formulated by Philip Gaskell with regard to the 'maske' of Milton's *Comus* (Gaskell, 1978), should we not trace these variations back to the diverse destinations, contemporary to one another, of the same text?

A second problem: that of the reasons and mechanisms that convey attempts at the restoration of the punctuation marks of oralisation during the eighteenth century. The case of Benjamin Franklin would be, from this point of view, exemplary. By imagining the diverse devices that would allow one to uphold the role of the public orator in the midst of a dispersed population, Franklin strives to reconcile the new definition of public and political space, which has the dimensions of a vast republic, with the traditional forcefulness

Orality Lost

of a live speech, addressed to an assembled citizenry (Melish, 1992). On the one hand, Franklin invites authors of 'public discourses', in their writings, to make use of genres most directly linked to orality: proverbs, dialogues, and letters (which belong to the oratory genre). On the other hand, the apprenticeship of reading aloud, which points out the duration of pauses and voice pitches, should become a fundamental element of the school curriculum. Finally, a reform of typographical conventions should make the oralisation of texts easier thanks to an 'expressive typography' that plays with italics, capital letters added to certain words, or new punctuation marks (for example, with the introduction into English of the inverted exclamation point or inverted question mark, proper to Spanish and which, placed at the beginning of a sentence, point out from the outset how one is to pitch one's voice). By mobilising these resources which he knew quite well from his own experience as a printer, Franklin brings printed discourse as closely as possible in line with oratorical performance and, by the same token, allows different orators to reproduce in identical fashion, and in different places, the original discourse. Thanks to reading out loud, thanks to 'expressive typography', the discourse of the 'publick Orator' will be reproduced as if it was 'present' in its very absence. In a manner contrary to Condorcet or Malesherbes, who were distrustful of the passions and emotions engendered by oratory rhetoric, and, because of this, full of praise for Gutenberg's invention, Franklin thinks it possible to surmount an apparently insoluble contradiction: how is one to organise around speech a public space which would not necessarily be enclosed within the confines of Antiquity's city-state?

'If we offend, it is with our good will. / That you should think, we come not to offend, / But with good will. To show our simple skill, / That is the true beginning of our end' (Shakespeare, 1600). The faulty pronunciation followed by Quince makes him say, in the prologue of the 'Comedy of Pyramus and Thisbe', the very opposite of what he would like to say – and what it would have been suitable to say. The play of faulty punctuation, which reverses the very meaning of the text, is played out on several occasions in Elizabethan literature. It indicates that the construction of meaning of texts depends on the forms which govern their inscription and their transmission (Chartier, 1994 and 1995). Against every critical approach that considers the materiality of texts and the circumstances of their performance to be without importance, Quince the clumsy reminds us that identifying the effects of meaning produced by forms (whether they be written, printed, or oral) is a necessity in order to understand, in their full historicity, the diverse appropriations of texts, whether literary or otherwise.

ROGER CHARTIER

BIBLIOGRAPHICAL REFERENCES

ANTONUCCI, Laura, 1989, 'La Scrittura giudicata. Perizie grafiche in processi romani del primo Seicento', *Scrittura e Civiltà* 13, pp. 491–534.

BORGES, Jorge Luis, 1975a, 'El espejo y la máscara', *El Libro de arena*, Buenos Aires, Emecé Editores.

BORGES, Jorge Luis, 1975b, 'William Shakespeare, Macbeth', *Prólogos con un prólogo de los prólogos*, Buenos Aires, Torres Aguero Editor, 1975, pp. 142–147.

BORGES, Jorge Luis, 1980, 'La Ceguera', *Siete Noches*, México, Fundo de Cultura Económica.

BOURDIEU, Pierre, 'Lecture, lecteurs, lettrés, littérature', *Choses dites*, Paris, Editions de Minuit, pp. 132–143.

BOTREL, Jean-François, 1993, *Libros, prensa y lectura en la España del siglo XIX*, Madrid, Fundación Germán Sánchez Ruipérez.

CATACH, Nina, 1968, *L'Orthographe française à l'époque de la Renaissance (auteurs, imprimeurs, ateliers d'imprimerie)*, Genève, Librairie Droz.

CATEDRA, Pedro et INFANTES, Victor, 1983, 'Estudio', *Los pliegos sueltos de Thomas Croft (siglo XVI)*, Valencia, Primus Calamus, Albatros ediciones, pp. 11–48.

CAVALLO, Guglielmo et CHARTIER, Roger (ed.), 1995, *Storia della lettura nel mondo occidentale*, Roma-Bari, Editori Laterza.

CERVANTES, Miguel de, 1605, *El Ingenioso Hidalgo Don Quijote de la Mancha*, Edición de John Jay Allen, Madrid, Cátedra, 1984.

CHARTIER, Roger, 1980, 'Loisir et sociabilité : lire à haute voix dans l'Europe moderne', *Littératures classiques*, 'La voix au XVIIe siècle', Patrick Dandrey (ed.), 12, pp. 127–147.

CHARTIER, Roger, 1992, *L'Ordre des livres. Lecteurs, auteurs, bibliothèques en Europe entre le XIVe et le XVIIIe siècle*, Aix-en-Provence, Alinéa.

CHARTIER, Roger, 1994, 'George Dandin, ou le social en représentation', *Annales. Histoire, Sciences Sociales*, mars-avril, no 2, pp. 277–309.

CHARTIER, Roger, 1995, *Forms and Meanings. Texts, Performances, and Audiences from Codex to Computer*, Philadelphia, The University of Pennsylvania Press.

DU FAIL, Noël, 1548, *Propos rustiques*, in *Conteurs français du XVIe siècle*, Paris, N.R.F., Bibliothèque de la Pléiade, 1965.

DUPONT, Florence, 1994, *L'Invention de la littérature. De l'ivresse grecque au livre latin*, Paris, La Découverte.

FLORES, R.M., 1975, *The Composition of the First and Second Madrid Editions of Don Quixote, Part I*, London, The Modern Humanities Research Association.

FOUCAULT, Michel, 1969, 'Qu'est-ce qu'un auteur?', *Bulletin de la Société française de Philosophie*, t. LXIV, juillet-septembre, pp. 73–104 (reprinted in *Dits et Ecrits 1954–1988*, Edition établie sous la direction de Daniel Defert et François Ewald avec la collaboration de Jacques Lagrange, Paris, Gallimard, 1994, *Tome I, 1954–1969*, pp. 789–821).

FOUCAULT, Michel, 1970, *L'Ordre du discours*, Paris, Gallimard.

FOX, Adam, 1994, 'Ballads, Libels and Popular Ridicule in Jacobean England', *Past and Present*, 145, pp. 47–83.

FRENK, Margit, 1981, '"Lectores y oídores". La difusión oral de la literatura en el Siglo de Oro', *Actas del Septimo Congreso de la Asociación Internacional de Hispanistas*, celebrado en Venecia del 25 al 30 de agosto de 1980, Giuseppe Bellini ed., Roma, Bulzoni Editore, Vol. I, pp. 101–123.

GARCÍA DE ENTERRÍA, María Cruz, 1973, *Sociedad y poesía de cordel en el Barroco*, Madrid, Taurus.

HALL, Gaston H., 1983, 'Ponctuation et dramaturgic chez Molière', *La Bibliographie matérielle*, présentée par Roger Laufer, table ronde organisée pour le CNRS par Jacques Petit, Paris, Editions du CNRS, pp. 125–141.

Orality Lost

HINMAN, Charlton, 1963, *The Printing and Proof-Reading of the First Folio of Shakespeare*, Oxford, Clarendon Press.

HOGGART, Richard, 1957, *The Uses of Literacy: Aspects of Working-Class Life with Special Reference to Publications and Entertainments*, London, Chatto and Windus.

IFE, B.W., 1985, *Reading and Fiction in Golden-Age Spain. A Platonist critique and some picaresque replies*, Cambridge, Cambridge University Press.

INFANTES, Víctor, 1992, 'Los pliegos sueltos poéticos : constitución tipográfica y contenido literario (1482–1600)', *En el Siglo de Oro. Estudios y textos de literatura aurea*, Potomac, Maryland, Scripta humanistica, pp. 47–58.

LOPE DE VEGA, 1609, *Arte nuevo de hacer comedias en este tiempo*, in *Lope de Vega Esencial*, Edición de Felipe Pedraza, Madrid, Esenciales Taurus, 1990, pp. 124–134.

McKENZIE, D.F., 1959, 'Compositor B's Role in the "Merchant of Venice" Q2 (1619)', *Studies in Bibliography*, 12, pp. 75–89.

MARCO, Joaquín, 1977, *Literatura popular en España en los siglos XVIII y XIX. Una aproximación a los pliegos de cordel)*, Madrid, Taurus.

MELISH, Jacob, 1992, *As Your Newspaper was Reading. La culture de la voix, la sphère publique et la politique de l'alphabétisation : le monde de la construction de limprimé de Benjamin Franklin*, mémoire de D.E.A., Paris, Ecole des Hautes Etudes en Sciences Sociales, dact.

MERLIN, Hélène, 1994, *Public et littérature en France au XVIIe siècle*, Paris, Les Belles Lettres.

MOLIERE, *L'Amour Médecin*, in *Oeuvres complètes*, Paris, N.R.F., Bibliothèque de la Pléiade, 1971, tome II, pp. 87–120.

MONER, Michel, *Cervantès conteur. Ecrits et paroles*, Madrid, Bibliorhèque de la Casa de Velazquez, 1989.

NELSON, William, 1976/77, 'From «Listen, Lording» to «Dear Readers»', *University of Toronto Quarterly. A Canadian Journal of the Humanities*, Volume XLVI, Number 2, pp. 110–124.

PETRUCCI, Armando, 1989, 'Scrivere per gli altri', *Scrittura e Civiltá*, 13, pp. 475–487.

RODRIGUEZ MOÑINO, Antonio, 1970, *Diccionario bibliogriáfico de pliegos sueltos poéticos (siglo XVI)*, Madrid, Castalia.

Romancero, 1994, Edición, prólogo y notas de Paloma Díaz-Mas, con un estudio preliminar de Samuel G. Armistead, Barcelona, Crítica.

RONSARD, 1565, *Abrégé de l'Art poétique françois*, in *Oeuvres complètes*, Paris, N.R.F., Bibliothèque de la Pléiade, tome II, pp. 995–1009.

RONSARD, 1572, *Les Quatre premiers livres de la Franciade. Au lecteur*, in *Oeuvres complètes*, op. cit., tome II, pp. 1009–1013.

SCHEID, John, and SVENBRO, Jesper, 1994, *Le métier de Zeus. Mythe du tissage et du tissu dans le monde gréco-romain*, Paris, Editions La Découverte.

SHAKESPEARE, William, 1600, *A Midsummer Night's Dream*, Edited by Harold F. Brooks, London and New York, Routledge, The Arden Edition of the Works of William Shakespeare, 1979, reprinted 1993.

SHAKESPEARE, William, 1611, *The Winter's Tale*, Edited by J.H.P. Pafford, London and New York, Routledge, The Arden Edition of the Works of William Shakespeare, 1963, reprinted 1994.

SPUFFORD, Margaret, 1984, *The Great Reclothing of Rural England: Petty Chapmen and their Wares in the Seventeenth Century*, London, The Hambledon Press.

TANSELLE, Thomas G., 1981, 'Analytical Bibliography and Renaissance Printing History', *Printing History*, Volume 3, Number 1, pp. 24–33.

TROVATO, Paolo, 1991, *Con ogni diligenza corretto. La stampa e le revisioni editoriali dei testi letterari italiani (1470–1570)*, Bologna, Il Mulino.

VELAY-VALLANTIN, Catherine, 1992, *Histoire des contes*, Paris, Fayard.

VEYRIN-FORRER, Jeanne, 'A la recherche des Précieuses', in *La lettre et le texte. Trente années de*

Roger Chartier

recherches sur l'histoire du livre, Paris, Collection de l'Ecole Normale Supérieure de Jeunes Filles, pp. 338–366.

VEYRIN-FORRER, Jeanne, 1989, 'Fabriquer un livre au XVIe siècle', *Histoire de l'Edition française*, Roger Chartier and Henri-Jean Martin (ed.), tome 1, *Le Livre conquérant Du Moyen Age au milieu du XVIIe siècle*, Paris, Fayard/Cercle de la Librairie, pp. 336–369.

VEYNE, Paul, 1983, *Les Grecs ont-ils cru à leurs mythes ? Essai sur l'imagination constituante*, Paris, Editions du Seuil.

WATT, Tessa, 1991, *Cheap Print and Popular Piety. 1550–1640*, Cambridge, Cambridge University Press.

ZANGER, Abby E., 1988, 'Paralyzing Performance : Sacrificing Theater on the Altar of Publication' *Stanford French Review*, Fall–Winter, pp. 169–185.

ZUMTHOR, Paul, 1987, *La Lettre et la voix. De la 'littérature médiévale'*, Paris, Editions du Seuil.

Part III
Practice

[9]

A Trade Union in Sixteenth-Century France[1]

By NATALIE ZEMON DAVIS

I

Labour agitation among European artisans goes back at least to the thirteenth century. Not only workers in the wholesale textile trades, but also the journeymen of cordwainers and saddlers, of skinners and tanners, even of cobblers and bakers, plotted together for higher wages and better conditions.[2] Yet details about these clandestine coalitions – their organization, their ritual, and their tactics – have been hard to come by. We know of them mostly from the masters' complaints and from governmental edicts forbidding them. Royal and city officials thought of journeymen's organizations as 'monopolies', as unjust in their efforts to force up wages as merchants who forced up the price of grain by hoarding it. To be sure, there are examples – especially in England – of open journeymen's guilds; and there are examples – especially in France – of open journeymen's confraternities. But their statutes are not very informative, for they include the legal religious and charitable activities, and disingenuously omit oaths and special agreements about wages or strikes.[3]

Until now, documents from the seventeenth century have been the earliest to reveal the dark secrets of the journeymen's organizations. Especially useful has been the testimony of a repentant ex-journeyman before the Faculty of Theology of the University of Paris in 1655.[4] Recently, however, I was lucky enough to come upon some documents giving a similarly detailed picture for the sixteenth century. Described there was the Company, as its members called it, of the printers' journeymen of Lyons. The source was a group of 18 journeymen from Lyons, testifying, not always so repentantly, before the Consistory and lieutenants of Protestant Geneva.[5]

[1] This is a slightly enlarged version of a paper presented on 10 June 1965 to the Canadian Political Science Association. The author is grateful to the American Association of University Women and the American Philosophical Society for grants which aided this research.
[2] G. Fagniez, *Etudes sur l'industrie et la classe industrielle à Paris au XIIIe et au XIVe siècle* (Paris, 1877), p. 76 and p. 76, n. 3; E. Levasseur, *Histoire des classes ouvrières et de l'industrie en France avant 1789* (2nd ed. Paris, 1900), I, 310–11, 314–15, 599–602; G. Unwin, *Industrial Organization in the Sixteenth and Seventeenth Centuries* (2nd ed. 1963), pp. 48–51; E. Lipson, *The Economic History of England* (12th ed. 1962), I, 393 ff.
[3] Lipson, *op. cit.* I, 401–2; Levasseur, *op. cit.* I, 399.
[4] *Ibid.* pp. 602–3 and, for the text of the testimony before the Faculty of Theology, pp. 703–7; E. Martin Saint-Léon, *Le compagnonnage, son histoire, ses coutumes, ses règlements et ses rites* (Paris, 1901), pp. 40–42; H. Hauser, 'Les compagnonnages d'arts et mériers à Dijon aux XVIIe et XVIIIe siècles', *Revue Bourguignonne*, XVII (1907, no. 4), 73–130. The 'MS. Constitutions of Masonry' of around 1400, described so well by D. Knoop and G. P. Jones (*The Genesis of Freemasonry* [Manchester, 1947]), apply to an organization which embraced masters *and* journeymen.
[5] These sources are described fully in my forthcoming book *Strikes and Salvation at Lyons, The Printers' Journeymen during the Reformation*. The sources are: Procès criminels de Genève, 1306, 1307, 1397 and Registres du Consistoire du Genève, vol. 24 (1567), 10r, 13r, 28v. Over a hundred years ago, E. H.

That such an organization existed among the printers' journeymen comes as no surprise. After all, the most celebrated strikes of sixteenth-century France were those which the printers' journeymen of Paris and Lyons carried on against their masters in 1539 and 1570. In a fine description of these events, written more than sixty-five years ago, Henri Hauser gave a brief sketch of what the organization behind them must have been like. Though not all of his predictions are borne out by the new evidence, the legal briefs and governmental hearings which he and later scholars have analysed show the public face and ideals of the group whose private face and values I have uncovered.[1]

Using all of this material together with information about the lives of many individual printers' journeymen, I want to present here the Company of the Griffarins. Since it is not necessarily a *typical* early trade union, I will make some suggestions about the extent to which it resembled the earlier and con-temporary workers' coalitions. I will also compare it to the highly developed *compagnonnages* of the seventeenth and eighteenth centuries – where, however, most of our information concerns other industries than printing.[2] When I am describing the Company of the Griffarins itself, I will ordinarily be talking about the period before 1573, because I want to hold certain factors constant. Before 1567 there was no prolonged serious economic crisis in printing in Lyons; by 1573 the industry was clearly in trouble.[3] Before 1573 publishers and master printers sided together against the journeymen; afterwards it was more of a three-way fight, with workers sometimes siding with masters against the publishers.[4] Before that date, Protestantism had won the support of the large majority of men in the Lyons publishing industry; whereas the journeymen began around 1566 to return to the Mother Church and after 1572 were a primarily Catholic group.[5]

Gaullieur gave a garbled reading of a few of the sentences in the Registres, 10r (*Etudes sur la typographie genevoise du XVe au XIXe siècle* [Geneva, 1855], p. 196, n. 1).

[1] H. Hauser, *Ouvriers du temps passé* (5th ed. Paris, 1927), ch. X. Among other descriptions since Hauser's first edition of 1899 are Marius Audin, 'Les grèves dans l'imprimerie à Lyon au seizième siècle', *Gutenberg-Jahrbuch* (1935), pp. 172–90, and D. Pottinger, *The French Book Trade in the Ancien Regime, 1500–1791* (Cambridge, Mass. 1958), pp. 262–8. L. Michon and Paul Chauvet have discovered further documents on the strikes; these are described in Chauvet's important work *Les Ouvriers du livre en France des origines à la Révolution de 1789* (Paris, 1959), ch. I.

[2] Chauvet, *ibid.* pp. 220–30, gives valuable information about the agitation of the Lyons printers' journeymen in the seventeenth and eighteenth centuries. Since no documents have been discovered on the rites and internal organization of the journeymen's Company at that date, we cannot know as yet to what extent it evolved along the lines of the later *compagnonnages*. On the other hand, Joseph Moxon's *Mechanick Exercises* of 1683–4 has preserved the rules and customs of a somewhat different kind of organization – the 'chapel' or individual shop organization of the London printers' journeymen (*Mechanick Exercises on the whole Art of Printing*, ed. H. Davis and H. Carter [2nd ed. 1962], pp. 323–9). Though sometimes negotiating disputes between the master and the individual shop, and having the mutual aid function, the chapel was not involved in industry-wide tactics of economic resistance (*ibid.* pp. 383–5).

[3] The first religious war, 1562–3, during which the king removed Lyons fairs to Chalons-sur-Saône, had a much more serious effect on luxury industries like silk than it did on book sales.

[4] After 1570 some Lyons publishers turned to printing *ateliers* in Geneva and elsewhere for cheaper rates. Lyons masters and journeymen joined together to oppose this.

[5] This is the subject of my forthcoming book, *Strikes and Salvation in Lyons*. The evidence is summarized in my article of the same title, appearing in the *Archiv für Reformationsgeschichte*, vol. 56 (no. 1, 1965), pp. 48–64.

50 NATALIE ZEMON DAVIS

Lyons' first press was set up in 1473. Seventy years later there were surely more than a hundred, with about 1,000 men involved in all levels of the industry.[1]

Everything was propitious for its expansion: Lyons' growing and cosmopolitan population, her four international fairs each year, religious and intellectual ferment which was increasing the demand for books. Nor were there guilds placing obstacles in the way of enterprising men. Lyons had long been a city of 'free work' (*travail libre*) – that is, a city in which no fee or masterpiece or guild membership was required of artisan or entrepreneur. If you had the capital, you could open up the shop. What *corporations* existed – and printing and book-selling had none until 1567 – were loose affairs, used by the Consulate for political purposes.[2] Such freedom also had its advantages for journeymen's coalitions. In fourteenth-century Florence, for instance, all men in the woollen industry had to be sworn members of the Arte della Lana, which was run by capitalist entrepreneurs. Thus, whenever journeymen carders or even master dyers wanted to set up a protective organization of their own, there were two authorities to crack down on them – the guild and the government.[3] In Lyons the printers' journeymen had only to trick the latter, and they were sometimes able to get away with murder – literally.

The printing industry was dominated by the great merchant-publishers of Lyons, who financed the printing of books without owning a shop or presses, and who then marketed the books throughout Europe. Rich and honoured, they sat on the town Consulate.

Up to about 1572, however, they had not yet squeezed out the independent publisher-printers. These were master craftsmen with enough capital to own and supply up to five or six presses and employ up to 25 workers and enough administrative skill to print and sell their own books. Most master printers had more modest establishments – one, maybe two presses, which they hoped that orders from the merchant-publishers would keep busy.

All the master printers seem to have felt that their margin of profit was too small. They could not blame their troubles on hard times, for the market was expanding. They might have blamed the merchant-publishers, who were winning the royal privileges to publish the really lucrative editions and who sometimes paid masters a penny for a printed page which they later sold for five.[4] For various reasons, however, up to the 1570's the masters stood

[1] The standard source is H. and J. Baudrier, *Bibliographie lyonnaise. Recherche sur les imprimeurs . . . de Lyon au XVI siècle* (12 vols. Lyons, 1895–1921) and *Tables* (2 vols. Geneva, 1950, Lyons, 1963). For further bibliography: L. Febvre and H. J. Martin, *L'apparition du livre* (Paris, 1958), pp. 515–16, 520–1, 523–8.

[2] Hauser, *Ouvriers*, pp. 110–17; N. Rondot, *L'ancien régime du travail à Lyon* (Lyons, 1897); Claude de Rubys, *Histoire véritable de la ville de Lyon* (Lyons, 1604), pp. 346–7. The only trades organized into sworn guilds until the end of the sixteenth century were those of the locksmiths and the barber-surgeons (for reasons of public health or safety). Sylvia Thrupp has recently stressed the great range in guild power from city to city in her article in the *Cambridge Economic History of Europe* (Cambridge, 1963), III, 242–54.

[3] N. Rodolico, 'The Struggle for the Right of Association in Fourteenth-Century Florence', *History*, VII, 2nd ser. (1922), 178 ff.; R. de Roover, *The Rise and Decline of the Medici Bank* (Cambridge, Mass. 1963), pp. 184–5.

[4] Of course, the merchant-publishers had heavy expenses for paper and transport to think about

with the publishers. When the publishers fined them for late work, they hollered at their journeymen for taking too many days off.[1]

In short, the major way the masters hoped to maintain or increase profits was to cut down on labour costs. They adopted the method – time-honoured among master craftsmen – of trying to replace some journeymen with unpaid apprentices.[2] They cut down on the traditional food-salary given their workers and, claiming that the journeymen were gluttons, tried to do away with it altogether.[3] The merchant-publishers for the most part could stay behind the scenes. When disputes became serious, they simply saw to it that the town Consulate always intervened on the side of the masters.[4]

The 'gluttons' in question were men who spent at least ten or twelve years working for wages as pressmen, typesetters, and proof-readers. Since one press and type *alone* cost almost a whole year's salary, most of them never became masters. They came to Lyons from all over – from peasant huts in nearby provinces; from artisan families in Paris and other cities; from Switzerland and Italy and Germany. Almost all of them were doing something different from their fathers before them, in a strange city, and in a trade that was relatively new. Thus they were eager for communal relationships in which they could take their rightful place and be accepted. Of course, some journeymen were natives of Lyons and some journeymen were the sons of printers; their distinctive role will be noted later.

The work the journeymen did also determined the kind of men they were. Standing up all day pulling and pushing a noisy press required great physical stamina. Typesetting and proof-reading required literacy, and between half and two-thirds of the journeymen could read and write.[5] Finally, printing

(Febvre and Martin, *op. cit.* pp. 162–73), but I here try to imagine possible interested views that the masters might have adopted.

[1] Bibliothèque Nationale, MSS. nouv. acquisitions français 8014, pp. 699–700.

[2] *Ibid.* pp. 693–4; Hauser, *Ouvriers*, p. 184; Chauvet, *op. cit.* pp. 24–5. In 1321 the fullers' journeymen of Paris accused their masters of taking on too many apprentices (Levasseur, *op. cit.* I, 313). Also see Lipson, *op. cit.* I, 316–18 on overuse of apprentice labour in fifteenth-century England. Article 3 of the 1587 'Orders concerning Printing' of the London Stationers' Company shows the same development in English printing (reprinted in E. Howe, *The Trade* [London, 1943], p. 8).

Some master printers and publisher-printers in Lyons also tried to increase profits by entrepreneurial techniques, such as short-term partnerships and specializing in certain kinds of editions.

[3] Archives municipales de Lyon, AA 151, 69r; B.N. MSS., n. acq. fr. 8014, pp. 691–2, 706. The first *known* cut-back occurred in 1536; but already in the 1520's Symphorien Champier reported that 'servants' in Lyons wanted to be treated as well as their masters and drink wine unmixed with water (*Ung petit livre de lantiquite . . . de Lyon: Ensemble de la rebeine . . .* [Lyons, 1530], reprinted in P. Allut, *Etude biographique . . . sur Symphorien Champier* [Lyons, 1859] p. 353). The custom of paying part of the journeymen's salary in food was followed in the Paris printing shops, where the masters complained that the workers were fussy about the quality and variety of the food and drink (Chauvet, *op. cit.* pp. 49–50).

[4] For instance, the publishers were not involved in the hearing about the strike before the Lieutenant-General, 2 July 1539 (Arch. mun. AA 51, 68v-70r), nor do they protest to the Consulate as do the master printers in 1540 (BB 57, 263r; BB 58, 117v). The wealthy merchant-publisher Hugues de La Porte was on the Consulate at the time and helped arrange a meeting between masters and publishers (BB 59, 297v-298r) as well as persuading the Consulate to subsidize and support the masters' legal appeals (BB 58, 116r). Only in 1570–2, when tension was beginning to mount between publishers and masters, did the former take the initiative in the conflict with the journeymen.

[5] In 1580, out of 115 printers' journeymen assembled to give power of attorney, 43 (about one-third) could not sign their names (Baudrier, *op. cit.* III, 1–4).

demanded disciplined co-operation: three to four men worked a press together, and pressmen, compositors, and correctors tried not to keep each other waiting. As the journeymen said themselves, 'we can't be compared to other artisans who work independently as they choose'.[1]

This solidarity was extended into the rest of their lives. They ate certain meals together at the master's table. Unmarried journeymen lived together. They spent free time together, drinking and talking at taverns, roaming the streets in large gangs, planning recreations of one kind or another.[2]

Their vocational experience also stimulated another trait which all the authorities called 'impudence',[3] but which we can describe as confidence or pride. Partly they were proud of their skills. Their learning may not have gone very deep – 'lightly tinted with letters' is how one disgusted editor described them [4] – but then the journeymen were comparing themselves with their fathers or other artisans, not with scholars. There is even a boastful tone in their talk of the 'incredible violence' of their work at the press.[5]

Their pride was also rooted in the conviction, shared by masters, publishers and many others, that printing was of enormous value to Christian society.[6] Minerva, 'the Mother of Printing and Goddess of Knowledge', was the central figure in a festival they organized and the journeymen proclaimed themselves the men who made her honour shine.[7] That their contemporaries did not agree that they should share quite so fully in the high repute of printing did not shake their faith. When the royal governor ordered their arrest as 'vagabonds' during a strike, they appealed on the grounds that they were not persons of such low quality.[8] When the king prescribed corporal punishment for their offences as for other persons doing physical labour, they protested that they laboured not out of coercion, as slaves, but 'as free men working voluntarily at an excellent and noble calling'.[9] Nor were they embarrassed by the fact that others had the capital while they did the work. 'Rather', they

---

[1] *Remonstrance et Mémoires, pour les Compagnons Imprimeurs, de Paris et Lyons: Opposans. Contre les Libraires Maistres Imprimeurs desdits lieux: Et adioutez* (N.p. [Lyons?], n.d. [1572], Bir-v. Though presented as a brief for journeymen from both Lyons and Paris, its heavy stress on and familiarity with the situation in Lyons show it to have been composed in that city. It is also based to a considerable extent on arguments and even phrases from journeymen briefs in Lyons in 1539 and 1540. Cf. July 1539 statement: 'in the Printing Industry, the work begins when everyone is together. When one or two are absent, the work stops' (Arch. mun. AA 151, 69r).

[2] In their study of the International Typographical Union, S. M. Lipset, M. Trow and J. Coleman stress the importance of the 'high-level of leisure-time social relations among printers' for the formation of printers' unions and active participation in them (*Union Democracy* [New York, 1962], pp. 27–9, 77 ff.).

[3] *Mémoire pour l'imprimerie* (Masters' complaint, 1572), Arch. mun. HH 98.

[4] Etienne Dolet, *Commentariorum Linguae Latinae Tomus Primus* (Lyons, 1536), col. 266.

[5] B.N. MSS., n. acq. fr. 8014, pp. 696–7; *Remonstrance*, A ir.

[6] As John T. Dunlop has pointed out (*Industrial Relations Systems* [New York, 1958], pp. 16–17), there must be some common ideology among the 'actors' in an industrial-relations system if it is to achieve any stability. In the Lyons printing industry, where there was so much disagreement about roles, belief in the importance of printing helped hold the 'actors' together. In shops where Protestant propaganda was being printed, the bond was intensified.

[7] *Recueil faict au vray de la chevauchee de l'asne faicte en le ville de Lyon . . . mil cinq cens soixante six . . .* in *Archives historiques et statistiques du Département du Rhône*, IX (1828–9), 418. This is one of their many references to the excellence of printing.

[8] B.N. MSS., n. acq. fr. 8014, pp. 701, 710–11.

[9] *Remonstrance*, B iiv.

said, 'the name Printer should truly be reserved for [us, since we] perform the greatest part of printing.' [1]

The camaraderie and the pride of the printers' journeymen were of great importance to the formation and development of the Company of the Griffarins. They also explain certain features of their work to which printers' journeymen did not object. They were not hostile to technological improvements in this 'admirable invention' (such as tympans to hold the paper in place, friskets for clean margins, and a pressing-stone that could be rolled [2]) even though these meant that jobs would end sooner and that their daily quota of printed pages would be raised. In fact, the daily quota, which was higher in Lyons than in Paris, played no part in the Griffarins' complaints until the 1570's.[3] The days off which they demanded were only one every two or three weeks. This is not excessive if one realizes that Lyons printing shops ran from 2 a.m. to 10 p.m. and that the journeymen were not agitating for shorter hours.[4] In other words, in between strikes, printers' journeymen worked hard and conscientiously – probably even more so when they and their masters were printing Protestant heresy.

What did trouble the printers' journeymen was that ownership was increasingly separating them from their masters in terms of income, responsibility for running the shop, and friendship. 'Given the quality of the parties involved', the workers said, 'there should be mutual and reciprocal love between us. Indeed, above all other Arts, the Masters and Journeymen [in printing] are or ought to be only onebody together, like a family and a fraternity.' [5]

This had been almost true in the early days of the industry – or so the journeymen often like to think, with a nostalgia characteristic of all European protest

---

[1] *Ibid.* A ir, B iir.

[2] Marius Audin, *Somme typographique* (Lyons, 1949), II, 88–93.

[3] Wages ordinarily began when the press began to work and stopped when it stopped (Arch. mun. AA 151, 70r). There was always the chance that an individual worker would then be given notice, though during a period of an increasing demand for books, this may not have been a serious problem. Around 1500 the output of a press was not much higher than in Gutenberg's day (300 sheets for 14 hours of work). By 1572 Parisian journeymen were expected to produce 2,650 sheets and Lyons journeymen, working 18–19 hours, 3,340 sheets (*Remonstrance*, B iv): the daily quota is not mentioned in the Griffarin testimony of the 1560's. In the *Remonstrance* of 1572, the Lyons journeymen propose that either they will take their meals out and this requirement be lowered, or the food-salary continue and they will produce the 3,340 sheets.
Of course, the classic case of medieval opposition to technological innovation – that of the fullers to the water-powered fulling machine (E. Carus-Wilson, 'The Woollen Industry', *Cambridge Economic History of Europe* [Cambridge, 1952], II, 410) – involved a much more drastic upset to the status and employment of the fullers.

[4] 'Les pauvres Compagnons . . . sont tenus de se trouver ès maisons de leurs maistres et commencer loeuvre à deux heures du matin jusqu' à dix heures du soir, tellement quils nont que quatre heures pour leur repos' (B.N. MSS., n. acq. fr. 8014, pp. 696–7). Thus, when there were two to three weeks of uninterrupted work, the journeymen needed a day off, 'que les uns appliquent à leur repos, les aultres a donner order à leurs affaires domestiques, les autres à leur Esbat et aucuns deux à Besongner si bon leur semble' (*ibid.* p. 697). Thirty-two years later, in 1572, though there had been no protest or strike on the issue of *hours*, they were down to 2 a.m. to 8 or 9 p.m. (*Remonstrance*, B iv). These hours are the longest on record for any craft of the period (cf. Hauser, *Ouvriers*, pp. 79–80), and there is evidence for agitation on hours in other crafts (Lipson, *op. cit.* I, 396). Only in the seventeenth century did the Lyons printers' journeymen begin to fight on hours, demanding 5 a.m. to 8 p.m. (Chauvet, *op. cit.* p. 221).

[5] B.N. MSS., n. acq. fr. 8014, p. 699; *Remonstrance*, B iir.

54   NATALIE ZEMON DAVIS

movements for centuries. There had been a Confraternity of the Printers, established at the Carmelite monastery, in which journeymen shared the leadership with masters on into the opening decade of the sixteenth century.[1] Shop life was still being improvised. The supply of skilled journeymen was still quite limited. Relations between masters and journeymen may well have been *comparatively* equable and brotherly. At any rate, the journeymen argued in later decades that they had 'old and ancient customs'· and 'rights', which their masters, through excessive avarice and desire to tyrannize, were now conspiring to destroy.[2]

As we go through the specific demands that the Griffarins made, we can see them defending their standard of living, but always on the assumption that they were just about as good as their masters. Take salary. The way the workers told it, the masters 'were trying to put them, their wives and children in the poor-house'.[3] Now it is true that married journeymen sometimes had a hard time making ends meet, but it is also true that, along with painters' journeymen and cabinet-makers' journeymen, they were the highest paid workers in Lyons.[4] That was no consolation, however, for, as they put it, the publishers and masters 'were acquiring every day great and honourable wealth at the price of [our] sweat and marvelous toil . . . yea, even at the price of [our] blood'.[5]

Or, take the food-salary. Governmental officials agreed with the journeymen in 1539 that their masters were trying to rob them both in regard to the quality of the food and in regard to the wages offered instead of food.[6] The journeymen could then have used this to bargain for some other demand. Instead they claimed the food-salary for the next thirty years: they did not want to be excluded from the master's table. Nor did they wish to be excluded from all decisions about who should be fired or when the shop should be open or closed.[7]

[1] Arch. mun. de Lyon, CC 23, 294*v*. Master Jacques Mareschal, alias Roland, one of the 'courriers' in 1518 (CC 55, 81*v*). Journeyman Richard Gentilhomme one of the 'courriers' in 1520 (CC 684, 3*r*). Already in 1514 Gentilhomme was separated from Roboam and other journeymen who were leaders of the new journeymen's organization (BB 83, 153*r*, 158*r*).

[2] B.N. MSS., n. acq. fr. 8014, pp. 691–4, 697. Specific references are made to the customary amount of 'vin, pain et pitance' (as the food-salary was called), to 'customary salaries', to the days off which 'lon a accoustume de longtemps et danciannetè . . . de prendre'. Similar themes in *Remonstrance*, A i*r-v*, B i*v*, C i*r*. The journeymen did not, however, imagine the early days as a complete Paradise. As they say in 1540, even the customary profit of their masters had been 'immoderate and excessive', though there would have been no dispute if the masters had just been satisfied with it and had maintained the journeymen in their 'rights' (B.N. MSS., n. acq. fr. 8014, p. 691).

[3] *Ibid.* p. 692.

[4] In 1539–40 the masters offered compositors and pressmen 8 sous tournois *per day* as total wages, without the food-salary (*ibid.* p. 706), Arch. mun. AA 151, 69*r*. (The figure given by Hauser, *Ouvriers*, p. 185,· is a misreading of AA 151, for 6 sous 6 deniers per day was only the offer made to ink-ballers.) 8 sous tournois was actually a little below the real value of their wages in money and nourishment. In 1548 painters' journeymen in Lyons were being paid 8 sous per day; cabinet-makers' journeymen 7 sous per day; unskilled labourers usually $2\frac{1}{2}$ sous, though up to $4\frac{1}{2}$ sous, per day.

[5] *Remonstrance*, A i*r*, but the same view expressed a little less colourfully in 1540, B.N. MSS., n. acq. fr. 8014, pp. 691–2.

[6] As is evident in the fact that both Lieutenant Jean du Peyrat in 1539 and the Parlement of Paris in 1540 supported the continuance of the food-salary, said the journeyman should be nourished 'reasonably and honestly' according to the amounts given in 1533–4, not those of the past few years (Arch. mun. AA 151, 69*v*; B.N. MSS., n. acq. fr. 8014, p. 715).

[7] *Ibid.* pp. 698, 706.

Perhaps nothing sums up the psychology of the situation better than the *atelier* where the master was literally the father. The fiery authoritarian Jean Moylin, alias de Cambrai, was a leader of the masters' cause even though his sons and nephews were among his journeymen. His relatives, most of whom were not to inherit the shop, repaid him in kind and became leaders of the journeymen's coalition.[1] At best, the only family relation that most masters were willing to have with their workers was that of a strong father to docile obedient sons.[2] But most journeymen wanted to be treated like adults and brothers.

The Company of the Griffarins was an attempt to provide its members with a new family, a new inheritance – that is, their own 'rules and ordinances of the printing industry' – and new weapons with which to fight for them. Did all such 'companies' of the fourteenth through sixteenth centuries emerge from similar circumstances? Clearly there were some differences, for coalitions are even found among bakers' and butchers' journeymen, that is, in trades where the skills, tools, shop size, character of the market, and governmental regulations all contrast with printing.[3] Only detailed research can answer this question. I speculate, however, that the Lyons printers' journeymen will be found distinctive in two ways. First, their collective work and social experience turned them to a union solution earlier than journeymen in other crafts who did their tasks singly.[4] Second, their intense pride, shared by only a few other artisans such as painters' journeymen, made them more resentful than most workers to loss of status and responsibility within the shop.

II

The first sign of the new Company was a series of restless street fights in 1514.[5] Twenty years later it was a large, disciplined organization. Among many

---

[1] Moylin's role: Arch. mun. AA 151, 68v; BB 57, 263r; BB 58, 117v. His son Gabriel and his nephew Mathieu Mouchet were active in defence of the journeymen (Baudrier, I, 283). His daughter Marguerite later married Pierre Compere, who was also a journeymen's leader in 1544 (*ibid.* I, 102). Two daughters married masters – Antoine Cercia and Jacques Berjon, whose son Jacques II was to become a Griffarin after his father's death (Procès criminels de Genève, 1397, 11r-12r). Galiot Thibout, a most militant Griffarin of the 1560's, was the son of master printer Guillaume Thibout of Paris (Procès criminels de Genève, 1307). Of course, some of these young men may not have fought with their own fathers, but may just have found it especially hard to except a role of 'subjection' in another shop.

[2] Thus, Hector Penet, a master who opposed the journeymen's claims from 1539 through 1565 (Arch. mun. AA 151, 68v; BB 57, 263r; Procès criminel de Genève, 1306), was able to stand up in court for a worker who presumably was loyal to him (Arch. dep. du Rhône, Registre des Sentences, B. travée 350, 1561–2).

[3] Bakers' journeymen in London (Lipson, *op. cit.* I, 394); butchers' journeymen in Lyons (Procès criminels de Genève, 1397, 2v).

[4] In Venice, where the first book was probably printed in 1469 and where Aldo Manuzio set up his shop in 1494, Manuzio complained already in 1504, 'Four times again, in my printing house, I have had to support the conspiracies and machinations of my workmen acting under the influence of cupidity' (quoted in C. Clair, *Christophe Plantin* [1960], p. 285).

[5] Arch. mun. BB 83, 153r, 158r – Roboam, later Captain of the Printers, one of those arrested. CC 677, April 1520, a fight between the printers and the fishermen of Saint Vincent, which may or may not have had an economic aspect. BB 42, 215r and BB 43, 13v – Master printer Jacques Roland, alias Mareschal, on watch and seized an armed journeyman, who was then rescued by the 'Captain of the Printers' and other journeymen.

problems that had been worked out was how to conceal their illegal doings from royal sergeants, the night watch, their masters and enemies. Small gatherings and initiations could be held in a journeyman's room or in one of the taverns that a few journeymen were running on the side.[1] But they had to find pretexts for large meetings and for leaders who could represent them publicly. 'Coalition under colour of religious confraternity' had long been the tactic of French artisans and was to be used by the *compagnonnages* of the seventeenth and eighteenth centuries. Henri Hauser thought the Lyons printing workers had also counted on this for their only camouflage, but the evidence suggests that this was not really the case.[2] For a while, one Griffarin said, there had been a 'confraternity', to which each member had given 4 sous per year for a mass. But it had no chapel associated with it and royal edicts banning such artisanal confraternities were an added inconvenience. Once Protestantism had made sufficient headway among the workers, even the common mass was ended.[3] For many years the Company of the Griffarins was a secular organization, thereby facilitating labour unity between Protestants and Catholics in its membership. Only in the late sixteenth and seventeenth centuries, under the tolerant encouragement of the Counter-Reformation, did the Lyons printers' journeymen make effective use of the confraternity.

The real disguises for the Company of the Griffarins were two old Lyons institutions – one, the recreational grouping, the other, the urban militia. Neighbourhood and craft groups put on parades, plays, and charivaris all through the year in Lyons. They were also called out by the Consulate to honour visiting dignitaries. Here was a fine excuse for captains and lieutenants and the collecting of funds. Indeed, the printers' journeymen enjoyed these affairs so much that they created a distinctive and celebrated recreational officer, named the Seigneur de la Coquille – that is, in printers' slang, the Lord of Misprint.[4]

---

[1] Two of the leaders in the 1539–44 conflict were also tavern-keepers – Barthélemy Frein and Pierre Chamarier (Baudrier, X, 349; I, 83) as was Roland Syrodet, an important Griffarin in the 1560's (*ibid.* I, 414; Arch. mun. CC 1174, 24v; Proc. crim. Gen. 1397, 15r). None of the testimony in Proc. crim. Gen. 1397 actually locates the ceremonies in an inn, however. Jean Berjon (5r), son of master Jacques, said 'quil a veu passer des compagnons Imprimeurs de la ville de Lyon de son jeune age estant cheulx son pere'. This certainly sounds as though the ceremony was held in a back room of the master's house; but that cannot have been true in all cases.

[2] Hauser, 'Compagnonnages', pp. 23–6; *Ouvriers*, p. 180. The term 'confrérie' is used during the years 1539–44 only in the Edict of Fontainebleau, article 5, and in the royal edict of Sept. 1544, where it could well apply only to Paris. Indeed, M. Chauvet's evidence (*Ouvriers*, p. 9) suggests that in Paris the coalition was early founded under pretext of confraternity. The local documents of the Lyons Consulate and the Sénéchaussée refer repeatedly to 'monopolies' and 'assemblies', but up to 1572 only once to 'confraternity'. This latter reference occurs in a May 1556 sentence of the Sénéchaussée, was addressed to both masters and journeymen ('Aussi deffenses leur soient faictes de ne faire aucunes monopoles sous couleur et pretexte des confrairies'); and could just as well have referred to the old Confraternity of the Printers, dominated by the masters, as to the journeymen's confraternity (Arch. dep. B. Sénéchaussée, Reg. de l'Audience, Feb.-Oct. 1556).

[3] Proc. crim. Gen. 1397, 19r. This is the only testimony which mentions that a confraternity had once existed. Odinet Basset, who had entered the Griffarins in the 1540's (14r), does not mention it. It is hard to believe there could have been much enthusiasm for this kind of disguise, when one realizes that many printers' journeymen were Protestant supporters by 1535 (see N. Z. Davis, 'The Protestant Printing Workers of Lyons in 1551', *Aspects de la propagande religieuse* [Geneva, 1957], pp. 247–57, and my forthcoming book *Strikes and Salvation in Lyons*).

[4] Among the extensive literature on popular festivals in Lyons, one can select the contemporary

The urban militia was built around neighbourhood units of ten men, who supplied their own arms. A gang of printers' journeymen could show up from one street or shop and volunteer. Known as good fighters, they were not turned down. Often officers of the Griffarins led their own *dizaines*. Thus a certain percentage of the journeymen had the occasion to bear arms legally.[1] Then when they were all assembled illegally in large armed bands, the royal sergeants and their aides did not 'dare to put a hand to them'. When they tried, they were beaten up themselves.[2]

This skillful manipulation of Lyons institutions depended on some men in the Company's leadership who knew the city well. Thus, although the root-lessness of most printers' journeymen in Lyons was the condition for the formation of their Company, the rootedness of a few of them was a condition for its successful operation. This condition was absent in nearby Geneva, a city of refugees, where in 1560 perhaps two printers' journeymen were natives and only a small percentage had lived there as long as ten years. This is one reason why printers' journeymen from Lyons failed to set up an enduring coalition there in the 1550's and 1560's, although economic and religious factors were very important as well.[3]

Once established, the Company of the Griffarins included in its membership pressmen, compositors, and proof-readers.[4] This unity was facilitated by their closely co-ordinated work, done under one roof, and the occasional lack of specialization in some shops. In contrast, in the textile industry in Lyons, where almost every stage was done at a separate establishment, the one coalition that I have discovered embraced dyers' journeymen only. Nevertheless, there might have been some strain within the Company, if the Griffarins had not shown themselves sensitive to the differences among the members. But they

---

remarks by Claude de Rubys, *op. cit.* pp. 499–503 and the excellent discussion of V. L. Saulnier, *Maurice Scève* (Paris, 1948), I, 194 ff., 328 ff. and *passim*. Though only two full texts of the festivals of the printers' journeymen before 1572 have been preserved (1566 and 1568), their role in the Entries is evident from 1533 on (*Le Ceremonial François* . . . ed. T. Godefroy [Paris, 1649]). In the Entry Parade of 1548, the captain who led the journeymen in front of Henri II was Guillaume Phyledier (Saulnier, *op. cit.* I, 334), who was to be a leader of the Griffarins by at least 1556 (Arch. dep. B. Sen., Reg. Aud., Feb.–Oct. 1556). His ensign for the Entry was Pierre Micollier, a journeymen's leader in 1544 (Baudrier, *op. cit.* I, 306).

[1] The *Etablies* of 1507, 1523, March 1536, 1557, 1561 and 1568, have numerous printers' journeymen on them (Arch. mun. EE 19–21, EE 24–25), among whom I have found almost all the men whom independent documents identify as Griffarin leaders. E.g. Roboam *dixainier* in 1523 (EE 20, 29v), Raymond de Trinc *dixainier* in 1536 (EE 21, 26v). Rollet Paté, 'capitaine des imprimeurs', is used with a band of 42 journeymen for emergency service in 1529 (M. C. and G. Guigue, *Bibliothèque historique du Lyonnais* [Lyons, 1886], pp. 288–9, 364, 368). The 1540 ban on weapon-carrying said that all printers' journeymen and apprentices in Lyons were not to bear weapons in town except in those cases where permitted by law or allowed by royal ordinance (B.N. MSS., n. acq. fr. 8014, p. 712).

[2] *Ibid.* p. 700; Arch. mun. AA 151, 68v.

[3] There was journeymen's agitation in Geneva (P. Chaix, *Recherches sur l'imprimerie à Genève de 1550 à 1564* [Geneva, 1954], pp. 18–29), but by 1567 the workers had failed to set up a secret company with oath (Proc. crim. Gen. 1397, 7v). This was due to the relative fairness of the 1560 Ordinances for Printing in Geneva (Chaix, *op. cit.* p. 26), the effectiveness of religious authorities in prosecuting such efforts, and other factors, discussed in my forthcoming book.

[4] This is evident not only from testimony about their demands and tactics, but from the names of members. For instance, in 1539–44, leaders Pierre Dumont, Barthélémy Frein and Roboam were respectively corrector, compositor, and pressman. In the 1560's corrector Jean Mairel, compositor Jullien Mouchet and pressman Jean Saulzion, alias Gros-Bonnet, were among those in the leadership.

did, as a 1544 statement to the Parlement of Paris shows: 'There are three kinds of journeymen in printing – compositors, correctors, and pressmen. As for the first and last, their work is manual ... but the art and skill of the correctors come from the mind, not from the work of hands.' Thus, since their work was not manual, the journeymen went on, proof-readers should be allowed to enter the shop and work on feast-days.[1]

The Company did not stretch, however, to include the scholars and poets who did periodic editorial work and specialized proof-reading (mathematics, music, Greek and the like). Such men had served no apprenticeship and had no desire to be considered artisans. Although some friendships grew up between editors and journeymen, the editors probably urged both sides to compromise during a dispute.[2] On the other hand, one small group of artisans of ambiguous status did play a role in the Company. These were journeymen who acquired, usually by rental, a press and type and printed almanacs and occasional pieces. Knowing that their period as masters was bound to be brief, they kept their ties and loyalty to the Company. It was on their presses that the journeymen's legal briefs and entertainments were printed.[3]

One joined the Company of the Griffarins at a secret ceremony in which one was 'passed as a Journeyman'. A young man who had apprenticed in Lyons was ordinarily passed at the end of apprenticeship. Men who had apprenticed and been working elsewhere would be urged by a friend or relative to join the Company.[4] Only journeymen who had already been received into

---

[1] B.N. MSS., n. acq. fr. 8014, p. 698. I have no evidence about whether compositors or pressmen or correctors took the initiative in the early organizing of the Company. Since 'les functions et charges des Compagnons sont tellement annexees et unies ensemble que l'absence ou retardement d'un seul fera cesser les autres' (*Remonstrance*, B iv), it is hard to single out in these shops the 'strategic workers' to which John Dunlop has called attention in union-formation ('The Development of Labor Organizations: A Theoretical Framework', reprinted in *Readings in Labor Economics*, ed. G. F. Bloom *et al.* [Homewood, Ill. 1963], 70–1).

After 1572 at least one typecaster was involved in the *recreational* activities of the Company. There does not seem to have been any joint economic agitation before or after 1572.

[2] For instance, while he was an editor for Sebastien Gryphe, Etiene Dolet went out drinking with Vincent Pillet (*Lavantnaissance de Claude Dolet* . . . [Lyons, 1539], p. 15), who was a Company leader in 1544 (Baudrier, *op. cit.* I, 342). Editor Charles Fontaine addressed a poem to Guillaume Phylledier in 1555 (*ibid.* IX, 29), who was a Griffarin leader (see n. 4, p. 56, above). I imagine that many editors, influenced by humanist moderation, agreed with the view of scholar Charles de Sainte Marthe, expressed in a 1540 poem to the masters and journeymen:

> 'Maistres, saichez Compagnons retenir,
> Vous Compaignons, leur debvez subvenir,
> Et cy apres cessent tous ces clameurs.
> Chassez de vous des noises les fauteurs
> A celle fin que puissez revenir
>   En bon accord.'

[3] For instance, Jullien Mouchet, alias des Femmes, was a Griffarin leader in 1565 and in 1571–2 (Proc. crim. Gen. 1307; Arch. mun. HH 98), but obtained permission to print an almanac in 1571 (Baudrier, I, *op. cit.* 125). Guillaume Testefort is another example. Such men are to be contrasted with Griffarins who unexpectedly became permanent masters, some of them (Barthélemy Frein) maintaining amicable relations with the Company, others (Jean Mairel) siding with the masters. Benson Soffer's theory of the 'autonomous' workman ('A Theory of Trade Union Development', *Labor History*, I [1960], 141–63) is not relevant to the situation before 1572, though it may be useful in considering the seventeenth-century printing industry.

[4] Proc. crim. Gen. 111: 'having arrived at Lyons, he addressed himself to his uncle, a printer, who said that he advised him to be passed as a journeyman and not to get mixed up with Forfants'.

a similar 'company' at Paris and thus knew the handshake and password were exempt from initiation, being accepted into the Griffarins at a simple banquet.[1] A candidate put in a request to the Captain. When approved by the Captain and certain other journeymen, he was given (or-could select) his 'godfathers', usually four of them. They gave him preliminary instruction on what the Griffarins called the 'rules' or 'laws' or 'ordinances' of the Printing Industry.[2]

Perhaps it was at this time that the journeymen learned what the name of the Company meant. This was not explained in the later ceremony, and in any case was not taken too seriously. The title was variously pronounced Golfarin, Gorfarin, Gourfarin, and Griffarin. It is the first which gives the key to its origin. Golfarin is an old French word for 'glutton'. It had been thrown at the journeymen often enough by masters and, according to one journeyman, by non-union workers,[3] until they had appropriated it as their name: the Company of the Gluttons. Undoubtedly it was especially appreciated at their banquets. From Golfarin the name became most frequently Griffarin – a neologism which suggested, however, claws or talons and thus the power of the Company.[4] This was all the glamour that the journeymen required in their title. The *compagnonnages* of the seventeenth century – in trades other than printing – referred to themselves more seriously as Compagnons de Devoir. They were the Enfants de Salomon or de Maître Jacques and their organization dated back to the building of Solomon's temple.[5] Printers' journeymen, in a new craft, were more realistic. Minerva was the Mother of Printing, but she never gave birth to the Company of the Griffarins.

After briefing came the banquet. All the officers of the company were there, some of the oldest journeymen, the 'godfathers', and the journeymen in the initiate's shop. The initiate paid the bill and somehow had to have enough money left for his entrance fee.[6] Then everyone retired to a back room. Here the godfathers sprinkled water and wine on the journeyman's head and gave him a new, usually vulgar name, which henceforth became his alias. A song was sung, profane expressions being sandwiched in between the 'O domino' and the 'de spiritu sancto' with which each verse began and ended. The words of this song have perished, but we can guess their tenor from a substitution made in the 1560's by conscientious Protestant members who feared blasphemy. While everyone else sang 'de spiritu sancto', they sang 'la grosse Margot', a well-known lady whom François Villon celebrated in one of his coarser poems.[7]

[1] *Ibid.* 22r. He had been received at Paris 'avec les frères' (perhaps the term used at Paris to refer to fellow members?). He and the other members from Paris did not have to pay for the Lyons banquet, at which they were exhorted to 'soustenir l'imprimerie'.

[2] *Ibid.* 3r, 11r, 10r, 5r.

[3] Proc. crim. Gen. 1307, interrogation of 11 Sept. 1565.

[4] On the whole, Griffarin appears more often than Golfarin in the sources, and I have therefore adopted it for the title. The fact that some of the leaders worked in the shop of Sebastien Gryphius, which was almost certainly the largest atelier in Lyons, may have had something to do with the name 'Griffarins.'

[5] Martin Saint-Léon, *op. cit.* pp. 2–10.

[6] In 1565 Jacques II Berjon paid 10 or 12 francs for his banquet (Proc. crim. Gen. 1397, 11r), or so he said. This is about two months' wages. Of course, journeymen could be passed together (*ibid.* 16r) which would cut down on the expenses for each initiate.

[7] This picture of the ceremony is pulled together from all the testimony in Proc. crim. Gen. 1397.

Thus fortified, the initiate took his membership oaths, some with his hands between the hands of one of the officers, others on the bare blade of a dagger. With the dagger he would maintain the ordinances of the Printing Industry to the death; if he broke his oath, the dagger would be the instrument of vengeance upon him. Often the weapon was given to the new member; he would need it for Company business. Since he would also need a means of identifying other Griffarins and members of the Paris Company, he was shown the special greeting and password: two right thumbs touch; one left little finger clasps the other; one right foot on the other's right foot; and then one journeyman bites the other's ear and whispers 'Vive les temps'.[1] (One wonders how such an operation could have been carried on in the midst of a street fight.) At the end, to fix the impression in his mind of these awe-inspiring events and to warn him of the punitive power of the Griffarins, the new Compagnon leaned over a table and was given three sword-whacks, called *assolia*, on his buttocks.[2]

These rites place printers' journeymen squarely in the tradition of the secret *compagnonnage* initiations of the seventeenth century.[3] The main difference between the ceremony of the Griffarins and those of the journeymen saddle-makers, shoe-makers, tailors, cutlers, and hatters revealed to the Paris theologians is complexity. The Griffarins' ceremony had fewer objects and ornaments for which to give high-flown explanations; and it parodied only baptism, not the mass as well. The printers' journeymen seem less devious in their coarseness and in their profanation. They took their oaths on a dagger; the later journey-men did it on the Bible. Finally, even Minerva herself would not have been allowed to attend a Griffarin initiation, whereas a godmother always participated in the seventeenth-century ceremonies. This reflects primarily the great role that hospitality was to play in the later *compagnonnages*.[4]

Mr Arly Allen called my attention to François Villon's poem 'Ballade de la Grosse Margot'. See Villon's *Oeuvres*, ed. Thuasne (Paris, 1923), I, 246 ff. and III, 691.

[1] One journeyman, who was reporting from hearsay only, said that 'Vivre la coquille' – 'Long live the misprint' – was an alternative password (Proc. crim. Gen. 1397, 1r). This seems unlikely because the Seigneur de la Coquille and his Suppôts were so well known that it would be too easy to guess such a password.

[2] 'Assolia' seems to come from the OF. 'assolir', to acquit, to absolve, to discharge from payment or obligation (F. Godefroy, *Dictionnaire de l'ancienne langue française*, I). Thus by receiving the sword-whacks in punishment, one is absolved. The O.E.D. gives 'assoil' and variations theoreof with the same set of meanings (I want to thank Prof. D. F. S. Thomson for his aid on this question). The Lyons 'assolia' thus explains the 'solace' described by Moxon as part of the 'ancient customs' of the English printing shop or chapel (*op. cit.* pp. 323 ff.). In the English case, however, the 'solace' could be blows *or* an equivalent fine, while in sixteenth-century Lyons, the Griffarin was absolved by blows only. In a 1712 initiation into a London chapel, the printer Thomas Gent was struck as he kneeled with a broadsword (E. Howe, *op. cit.* p. 21). I have not come across this physical blow in any other initiation ceremony. It was not mentioned in the testimony before the Paris Faculty of Theology. The penalties in the seventeenth-eighteenth century *compagnonnages* in Dijon were monetary. Clearly, the Griffarins' concept of punishment was primitive. The *assolia* may have been part of the rites of medieval journey-men's coalitions. It was not, however, part of the rites of the medieval masons (masters and journeymen).

[3] This would have surprised Henri Hauser, who doubted that the printers' journeymen resembled the later *compagnonnages* in this regard and, on the whole, failed to understand the significance of initiation rites in the development of the labour movement (Hauser, *Ouvriers*, p. 176, n. 1; 'Compagnonnages', pp. 28–30).

[4] On the seventeenth-century testimony, see Levasseur, *op. cit.* I, 703–7. On the uses of 'hospitality', see below, p. 62.

The heart of the Griffarin ceremony had been the oaths. To the extent that the members took these in dead earnestness, the Company would hope to succeed in imposing on its craft the 'order' which the journeymen had sworn to maintain. He swore to do no wrong to master or fellow journeyman. He swore not to work for a master for wages less than had been agreed upon by the Company. He swore not to take a job from which another journeyman had been unjustly fired. He swore not to work for a master while a fellow journeyman had an unresolved dispute with him. Then there were oaths about the Forfants, as the Griffarins called workers who were never initiated into the Company. One was not to associate with them or work in a shop with them. In a fight one would support a fellow Griffarin against the Forfants, even if one's father or brother was a Forfant. Such was the loyalty which the Company exacted from its members. Finally, the journeymen swore to reveal nothing of what had gone on at the ceremony to anyone.[1]

After the ceremony came the day-to-day struggles in which the oaths were to take on their meaning. Even the oath to do no wrong to master or fellow journeyman was not ignored. In regard to fellow journeymen, it was probably meant to discourage personal fights. It *may* also have been intended to maintain standards of work in the shop. The only case to which we know certainly that this oath applied is theft. Filching material, for instance, was an old habit of unsupervised artisans in the textile crafts, but it sometimes happened within the more factory-like arrangements of the printing shop. One printing worker, admitting to authorities that he had walked off with five galleys of type, said when 'he considered carefully how much work he had done, he did not find that he owed [his master] anything at all'.[2] This individualistic tactic was wrong, according to the Company of the Griffarins. A member who saw a fellow journeyman doing such a thing was to warn him two or three times. If he persisted, the master was told and the offender was given *assolia* and banned temporarily from the Company.[3] On the other hand, concern for good behaviour was nowhere near as strong with the Griffarins as it was to be in London printing chapels of the seventeenth century or in the later French *compagnonnages*. Indeed, the Griffarins had no scruples about permitting a mass assault on a master's house, with stone-throwing and cursing, in order to regain a sword of disputed ownership.[4]

Wages and conditions were, of course, the important issues. In the *compagnonnages* of the seventeenth and eighteenth centuries, the crucial weapon against the master was the complete control of hiring. Elaborate procedures,

---

[1] Oaths drawn from all the testimony in Proc. crim. Gen. 1397. There are tiny variations in phrasing from testimony to testimony, whereas the actual wording was presumably fixed.

[2] Chaix, *op. cit.* pp. 238–9. There are other cases of theft from the master. E.g. in 1565 master Etienne Servain accused journeyman Jean Bollier, alias Le Bourguignon (recently passed a Griffarin, Proc. crim. Gen. 1397, 9*v*) of leaving his job with stolen books and clothes (Proc. crim. Gen. 1307).

[3] Proc. crim. Gen. 1397, 8*r*, 18*v*, 6*r*, 7*r*. This punishment was actually given to Jacques Ours, native of Chambéry, who had stolen a coffer and money while working as a printers' jouneymen in Paris. The journeymen of Paris wrote to the Company in Lyons, where Ours was then working, and action was taken against him (8*r*).

[4] Morality in the chapel, Moxon, *op. cit.* pp. 324–6; in the later *compagnonnages*, Martin Saint-Léon, *op. cit.* pp. 57–9. The attack on master Hector Penet's house, Procès criminel de Genève, 1306.

including hospitality at a special inn for a journeyman coming to a new town, were worked out to maintain this hold. With the Griffarins, in contrast, there was no attempt to arrange in detail the hiring of each member. Rather the journeyman was presumably told the agreed-upon salary scale, what masters were on the blacklist for unfair firings, what shops were dominated by non-union workers and the like. Then he would find his own job.[1]

The tactic upon which the Griffarins depended much more heavily than the later *compagnonnages* was the strike – shop-wide and in serious situations, such as 1539 and 1570, industry-wide. When something went wrong within a shop – say, the master put apprentices to typesetting or pulling the press – the journeymen would ask him three times to change his mind. If he remained obdurate, one journeyman would signal 'tric, tric' and the whole shop would walk out, either for the day or until the dispute was ended. During that time no Griffarin would accept a job in the shop. Any apprentices who refused to leave would be beaten until they accommodated.[2]

At all times there was the problem of the men whom the masters described as 'the good journeymen who wish to do their duty and work'.[3] The Griffarins called them Forfants – rogues, imposters, rascals – an epithet from the Italian, which was felt by contemporaries to be as nasty and insulting as 'scabs'.[4] Since they had not been passed as journeymen, they were not authentic journeymen at all. 'No matter what one pays them or how one treats them,' said one Griffarin, 'they don't make trouble.' 'They work for beggar's pay.'[5]

The Forfants were a minority of the workers in the Lyons printing industry, only about 25 per cent in 1539.[6] It is hard to discover exactly what factors might lead journeymen to stay out of the Company. Apprenticing in a Forfant shop may have had some effect. But they were not forced into the category of Forfants because the Company would not accept them. The Griffarins ordinarily welcomed Protestants and Catholics from all countries. Moreover,

---

[1] On hospitality, the 'Mère' and 'Père' at the special inn, and other procedures for controlling hiring, see Hauser, 'Compagnonnages', pp. 42–51; Martin Saint-Léon, *op. cit.* pp. 50–5. Rudimentary efforts to control hiring are found already in 1285 among the weavers' journeymen of Rouen (Levasseur, *op. cit.* I, 314). The contrasting Lyons practice is evident from Proc. crim. Gen. 1397 (see especially 11r) and in the masters' complaints, where no mention is made of hiring control. In the last quarter of the century, when the food-salary had been ended in Lyons, the number of *imprimeurs-taverniers* among the journeymen increased. Though undoubtedly printing workers stayed at their inns, there is no clear evidence from the seventeenth century that the journeymen tried to organize all hiring (see Chauvet, *op. cit.* pp. 220–8).

[2] Composite portrait from Arch. mun. AA 151; B.N. MSS., n. acq. fr. 8014; and Proc. crim. Gen. 1397, especially 7r, 10r, 12r and 18r ('si on ne leur voulait bailler ce qu'ilz demanderoient par trois fois, quilz se debauchassent'). The word 'tric' was not a secret one, and was well known to masters and authorities. The printers' journeymen used it *both* for days-off that they took when they needed them for rest (B.N. MSS., n. acq. fr. 8014, p. 697) *and* for walking out because of a dispute. Hauser, *Ouvriers*, p. 180, n. 1, speculated that 'tric' came from the Dutch 'trekk'. It seems to me that there are several other possible origins, such as the Latin and Provençal roots of 'tricher', which can suggest doing a playful trick as well as deception. It also may be related to the French 'trictrac'.

[3] Arch. mun. AA 151, 69r; HH 98.

[4] E. Huguet, *Dictionnaire de la langue française du 16e siècle* (Paris, 1950), IV, 162.

[5] Proc. crim. Gen. 1397, 12r, 3r.

[6] The masters estimated that a band of around 300 striking journeymen was marching through Lyons during 1539 (B.N. MSS., n. acq. fr. 8014, p. 700). The journeymen estimated 400–500 in their camp (p. 694).

these were decades of economic expansion, and the printers' journeymen felt proud of the numbers of men in their honourable calling. Thus, rather than adopting special measures to keep down the labour supply as did the exclusive *compagnonnages* of the later centuries and as the printers' journeymen were to do to some extent themselves in the seventeenth century, the Company at this date preferred to receive members and then keep them to their Ordinances for the Printing Industry.[1] The only exception to this policy was in the mid-1560's. For a few years, unemployment in Geneva sent a group of printers to Lyons, several of whom had apprenticed in Geneva. Most of them were willing to work for beggars' pay, while one who was 'passed as a journeyman' broke his oath by supporting a Forfant against a Griffarin. The result was that the Company, which had Protestants in its leadership, would not receive men who had apprenticed in Geneva even if they applied. This was a measure against potential Forfants, not against foreigners.[2]

Whatever situations created Forfants, they did not lead to any special rules, dues or ceremonies among that group.[3] They were not, in other words, a rival 'rite' such as that which split the *compagnonnages* of the late seventeenth century. For safety's sake, Forfants did walk the street together and were possibly armed. They had good reason, for the Griffarins frequently set upon them, hamstringing being considered an especially good punishment for a Forfant.[4]

In their violent attacks on scabs and unco-operative apprentices, the Griffarins were following a pattern of action familiar to journeymen's coalitions since the fourteenth century.[5] Yet theirs was violence with a difference. First, it was not diffuse, chaotic, spur-of-the-moment violence. They had learned their discipline around the presses and were capable of strategic armed marches which did *not* end in bloodshed. When they did attack, they did not intend to kill, but just to frighten and wound.[6] Further, some of their

[1] The geographical diversity of the Griffarins is evident just from the men testifiying in 1567. Nor had all Griffarins worked only in Paris or Lyons: Galiot Thibout had worked at Orléans (Proc. crim. Gen. 1307) and his fellow Griffarin Nicolas Le Rouge (*ibid.*) had worked in his home town of Troyes (Reg. Consistoire de Genève, vol. 19 (1562), 65*v*).

While in *1653*, the Lyons printers' journeymen were demanding that masters prefer them to all journeymen who come to the city from other provinces and towns (Chauvet, *op. cit.* p. 221), they make no such demands before 1572. The first sign of a change in attitude was in the *Remonstrance* of 1572, when the journeymen argued that it is more than reasonable that journeymen who have apprenticed in Paris and Lyons be preferred 'tant pour un honneste debvoir que pour une police bien reglée, à cause de plusieurs scandales qui concernent le fait d'Imprimerie' (A iiv–B ir). In the same brief the journeymen *regretted* that the number of printers' journeymen was declining.

Even their actions regarding the apprentices do not seem consciously geared toward cutting down on the supply of paid labour. The journeymen asked that the number of apprentices per press be limited (B.N. MSS., n. acq. fr. 8014, pp. 693–5) because the masters were using this unpaid labour at journeymen's tasks. They did not request that the length of apprenticeship be fixed by law until the *Remonstrance* of 1572 (B iir).

[2] This whole story emerges from Proc. crim. Gen. 1397, and I have treated it in detail in my forthcoming book.

[3] *Ibid.* 12*v*, 23*r*.

[4] *Ibid.* 3*v*, 13*v*; Proc. crim. Gen. 1307, testimony of Gabriel Cartier and of Thibout, 11 Sept. 1565.

[5] Cordwainers' journeymen in Lipson, *op. cit.* I, 406–7. Mason's journeymen in D. Knoop and G. P. Jones, *The Medieval Mason* (Manchester, 1933), p. 151. I am grateful to my students Donna Rowland and Michael Spence for calling these examples to my attention.

[6] Some of the masters, such as Etienne Servain, and the Geneva authorities believed that the Griffarins

64   NATALIE ZEMON DAVIS

seemingly purposeless fights with men outside the printing craft turn out to
have been planned: as one journeyman said, 'Griffarins have people, like
butchers and dyers, ready to rush on the Forfants and [the Griffarins] return
like service to the butchers and dyers'.[1]

The bellicosity of the printers' journeymen was also informed with literacy
and tempered by contact with intellectual values. At least they tried to come
to terms with their masters before walking out of the shop. They proposed
committees of journeymen, masters, and burgers to negotiate salary disputes.[2]
And finally, more than any other group of journeymen of their time, they
used the courts to gain their cause. They appealed royal edicts to the Parlement
repeatedly, even when the king had explicitly forbidden them to do so. They
played off rival jurisdictions in Lyons in hopes of winning better decisions.[3]
The Company also kept an archive of relevant decisions and edicts and, though
it hired lawyers to present the briefs, its officers played an important role in
determining strategy and drawing up briefs.[4]

All of these activities took money. The Company's treasury was made up
primarily of a rather high entrance fee, the exact amount of which was varied
according to ability to pay.[5] In times of emergency, a fee of 4 to 6 sous was
collected from the members each week.[6] Such funds were used for legal appeals,
for the expenses of Griffarins arrested in the course of Company action, and
possibly for a strike fund. The strike of 1539, for instance, had lasted three to
four months and Lyons' new poor-relief organization, never tender toward
healthy beggars, was not going to keep the wives of strikers on its rolls for very

planned to kill Forfants (Proc. crim. Gen. 1307), but I cannot see that they intended to go beyond the
wound of hamstringing. Of course, these 'moderate' intentions were not much consolation to the widow
of Aymé Nesme, a Forfant who died from his wounds (*ibid.*).

[1] Proc. crim. Gen. 1397, 2v. This explains, for instance, the Consulate's warning 'A esté enjoinct
aux capitaines des imprimeurs et des taincturiers présens de n'esmouvoir noyses les unes bandes contre
les aultres les jours des entrées' (*Entree du Roy Henri II . . . à Lyon . . . Relations et documents . . .* , ed. G.
Guigue [Lyons, 1927], p. 182). Also the fight between printers' journeymen and some dyers in 1550
(Arch. dep. Rhône, B. Reg. des sentences, Travée 350, 1551–2) and between them and the velvet-makers
in 1552 (J. Guéraud, *La chronique lyonnaise*, ed. J. Tricou (Lyons, 1929), pp. 61–2).

[2] B.N. MSS., n. acq. fr. 8014, p. 696. *Remonstrance*, B iv – B iir.

[3] Arch. dep. Rhône, B. Sen., Reg. Aud. Feb.–Oct. 1556: the journeymen ask that the case be
removed from the Sénéchaussée to the old temporal court of the Archbishop of Lyons 'attendu qu'ils
sont domicillez et ont femme et enfans en ceste ville'. This at a time when most of the leaders (if not all)
were Protestant!

[4] The Company's collection of documents is evident from the *Remonstrance* (A iv), where there are
quotes from various decisions 'qu'on a en main'. The Paris company had one as well (Chauvet, *op. cit.*
pp. 485–7). The journeymen's role in determining the content and phrasing of briefs is clear from a
comparison of their statements at the hearing of 2 July 1539, where no lawyer was present (Arch.
mun. AA 151, 68v – 69r), with Jacques Du Puy's brief presented for them to Parlement some months
later (B.N. MSS., n. acq. fr. 8014). On differences in strategy between lawyer and journeymen, see
ibid. p. 701.

[5] Within a two-year period, 1563–5, the regular entrance fee was 2 *écus* (about a month's wages),
but some men were allowed to pay 1 *écu* because they could not afford more (Proc. crim. Gen. 1397,
3r, 7v, 8r, 9r, 10r, 12v).

[6] Arch. mun. HH 98; Proc. crim. Gen. 1307, testimony of 14 Sept. and 3 Oct. During the emergency
collection of 1565, due to the trouble following a street battle, journeymen who were not working
did not have to contribute (*ibid.*). Jean Berjon's impression that 'ils font une cuilliette toutes les sepmay-
nes' (Proc. crim Gen. 1397, 5v) seems to be based on the emergency collection. He said he had not
actually been passed a journeyman himself, and none who had reported a *regular* weekly contribution.

long.[1] In ordinary times, the Company's treasury gave help to sick and old journeymen and to those out of work. Even the orphans of journeymen sometimes got aid. In many of these cases, printers' journeymen could and probably did turn to the Aumône-Générale. The Aumône's funds were limited, however, and the journeymen suspected that the rectors were not always fair in assaying their needs. Thus the mutual aid provided by the Griffarins was genuinely appreciated.[2]

Of course, the master printers and publishers of Lyons liked to think that the journeymen's coalition did not really have the support of its members. A few mutinous bullies, they claimed, were keeping the rest in line.[3] Though fear of *assolia* and of ostracism played their part in holding men to the Company, it was not run by a small clique. By the 1560's there is sign of an *élite* among the officers – two of them were relatives of leaders of 20 years before [4] – but the members still had some say in Company policy. In addition to their own meetings, the officers called periodic assemblies for discussion. These must have been lively, since on some issues (such as the treatment of Forfants in the early summer of 1565) there were divergent views within the Company.[5] Officers themselves were not immune from punishment: treasurer Julien Mouchet was ostracized for a while and then returned to lead the agitation of 1571–2.[6]

Indeed, members were sufficiently loyal that when the Reformed Consistories of Lyons and Geneva insisted that Protestant Griffarins break their oaths, most of them preferred to break with the Reformed Church. The Company of the Griffarins had given them traditions, fellowship, help when they were sick, and some control over their worldly destiny. In fact, the Company had achieved real gains: though factors like the price rise were outside their power, they kept their wages at a level that made the masters and publishers squawk to

---

[1] *Ibid.* 9r. In July 1539 rector Jean Daulhon complained to the lieutenant-general of the Sénéchaussée that the wife and children of the printers' journeymen were coming to the Aumôme saying they were dying of hunger. The Aumône was now overcharged (Arch. mun. AA 151, 69r). I checked through the minutes of the Aumône for the entire year of 1539 and found exactly one reference to the wife of a printers' journeymen (Archives de la Charité, E 5, p. 410): Claude, wife of Jacques l'imprimeur, given 'une aumône' for one month on 15 June.

[2] Proc. crim. Gen. 1397, 5v, 7r–v, 9v–10r, 12v. Two of those testifying had actually received such aid from the Company, though they had not been members long. On the journeymen's suspicions of the fairness of the rectors of the Aumône-Générale, see B.N. MSS., n. acq. fr. 8014, p. 695.

[3] Arch. mun. HH 98.

[4] Julien Mouchet, alias des Femmes, treasurer in the 1560's (Proc. crim. Gen. 1397, 9r) and Pierre Venicy, who presented the sword in one of the ceremonies (Reg. Consist. Gen. vol. 24 (1567), 10r) were relatives of Mathieu Mouchet and Simon Venicy, leaders in 1539–44. Exactly how the captain, lieutenant, ensign, and recreational officer were chosen is unknown, though, from the names we possess from the 1520's on, the captain changed quite often. Jacques Berjon simply said 'quatre des plus apparens et principaulx dentre eux ont le gouvernment' (Proc. crim. Gen. 1397, 11v). After 1572, leaders such as Guillaume Testefort and Jean Saulzion seem to retain their prominence for longer periods.

[5] Proc. crim. Gen. 1306; Jean Bollier had attended an assembly of about 20 for the 'accord', but had not attended the others. The dispute among the Griffarins in 1565 followed the serious wounding of Forfant Aymé Nesme and concerned the extent to which an 'accord' should be made between the two groups. Another sign of contact between members and officers, beside the banquets, is the large numbers of journeymen who accompanied leaders to hearings: six named journeymen 'et plusieurs autres en grand nombre' to the hearing of May 1556 (Arch. dep. Rh. B. Sen., Reg. Aud. Feb.-Oct. 1556).

[6] Arch. mun. HH 98.

the king and look for cheap labour elsewhere, and up to 1572 the journeymen were able to hold on to the food-salary.[1] Their demands did go well beyond this, of course, and they still considered themselves poor; but the journeymen did not suffer the constant frustration that can transform such a movement into a revolutionary one.

For revolutionary in the full sense the printers' journeymen were not. Slightly fantastic though their image was of the golden age of printing, when they said gentleman had worked as printers' journeymen, no egalitarian or communistic millennium in the future danced before their eyes.[2] In fact the Anabaptist solution never appealed to them even when they became uneasy in the Reformed Church. Their sense of worth and their radical view of the relative importance of labour to capital were almost always expressed in short-term demands confined to their own *métier*. Only in 1529–34, still formative years for the Company, did they come close to a revolutionary mood as far as secular issues were concerned. In 1529 they had *not* participated in the Grande Rebeine of Lyons, disorganized but serious grain rioting primarily by unskilled labourers, women and children. Instead they had volunteered to help the Consulate restore order and requisition grain for a public granary for the poor.[3] When the Consulate failed to make good on the latter promise, the printers' journeymen became 'seditious'. Together with the dyers' journeymen, they led armed marches through a Lyons stricken with famine and epidemic. Their placards, with words 'heavily insulting' to the authorities, have not survived; but once the Consulate had responded by creating the Aumône-Générale, the agitation of the printers' journeymen stopped.[4] After this, they did not lose interest in problems outside the printing shop: large numbers of them participated in efforts to change Lyons' religious institutions, and their recreations often included quips on the political and religious scene.[5] But the apparatus of the Company itself – its oaths, its punishments and its treasury – was used for concrete issues in printing. When they beat up the scabs in the butchers' and dyers' trade, they were returning a favour, not

[1] Audin, *op. cit.* pp. 176, 186ff.; B.N., MSS., n. acq. fr. 8014, p. 715; Chauvet, *op. cit.* pp. 68–75, on the victories of 1572.

[2] *Remonstrance*, C iv; before 1572, however, I have not come across this particular formulation. I discuss the attitude of the printers' journeymen toward radical religious solutions in my forthcoming book. It would be most interesting to compare the attitudes of sixteenth-century German miners with those of the printers' journeymen in these regards.

[3] Guigue, *Bibliothèque historique*, gives all the documents from which a vocational distribution of the rioters can be worked out as well as the role of the printers' journeymen in the special troops clearly seen. The lieutenant-general announced that the latter were 'to search the granaries of the town and be powerful enough to break into them if necessary' (Champier, *op. cit.* 367).

[4] H. Hauser, 'Etude critique sur la Rebeine de Lyon', *Revue historique*, LXI (1986), 301–2, 301, n.1, 302, n.1 (quoting documents from Arch. mun. BB 49). On the formation of the Aumône-Générale, see Henri de Boissieu, 'L'Aumône-Générale de 1534–1562', *Revue d'histoire de Lyon*, III (1909), 43–57.

[5] For instance, the relations between peace and the cultivation of the arts and sciences was the theme of their 1559 display at the celebration of the peace of Cateau-Cambrésis (G. Paradin, *Mémoires de l'histoire de Lyon* [Lyons, 1573], p. 361). Peace and orthodoxy are both themes of the rather special *Discours du temps passé et du present* which they performed in 1568 (L. Scheler, 'La Confession publique des imprimeurs lyonnais en 1568', *Bibliothèque d'humanisme et renaissance*, XXI [1959], 350–63. M. Scheler, who discovered this valuable pamphlet, did not realize that these festivals were put on by journeymen, rather than masters or publishers).

forwarding a labour federation. They noticed that there was injustice in other crafts,[1] but their identification was wholly with the 'estate of printing.'

III

Until we have new documents on the journeymen's coalitions of the thirteenth through sixteenth centuries, we cannot estimate exactly the place of the Company of the Griffarins in the history of the labour movement. Several suggestions emerge from this study, however. In the first place, this is a particularly clear case of a journeymen's coalition which is not primarily a reaction to craft guilds controlled 'unfairly' by masters or industrial entrepreneurs. Journeymen's coalitions were a response to life, shop experiences and work as wage-earners, with craft guilds sometimes a reinforcing factor.

Secondly, craft guilds were not necessarily the institutional model or antecedent for journeymen's coalitions. Indeed, many English journeymen's coalitions lost their efficacy because they had modelled themselves too closely upon the craft guild.[2] Journeymen's coalitions were organizations of economic resistance with some tactics all their own, and some shared with other groups. The strike, for instance, was a tactic also used by peasants.[3] Journeymen's coalitions were clandestine and disapproved and thus had to depend for their cohesiveness and success on secret oaths and initiation ceremonies. The *conjuratio* is a form which dates back to the late Roman Empire and which was readily turned to for communal uprisings and illegal combinations of all kinds. The initiation rite is, of course, much older and is a widespread social practice.[4] The blend of primitive and Christian elements in the Griffarins' ceremony could even have reached them from peasant sources, though more probably it derived from earlier journeymen's coalitions. Banquets, recreations, and mutual aid were activities which journeymen's organizations could have adopted from religious confraternities as well as from craft guilds.

Journeymen's coalitions were not all alike, as we have seen. The French *compagnonnages* of the seventeenth and eighteenth centuries with their elaborate rites were exclusive in membership, developed hierarchies within their group, and focused on techniques to restrict the labour supply.[5] These are often thought to be the inevitable concomitants of the secret labour-society, but the Company of the Griffarins up to 1572 retained relatively simple rites, welcomed new members, did not create grades of membership, and focused on the work

---

[1] 'Si l'on a iamais remarqué en aucuns estatz, et mestiers; les Maistres et superieurs tascher par infinis moyens de subjuger, assubiectir et traiter avec toute rigueur et servitude les Compagnons et domestiques de leur vacation: Cela a esté praticqué de tout temps et presentement en l'art de l'Imprimerie?' (*Remonstrance*, A i*r*).

[2] Lipson, *op. cit.* I, 407–10.

[3] R. H. Hilton, 'Peasant Movements in England before 1381', *Essays in Economic History*, ed. E. M. Carus-Wilson (1962), II, 82.

[4] Thrupp, 'Gilds', *C.E.H.* III, 235. For a valuable discussion of ceremonies, see E. J. Hobsbawm's chapter 'Ritual in Social Movements', in his *Primitive Rebels* (Manchester, 1959).

[5] Prof. Emanual Chill of the City College of New York has been working on the development of the *compagnonnage* from the sixteenth through the eighteenth century and also believes that the seventeenth century 'probably witnesses a crystallization of [earlier] artisanal traditions and a contraction of the *compagnonnage* into exclusivist élites' (letter of June, 1965).

68   NATALIE ZEMON DAVIS

stoppage to get its way. In part these differences were due to the different context in which the coalitions were operating: in the seventeenth century, when printing in Lyons was not expanding and was more tightly regulated than before, the journeymen became hostile to all foreign workers and would not receive them into their group. In part, however, the differences were due to differences in craft: the printers' pride and special camaraderie kept them from joining the 'rites', such as the Enfants de Maître Jacques, which embraced several crafts.

Readers familiar with the development of trade unions in the English printing industry may well be wondering why a 'Company of the Griffarins' did not spring up in London.[1] There were differences between the two cities, of course, the existence of the powerful Company of Stationers being an especially important one. Yet the industrial and technological forces described above – if my explanation has been valid – should have turned out some proud and 'mutinous' journeymen. The answer *may* be that there was such a coalition in London in the sixteenth century, but that the shrewd labour policy of the master printers helped transform it into the relatively harmless 'chapel' of the seventeenth century. The petitions which the London journeymen presented to the Privy Council or to the Stationers' Court from 1578 onward could have required no more organization than that allowed them as members of the Stationers' Company.[2] It is the ceremonies and customs of the seventeenth century chapel which give pause. There, in an organization confined to the single shop and approved by the master printer, new journeymen were given godfathers, were baptized, and were given their 'solaces' (that is, *assolia*) on the buttocks with a sword.[3] Here, in my view, is the residue of ceremonies from a sixteenth-century journeymen's coalition which had grown out of contact between continental and English printing workers. I speculate that there occurred in London what can be traced in detail in the printing *atelier* of the great Antwerp industrialist Christophe Plantin. Having had trouble with his workers, he took what he could use from their coalition – the baptism, the banquet, the oath, the mutual aid, the incipient concern for discipline and morality in the shop – and set up a 'company union'.[4] The French master printers did not have the wit to imitate the Plantin chapel for more than a

---

[1] See the useful discussions of E. Howe, *The London Compositor* (1947), p. 22 and A. E. Musson, *The Typographical Association* (1954), pp. 8–14. Both discuss the chapel and Mr Musson discusses also (p. 9) their undoubted utilization by the journeymen of their role in the Stationers' Company. Mr Howe concludes 'it is unlikely, however, that there was any organized union of the principal chapels in the London trade much before 1800' (p. 22). Mr Musson says (p. 12) 'there is no concrete evidence, however, of trade societies in the printing trade till towards the end of the eighteenth century'.

[2] C. Blagden, *The Stationers' Company* (1960), pp. 66, 123–4, 151; Musson, *op. cit.* p. 8.

[3] Moxon, *op. cit.* pp. 323 ff. Howe, *Compositor*, p. 27. See p. 62, n. 2 above for the etymology of *assolia* and *solaces*.

[4] M. Sabbe, 'Dans les ateliers de Plantin. Règlement du travail, discipline et prévoyance sociale', *Gutenberg Jahrbuch* (1937), pp. 174–92; Chauvet, *op. cit.* pp. 423–6, 440–5. Evidence of the baptismal ceremony and the oath, which is now 'safe' because it is made with the master's knowledge and before a group which did not negotiate salary with the master, comes from the opening of the seventeenth century. Yet they surely go back to the other innovations and rulings Plantin had instituted by 1583. M. Chauvet also concludes that the Plantin chapel was a 'syndicat maison' (p. 426).

A FRENCH TRADE UNION   69

hundred years; the London masters saw its advantages right away. Not until the eighteenth century did the English printers' journeymen try to unite again in an independent organization.[1]

By that date, certain features of the Company of the Griffarins had become archaic. Yet the spirit with which they met their new condition of life has not. The quest for a sense of family and brotherliness is often thought of as a vestigial survival from the pre-capitalist past. Rather I think we should see it as permanently creative in societies where impersonal contractual relationships threaten to dominate. We cannot consign to the past the sentiment which led the printers' journeymen to say that they 'laboured not as slaves, but as free men, working voluntarily at an excellent and noble calling'.

University of Toronto

---

[1] The evidence for the French 'chapelles' comes from the eighteenth century (*ibid.* pp. 437–8). It is true that the Company of the Griffarins had some shop organization, since work stoppages were ordinarily on a shop basis. But the ceremonies always included Griffarin officers and godfathers who were not necessarily in the shop, along with the journeymen from the shop; and the treasury as well as the assembly were not organized around the shop. The chapel later became the unit around which modern trade unions were to be built; but this should not obscure the diference between it and the true journeymen's coalition.

The views expressed in the text here are really suggestions for further research. It *may* be, for instance, that Plantin was imitating an institutional form which the English masters had pioneered. The word 'chapel' may have an English rather than a French origin (Howe, *Compositor*, p. 22). On Plantin's connexion with the London book trade, see Clair, *op. cit.* pp. 208–10.

[10]

Inquisitional Trials and Printing-Workers in Sixteenth-Century Spain

by

CLIVE GRIFFIN

A T THE END OF AUGUST 1565 a young Frenchman, known in Spain as Antonio de La Bastida, was languishing in the bishop's prison at Sigüenza on suspicion of heresy.[1] Some eight months earlier he and more than a dozen work-mates in that small Castilian town had been sitting round their master's fire one winter's night after the day's work was over. They had begun discussing matters loosely connected with those Reformation beliefs which were circulating north of the Pyrenees and which in Spain were condemned without distinction as *luteranismo* or 'Lutheran heresies'. Religion had arisen as a topic of conversation for two reasons. One of La Bastida's colleagues, named Juan de Villareal, had begun by recounting the story of a journey to the Low Countries on which he had met a Flemish colleague, a fervent *luterano*, who had shocked him by openly rejoicing at the death of Henry II of France. This Fleming had explained to Villareal that the news was a cause for celebration because the French king had been an implacable enemy of the Huguenots.[2] The conversation between the Sigüenza workers then turned for some reason to 'the saintly Brother Diego who, they claim, saved his Majesty the Prince', that is to say to the subject of Fray Diego of Alcalá — the '*santo sanador*', or healing saint — whose incorrupt corpse was venerated by successive Spanish monarchs.[3] In 1562 Carlos, son of Philip II, had been on the point of death after falling down a staircase in the university town of Alcalá de Henares, some said in pursuit of

[1] Archivo Diocesano, Cuenca (henceforth: 'ADC'), Inquisición, legajo 235, expediente 3032B, trial of Antonio de La Bastida (henceforth: 'trial of La Bastida'), 77 unfoliated folios. I translate into English all quotations from the original Spanish and Portuguese documents, but retain the versions of foreign names recorded by the secretaries to the Spanish and Portuguese Inquisitions. I wish to acknowledge the grant awarded to me by the British Academy which enabled me to undertake the research for this study. I would also like to thank Jonathan Mallinson, Mark Greengrass, Father Dimas Pérez Ramírez and Javier Triguero of the Archivo Diocesano, Cuenca, and María Dolores Alonso of the Archivo Histórico Nacional, Madrid (henceforth: 'AHN').
[2] Trial of La Bastida, fols [5]ʳᵛ, [10]ʳ, [22]ʳ, [36]ʳᵛ, and [48]ʳᵛ. Henry II died on 10 July 1559 from wounds sustained in a tournament held in Paris to celebrate the marriages of Philip II to Elizabeth of Valois, the eldest daughter of the French king, and of the Duke of Savoy to Margaret, Henry's sister. These alliances sealed the peace treaty signed between France and Spain at Cateau-Cambrésis. Henry's wounds proved fatal despite the intervention of the famous anatomist Andreas Vesalius. The Huguenots considered Henry's death to be divine punishment for his persecution of them; see R. J. Knecht, *The Rise and Fall of Renaissance France, 1483–1610* (London, 1996), p. 286.
[3] Trial of La Bastida, fol. [37]ʳ.

a common wench who had caught his eye. The prince's head wound was so serious that Andreas Vesalius was summoned to his bedside only to be prevented in the nick of time by his Spanish colleagues from trepanning the prince, an operation which would undoubtedly have proved fatal. Instead, the remains of Fray Diego were brought to the patient's bedchamber, the prince touched them and then covered his terribly infected face with his hands. His miraculous recovery dated from that moment.[4] La Bastida would have had first-hand knowledge of these events because he was working at Alcalá at that time.

La Bastida was usually careful to keep his own counsel. However, he had a reputation as a drinker and a trencherman, and wine doubtless loosened his tongue that evening as he chatted with his colleagues after dinner, for he decided to share with them his own views about the matters they had been discussing. He was to pay a high price for this indiscretion. He first voiced his doubts about Fray Diego's cure of Prince Carlos, saying that many figures revered in Spain as saints were nothing of the sort. He added for good measure the unconnected opinion that any bishop was as powerful in his own diocese as was the Pope in Rome, and that St Peter had never held the latter position but had merely been Bishop of Antioch.[5] When La Bastida was eventually denounced to the authorities two further accusations against him were added: his work-mates had noticed his sympathy for a *luterano* position when they had been lamenting the assassination of the leader of the Catholic faction in France, the Duc de Guise (February 1563), and he had been reluctant to celebrate a certain Catholic victory over the Huguenots in that country.[6]

On 20 April 1565 Villareal and another of La Bastida's colleagues, Alonso Martínez, denounced him to the ecclesiastical authorities of Sigüenza.[7] They offered no explanation for their delay of some three months in doing so, but it transpires that, after their conversation the previous winter, Villareal and La Bastida had quarrelled over a game of cards, while Martínez owed the Frenchman money.[8] It is therefore possible that their motives were not unmixed. However, it is equally possible that those two humble artisans were merely acting as so many Spaniards did at that time when the Church,

---

[4] When the prince recovered, he importuned his father to pressurize the Pope into canonizing Fray Diego (d. 1463), but this end was not achieved until 1588. There was a debate in Spain in the 1560s about whether Fray Diego's intervention or the doctors' skill lay behind Carlos's recovery, which appears to be reflected in La Bastida's argument with his work-mates; see L. J. Andrew Villalon, 'Putting Don Carlos Together Again: Treatment of a Head Injury in Sixteenth-Century Spain', *Sixteenth Century Journal*, 26 (1995), 347–65.

[5] Trial of La Bastida, fol. [5]ʳ⁻ᵛ. The theologians consulted by the Cuenca Inquisition about these accusations judged La Bastida's views on the power of bishops and Saint Peter to be heretical, but they did not criticize his scepticism of popular saints not officially endorsed by the Church (trial of La Bastida, fol. [45]ʳ).

[6] Trial of La Bastida, fol. [10]ʳ.

[7] Trial of La Bastida, fol. [5]ʳ⁻ᵛ.

[8] Trial of La Bastida, fols [8]ᵛ and [36]ᵛ.

24   *Inquisitional Trials in Sixteenth-Century Spain*

the Inquisition, and the secular authorities were mounting a vigorous propaganda campaign to root out all trace of Protestant heresy in Spain. The 1560s were the key decade in that campaign and the vast majority of Spaniards, high and low, saw heresy lurking behind many an ill-informed or casual comment.

The 1560s were indeed a fraught period for Spain: in Spanish eyes, a Protestant Jezebel sat upon the English throne threatening the sea route to Spanish possessions in the Low Countries, while religious divisions were throwing those possessions into turmoil. The inroads made by Islam in the western Mediterranean were an ever-present threat, and Spain's own Moorish population — the nominally Christianized *moriscos* — were perceived as a dangerous fifth-column within the country. Indeed, the *moriscos* were to revolt in 1568, contributing to one of the worst periods of crisis in sixteenth-century Spanish history. But it was France, on Spain's very borders, which presented the most immediate threat, for the neighbouring kingdom was racked by the Wars of Religion, proof if any were needed of the urgent need to defend Spain from the civil strife which followed in the wake of Reformation ideas. For many decades large numbers of Frenchmen had been crossing the Pyrenees in search of work and by the 1560s they constituted an extraordinarily high percentage of the population in certain regions of the country. They were to fall victim to the Inquisition in disproportionately· large numbers.

Despite the general atmosphere of panic, Iberian Spain was in fact never seriously threatened by Protestant ideas; most Spaniards had no direct contact with them, and those who did almost invariably rejected them out of hand. But there was in Spain a general perception that the country was the last bastion of Catholic orthodoxy, beset by agents bent on infiltrating Protestant ideas and books into Spain to sow heresy, dissent and social discord. The unearthing of the famous *luterano* cells in the major cities of Valladolid and Seville in the late 1550s greatly enhanced this perception. Protestant ideas came from abroad, and by the 1560s all foreigners were falling under suspicion. Juan de Villareal's testimony is eloquent: 'Because the said La Bastida is a foreigner, I do not consider him to be a good Christian.'[9] In this atmosphere of near-hysteria any apparently unorthodox remark was dangerous, but it was especially so if uttered by somebody from the '*nación sospechosa*', or suspect country, of which La Bastida was a native. As Dr Daza, La Bastida's prosecutor at Sigüenza, put it: 'Heresy is once again rife in the Kingdom of France where the accused was born and

---

[9] Trial of La Bastida, fol. [36]ᵛ. For Spanish xenophobia at this time see Miguel Jiménez Monteserín, 'Los luteranos ante el tribunal de la Inquisición de Cuenca, 1525–1600', in *La Inquisición española: nueva visión, nuevos horizontes*, ed. by Joaquín Pérez Villanueva (Madrid, 1980), pp. 689–736 (especially p. 699), and Jaime Contreras, *El Santo Oficio de la Inquisición de Galicia (poder, sociedad y cultura)* (Madrid, 1982), p. 16.

brought up; he is thus deeply suspect.' Bachelor Santos, the Cuenca prosecutor, shared his colleague's view: 'As this man is French, it is all the more probable that he is guilty.'[10] When La Bastida came to defend himself against the charge of heresy, he was acutely conscious of the danger represented by his origins, and he therefore claimed somewhat implausibly: 'If my being a Frenchman is what is making the prosecution so suspicious of me, let me say that I have lived in Spain for eleven years and can no longer speak my native tongue [. . .]. I now consider myself a Spaniard rather than a Frenchman.'[11]

When La Bastida was denounced to him, the Sigüenza prosecutor initially sat on his hands. Then, after four months of inactivity, he suddenly set the inquisitorial wheels in motion: an order for the Frenchman's arrest was issued on 28 August, the following day he underwent his first interrogation, and his possessions were confiscated from his master's house where he lodged. The ever-present figures of Juan de Villareal and Alonso Martínez certified that these items all belonged to La Bastida, repeated their earlier accusations against him, and swore that personal malice was not the motive for their testimony.[12] La Bastida thus suddenly found himself not only deprived of his freedom and all his worldly goods but also, as he subsequently protested, robbed of the good reputation he had enjoyed in Sigüenza ever since arriving to work in that town almost a year previously; for the rumour soon spread that, despite all his outward signs of orthodoxy, he was really an accursed heretic. He understandably feared the inquisitorial process in which he found himself caught up, and his terror increased on 30 August when, somewhat unusually, the charges against which he would have to defend himself were formally communicated to him. He determined to escape while he still had the chance.[13] That same night he filed through his shackles, breaking out of his cell at dawn and making for Alcalá where he doubtless still had friends. He made good time to Baides, a small village some twelve miles from Sigüenza on the main route from Zaragoza to Toledo, but as the sun grew hotter thirst forced him to break cover and go down to the river Henares where he was spotted by a band of horsemen travelling to Madrid from Sigüenza. They immediately recognized him, for a hue and cry had been raised as soon as his escape from prison had been discovered, and everybody in the area was on the lookout. As soon as they

---

[10] Trial of La Bastida, fols [18]ʳ and [56]ʳ.
[11] Trial of La Bastida, fols [59]ʳ–[60]ʳ. French immigrants to Spain were particularly vulnerable to persecution by the Inquisition, especially in Aragon and Catalonia; see Elisabeth Balancy, 'Les Immigrés français devant le Tribunal de l'Inquisition de Barcelone (1552–1692)', in *Les Français en Espagne à l'époque moderne (XVIe-XVIIIe siècles)*, ed. by Jean-Pierre Amalric and Gérard Chastagnaret (Paris, 1990), pp. 45–69, and William Monter, *Frontiers of Heresy: The Spanish Inquisition from the Basque Lands to Sicily* (Cambridge, 1990), pp. 45, 106–07, and 234–35.
[12] Trial of La Bastida, fols [10]ʳ–[11]ʳ.
[13] The Inquisition's archives are full of complaints made to headquarters by the regional tribunals about the sorry state of their prisons, the corruption of their employees, and the frequency with which prisoners escaped.

26   *Inquisitional Trials in Sixteenth-Century Spain*

saw him in the distance they shouted, 'There goes the *luterano*', a cry which speaks volumes about the atmosphere in Spain in those years.[14] La Bastida tried to get away up the rocky hillside and in desperation hid in a tree, but he was surrounded, forced to surrender, and returned to Sigüenza after his few hours of liberty.

Back in that town, his trial began in earnest, the prosecutor interpreting his bid for freedom as evidence of his guilt. La Bastida reluctantly confessed that the file with which he removed his shackles had, in classic fashion, been smuggled into his cell in some food by a serving-boy called Cebrianillo who worked, as La Bastida did himself, for a man called Sebastián Martínez.[15] Like almost all those who found themselves on trial for heresy, he began by denying the charge of having uttered heretical 'propositions'.[16] He claimed that, if he had said anything which smacked of heresy, it was because 'I am a young, ignorant lad [. . .] and because I didn't realize that there were any errors or heresy in what I said, for I have never received any instruction in such matters'.[17] Nevertheless, several witnesses asserted that an intelligent and literate person like him would never have voiced *luterano* beliefs through mere ignorance.[18] Work-mates who had known La Bastida long before he had been employed at Sigüenza were summoned to give testimony at his trial, witnessing to his good character and devout behaviour. According to them, he was an exemplary young man who did not share the vices they said were common in others of his age: he was a hard worker, responsible, modest in speech and action, and assiduous in observing fasts, jubilees, and all the festivals of the Church.[19]

At this period Sigüenza came under the jurisdiction of the Cuenca tribunal of the Inquisition and so, given the seriousness of the denunciations made against the prisoner, all the papers concerning him were sent to Francisco de

---

[14] Trial of La Bastida, fol. [12]ʳ.

[15] Trial of La Bastida, fol. [13]ᵛ.

[16] 'Propositions' were erroneous statements about the faith which were not necessarily formally heretical but nevertheless did not conform to orthodoxy as defined by the Church; see Nicholas Griffiths, 'Popular Religious Scepticism and Idiosyncrasy in Post-Tridentine Cuenca', in *Faith and Fanaticism: Religious Fervour in Early Modern Spain*, ed. by Lesley K. Twomey, Robert Hooworth-Smith, and Michael Truman (Ashgate, 1997), pp. 95–126 (p. 96).

[17] Trial of La Bastida, fol. [17]ʳ. Although La Bastida was twenty-five or twenty-six years old when arrested, all the witnesses in his trial stress his youth, referring to him as 'a young lad'. The Inquisition tended to be lenient with the young or the ignorant who were able to persuade it that they were genuinely contrite. For example, in 1571 the Toledo tribunal showed clemency to Juan Gómez, a Galician agricultural labourer, on the grounds that, although he had uttered 'propositions', he 'seemed to have pronounced them innocently and as a man of little understanding' (AHN, Inquisición, legajo 99, caja 2, expediente 18, fol. [35]ʳ); similarly, the Flemish typesetter Enrique Loe, Loc, Loher or Loye was not dealt with harshly because he was still under twenty-five years of age and had shown evidence of contrition (AHN, Inquisición, legajo 111, expediente 13, unfoliated (henceforth 'trial of Enrique Loe'), fol. [27]ʳ).

[18] The defence La Bastida drew up in prison shows that he could write Spanish well, although one of the witnesses in his trial maintained that he spoke it with a foreign accent (trial of La Bastida, fols [19]ʳ, [22]ʳ, and [59]ʳ–[60]ʳ).

[19] Trial of La Bastida, fols [24]ʳ–[31]ʳ.

Ayanz, Inquisitor of Cuenca.[20] Ayanz went through them with his theological advisers and, considering that the case warranted further investigation, ordered La Bastida to be sent to him from Sigüenza under escort. Once in Cuenca, the Frenchman was put in a cell with a village priest named Juan García who was facing charges of seducing his female confessants. The two immediately set about planning their escape, La Bastida apparently hoping to flee Spain and find work in Venice, but just before they could put their scheme into effect, La Bastida was transferred to a more secure cell.[21] García, however, managed to get away (in December 1565) and was on the run for several weeks. When he was eventually recaptured, he confessed to their plans, doubtless in an attempt to attract the Inquisition's clemency.[22] He also offered a detailed description of his cell-mate's behaviour in prison. La Bastida, he maintained, had been sunk in despair: 'He did nothing but weep and put his head into the sunlight which came through the window and test the bars to see if there was any chance of his squeezing through [. . .]; he said that if he couldn't escape he'd hang himself.' Naturally, one cannot necessarily believe everything the Inquisition's prisoners said, but it is probable that what Juan García testified was true and that La Bastida did, indeed, confide to him that 'he would willingly wear a *sanbenito* [the garment imposed by the Inquisition on penitents], suffer two hundred lashes, or serve as a galley slave for three or four years as long as he could avoid being put to death'.[23] It is likewise difficult to explain why García should have invented La Bastida's claim to him that, far from being a Huguenot, he had gone to Spain expressly to get away from the excesses of the French Protestants.[24]

La Bastida was apparently terrified, assuming that he was going to be burnt alive by the Cuenca Inquisition, but if so he exaggerated the danger in

[20] Ayanz had to send far and wide for witness statements in the subsequent trial because, after fulfilling his contract in Sigüenza, Sebastián Martínez had returned to Valladolid with some of his workforce, including Villareal and Alonso Martínez. Others of the companions who had chatted round the hearth that winter's night in Sigüenza were no longer to be found either there or at Valladolid. This is the case, for example, with two Frenchmen: Felipe Arnaut and Isac de Ribera. The former had returned to France and the latter had gone on to Alcalá de Henares where we find him working several years later.
[21] Trial of La Bastida, fol. [66]ʳ. Among those with Reformist sympathies Venice had long enjoyed the reputation of being a haven of tolerance. A French Calvinist who was astonished to be arrested there in 1570 said that he had assumed that it was 'a free place where everybody can live as they please'. By this time, and even some years earlier when La Bastida set his sights on it, religious tolerance was, however, a thing of the past in Venice; see John Martin, *Venice's Hidden Enemies: Italian Heretics in a Renaissance City* (Berkeley, 1993), pp. 185–86 and 219.
[22] García, priest of the small village of Tinajas, was a seasoned escaper but he implausibly accused La Bastida of having taught him how to escape (trial of La Bastida, fols [40]ʳ–[42]ʳ, [63]ᵛ, [65]ᵛ–[66]ᵛ, and [69]ᵛ). He was put to the torture, eventually absolved in Cuenca Cathedral, and sentenced to confinement in a monastery for three years. Only fragments of his trial survive (ADC, Inquisición, legajo 761, expediente 877). Further details about this wayward priest and his brother Pedro García are to be found in ADC, Inquisición, libro 333B, fol. 211ʳ, and libro 356, fols 280ᵛ–81ᵛ, as well as in AHN, Inquisición, legajo 2544, caja 1, expediente 43, fol. [1]ʳ, and expediente 52, fol. [1]ʳ. I am indebted to Adelina Sarrión Mora for her advice about cases of solicitation in the confessional.
[23] Trial of La Bastida, fol. [40]ʳ⁻ᵛ.
[24] Trial of La Bastida, fol. [41]ʳ⁻ᵛ. For Catholic immigrants from France going to Spain in search of a safe haven from Protestantism in their own country, see Jiménez Monteserín, 'Los luteranos', p. 703.

which he found himself. Inquisitor Ayanz tried, as was normal in such cases, to discover whether there were any firmly-held heretical convictions lying behind what La Bastida had said at Sigüenza, but was also conscious that the Frenchman was frightened out of his wits whenever he interrogated him. He accordingly allowed him pen and paper to write his defence and confession in his cell; fortunately this document survives. From it we can deduce that the comments La Bastida made in Sigüenza that fateful night were not the product of a well thought-out theological position nor the result of a careful study of Protestant literature; rather, he was merely mouthing what he had picked up from two compatriots. One was a sailor from Rouen whom he had happened to bump into at the Seville docks, and the other a young French Huguenot with whom he had worked for a considerable period both at Seville and Toledo and who had attempted to convert him from Catholicism. Ayanz ordered the defendant to be put to the torture but no confession of his having been a secret *luterano* could be extracted from him. La Bastida showed the requisite contrition, and Ayanz evidently accepted his defence that he was merely an ignorant youth. In March 1566, accompanied in Cuenca Cathedral by a motley crew — the errant priest Juan García, a Flemish herbalist, and a miller from Cuenca — he abjured his errors and was banished in perpetuity from that district.[25]

La Bastida's case differs in only one major respect from that of many another immigrant at this time whose behaviour was considered by his Spanish neighbours or work-mates to be dangerously different from their own or whose casual remarks were interpreted as unorthodox when the witch-hunt for *luteranos* was at its height. What distinguished La Bastida's case is that he was a printing-worker, and his trial papers prove a rich source of information for historians of the book, in particular because we otherwise know so little about the humble artisans employed in sixteenth-century Spanish presses. This dearth of information can be attributed to the fact that, although printing-workers occasionally make an appearance in legal documents conserved in local Archivos de Protocolos, such sources provide scant detail about their place of origin, professional training, and careers, and none at all about their social and family origins, their educational background, their opinions and aspirations, or about the life they led as printing-workers in Spain.

It has long been known that inquisitional trials can teach us a good deal about the lives of what French historians call the *menu peuple*. However, as far as I am aware, historians of the book have not quarried in any systematic fashion the surviving trial-records of the Spanish and Portuguese Inquisitions,

---

[25] For information on the other penitents at this ceremony see ADC, Inquisición, libro 333B, fols 98^r and 237^v.

together with the very full runs of their surviving correspondence.[26] However, these papers cast important light on the lives of printing-workers in several ways. First, by the 1560s the Holy Office in Spain was obliging all defendants suspected of heresy to pronounce a *discurso de la vida*, a potted account of their life history which was, in fact, constituted by a series of connected answers to a standard questionnaire nowhere explicitly mentioned in the records. Second, as the arrested printing-workers responded to questions about their religious convictions and how and when they acquired them, they often made casual mention of their careers; for instance, about their having printed a particular edition or about who were their work-mates in a particular press. Third, once the interrogations had been concluded, they were encouraged to 'unburden their consciences', as the inquisitors put it, by denouncing others of their acquaintance who shared their heretical beliefs; when they did so, they often described a wide network of itinerant printers and printing-workers, also sometimes commenting on when and where they had met them. This testimony can provide information about unknown printers and presses, about hitherto unknown editions, and about a host of otherwise anonymous printing-workers. Naturally, the defendants in these trials feared for their lives; they often tried to conceal certain episodes in their past while putting a positive gloss on others as they strove to guess how much the inquisitors already knew about them, who among their acquaintances had denounced them to the Holy Office, and on suspicion of what crime. Under these circumstances truth must frequently have been a casualty.[27] However, a good deal of the most interesting information provided by these trials to the historian of the book is probably reliable, either because it occurs in passages of the trial in which it is difficult to imagine why defendants

---

[26] A handful of inquisitorial trials of sixteenth-century printers or printing-workers in the Spanish-speaking world have been studied or transcribed; for example, José Goñi Gatzambide, 'El impresor Miguel de Eguía procesado por la Inquisición', *Hispania Sacra*, 1 (1948), 35–88, examines the trial of a Spanish printer, while Francisco Fernández de Castillo, *Libros y libreros en el siglo XVI*, 2nd edn (Mexico City, 1982), and the first volume of Juan Pascoe, *La obra de Enrico Martínez*, 2 vols (Tacámbaro [Mexico], 1996–), reproduce the trials of printers and booksellers in Mexico. Cristóbal Pérez Pastor refers in passing to the inquisitorial trials of several printing-workers; for example, in his *La imprenta en Toledo: descripción bibliográfica de las obras impresas en la imperial ciudad desde 1483 hasta nuestros días* (Madrid, 1887; repr. Toledo, 1984), p. xix, he mentions the trial of 'Pierre de Ruen', the Pierre de Ribera to whom I refer below; and in his *La imprenta en Medina del Campo* (Madrid, 1895; repr. Salamanca, 1992, with a preface by Pedro M. Cátedra), pp. 435–36, he returns to the same trial, adding a reference on p. 439 to that of the French typesetter 'Pierres de Reims', the Pierre de Rinz I mention below. But Pérez Pastor undertook no systematic study of these cases. The present article is a first attempt to exploit the archives of the Spanish and Portuguese Inquisitions for a study of such humble printing-workers. It constitutes part of a future book about what is revealed of the world of the Iberian book in the sixteenth century by the records of the Holy Office's headquarters in Madrid and Lisbon, and those of the various provincial tribunals. Important starting points have been provided by Ernst Schäfer, *Beiträge zur Geschichte des spanischen Protestantismus und der Inquisition im 16. Jahrhunderts, nach den Original-Akten in Madrid und Simancas*, 3 vols (Gütersloh, 1902; repr. Aalen, 1969), and Julián Martín Abad, *La imprenta en Alcalá de Henares (1502–1600)*, 3 vols (Madrid, 1991).

[27] In their *discursos de la vida* printing-workers tried by the Inquisition tended to pass over in silence their acquaintance with suspect cities like Antwerp, Lyon, Geneva or La Rochelle; it was only under interrogation that they let slip the fact that they had lived and worked in such places.

30   *Inquisitional Trials in Sixteenth-Century Spain*

should have wanted to mislead their interrogators, or because they unwittingly damned themselves by their testimony where, had they been more alive to the importance the prosecution attached to what they were saying, they would undoubtedly have lied. The following is the *discurso de la vida* provided by La Bastida to the Cuenca tribunal in September 1565.[28]

When questioned, he said his name was Antonio de La Bastida and that he was a native of France, born in Albi and 25 years of age, a printing-worker by trade, currently resident in the town of Sigüenza.

Parents

Hernando de La Bastida, servant to the Bishop of Albi, deceased. Margarita de Reualer, his wife, resident at Albi.

Paternal grandparents

Juan de La Bastida, merchant, citizen of Anges [Angers?], deceased. Luysa de Narbona, native of Narbonne, deceased.

Maternal grandparents

The defendant said that he did not know their names.

Paternal uncles and aunts

Giles de La Bastida, formerly canon of the church of Santa Cecilia at Albi, deceased.[29] Catalina de Ribaleri, citizen of Albi, wife of Berenguel Landes, merchant.

Maternal uncles and aunts

Elena de Ribaleri, widow of Antonio de La Costa.

Brothers and sisters

He said he had none. The defendant said that he was unmarried and had no children.

When questioned, he said that all his aforementioned family was of old Christian stock without taint of Moorish or Jewish blood, nor had any of them, himself included, ever been apprehended or sentenced by the Holy Office.

He knew how to cross himself, and recite fluently in Latin the Lord's Prayer, Ave Maria, Salve Regina, and the Ego Peccator.

When questioned, he said that he was baptized and confirmed as a Catholic and that he went to Mass, confessing at the times stipulated by the Church, and last Lent he confessed at Sigüenza to Bachelor Manjón,[30] a cleric from that town, and received the Holy Sacrament in Sigüenza Cathedral, and subsequently, when the Jubilee was proclaimed last August, he confessed to the aforementioned Bachelor Manjón and received the Holy Sacrament in order to gain the said Jubilee, and in Lent of [fifteen] sixty-four he confessed at León to a Franciscan friar whose name he cannot recall and received the Holy Sacrament in León Cathedral, and the previous Lent he confessed in Seville to a priest from Seville Cathedral whose name he does not know; he has no certificates of confession from any of these occasions.

When questioned, he said that he could read and write and that he began to learn the *Art* of Antonio[31] at Toulouse but did not continue his studies because he was put

---

[28] Trial of La Bastida, fols [46]ʳ–[48]ʳ.
[29] i.e. the Cathedral of Sainte Cécile.
[30] See below, n. 77.
[31] i.e. he began studying Latin using Antonio de Nebrija's *Introductiones latinae*, generally known in Spain as the 'Artes'.

to work in a printing-press, and that it was his cousin Symon Landes who taught him in Albi how to read and write.

Asked to give his *discurso de la vida*, he said that he grew up in his father's house at Albi living there until he was seven or eight, and when he was that age a bookseller from Albi called Juan (he does not remember his surname) took him to Toulouse at his father's request to study Latin at the Colegio de Lesquila,[32] and when he had been there for about six months, the defendant's father died, so he abandoned his studies as soon as he learnt of his decease and was bound apprentice for a period of five years to the printer Jaques Colonyés[33] to learn the art of pulling the bar, and at the end of those five years he came to Spain in [fifteen] fifty-four with Juan Mole who was married to a woman in Toledo and was a type-caster by trade;[34] they came to Zaragoza where the defendant worked at his trade in the house of the printer Pedro Bernuz[35] for eight or nine months, and from there he came to Valencia and worked for some six months in the house of the Flemish printer Juan de Mey,[36] and then for seven or eight months more in the house of Antonio de Sanauje[37] who was at that time a printer and bookseller, and from Valencia he returned to Zaragoza working for about two months there in the house of the printer Esteuan de Nágera,[38]

[32] i.e. the Collège d'Esquille, one of the small colleges of Toulouse University. This college was disbanded shortly after La Bastida's time there, but some of its buildings still survive in the Rue du Taur.

[33] i.e. Jacques Colomiés I. The Colomiés dynasty of printers was famous for publishing Catholic propaganda; see *Histoire de l'édition française*, ed. by Henri-Jean Martin and Roger Chartier, 4 vols (Paris, 1983–86), I, p. 353. The French typesetter Pierre de Rinz, who was tried for heresy at Toledo, had similarly worked at Toulouse for Jacques Colomiés I before going to Spain (AHN, Inquisición, legajo 112, expediente 6, unfoliated (henceforth 'trial of Pierre de Rinz'), fol. [7]').

[34] This 'Juan Mole' was probably the 'Juan Molot', or 'Juan Molo, the printer', who was a member of a *luterano* cell of French printers of playing-cards tried at Toledo in 1564 and who managed to escape from the Inquisition when he learnt that his comrades had been apprehended; see Ernst Schäfer, 'Die Vereinigung französischer Protestanten zu Toledo um die Mitte des 16. Jahrhunderts', *Zeitschrift für Kirchengeschichte*, 21 (1900–01), 399–434 (p. 406), and Juan Blázquez Miguel, *La Inquisición en Castilla-La Mancha*, Universidad de Córdoba, Monografías, 86 (Madrid, 1986), pp. 151–52. This same man was also referred to by the French binder and bookseller João de Leão (Jean de Lyon), who was tried three times by the Lisbon Inquisition and eventually executed there in 1574. João had met Molo at Granada in about 1561 or 1562, later describing him, in terms very similar to those used by La Bastida, as 'Johan Mola of Paris who is a type-caster married to a woman in Toledo': Instituto dos Arquivos Nacionais/Torre do Tombo, Lisbon, Inquisição de Lisboa, processo 1366, the three trials of João de Leão (henceforth 'trials of João de Leão'), fol. 257'.

[35] Pedro Bernuz printed at Zaragoza from 1540 to 1571; see Juan Delgado Casado, *Diccionario de impresores españoles (siglos XV–XVII)*, 2 vols (Madrid, 1996), I, pp. 67–68. Enrique Loe, the Flemish typesetter tried for heresy at Toledo, also worked in Bernuz's press on arrival in Spain (trial of Enrique Loe, fol. [6]').

[36] Juan Mey, or Jan van Mey, printed at Valencia from 1543 until 1555; see Delgado Casado, *Diccionario*, I, pp. 454–55.

[37] Antonio de Sanahuja worked as a bookseller at Valencia from 1544 to at least 1557. In 1554 he established his own press, but his production was small and the last known edition he produced was dated 1556. As both bookseller and printer he was closely associated with Juan Mey; see Delgado Casado, *Diccionario*, II, pp. 627–28. La Bastida's statement indicates that he knew of Sanahuja's later abandonment of the craft of printing. João de Leão had worked as a binder for Sanahuja from about 1557 to 1561 (trials of João de Leão, fol. 16').

[38] Esteban de Nájera was a member of a printing dynasty, who ran a press in Zaragoza from 1550 until 1555; see Delgado Casado, *Diccionario*, II, p. 483. In La Bastida's trial, Esteban's brother, Diego, testified in favour of the Frenchman, maintaining that he had met him some eight years previously when La Bastida had worked for about a month in Esteban's press at Zaragoza. At that time La Bastida had just arrived in Spain and was 'a very young lad whose beard had not yet begun to grow'. Diego ran into him again at Sigüenza when he joined the team that Sebastián Martínez had formed to print liturgical books for that diocese (trial of La Bastida, fols [24]'–[25]').

32　　　*Inquisitional Trials in Sixteenth-Century Spain*

and afterwards he returned to Valencia but could find no work there, and after a week he went to Salamanca and worked there for a year in Andrés de Portonaris's house[39] and from time to time in that of Juan de Cánova,[40] and from there he went to Medina del Campo but could find no work and travelled to Alcalá de Henares where there was no work to be had either, and went to Toledo where there was no work, and returned to Zaragoza where he could find no work, and went back to Valencia where he was employed for nine months in the house of the wife of the late Juan de Mey,[41] and then because the plague struck Valencia[42] the defendant went to Barcelona where he worked for eight or nine months in a press owned by a doctor, a bookseller, and a schoolteacher,[43] and he fell ill there and returned to the town of Albi where he stayed in his mother's house for three months, and after that he went to Lyon in France where he worked for a year in Teobaldo Pagano's press,[44] and when peace was declared between Spain and France he went to Paris for a fortnight to see the celebrations,[45] and on his way back to the region of his birth he met a nephew of Don Juan García, a Valencia merchant, and came with him to Valencia and was employed as his servant for six months, and then he returned to Zaragoza, going back to Valencia and working for four months in the house of the printer Juan Navarro[46] and another four in the house of the wife of the aforementioned Juan de

[39] The Italian printer Andrea de Portonariis ran a press at Salamanca from 1547 until 1568; see Lorenzo Ruiz Fidalgo, *La imprenta en Salamanca (1501–1600)*, 3 vols (Madrid, 1994), I, pp. 65–73. At least two other immigrant printing-workers tried for heresy at Toledo had worked in his press: the French typesetter Juan Franco, whose two trials are: Universitäts-und Landesbibliothek Sachsen-Anhalt, Martin-Luther-Universität, Halle-Wittenberg (henceforth, 'ULHW'), Inquisitionakten Handschriften, Yc 2⁰ 20 (3), fols 130ʳ–76ʳ (henceforth 'trials of Juan Franco'), see here fols 131ʳ, 139ᵛ, and 154ᵛ; and the French typesetter Pierre de Ribera whose trial is AHN, Inquisición, legajo 112, expediente 8, unfoliated (henceforth 'trial of Pierre de Ribera'), see here fol. [15]ʳ.
[40] Juan de Cánova printed at Salamanca from 1553 to 1569; see Ruiz Fidalgo, *La imprenta en Salamanca*, I, pp. 76–80. Cánova employed not only La Bastida but also the Flemish typesetter Enrique Loe who, as we have seen, was later tried for heresy at Toledo (trial of Enrique Loe, fol. [6]ʳ), whilst his father Alejandro de Cánova employed Juan Franco (trials of Juan Franco, fol. 136ʳ).
[41] Juan Mey died in 1555. His widow Jerónima de Gales ran the press until she married another printer in 1568; see Delgado Casado, *Diccionario*, I, pp. 451–52. She appears to have been one of the few women who we can be reasonably sure worked in the presses they managed; see Clive Griffin, 'Brígida Maldonado "ynprimidora" sevillana, viuda de Juan Cromberger', *Archivo Hispalense*, no. 233 (1993), 83–117 (p. 87).
[42] Doubtless the plague which ravaged that city in 1557 and 1558.
[43] I am not able reliably to identify this Barcelona press, although the schoolmaster appears to have been a man called Escobar to whom La Bastida refers later in his trial (fol. [60]ᵛ). It is possible that this man was Francesc Escobar who was associated with the French printer, bookseller, publisher and author Claudi Bornat who was active in Barcelona from 1556 to 1575. La Bastida may even be referring here to this printer because Bornat occasionally styled himself as bookseller at that time and entered into partnership with Escobar and Onofre Bruguera (both said to be 'artium et medicine doctores') to print books; see Josep-Maria Madurell i Marimon, *Claudi Bornat* (Barcelona, 1973), p. 138.
[44] The Protestant printer Thibaud Payen was active at Lyon between 1534 and 1570; see Henri Louis Baudrier, *Bibliographie lyonnaise: recherches sur les imprimeurs, libraires, relieurs et fondeurs de lettres de Lyon au XVIᵉ siècle*, 12 vols (Lyon, Paris, Geneva, Lille, 1895–1950), IV, pp. 206–90. Payen had employed at least two of the French printing-workers later tried for heresy by the Toledo Inquisition: Pierre de Rinz (trial of Pierre de Rinz, fol. [7]ᵛ), and Pierre Reigner, whose trial is AHN, Inquisición, legajo 112, expediente 5, unfoliated (henceforth 'trial of Pierre Reigner'), see here fol. [21]ᵛ.
[45] The Treaty of Cateau-Cambrésis was signed in April 1559. The royal marriages which crowned this treaty were celebrated in Paris in July of that year, and the public festivities associated with them are doubtless what La Bastida attended. If this is the case it is not surprising that he should have had views about Juan de Villareal's account of reactions to Henry II's death (see p. 22 above and n. 2) because he had himself been in Paris when it occurred.
[46] Juan Navarro ran his press at Valencia from at least 1532 to 1543; books were subsequently signed from 1552 to 1583 'in Juan Navarro's house' but it is not known who managed the press during that period; see Delgado Casado, *Diccionario*, II, pp. 484–85.

Mey, and then he went to Granada where he worked for fourteen months in Councillor García de Briones's press,[47] and from there he went to Córdoba where he worked for three months in the house of the printer Juan Baptista,[48] and then he set off for Seville, but on the way he fell in with some gentlemen who were travelling to the Indies, and he accompanied them to Jerez [de la Frontera] working in their employ as a servant for three months, and he returned to Seville and worked for a year in the house of the printer Sebastián de Trugillo,[49] and from there he came to Toledo where he worked for three months in the house of the printer Juan de Ayala,[50] and from there he went to Alcalá de Henares where he worked for three months in the house of the printer Andrés de Angulo,[51] and from there he went to Madrid where he stayed for about a month wandering around,[52] and afterwards he went to Burgos and worked for four months in the house of Felipe de Junta,[53] and from there he went to León where he worked for a year in the house of the printer Pedro de Celada printing breviaries for that bishopric,[54] and from there he returned to Burgos where he spent another two months in Felipe de Junta's house, and from there he went to Berlanga where he was three months in Canon Robles's house working on a book called 'a centurio' which Diego de Córdova from Burgo de Osma was printing,[55] and from there he went to Sigüenza where he has been about

[47] At least two editions are known to have been issued in 1563 and 1564 from the press that Elio Antonio de Lebrija, the grandson of the great Spanish humanist Antonio de Nebrija (or Lebrija), ran at Granada with García de Briones, but this partnership was short-lived; see Antonio Gallego Morell, *Cinco impresores granadinos de los siglos XVI y XVII* (Granada, 1970), p. 43.

[48] Juan Bautista Escudero set up the first press in the city of Córdoba; he printed there between 1556 and 1583, specializing in the sort of liturgical editions on which La Bastida would also work at Burgos, León, and Sigüenza; see Delgado Casado, *Diccionario*, I, pp. 205–06.

[49] Sebastián Trujillo is said to have printed at Seville from the early 1540s until 1569; see Delgado Casado, *Diccionario*, II, pp. 682–84. However, he must have died before 1569 because some two years earlier it was his widow Ana de la Peña who employed another of the French printing-workers later tried at Toledo, the typesetter Pierre de Rinz (trial of Pierre de Rinz, fol. [7]'). For his part, La Bastida was certainly working in this press during the spring of 1563 when Trujillo was still alive (trial of La Bastida, fol. [46]').

[50] La Bastida must be referring here to Juan de Ayala Cano, son of the better-known Toledo printer Juan de Ayala. Ayala Cano probably worked at Toledo between 1556 and 1576; see Delgado Casado, *Diccionario*, I, pp. 49–50. Ayala Cano also employed the Flemish typesetter Enrique Loe who was later tried in that city (trial of Enrique Loe, fols [5]' and [6]').

[51] Andrés de Angulo ran a press at Alcalá from 1560 to 1578; see Martín Abad, *La imprenta en Alcalá de Henares*, I, pp. 104–06. Martín Abad notes that Pierre de Rinz, Enrique Loe, and the Parisian typesetter Guillermo Herlin, all of whom feature in this article, were employed by Angulo. When a royal commission visited the Alcalá presses in December 1572 the team working in Angulo's press consisted of four compositors, five pullers, four beaters, and a type-caster (there were six Spaniards, six Frenchmen, one Fleming, and one Portuguese); unfortunately their names were not recorded (AHN, Universidades, legajo 135, caja 1, unnumbered expediente, fols [5]'–[6]'). I am grateful to Julián Martín Abad for giving me the archival reference to this document, discovered in the AHN by Ramón González Navarro.

[52] Madrid became the capital in 1561; La Bastida visited it shortly afterwards. He would not have gone there in search of work as a printer because the first press was not set up there until 1566.

[53] Felipe de Junta, a relation of the famous Giuntas of Florence, Venice, and Lyon, ran his press at Burgos from 1560 to 1596; see Delgado Casado, *Diccionario*, I, pp. 351–52.

[54] Little is known about Celada, but Delgado Casado, *Diccionario*, I, pp. 139–40, suggests that he was active between 1548 and 1556. However, this period must be extended because the breviary which La Bastida worked on in Celada's press at León must have been the *Breviarium Legionense* signed on 1 April 1564; see Antonio Odriozola, *Catálogo de libros litúrgicos, españoles y portugueses, impresos en los siglos XV y XVI* (Pontevedra, 1996), p. 217, no. 223. No copy is now known.

[55] This book was Francisco de Robles's *Copia sive ratio accentuum omnium fere dictionum difficilium, tam linguae latinae, quam hebraicae, nonnullarumque graecarum*. It was printed in 1564/5 by Diego de Córdoba at Berlanga in the house of the author's brother, Canon Juan de Robles, who corrected the proofs.

34   *Inquisitional Trials in Sixteenth-Century Spain*

a year printing works for that bishopric in the house of the printer Sebastián Martýnez,[56] whence they have now brought him prisoner to this Holy Office.

This autobiographical sketch enables us to reconstruct quite precisely La Bastida's travels through France and Spain (see Figure 1). What he says about himself here and at other moments of his trial, together with his colleagues' testimony about him, paints a picture of someone who was in most respects typical of those immigrants who worked in the Spanish presses of the period. They were in the main young and footloose bachelors, which may explain why La Bastida and the French binder João de Leão (Jean de Lyon) both pointed out that their friend and compatriot 'Juan Molo' was married to a woman in Toledo, for such a situation was unusual among them. These immigrant workers differed notably in their intellectual background and professional training from their Spanish counterparts. For instance, although La Bastida was a pressman, not a compositor, he could read and write both French and Spanish (he left several pages of testimony written in his own hand in perfect Castilian); he even claimed to have begun to study Latin in Toulouse before circumstances obliged him to make his way in the world.

In this way La Bastida resembles other French printing-workers encountered in the papers of the Spanish Inquisition. Pierre de Rinz, for example, was working as a compositor in Andrés de Angulo's press at Alcalá de Henares when he was arrested in 1569 on the orders of the Toledo tribunal of the Inquisition. He was the illegitimate son of a priest from Reims and had been sent by his father to study Latin and philosophy in Paris until, as had happened with La Bastida, his father died and the money ran out. His brother-in-law, a Calvinist bookseller who was in correspondence with the Protestant leader Louis, Prince of Condé, then took him to Geneva and apprenticed him to Robert Estienne's agent there, the printer Thomas

---

[56] Sebastián Martínez printed mainly at Valladolid (1550–66) and Alcalá de Henares (1562–76), although he also set up presses for short periods in Palencia and Sigüenza; see Martín Abad, *La imprenta en Alcalá de Henares*, I, pp. 106–09, and Delgado Casado, *Diccionario*, I, pp. 436–38. He is not to be confused with the Alcalá cleric and typesetter of the same name burnt at the Seville *auto de fe* of 1562 for writing, printing, and distributing heretical propaganda (AHN, Inquisición, legajo 2075, expediente 2). Between 1561 and 1565 the first of these men printed mainly liturgical editions at Sigüenza for the local bishop Pedro de la Gasca. The editions on which La Bastida would have worked there were the *Officium totius Hebdomade Sancte. Iuxta consuetudinem alme ecclesie Seguntine* (1564) and the *Manuale Seguntinum* (1565); see Odriozola, *Catálogo de libros litúrgicos*, pp. 423 and 385, nos 598 and 534. Father Felipe Pérez Rato, Canon Archivist of the Cathedral of Sigüenza, kindly informs me that the *Passionarium et Matutinale festorum: Nativitatis Domini et Resurrectionis: et Corporis christi. Iuxta consuetudinem alme ecclesie Seguntine*, which I have not seen and which is dated by Odriozola to 1565, was actually printed by Sebastián Martínez in 1563; see Odriozola, *Catálogo de libros litúrgicos*, pp. 423–24, no. 599. The royal commission which visited the Alcalá presses found only three men working there for Martínez in 1572: a Portuguese compositor called Manuel, a Flemish puller called Quirin, and Juan de Pla, a Catalan beater (AHN, Universidades, legajo 135, caja 1, unnumbered expediente, fol. [7]ʳᵛ). The first of these was doubtless the 'Alonso Manuel portugués' who in March 1570 had been employed in the Alcalá press of Juan de Villanueva (trial of Enrique Loe, fols [16]ʳ, [18]ᵛ, and [34]ʳ).

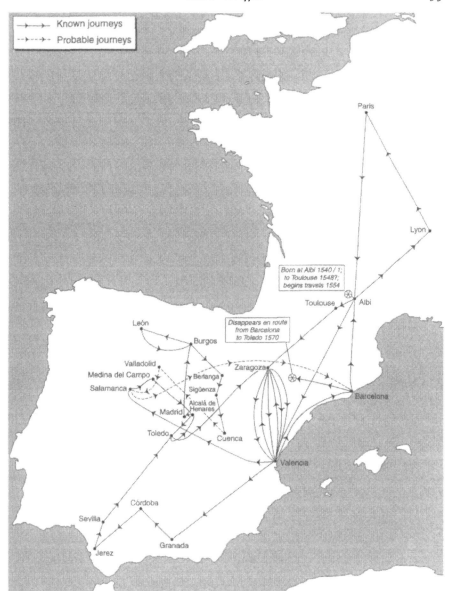

FIGURE I. The travels of Antonio de La Bastida, 1540–70

Courteau, who was associated with Oporinus and was well known in Reformist circles.[57] As Natalie Zemon Davis has shown, French *compagnons-imprimeurs* who worked in the sixteenth-century presses of Lyon

[57] Trial of Pierre de Rinz, fol. [7]ʳ.

36   *Inquisitional Trials in Sixteenth-Century Spain*

tended to have an elevated opinion of themselves because their craft required mastery of revolutionary techniques and because they were in day-to-day contact with a culture of the written word.[58] Although they may not have completed their studies, many of the foreign artisans who worked in the Spanish presses of the period seem to have shared that sense of superiority not only in comparison with those engaged in other crafts but with their fellow printing-workers of Spanish origin. Some of these Spaniards were clearly impressed by them, as is witnessed by Alonso Martínez, one of La Bastida's Spanish work-mates at Sigüenza, who says of him: 'He knew how to read and write Latin and the vernacular and he boasted that he could read some of the things in those languages that we were printing, saying that he could understand them.'[59] Pierre de Rinz was similarly proud of his knowledge of Latin: his fellow-workers recount how he would back up his tendentious views on religious matters by quoting the Bible and theologians, a habit which made the inquisitors extremely suspicious of him, especially when he began to argue doctrinal points with them.

But these trials show that although many French printing-workers in Spain were very concerned about intellectual debates, especially on the subject of religion, they lived only on the margins of the book-culture from which, ironically, they earned their daily bread. Their contact with that culture was often only superficial. For example, Pierre de Rinz had strong opinions on matters of faith, but rather than expressing conclusions reached after a study of printed material, it seems that he merely repeated what he had picked up from discussions he had overheard between authors or students who had happened to visit the presses in which he was employed.[60] Juan Franco, another French printing-worker tried at Toledo in those years, was characteristic of somebody who had daily contact with a book-culture to which he nevertheless had only limited access, acquiring his unorthodox ideas second-hand. When he was employed in Andrea de Portonariis's Salamanca press, Franco had encountered 'one Maître Jac Bofeo who was

[58] Natalie Zemon Davis, 'Strikes and Salvation at Lyon', in her *Society and Culture in Early Modern France* (Oxford, 1987), pp. 1–16 (p. 5), maintains that although the Lyon *compagnons* had little real education, they were fiercely proud of what learning they had acquired, comparing it favourably with the poor level of education of their fathers or of other artisans in the city.
[59] Trial of La Bastida, fol. [23]ʳ. Other witnesses were less impressed, saying: 'He is not a man with any solid learning [. . .], neither a theologian nor a Latinist' (fols [22]ʳ, [26]ᵛ, and [29]ʳ). Cf. Davis, 'Strikes and Salvation', p. 5: 'About two-thirds of [the printing-workers of Lyon] could read and write.' The Alonso Martínez who was employed by Sebastián Martínez at Sigüenza appears to be the man of the same name who was working as a bookseller and printer at Valladolid in 1561; in 1566 he was again associated with Sebastián Martínez in that town when he witnessed the latter's sale of a press to his old employee Bernardino de Santo Domingo: see Archivo Histórico Provincial de Valladolid (henceforth 'AHPV'), Protocolos, legajo 144, fol. 211ʳ. I am indebted to Anastasio Rojo Vega for this information and for a copy of the document from the same archive mentioned below in n. 97. Although in 1563 Alonso Martínez figured as the husband of Ana Requejo, receiving the promise of a dowry of 150,000 *maravedíes*, three years later La Bastida described him, possibly vindictively, as *amancebado*, or living with his mistress: see AHPV, Protocolos, legajo 147, fol. 1911ʳ, and trial of La Bastida, fol. [70]ᵛ.
[60] Trial of Pierre de Rinz, fol. [10]ʳ.

working as a proof-corrector on the "libro de justicia et jure" of Fray Domingo de Soto [. . .] and, as the aforementioned Maître Jac Bofeo was discussing Purgatory because this book dealt with it, the said Maître Jac claimed that Purgatory was nowhere mentioned in the Bible'.[61] We learn about many other similar cases of contact between semi-educated printing-workers and the intellectuals they came across in the presses. For example, we have a record of the relationship between some French workers and a Parisian professor who passed through Alcalá in 1568, got to know some of his compatriots employed in a press there, and took them out into the countryside to discuss the 'New Religion' with them.[62] In all these cases it is clear that the workers acquired their religious convictions not through reading but through listening and discussion.[63]

These workers' intellectual concerns appear to have been centred on religion, and reflect Reformist views which they had assimilated in the various cities in which they had worked before crossing into Spain. Their opinions were those we would expect to find among immigrants from northern Europe tried by the Inquisition in those years. For example, they question papal power, the efficacy of indulgences, pilgrimages, fasting, saints and holy images, the Real Presence of Christ's body in the consecrated host, the existence of Purgatory, the necessity of priestly confession, and, more generally, the morality of the Catholic clergy. At work in the presses they hummed Clément Marot's vernacular versions of the Psalms, and in their free time they went in groups into the countryside where they could sing them aloud far from prying ears. But some of them were also discriminating, not being content merely to parrot ideas current among their Reform-minded colleagues. The Flemish compositor Enrique Loe, for instance, who was notorious in the Alcalá presses for his drunkenness, had served as an altar-boy in his native Antwerp, and was later so racked by doubt about whether he had committed a grave sin by drinking two *maravedíes'*-worth

<hr/>

[61] Trials of Juan Franco, fol. 154ᵛ. In at least the period 1554–56 'Iacobus Boffaeus' played a major role in the editing and printing of many Latin, Greek, and vernacular editions produced at Salamanca by Andrea de Portonariis. He may well have worked there longer because we find a contribution of his in a book printed by Juan de Cánova as late as 1558; see Ruiz Fidalgo, *La imprenta en Salamanca*, I, p. 68, and nos 417, 421, 430, 432, 445, 447, 448, 454, 462; and II, no. 507. I am grateful to Vicente Bécares for alerting me to the identity of this important member of the world of printing in Salamanca.
[62] Trial of Pierre de Rinz, fols [18]ᵛ–[19]ʳ. The French professor, Mathieu Bossulus, taught rhetoric at Valencia University in at least 1564 and 1565, a work of his appearing in that city in 1566. Juan de Mariana would say of him, 'Disguising his true opinions, this heretic taught first for some time at Valencia del Cid and subsequently at Paris'; see Amparo Felipó, *La Universidad de Valencia durante el siglo XVI (1499–1611)*, Monografías y Fuentes, 18 (Valencia, 1993), p. 94, and J. M. de Bujanda, *Index d'Anvers 1569, 1570, 1571*, Index des livres interdits, 7 (Sherbrooke and Geneva, 1988), p. 60. It has been claimed that Philip II chose Bossulus as Prince Carlos's tutor; see *Archives biographiques françaises*, ed. by Susan Bradley, (London, Paris, Munich, New York, 1988), microfiche 130, pp. 127–28.
[63] An exception was Benito Dulcet, a type-caster from Lyon, who was denounced at Toledo and Barcelona as a heretic and sentenced in 1571 to three years at the oar. The Barcelona inquisitors recorded that, when he was apprehended, 'a book of the Lutheran sect was found in his coat pocket' (AHN, Inquisición, libro 730, fol. 136ᵛ; I am grateful to Anne Dubet for kindly transcribing this document for me).

38   *Inquisitional Trials in Sixteenth-Century Spain*

of wine before taking communion on his wedding morning that he was anxiously consulting work-mates about it many years after the event. Pierre de Rinz accepted many of the teachings he had heard from preachers in Geneva, where he lived across the street from Jean Calvin, but rejected some Calvinist doctrines, drawing quite fine theological distinctions between them.[64]

The trials allow us to glimpse the background and intellectual concerns of these printing-workers albeit filtered, and thus distorted, through the eyes of the inquisitors and their secretaries.[65] They are also full of chance details and asides about their work and the presses, thus casting valuable light on their professional lives. We can study these under four separate headings.

First, the trial papers offer details of the defendants' professional training. As we saw in La Bastida's *discurso de la vida*, he served a full five-year apprenticeship as a puller at Toulouse. This may explain why he found employment in Spanish presses printing liturgical editions, because such books were normally produced in red and black, and so, given the techniques of two-ink printing at the time, such work demanded skilled pressmen.[66] We know that the workers contracted by Sebastián Martínez for his Sigüenza office in 1564 and 1565 were engaged in the printing of liturgical works for the bishop of that diocese and, indeed, this could be the reason why the ecclesiastical prosecutor in that town did nothing about La Bastida's case for such a long time after receiving denunciations against him: quite simply he waited until all the books needed by the diocese had been finished before arresting such a skilled member of the team printing them. However, La Bastida's long period of training was not typical of the immigrant workers who appear in these trials. In most of the cases I have examined, foreign printing-workers operating in Spain had not served a complete apprenticeship before crossing the Pyrenees. Nevertheless, when they were arrested most of them were employed as compositors, that is to say in one of the most highly-prized specialities in the industry. As we have seen, the young Pierre de Rinz had been bound to a Genevan printer, yet after serving only seven months of his apprenticeship he fled from his master. Enrique Loe came from a family of Antwerp typographers but had been employed in his

---

[64] Trial of Enrique Loe, fols [7]ᵛ and [28]ʳ; trial of Pierre de Rinz, fols [8]ᵛ and [18]ʳ. It is, of course, impossible to be absolutely certain that the defendants were telling the inquisitors the truth about these matters.

[65] See Contreras, *El Santo Oficio de la Inquisición de Galicia*, pp. 571–76.

[66] La Bastida alluded to his craft when he tried to persuade his interrogator at Sigüenza that nobody smuggled into his cell the file he had used in his escape from the bishop's prison there. He claimed that, 'I was arrested and taken off to prison so unexpectedly when I was filing the points pressmen use to make holes in the paper, that I just slipped the file into my breeches' (trial of La Bastida, fol. [13]ʳ). This was a lie, but a plausible one because it reflected how necessary it was for the pressman to keep these guide points sharp; if the book on which he was working used two different coloured inks, as did many liturgical editions, once all the sheets in the edition had been printed in one colour he needed to be able to lay them back on the press with great precision so that the second colour was printed in exactly the right place without overprinting the first.

native city as a simple serving-boy in a press before he went to Spain. Neither of them had worked long enough in any Spanish press to have served an apprenticeship in their adopted country, yet when they were arrested they were both working as compositors.[67] In France guilds and associations of *compagnons-imprimeurs* attempted to impose strict regulations about the qualifications of those employed in the presses. In Spain labour in the industry was unregulated, and it was quite normal for a worker to find employment as a compositor without having served the period of training that was necessary in, for example, Paris or Lyon. While, at least in theory, the *compagnons* of Lyon had to be able to read and write French, and even know some Latin, it was not unusual in Spain to find that printers and even booksellers were illiterate.[68] This may go some way towards explaining the poor quality and numerous misprints of many Spanish editions of this time.

Second, the trial records reveal how important team work was in the presses of the period. In Spain, among young, itinerant, rootless and frequently foreign craftsmen, this created a strong sense of solidarity which could be reinforced by their sharing Reformist religious views. As a rule three workers were needed to operate a sixteenth-century press: a compositor, a beater, and a puller (in Spain the master-printer frequently doubled up as proof-corrector). The team had to synchronize their work to maintain a steady rhythm of production, and this meant that each worker was dependent upon his companions. As Enrique Loe said when he was accused of not respecting the festivals of the Church, 'it is true that I worked on holy days but this was because I had no alternative, for if I had insisted on resting, my two work-mates would have had to do the same'.[69] One night, as they lay in bed in the Toledo press where they were working together, a fellow-Frenchman confessed to La Bastida that he was a secret Protestant. He got cold feet the next morning, fearing that this admission might lead to his being denounced to the Inquisition, and he immediately fled the city. As a consequence La Bastida lost his job 'because, as one of the team went missing, there was no work'. As soon as one member of the team disappeared, production stopped.[70]

This interdependence in the workplace was reflected in the sense of comradeship which emerges from the inquisitional documents. At Sigüenza, for example, the workers were given board and lodging by their master in his house. In their free time they went to Mass together, visited a local

---

[67] Trial of Pierre de Rinz, fols [7]ᵛ–[8]ʳ, and trial of Enrique Loe, fol. [6]ʳ⁻ᵛ.

[68] Hugo de Mena, a printer from Paris who ran a press in Granada, boasted in 1573 that all his employees could read and write Latin; they all seem to have been foreigners. René Rabut, another French printer working at Granada at that period and known personally to La Bastida, was himself illiterate; see Juan Martínez Ruiz, 'Visita a las imprentas granadinas de Antonio de Nebrija, Hugo de Mena y René Rabut en el año 1573', *Revista de Dialectología y Tradiciones Populares*, 24 (1968), 75–110 (p. 79).

[69] Trial of Enrique Loe, fol. [13]ʳ.

[70] Trial of La Bastida, fol. [59]ʳ.

40   *Inquisitional Trials in Sixteenth-Century Spain*

hermitage outside the town as a group, all took part together in local religious processions, and, in particular, spent their time talking to each other. Their conversation included news from France and politics, but seems to have been dominated by religion. When La Bastida was employed in the Seville office of Sebastián Trujillo, he went to see the various sights of the city with his work-mates, and together they spoke to French sailors whose ships had tied up at the docks.[71] In Barcelona the printing-workers employed in a single press all went out of the city together to picnic at Monjuich, ate meat there on days of abstinence and, as ever, discussed religious matters;[72] those employed in the Alcalá presses went for country walks together;[73] and wherever printing-workers met they drank together in taverns or in private. Not only because of the solidarity which was a result of labour practices but also because they were itinerant foreigners who found themselves surrounded by an atmosphere of extreme xenophobia, it appears that the French printing-workers lived in a closed world where all their friends and acquaintances were associated with the business of printing. Moreover, as was typical in the printing industry everywhere at the time, the long day worked in the Spanish presses meant that employees had little free time to meet anybody not belonging to that world.[74] The French printing-workers even seem to have identified with their master's interests: when the Frenchman Pierre Reigner was employed as a typesetter in a press at Barcelona, he discovered that a compatriot of his working for another printer in the same city had purloined type from Reigner's master; he confronted him in the street and risked his own life in the ensuing fight.[75] The only things which seem to have challenged the sense of solidarity among printing-workers were quarrels over women, cards, or religion. This can be seen from La Bastida's case: he was denounced to the Inquisition by the Spaniards who had laboured and lived alongside him in the Sigüenza press despite the fact that they later testified that they had always thought of him as a good friend, colleague, and worker.[76] But it is probable that at least some Spanish presses would have witnessed few disputes over religious matters because both master and workers were immigrants who shared

---

[71] Trial of La Bastida, fols [48]ᵛ–[49]ʳ.
[72] Trial of Isabel Reigner, ULHW, Inquisitionakten Handschriften, Yc 2° 20 (3), fols 179ʳ–232ʳ (henceforth 'trial of Isabel Reigner'), see here fol. 195ᵛ.
[73] Trial of Pierre de Rinz, fol. [18]ʳ.
[74] In the defence La Bastida wrote in his cell at Cuenca, he named sixty-nine people living in fifteen Spanish towns who knew him well and who would attest to his orthodoxy: sixty were printers, members of their families, or printing-workers; three were booksellers; two were merchants; one was a priest; and the occupation of the remaining three was not recorded (trial of La Bastida, fol. [60]ʳ⁻ᵛ).
[75] Trial of Pierre Reigner, loose sheet containing his defence written in French.
[76] Alonso Martínez maintained that he had always considered La Bastida a close companion (trial of La Bastida, fol. [11]ᵛ). When Matías Gast, a printer at Salamanca, wrote to Plantin in 1574 asking him to recruit a type-caster for him in Flanders, he was very conscious of the danger of having a heretic in his press: 'Above all you must understand that I do not want a drunkard or anybody sympathetic to heresy'; see *Correspondence de Christophe Plantin*, ed. by Max Rooses and Jan Denucé, 8 vols (Antwerp and The Hague, 1883–1918), IV, pp. 117–19.

similar Reformist ideas. Indeed, so numerous were Frenchmen in Spain's printing industry that at this time some presses would have been entirely French- rather than Spanish-speaking.

Third, the Inquisition's papers contain many incidental details which provide information about the history of Spanish printing. For example, the poor proof-reading of sixteenth-century Spanish books is notorious, and was much commented upon at the time. But it was essential to avoid errata in some editions, particularly in liturgical books. From La Bastida's trial we learn that a university graduate, Diego de Manjón, who regularly heard La Bastida's confessions, acted as proof-corrector for the liturgical editions printed at Sigüenza.[77] As we have seen, another trial gives the name and certain views of the proof-corrector of an edition, now lost, of Domingo de Soto's *De iustitia et iure libri decem*, printed at Salamanca.[78] The documents also enable us to amend the history of several Spanish presses which has hitherto been based upon an analysis of their surviving production. For example, it had been thought that the printer Pedro de Celada worked at León until 1556; La Bastida's trial papers show that he was in fact still active in the industry there years later.[79] The same goes for the Valencian printer Juan Navarro. It was thought that he ceased to print personally in 1543 despite several later editions the colophons of which state that they were printed in his house. La Bastida's trial indicates that Navarro was in fact printing many years later, his sons also being printers.[80] On the other hand, these documents allow us to date the Seville printer Sebastián Trujillo's death earlier than has hitherto been thought.[81] The inquisitorial papers similarly cast light on such matters as how long it took to print certain editions, and the fact that a printer like Sebastián Martínez, who was based at Valladolid, not only set up a branch office at Sigüenza specifically to print a series of liturgical editions for that diocese, but was loyally accompanied to Sigüenza by a number of his employees, who returned with him to Valladolid once the job had been completed.[82] But not all his employees had

---

[77] Manjón testified in favour of La Bastida (trial of La Bastida, fols [29]ʳ–[30]ʳ), because he knew the Frenchman well, having worked alongside him for several months at Sigüenza. It was usual in Spain for the ecclesiastical authorities who commissioned the printing of liturgical editions to provide a canon or reliable cleric to check the proofs; see Clive Griffin, *Los Cromberger: la historia de una imprenta del siglo XVI en Sevilla y Méjico* (Madrid, 1991), p. 150. Bachelor Manjón had doubtless been appointed by the ecclesiastical authorities at Sigüenza to do this work in Sebastián Martínez's press.

[78] Trials of Juan Franco, fol. 154ᵛ.

[79] Trial of La Bastida, fol. [46]ʳ. See n. 54 above.

[80] Trial of La Bastida, fol. [60]ʳ.

[81] See above, n. 49.

[82] La Bastida implies that the printing of Francisco de Robles's *Copia sive ratio* (see n. 55 above) took three months. As it was an octavo book set in small types and consisting of sixteen sheets, this is plausible. The two copies held in the Biblioteca Nacional at Madrid represent different states and contain different dates on the title-page: R/9200, 'Anno Domini. 1564. Kalen. Decembris.'; R/16289, 'Anno Domini. 1565. X. Kal. Martij.'. The colophon of both contains the date '1564' and, according to the preliminaries, the licence for printing was issued in May of that year. I am grateful to Klaus Wagner for his help with the study of this edition.

42   *Inquisitional Trials in Sixteenth-Century Spain*

previously worked for him at Valladolid; when in Sigüenza he contracted some itinerant craftsmen to work on just one of these books, while others were contracted to print the whole series.

My fourth and final general conclusion extracted from these trials is that La Bastida and his companions led extraordinarily peripatetic lives.[83] The similarity of working practices in the printing industry throughout Europe meant that itinerant craftsmen found no difficulty in fitting in with the operation of any press. The documents also show that the foreign printing-workers who went to Spain had constantly to travel from one press to another in search of employment. La Bastida was not untypical in being contracted by no fewer than seventeen different presses located in thirteen Spanish towns, and he returned more than once to work again in some of those presses. Not only that, but he was not averse to abandoning his craft to work as a servant to earn his daily bread.[84] The contracts he was given to work as a puller varied in length, but they were seldom for more than a year. Sometimes they were only for the production of a single book and, once it was finished, he had to look for employment elsewhere. He must have walked thousands of miles across Castile, Aragon and Andalusia, not to mention his journeys through France in search of work, a place to convalesce from illness, or simply entertainment, such as his trip from Lyon to Paris to witness the celebrations of the Peace of Cateau-Cambrésis. Itinerant printing-workers needed to know where work was likely to be available; their resulting informal information network can be partially reconstructed from the mass of documents conserved in Iberian archives. For example, Diego de Nájera not only knew La Bastida because he worked alongside him in Sigüenza and had first met him many years previously in the press run by Nájera's brother at Zaragoza, but he was also able to confirm what the Frenchman had told the Cuenca inquisitors about his peripatetic life, because comrades whom Nájera had met on his own travels round Spain had kept him abreast of La Bastida's career.[85] These printing-workers all knew each other, news and gossip travelling rapidly among them from mouth to mouth or, on occasion, through the letters they sent each other.[86] This network clearly provided some with an early warning of the Inquisition's interest in

[83] La Bastida's journeys overland are illustrated in the map which accompanies this article (Figure 1, above). He may in fact occasionally have travelled by boat, but there were few navigable rivers in Spain.
[84] Young Frenchmen frequently sought work as domestic servants in Spain; see Jiménez Monteserín, 'Los luteranos', p. 702. Many years earlier the famous Martin Guerre had left his village near Pamiers to find work as a lackey in Burgos; see Natalie Zemon Davis, *The Return of Martin Guerre* (Harmondsworth, 1985), p. 24.
[85] Trial of La Bastida, fol. [24]ʳ.
[86] In 1572 the Antwerp compositor Pedro Alberto, who had been tried for heresy and had appeared at the Toledo *auto de fe* of June 1570 alongside fellow members of the world of the book including several mentioned in this article (Pierre de Rinz, Guillermo Herlin, Pedro Flamenco, and Isac de Ribera), told the inquisitors of the Lisbon tribunal how he and other foreign printing-workers and booksellers in the Iberian Peninsula kept in touch by letter (trials of João de Leão, fols 134ᵛ–35ʳ).

them, and consequently they changed their identity or vanished.[87] In its turn, the Holy Office made use of the network to track down suspects: it only had to send an agent to any printing centre to pick up a wealth of information about the people it wished to interview. Printers and their employees invariably knew the whereabouts of anybody with whom they had at some time worked, or, at the very least, knew somebody who did.[88]

We may well wonder why, given the risk they ran during a period of fierce Spanish xenophobia, all these foreign printing-workers came to Spain in the first place. We have already seen that Spain offered job opportunities to men who had not served long apprenticeships in the printing industries of their countries of origin. It may also be the case that some of them, La Bastida included, were orthodox Catholics who considered Spain to be a safe haven at a time of religious strife in Flanders and France; we should not, for instance, forget that La Bastida's father had worked for the Bishop of Albi and that one of his uncles had been a canon of Albi cathedral. Moreover, Spain had traditionally been the destination for thousands of men emigrating from north of the Pyrenees in search of work, and to enterprising young Frenchmen who found themselves caught up in the bloody civil wars of the 1560s, Spain offered the promise of a more stable future. However, what must have been particularly attractive to foreign artisans and even unskilled farm workers was the demand for labour and the relatively high wages to be earned in Spain.[89] As can be seen from La Bastida's *discurso de la vida*, there were periods when work was in short supply even there, but when his career is compared with those of other printing-workers who spent a desperate youth searching for employment in France before travelling south, we can readily appreciate how attractive Spain would have seemed to them and how that pull was strong enough to persuade even those sympathetic to the 'New Religion' that the risk of being apprehended by the Spanish Inquisition was worth running.[90] As Pedro de Güerta, a Flemish peddler of printed holy

---

[87] João de Leão smuggled letters out of the Inquisition's prison at Lisbon warning fellow-heretics engaged in printing and bookselling about the Holy Office's interest in them (trials of João de Leão, fol 122ʳ⁻ᵛ).

[88] In general, immigrant printing-workers fell under suspicion because they were foreigners who, given their itinerant way of life and their craft, had worked in Reformist centres where they had come into contact with heretical ideas. The Holy Office does not seem to have been particularly concerned about what books they had printed there. Nevertheless, on occasion the inquisitors showed some interest in the printing of particular books, as happened, for example, when they accused Enrique Loe of having helped to print a vernacular Bible at Antwerp (trial of Enrique Loe, fol. [3]ʳ).

[89] Balancy, 'Les Immigrés français', p. 48.

[90] Pierre de Rinz, although an experienced printing-worker before emigrating to Spain, had to take work as a servant in the Château de Sancerre and then join up as a soldier because he could find no other work in France (trial of Pierre de Rinz, fol. [7]ʳ). Even the famous Lyon printer Sebastien Gryphe followed the flag at one stage because he had no capital to set up as a printer; see Martin and Chartier, *Histoire de l'édition française*, I, p. 262. When suspects were apprehended by the Spanish Inquisition their possessions were inventoried. Although the printing-workers who went to Spain seem to have been attracted by the relatively high wages to be earned there, when they were arrested they seldom owned anything more than the worn clothes they stood up in, a few coins, and the old sword they carried on their journeys round the country.

44   *Inquisitional Trials in Sixteenth-Century Spain*

pictures and friend of several foreign printing-workers tried by the Holy Office, was to say, in Spain it was a question of earning good wages and keeping your mouth shut.[91] Some unfortunate immigrants did not heed this advice, and came to rue the day they decided to cross the Pyrenees.

One final observation can be made about these records. Not only were foreign printing-workers prepared to run the risk of spending many years living in Spain; some, at least, remained in the country even after their trials and having as a consequence served time in prison or the galleys.[92] Adrián de Alkmaar, from what is now northern Holland, was accused in 1562 of *luteranismo*, sentenced by the Zaragoza Inquisition to a flogging, and dispatched to the galleys for four years.[93] When the ship to which he had been condemned went down, he managed to swim to safety and escape but, rather than returning to the Low Countries, he found work in Pierre Reigner's Barcelona press under the assumed name of 'Alejandro'. He subsequently left Catalonia and travelled south, working as a typesetter in at least Toledo and Alcalá de Henares. He was denounced in Toledo, arrested, tried there in 1570, and returned to the galleys.[94]

Adrián was a victim of the accusations made to the Toledo inquisitors in 1569 and 1570 by a Parisian Huguenot named Guillermo Herlin. Among the dozens of former colleagues denounced by this sinister figure was La Bastida, who must also have stayed in Spain long after his unhappy experiences in Sigüenza and Cuenca. Herlín's denunciations sowed panic among the foreign printing-workers of Alcalá de Henares where he had worked as a

---

[91] Trial of Pedro Flamenco: ULHW, Inquisitionakten Handschriften, Yc 2° 20 (3), fol. 236ʳ; Güerta was generally known in Spain as 'Pedro Flamenco'. A Huguenot printing-worker who seems to have followed this advice for some time was Isac de Ribera, who worked with La Bastida at Sigüenza without falling under suspicion. Later, however, he was denounced for having declared himself a *luterano* while working at Alcalá, and he appeared at the Toledo *auto de fe* of June 1570 (Biblioteca de Palacio, Madrid, MS II/1846, fol. 64ᵛ [olim 147ᵛ]; I am grateful to Jean-Pierre Dedieu for this reference and to María Luisa López-Vidriero for facilitating my examination of this document). In 1573 Toledo forbade Isac de Ribera to leave Castile; some five years later he was detained by agents of the Inquisition while attempting to make his way back to France, as a result of which he was tried at Zaragoza and returned to the Toledo Inquisition (AHN, Inquisición, libro 988, fol. 348ʳ). His Toledo and Zaragoza trial papers have disappeared, but we know that he was from Lyon and that before emigrating to Spain he had been employed in Robert Estienne's Genevan press (trial of Pierre de Rinz, fol. [20]ʳ, and trial of Enrique Loe, fol. [10]ʳ). He may well have been the Isaac de Rovière who, in 1562, had been tried at Geneva for deserting his master in Lyon and fleeing to Switzerland; see Paul Chaix, *Recherches sur l'imprimerie à Genève de 1550 à 1564: Etude bibliographique, économique et littéraire*, Travaux d'Humanisme et Renaissance, 16 (Geneva, 1954), pp. 221 and 238. Although many foreign printing-workers must have kept their Reformist sympathies to themselves, being careful to show only a face of the strictest orthodoxy when they were in Spain, there is little evidence that most Spaniards employed at this time in the printing industry were anything but genuinely orthodox. Indeed, La Bastida's employer at Córdoba, Juan Bautista Escudero, turns out to have been an agent of the Holy Office (trial of Pierre de Ribera, fol. [18]ʳ).

[92] The Spanish Inquisition frequently forbade ex-prisoners to leave the kingdom in which they had been tried, but in practice it proved impossible to police such orders effectively.

[93] AHN, Inquisición, libro 988, fol. 97ʳ. Adrián was generally known in Spain as 'Adrián Gaspar'.

[94] Trial of Isabel Reigner, fols 195ᵛ and 215ʳ; trial of Enrique Loe, fol. [28]ʳ; trial of Pierre de Ribera, fol. [8]ʳ; and AHN, Inquisición, legajo 2105, expediente 8, fol. [2]ʳ.

typesetter and where he was arrested by agents of the Holy Office. Many of his work-mates there immediately fled the town, some to the nearby city of Toledo, others as far afield as Catalonia or Andalusia. Acting on information supplied to them by Herlin, the Toledo inquisitors requested the Valladolid tribunal to search for and detain La Bastida; the Valladolid inquisitors summoned the Frenchman's old employer, Sebastián Martínez, and learnt from him that La Bastida was no longer in that city but had moved on to Salamanca. They reported back to Toledo, adding that they had learnt that La Bastida already had a criminal record in Cuenca.[95] Although he was assiduously sought in northern Castile, La Bastida proved elusive, but was eventually tracked down and apprehended many miles away in Barcelona. The inquisitors of that city informed their Toledo colleagues that, when he was arrested, a written certificate of his having recanted heretical opinions was found sewn into the lining of his breeches. This document had doubtless been issued by the Cuenca tribunal in 1566.[96] The Toledo inquisitors immediately dispatched an agent to Catalonia to escort the detainee back under guard to their prison together with the French master-printer Pierre Reigner and his wife Isabel who had also been accused of heresy by Herlin. After long trials at Toledo, the naïve and elderly Pierre was condemned to six years in the galleys where he doubtless perished; Isabel's end was less protracted, for she was condemned to the flames in Toledo. For his part, La Bastida had learnt from his previous experience at the hands of the Inquisition. He was aware that, as he now stood accused for a second time of heresy after having abjured such beliefs some years earlier at Cuenca, he would be treated by the Toledo tribunal as a relapsed heretic and, if found guilty, would run the risk of ending his days at the stake. He drew the obvious conclusion: he gave his escort the slip on the way from Barcelona to Toledo, disappeared into the night, and nothing more was heard of him by the Spanish Inquisition.[97]

Oxford

[95] Letter from the Valladolid tribunal to Toledo dated 3 March 1570, contained in the trial of Pierre de Ribera, fol. [7]ʳ⁻ᵛ.
[96] Letter from the Barcelona tribunal to headquarters in Madrid dated 8 July 1570: AHN, Inquisición, libro 737, fol. 202ʳ; and letter from the same tribunal to Toledo dated 27 June 1570, contained in the trial of Pierre Reigner, fol. [12]ʳ.
[97] Trial of Pierre Reigner, fol. [14]ᵛ. The Antonio Bastida apprehended by the Holy Office at Perpignan in 1582 and sentenced to seven years at the oar is not the person studied in the present article (AHN, Inquisición, libro 730, fols 389ᵛ–90ʳ, and libro 1158, fol. 117ʳ). However, it is quite possible that 'the Frenchman Antonio La Bastida' mentioned in the will of his wife Catalina de Cortegana, dated 26 April 1572, was the pressman from Albi (AHPV, Protocolos, legajo 515, unfoliated). If this is the case, La Bastida would have married, probably in Valladolid, between his banishment from the district of Cuenca in March 1566 and the order for his arrest issued by the Toledo tribunal in February 1570.

[11]

Printers of the Mind: Some Notes on Bibliographical Theories and Printing-House Practices

by

D. F. McKENZIE*

I

IN RECENT YEARS WE HAVE ALL COME TO RECOGNIZE THE NEED FOR what might be called 'scientific' investigation in bibliography, a phrase which at its best implies, as Professor Bowers has succinctly put it, a strict regard for certain fixed bounds of physical fact and logical probability.[1] The achievements resulting from such a concern are clear and important. In descriptive bibliography we have gained a new, accurate and rational vocabulary, and formulae that are both economic and unambiguous. In analytical bibliography — with which I am principally concerned — we have been taught to use the critical tools of comparison and analysis in a new way; and the importance of establishing press variants by collation, of detecting setting by formes, of distinguishing between compositors by spellings or impressions by press-figures is no longer questioned. Scientific bibliography, complete with its laboratory aids, has become a new orthodoxy.

Yet, as T. S. Eliot puts it, *All our knowledge brings us nearer to our ignorance.* In the very act of opening our eyes to new and exciting

* This paper was originally given in a very much shorter form as a lecture at the University of Illinois, the University of Virginia, and the University of California (Los Angeles) in May 1963. In revising it I have tried to take account of more recent work but I am very conscious of the injustices I am doubtless doing to those whom I quote out of context. May I plead lack of space and offer the reflection that although methodological discussion has a way of seeming unfair to those criticised, it's only a form of intellectual house-keeping, dependent upon and tributary to the greater work of others? Mottos for the day might be: "Profound truths are not to be expected of methodology" (Sir Karl Popper) and "Methodology is at best a short-cut for the inexperienced" (R. C. Bald).

1. *Textual and Literary Criticism* (1959), p. 115.

possibilities, our discoveries raise fresh problems of understanding and breed an awareness of our limitations. In particular, the detailed relation of analytical bibliography to the editing of seventeenth- and eighteenth-century texts depends upon a number of assumptions about printing-house conditions that are only now beginning to be tested. Indeed, if I were to give this paper an epigraph, it might well be that quoted by Sir Karl Popper from Black's *Lectures on the Elements of Chemistry* published in 1803: "A nice adaptation of conditions will make almost any hypothesis agree with the phenomena. This will please the imagination, but does not advance our knowledge."[2] Our ignorance about printing-house conditions in the 17th and 18th centuries has left us disastrously free to devise them according to need; and we have at times compounded our errors by giving a spurious air of 'scientific' definitiveness to our conclusions.

There has of course been nothing morally reprehensible in this, for 'scientific' in such a use has meant little more than an honesty of method in respect to the physical phenomena available for study.[3] As in the physical and natural sciences, at least in their more elementary stages of observation and classification, it has, as I have indicated, simply meant placing the stress in the first instance on a finite number of particulars and drawing a conclusion from them. And since bibliographers very rarely have anything to work on but the physical evidence of the books themselves it has seemed only natural that any methodology should work within these limitations and seek its exactitude by describing and relating only the observable facts of the paper and the marks it bears.

Some distinguished bibliographers, it is true, have had their doubts. R. C. Bald remarked that "whatever bibliography may or may not be, it is not an exact science, if one understands by an 'exact' science a branch of study which arrives at its conclusions through experiment and observation and can reproduce the conditions of an experiment so that the results can be repeated and checked at any time ("Evidence and Inference," pp. 2-3). And R. B. McKerrow, late in life and writing

---

2. Quoted at p. 82 of *The Logic of Scientific Discovery* (Harper Torchbook edition, 1965).

3. Bibliographers' use of the word may be consulted at the following points: W. W. Greg, *Collected Papers*, ed. J. C. Maxwell (1966), pp. 76, 220-3; R. B. McKerrow, *Prolegomena for the Oxford Shakespeare* (1939), pp. vi-viii; R. C. Bald, "Evidence and Inference in Bibliography," reprinted in *A Mirror for Modern Scholars*, ed. Lester A. Beaurline (1966), pp. 2-3; Fredson Bowers, *On Editing Shakespeare* (1955), pp. 41, 95, 99, 124; *Textual and Literary Criticism*, pp. 70, 81, 96, 100-1, 115; *Bibliography and Textual Criticism* (1964), pp. 72, 74, 90; J. Hazel Smith, "The Composition of the Quarto of *Much Ado about Nothing*," *SB*, XVI (1963), 10.

more particularly of textual criticism, made much the same point and added the comment that "Nothing can be gained, and much may be lost, by a pretence of deriving results of scientific accuracy from data which are admittedly uncertain and incomplete" (*Prolegomena*, p. vii). It is this last point which I wish to take up.

The effect of Bald's suggestion that bibliography "cannot claim for its conclusions the same universal validity as belongs to those of the exact sciences" is simply that we should rest content with a very different order of certainty but take the precaution of scrutinizing more frequently than we do the procedures of bibliographical scholarship. McKerrow's comment, however, runs far beyond his intention and offers a radical criticism of the very bases of all knowledge inductively derived. It is not that bibliographical inquiry differs in any essential respect from 'scientific' inquiry as described, but that the method common to both is itself logically unsound. Bibliography, as it happens, is a convenient area in which to demonstrate its unsoundness.

For whatever the short-term advantages, to assume, as we have been asked to do, that analytical bibliography must be empirically based, and to limit our knowledge to that which may be derived by inductive inference from direct observations, is to invite the obvious objection that no finite number of observations can ever justify a generalization. Bertrand Russell remarked that so far as he could see induction was a mere method of making plausible guesses. "It is far from obvious, from a logical point of view," writes Sir Karl Popper, "that we are justified in inferring universal statements from singular ones, no matter how numerous; for any conclusion drawn in this way may always turn out to be false: no matter how many instances of white swans we may have observed, this does not justify the conclusion that *all* swans are white" (*Scientific Discovery*, p. 27). David Hume had made essentially the same point: "Even after the observation of the frequent conjunction of objects, we have no reason to draw any inference of any object beyond those of which we have had experience."[4] And more graphically the Lilliputians' ignorance is ironically exposed: "Besides, our histories of six thousand moons make no mention of any other regions than the two great empires of Lilliput and Blefescu."

Nor is it simply that there is no logical way of arriving at general truths from the examination of sampled cases. To observe at all is to bestow meaning of some kind on the thing observed; to gather particular pieces of evidence is to seek those relevant to some preconceived

---

4. *Treatise of Human Nature*, Book I, part iii, sec. 12.

notion of their utility.[5] But the main point is that any general laws derived by the inductive method remain highly vulnerable to fresh evidence. Where the known particulars are few, this risk will be greatest.

The inductivist in all subjects may of course freely admit that *incompleteness* is almost invariably a characteristic of his evidence and that his conclusions may therefore be subject to modification when new evidence comes to hand. Looked at in this way the inductive process carries a burden of assumed truth waiting to be converted into proven error: knowledge, that is, comes with the act of disproof. And until that moment arrives we may be offered conclusions that lay claim only to some degree of 'reliability' or 'probability,' based on reasonable assumptions about the comprehensiveness of the evidence used and about the predictability of past or 'normal' examples into the future.[6]

Even such a qualified attitude, however, is still inadequate to the demands of bibliography. For one thing, I doubt that 'normality,' in any serious and extended sense, is a meaningful concept.[7] For another,

5. The point is neatly made by Robert K. Turner, "Reappearing Types as Bibliographical Evidence," *SB*, XIX (1966), 198: "hypothesis is essential to observation." Professor Hinman has a relevant paragraph: "When I first learned from the indisputable evidence furnished by individual types that the Folio was indeed set throughout by formes rather than by successive pages, I was probably as much surprised as anyone else. But should I have been? To *prove* setting by formes required evidence not adduced before; but not to have suspected it sooner was to have failed to see facts — or at least the probable implications of a complex of related facts — that had long been staring us all in the face, so to speak." The point is made "in order to suggest a not unimportant general principle of bibliographical investigation" — *Printing and Proof-Reading of the Shakespeare First Folio* (1963), I, 50-51.

6. The difficulties created by limited criteria are indicated by Antonin Hruby in "A Quantitative Solution to the Ambiguity of Three Texts," *SB*, XVIII (1965), 153-4; and Professor Bowers warns of the inadequacy and dangers of inferential arguments in "Some Relations of Bibliography to Editorial Problems," *SB*, III (1950), 54, 57. Professor Bowers' most thorough and

challenging investigation of the problem is offered in chapter III of *Bibliography and Textual Criticism*. He suggests three orders of certainty, "the demonstrable, the probable, and the possible" (p. 77), and stresses the importance of "the postulate of normality" as a necessary curb on the number of plausible conjectures that human ingenuity might otherwise devise (pp. 64, 70, 72). See also Hinman, "The Prentice Hand in the Tragedies of the Shakespeare First Folio: Compositor E," *SB*, IX (1957), 3.

7. Professor Bowers remarks: "No one can argue that we know all about the printing processes of the past, and it is just as obvious from time to time this postulate of normality has fostered incorrect explanations based on imperfect evidence." (*Bibliography and Textual Criticism*, p. 72). The cautionary note is justified, not because the elementary physical actions of setting, transferring, imposing, inking, proofing, printing from, or distributing type differed from century to century, nor even because the kinds of work and sizes of shops differed, but because the amount of work done and the relations between those performing it differed from day to day. "Normality" in one sense is limited, though within its limitations valuable; in the other sense it doesn't exist.

BIBLIOGRAPHICAL THEORIES   5

even granting the inductivists' case, I doubt whether bibliography has yet either the body of documentary evidence or the fund of experimental proof necessary to bring most of its conclusions within a usefully narrow range of probabilities. Under present conditions, therefore, we are tempted either to over-stress the few 'proofs' achieved (by restricting further inquiry to a demonstration of their 'normality' and so asking that new conclusions be consistent with it), or conversely (in the greater number of cases where we have little developed knowledge of the causative conditions) to tolerate any number of 'probable' explanations for the same limited range of phenomena. Neither alternative is a particularly happy one. The first protects us from open-ended speculation by a crippling limitation of the subject; the second, although it characterizes the subject as practised, is rarely capable of conclusive demonstrations.[8]

But there is another way of looking at the whole problem; nor does it involve any question-begging distinctions between bibliography and 'science,' for it applies equally to both. It simply consists in recognizing the present situation of multiple 'probabilities' as the desirable one and regarding them as hypotheses to be tested *deductively*. I am naturally tempted to it because the productive conditions in early printing houses display an incredible variety which, if it is to be re-conceived at all, demands an imaginative facility in devising hypotheses;[9] and also because bibliographers, as a matter of fact, are becoming increasingly concerned to trace processes involving complex relationships less susceptible of conclusive demonstration. More seriously, deductive reasoning (by which a general hypothesis dictates particular possibilities or 'predictions' and rules out others) does offer a sound way to knowledge. Like induction, it is open to logical objection, for no amount of positive evidence can ever conclusively confirm an hypoth-

8. "The subject as practised": it could be urged that no science is a disembodied activity, but only the activities of its practitioners, and that it is defined less by its body of commonly accepted knowledge than by the dynamics of difference. Robert K. Turner's "The Composition of the *Insatiate Countess* Q2," *SB*, XII (1958), 198-203, for example, does not offer mechanical demonstration and proof from the physical and inexorable evidence of the printing house so much as a proliferation of unrelated, arbitrary hypotheses to explain away inconsistencies.

9. May I recall what Greg said of Professor Dover Wilson? "He is of imagination all compact. And imagination, I would remind you, is the highest gift in scientific investigation, even if at times it may be the deepest pitfall." (*Collected Papers*, p. 217). I have myself a pleasant recollection of meeting Professor Dover Wilson in May 1958. "I always believe," he said, "that if you have a good idea you should send it out into the world. If it survives, fine. If it doesn't, then at least you *know* it's wrong." The serious implications of that last phrase are only now beginning to dawn on me.

6   STUDIES IN BIBLIOGRAPHY

esis; but one piece of negative evidence, one contradictory occurrence, will conclusively falsify it.

These comments are philosophic commonplaces and stated so baldly must seem slightly naive. Yet they do serve to point quite sharply to the two main directions open to bibliographical inquiry. If bibliographers wish to persist as inductivists then they must diligently search out the historical facts which will alone provide a fairly accurate definition of 'normality' and offer these as a corrective to the logical defects inherent in the method. Alternatively they may confess outright the partial and theoretic nature of bibliographical knowledge, proceed deductively, and at the same time practise a new and rigorous scepticism.

In fact the nature of 'normality' as so far revealed by historical evidence suggests that the 'norm' comprised conditions of such an irrecoverable complexity that we must in any case adopt the latter course. If the 'scientific' proofs offered in some recent bibliographical analyses of older books were seen philosophically for the conjectures they are, we should I think be nearer the true spirit of scientific inquiry and the humility that always accompanies an awareness of the possibility of fresh evidence and therefore of falsification. The subject would not then be circumscribed by the demand for demonstrable proofs; rather it would be expanded in its hospitality to new ideas and in its search for fresh historical evidence in the service of disproof. Such a method would be, in the best sense, scientific.

In the following section I wish to offer some varieties of fresh evidence. Its main implication is that the very fixity of the physical bounds within which we are asked to work is inimical to the development of a sound methodology — first, because if the stress is laid on 'proof' then the small number of paradigms available to us unreasonably restricts the subject; second, because in the present state of our knowledge the finite particulars with which we must work are too few and therefore permit too many alternative generalizations to be induced from them; third, because the conception of 'normality' as a corrective to the undisciplined proliferation of generalizations misrepresents the nature of the printing process; fourth, because induction is necessarily an inconclusive method of inquiry. The evidence is consistent with my belief that we should normally proceed in our inquiries by the hypothetico-deductive method which welcomes conjectures in the positive knowledge that productive conditions were extraordinarily complex and unpredictable, but which also insists that such conjectures be scrutinized with the greatest rigour and, if refuted, rejected.

BIBLIOGRAPHICAL THEORIES   7

II

When the University of Cambridge set up its printing house in 1696, nearly all the records relating to the erection of the building, and then subsequently to its operation throughout the next decade, were preserved. The annual press accounts show clearly the kinds of expenditure involved in running a small printing house; and the workmen's vouchers for composition, correction and presswork, together with the joiners', smiths', glaziers', plumbers', typefounders', fellmongers', carriers', and printers'-suppliers' bills, reveal the week-by-week operations of a printing house in a detail which is, I believe, unparalleled. In addition the Minute Book of the curators of the Press provides direct evidence of printing charges and edition sizes over the period.[10] With such a wealth of primary documentary material it has been a simple matter to construct detailed production charts for the books printed, showing their progress sheet by sheet and recording the exact division of work between different compositors, correctors and pressmen. It has been a simple matter also to offer definitive details on the wages earned and the actual amount of work done by compositors and press-crews, and to construct work-flow diagrams illustrating the disposition and organization of work within the printing house as a whole on all books and ephemera in production over any one period. It must suffice for the moment simply to observe that the patterns which emerge seem to me to be of such an unpredictable complexity, even for such a small printing shop, that no amount of inference from what we think of as bibliographical evidence could ever have led to their reconstruction. To this Cambridge evidence we may now add the invaluable record of work done in the Bowyers' printing house over the years 1730-9. The ledger which records this work is in the possession of the Grolier Club of New York and is to be edited for the London Bibliographical Society by Mr Keith Maslen. The details which it gives of compositors' and pressmen's work, sometimes week by week, also permit the accurate reconstruction of working conditions, whether for one book or for the printing house as a whole. As Mr Maslen has remarked, "Work patterns are more complex at the bigger and busier London house, but in broad outline the picture is unchanged."[11]

10. The primary records are printed in volume II of my *Cambridge University Press, 1696-1712* (1966).

11. *AUMLA* (May, 1967), p. 109. Dr J. D. Fleeman's discovery of the Bowyer ledger was reported in *The Times Literary Supplement*, 19 Dec. 1963, p. 1056, and some of its details were put to use in his note "William Somervile's 'The Chace,' 1735," *PBSA*, LVIII (1966), 1-7.

8   STUDIES IN BIBLIOGRAPHY

Let me now look briefly at our ruling assumptions about the amount of work that a compositor and pressman might get through in an hour, day, or week. On these points, however carefully we qualify it, the evidence such as we have leads us to suppose a maximum setting rate of something like 1000 ens or letters an hour by one man and a printing rate of 250 impressions an hour at full press.[12] Taking each of these figures as averages which allow for imposition, proofing, correction, make-ready, washing and distribution, we may then, to estimate daily production, multiply by twelve to get as totals 12,000 ens and 3000 impressions. Finally, for weekly totals, we multiply by six to get figures of 72,000 ens and 18,000 impressions. These totals, we allow, are probably too high, but translating them cautiously into terms of actual book production, we might say that a quarto of five to six sheets, each containing some 10,000 to 12,000 ens and printed in an edition of 1200 to 1500 copies, would take about a week to produce if only one compositor and one full press were at work on it. Given the conditions mentioned, the logic is impeccable. Nor is it, as a method, foolish simply because we cannot know of occasional human aberrations from these norms. Yet I cannot forbear a quotation from George Eliot's *Daniel Deronda*:

Men may dream in demonstrations, and cut out an illusory world in the shape of axioms, definitions, and propositions, with a final exclusion of fact signed Q.E.D. No formulas for thinking will save us mortals from mistake in our imperfect apprehension of the matter to be thought about . . . [and] the unemotional intellect may carry us into a mathematical dreamland where nothing *is* but what is not.

The Cambridge and Bowyer papers (and they are not the only ones) make it quite clear that wages and therefore output, since the men were on piece-rates, varied considerably as between one man and another. It is not just a matter of occasional lapses or minor disparities to be cautiously conceded; it is a fundamental fact that should radically alter our whole conception of 'norms'. Moreover, any one man's income and therefore his actual output might fluctuate greatly week by week. Taking the Cambridge compositors first, one of them (John Délié) averaged 13s.5d. a week over one period of 59 weeks, and only 9s.9d. over a further period of 80 weeks. Yet on 11 May 1700 he was

---

12. Professor Hinman conveniently summarizes the evidence and offers some very careful qualifications of it in *Printing and Proof-Reading* I, 39-47. Although his method and purposes must in fact assume a norm, he is quite clear about the foolishness of trying to pretend that there may not have been considerable variation from it (cf. I, 46).

paid at the rate of £1.6s.8d. a week for setting in two weeks eight sheets of a book which required a daily average of 10,240 ens plus marginal notes. William Bertram averaged 10s.8d. over one period of 78 weeks and 10s. over another period of 47 weeks. Clement Knell and John Muckeus were content to average just over 13s. a week for long periods, and William Great 10s.3d. The only compositor to show sustained application at a high level was Thomas Pokins. His average weekly income over a period of two full years was £1.1s.5d. Yet in the five weeks up to 6 June 1702 he set some 318,000 ens, giving a daily average of 10,600, and his reward for this work was just on £1.7s.11d. a week. To reinforce the implications of these comments on the fluctuations in wages earned, we have only to look at the amount of work actually done in ens per day. Pokins's averages throughout 1702 were 6,307 (not 10,000 or 12,000) ens a day or 37,842 (not 72,000) a week. The next best daily averages for any lengthy period were those of Bertram with 5,700 ens and Knell with 5,603. Often the daily totals were well below these figures, and all of them of course are well below even such an elastic hypothetical norm as 10,000 to 12,000 ens a day. A glance at appendix II (d) below will show a similar variation of performance within the Bowyers' shop. The wages for the two-week period range from as much as £3.15s.0d. to as little as 8s.2d. And this personal variation as between compositors may be paralleled by comparable fluctuations in the amount of work done at various periods throughout the year. Strahan's ledgers, although they do not yield the same detail, also show great fluctuations in the total wages he paid out week by week (B. M. Add. MS. 48,801). And the records of the Plantin-Moretus Museum, the Oxford University Press, and even the "Case-Book" of John Wilson, printer in Kilmarnock in 1803, tell the same story.[13]

13. I must express my gratitude to Dr Léon Voet, Curator of the Plantin-Moretus Museum for supplying me with photocopies of entries from the *Mémorial des Ouvriers* for the months of Jan.-Mar. 1622. Dr Voet has brought together much valuable information in "The Making of Books in the Renaissance as told by the Archives of the Plantin-Moretus Museum," *PaGA*, X, no. 2 (Dec. 1965), 33-62. The most relevant Oxford document is a "Bill Book" for the years 1769-72 which I cite by courtesy of the Printer to the University. John Wilson's "Case-Book" was brought to my attention by Miss Frances M. Thomson who is preparing an edition of it. I should also mention Mr Rollo G. Silver's contributions to this journal, especially "Mathew Carey's Printing Equipment," *SB*, XIX (1966), 85-122, which form a valuable addition to the primary documentation on early printing houses. There is a more general point to be made. Greg, recognizing the level of generality that any respectable discipline must seek, insisted that bibliography comprehend manuscript as well as printed texts. Similarly it might be argued that ancient and modern book production should not be too readily separated. Mr Simon Nowell-Smith has shown in his 1966 Lyell Lectures how more recent books can be usefully (and disturbingly

Turning now to presswork, we have precisely the same situation. One of the better performances at full press in Cambridge was that of Jonathan Cotton and Robert Ponder during the week ending 24 February 1700 when for £1.4s.6d. each they worked off 10,350 sheets on four different books, averaging well over 3,400 impressions a day. But such figures and therefore such high incomes were quite exceptional. Albert Coldenhoff, working by himself at half press, earned on average 13s.3d. a week over a period of 67 weeks, and other average weekly wages earned by various workmen at half press were, in round figures, 11s., 12s., 15s. and 18s. At full press the average receipts show the same kind of range. If instead of wage bills we again look at the actual amount of work done, we can point to Thomas Green's single-handed production of 8,250 impressions one week, and only 4,750 the next; or to the work of Ponder and John Quinny who printed the following numbers of impressions week by week from mid-June to mid-July 1700: 15,200; 13,800; 9,700; 12,700; 10,700; 17,000 and so on. The hypothetical norm, you may recall, was 18,000.

Well, conclusions? Simply that our hypothetical figures are too high? Certainly that seems to be true, but the implications are I think more far-reaching. One is that we have perhaps failed in our historical sense, too readily imputing our own twentieth-century ideas and interests and the assumptions of our own society — especially our economic assumptions — to men whose attitudes to work were quite different from ours. We cannot afford to disregard contemporary social conditions and pre-Industrial Revolution attitudes. One careers adviser pointed out in 1747 that many pressmen played a great part of the time, and Benjamin Franklin took much the same jaundiced view of the British workman. As one economic historian puts it, "the conditions of life and habits of the people were all against the monotony of regular employment;" and again: "Contemporary evidence indicates that few cared to take advantage of their opportunities." The mass of labourers, said Sir William Temple, work only to relieve the present want.[14] Our society today reacts to the stimulus of high wages because modern society can satisfy a wide range of wants. But if wants don't increase, there is little point in working for anything beyond the bare necessities, and good wages will only suggest to a workman "an oppor-

---

for such concepts as "edition" and "issue") documented from publishers' archives. The growth of such bibliographical work in the modern period will, if the subject is to keep its integrity, enforce a greater

realism in discussing the productive conditions for earlier books.

14. For these references see *Cambridge University Press* I, 89-92, 139-40.

BIBLIOGRAPHICAL THEORIES   11

tunity to avoid part of his toil."[15] An anonymous writer of 1728 makes the point well: "People in low life who work only for their daily bread, if they can get it by three days work in a week, will many of them make holiday the other three *or set their own price on their labour*" (my italics).[16] One of the reasons why Elizabethan printers tried so often to exceed their allowed number of apprentices may have been that apprentices could be commanded to work regularly where journeymen could not.[17] So although we may today think of piece-rates as an incentive, it would seem that in the 17th and 18th centuries they were the employers' best protection from men who had no intention of working any harder than necessary for food and drink. A journeyman's output, that is, was conditioned largely by what he was able or willing to earn. As Moxon revealingly says, "they are by Contract with the Master Printer paid proportionably *for what they undertake to Earn* every working day, be it half a Crown, two Shillings, three Shillings, four Shillings, &c." (my italics). That is, he speaks quite casually of a performance difference of one hundred per cent.[18]

15. E. S. Furniss, *The Position of the Laborer in a System of Nationalism* (1920), p. 234. Furniss remarks that "The English laborer . . . responded, when prices fell or wages rose, so that he could satisfy his wants with diminished effort, by 'keeping holiday the remainder of his time'." (p. 235). The contemporary evidence cited by Furniss is full and detailed. D.C. Coleman, in "Labour in the English Economy of the 17th Century," *Economic History Review*, 2nd ser. VIII (1956), 280-95, points out that modern writers have underrated the recurrent problem of unemployment and comments that half-employment was often the rule. He cites Thomas Manly's note of 1669 that "They work so much fewer days by how much the more they exact in wages;" remarks that this was said of "agricultural workers and of industrial, of urban as well as of rural;" and adds "Irregularity of work . . . was not confined to the working week. The working day at one end of the scale, the working year at the other, were both very different from their counterparts in the modern industrialized community" (p. 291).

16. *Some Thoughts on the Interest of Money* (1728), cited by Furniss.

17. Such an argument was in fact used in litigation in 1592 when Benjamin Prince, a journeyman employed by John Legate, said he need only do what he could whereas Parker, an apprentice, had to do as his master bade him. See "Notes on Printing at Cambridge, *c.* 1590," *Trans. Cambridge Bibliographical Society*, III (1959), 102. The whole question of full or partial employment, however, needs to be related to the evidence we have of journeymen's grievances. It may be that under conditions of widespread unemployment an increase in part-time work is to be expected rather than a severe restriction of the labour force to the few men of highest efficiency.

18. *Mechanick Exercises*, ed. H. Davis and H. Carter (1958), p. 327; see also p. 328 for the phrase "their *Contracted Task*." Professor Hinman (*Printing and Proof-Reading*, I, 42-45) considers some of the evidence for daily output at press and case (e.g. the Gay-Purslowe contract of 1631, Moxon, Richardson's figures of 1756, and early 19th-century rates for setting). He clearly considers the figures rather high and suggests that they were not consistently attained. I am sure he is right, notwithstanding abundant evidence elsewhere for

The significance of this system of individual contracts — operating as far back as 1631 and even, I would claim, 1591 — has I think been overlooked. What it meant in effect was that a workman need work no harder than he had contracted to do, and only if he fell behind his contracted figure and then kept another waiting might he have to make good his colleague's loss of work. It was the master's job to accommodate these variables, not the workmen's. That the master had to make payments and organize production schedules on the assumption that men worked at *different* speeds is quite consistent with the Cambridge and Bowyer evidence and any other that I have seen; nor is it, so far as I know, inconsistent with any of the classically 'demonstrable' bibliographical proofs. But its consequence — the normality of non-uniformity — is an uncomfortable one for any methodology.

It might be thought that the fluctuations in output which I have noted are — in part at least — to be expected if there were too little material to keep the men working at high capacity week after week, a state of affairs all too likely in a small provincial academic press. Yet, once more, the evidence available shows a similar pattern at other presses. In fact, both the Cambridge and Bowyer records suggest that fluctuations in the volume of work would be reflected more readily in the number of workmen employed than in the actual level of work done by any one man.[19]

---

high press output — see "Notes on Printing at Cambridge," p. 101 n., where a number of references are collected. Testimonies for 1592 claim 2500 impressions as the normal daily amount worked off for 3s.4d. per press-crew. But it is also stated that under the rules of the London Company a pressman was to have his full contracted wages if on any day, by agreement with the master, fewer sheets were printed. Several 19th-century ones could be added, but Blackwell's estimate of 2500 impressions per day, cited by Mr Rollo G. Silver, is among the most important ("Mathew Carey's Printing Equipment," p. 102). The real point, however, is not that these figures were norms, except perhaps for very large edition quantities, but the accepted maxima. The evidence is consistent with the hypothesis of extreme variability within the limits indicated, but any "norm" derived from the evidence can be repeatedly falsified and its predictive value thereby seriously impaired. It may be noted that Plantin's pressmen and compositors received differential payments, as did those of Crownfield and Bowyer, for formes of varying difficulty, and in 1592 differential rates applied to presswork according to the size of type.

19. The point about fluctuations in the number of workmen is admirably made, in the case of Plantin, by the charts in Raymond de Roover's "The Business Organization of the Plantin Press in the Setting of Sixteenth Century Antwerp," *De Gulden Passer*, XXXIV (1956), 104-20. The figures there given show the absolute variations, but in addition the ratios of workmen to presses and of compositors to pressmen may be easily calculated as at January in every year from 1564 to 1589. To take two years: on 4 Jan. 1572 there were 13 presses in use, 23 pressmen, 23 compositors, and 7 other employees; on 2 Jan. 1574 there were 16 presses in use, 32 pressmen, 20 compositors, and 4 other employees. The smaller English

BIBLIOGRAPHICAL THEORIES   13

Where output varies so markedly from man to man and period to period, any reliance on 'norms' would seem to imply an almost irresponsibly large burden of probable error; polite concessions to occasional departures may serve a while as palliatives but general statements that can be so persistently falsified whenever any concrete evidence appears to test them are poor premises for advanced argument. Moreover, I have for simplicity here dealt mainly in averages; the actual figures are infinitely more varied and any attempt to trace the total complex patterns week by week, even with all the documentary evidence, is like trying to record the changing images of a kaleidoscope in the hands of a wilful child.

So far I have discussed, too, only the most elementary variables, and have left aside all question of edition sizes or the ways in which work was organized. Assumptions about the edition sizes of early books usually take account of the 1587 ordinance of the Stationers' Company which, with one or two exceptions, forbade the printing of more than 1250 or 1500 copies of any book from the same setting of type, although as McKerrow remarks "we have no certain knowledge of how long or how carefully the rule was observed."[20] And occasionally edition sizes have been related to the bibliographical evidence of skeleton formes, since it is understood "as a general principle that in any book printed on a single press two sets of headlines will appear only if the book was printed in an edition large enough for composition to keep ahead of presswork."[21] For the later 17th century and the 18th century the problem of variability in edition size is acknowledged to be more complex. Yet even in the early 1590's a pressman, Simon Stafford, giving evidence in court, pointed out that the number of sheets printed in any one day might vary considerably, reflecting different edition sizes, since "they had diverse numbers upon Severall bookes and the

shops could not have tolerated this degree of fluctuation, but where the records survive the ratios of compositors to pressmen to presses can be shown to have varied quite markedly. The Cambridge and Bowyer presses illustrate a disturbingly large variance in weekly, monthly and annual levels of production; Strahan's and Charles Ackers' output differed significantly from one year to the next; and the charts given of Oxford printing in F. Madan's *The Oxford University Press: a Brief Account* (1908), although based only on surviving works, are a graphic corrective to an overreliance on "norms." I know of no direct evidence that obliges us to exempt Elizabethan and Jacobean printers from such fluctuations, although the legal limitation on the number of printers has tempted some to assume continuous output at maximum levels. There is much evidence that some Elizabethan printers constantly lacked work.

20. *Introduction to Bibliography* (1928), p. 132.

21. Hinman, "New Uses for Headlines as Bibliographical Evidence," *English Institute Annual, 1941* (1942), p. 209.

numbers did alter."[22] At Cambridge in the early 1700's sermons were printed on average in 650 copies, the minimum being 400 and the maximum 1150. But the mean, as distinct from the average, was nearer 500 copies. One book of theological controversy was printed in a first edition of 750; a second edition of 1000; a third edition of 2000; and a fourth edition of 1250. Yet another of the same author's books ran through three editions in the order of 750, 500 and 500; and another was printed in two editions of 1000 copies each. Other figures for edition sizes of books on a fairly wide range of subjects are: 350, 500, 522, 550, 700, 820, 1050, 1150, 1250, 1500 and 3000. Again the Bowyer papers show a similar variation, apparent even in the Voltaire editions cited in appendix II (g). And the same point is made by the edition sizes given in Strahan's and Ackers' ledgers, and more particularly in those I quote both for the part issues of *A New General Collection of Voyages and Travels* and the monthly numbers of *The London Magazine*. Quite apart therefore from these figures invalidating any hypothetical norm (for any particular case, given the degree of variation, would seldom correspond to the assumptions of a guiding hypothesis), the need for a master printer to juggle with such varying totals, as well as the varying abilities of his workmen, reinforces what has been merely hinted at so far about work organization.

Normally in bibliographical analysis we are concerned with a particular book, usually a work to be edited, and that great range of printing which our literary interests have not led us to examine must be largely ignored. This is as it should be for life is short and, as Professor Todd has indicated in a disarmingly amusing note, some books are more valuable than others.[23] But the consequences of such selectivity cannot be ignored if bibliography, as the study of the transmission of literary documents, is to continue to lay claim to the serious intellectual status that Greg established for it. I shall return to this point. Meantime I wish to look briefly at a very common assumption, though not a universal one, in bibliographical analysis. It is the assumption that even if the whole resources of a house were not directed towards printing the book under examination, at least one compositor and one

22. "Notes on Printing at Cambridge," p. 101. See also P. Hernlund, "William Strahan's Ledgers: Standard Charges for Printing, 1738-1785," *SB*, XX (1967), 89-111, esp. p. 104 where the frequencies of certain edition sizes are given. Professor Hinman notes the folly of setting edition sizes to suit bibliographical equations (*Printing and Proof-Reading*, I, 40), but bibliographers sometimes forget that the number printed is a marketing decision which bears no relation whatever to printing conditions, although a master would of course be concerned to apportion all the work on hand in the most economic way.

23. "The Degressive Principle," *Times Literary Supplement*, 1 Sept. 1966, p. 781.

press-crew would be set to work fairly consistently on it.[24] Under these conditions we might expect five to six sheets a week to be completed.

Again, however, should we not take pause? The occasional prospectus might serve to put us on our guard, for few require printing times of anything like even five sheets a week. And in fact some surviving Cambridge agreements offer delivery times of — as near as matters — one sheet a week. Out of some 36 books of ten or more sheets produced between 1698 and 1705, only 7 were printed at an average rate of more than 2 sheets a week. *Suidas*, the Greek lexicon, was printed at the rate of $3\frac{1}{2}$ sheets a week, and the remainder of this group of 7 books progress on average at a rate of between 2 and 3 sheets a week each. For 14 books the average was between 1 and 2 sheets, and for 15 books it was no higher than a single sheet and often it was less than that. The Cambridge evidence cannot be discounted by noting that some of these books required careful correction, for the evidence from the Bowyer and Ackers ledgers points exactly the same way.[25] Nor does there seem to be any necessarily significant relationship between the total amount of work on hand and the rate of progress for any one book.

The force of these examples is simply that the Cambridge and Bowyer presses, like any other printing house today or any other printing house before them, followed the principle of concurrent production. Obviously the variety of runs gave greater flexibility in the organization of presswork and permitted more economical use of the

---

24. I hope it will be agreed without my listing references that such an assumption is widespread. Professor Todd at least agrees, for he once wrote, in iconoclastic vein: "Implicit in most accounts of presswork on hand-printed books is the convenient assumption that, at a given time, the entire resources of the shop are devoted to the production of a single work . . .". — "Concurrent Printing: An Analysis of Dodsley's *Collection of Poems by Several Hands*," *PBSA*, XLVI (1952), 45. Jobbing work may be invoked as a convenient way of explaining apparent delay, but even in Professor Hinman's discussion of the First Folio, which takes some account of other works printed by Jaggard in 1621-3 (see I, 16-24), the fundamental work patterns are traced in isolation from the other work on hand as though the Folio contained in itself all the evidence

of its production.

25. The Bowyer books tabled in appendix II (g) may serve as examples. The several editions of Voltaire were printed quite quickly (nos. 1-4); the 20 sheets of Baxter, a more difficult text, and the $17\frac{1}{2}$ sheets of Spenser, both took 33 weeks (nos. 5 and 6); Lobb's 34 sheets, on the other hand, were finished in only 29 weeks; more direct evidence of the different speeds of work on different books can be seen in appendix II (a) — (f). For Ackers, see *A Ledger of Charles Ackers, Printer of 'The London Magazine'* (1968), p. 19. Few printers, however, were as slow as Nicholas Okes was with one work: in five years he had printed only 6 sheets of a book called *Speculum Animae* — Jackson, *Records of the Court of the Stationers' Company, 1602-1640* (1957), p. 180.

several sizes of type available; but, however efficiently *total* production was organized, the system inevitably meant that individual books took longer to print than we might have thought likely, just as most books today take far longer than the productive capacity of the machinery would lead us to expect.

The important point, however, was made by Professor Todd many years ago. Under conditions of concurrent production, he remarked, "the book is only one of several components in a more extensive enterprise, and thus exhibits only a portion of the information necessary for its analysis. Until the other portions have been located and the various pieces reassembled in the pattern originally devised the puzzle will remain unsolvable" ("Concurrent Printing," pp. 45-6, 56). And again: "in instances of concurrent printing the bibliographer must examine all the books so related before attempting the analysis of any. To do less than this . . . is to learn little or nothing at all." These remarks cannot be repeated too often, but unfortunately Professor Todd's qualifying comments have tended to minimize their application to "the larger establishments of the eighteenth century [where] the facilities were certainly adequate for simultaneous work on several projects, involving, in some instances, independent groups of compositors and pressmen, in others, the same group intermittently employed, first on a few sheets of one book, then on a few of another." And his more immediate concern, the interpretation of press figures, whose "very presence implies unsystematic piecework engaged in conjunction with other miscellaneous endeavours," has also perhaps encouraged the belief that concurrent production may very well have been a feature of large printing houses in the 18th century but not of smaller and earlier ones.[26]

Such a view must be abandoned. No amount of historical quibbling can neutralize the plain facts of the Cambridge documents: an earlier and smaller printing house, never using more than two presses, often one and a half, and occasionally only one, habitually printed several books concurrently. So far as I am aware there is no primary evidence whatever to show that any printing house of the 16th, 17th or 18th centuries did not do likewise.

26. Professor Todd later wrote of concurrent printing as a practice "extraordinary in the seventeenth century" but "commonplace in the eighteenth" — "Bibliography and the Editorial Problem in the Eighteenth Century," *SB*, IV (1951-2), 46. G. Thomas Tanselle, "Press Figures in America," *SB*, XIX (1966), 129-30, also writes of the need for fuller information on all books being handled within a shop at one time.

Our mistake here I think goes back to a misreading of an observation by McKerrow. He remarked that "for a printing house to be carried on economically there must be a definite correspondence between rate of composition and the output of the machine room."[27] Notice how all-inclusive his terms are: printing house, machine room. I should like to offer now two quotations which take their origin in McKerrow, and I should like you to notice how in each case McKerrow's valid general statement is transformed into an invalid particular statement. First, Professor Turner:

In the Elizabethan printing shops, a cardinal principle of efficient operation was, we suppose, that composition and presswork should proceed at the same rate. If material could be set into type faster than the press could run it off, compositors had to waste time; conversely, if presswork went faster than composition, the pressmen would stand idle. Given pressmen and compositors of reasonable skill, the chief factor determining the speed of the presswork was the size of the edition . . .

at this point we become involved in a particular statement

. . . and the chief factor determining the speed of composition was the amount and difficulty of the text material to be set into each forme. Ideally one forme ought to be machined in the time required to distribute the immediately preceding forme and to set and impose the next, and in the case of books which got a great deal of text into each forme, as the [Shakespeare] Folio did, this ideal relationship could be approached only if two compositors could set simultaneously.[28]

Professor Hinman asks:

What plan would ensure the most satisfactory ratio between the time necessary to *set* one forme of the contemplated book into type and the time needed to *print off* the desired number of copies of such a forme? — for an efficient balance between composition and presswork was one of the prime requirements of successful printing house operations in the earlier seventeenth century. (*Printing and Proof-Reading*, I, 45n.)

This last is a quite different and seriously distorting assumption: that an economic relationship between composition and presswork is necessary on any *one* book for the business as a whole to be successful. The position is really so much more complex; indeed the more variables a printer has to juggle — in numbers of compositors and full or half press-crews, in their individual capacities, in edition sizes, in the num-

27. "Edward Allde as a Typical Trade Printer," *Library*, 4th ser. (1929), 143.

28. "Analytical Bibliography and Shakespeare's Text," *MP*, LXII (1964), 55.

ber of books on hand, and in the demand for ephemera — the more chance he has of making them compatible and therefore of making his business as a whole economically successful.[29]

Such a conclusion is not inconsistent with the figures given earlier to demonstrate the variable levels of production achieved by a printing house; they simply reinforce the point that an 'economic' disposition of men and materials could only be achieved complexly — and that the fine considerations of timing implied by many studies devoted to the analysis of a single work may be a world away from the reality. Relax the time scheme ever so slightly, and a whole house of bibliographical cards comes tumbling down. In particular the correlations often traced between edition size, number of compositors, skeleton formes and presses, must look very different if translated to a context of concurrent printing. But I anticipate.

If concurrent production was much the most efficient way of running a printing house, as distinct from the most efficient method of producing a single book, how then, under these conditions, was work apportioned? What kind of range does a compositor's work, for example, show week by week? Although it was by no means rare at Cambridge for a compositor to have a monopoly on any one book, the work was usually shared. Of a sample of 118 Cambridge books, only 50, or 42%, were set by a single compositor; and if we except very short works like sermons, the percentage drops to 24. Moreover it was unusual for a compositor to work for any long period on one book to the exclusion of all others — usually he would be setting type for two or three concurrently. Of the 13 compositors whose work for Bowyer over a two-week period early in 1732 is recorded in appendix II (d), only *one* was engaged on one book alone.

Undoubtedly the main considerations determining the allocation of work were simply a compositor's freedom to do it and the availability of type. If a compositor had no other work on hand he would be transferred to any that might be offering and for which type was available. For normally, even when two or more compositors worked on a book, they did not work together setting sheet and sheet about. What usually happened was that one took over where the other left off and then composed as many sheets as the master found convenient or

29. Stower, *The Printer's Grammar* (1808), p. 376, makes the point: "Compositors and pressmen are at all times dependent on each other; they therefore demand the *constant attention of the overseer* [my italics] in order that nothing may occur to cause a stoppage or standing still to either party." In a smaller office this concern for oversight and disposition of the work on hand would naturally have been the master's.

as other commitments allowed. A quarto edition of Virgil may be cited to make the point. Bertram set sheets A-E, then Crownfield took over and set F-3R, next Michaëlis set 3S-3Z, Bertram then resumed setting, continuing to 4F, Délié was brought in to set 4G, Crownfield took over once more with 4H and finally, after Crownfield had retired at 4O, Bertram set to 4R and finished off the book. Although four compositors were involved, and although Crownfield worked on two sections of the book and Bertram on three, on no occasion were any two men setting simultaneously. Nor incidentally would it be true to say that they were setting alternately. And it would certainly be quite wrong to assume that work was divided so that the book might be printed more quickly. Meantime of course each Cambridge compositor was also concurrently engaged on some other book or books.[30] In appendix II (g) examples 2 and 4, Bowyer's two English editions of Voltaire, show the same pattern of work. Whereas the printing house printed, and individual compositors normally set, several works concurrently, the composition of any one book would therefore usually be a simple matter of progression from sheet to sheet, or from one group of sheets to another, by consecutive compositors. It follows that the compositorial pattern within any such book will rarely offer adequate evidence in itself of the productive conditions but will have been determined by, and will reflect the exigencies of, the general pattern of work in the printing house as a whole over a period of months or even years.

Turning now to the other half of the equation — presswork — we must again affirm that the most efficient disposition of work, given the variables to be reconciled, could be achieved only by a highly flexible system. As with composition, the actual manner in which work was apportioned to the men would have depended in part on the number of men employed and the amount of work on hand. But regardless of the size of the plant it seems unlikely that a particular press consistently served the compositor or compositors setting a particular book. At Cambridge, it is quite clear, any press-crew might get any sheet of any book to print off, and consequently it was rare for any book of more than two or three sheets to be printed solely at one press. The production tables for books printed at Cambridge show quite conclusively that the use of two press-crews was a perfectly normal procedure and had nothing whatever to do with increasing the speed of production. If a forme was ready for printing, it went to whichever

30. See Table 11, *Cambridge University Press*, I, 106-7. For Bowyer, see appendix II (e) where, of 14 compositors listed for the two-week period, only one (C. Knell) worked on a single book.

crew was ready to take it, although usually it seems that a sheet would be printed and perfected by the same crew. The position in the Bowyers' shop is much more complex, for it is clear that *formes*, not just sheets, might be sent to any press which happened to be free and that any sheet might well be printed at one press and perfected at another. Again the Voltaire and Baxter examples in appendix II (g) make it plain that this practice was very common.

In a large shop the distribution of work is likely to be more complex simply because there are more routes open for a book to take; but in both large and small shops there is such strong evidence of fluctuations in the number and strength of press-crews that a pattern of work must very often reflect such changes too. At Cambridge there was considerable variety in the number and composition of the press-crews, ranging from half press only during the first half of 1699, to full press only during the second half of the same year and a good part of 1700, and various combinations of half and full press during other years. Only for a brief period in 1701 were two full presses in operation simultaneously; but we find (unexpectedly, for the usual arrangement we might think would be for the two men to work together at a single press) two half presses at work during 1705, 1706 and part of 1709. There were frequent changes in the composition of the crews during the period from 1699 until early 1702. In later years the normal arrangement — if you will permit the term — was one full press and one half press. But the varying patterns make it extremely difficult to assume a norm. So too in the Bowyers' shop: 3 presses were in use between 24 Dec. 1731 and 15 Jan. 1732; 4 between 17 Jan. and 29 Jan.; 4 (but only 3½ crews) between 31 Jan. and 12 Feb.; 5 between 14 Feb. and 26 Feb.; and 6 (but possibly only 4 full and 2 half crews) between 28 Feb. and 18 Mar. (Just to complicate matters further for the analyst, press no. 7 was in use throughout the whole of this period and the press figure 7 appears on some of the sheets which it printed, but at no time were there as many as seven presses in use.)

So a press-crew, just like a compositor only more so, would usually be working on several books at a time, with "All work to be taken in Turn, as brought to the Press, except in such Work as may require Dispatch, or the Compositor will want the Letter . . .".[31] The simplest way of using the crews most efficiently was not to try to maintain a strict relationship between a particular compositor and a particular press — the varying edition sizes and varying output of the men would

31. Rules of a London chapel in 1734, printed by Ellic Howe, *The London Compositor* (1947), p. 31.

have made this very difficult — but, given the presswork which was offering, to apportion it so that each crew always had something to go on with. This was the easiest way of accommodating the varying runs required for the different books in production at the same time. In thinking otherwise we may also have under-estimated the flexibility of the common press itself as a machine. Each press had several friskets, ready cut to common formats. It was a very simple matter to change them over; and since the sheets were printed wet on a sopping tympan, the type bit deep into the paper and careful make-ready was unnecessary — certainly it did not need the care of the modern kiss-impression. Technically there was no reason therefore why the press should not work to a number of compositors setting several different books, perhaps within one day, certainly within one week.

It is more than time now for us to re-unite the two halves of McKerrow's equation — the 'rate of composition' and 'the output of the machine room'. We have seen that, both at Cambridge and in the Bowyers' shop, books were produced concurrently. This meant not only that several books were in production at the same time but that each workman, whether at press or case, was often engaged on several books more or less at once. If we are correctly to reconstruct the detailed operations of a printing house — even a very small one — or a true account of the printing of any one book, we must therefore do it in a way that shows the complete pattern of work in its full complexity.

The diagrams given in appendix I (a) and (b) are an attempt to do this. They show precisely how all work on hand at Cambridge was allocated between 26 Dec. 1701 and 28 Feb. 1702 and convey some impression of the flow of work.[32] Again I am tempted to quote George Eliot and say that the sheets seem to follow only what she calls "the play of inward stimulus that sends one hither and thither in a network of possible paths." *Suidas*, an exceptional case, demanded the almost undivided attention of four compositors working in pairs on each volume; and Crownfield, Bertram and Pokins spread their work over two to three books each. When we look at the distribution of work to the different press-crews, we note that with one exception every compositor or pair of compositors sent work to both presses; and, moreover, that the work composed during these weeks was in many cases

32. The two charts may be compared to those given as Table 15 in *The Cambridge University Press*. Taken together, the five charts show completely different patterns of work at five distinct stages of a continuous working period of five months, although many of the men and books involved are the same.

printed by any of four different press-crews. If we take a single book —
Psyche, either volume of *Suidas,* or Whiston's *Short View* — the point
to be made is much the same, that the various sheets of any particular
book were likely as not printed at more than one press. The details
given for the Bowyer shop in appendix II (a) to (e) cover two distinct
periods: first, from 26 Dec. 1730 to 6 Feb. 1731, and second, from 31
Jan. to 26 Feb. 1732. Their testimony in witnessing to the disposition
of work is consistent with that of the Cambridge records but the relationships revealed between the several productive units, whether compositors or pressmen, are very much more complex. The information
given reveals, for example, the number of *pages* set by each compositor, the edition size, and the number of *formes* printed by each press;
in the case of appendix II (a) we can also see the peculiar arrangements between presses 1, 3 and 7 for printing and reprinting the
Defence of the Present Administration. I take this evidence to be quite
conclusive. It shows that the essential procedures for the distribution
of work were the same for a larger and later shop as they were for an
earlier printing house with only two (or more commonly one and a
half) active presses. It shows that although we should doubtless be
right to assume — allowing for certain social attitudes and conditions
we have mentioned — that composition and presswork *as a whole* were
fairly economically balanced, it would be quite wrong to conclude that
this balance was either necessary or possible for work on any individual book.

III

The more substantial matters discussed in the preceding section —
workmen's output, edition sizes, and the relationship between composition and presswork under conditions of concurrent production — must
now serve as a prelude to notes on a number of bibliographical procedures that imply quite different productive conditions. If the evidence
of part II withstands challenge, it must I think be held to falsify several
current hypotheses. It is not easy to summarize these but the ones I
have in mind relate particularly to compositors' measures, cast-off copy,
skeleton formes, proof-correction and press figures.

If one assumes that a compositor usually worked on only one book
at a time he would have had no need to alter the measure to which he
had set his composing stick. Changes in line measurement within any
one book might therefore be taken to indicate an abnormal interruption, after which the stick was reset to a slightly different measure, or

the presence of a second compositor.[33] Professor Bowers cites, for example, Bellon's *The Mock-Duellist* (1675) in which sheets B-F are set with a 120 mm. measure and sheets G-I with a measure of 121 mm. "In such a book the inference is probably that with sheet G another compositor . . . took over the work. In general, one is likely to conjecture that any interruption of the printing sufficient to cause a single compositor to adjust his stick again after working on some other book would most likely have been sufficient to cause the skeleton-formes to be broken up . . ." ("Bibliographical Evidence," p. 157). These conclusions must, however, seem misplaced if one begins from a different premise. If we assume concurrent production, for example, then the likelihood of measures reflecting the division of work among compositors will be small. In the first place, production times were too long; and in the second place, compositors working on several books at a time, often in quite different sizes of type, would have had to change their measure constantly. As it happens, these propositions are consistent with the Cambridge evidence, whereas analysis of a few of the Cambridge books suggests that it would be impossible to judge how compositorial work was divided on any of them from the evidence of measures. Not only do the widths of type-pages set by the same compositor vary, but different compositors are often found setting to an identical measure, and interruptions are routine. The general practice inferred from limited physical evidence and the underlying assumption about work method remain mutually consistent, but in most cases they are likely to be quite wrong.

One of the more delicate exercises in advanced analytical bibliography is tracing the pattern of skeleton formes as evidenced by running titles in order to determine the order of presswork and, it might be claimed, the number of presses used. This pattern may be related by a time scale to another showing compositorial stints, or it may of itself be taken to imply a certain number of compositors at work on the book. The relationship indicated between composition and presswork may then be employed as an analytical tool in determining such things

33. Bowers, "Bibliographical E v i d e n c e from the Printer's Measure," *SB*, II (1949-50), 153-67, esp. pp. 155-6: "The most elementary and easily discerned cases which can be determined by measurement occur when . . . printing of a book is so materially interrupted that when work is resumed a different measure is inadvertently employed." See also "Purposes of Descriptive Bibliography, with Some Remarks on Methods", *Library*, 5th ser. (1953), p. 18 n., and "Underprinting in Mary Pix, *The Spanish Wives* (1696)," *Library*, 5th ser. (1954), p. 248. John Smith, *The Printer's Grammar* (1755), pp. 197-8, suggests other reasons why measures, ostensibly the same, might differ. For Moxon, see *Mechanick Exercises*, p. 203.

as nature of copy, methods of setting, edition size and proofing procedures. Implicit in all such analyses is the fundamental assumption that composition and presswork on a particular book would normally seek a condition of balance. This is a difficult area in which to order the work done while being fair to the arguments of those who have used such evidence; nor am I confident that I fully understand the analytical principles used. But the subject is important and even at the risk of misrepresentation demands discussion.

The pioneer study in the use of headlines, as in much else, was written by Professor Bowers over thirty years ago.[34] The association of sets of headlines with skeleton formes is now so well evidenced that it may be taken for granted, and, as Professor Bowers has also remarked, "the basic principles of the printer's use of headlines did not differ markedly in any period when books were printed by hand."[35] Where a single skeleton was used for both formes of a sheet,

> the press was idle while the forme just off the press was being washed and stripped and its skeleton was being transferred to the type pages which were next to be printed. . . . Some printers used two skeletons, each with its own set of headlines. Thus while one forme was on the press, the skeleton was being stripped from an already printed forme and imposed about the type pages next to be printed. Since the transfer of this second skeleton could take place while the press was printing the first, there was no delay at all between the time a forme was removed from the press and the time the new one was planked down on the bed (pp. 188-9).

The phrase 'the press was idle' is perhaps misleading since under conditions of concurrent printing the press would not be 'idle' at all but employed on another book. It has however had considerable repercussions and a great many bibliographical arguments have been constructed on the assumption that this inferred idleness could not have been the norm and must have been avoided in order to secure a balanced relationship of composition and presswork. So Professor Turner: "In order to effect the minimum press delay, the formes . . . would have had to go through the press in the following order . . .".[36] ". . . in one-skeleton work the press was forced to stand idle . . .".[37]

34. "Notes on Running-Titles as Bibliographical Evidence," *Library*, 4th ser. (1938), pp. 318-22. In 1909 A. W. Pollard had drawn attention to the recurrent headlines in Folio 2 *Henry IV* (*Shakespeare Folios and Quartos*, pp. 134-5).

35. "The Headline in Early Books," *English Institute Annual, 1941* (1942), p. 187.

36. "The Composition of *The Insatiate Countess*, Q2," *SB*, XII (1958), 202.

37. "The Printing of Beaumont and Fletcher's *The Maid's Tragedy*, Q1 (1619)," *SB*, XIII (1960), 201; see also pp. 202, 204, 208 for assumptions about timing.

BIBLIOGRAPHICAL THEORIES   25

"There is every reason to believe that press delays were abhorrent to the 17th-century printer" (*"The Maid's Tragedy,"* p. 217). ". . . a compositor would not change from setting by formes to *seriatim* setting without risking a press delay unless he was ahead of his press . . ."[38] ". . . the adoption of one-skeleton printing for several formes, and the resultant press delays . . ." (*"Philaster,"* p. 28). "If we assume that two skeletons would have been employed in the most efficient manner . . ."[39] ". . . working on the assumption that composition and press-work could stay more-or-less in balance . . ."[40] ". . . two formes . . . would not have been machined concurrently, for had they been, a delay in presswork would have resulted."[41]

Professor Hinman, however, extended the argument by pointing out that if a book were printed in a very small edition, printing would be so well ahead of setting that a second skeleton would be of little use.

The press will inevitably be obliged to stand idle periodically, waiting for the compositor to get new material for it. In such circumstances, of course, there would be no point in accelerating presswork speed further by the use of two skeletons; for although the use of two skeletons can speed up press-work, it cannot increase composition speed: however many skeletons are employed, the same number of impositions will be required ("New Uses for Headlines," p. 209).

Professor Hinman then suggests that if the edition were a very large one, however, the reverse might be true. Printing would take longer than setting and the pressmen might well seek to avoid delays and restore the balance by using two skeletons. Hence Professor Bowers has subsequently stated that "certain assumptions can be made about the rate of compositorial to press speed and thus about the number of

38. "The Printing of *Philaster* Q1 and Q2," *Library*, 5th ser. (1960), p. 22.

39. *Ibid.* In the article from which the last three quotations are drawn, Professor Turner suggests that "the erratic time-relationship" and therefore the imbalance in the relationship of composition and presswork may reflect variable copy, extra help with distribution, or indicate that "typesetting was attended by serious difficulties" — the textual implications of the latter inference are important.

40. "Printing Methods and Textual Problems in *A Midsummer Night's Dream,* Q1,"

SB, XV (1962), 46.

41. "The Printers of the Beaumont and Fletcher Folio of 1647, Section 2," *SB*. XX (1967), 37. Another point of view on this whole question of delay is that of A. K. McIlwraith: "It seems that printers . . . were sometimes willing to interrupt their work for quite a slight cause. This in turn suggests that time was not at a premium, and casts some doubt on any argument which rests on the assumption that speed was economically important." See "Marginalia on Press-corrections," *Library*, 5th ser. (1950), p. 244.

copies printed";[42] and Professor Williams has remarked that "in a small edition press time would be briefer than composition time and the compositor would always be concerned lest he fall behind and so delay his press."[43]

Yet another application was indicated by Professor Hinman when he noted that skeleton formes "have an intimate connection with various possible methods of stop-press correction" ("New Uses for Headlines," p. 222). Applying this principle in a re-examination of the proofing of *Lear*, Professor Bowers wrote:

With one-skeleton printing there is nothing for the press to work on when the forme is removed for correction. The most obvious thing to do with two skeletons is to plug this gap by putting the second forme on the press and pulling its proofs so that correction in the type can be made at leisure without further halting the press.[44]

At the same time he offered a succinct restatement of the basic position:

Two-skeleton printing was an extension of one-skeleton, devised to secure relatively continuous presswork by avoiding the major delay at the press which occurred when a new forme was imposed for printing.[45]

The temporal relationship between composition and presswork here assumed is however capable of many permutations. One might start with evidence of presswork and seek signs of, or infer, compensating adjustments in composition; alternatively, one might begin with some knowledge of the speed of composition and then try to trace evidence of presswork to match. In the first case the evidence of press-

42. "Purposes of Descriptive Bibliography," p. 18 n. Elsewhere Professor Bowers brings together in a single sentence many of the considerations raised here: "On the evidence of spelling, only one compositor set (*) B-D, but with about half a normal edition-sheet, he could not have kept up with the press and therefore would not have imposed with two skeleton-formes." — "The Variant Sheets in John Banks's *Cyrus the Great*, 1696," *SB*, IV (1951-2), 179.

43. "Setting by Formes in Quarto Printing," *SB*, XI (1958), 49. The compositor was unlikely to have been "concerned" at the imbalance, since the reason for it (edition size) was none of his making. It is

also salutary to observe that the words '*his press*,' as in Professor Turner's article cited in note 38, show the unconscious hardening of assumption into self-evident truth.

44. "An Examination of the Method of Proof Correction in *Lear*," *Library*, 5th ser. (1947), p. 29.

45. *Ibid.*, p. 28. In "Elizabethan Proofing," *Joseph Quincy Adams Memorial Studies* (1948), pp. 571-86, Professor Bowers added "I feel that this was the major delay which was circumvented and that a certain reduction possible in the time for press-correction was only a minor consideration." (p. 574).

work will almost invariably be in the shape of skeleton formes, although their interpretation may not always be straightforward.

Do they, for example, indicate one press or two? Professor Bowers
long ago remarked that "the evidence of running-titles to determine
the number of presses is often dubious in the extreme and its application hazardous."[46] And Greg expressed some doubt about the equation
of skeleton formes with presses.[47] Yet such equations have been made.
Professor Price, writing of *Your Five Gallants*, claimed that "in 1607
[Eld] had at least two presses, as the running-titles . . . show." And
again, writing of *Michaelmas Term*, "the series of running-titles seem
to imply that at least four presses worked on the book."[48] Professor
Bowers: "Since regularly alternating two-skeleton formes produce
maximum efficiency for one-press work, the staggered appearance of
three skeletons . . . suggests the use of two presses." On this assumption, it becomes possible to observe a "mathematical regularity of
transfer between the presses according to a fixed and efficient system";
hence "the three-skeleton pattern . . . is *proof* of two-press printing"
(my italics).[49] And again: "The analysis of running titles reveals that
two presses printed Q2 [*Hamlet*]," each press being served by a different compositor.[50] It is not surprising then to find others writing of
"a normal pattern for two-compositor work in which each man serves
a different press."[51] And writing of *The Revenger's Tragedy*, Professor
Price noted that the four skeletons present suggest two presses, adding
that elsewhere "Eld's pressmen clearly revealed their use of two presses
by printing on different stocks of paper."[52]

46. "Notes on Running-Titles," p. 331. In
a later note, Professor Bowers states that
"running-titles will almost inevitably reveal
simultaneous setting and printing of different portions of a book" — *Principles of
Bibliographical Description* (1949), p. 125.

47. *The Variants in the First Quarto of
'King Lear'* (1940), pp. 48-9.

48. "The First Edition of *Your Five Gallants* and of *Michaelmas Term*," *Library*,
5th ser. (1953), pp. 23, 28. Professor Price
believes that *Michaelmas Term* was printed
partly by Purfoote and partly by Allde:
"In [its] printing, one skeleton was used
for gatherings A and B, two for C-I, one
press doing the inner, the other the outer,
formes; but for gatherings H and I, the
presses twice interchanged the formes" (p.
29).

49. "Underprinting in *The Spanish
Wives*," p. 254. Each press is said to have
printed and perfected its sheet with the
one skeleton forme.

50. "The Textual Relation of Q2 to Q1
Hamlet (I)," *SB*, VIII (1956), 46. See also
"The Printing of *Hamlet* Q2," *SB*, VII
(1955), 42.

51. Cantrell and Williams, "Roberts'
Compositors in *Titus Andronicus* Q2" *SB*,
VIII (1956), 28. They add: "The book was
printed throughout with one skeleton-
forme, and so necessarily on one press . . .".

52. "The Authorship and Bibliography of
The Revenger's Tragedy," *Library*, 5th ser.
(1960), p. 273. Quite apart from the question of skeleton formes, the inference from
paper might be queried. It is just as simple

The attractive simplicity of Professor Bowers' initial proposition about skeleton formes is no longer easy to discern. Nevertheless it has been repeatedly put to use in order to determine also the number of compositors engaged on a book. In an article on the printing of *Romeo and Juliet* Q2, for example, we are told that "variant compositorial characteristics suggest the presence of two compositors" and are assured that "the *mechanical evidence of presswork corroborates* that suggestion" (my italics). The quarto was printed from two skeletons recurring in regular sequence. The writers continue: "This evidence from running titles can be explained only with great difficulty as accompanying the work of one compositor; but a reasonable explanation may be offered by resorting to the hypothesis of a second press, and *thus of a second compositor*" (my italics).[53] Earlier, Professor Bowers had remarked that "printing by two presses must necessarily require the services of two compositors" ("Bibliographical Evidence," p. 166 n. 13). Again that a "general alternation involving the use of four skeleton formes is inexplicable for printing with one press; yet if we hypothesize two presses it follows that there must have been more than one compositor."[54] In another case, where only one skeleton-forme was used, "the running-title pattern indicates no second workman."[55] Professor Turner has written: "One skeleton ordinarily means one compositor; two may mean two setting simultaneously . . .".[56] But the clearest example of skeleton formes in relation to composition is offered by *Hamlet* Q2, in which "compositor X served one press and

to assume that that the heaps were told out by the warehouseman (or boy) from alternate bundles as required for each successive signature. Otherwise it must be assumed that each press knew in advance precisely what proportion of the edition it would print and had on hand all the white paper it would need to complete that work.

53. Cantrell and Williams, "The Printing of the Second Quarto of *Romeo and Juliet* (1599)," *SB*, IX (1957), 107, 113-4.

54. "Shakespeare's Text and the Bibliographical Method," *SB*, VI (1954), 79.

55. Cantrell and Williams, "Roberts' Compositors in *Titus Andronicus*," p. 28: "The problem of *Titus* Q2 is further complicated by the fact that in the reprint X and Y did not combine to set their mate-

rial in a normal pattern for two-compositor work in which each man serves a different press. In fact, the peculiar feature of *Titus* is that there should be a second compositor at all. *The running-title pattern indicates no such second workman*" (my italics).

56. "The Text of Heywood's *The Fair Maid of the West*," *Library*, 5th ser. (1967), p. 302. In "The Printing of *A King and No King* Q1," *SB*, XVIII (1965), 258, Professor Turner had assumed that a single skeleton printing sheets A-F implied one compositor, and that a second skeleton introduced at G implied another, and quicker, one — although apart from signings there were otherwise "no means to distinguish the work of the two compositors" (n. 12). See also Hinman, *Printing and Proof-Reading* II, 522 n.l.

imposed his formes for that press, whereas compositor Y served a second press and, correspondingly, imposed his own distinct formes for that press." These observations led Professor Bowers to remark that "when, as in *Hamlet*, the spelling tests for compositors equate so precisely with what one may conjecture to have been their stints from the evidence of running-titles, we may be somewhat more confident in the future about roughing-out two-compositor work in books on this running-title evidence" ("Printing *Hamlet* Q2," pp. 41-42).

There would appear to be enough flexibility in the principle to allow its reverse application, for, as in the case of *Romeo and Juliet*, two skeletons may become two presses if there is some slight evidence of two compositors (and hence "corroborate" the suggestion that there *are* two compositors). But since compositors have left no skeletons they are less easy to detect than headlines, and there are therefore fewer cases of presswork conditions being inferred from the prior evidence of composition.

By now I hope I have, at the very least, made clear by selection and juxtaposition the multiple and often confusingly diverse general statements inferred from the number and order of skeleton formes,[57] and laid bare the fundamental assumptions about desirable ratios between compositors and press-crews. It simply remains to ask how reliable such analyses would turn out to be if tested by analogy (a fair enough procedure, since their authors imply extended application by analogy).

Two Cambridge books may serve: Beaumont's *Psyche* (1702), a folio in fours, and Newton's *Principia* (1713), a quarto (*Cambridge University Press*, I, 126-7, 219-21). To take *Psyche* first, and in particular the quires 2E-2Z which can be related to full work-flow charts,[58] we may observe that the edition was 750; that only one compositor worked on it at a time (Bertram set 2E-2F, 2K-2Q1/2, 2T1/2-2Z; Crownfield 2G-2I, 2Q1/2-2T1/2); that four skeleton formes were in regular use; and that setting and printing of these 19 quires, or 38 sheets, took about 20 weeks in all (from mid September 1701 to 31 Jan. 1702). All I wish to establish now is the futility of attempting to infer any direct

---

57. In some cases two skeletons, regardless of edition size or speed of composition, may be evidence not of increased speed of production, but of a *slower* than normal rate of production, simply because it can be a very convenient way of keeping type safely standing whether before or after printing (either to allow of proofing in the sheet,

or to defer distribution). Stower, *Printer's Grammar*, p. 474: "Forms will sometimes remain a considerable length of time before they are put to press."

58. *Ibid.*, Table 15, but continued below in appendix I (a) and (b).

correlation of presswork with these conditions from the four skeleton formes. Two quires set by different compositors (2F-2G), and with identical forme patterns, were both printed at the same full press; two quires set by the same compositor (2K-2L), but with utterly different forme patterns, were both printed by the same half press; two quires set by the same compositor (2O-2P), and with identical forme patterns, were both printed at the same half press; all four skeletons appear in quire 2T, one sheet of which was printed at one full press and the other sheet of which was printed at another full press; all four skeletons appear in quire 2U, one sheet of which was printed at full press and the other sheet of which was printed at half press. And yet if this evidence were not available it would be perfectly respectable to infer that this regular use of four skeletons might mean either (a) a large edition; or (b) two compositors, if not three; or (c) at least one full press in continuous operation.

Newton's *Principia* is a little easier to deal with since it is a quarto, and although there are four skeletons in all, only two of these were in use at any one time. The first printed most outer formes in sheets C-2P, the second most inner formes; in 2Q-2V their roles were reversed. New skeletons were constructed for 2X, one printing all inner formes to 3P, the other all outer formes. Under these very straightforward conditions, we might normally infer one of the following:

(a)   There was a single compositor, but the press was evidently lagging behind composition; therefore two skeletons were used to save imposition time. We might also infer a fairly large edition.

(b)   The edition was probably small and presswork regularly ahead of composition — especially since the text was in Latin and cuts had to be accommodated within it; but nothing would be gained by the use of two skeletons under such conditions unless, say, two compositors were at work.

(c)   The reversal of skeletons at 2Q is probably insignificant, but a serious interruption undoubtedly occurred after the printing of 2V when the first two skeletons were broken up.

I trust that this example is thought to be no worse for its approximations than most such arguments, but it seems to me to point up once more the nature of our guiding assumptions about skeleton formes and the relationship of composition to presswork. In doing so it also indicates the likely error in our general statements on these matters since their claim to represent the truth can be falsified by contradictory case-studies. If, as for many books, there were no external evidence to control speculation, any of the explanations given above, suitably

BIBLIOGRAPHICAL THEORIES   31

sophisticated, could be employed in a publishable account of the printing of the *Principia*. The facts of the matter are: the edition was 700; only one compositor at a time worked on the book (Pokins set B, 2Q-3R, a-d; Délié C-2P) ; the book was printed at both full press (49 sheets) and half press (17 sheets) without these conditions in any way being reflected in the number or order of skeletons; when there were changes in skeletons, press conditions remained constant; a delay of some months in 1712 is unmarked by the skeletons; the mere reversal of skeletons at 2Q was preceded by a delay of 11 months; the creation of entirely new skeletons for 2X may have been related to a delay of about 3 months; the first pair of skeletons were in use for over 2 years, the second for 1½ years; printing of the 66 sheets in the book extended from October 1709 until May 1713.[59]

I have not examined the skeleton formes in Bowyer books, but the fact that the sheets in them were often printed at one press and perfected at another must render very complex indeed any analysis seeking to relate compositors, formes and presses — even with the help of press figures. It cannot be assumed that other and earlier presses did *not* do likewise (without the figures); it is just that we happen to know for certain in some cases what the Bowyers did.

I wish now to broaden the argument a little by adverting to the Shakespeare First Folio and by offering yet another case-study. When Professor Hinman writes:

Long sequences of Folio formes were often set by two compositors setting simultaneously; yet one press regularly printed off these formes as rapidly as they were set. Now, unless our estimates are badly at fault, this would not have been possible if the edition had consisted of many *more* than about 1,200 copies. Nor on the other hand could two compositors (and no more than two seem ever to have set type for the Folio at any given time) have kept even one press continuously busy if the edition had been of appreciably *less* than 1,200 copies . . .[60]

59. We might stand to gain clarity if, when discussing changes in the pattern of skeletons, we were to abandon the term "interruption" with its assumptions about timing and its implications of delay. Normally what we are observing is simply a discontinuity.

60. *Printing and Proof-Reading* I, 46. See also I, 124 where the same point is made and Professor Hinman cites Moxon: "It is also Customary in some Printing Houses that if the Compositer or Press-man make either the other stand still through the neglect of their contracted Task, that then he who neglected, shall pay him that stands still as much as if he had Wrought." Professor Hinman seems to imply that if a forme were machined in appreciably *less* time than one could be set the press would stand idle and the compositors would have to reimburse the pressmen. But this can hardly have been so. It was the master's job to worry about these things; Moxon is only concerned with 'neglect' of a 'contracted Task.'

When Professor Hinman makes this point, he is deducing the probable size of the edition from an hypothesis about timing. The tentative nature of this deduction is made very clear and Professor Hinman's scholarship is of such excellence that it is seldom possible to offer views that he has not already entertained. Yet there can be no mistaking the main import of the above passage: two compositors and one press working on the Folio alone yield 1200 edition-sheets a day. Obviously, without full information about all other work on hand, one cannot falsify Professor Hinman's argument or its implication that the printing of the Folio was, by and large, a self-contained operation. Nor, without such evidence, can one prove it. But it may be salutary to consider its status as a general proposition which is likely to be true for other books of the period. For, as Professor Hinman himself says,

Because the Folio was a book it must have been produced by methods which, in part at least, were followed in the making of other books; and investigative techniques that are of value in the study of the printing of the Folio should be useful in other studies too (*Printing and Proof-Reading*, I, 13).

Now if roughly comparable books show quite different conditions of production, the above hypothesis about timing and the deduction from it about edition size will be weakened. More, its proven inability to predict the other possibilities will severely limit its standing as a statement of general application.

Volume I of the 1705 Cambridge-printed edition of the Greek lexicon *Suidas* is perhaps a book that is "roughly comparable" (*The Cambridge University Press*, I, 224-33). It is a folio in fours, with some 954 pages, about 8,500 ens per forme set double column in English Greek and English Latin with Long Primer footnotes; being started by 1 Nov. 1701 and finished by 4 Sep. 1703, it took some 22 months to print: the edition size was 1500 (150 large-paper copies, 1350 small-paper); it was set throughout by two compositors working simultaneously on each forme; 1661½ sheets were printed at full press and 72 at half press. The Shakespeare volume is a folio in sixes, contains just under 900 pages, has about 10,600 ens per forme set double column in Pica English; according to Professor Hinman's table it took about 18½ months to print but if we add the 2½ months given as the possible length of an interruption, the total would be 21 months; and Professor Hinman suggests an edition of about 1200 on the assumption that two compositors and one press were working on it more or less continuously. It would be foolish to think of these two books as being any more than only very roughly comparable; the Shakespeare Folio is in English, not Greek and Latin, and has 22 fewer sheets than the *Suidas* volume. Yet the Folio has slightly more ens to the sheet and *Suidas* took slightly longer to print, so that in the quantitative matters of bulk, relation of composition to presswork, printing time, and edition size, the two books are not perhaps so very different.

When we discover, however, that throughout exactly the same period as the one in which the first volume of *Suidas* was being printed the identical one-and-a-half presses that printed it also served three to four other compositors, two of them often working simultaneously, to print another 1500 copies of the *second* volume of *Suidas* — yet another Shakespeare Folio as it were — as well as 20 other books whole or in part and at least 23 smaller jobs, then we might be forgiven for thinking that Professor Hinman's estimate *is* badly at fault. Nevertheless my point is not that his equation (two compositors and one press yield 1200 edition-sheets a day) is wrong — indeed, under some conditions it might well be exact — but that it seriously misrepresents the general conditions of book production.[61]

61. Although I am not really concerned to query Professor Hinman's estimate of the edition size of the Folio, it is possible to offer more precise estimates on costs than either Greg or Willoughby has given. Such a note in itself may be of interest, but my purpose is larger: to show how costing *methods* current in 1700 can be applied to the 1620's. It so happens that Cantrell Legge the Cambridge printer has left a very detailed "direction to value most Bookes by the charge of the Printer & Stationer. as paper was sould Anno Dni: 1622" (Cambridge University Archives Mss. 33.2.95 and 33.6.8). The Folio contains about 227 sheets. At the highest of Legge's 1622 prices, for paper and printing of the best quality, it would have cost 13s.4d. per ream. For average quality the cost would probably have been nearer, in all, to 10s. or 11s. per ream. At the first of these prices, an edition of 500 copies would have cost £151.6s.8d. to produce; for an edition of 1000 copies the cost would have been £302.13s.4d.; for 1250 copies it would have been £378.6s.8d. Legge indicates that the Stationers' mark-up was usually twice as much again as the prime costs for paper and printing ("So they gaine clearly for euery 12s. laid out 1-5-0 The like proportion you may make of all other english, & forraine bookes"). However many were printed, the unit cost per copy of the Folio, accounting paper and printing at the highest price (13s.4d. per ream printed), would be 6s.0d. A normal mark-up would therefore give a selling price of 18s. (not far off Steevens' £1.0s.0d.). The maximum possible return therefore to the four partners would be £300 for 500 copies selling at 18s. each; £600 for 1000 copies; and £750 for 1250 copies. These figures are crude, but they are not so wrong as to be irrelevant. If 500 copies were printed, given a two-year printing period, the investment would yield roughly 100% per annum, if 1000 copies were printed it would have been 200% per annum. But since a good proportion of the prime costs would not have had to be met until printing was well advanced, nor the balance paid until after printing had finished, a substantial part of the "investment" monies could have been met from the income from sales. Even the lowest of these returns (on an edition of 500) would have justified the venture.

It may also be noted that the amount

If I am right, and there is miscalculation somewhere, the reason for it probably lies in an inference drawn from skeleton formes, and its consequences return us to the subject of concurrent printing. For the purity of Professor Hinman's argument virtually commits him to the view that the Folio was printed on one press, "the Folio press." Apart from 18 quires near the beginning, the Folio is a one-skeleton and therefore, it is claimed, a one-press book: ". . . throughout most of the book, indeed, two-press work was manifestly impossible, the same skeleton having been used in successive formes . . .".[62] Professor Hinman here means that two presses cannot have been in simultaneous use, but as he says at another point:

Only one press *at a time* can possibly have been used, and it is but reasonable to suppose that the successive Folio formes, once set, were ordinarily delivered to the same pressmen and printed at the same "Folio" press.[63]

---

regularly allowed to retailers was 3s. in the £. ("Notes on Printing at Cambridge," p. 103).

It is possible to refine the figures further. Legge priced the best paper at 5s.6d. per ream; printing would therefore have cost 7s.10d. per ream. Gay's contract with Purslowe allowed 8s. per week for 3000 impressions per day; this meant, for a full press, 16s. per week for 18,000 impressions (or 18 reams perfected) ; this gives a price of roughly 10½d. per ream. Presswork on the Folio might therefore be set at 11d. per ream. Now, applying methods customary in 1700, allowing for correction at one-sixth the rate for composition, and adding the "printer's thirds" for over-heads, the detailed costs of printing may be outlined as follows:

Presswork	11d.
Composition	3s. 8d.
Correction	8d.
	5s. 3d.
Add for overheads	2s. 7d.
Cost of printing per ream	7s.10d.
Add cost of paper	5s. 6d.
Total price for paper and printing per ream	13s. 4d.

62. *Printing and Proof-Reading* II, 438. Two skeletons were used in quires F-X, a-b. See also I, 125-6: "One of the most striking facts about the Folio is that only one set of rules appears throughout most of the book; and the *continuous* use of the same rules can be satisfactorily accounted for only if presswork could keep *continuously* abreast of composition without difficulty. [A footnote adds: "Otherwise *two* sets of rules — two 'skeletons' — would almost certainly have been used."] Evidence from rules alone therefore establishes the very strong likelihood that the Folio press regularly worked off one forme as fast as the immediately succeeding forme was set."

63. *Ibid.*, I, 123. At this point Professor Hinman also writes: "Each successive forme [in 'o'] had been printed off and was ready for distribution by the time compositorial work for the next forme but one was undertaken." The distribution pattern shows that this was so, but I fail to see its relevance to *speed* of presswork; it simply means that setting did not go forward until the last forme but one was distributed. Professor Hinman mentions the possibility that composition was quite regularly interrupted on the completion of each new forme "to allow the press to catch up" but rejects the idea with the words "of such a practice there is neither evidence *nor any shadow of likelihood*" (my italics). The same *sequence* may be followed at variable *speeds*.

Moreover, two compositors working together and serving this one press are thought to represent an ideally self-sufficient relationship for an edition of about 1200 copies, and since apparently this is the condition more frequently found,

it seems clear that the printing of the Shakespeare collection was planned as a self-contained operation, one that could be economically conducted altogether apart from the other printing tasks with which the establishment was concerned. Yet the plan was by no means inflexible. It allowed for the concurrent production of other *occasional* work. First of all, however, it provided for the independent printing of Shakespeare's plays (I, 75).

Professor Hinman's main stress here, and his concession, are the crux of the matter. At times of course most analytical bibliographers working in this field have to confess an *imbalance* of composition and presswork on a book, either implicitly by failing to pursue the point or explicitly by marking breaks in an otherwise apparently consistent pattern. When this happens, some odd jobbing at case or press is a likely and convenient suggestion to restore the ratio and avoid idleness. This opportunistic resort to a theory of concurrent printing need not be documented at length but it is important to note its circumstantial origins. For much of the Shakespeare Folio, set by one man, there is persistent evidence that the economic considerations behind the plan (at least in the form suggested) did not apply; and to explain the apparent imbalance Professor Hinman allows that 'the Folio press' must have engaged in some concurrent printing:

It would be rash to suggest that, if only one compositor at a time set type for the Folio, the Folio press (as for convenience we may call it) must always have stood idle half the time. It could have been used to print other, non-Folio matter — if only this other matter were available. And doubtless it sometimes was; but not always, not regularly (I, 74).

And again:

Fairly often, therefore, though rarely for long, the rate at which composition for the Folio normally progressed was halved, and accordingly the full-time services of the press were not required for Folio printing. But we need not suppose that press time was therefore wasted. It is in the highest degree probable that, on at least most of these occasions, both the Folio press and one of the Folio compositors were used to produce other work — presumably job work . . .[64]

64. *Ibid.*, I, 75. At I, 153 we find: "Whether one or two skeletons were used in such a book probably depended upon the composition-presswork relationship." See also I, 28 n.l, 49, 364; II, 490-1, 524.

If I now seem to labour a point it is simply because Professor Hinman's account of the printing process reflects and therefore lends massive authority to the erroneous assumption that a book was normally put into production as an independent unit. The single skeleton forme, its association with 'the Folio press', the suggested edition size, the 'economic' balance between compositors and press-crew, all combine to reinforce this view. What is offered as exceptional — occasional concurrent printing — other evidence would suggest to be normal; what is offered as normal — a self-contained operation — is elsewhere exceedingly rare. Neither the Cambridge nor Bowyer papers would permit such inferences to be drawn from skeleton formes; neither would permit such assumptions to be made about the operations of a single press; neither would be consistent with the general economic argument put forward. Nor is it, I think, a matter of proven historical difference, as though the early 17th century were doing something that the 18th century no longer found necessary. For no differences have been constated that cannot be seriously questioned by exposing the primary assumptions. Noting at one point that most of the Folio was printed by a single press, Professor Hinman revealingly adds:

Or, conceivably, by two presses working alternately on different formes; but this, for all practical purposes, would amount to the same thing.[65]

With all respect, one is obliged to say that 'for all *practical* purposes' it would not. The moment we admit the possibility of two presses we halve the work of one of them on the Folio and concede that each is concurrently printing other books as well. The problems of calculating the ratio between compositors and press-crews are doubled, for the ratio must be assessed for each crew and the assessment must take full account of all other work on hand. The pattern of work becomes far more complex as the various edition-sheets for different books are printed off one with another at the two presses. For some limited *theoretic* purposes the ratios abstracted by Professor Hinman may be sound, but his evidence, as he concedes, is consistent with normal conditions of concurrent printing at press, and much of the time with concurrent work at case.

65. *Ibid.*, I, 123. See also I, 49: ". . . one compositor (and hence, it may be added, two or more compositors setting alternately; for this would amount to much the same thing) . . .". One should add that even without prejudice to the main thesis of balanced work on the Folio alone, Professor Hinman's masterly account of the work done on the Folio concurrently with other books makes it quite clear that a 'norm' of concurrent printing, as shown for the 1700's or 1730's, also applied to the 1620's.

BIBLIOGRAPHICAL THEORIES   37

The implications of assumptions which seem to be so much at odds with usual printing conditions do not end here:

It is demonstrable, that a single press could (and did) print off a Folio forme at least as fast as *two* compositors working simultaneously, one on each of its two pages, could set such a forme. Hence there can be no doubt that composition by one compositor ordinarily took at least twice as long as the machining of the forme.[66]

Under the latter conditions 'there would be a gross imbalance between composition and presswork', under the former 'a highly efficient ratio'. Professor Hinman makes much of the economic reasons for simultaneous setting, and hence setting by formes:

With some emphasis let it be said, for the point is vital, that casting off copy would make possible *the simultaneous setting of different Folio pages by different compositors*. Hence Jaggard might well have undertaken it even if his supplies of type had been unlimited (I, 74).

Again, an economic ratio of composition and presswork for the Folio

could be effected, and effected economically, if two compositors worked simultaneously on its various formes — and Jaggard probably cast off the copy for it with precisely this end in view (I, 75).

By displacing type-shortage as the primary reason for casting off copy, and substituting an economic relationship dependent on assumptions about timing, Professor Hinman not only diminishes the classical status of his own major demonstration but starts a bibliographical hare. The constant factor throughout the Folio is shortage of type because of the method of quiring, and Professor Hinman himself makes it clear that this "may have made it more or less mandatory to set the Folio by formes." His attempt to give an extended generality to his brilliant particular and practical proof from type-shortages misrepresents the general conditions of work, not only in Jaggard's shop but in the period as a whole.

For this again is my immediate concern: the encouragement given to the view that even where there is no conclusive evidence of type-shortages, revealed by the presence of identical sorts in both formes of a sheet or in the first half of a quire, we may have setting by formes. In such cases reliance is usually placed on a 'pattern of distribution' — evidence which is used with most admirable insight and control by Professor Hinman but which, in lesser hands, and in quarto printing,

---

66. *Ibid.*, I, 74 n.2. The demonstration referred to is, I think, that given at I, 123-4; see note 63 above.

may prove very tricky indeed. In a folio of course the major production unit was the quire and (now that Professor Hinman has pointed it out) it is obvious enough why in a folio in sixes type should be inadequate for normal page-by-page setting. In a quarto, however, the reasons are far from clear, and despite Professor Turner's assurance that "it begins to appear that [Elizabethan play quartos] were *more often than not* composed by formes" (my italics) ("Printing *King and No King*", p. 255), a certain scepticism ought perhaps still to be exercised. Professor Williams, for example, arguing that the quarto *Epicedium* (1594) was so composed, implied considerable concern on the compositor's part at setting vv for w, an assessment by the compositor of the number of w's required for the work, a count of those available to him in the case, and a decision to set by formes for this one reason despite attendant complications. In another case "Random mixing of roman and italic forms of 'k', 'K', 'S' and 'Q' . . . are common in the quarto and are without significance. The shortage of lower-case 'w', on the other hand, discloses a pattern throughout the quarto."[67] But one may fairly ask whether it is safe to prove a case by accepting only such limited 'patterned' evidence. The idea that a 'pattern' must be significant because it appears to indicate a regular method of work is one of the most perniciously seductive presuppositions of current bibliographical analysis. The conflicting evidence of 'k' is disregarded in part because it "violates the order of imposition and printing as disclosed by the running-title evidence." For "evidence from running titles indicates that outer B preceded inner through the press." This of course is merely a further assumption given the status of proof (and then applied as such) because the skeleton formes *can*, but arbitrarily, be ordered in a pattern.

In the Shakespeare Folio, Professor Hinman noted, "As a rule . . . no forme has types in common with either the forme immediately preceding or that immediately following it" (*Printing and Proof-Reading*, I, p. 81); and the sequential relation of setting, printing, and distribution here implied has been adapted for the quartos. Professor Turner had earlier given it shape when, writing of *Philaster*, he observed

that types which originally appear in B (o) reappear through sheet C; whereas types which originally appear in B (i) do not reappear in sheet C

---

67. "Setting by Formes in Quarto Printing," p. 42. The second quarto referred to   is *The First Part of The Contention* (1594).

but do reappear in sheet D. Therefore, B (i) must have been distributed after B (o) and doubtless followed it through the press.[68]

Mr John Hazel Smith, discussing *Much Ado*, offers a similar argument: "The precedence of A (i) is proved by three italic types (B_1, B_2, d_1) from that forme which are then divided between the formes of B." And again:

That *Much Ado* is composed by formes will be abundantly clear later. It is already indicated by the types (B_1, B_2, d_1) which appear in two adjacent sheets: under seriatim composition it would be very rare to find, as we find several times in this quarto, on the first or second page of a second sheet a type from either forme of a first sheet (p. 11).

And Professor Turner's subsequent formulation gives the principle a usefully definitive form:

in a quarto set by formes, type from the first forme of each sheet normally reappears in both formes of the succeeding sheet, but type from the second forme only in the second forme of the succeeding sheet.[69]

Mr Smith's study is probably the least fortunate example of an attempt to prove setting by formes in a quarto by "applying scientific bibliographical methods," for Professor Hinman has since pronounced it wrong.[70] But the irony is that the methods used by Mr Smith *were* those "illustrated by the work of Charlton Hinman on the Shakespeare First Folio and by George W. Williams and Robert K. Turner, Jr, on

68. "The Printing of *Philaster*," p. 22. See also "Printing Methods in *A Midsummer Night's Dream*" where Professor Turner argues that if type from B (o) is found in both formes of sheet C, and type from B (i) is found only in part of C (i), and if type from C (o) is found in both formes of D, and type from C (i) is found only in D (i), then, "when type reappears in this manner, composition cannot have been *seriatim*" (p. 36). The following remarks make it clear that Professor Turner means cannot have been *seriatim* "without press delays." The fundamental argument is not bibliographical in the sense that Professor Hinman's is.

69. "The Printing of *A King and No King*," p. 258. See also, in "Printing Meth-

ods in *A Midsummer Night's Dream*," Professor Turner's suggestion that "It seems likely that the compositor, working on the assumption that composition and press-work could stay more or less in balance, originally intended to follow the conventional procedure for setting by formes — to compose two formes, distribute the first, set the third, distribute the second, [set the fourth] and so on." (p. 46).

70. "Shakespeare's Texts — Then, Now and Tomorrow," SS, XVIII (1965), 31. It is also pointed out there that, before *Richard II*, "no first quarto has hitherto yielded such entirely conclusive evidence of setting by formes as the Folio does throughout" (p. 28).

other Renaissance quartos" ("Compositor of *Much Ado*", p. 10). And some of these methods are not, inherently, very reliable.[71]

The comment called for here can only be a very general and cautionary one. Neither the Cambridge nor Bowyer records offer much positive evidence of setting by formes; although their combined testimony does demonstrate the rarity of such a practice for books other than page-for-page reprints and must therefore give us pause. We must recall too that neither Moxon, Stower, nor any other early grammar mentions casting off as a means of enabling work to be set by formes. In every case it is, as Stower puts it in his index, a "manner of calculating in order to ascertain the number of sheets a manuscript will make, the size of the letter being fixed on"[72] — that is, a device for costing, and for determining the paper required, not for organizing work. Nowadays we call it estimating. As Professor Hinman observes, actual casting off for setting would not have been undertaken without good reason, although it is true that the difficulties may have been overestimated for verse plays as distinct from full prose works (*Printing and Proof-Reading*, I, 73). But if, as is claimed, "the practice was by no means uncommon" and "is to be seen in first quartos that issued from many different printing houses, over a wide stretch of years" ("Shakespeare's Texts," p. 31), it is to be hoped that firmer controls will be applied in its demonstration than have hitherto been evident. In particular, arguments heavily reliant on time-schemes will rarely command that ready assent which was given to Professor Hinman's initial proof that the Folio *must* have been set by formes.[73] On the face of it, the most important reason for setting by formes in quarto is unlikely to have been urgency, nor even an unusually small fount, but a fount *depleted* because of concurrent printing — for if work overlapped on two or more books using the same fount of type, setting by formes would offer a method of making some progress with all. Professor Hinman has again led the way in showing how, in Jaggard's shop, concurrent setting of other books, reduced the supply of type for the Folio.

71. See Turner, "Printing Methods in *A Midsummer Night's Dream*," p. 39: "By itself the testimony of shortage is, I believe, less reliable than any other bibliographical technique."

72. *Printer's Grammar*, index. See also Moxon, *Mechanick Exercises*, p. 239: "*Counting* or *Casting off Copy* . . . is to examine and find how much either of *Printed Copy* will *Come-in* into any intended number of *Sheets* of a different *Body* or *Measure* from the *Copy*; or how much *Written Copy* will make an intended number of *Sheets* of any assigned *Body* and *Measure*."

73. "Cast-off Copy for the First Folio of Shakespeare," *SQ*, VI (1953), 259-73.

If copy is cast off for a quarto text, there is no compelling reason why any sheet should not be printed in any order — say, H, F, A, C, D, B, E, G. One might expect and assume a straightforward progression through the book, but there is no compelling reason for it. But *order* of formes through the press is an important ingredient in much bibliographical work. Where there is detectable damage in the course of printing (whether to types, headlines, rules or ornaments) it may be quite possible to prove order, and in some cases a precedent forme, at least within the same sheet, may be determined by using the Martin-Povey lamp. I am not sure whether it is evidence of this kind that led Professor Turner to write that "information about presswork, specifically the order of the formes through the press, is relatively easy to obtain and is based on evidence that is the least controvertible" ("Beaumont and Fletcher Folio", p. 36), but, so far as I can tell, order has. usually been determined, not according to such evidence, but according to a *pattern* of headline recurrences. "Evidence from running titles indicates that outer B preceded inner through the press" (Williams, "Setting by Formes", p. 43) is a familiar form of wording; or "on the evidence of running titles, it is clear that B (o) was machined before B (i)". I confess that I have never understood what was meant when I have read such a phrase, and again I suspect that priority is based on assumptions about timing, and inferences drawn from variants, from a pattern of alternating skeletons, or from reappearing types which permit a hypothesis about distribution. In any case, whatever the internal patterns which some physical features may take within a book, there is little reason to elucidate them by constructing a time-scheme or by supposing the successive printing of all formes of the same book. I know of no evidence that obliges us to think of one sheet (or forme) being followed immediately on the press by another of the same book. There is some case for it when perfecting, none between sheets. There is too much evidence in the Cambridge books of perfectly regular patterns sustained under the most diverse conditions of concurrent printing. It is not always easy to tell when an apparently general statement is really only a singular one made of a particular book, but if it is generally true, as Professor Turner says, that "to prove the order of printing is usually to prove the order of composition of the formes" ("Beaumont and Fletcher Folio", p. 37), important textual consequences may follow from the initial assumptions.[74]

74. Another theory that one should like to have some external evidence for is that which closely associates a compositor with a particular set of type cases. Professor

It is perhaps worth looking briefly at one Cambridge book, Bennet's *Answer to the Dissenters Pleas* (2nd ed., 1700). Its testimony is not all that important, since it is a page-for-page reprint, yet it does show quite vividly that, once copy is cast off, any sequence of setting and printing might be followed. The sheets were composed as follows: Bertram set E, K by 13 Jan. 1700; B, H, S by 20 Jan.; Knell set C by 26 Jan.; Bertram D, L, U and X/* by 10 Feb.; Knell completed F, G½ between 20 Jan. and 17 Feb.; G½, I by 24 Feb.; Bertram P, Q, R by 24 Feb.; N, O, T by 2 Mar.; Knell A, M by 9 Mar. The order of printing appears to have been: E, H, K, B, L, S, U, C, D, F, X/*, G, I, R, Q, N, O, P, A, M, T (*Cambridge University Press*, I, 192-3).

The Cambridge papers, if not those of the Bowyers, provide very clear evidence of regular proof-correction of all books printed. Such a practice may have been slightly unusual as many of the books were classical texts and the press prided itself on its accuracy, yet I think not, for London houses in the 18th century, like Cambridge, regularly set as their price for proofing one-sixth of the rate of composition.[75] There is considerable doubt, however, about the validity of applying 18th-century evidence to Elizabethan books; even Moxon's testimony from the later 17th century has been rejected as irrelevant to the earlier period. If this is so, then the 'norms' used to introduce some measure of probability into analytical accounts of the proofing and printing of earlier books will themselves be only inferential. Moxon, we may recall, notes that:

The *Press-man* is to make a *Proof* so oft as occasion requires . . . The *Compositer* having brought the *Form* to the *Press*, lays it down on the *Press-stone*, and the *Press-man* . . . *Pulls* the *Proof-sheet* . . . carries the *Form* again to the *Correcting-stone* and lays it down: And the *Proof* he carries to the *Compositers Case* [pp. 302-3].

And the *Compositer* gives the *Correcter* the *Proof* and his *Copy* to *Correct* it by: which being *Corrected*, the *Correcter* gives it again to the *Compositer* to *Correct* the *Form* by [p. 233].

Having corrected it, the compositor

Hinman offers a very fine discussion of the question and has much contributory evidence for identifying compositors from type-groupings where distinctive spellings are lacking. See also Turner, "Reappearing Types," pp. 200-3. I have not examined Cambridge or Bowyer books for evidence of this kind.

75. So Richardson, advising Oxford to do "as the London Printers do, reckon at the rate of 2d in the shilling for the Press Correctors, of what is paid the Compositors." — quoted by I. G. Philip, *Blackstone and the Reform of the Oxford University Press* (1957), p. 40.

carries the *Form* to the *Press*, and lays it on the *Stone* for a *Second Proof*, and sometimes for a *Third Proof*; which having *Corrected*, he at last brings the *Form* to the *Press*, and again lays it on the *Stone* . . . After all this *Correcting* a *Revise* is made, and if any *Faults* are found in any *Quarter* of it, or in all the *Quarters*, he calls to the *Press-man* to *Unlock* that *Quarter*, or the whole *Form*, that he may *Correct* those *Faults* . . . [pp. 238-9].

And before continuing printing, the pressman will check

4*thly*, That no *Letters* or *Spaces* lye in the *White-lines* of the *Form*; which may happen if the *Compositer* have *Corrected* any thing since the *Form* was laid on the *Press*, and the *Compositer* through oversight pickt them not all up [p. 269].

Professor Bowers has remarked, however, that

Moxon describes a method of pulling proofs that interrupted the printing whenever a forme to be proofed was prepared. The delay would not be equally serious, but on the evidence this does not seem to have been the usual Elizabethan practice (*Bibliography and Textual Criticism*, p. 103 n. 1).

To make this point is to stress again the primary importance of continuous printing at press. Professor Hinman would doubtless agree, for he says that

The proof-correction practices spoken of by Moxon may have been common in his day, but they were certainly not so in the 1620's (*Printing and Proof-Reading*, I, 228 n. 1).

But Professor Hinman's basic reason for rejecting Moxon's account as in any way relevant to the 1620's has little to do with timing. It is rather the many self-evident errors that survive in the printed text. Discussing – and dismissing – in a footnote the idea that regular proofing may have preceded that established by a collation of the variants he has observed, Professor Hinman notes:

there are far too many obvious errors of all kinds in far too many Folio pages to allow us to think that any such preliminary reading as may have been done for this book, whether with or without benefit of some kind of printed proof, and whether by compositor or by an official 'corrector of the press', ever amounted to much (I, 228 n. 2).

It is a view that in general Professor Bowers would probably – and reciprocally – endorse, since he has observed that

The automatic assumption is surely wrong that every forme of cheap commercial printing was necessarily proof-read. Any editor of Elizabethan play quartos is familiar with some formes in which the typographical errors are so gross as to make it seem impossible to suppose that these formes had been read (*Bibliography and Textual Criticism*, p. 126).

It may seem singularly fool-hardy not to follow such authority, but I am constrained to persist in a certain incredulity. Professor Hinman's failure to list the 'many obvious errors of all kinds' at least makes one's task of qualification a little easier since he has not, in this case, sufficiently illustrated, let alone proved, his point. If Moxon, and proofing practices so well evidenced elsewhere in the century and beyond it, are to be displaced as the 'norm', the question would seem to demand rather fuller discussion than I have yet seen devoted to it.

The view that Professor Hinman is concerned to question is, essentially, Greg's — that in the Folio "the printer was not indifferent to the accuracy of his text."[76] And it may well be that if we *were* "once possessed of a full record of the press variants in the First Folio" (*Printing and Proof-Reading*, I, 227), such a view might have to be altered. Professor Hinman's labours of collation leave him in no doubt that now "there is in fact considerably more evidence that the printer *was* largely indifferent to the accuracy of his text" (I, 227). Yet such a conclusion is scarcely judicious; there is a great difference between the truth and the whole truth, between "a *full* record of the press variants" and a full record of the *surviving* press variants.[77]

This is not just a quibble. Traditionally the stages of proof-correction have been at least three: galley (whether page- or slip-), revises, and, as a last resort, stop-press. And let us not forget that the manuscript copy precedes all three. Now it is incontestable that these several stages can be found in increasing frequency as one moves from manuscript (how much of that survives?), to page-proofs (very few of these), to revises (slightly more of these — if some of our surviving 'proof' sheets can be so considered), to stop-press (hundreds of these). Each successive stage supersedes the previous one; once the unique copy has been set and checked, it can be disposed of, once the single galley proof has been read and checked, it can be disposed of, once the revise has been read and checked, it can be disposed of, but once printing has started, the multiple copies are preserved and of course they are available for consultation in those portions of the edition still extant. It

76. *The Shakespeare First Folio* (1955), p. 464.

77. All the statement means is that some evidence of correction has survived; it leaves quite open the possibility that invariant formes already embody corrections, and that even where formes are variant the 'uncorrected' states may be intermediate ones.

BIBLIOGRAPHICAL THEORIES

only remains to note that the principle of increasing frequency persists even here, for, as Professor Hinman has observed in the case of the Folio, the earlier 'uncorrected' state is likely to be preserved in about ten per cent of copies, and the later and latest, press-corrected, states in ninety per cent of surviving copies; these last therefore will be the ones most frequently observed. We must of course work from what we have to what we have not, but our chances of going the full distance and thereby establishing 'a full record of the press variants' — if these are taken to include all stages of proofing — are very remote indeed. When such evidence (of its very nature) demanded to be discarded, it is difficult to see why one should assume that it never existed.[78]

But one may consider the point in another way: it is easy after repeated and intense scrutiny to discover 'obvious' misprints, and it is also very easy to miss them. Each year I put some four or five senior and intelligent students through the rudiments of type-setting and when they come to correct their work they almost invariably have to do it in two or three stages because these latter-day John Leasons have failed to correct all the 'obvious' errors the first time through. Yet there *was* a first time (see *Printing and Proof-Reading*, I, 233). It is true that the more experienced students make fewer mistakes, but it is again remarkable how many of these mistakes my latter-day John Shakespeares overlook in their first attempt at correction. Much the same point is made of course by Professor Hinman when speaking of sections of plays set by Compositor E, sections "which were subjected to much *more* proof-reading than others — yet only to very *careless* proof-reading, since a great many errors nonetheless escaped uncorrected in these plays" (I, 233). Errors, that is, persist through one or more stages of proof-reading; the much-proofed page from *Antony and Cleopatra* leaves errors uncorrected.[79] The existence of some formes in three or more states indicates that at one or more stages of correction errors were missed which were later thought serious enough

---

78. Instances of an 'uncorrected' state surviving in a single copy point to the dangers we run if we too readily equate invariant formes with uncorrected ones. The 'uncorrected' states, being earlier, are likely to be fewer and in most cases may have disappeared completely. In "A Proof-sheet in *An Humorous Day's Mirth* (1599) printed by Valentine Sims," *Library*, 5th ser (1966), pp. 155-7, A. Yamada notes that "out of fifteen copies examined, the Bute copy alone retains the uncorrected readings on the outer forme of G, and all the other copies have the forme in the corrected state." (p. 155). Of twenty copies of Tailor's *The Hogge hath lost his Pearle* (1614), only one has inner and outer E in their 'uncorrected' states.

79. Stower said that it should be "an invariable rule" to demand a *second* revise, "particularly with foul compositors, as no sort of dependence can be placed on them" (*Printer's Grammar*, p. 382).

to alter. Greg's list of misprints in Q1 *Lear,* based on the corrected state of the sheets and therefore taking no account of the original errors that were subsequently altered, is most revealing in this connection (*Variants,* pp. 63-79). Professor Hinman's new evidence from variants introduced at a relatively late stage of the Folio's production does not dispose of Greg's judgement. The 'obvious errors' have been there since 1623 and Greg, who had as good an eye for them as anyone, still thought that "the printer was not indifferent to the accuracy of his text", and that "he took what were thought in his day to be reasonable precautions, and went to some trouble, to reach a moderate standard in the execution of what may not have been at all times an easy task" (*Shakespeare First Folio,* p. 464).

There is of course another way of looking at the problem — and I must repeat that I am really only concerned with questions of method and that like Troubleall I merely wish to ask 'by what warrant' certain inferences are given the standing of general statements. So, *a priori,* one might ask whether it is likely that the essentially trivial corrections noted by Professor Hinman would have been made at all if the printer were indifferent to the accuracy of his text? Or, to put it yet another way, is it likely that a printer who put up with so many bibliographically serious delays at press in order to correct minor blemishes would fail to observe routine correction procedures in order to avoid major infidelities and the prospect of really serious delays in the last stages of production? Which brings us back to Moxon.

It is not I hope gratuitously irresponsible to suggest that none of the evidence presented from the Folio demonstrates conclusively that the procedures which Moxon describes were 'essentially different' from those of the 1620's. At the very least, the *"Proofe,* and *Reuiewes"* pulled by Jaggard for Brooke's *Catalogue* testify to the currency of Moxon's terms at this time, and in Jaggard's shop (McKerrow, *Introduction,* p. 207). We must grant that the copy for the Folio has disappeared; we must grant that the foul proofs have disappeared; but what does remain in evidence corresponds exactly to that which we should expect to find at the later stages of correction as outlined by Moxon. And it is precisely at these stages of correction that copy is *not* consulted. That phase is well behind, and even if some errors have persisted it is not to be expected that substantive matters will *now* command 'painstaking' attention. But it *is* to be expected that typographical infelicities — the things that catch (and for long curiously avoid) a pressman's eye through the repeated pullings — will be picked up from time to time. Turned letters, lifting spaces, uneven inking, badly defective letters — these are precisely the things which at this stage the beater, who "peruses the *Heap*" (*Mechanick Exercises*, p. 292), was deputed to look for. He takes care

to see if no accidents have befallen the *Form*, viz. that no *Letters, Quadrats* or *Furniture* &c. Rise, that no *Letters* are *Batter'd* . . . that no *Pick* be got into the *Form*, or any other accident that may deface the beauty of the Work . . . (p. 303)

Rising letters, quadrats and furniture, and probably loose spacing, are fixed by the pressman, who has a bodkin for the purpose; but if letters are to be replaced, "he *Unlocks* the *Quarter* they are in, and desires the *Compositer* to put in others in their room" (p. 304). None of this is inconsistent with what we find in the Folio; indeed Professor Hinman's variants are clear evidence that Jaggard's beater was doing exactly what Moxon demands — turning out a book that was not marred by too many purely typographical blemishes.

Let us now recall too what Moxon says of revises and of correction at press: the forme, being now on the bed of the press, *is left there*, "and if any *Faults* are found in any *Quarter* of it [the Compositor] calls to the *Press-man* to *Unlock* that *Quarter* . . . that he may Correct those *Faults*" (pp. 238-9). There are several points here: the kind of corrections documented for the Folio are unlikely to have required removal of the forme from the press. At this stage, even after as many as three proofs, a revise is pulled — but now the forme is virtually ready for printing and the likelihood is great that printing will begin while the revise is being looked at. The single copy of the revise is likely to be a pull of the full forme; in the case of the white-paper forme its chances of being preserved are negligible, but in the case of the perfecting forme this single marked sheet has a greater chance of being placed on the heap and eventually bound. Although the revise will be of the full forme, Moxon suggests that it might be attended to in sections, or quarters, so that the pressman might unlock only so much of the forme as is necessary, perhaps only a page in the case of the Folio. In many cases in the Folio both pages must have been unlocked and corrected together, yet Moxon's wording does hint that the revise itself might be read in sections. I find it most interesting therefore that Professor Hinman should write: "Four actual proof-sheets for the Folio have survived — although . . . they ought perhaps rather to be called proof *pages*"; and "the essential proof-reading unit, so to speak, was rather the single page than the complete forme" (*Printing and Proof-Reading*, I, 233, 234). I wonder, however, whether these four proof pages should not perhaps be referred to as revises to distinguish them from the first and substantial stage of correction as well as from the last and accidental one.

In any case, however cursory we may think the Folio by our own standards and in the absence of author-correction, it would seem premature to conclude that what so closely corresponds to revises and stop-press correction as described by Moxon was not preceded by the routine proofing procedures which he also outlines. These may have been deficient in execution, but I cannot think that Professor Hinman's inferences justify the view that "the method of printing and proofing adopted", whether in the Folio or beyond it in the earlier 17th century, "was essentially different . . . from the method described by Moxon some sixty years later" (I, 228).

Professor Hinman, in another context, also discounts the testimony of Ashley's translation of Le Roy (1594), "since Le Roy was not a professional printer" (I, 41). Ashley writes of the pressman who is pulling:

taking the barre in his hand, he pulleth as hard as he can vntill the leafe be imprinted on one side, on which they bestowe halfe the day; and the other halfe, on the other side; yelding in a day twelue hundred and fiftie sheetes, or thirteen hundred imprinted. But before they do this, they make two or three proofes, which are reuiewed: and on this correction continew the rest.[80]

The late Mr Kenneth Povey found reason to believe that Ashley had expert help in making his translation; and it may be further noted that Jaggard's precise use of the word "*Reuiewes*", both as a noun and as a verb in the phrase "viewed, reuiewed, directed, corrected", suggests that Ashley's use of the word "reuiewed" was not idle. Ashley is at one with both Jaggard and Moxon in suggesting that, first, there might be two or three proofs and, next, a 'reuiew' or revise. Even the phrase "continew the rest" could relate to a process of continuous printing, stopped to make the late changes found in the revise, and then resumed. Mr Povey used Allde's 1624 edition of Massinger's *The Bond-man* as a test case, and found all the variants reconcilable with an orderly routine of proof-correcting and perfecting described by Moxon. He suggested, moreover, that

since Ashley's concise account is fully confirmed by Moxon, it might well

80. Quoted by K. Povey, "Variant Formes in Elizabethan Printing," *Library*, 5th ser. (1955), p. 42.

be adopted as the credo of students of Elizabethan printing-methods in preference to any modern construction (p. 43).

Nowhere perhaps so much as in the consideration of skeleton formes and proof-correction procedures are modern constructions so crippled by the absence of primary evidence and so vulnerable therefore to the general objections that may be made to all inductive methods. One recalls Black: "a nice adaptation of conditions will make almost any hypothesis agree with the phenomena." It is doubly a pity, however, when writers adapt conditions to suit their theories and then find themselves obliged to discount the testimony of such an excellent palmer as Moxon.

But much the same may be said of many studies of 18th-century printing which have been conducted on the assumption that conditions then were essentially different from those of the preceding century. My own major argument in this paper is of course that productive conditions were constantly changing, not just from century to century in different houses, but from day to day in the same house, simply because concurrent printing has been the universal practice for the last 400 years. If I am right, this fundamental fact poses more problems for analytical bibliography than any minor period differences. These there certainly were, and they must be carefully charted, but we must beware of that ostensibly sophisticated historical relativism which insists on making fine distinctions between periods when virtually nothing certain is known about either element of the comparison. When, for example, Professor Todd writes that

whenever books contain press figures their very presence implies unsystematic piecework engaged in conjunction with other miscellaneous endeavours. For labour which is predetermined, controlled, and properly recorded by the overseer . . . the figures become superfluous and accordingly disappear ("Concurrent Printing", p. 56).

the implication is that we are here dealing with quite distinctive conditions; but this, as the song says, ain't necessarily so. Whatever the variables, labour was always predetermined, controlled, and properly recorded, whether on piece rates or not. Crownfield's disposition of work, usually without figures, was no different from the Bowyers' with figures, and Stower's "Plan of a Book for checking Compositors' and Pressmen's Bills" assumes exactly the same conditions a hundred years later when press figures are on their way out (*Printer's Grammar*, p. 435). The procedures have always been the same — only the methods of recording them have differed.

I cannot here attempt to describe the thick web of theory spun around press figures.[81] In their incredible and perplexing variety they are eloquent witnesses to the customary conditions of presswork in any printing house, and perhaps only an imagination as fertile as Professor Todd's, and a mind as subtle, could have penetrated their mysteries. On their usefulness, let him speak:

> Contrary to McKerrow's prediction that [press figures] would prove to be of little importance, recent investigation has shown that they may be interpreted as signs of cancellation, variant states, half- or full-press operation (indicating the employment of one or two men at the machine), type pages arranged within the forme in some irregular pattern, sheets impressed in some abnormal order, an impression of the formes for each sheet by one man working both formes in succession, or two men working both simultaneously, impressions interrupted for one reason or another, reimpressions or resettings of the book, in whole or in part, copy distributed among several shops, overprints involving an increase in the number of sheets machined for certain gatherings in order to meet an unanticipated demand for copies, and underprints consisting of a decrease in the number of sheets in order to reduce the issue and speed its publication ("Editorial Problem in the Eighteenth Century", p. 47).

Much bibliographical writing, like that in any new subject, has a strong proselytizing strain which is apt to show itself in a slight tendency to rhetorical overstatement and the premature elevation of particular observations to the status of general truths. One or two pieces of information that have become available since Professor Todd wrote the above account do call for its qualification; I present them now only to carry forward my general argument that the 'empirical' method, with its reliance on 'direct observation',[82] might lead us wildly astray. Press figures, as Professor Todd has indubitably shown, are of enormous value in revealing conditions normally concealed, but they still need theories to make them work and the theories so far applied have been largely without benefit of primary evidence from the printing house itself.

As I have indicated elsewhere, Cambridge pressmen in the early 18th century did not normally use press figures, and the first two volumes of *Suidas* are the only two books of the period in which they appear (*Cambridge University Press*, I, 128-32). This exception is wholly due to the employment of John Terrill who came up from

81. A useful reference list is given in Tanselle, "Press Figures in America," p. 126 notes 10 and 11.

82. See Todd, "Observations on . . . Press Figures," *SB*, III (1950-51), 173.

BIBLIOGRAPHICAL THEORIES 51

London towards the end of November 1701 and who left Cambridge again on 15 May 1703. Terrill's bills for presswork match the figures exactly and make it perfectly clear that, in this case, the figures represent a man, specifically Terrill, not a press. Terrill did not always use a figure, nor keep to the same one; and it is certain that here in the Cambridge house his use of a figure was a purely personal and optional matter. His main reason for using one at all would seem to have been that the first two volumes of *Suidas* were being printed concurrently and as they were independently signed 'Suidas the quire G' or 'Suidas G1' might refer to either or both volumes. So Terrill played safe by marking the sheets that he printed, although he thought it necessary to figure only one forme in each sheet. In this, his practice was consistent with that recommended by Savage in 1841 but not with that followed by the Bowyers in the 1730's.[83] Terrill's main concern seems to have been merely to use some idiosyncratic mark, and once the work had been paid for any other might serve as well. It is not surprising therefore to discover that Terrill used two different figures (* and ‡) in both volumes. The first (*) was used between the end of November 1701 and 28 Feb. 1702; during this period Terrill worked under markedly different conditions at different times — first with Brown at full press and then alone at half press — yet he used the same figure throughout. From 28 Feb. until 2 May 1702 he worked with Ponder without a figure. Thereafter, until his departure on 15 May 1703, Terrill used the second figure (‡), again in both volumes, to mark almost every sheet on which he worked. When he left, the figure disappeared.

Clearly the consistent use of one figure in one part of a book and of another figure in another part has in this case nothing whatever to do with simultaneous — or even successive — printing of each portion at different presses. Nor has the incidence of variously figured and unfigured sheets anything whatever to do with printing at full or at half press. If, even occasionally, a pressman was personally responsible for his choice of figure, as here, this would go far to account for the many idiosyncratic numbers or marks adopted in some books and their apparently haphazard arrangement. And if, even occasionally, a figure represents a man rather than a press, it is formally possible to argue that a sheet which shows varying figures in copy to copy simply reflects changes in the press-crew part-way through a single impression and not distinct impressions.

83. Savage, *Dictionary of the Art of Printing* (1841), p. 814.

Indeed, whether a figure indicates a pressman or a press, such variation is in any case to be expected in books printed in very large editions. *The London Magazine,* for example, was printed for a time in 8000 copies. Since it comprised three and a half sheets, its printing would have kept three full presses wholly engaged for more than a week. Over such a time span — longer if the presses were required to do other work too, as Ackers' were — it is highly probable that changes would occur in the conditions under which *the single impression* would be completed. Changes of men, as well as changes of press, part-way through printing might well be reflected by new figures yet none of them be bibliographically significant — or at least no more bibliographically significant than the daily discontinuities incident to all printing in large editions. Naturally such evidence would rarely be left to stand alone; at the very least it would set one searching for new skeletons, partial re-settings, advertisements and so on; my point is the quite simple one that the relationship between variant states and distinct impressions must be very carefully assessed if the general conditions of work are not to be misrepresented.

But, as Dr Fleeman has already shown, there is quite conclusive evidence in the Bowyer ledger to associate press figures with a *press* not a man, evidence which can be corroborated by reference to the printed books themselves.[84] Bowyer numbered his presses and his accounts usually show, by their numbers and crews, the presses at which work was done. If a press-crew had a press of its own at which it regularly worked — and there is some evidence that this was so in Cambridge in 1740 — then the distinction between men and machines would virtually disappear;[85] but the Bowyer papers offer us no such simple resolution. In the examples of Bowyer books listed in appendix II (g), the figures and/or presses and/or crews can be lined up with a certitude unparalleled in any purely inferential construction. Yet it is most important to note, first, how many discrepancies there are between the records and the printed figures (especially in No. 5); second, the difficulty of assuming continuity of press-crews for any one figure; third, the irrelevance of the highest figure printed, although it designates a press, to the actual number of presses in use; fourth, that the occasional failures to figure a forme are in fact oversights and do not represent work done at a notionally blank press. It is another example of the by now familiar paradox: primary evidence definitely restricts

84. "William Somervile's 'The Chace,' 1735," *loc. cit.*

85. *Cambridge University Press,* I, 125, but see also I, 131 n.1, and Tanselle, "Press Figures in America," p. 127 n.13.

the generality of many statements hitherto made about the interpretation of press figures; yet it reveals such diversity of conditions in their use that almost any answer might well be true for any particular book. It is another warning that, as Professor Todd has put it, "any theory envisaging a uniform procedure in an unorganized, *laissez-faire* handicraft must be regarded with suspicion" ("Observations on Press Figures", p. 173). When therefore the writer of a review article in the *Times Literary Supplement* took Mrs Russell to task for not adequately listing press figures in her bibliography of Cowper, and suggested that the printers of certain editions might be identified by the pattern of press figures, or that because the figures 3 and 6 recur in Bensley's editions of Cowper these editions were always placed in the care of the same pressmen, the arguments may be much less 'advanced' than they seem.[86] In the light of complexities discovered by *any* primary documentation so far unearthed, such an ostensibly direct frontal assault turns out to be no more than a rear-guard action in defence of a much too simplistic and now obsolescent bibliographical method.

IV

I should not wish to deny that significant changes occurred in printing and publishing between the years 1500 and 1800; but on two counts I wish to offer some resistance to the evasive tactics of those who would for their part deny the relevance of conditions in any one period to those in another. Of course 1586 is not 1623, nor 1683, 1695, 1701, 1731, nor 1790. Yet just as Greg has argued that bibliography, as the study of the transmission of literary texts, comprehends manuscripts as well as printed books, so I wish to argue that the integrity of the subject can best be preserved and a sound methodology evolved only if we stress the *similarity* of conditions in all periods. *Then* fine distinctions may be entertained, not as period differences but as the inevitable result of variables which will differ from day to day and house to house. My second reason for resisting the too ready rejection of analogy is that very little fundamental research has been done on the history of printing. History is never so gross as when it's being formulated to serve a theory; and bibliographers with their eyes closest to the internal physical evidence have, on the whole, seen least of what lies beyond it.

The familiar picture of 'Elizabethan' printers, restricted in number, presses, edition quantities, and apprentices, and therefore con-

---

86. "Of Text and Type," *Times Literary Supplement*, 24 Feb. 1966, pp. 233-5.

stantly under pressure, and operating an essentially uncomplicated, balanced production schedule, is attractive in its simplicity. But in its generalized form such a picture is also apt to be dangerously misleading. Simpson, discussing the limitation of presses, once wrote that "When a printer with at most two presses had a book on the stocks, he could do nothing else until he had printed it off."[87] Such a view, so stated, now seems extremely naive, although something like it is implied in many studies even today. The documentation that exists for a shop of comparable size in 1700, printing books in editions no larger than those permitted in 1587, makes it clear that productive conditions of enormous complexity involving as many as ten or a dozen jobs at any one time were normal in a small two-press house.

But even the *size* of 'Elizabethan' shops has perhaps been a little too readily set at one or two presses, and the 'strict limitation' on their numbers over-stressed. The evidence would appear to be straightforward, but is it? Were there really too few printers and presses for the work available, or too many? In 1582, at a time of complaints from journeymen about lack of work, Christopher Barker said that the number of printing houses then in London (22) could be more than halved and the needs of the whole kingdom still met.[88] In 1583 the complaint of the 'poor men' of the Company was that they had too little work, and Commissioners appointed to look into the trade recommended that some privileged books be released to the poor for printing, a practice continued by the several Stocks of the Stationers' Company throughout the 17th century to assist printers who were short of work (Greg, *Companion*, pp. 21, 128). In May 1583 there were 23 master printers, possessing in all 53 presses: Barker had 5, Wolf 5, Day and Denham 4 each, and six others 3 apiece.[89] Although the Commissioners of 1583 recommended that no more presses be set up without license, their recommendation in respect of the existing presses was simply

That euerie printer keping presses be restrained to a reasonable number of presses according to his qualitie and store of worke, as for example the the Quenes printer hauing but .v. presses, and the lawe printer but twoo, we think it not reason that Wolf haue .v. but to restraine him and such other to one or two by discretion till his stoare of worke shall require moe (Greg, *Companion*, p. 131).

87. *Proof-Reading in the Sixteenth, Seventeenth and Eighteenth Centuries* (1935), p. 46.

88. Greg, *A Companion to Arber* (1967),

p. 26. I shall normally cite Greg's calendar instead of the originals.

89. Arber, *Transcript of the Registers of the Stationers' Company*, I, 248.

BIBLIOGRAPHICAL THEORIES   55

Could anything more permissive be desired? The Star Chamber decree of 1586 forbade the erection of new presses "tyll the excessive multy-tude of Prynters havinge presses already sett up, be abated" (Greg, *Companion*, p. 41). A statement of the position the following month shows that the number of printers had risen to 25 and that Barker had increased the number of his presses to 6 (Arber, *Transcript*, V, lii). Apart from isolated cases of surreptitious printing punished by seizure of equipment, and apart from the normal licensing of those who suc-ceeded to the select company of master printers, there is nothing to show how this positive abatement in the number of presses was pro-cured. For the next twenty-nine years, there is little primary evidence at all to show in what measure the conditions of 1586 had ceased to apply. Indeed, apart from the recurrent fuss over privileges, there is evidence of a general relaxation.

When in 1613-15 the unemployed journeymen again complained about their inability to set up presses, they saw that a necessary condi-tion of such a freedom would be access to privileged copies — otherwise there would be little work.[90] The master printers for their part were worried, or made a pretence of being so, at the "multitude of Presses that are erected among them" and by a self-denying ordinance agreed that, the King's Printer apart, fourteen of them should have 2 presses each and five of them 1.[91] Since the number of printers was 20 in all, such a rule can only mean that many of them had retained from a much earlier period, or set up over the last few years, far *more* presses than the numbers now set down. And since the number of printers did remain fairly constant, the agreement can only have been designed to secure a slightly more equitable distribution of work among these very printers; it implied, therefore, considerable *under*-production in the *smaller* shops.

Are we to take it that this decision by the Court of Assistants was immediately enforced? There is no evidence of it. *Eight years later*, on 5 July 1623,

90. Greg, *Companion*, pp. 52-3. This point is made time and again. Wood's petition of 1621 makes it clear that even of those with presses some were rich and some were poor: "the rich men of the Company by the power of their ordinances, dispose of all things in priuilege to their owne perticular benefits for the most part, and the poore Masters, and Iourney-men Printers haue little, and some of them no worke at all from the Company . . ."

(Greg, *Companion*, p. 170). Lownes, Pur-foote, Jaggard and Beale — "those foure rich Printers" — are most complained against for the privileges they hold and the punitive actions they can take against offendors, empowered as they are both by ordinance and their high position in the Company.

91. Jackson, *Records of the Court of the Stationers' Company*, p. 75.

Whereas the m^r printers of this Company, according to a former order haue reformed themselues for the number of presses that eueryone is to haue and accordingly haue brought in their barres to shewe their Conformitie there-vnto. . . (Jackson, p. 158).

again it is set down down that, the King's Printer excluded, fourteen printers should have only 2 presses each and five of them 1. Augustine Matthews was one of these five, but it is clear from another entry that he had more than one press (Jackson, p. 159). By September the following year the order had still not been put into effect and an inspec-torial party was authorized to dismantle any excess presses.[92] By 7 Feb. 1625 the Court was prepared to give up:

It is ordered that if the m^r Printers doe not Conforme themselues to the number of presses as hath ben agreed of by former orders and bring in their barres before o^r ladye day next, *Then those that are already brought in to be deliu'ed backe againe* [my italics] (Jackson, p. 173).

In 1637, after being restricted to one press ever since 1586, the Cambridge printer was graciously allowed a second. When in 1632 Roger Daniel had moved in he took over:

Six printing presses, five copper plates, six bankes, seven great stones, one muller, thirteen frames to set cases on . . . six and fifty paire and an halfe of cases for letters made of mettle and one case for wooden letters, five and twenty chases, twenty gallies, fifty paper and letter bords, . . . (Roberts, p. 50).

The Star Chamber decree of 1637, reporting that of 1586 as defective in some particulars so that divers abuses had arisen to the prejudice of the public, attempted to keep the number of master printers down to 20 (there were 22), but the number of presses, always more difficult to restrict, was allowed to rise (Greg, *Companion*, p. 105). By 1649 there were apparently some 60 printers in London and by 1660 the number had increased to 70, though it is doubtful whether there were so many printing houses. The Licensing Act of 1662 provided that no more printers be licensed until the number had fallen again to 20, but nothing was done to enforce the ruling and for the next thirty years it was openly ignored.[93] In 1668, after the great fire, there were 65 presses in 26 houses, the King's Printer having 6, two others 5

92. Jackson, p. 169. The search uncovered a press operated by George Woods; it was dismantled. Woods of course had no right to a press at all.

93. Plant, *The English Book Trade* (1939), p. 84; Howe, *London Compositor*, p. 33.

each, another 4, seven had 3, nine had 2, and six had 1.[94] Negus in 1724 listed 75 London houses and 28 in the provinces. Mr Ellic Howe comments: "There was, therefore, no great expansion in the trade compared with its state seventy years previously" (*London Compositor*, p. 33). By 1785 there were 124 printers; in 1808 "not more than 130", although Stower in the same year listed 216; by 1818 the total in London was 233.[95]

All I wish to ask now is whether there is much conclusive evidence that 'Elizabethan' conditions in any one printing house were utterly distinctive from those common in the 18th century? Expansion of the trade there undoubtedly was but except in a very few cases (Watts in the 1720's, Bowyer, Richardson and Strahan mid-century — a half dozen at most out of upwards of a hundred?) what we get in the 18th century is proliferation, multiple establishments, not an exceptional growth in any one. The fundamental conditions of work in each remain unchanged. Or again, if it is urged that the multi-press shops of the 18th century have few parallels in the early 17th century, one is entitled to ask quite directly how Ackers' and the Bowyers' three-, four-, and five-press shops of the 1730's differ from those of Barker, Wolf, Day, Denham, all of whom had more than three presses, and the other six printers who in 1583 had three presses each. Or one might ask how significantly, in terms of size, either group differs from those listed in 1668 (eleven of whom had three or more presses). And even if it is conceded that none of the printers limited to two presses in 1615 and 1623 would have grossly exceeded this number, a certain scepticism is still permissible since there is no evidence at all that they conformed to the ruling and much that they refused to. Or take the question the other way round: grant for the moment that most Elizabethan shops were two-press or one-press houses; it may then be asked what the distribution of presses was within 18th-century houses. How many had two, how many had only one? In the second week of October 1732 even Bowyer had only two (See appendix II (f).). For the rest, no one knows, and even press figures may not tell us.

Is the problem any simpler if we look at edition quantities? It is true that these were limited by regulation in Elizabethan-Jacobean

94. Plomer, *A Short History of English Printing, 1476-1900* (1915), pp. 185-8; Howe (p. 33) gives the figure as 35.

95. *Ibid.*, pp. 132-3. Professor Todd states that "By the end of the eighteenth century the personnel of the trade numbered no less than 2815" ("Observations on . . . Press Figures," p. 179). But this figure relates to 1818, not to the previous century, and its user implies that the number of master printers had virtually doubled in the previous 10 years — see Howe, p. 132.

times and not in the 18th century. Yet two points must be kept in mind. First, very few books printed in the 18th century, apart from some newspapers and periodicals about which some firm figures are at last available, ever in fact exceeded the limits for editions laid down in 1587 and liberalized in 1637. Neither the Cambridge, Bowyer, Woodfall, nor Strahan documents suggest that for any one edition, however many impressions it might comprehend, there is any very gross disparity between Elizabethan and 18th-century conditions in this matter. Out of some 514 books printed by Strahan between 1738 and 1785, only 43 were printed in 2000 copies or more, and of these only 15 were in editions of 3000 or more (Hernlund, "Strahan's Ledgers", p. 104). The edition quantities I cite for Dyche's *Guide to the English Tongue* may be more in keeping with some statements I have seen about expansion of the trade in the 18th century — and with others implying trade restriction and small editions in the 17th century. In any case it leads me to my second point: the prodigious numbers of certain books that were produced in the earlier period. Professor Todd once remarked that "a certain discretion common to most authorities, including bibliographers, moves us to view the unknown as unmentionable". And the loss of much ephemera of the 16th and 17th centuries (almanacks, school texts, and many other books required in multiple editions by the several Stocks of the Stationers' Company) has perhaps made us unmindful of the volume of such work. The late Cyprian Blagden's analysis of the distribution of almanacks in the second half of the 17th century, only one aspect of such printing, is a useful corrective.[96] For the earlier period odd cases reveal substantial printings: the 4000 copies of the Psalms in metre, for example, printed by Frank and Hill in 1585; the 10,000 copies of the ABC and Little Catechism printed the same year by Dunn and Robinson (Greg, *Companion*, p. 37). In three years, during the early 1630's the Cambridge printers provided for the London Company 18,000 *Pueriles Sententiae*, 12,000 Aesop's *Fables*, 6000 *Pueriles Confabulationes*, 6000 copies of Mantuan, and at least seven other books in 3000 copies or more (Roberts, p. 51). But the major evidence of large editions, far in excess presumably of the limits set, is the complaints from journeymen. The Company regulations of 1587, designed for the benefit of the journeymen, sought to provide further work by restricting the use of standing formes and by limiting impressions to 1500 copies of some books and 3000 of others (Greg, *Companion*, p.

96. "The Distribution of Almanacks in the Second Half of the Seventeenth Century," *SB*, XI (1958), 107-16.

BIBLIOGRAPHICAL THEORIES

43). These were of course Company regulations enforced, if at all, by those least likely to gain from them. The workmen are further complaining in 1614, and in 1635 an organized protest is made about the extraordinary number of books printed at one impression and the abuse of standing formes. The alleviation of the journeymen's distress may have been procured by the restriction of standing formes to the Psalter, Grammar and Accidence, Almanacks and Prognostications, but one doubts it.[97] The 1635 provision that no nonpareil books exceed 5000 copies, no brevier exceed 3000 (6000 in some cases), and that all others be kept to editions of 1500 or 2000 (3000 with permission), suggests that multiple impressions and large editions were hardly the prerogative of the 18th century (Greg, *Companion*, p. 95).

Professor Todd has probably done most to set the general attitude towards 18th-century printing and thereby also to imply that conditions in the earlier periods were considerably different. He writes:

[Eighteenth-century books] are the products of conditions of greater complexity than those which apply to earlier periods, and therefore occasionally require supplemental techniques for their analysis. It has not been sufficiently realized that printing, in this century, has progressed beyond the era of the simple handicraft and now represents one of mass production, where not a few but hundreds of pages of type may be retained and repeatedly returned to press, where not one or two individuals but batteries of pressmen and compositors may produce, in a matter of hours, editions running into thousands of copies, where not one but several books may be put to press concurrently by the same personnel. These practices, though extraordinary in the seventeenth century have become commonplace in the eighteenth . . . ("Editorial Problem in the Eighteenth Century", p. 46).

And elsewhere:

Before the expiration of the Licensing Act in 1695 the process of bookmaking was undoubtedly less confused than afterwards: only thirty-five master printers were authorized to practise the trade, and most of these, we may be sure, conformed to the regulation limiting the number of presses and apprentices for each shop. . . . After 1695, though, the conditions for disorder increase in approximately the same ratio as the means for detecting it disappear ("Observations on Press Figures", p. 179).

97. The articles of 1635 (Greg, *Companion*, pp. 94-5) were still being ignored in 1637 (*Ibid.*, p. 102). The trouble was partly that their enforcement was left to the men whose interests they were least calculated to advance. So one finds the journeymen continuing to complain that the orders of 1586-7 and those of 1635 had not been fulfilled and pleading that they be recorded in some court of justice so that they could be sued upon before a competent judge (*Ibid.*, p. 326). The complaints come to a head again in 1645.

Professor Todd is undoubtedly right that *some* 18th-century books are the products of conditions of greater complexity: any increase in size will increase the number of variables. Undoubtedly too in the largest houses a good deal of type was kept standing, although it would be interesting to go into the economics of such a practice. For the rest, the case for any really radical difference between the centuries would seem to have been over-stated. Perhaps a fine historical exactitude will be possible when more primary documentation has been published and some serious thought given to its economic implications.

V

Plus ça change, plus c'est la même chose. It's the only way I can explain the central paradox of this paper: that all printing houses were alike in being different. Despite my misgivings about 'norms' I have tried to suggest that all printing houses were more alike over the years than many bibliographers are prepared to allow: in size of plant, variability of work force, edition quantities printed, use of standing formes, proofing procedures, and most important of all in printing several jobs concurrently. I have stressed the supreme importance of primary evidence and I have tried to use it to expose and curb what I take to be erroneous inferences. In doing so, I have also tried to demonstrate more generally some weaknesses inherent in the inductive method. When the standing of general statements is damaged by contrary examples, the inductivist usually seeks a safe retreat in some form of historical relativism; I have tried to show how naive this can be. I am sure that Professor Hinman is right, though my sense pursues not his, when he stresses the importance of the new knowledge which will come "in the light of information about printing-house personnel and printing-house methods that is only now becoming known" ("Shakespeare's Texts", p. 26).

Bright lights will cast deep shadows, and I must confess to a feeling of mild despondency about the prospects for analytical bibliography: limited demonstrations there may certainly be, although they may require a life-time's devotion to make them; wherever full primary evidence has become available it has revealed a geometry of such complexity that even an expert in cybernetics, primed with all the facts, would have little chance of discerning it. But, as Nestor says, "In the reproof of Chance lies the true proof of men". Bibliography will simply have to prove itself adequate to conditions of far greater complexity than it has hitherto entertained. To do so, it will inevitably be obliged to use multiple and ingenious hypotheses, to move from induction to deduction, simply because a narrow range of theories is less likely to embrace the complex possibilities of organization within even a quite small printing house. A cynic might observe that the subject is already characterized by multiple and ingenious hypotheses, but too many of these have been allowed to harden into 'truth'. A franker acceptance of deductive procedures would bring a healthy critical spirit into the subject by insisting on the rigorous testing of hypotheses, and the prime method of falsification — adducing contrary particulars — would impose a sound curb on premature generalizations. It may be little pleasure "to observe how much paper is wasted in confutation", but bibliography might grow the more securely if we retained a stronger assurance of its hypothetical nature.

There is, however, a final paradox. Bibliography has nothing to do with bibliographies, and I only hope that new knowledge about productive conditions will prove disturbing enough to widen the gap between the two. The essential task of the bibliographer is to establish the facts of transmission for a particular text, and he will use *all* relevant evidence to determine the bibliographical truth. Author and subject bibliographies have a completely different function and it would be preposterous now to demand of them any great bibliographical sophistication. This would appear to be an argument in favour of degressive bibliography. Not at all; the phrase is meaningless. Booklisting may be as degressive as it wishes, bibliography never. Greg made the point so clearly that it's surprising to find that there is still any fuss about it; if any notice had been taken, we should have less half-baked bibliography and cheaper book-lists.[98]

But finally, if our basic premise is that bibliography should serve literature or the criticism of literature, it may be thought to do this best, not by disappearing into its own minutiae, but by pursuing the study of printing history to the point where analysis can usefully begin, or by returning — and this is the paradox — to the more directly useful, if less sophisticated, activity of enumerative 'bibliography'. This it is which gave us the Pollard and Redgrave and Wing *S.T.C.*s, both of which have been of inestimable service to the study of history, life, thought — and bibliography — in the 16th and 17th centuries. It will be a pity if history, life, thought — and bibliography — in the 18th century are long deprived of a comparable service.

98. *Collected Papers*, pp. 76-77, 222-3, 240. The arguments from expediency given in *The Times Literary Supplement* during August-September 1966 seem to me to be beside the point.

Note to the appendices: The information offered in the following appendices is intended merely to provide supporting evidence for the argument of this paper. It is not offered as a contribution to the detailed bibliographical study of either the books or the printing houses mentioned in it. The original documents referring to the Cambridge University Press are printed in my *Cambridge University Press, 1696-1712: A Bibliographical Study* (1966) : the two charts printed here continue those given as Table 15 in that book. The details of the Bowyer printing house are taken from the Bowyers' record of composition and presswork over the years 1730 to 1739; the volume in which this work is recorded is in the possession of The Grolier Club and is being edited for publication by Mr Keith Maslen. An edition of the ledger of Charles Ackers, printer of *The London Magazine*, was recently published by the Oxford Bibliographical Society. The appendices are long, but I have deliberately multiplied the examples to illustrate fully the variety of conditions under which the books mentioned came to be made, by different men, at different periods, and in different places.

BIBLIOGRAPHICAL THEORIES   63

APPENDIX I (a)

Cambridge University Press: Work done by Compositors and Pressmen
26 December 1701 – 31 January 1702

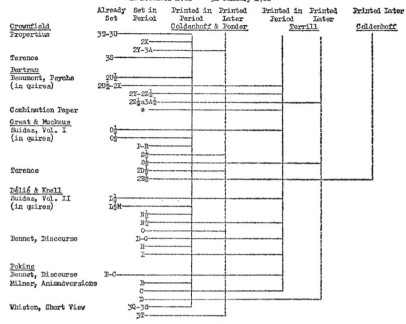

APPENDIX I (b)

Cambridge University Press: Work done by Compositors and Pressmen
1 – 28 February 1702

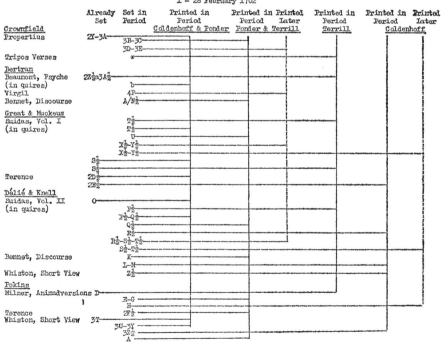

64

STUDIES IN BIBLIOGRAPHY

APPENDIX II (a)

William Bowyer's Press: Work done by Compositors and Pressmen
26 December 1730 — 16 January 1731

Books and Compositors	Edition Size	Press 1 W. Diggle J. Mazemore	Press 3 R. Collyer R. Franklin	Press 7 J. Clarke S. Peacock
1. Baxter, *Winter Evening Tales* [Already set]	750		A_2	
2. Clarke, *Sermons* J. Nutt: $P_{10}, Q_{10}, R_{10}, S_{10}, B_{12}, C_8$ B_4, I_5, K_6 P. James: $P_6, Q_6, R_6, S_6,$	1500	S_1		S_1, P_2, Q_2 R_1
3. *Defence of Present Admin.* J. Hart: $A_{1½}, B_{1½}$ C. Micklewright: $C_{1½}, D_{1½}$ J. Nutt: Reimposing 6 formes	1st ed. 2500 2nd ed. 500	1st edition A, B 500 + 500 C, D 500 A, C 1500	1st edition B, D 1500 C, D 500 2nd edition A, C 500	2nd edition B, D 500
4. *Distilling* J. Hart: A_4 J. Nutt: I_{13}, K_{10}, A_{12} P. James: I_5, K_6	1000	I_2, K_1	H_2, K_1	
5. *Foedera* vol. XVIII C. Micklewright: $12O$	500	$12L_2, 12M_2$	$12N_2$	
6. Freind, *Hippocrates* D. Redmaine: $3I — 3M$	500 +80	$3F_1, 3G_1, 3H_1$	$3F_1, 3G_1, 3H_1$	
7. *Greek Grammar* D. Redmaine: $2A_{1½}$	1500		X_1	
8. Gyles, *Catalogue* R. Bell: π (folio page)	100 (½ sheets)		π	
9. *Marmora Oxonia* J. Hart: $7K_2, 7L_4, 7M_2$	300 + 6	$7K_1, 8I_1$	$7I_2, 7K_1$	
10. Marshall, *Proposals* [Already set?]	1500		π	
11. Marshall, *Receipts* J. Nutt: 2 Great Primer	1000		π --	
12. Peyton, *Catastrophe* R. Bell: $G½ — K½$	750	G_1	E_1, F_1	$H_1, I_1, K_1, A_1·$
13. *Philosophical Transactions* R. Holmes) T. Hart) $4G — 4T$	750	$4H_2, 4I_1, 4L_1,$ $4M_1, 4N_2, 4O_2$	$4G_2, 4I_1, 4L_1,$ $4M_1, 4P_2, 4Q_2$	$4K_2$
14. Rapin de Thoyras, *History* J. Hart: [No. 53] H6, I6, K6, L6, M6, N6 [No. 47] 2 sheets 4 pages R. Bell: [No. 53] H6, I6, K6, L6, M6, N6	750		Covers 250 (½ sheet)	
15. Regnault, *Phil. Conversations* D. Gaylord: B, C, D, E_7, F, G, H C. Micklewright: E_9	1000	B_1, C_1, D_1	$B_1, C_1, D_1,$ E_2	
16. St George's Chapel, *Hymns* J. Nutt: π [printed later]	500			
17. Wade, *Horace* R. Holmes) T. Hart) Title ½ sheet J. Nutt: Reimposing 3 castrated sheets in 4°	250 +24	$A_{1½}$ A_2 (4°)	$X_{1½}$ X_2 (4°)	cancelled leaf
18. Wake, *Catechism* D. Redmaine: Index ½ J. Hart: Index ½ D. Gaylord: Index 4 pages	3000		O_2	

Note: As Clarke and Peacock received only one week's copy money, press 7 was presumably in use for only one of the three weeks. During this three-week period, compositors' and pressmen's earnings were: (a) Compositors: Bell £1. 9. 7.; Gaylord £1.18.10.; J. Hart £2. 9. 7.; T. Hart and R. Holmes £4.15.0.; James (unrecorded: James was still an apprentice); Micklewright £1.13. 7.; Nutt (unrecorded: Nutt was still an apprentice); Redmaine £1.17. 3.; (b) Pressmen: Diggle and Mazemore £2.18. 3.; Collyer and Franklin £3.19. 3.; Clarke and Peacock £1.10. 1. (In this and the following tables fractions of a penny have been disregarded.)

BIBLIOGRAPHICAL THEORIES   65

APPENDIX II (b)

William Bowyer's Press: Work done by Compositors and Pressmen

18 — 30 January 1731

Books and Compositors	Edition Size	Press 1 [W. Diggle J. Mazemore]	Press 2 T. Farmer ?. Wardman	Press 3 R. Collyer R. Franklin	Press 5 [unnamed]	Press 7 J. Clarke S. Peacock
1. *Address* C. Micklewright: (4 settings)	8000	1250	3750	2000		1000
2. *Advice to Poultney [= Poem in Defence of Walpole]* J. Nutt: Great Primer ½ sheet	100 +12		π½			
3. Clarke, *Sermons* P. James: C8, D4, F4, F6, G10, H6, I4 J. Nutt: D12, E12, F10, G8, H10, I12	1500		C2, F1, G1, H1	R1, E1	H2, G1	D2, E1, F1
4. Du Pin, *Proposals* D. Redmaine: 4 pages	500	π				
5. Du Pin, *Receipts* J. Nutt: 2 Great Primer	500	π				
6. *Ellen Foord's Case* C. Micklewright: [printed later]	712					
7. Freind, *Hippocrates* [Already set]	500 +80	3K1	3I1, 3K1			3I1
8. *Greek Grammar* D. Redmaine: 2B	1500			Y1		
9. Lobb, *Treatise of Small Pox* D. Redmaine: B [printed later]	750					
10. *Marmora Oxonia* J. Hart: 7M2, 7N2	300 + 6			7L1	7M1	7L1, 7M1
11. Marshall, *Sermons* C. Micklewright: E11, G3, H3, I6, K8, L7 J. Lewis: E5, F16, G13, H11, I10, K8, L9	800	F1, H1	G1, F1, G1	B1, C1, G1, I1	H1	B1, D2, E2, I1
12. *Parliamentary Votes* D. Redmaine: 1 and 2 R. Bell:	1000 +1250	B1, D1½, E1½, F1½, G1½, H1½, I1½		A1	A1	B1
13. *Philosophical Transactions* T. Hart) R. Holmes) 4U–5G	750	5A1	4R1, 4S1, 4T1, 4X1, 4Y1, 4Z1, 5C1	4X1, 5B1, 5C1	4U1, 4X1, 4Z1, 5B1, 5D1, 5E1	4R1, 4S1, 4T1, 4U1, 5A1, 5D1, 5E1
14. Rapin de Thoyras, *History* R. Bell: [No. 47] O4, Y4, Z4, Wrappers 2 pages J. Hart: [No. 47] O6, Y6, Wrappers 2 pages I. Grainger: H4, I4, K4, L4, M4, N4, O6, Y6, Z8, 2A8	750	M1	H1, L1, M1, N1	H1, I1, N1	I1, K1, L1	N1
15. Regnault, *Phil. Conversations* D. Gaylord: K8, L — O, P8 I. Grainger: I, K8	1000	K1	I1, K1	F1, G1, H2, I1, L1		F1, G1, L1
16. St George's Chapel, *Hymns* [Already set]	500					π
17. Skerret, *Sermon* D. Redmaine: 4 pages	250	Title				
18. *State of National Debt* R. Bell: A — D, Broadside	750		Broadside		A1, B1, C1, D1	
19. *Warrington's Case* J. Hart: [printed later]	800 +50					

Note: Diggle and Mazemore also claimed for '19 Rm Malt Rules @2s.8d. per Rm, Altering 10 shts. Sign. at 3d.' and '18 Rm. 5 qrs. of Gr. Malt. Bv @ 3s. per sht. & Altering 28 signatures @ 2d. each.'. During this two-week period, compositors' and pressmen's earnings were: (a) Compositors: Bell £2.19. 2.; Gaylord £1.10. 2.; Grainger £2. 0. 0.; J. Hart £1. 6.11.; T. Hart and R. Holmes £2.12.4.; James (unrecorded); Lewis £1. 2. 8.; Micklewright £1.10. 4.; Nutt (unrecorded); Redmaine £1.18. 2.; (b) Pressmen: Diggle and Mazemore £4.15. 5-[?]; Farmer and Wardman £2. 4. 5.; Collyer and Franklin £2. 7.11.; Press 5 (unnamed) £1.16. 6.; Clarke and Peacock £2.13. 0.

APPENDIX II (c)

William Bowyer's Press: Work done by Compositors and Pressmen
1 — 6 February 1731

Books and Compositors	*Edition Size*	[*Press 1* unnamed]	[*Press 2* unnamed]	[*Press 3* unnamed]	[*Press 7* unnamed]
1. Clarke, *Sermons* T. Hart) – R. Holmes) M6, N7, O7 P. James: I2, K8, L5, M4, N3, O3 J. Nutt: K8, L11, M6, N6, O6	1500	H1, K1, L1, M1	I1, K1, M1, N1	I1, L1, N1	
2. *Distilling* [Already set]	1000		A2		
3. *Ellen Foord's Case* [Already set]	100 + 12 +400 +100 +100	*			
4. *Islington Lodgers' Bills* J. Nutt:	500				*
5. *Letter from the West* D. Gaylord: A½, B½, C½ [printed later]	6				
6. Lobb, *Treatise of Small Pox* [Already set]	750		B1		B1
7. Marshall, *Sermons* J. Lewis: M13, N7, O7, P10 C. Micklewright: M3, N9, O9, P6	800		K1, M1	L2 500 Titles	K1, L1, M1, N2
8. Moss, *Sermons* J. Hart: B [printed later]	1000				
9. Newcome, *Evidence of Christian Religion* T. Hart) B [Specimen only? R. Holmes) Presswork unrecorded]	?				
10. *Parliamentary Votes* J. Hart: 10 — 14	1250 1000	K½, L½, M½, N½, O½			
11. Parsons, *Bills* J. Nutt: [printed later]	1000				
12. *Pension Bills* J. Hart; 1 sheet English	750		1 forme		1 forme
13. *Philosophical Transactions* T. Hart) R. Holmes) 5H, 5I, 3I, 3K1	750	5F1, 5H1	5H1	5G1	5F1, 5G1
14. Rapin de Thoyras, *History* R. Bell: 2A8, 2B8	750		Z1	Y2, Z1, 2A1	O2
15. Regnault, *Phil. Conversations* D. Gaylord: P8, Q	1000	M1		N1	M1, N1
16. *Swedish Dictionary Proposals* Compositor unrecorded: ½ sheet	50 +6		1 forme		
17. *Warrington's Case* [Already set]	800 +50		1 forme		1 forme
18. Wesley, *Prolegomena* J. Hart: B [Specimen only? Presswork unrecorded]	?				

Note: During this one-week period, compositors' and pressmen's earnings were: (a) Compositors: Bell 9s.7d.; Gaylord 15s.10d.; J. Hart £2. 1.11.; T. Hart and R. Holmes £1.13.11.; James 7s.9d.; Lewis 11s.7d.; Micklewright 8s.6d.,; Nutt 11s.6d. [?]; (b) Pressmen: Press 1 £2. 1. 3.; Press 2 £1. 9. 1.; Press 3 £1. 2. 9.; Press 7 £1. 6.10.

BIBLIOGRAPHICAL THEORIES   67

APPENDIX II (d)

William Bowyer's Printing House: Composition and Presswork

31 January — 12 February 1732

1. *Composition*	*Work Done*	*Earnings*
I. Lance	Evidence of Christian Religion O, P, Q, R and making up three formes	13. 8.
R. Dennett	Bill for Sugar Colonies 2 sheets Remarks on Lives of the Saints B, C, D, E, F, G, H4 Life of Cleveland, vol. I Title	£3. 0. 7.
B. Baddam	Cocks's Catalogue M1, N8 Charitable Corporations D Hymns for St Dunstan's Sacrament A, B, C, E, F4	£1. 6.11.
B. Tarrott	Charles XII F4 Letter to Member of Parliament 2 sheets Sacrament D half sheet	14. 8.
D. Gaylord	Calmet's Dictionary 3Z, 4A, 4B, 4C Articles of Limerick A, B and over-running several times Charles XII M, N, O4	£2. 6.11.
G. Grantham	Gyles's Catalogue Voyages 6O2, Q2, R2, U4, Y2, A4	8. 2.
G. Hills	Charitable Corporations A, B4, [C6] Charles XII F4 Tully's Offices L12, M12	£1.11. 8.
C. Micklewright	Votes 18, 19, 20, 21, 22 Tully's Offices L12, M12, N12	£2.12. 6.
J. Morgan	Charles XII C5, D8, E5, F8, G8, H4 Hutchinson B Gentleman Farrier	£1. 7. 8.
R. Holmes	Scripture Vindicated D6, E, F, G, H, I, K, L Proposals for Hippocrates	£1.10. 4.
T. Hart	Votes 14, 15, 16, 17 Memoria Technica M, N, O Wesley's Job Y, Z and correcting Y	£2.10. 8.
T. Allestree	Gyles's Catalogue A4 Voyages 6O2, 6P4, 6S2, 6X2, 6Z2, 7B4, 7C2	£1. 7. 2.
J. Nutt	Moss's Sermons B, C, D, E, F Charles XII B, C11, D8, E11, F8, G8, H12, I Scheme to Pay National Debt 2 pages ditto imposing 3 half sheets Hymns for St George ye Martyr Greek quarto page of Mr Dwight An English folio page	[£3.15. 0.]

68   STUDIES IN BIBLIOGRAPHY

2. Presswork

No.	Job	*Press 1* S. Peacock H. Perry	*Press 2* [unnamed]	*Press 3* R. Franklin T. Reynolds	*Press 7* J. Flower
500	Receipts for Lysias	π			
350) 24)	Voyages	6C1, 6H2, 6D1, 6F1, 6E1, 6G1, 6I1, 6O1, 6N1, 6P1, 6S1, 6Q1	6C1, 6F1, 6G1, 6K2, 6L2, 6O1, 6R2, 6T1, 6Q1	6D1, 6E1, 6T1, 6M1, 6N1, 6P1	
500	Cocks's Catalogue	I	K1	L1, M1, N1	Y
500	Scripture Vindicated		D1	C, E, F, H	
500	Remarks on Lives of the Saints	B1	C2, D1	B1, D1, E1	
500	Proposals for Hippocrates		One forme		
400	Wesley's Job	Y1			
100) 400) 100)	Proposals for Lysias			π	
750	Gyles's Catalogue	¼ sheet	S1	T1, U1	
750	Sacrament	A1			B
750	Remarks on Scandal	A, B	C1, D1		[A]
750	Cock and Bull	B			
700) 64)	Spenser	G1			
1000	Bill for Sugar Colonies	A2	B1	[B1]	
1000	Moss's Sermons	A1, E2, G1, H1, L1	F1	A1, G1, H1	I1
1000	Memoria Technica		K, L		
1000	Charles XII	L1, M1, O1/4	M1, N1	N1	
1000	Charitable Corporations	A1, B1, C1	A1, C1, D1	B1	
1000	Chirurg. Instit.	A1, 2C1	A1, R a page	2C1	
1000	Calmet		B1, C1	B1, C1	
1500	Greek Grammar		A1		
1500	Hymns for St Dunstan's			π	
1500	Tully's Offices	I1		I1	L1, M1
1500	Life of Cleveland	Titles			
2000	Votes	O, Q1, T, X1	P1, R1, U1, Y1	O1, S1, X1, Y1	
	Earnings:	£3.19. 5.	£3.10. 3.	£3. 2. 2.	14. 0.

APPENDIX II (e)

William Bowyer's Printing House: **Composition and Presswork**

14 — 26 February 1732

1. Composition	Work Done	Earnings
D. Redmaine	Bankrupts' Bill A, B Votes 28, 29, 30, 31, 32 Spenser H, I, K Injured Innocence G8, H4	£3. 5. 4.
R. Dennett	Remarks on Lives of the Saints H4, I, K Injured Innocence I2, K8 Voyages 7O, 7P2	£1.11. 8.
B. Baddam } B. Tarrott }	Sacrament F4, G8, H8, I8, K8 Letter to Archbishop 7 half-sheets Gentleman Farrier C, D, E, F	£2. 7. 2.
G. Hills } C. Micklewright }	Tully's Offices N12, O Ditto Brevier Index P12 Bankrupts' Bill C, D, E, F Life of Cecil A, B	£3. 9. 0.
R. Holmes	Scripture Vindicated, Part II M, N, O, P, Q, R, S Evidence of Christian Religion S, T, U1/4, Title ¼	£1.11. 1.
G. Grantham	Voyages 7E1, 7G3, 7H2, 7K2, 7L4, 7M3, 7Q2, 7R3, 7T2, 7U2 Injured Innocence H4, I6	£1.18. 2.

BIBLIOGRAPHICAL THEORIES   69

D. Gaylord	Calmet's Dictionary 4D, 4E, 4F, 4G, 4H Charles XII F8, Correcting N	£1.15. 2.
C. Knell	Voyages 6S2, 6T2, 6Z2, 7C2, 7D4, 7E1, 7H2, 7I1, 7M1, 7N4, 7R1, 7S4, 7T1	£1.17. 1.
G. Karver	Cocks's Catalogue M7 Chiselden's Syllabus Cock and Bull 3 half-sheets Hutchinson C8	£1.13. 9.
W. Diggle	Voyages 6B2, 6T2, 6X2, 6Y2, 7E2, 7F1, 7G1, 7I3, 7K2, 7P2, 7Q2 Nelson quarter-sheet	£1.12. 2.
T. Hart	Votes 23, 24, 25 Wesley's Job 2A, 2B, 2C2 Correcting Z, 2A Mr Chishull's half-sheet Memoria Technica P Bill for Parton Pier	£3. 0. 8.
J. Nutt	Moss's Sermons A, a, G, H, I ditto 2F half-sheet, vol. I Chiselden one page Two Great Primer receipts	£1.12. 6.

2. Presswork

No.	Job	*Press 1* S. Peacock H. Perry	*Press 2* H. Davis J. Mazemore	*Press 3* R. Franklin T. Reynolds	*Press 5* E. Vicaris W. King	*Press 7* R. Collyer
400	Vie de Thou					r
250	Owen				Title	
300	Hutchinson	B1, E1, G1	B1, C1, D1, E1, F1, G1 ¼ sheet	C1, E1		D1, F1, G1
300	Wooton					
500	Lives of Saints	G1				
350 / 24	Voyages	6Z2, 7C1, 7E1, 7G1, 7H1, 7I1, 7L1	6U2, 7A1, 7F1, 7K2, 7L1	6X1, 6Y1, 7A1, 7D2	6S1, 6T1, 6X1, 7B2, 7C1	7F1, 7H1
450 / 50	Job	Z1	Z1, 2A1	2A1		
500	Evidence of Christian Religion	R	P1	O1, T1	Q, S	
500	Scripture Vindicated	O	G1, I1, K1	L1, P1		M, N
500	Remarks on Lives of the Saints			C1, F2	E1, H2	G
500	Receipts for Hippocrates	r				
750	Cock and Bull	C, D	Title			
750	Sacrament	H, K		G1, I1	B1, C1, E1, F1	
750	Letter to Archbishop			B1, C1, D1		
700 / 64	Spenser	H1			B1, C1, E1, F1	
1500	Greek Grammar	2N				
1000	Calmet's Dictionary		D1, E1	D1, E1		
1000	Moss's Sermons	a2, I1, L1	L1		K1	K1, 2F
1000	Gentleman Farrier					A1
1000	Memoria Technica	M	N1, O			
1250	Bankrupts Bill	A1, B1, C1, D1, E1	A1, C1, E1, F1	F1, D1		[B1]
1500	Tully's Offices	K	N1	K1, M1	K1	N1
2000	Injured Innocence		G1, H1	I1		
2000	Votes	Z1, 2A1, 2B1, 2E1, 2H1	Z1, 2C1, 2D1, 2F1, 2H1	2A1, 2C1, 2E1, 2G1, [2F1]		
4250	Nelson	¼ sheet				
	Earnings:	£4. 1. 8.	£3.14. 9.	£3. 5. 8.	£1. 9. 6.	£1. 2. 4.

APPENDIX II (f)

William Bowyer's Printing House: Composition and Presswork

8 — 14 October 1732

1. *Composition*	*Work Done*	*Earnings*
P. Grantham	Bacon's Letters X, Y	9. 1
M. Newsted	Clifton's State of Physick A, a, b	18. 1.
O. Nelson	Rosalinda D, E, F	18. 1.
R. Holmes	Fryar Bacon 3G, 3H, 3I, 3K, 3L, 3M 1 page	£1. 1. 5.
T. Clark	Essay on Colonies B, C, D, E	£1. 0. 1.
D. Gaylord	Thuanus Part VI 6A, 6B, C 2 pages	£1. 0. 1.

2. *Presswork*		[*Press 1*]	[*Press 2*]
6000	Latin Testament	L	
300	Chiselden's Tables	XXV, XXVI	
1500	Swift's Miscellany	B1	B1
100	Middleton's Sermon	Titles	
750			
150 }Thuanus		6A2	3R2, 3S2
5			
1000	Rosalinda		B2
220 }Fryar Bacon			3D2, 3F2, 3G2
30			
500 }Clifton's State of Physick			M2, N2
25			
200 }Bacon's Letters			S2
25			
	Receipts for Duke of Somerset		π
Earnings:		£1.15. 8.	£1.12. 6.

Note: Neither the names of the crews nor the numbers of the presses used are given, but payments of copy-money show that two full crews were employed. Each man at press 1 therefore received 17s.10d. and each man at press 2 received 16s.3d.

APPENDIX II (g)

Books Printed by William Bowyer: Some Case-Histories

1. Voltaire, *Histoire de Charles XII*. [London, 1731.]

12°:   A — P⁶ (all printed by Bowyer)   Copy: BM. 10761.df.14.

Production: 7½ sheets; edition 750; composition 5s.3d. per half sheet; presswork 1s.9d. per half sheet; price per sheet 24s.; finished by 13 Jan. 1732; volume I only printed by Bowyer. On this and the next three items, see the article by K.I.D. Maslen, *The Library*, 5th ser. XIV (1959), 287-93. (The date of completion, 13 Jan., is derived from the Bowyer Paper Stock Ledger. Bowyer's account of work done covers the entire period from 26 Dec. 1731-29 Jan. 1732, hence the later date given below.)

Composition: A — P, T. Hart 29 Jan.

Presswork: A, *1* (Diggle/Peacock) 29 Jan.; B, C, *3* (Franklin/Reynolds) 29 Jan.; D, *1* (Diggle/Peacock) 29 Jan.; E, F, *3* (Franklin/Reynolds) 29 Jan.; G-M, *1* (Diggle/Peacock) 29 Jan.; N, O, *2* (unnamed) 29 Jan.; P, *3* (Franklin/Reynolds) 29 Jan.

Figures: 1 — A4, D3v, G6v, H6v, I3v, K6, L3v, M4v
2 — N6v, O3v
3 — B6v, F6v, P4v
Note: Franklin's and Reynolds' failure to figure C and E.

2. Voltaire, *History of Charles XII*. London, 1732.

8°:   A1 B — N⁸ O1 (all printed by Bowyer)   Copy: BM. 153. p. 23.

Production: 12¼ sheets; edition 1000; composition 6s.; presswork 4s.; price per sheet 18s.; begun by 29 Jan. 1732; finished by 26 Feb. 1732; first 12¼ sheets only printed by Bowyer.

BIBLIOGRAPHICAL THEORIES   71

Composition: K, L, Lane 29 Jan.; B, C11, Nutt 12 Feb.; C5, D8, Morgan 12 Feb.; D8, E11, Nutt 12 Feb; E5, F8, Morgan 12 Feb.; F8, G8, Nutt 12 Feb.; G8, H4, Morgan 12 Feb.; H12, I, Nutt 12 Feb.; M, N, O4, Gaylord 12 Feb.; correcting in N, Gaylord 26 Feb.

              Note: F may have been set twice. In addition to the claims listed above, the following are recorded: F4, Hills 12 Feb.; F4, Tarrott 12 Feb.; F8, Gaylord 26 Feb.

Presswork: Bi, Bo, 2 (unnamed) 29 Jan.; Ci, Co, 1 (Diggle/Peacock) 29 Jan.; Di, 2 (unnamed) 29 Jan.; Do, Eo, 3 (Franklin/Reynolds) 29 Jan.; Ei, 1 (Diggle/Peacock) 29 Jan.; Fi, 2 (unnamed) 29 Jan.; Fo, 7 (Franklin/Reynolds) 29 Jan.; Gi, 1 (Diggle/Peacock) 29 Jan.; Go, Ho, 2 (unnamed) 29 Jan.; Ko, 2 (unnamed) 29 Jan.; Ki, Li, 7 (Jones/Perry) 29 Jan.; Lo, Mi, 1 (Peacock/Perry) 12 Feb.; Mo, Ni, 2 (unnamed) 12 Feb.; No, 3 (Franklin/Reynolds) 12 Feb.; A/O, 1 (Peacock/Perry) 12 Feb.

Figures: 1 — C1v, C8v, E7v, G1v, L6v, M7v
              2 — B7, B8, D1v, F8, H2v, K7, M7, N8
              3 — D7, E7, G7, I8, I8v, N8v
              7 — F8v, H5v, K5v, L5v

              Note: Go claimed by 2 but figured 3; the changes of crew for presses 1 and 7; the same crew worked both presses 3 and 7 within the same period, so that both cannot have been in use at once.

3. Voltaire, *Histoire de Charles XII* ('Seconde Edition, révùe corrigée / par l'Auteur'). [London, 1732.]

8°:   A – K8 L4 (all printed by Bowyer)   Copy: BM. 611.c.12 (1).

Production: 10½ sheets; edition 1000; composition 8s.; presswork 4s.; price per sheet 21s.; begun by 18 Mar. 1732; finished by 8 April 1702; first 10½ sheets only printed by Bowyer.

Composition: A–H, Dennett 18 Mar.; I, K, Dennett/Tarrott 25 Mar.; L½, T. Hart 25 Mar.

Presswork: (None of the crews is named) Ai, Ao, 7 – 18 Mar.; Bi, 5 – 18 Mar.; Bo, Ci, 3 – 18 Mar.; Co, 1 – 18 Mar.; Do, 3 – 18 Mar.; Di, 7 – 18 Mar.; Ei, 4 – 18 Mar.; Eo, 1 – 18 Mar.; Fi, 3 – 18 Mar.; Fo, 7 – 8 Apr.; Gi, 3 – 8 Apr.; Go, Ho, 7 – 8 Apr.; Hi, 2 – 8 Apr.; Ii, 3 – 8 Apr.; Io, 7 – 8 Apr.; Ko, 4 – 8 Apr.; Ki, L, 2 – 8 Apr.

Figures: 1 — C7, E7
              2 — H8, K1v, L3v
              3 — B7, C8, F8, G8, I7v
              4 — E6, K2v
              5 — B8
              7 — A2v, A3v, D1v, F2v, G2v, H7, I5

              Note: Fo was also claimed by press 2 on 18 Mar.; Do (press 3) unfigured.

4. Voltaire, *History of Charles XII* ('The Second Edition, Corrected.'). London, 1732.

8°:   A6 B – N8 (all printed by Bowyer)   Copy: BM. 10761.bb.39.

Production: 12 sheets; edition 2000; composition 6s.; presswork 8s.; price per sheet 28s.; finished by 18 Mar. 1732 (as all claims are dated 18 Mar., dates are omitted from the tables of composition and presswork given below); sheets B – N only printed by Bowyer.

Composition: B16, C4, Grantham; C6, Knell; C6, D2, Allestree; D11, Grantham; D3, E6, Knell; E6, Allestree; E4, F7, Grantham; F5, Knell; F4, G4, Allestree; G8, Grantham; G4, H4, Allestree; H4, Knell; H8, I10, Grantham; I2, Allestree; I4, K4, Knell; K8, Grantham; K4, L3, Allestree; L7, Knell; L6, M6, Grantham; M8, Allestree; M1, Nutt; M1, N4, Knell; N8, Grantham; N4, T. Hart.

Presswork: (None of the crews is named) Bo, 4; Bi, 2; Co, 3; Ci, Do, 7; Di, Eo, 1; Ei Fi, 2; Fo, Go, 3; Gi, 4; Hi, 3; Ho, 2; Ii, 1; Io, Ki, 7; Ko, Lo, 3; Li, 1; Mi, 7; Mo, Ni, 2; No, 1.

Figures: 1 — D7v, E7, L8, N8v
              2 — B8, E1v, F5v, H2v, M2v, N1v
              3 — C8v, F7, G8v, H7v, L7
              4 — B2v, G1v
              7 — C1v, D7, I2v, K1v, M1v
              Note: Ii (press 1) and Ko (press 3) are unfigured.

5. Baxter, *Glossarium Antiquitatum Britannicarum*. London, 1733.

8°:   A4 a8 B – T8 U4   Copy: BM. 7708.b.5.

Production: 20 sheets; edition 500; composition 10s.; presswork 2s.4d.; price per sheet 22s.; begun by 10 Oct. 1732; finished by 2 June 1733.

72　　　　　　　　STUDIES IN BIBLIOGRAPHY

Composition:　　(Thomas Hart set the text unaided except as noted for the 8 pages of C) B, 7 Oct.; C8, Hart/Micklewright 11 Nov.; C8, D, 25 Nov.; E, F8, 2 Dec.; F8, G, 9 Dec.; H8, 20 Jan.; H8, I8, 27 Jan.; I8, K, L8, 24 Feb.; L8, 3 Mar.; M8, 10 Mar.; M8, N8, 17 Mar.; N8, O, 24 Mar.; P, Q, R, 14 Apr.; S, T8, 28 Apr.; T8, 5 May; U8, 12 May; A, a, 26 May.

Presswork:　　　Bo, 2 (Mazemore/Peacock) 11 Nov.; Bi, *1* (Classon/Diggle) 11 Nov.; Co, *3* (Bradley/Vicaris) 2 Dec.; Ci, Di, Do, *1* (Classon/Diggle) 2 Dec.; Eo, 2 (Mazemore/Peacock) 9 Dec.; Ei, *1* (Classon/Diggle) 9 Dec.; Fi, Fo, 2 (Mazemore/Peacock) 23 Dec.; Gi, *3* (Dennis/Duff); Go, Hi, Ho, 2 (Mazemore/Peacock) 27 Jan.; Ii, Io, 2 (unnamed) 24 Feb.; Ki, Ko, *1* (Diggle/Reynolds) 3 Mar.; Li, *3* (Dennis/Duff) 24 Mar.; Ni, 2 (Clarke/Mazemore) 24 Mar.; No, 7 (Jones/Needham) 24 Mar.; Oi, 7 (Jones/Needham) 14 Apr.; Oo, *3* (Duff/Mazemore) 14 Apr.; Pi, 2 (Clarke/Dennis) 14 Apr.; Po, Qi, *1* (Milburne/Reynolds) 14 Apr.; Qo, 3 (Duff/Mazemore) 14 Apr.; Ri, Ro, 2 (Clarke/Jones) 28 Apr.; Si, *1* (Classon alone) 28 Apr.; So, *3* (Duff/Mazemore) 28 Apr.; T (unrecorded); A/Ui, *1* (unnamed) 26 May; A/Uo, 2 (unnamed) 26 May; ai, ao, 7 (Brooker/Clarke) 2 June.

Figures:　　　　1 — A3v, C1v, D3v, E7v, K8, K8v
　　　　　　　　2 — a5, a6, B8v, F7, F8, G4v, H1v, H7, I7, I8, L2v, P7v, R7v, U3v
　　　　　　　　3 — C8v, L7v, M7v, M8v, O8v, Q7, S6v, T7v, T8v
　　　　　　　　5 — G5v
　　　　　　　　7 — N7, O7v

　　　　　　　　Note: Press 1 failed to figure Bi, Po, Qi, Si; Press 2 failed to figure Eo, Ni, Ro; Press 3 printed Gi but the forme is figured 5; both ai and ao were printed by Press 2 but both are figured 7; the changing composition of the crews at each press:

　　　　　　　　Press 1: (a) Classon/Diggle (b) Diggle/Reynolds (c) Milburne/Reynolds (d) Classon alone (e) unnamed
　　　　　　　　Press 2: (a) Mazemore/Peacock (b) unnamed (c) Clarke/Mazemore (d) Clarke/Dennis (e) Clarke/Jones (f) unnamed
　　　　　　　　Press 3: (a) Bradley/Vicaris (b) Dennis/Duff (c) Duff/Mazemore
　　　　　　　　Press 7: (a) Jones/Needham (b) Brooker/Clarke

6. Spenser, *The Shepherd's Calendar*, ed. J. Ball. London, 1732.

8°:　　A8 al B — Q8 R6 (–R6)　　　　　　　　　　　　Copy: BM. 11607.f.7.

Production:　　17½ sheets; edition 700 Demy, 60 Royal, 4 Writing Royal; composition 5s.6d.; presswork 2s.6d.; price per sheet 20s.; begun by 27 Nov. 1731; finished by 10 June 1732.

Composition:　　(Daniel Redmaine set the whole text except probably for P, A, a) B8, 27 Nov.; B8, C, D, 24 Dec.; E — G, 29 Jan.; H — K, 26 Feb.; L — O, 18 Mar.; P (unrecorded unless it be George Karver's claim below); Q, 25 Mar.; R, 8 Apr.; *1* sheet [=P?], 6 pages, Karver 27 May; 4 pages, Grantham, 10 June.

Presswork:　　　Bi, 2 (Davies/Mazemore) 24 Dec.; Bo, Ci, *1* (Diggle/Peacock) 24 Dec.; Co, *3* (Diggle/Peacock) 24 Dec.; Do, 2 (unnamed) 29 Jan.; Di, Eo, *1* (Diggle/Peacock) 29 Jan.; Ei, Fo, 2 (unnamed) 29 Jan.; Fi, *1* (Franklin/Reynolds) 29 Jan.; Gi, *1* (Peacock/Perry) 12 Feb.; Go (unrecorded, but figured 7); Ho (unrecorded, but figured 5); Hi, *1* (Peacock/Perry) 26 Feb.; Io, Ii, 2 (unnamed) 18 Mar.; Ki, *3* (unnamed) 18 Mar.; Ko, Li, Lo, *1* (unnamed) 18 Mar.; Mo, 2 (unnamed) 18 Mar.; Mi, No, *4* (unnamed) 18 Mar.; Ni, *1* (unnamed) 18 Mar.; Oo, 7 (unnamed) 25 Mar.; Oi, Po, *4* (unnamed) 25 Mar.; Pi, Qi, Qo, *1* (unnamed) 25 Mar.; Ri, 2 (unnamed) 25 Mar.; Ro, 7 (unnamed) 25 Mar.; Ai, 7 (Jones/Perry) 10 June; Ao, a, 2 (Hardicke/Mazemore) 10 June.

Figures:　　　　1 — B2v, C7v, D6, E2v, G7v, H1v, K2v, L4v, L5v, P2v, Q7
　　　　　　　　2 — A7, D2v, E1v, F2v, I2v, I8, Q3v, R4
　　　　　　　　3 — C7, K8
　　　　　　　　4 — M8, O3v, P6
　　　　　　　　5 — H2v
　　　　　　　　7 — A7v, B6, G8v, O2v

　　　　　　　　Note: Bi claimed by 2 (Davies/Mazemore) but figured 7; Franklin's and Reynolds' failure to figure Fi; the failure of press 2 to figure Mo; the failure of presses 1 and 4 to figure Ni and No; Qi claimed by 1 but figured 2; the failure of press 7 to figure Ro; Diggle and Peacock worked both presses 1 and 3 within the same period.

7. T. Lobb, *A Treatise of the Small Pox*. London, 1731

8°:　　A4 a — c6 B — 2H8 2I6 (— 2I6)　　　　　　　　Copy: BM. 1174.h.4

Production:　　34 sheets; edition 750; composition 8s.; presswork 3s.6d.; price per sheet 18s.; begun by 30 Jan. 1731; finished by 14 Aug. 1731.

BIBLIOGRAPHICAL THEORIES   73

Composition: B, Redmaine 30 Jan.; C, D, E8, H8, correcting C, Redmaine 20 Feb.; E8, F, G, Hart/Holmes 20 Feb.; H8, I, K8, Hart 6 Mar.; L-O, Hart/Holmes 20 Mar.; P-S, Hart/Holmes 3 Apr.; T-Y, Z4, Hart/Holmes 17 Apr.; X12 [sic = Z12?], Morgan 17 Apr.; 2A, 2B, 2C8, Hart/Holmes 1 May; 2C8, Hart/Holmes 15 May; 2D8, Hart 29 May; 2D8, Holmes 20 May; 2E12, Holmes 5 June; 2E4, 2F-2H, 2I4, Holmes 26 June; a, b, Imperfection B, 2I4, Holmes 17 July; 2I4, A, c, Holmes 31 July.

Presswork: Bi, 7 (unnamed) 6 Feb.; Bo, 2 (unnamed) 6 Feb.; Ci (no record); Co, 7 (unnamed) 20 Feb.; Di, 2 (unnamed) 20 Feb.; Do, 3 (unnamed) 6 Mar.; Ei, 7 (unnamed) 20 Feb.; Eo, 1 (unnamed) 20 Feb.; Fi, Fo, 7 (unnamed) 20 Feb.; Gi, 1 (unnamed) 6 Mar.; Go, 3 (unnamed) 6 Mar.; Hi, 3 (unnamed) 6 Mar.; Ho, 7 (unnamed) 6 Mar.; Ii, 3 (unnamed) 6 Mar.; Io, Ki, 2 (Clarke/Ward) 20 Mar.; Ko, 3 (Collyer/Franklin) 20 Mar.; Lo, 2 (Clarke/Ward) 20 Mar.; Li, Mi, Mo, 1 (Diggle/Mazemore) 20 Mar.; Ni, 7 (Farmer/Peacock) 20 Mar.; No. 3 (Collyer/Franklin) 20 Mar.; Oi, 7 (unnamed) 3 Apr.; Oo, 3 (unnamed) 3 Apr.; Pi, 2 (unnamed) 3 Apr.; Po, Qi, 3 (unnamed) 3 Apr.; Qo, Ro, 2 (unnamed) 3 Apr.; Ri, 1 (unnamed) 3 Apr.; Si, 1 (Diggle/Mazemore) 17 Apr.; So, Ti, 3 (Franklin/Reynolds) 17 Apr.; To, 7 (Farmer/Peacock) 17 Apr.; Ui, 1 (Diggle/Mazemore) 17 Apr.; Uo, Xo, 2 (Clarke/Ward) 17 Apr.; Xi, 3 (Franklin/Reynolds) 17 Apr.; Yi, 1 (Diggle/Mazemore) 1 May; Yo, 3 (Franklin/Reynolds) 1 May; Zi, 2Ai, 2Ao, 7 (Farmer/Peacock) 1 May; 2B (no record); 2Co, 3 (Franklin/Reynolds) 5 June; 2Ci, 2Do, 7 (Farmer/Peacock) 5 June; 2Di, 2 (Clarke) 5 June; 2Ei, 2Eo, 2Fo, 7 (Farmer/Peacock) 26 June; 2Fi, 2Gi, 3 (Franklin/Reynolds) 26 June; 2Go, 7 (Farmer/Peacock) 26 June; 2Hi, 2Ho, 1 (Clarke/Diggle) 17 July; 2I (not recorded); ai, 7 (Farmer/Peacock) 31 July; A, ao, bi, bo, 1 (Clarke/Diggle) 31 July; co, 3 (Franklin/Reynolds) 31 July; 1000 loose titles, 2 (Clarke/Davies) 14 Aug.

Figures: 1 — a8v, b2v, c8, E7, G8, I2v, L8, M4v, M5v, R7v, S1v, U8, 2H7v

2 — B7, K8, L7, P7v, Q8v, U5, X8v, Z7, 2D7v

3 — c7, D7, G7, H7v, K7, O2v, P7, Q7v, S7, T8, Y7, 2F7v, 2G7v

7 — a5v, B8, C7, E8, F6v, F7v, H8v, N3v, O8, T5, 2A8, 2B1v, 2B7, 2C7v, 2E2v, 2F4v, 2H6v, 2I4

8. *A Defence of the Present Administration.* London, 1731

[8°: A — D4]   Copy: not located

Production: 2 sheets; edition 3000; composition 5s.6d. per sheet; presswork 1s.2d. per 500, 3s. per 1500; price per sheet 16s. for the first 1000 and 5s. per ream for the rest; finished by 16 Jan. 1731.

Composition: A, B, J. Hart 16 Jan.; C, D, Micklewright 16 Jan.

Presswork: 'first edition':
Press 1 (Diggle/Mazemore) A, B, D, 500; A, C, 1500; A, B, C 500
Press 3 (Collyer/Franklin) C, 500; B, D 1500; D 500
'second edition':
Press 3 (Collyer/Franklin) A, C 500
Press 7 (Clarke/Peacock) B, D 500

9. E. Peyton, *Catastrophe of the Stuarts.* London, 1731

8°: A² B — I4 K²   Copy: BM. 110.e.23

Production: 4½ sheets; edition 750; composition 8s. per sheet; presswork 3s. per sheet; price per sheet 18s.; begun by 24 Dec. 1730; finished by 16 Jan. 1731.

Composition: B — F, Grainger 24 Dec.; G — K, Bell 16 Jan.

Presswork: B, C, 1 (Diggle/Mazemore) 24 Dec.; D, 3 (Collyer/Franklin) 24 Dec.; E, F, 3 (Collyer/Franklin) 16 Jan.; G, 1 (Diggle/Mazemore) 16 Jan.; H — K/A, 7 (Clarke/Peacock) 16 Jan.

Figures: 1 — B4, C2v, G1v

2 — F4

7 — H4v, I3v, K1v

Note: The evidence that Bowyer printed this pamphlet is of more than passing interest, for on Wednesday 27 Jan. 1731 its printer and publisher were taken into custody for publishing a libel. The bookseller, Charles Davis, was bound in a recognizance to appear at the King's Bench, which recognizance was continued for a period of 12 months, when he was discharged without penalty (*Whitehall Evening Post*, No. 1921, 28 — 30 Jan. 1731). Bowyer debits Davis with the printing costs, but the imprint reads 'Printed for T. Warner'.

10. Regnault, *Philosophical Conversations.* 3 vols. London, 1731

   vol. 1 — 8°: A⁸ (—A8) B — 2C⁸ 2D⁸ (— 2D8)

   vol. 2 — 8°: A² . . . Q — 2D⁸ (all printed by Bowyer)

                                  Copy: BM. 536.h.6-7

Production: vol. 1 — 26 sheets; vol. 2 — 12 sheets; 38 sheets in all; edition 1000; composition 6s.; presswork 4s.; price per sheet 22s.; begun by 16 Jan. 1731; finished by 26 June 1731; in vol. 2 sheets A and Q — 2D only printed by Bowyer.

Composition: vol. 1: B — D, Gaylord 16 Jan.; E9, Micklewright 16 Jan.; E7, F — H, Gaylord 16 Jan.; I, K8, Grainger 30 Jan.; K8, L — O, P8, Gaylord 30 Jan.; P8, Q, Gaylord 6 Feb.; R — X, Y8, Gaylord 20 Feb.; Y8, Gaylord 6 Mar.; Z, 2A, 2B, Gaylord 20 Mar.; 2C, 2D8, Bell/Gaylord 1 May; A8, Gaylord 29 May.

                  vol. 2: Q, Bell 3 Apr.; R — X, Bell/Gaylord 1 May; Y — 2D, Bell/Gaylord 15 May; 16 pages Long Primer, Bell 29 May; two titles, Bell 26 June.

Presswork: vol. 1: Bi, *3* (Collyer/Franklin) 16 Jan.; Bo, Co, *1* (Diggle/Mazemore) 16 Jan.; Ci, Do, *3* (Collyer/Franklin) 16 Jan.; Di, *1* (Diggle/Mazemore) 16 Jan.; Ei, Eo, *3* (Collyer/Franklin) 16 Jan.; Fo, *3* (Collyer/Franklin) 30 Jan.; Fi, Gi, *7* (Clarke/Peacock) 30 Jan.; Hi, Ho, Ii, *3* (Collyer/Franklin) 30 Jan.; Io, Ki, *2* (Farmer/Wardman) 30 Jan.; Ko, *1* (Diggle/Mazemore) 30 Jan.; Li, *3* (Collyer/Franklin) 30 Jan.; Lo, *7* (Clarke/Peacock) 30 Jan.; Mi, *1* (unnamed) 6 Feb.; Mo, Ni, *7* (unnamed) 6 Feb.; No, *3* (unnamed) 6 Feb.; Oi, *1* (unnamed) 20 Feb.; Oo, Po, *2* (unnamed) 20 Feb.; Pi, Qi, *7* (unnamed) 20 Feb.; Qo, *3* (unnamed) 6 Mar.; Ri, *2* (unnamed) 6 Mar.; Ro, Si, *7* (unnamed) 6 Mar.; So, To, *3* (unnamed) 6 Mar.; Ti, *2* (unnamed) 6 Mar.; Ui, Uo, *1* (Diggle/Mazemore) 20 Mar.; Xi, *3* (Collyer/Franklin) 20 Mar.; Xo, *7* (Farmer/Peacock) 20 Mar.; Yo, *2* (unnamed) 3 Apr.; Yi, Zi, *7* (unnamed) 3 Apr.; Zo, *3* (unnamed) 3 Apr.; 2Ai, *7* (Farmer/Peacock) 17 Apr.; 2Ao, *3* (Franklin/Reynolds) 17 Apr.; 2Bo, *3* (Franklin/Reynolds) 1 May; 2Bi, 2Ci, *7* (Farmer/Peacock) 1 May; 2D, A (unrecorded).

               vol. 2: Qi, *1* (Diggle/Mazemore) 1 May; Qo, Ri, *3* (Franklin/Reynolds) 1 May; Ro, *1* (Diggle/Mazemore) 1 May; So, Ti, *3* (unnamed) 15 May; To, *1* (unnamed) 15 May; Uo, *3* (unnamed) 15 May; Ui, Xi, Yi, Zi, *7* (unnamed) 15 May; Xo, Yo, Zo, *7* (unnamed) 29 May; 2Ai, *2* (unnamed) 29 May; 2Ao, *3* (Franklin/Reynolds) 29 May; 2B (unrecorded); 2Co, *1* (unnamed) 29 May; 2Ci, *2* (unnamed) 29 May; 2Di, *3* (Franklin/Reynolds) 26 June; 2Do, *3* (Farmer/Peacock) 26 June; 'A3' and titles to vols 1, 2 and 3 also claimed by Diggle alone at press *1*.

Figures: vol. 1: 1 — A7, B7, C7, D8, K7, L8v, M1v, N2v, R7, T1v, U6, U7
                         2 — C7v, I6v, K5v, O8v, R8, X7v, Y8v,
                         3 — F7, G7, H7, I8, O8, Q7, S5, Z8v, 2A7
                         7 — F5v, G5v, L7v, M5, N7v, P2v, Q8, S5v, T7, X8v, Y8, Z3v, 2A7v, 2B1v, 2C7v

           vol. 2: 1 — Q1v, R2v, T2v, Z1v, 2C8v
                         2 — U7v, Y7v, 2A6, 2C6
                         3 — U7, 2D5v
                         7 — S3v, X3v, Y5, 2B1v, 2B2v

APPENDIX III

(a) Edition Sizes of Part Issues of

Astley's *A New General Collection of Voyages and Travels* (1743-47)

(Printed by Charles Ackers)

Volume	Part Nos.		Edition		Reprints		Total Edition
I	1	sig. B	1750	+	350	+ 1000	3100
		sig. C	2000	+	1100		3100
		sig. D	2000	+	1100		3100
	2		2000	+	1000		3000
	3		2000	+	1000		3000
	4 — 33						2500
II	34 — 79						2250
III	80 — 85						2250
	86 — 103						1750
	104 — 117						1500
VI	118 — 164						1500

Note: Ackers also printed 35,000 Proposals for this Collection.

BIBLIOGRAPHICAL THEORIES   75

(b)   Edition Sizes of *The London Magazine*

1732 — 1747

(Printed by Charles Ackers)

Monthly Numbers	1st Edition	Reprint	Total
Apr. 1732 — Dec. 1732	[2500]	1500	[4000]
Jan. 1733 — May 1733	4000	1250	5250
Jun. 1733 — Jul. 1733	4000	1500	5500
Aug. 1733	4500	1250	5750
Sep. 1733 — Oct. 1733	5000	1250	6250
Nov. 1733	5000	1000	6000
Dec. 1733 — May 1734	6000		6000
Jun. 1734 — Dec. 1734	6250		6250
Jan. 1735 — Dec. 1736	7000		7000
Jan. 1737 — May 1737	6000		6000
Jun. 1737 — Jul. 1737	6000	1000	7000
Aug. 1737	6000		6000
Sep. 1737	6500		6500
Oct. 1737 — Jul. 1739	7000		7000
Aug. 1739 — Dec. 1740	8000		8000
Jan. 1741 — Dec. 1741	7500		7500
Jan. 1742	7000	1000	8000
Feb. 1742 — Jul. 1743	8000		8000
Aug. 1743 — Dec. 1743	7500		7500
Jan. 1744 — Jan. 1747	7000		7000
Feb. 1747 — Dec. 1747	7500		7500

(c)   Edition Sizes of T. Dyche's *A Guide to the English Tongue*

(Printed by Charles Ackers)

4 Dec. 1733	19th ed.	10,000
4 Nov. 1734	20th ed.	10,000
5 May 1735	21st ed.	10,000
11 Oct. 1735	22nd ed.	10,000
23 Sep. 1736	23rd ed.	10,000
11 May 1737	24th ed.	10,000
28 Jan. 1738	24th ed. [sic]	15,000
19 Jul. 1738	'a new Edition'	10,000
26 Jan. 1739	'a new Edition'	10,000
17 Jul. 1739	'a new Edition'	5,000
25 Oct. 1739	'a new Edition'	10,000
3 Oct. 1740	'a new Edition'	20,000
17 Jun. 1741	'a new Edition'	20,000
3 May 1742	'a new Edition'	20,000
14 May 1743	'a new Edition'	5,000
18 Aug. 1743	'a new Edition'	10,000
6 Jan. 1744	'a new Edition'	5,000
12 May 1744	30th ed.	5,000
9 Aug. 1744	'a new Edition'	5,000
23 Oct. 1744	'a new Edit'	5,000
10 Jan. 1745	'a new Edition'	5,000
16 Mar. 1745	'a new Edition'	5,000
7 Jun. 1745	'a new Edit.'	5,000
10 Sep. 1745	'a new Edit.'	5,000
14 Dec. 1745	'a new Edition'	5,000
12 Apr. 1746	'a new Edit.'	5,000
4 Jul. 1746	'a new Edit.'	5,000
13 Oct. 1746	'a new Edit.'	10,000
13 Feb. 1747	35th ed.	5,000
27 Apr. 1747	'a new Edition'	5,000
29 Jul. 1747	'a new Edition'	5,000
2 Nov. 1747	'a new Edition'	5,000
1 Feb. 1748	'a new Edition'	5,000

Part IV
Selling

[12]

'Omnium totius orbis emporiorum compendium': the Frankfurt fair in the early modern period

JOHN L. FLOOD

BETWEEN 19 AND 23 October 2005, 284,838 people descended on the exhibition grounds at Frankfurt am Main to visit the annual Frankfurt Book Fair, the most important regular event in the publishing world's calendar. The association of publishing with Frankfurt has a long history — though not quite so long as one might imagine. Indeed, given the city's important role in the book trade, especially in the sixteenth century, it seems almost a paradox that it was such a relative latecomer as far as the introduction of printing was concerned. Leaving aside the short-lived press of Beatus Murner in the Franciscan friary at Frankfurt in 1511/12, the first printer in the city was Christian Egenolph who arrived from Strasbourg in December 1530, to remain until his death in 1555.[1] This was three quarters of a century after the earliest printing at nearby Mainz, and in the meantime printing had established itself in many major German cities and abroad, beginning with Bamberg (*c.*1459), Strasbourg (1459/60), Cologne (1464/5), Rome (1467), Augsburg (1468), Venice (1469), Basle (1468/70), Nuremberg (1470), Paris (1476) — and even distant London. Only after Egenolph established the first long-term printing shop in Frankfurt did others recognize its favourable position; it then eclipsed the previous centres of the German book trade like Augsburg, Nuremberg, Basle, Strasbourg and (since the 1520s) Wittenberg in importance. Frankfurt really came into its own as a printing and publishing centre only in the second half of the sixteenth century, and already soon after 1600 it was overtaken by Leipzig. Among the men who made Frankfurt what it was were, besides Egenolph, Peter Braubach, Hermann Gülfferich, the publisher Sigmund Feyerabend and a bevy of printers associated with him, and André Wechel, a refugee from France following the 1572 St Bartholomew's Day massacre.[2]

Although, like most German cities, Frankfurt was a small place, with 15,000 inhabitants in 1475, it had long been an important town. The medieval kings and emperors, who had no fixed capital, are known to have

2 FAIRS, MARKETS AND THE ITINERANT BOOK TRADE

visited it some 300 times before 1378, and right down until 1806 it was here that the election of the emperor generally took place, and from 1563 onwards he was crowned here, too. In 1372 it had become an imperial free city, owing allegiance directly to the emperor and with the right to levy its own taxes and make its own laws. Its convenient location enabled it to become a centre of trade at an early date. A market is attested already in the eighth century. A privilege was granted for an autumn fair in 1240, though its origins probably go back even to the twelfth century, and a charter for a spring fair was granted by Emperor Ludwig IV (Ludwig der Bayer) in 1330. Frankfurt's chief asset was its location in the centre of Germany, almost equidistant from Lübeck, Venice, Vienna, Lyon, Paris, Antwerp and Amsterdam; no wonder, then, that merchants preferred to meet on the banks of the Main, rather than travel in person all the way to the extremities of Europe. Frankfurt lay on major trade routes linking Lüneburg, Hamburg and Lübeck, with Scandinavia and the Baltic beyond, with Nuremberg and Prague in the east, Regensburg and Vienna on the Danube, and Augsburg, Venice and Italy in the south. Nevertheless, road transport was difficult and slow — five miles a day is said to have been average for a heavy wagon, and even sending a letter by messenger took many days: it counted as exceptionally fast for a letter to take only nine days from Frankfurt to Lübeck, and three weeks would have been more usual.[3] Crucial to Frankfurt's commercial importance was its favourable position on the chief waterways, close to where the River Main joins the Rhine. On the Main lie the ecclesiastical centres of Bamberg and Würzburg and the small imperial free city of Schweinfurt. The Rhine links Basle, Strasbourg, Worms, Mainz, Cologne and the Netherlands, and affords access to the North Sea. Water transport was ideal for heavy barrels of books. Christopher Plantin, for instance, would send his books by wagon from Antwerp to Cologne, where his colleague Maternus Cholinus would arrange onward transport up the Rhine to Frankfurt.[4] On arrival at the Main quayside they could be rolled to the nearby Buchgasse or Büchergasse ('Book Lane') (Fig. 1), a name first attested in 1518, between the river bank, the city walls and the church of St. Leonhard.[5] (Fig. 2)

Yet, for all its convenience, transport on water was still difficult and hazardous and hampered by restrictive practices which would only be abolished through the efforts of Napoleon and Prussia in the nineteenth century. In the early modern period Germany was not the unified country it is today. The Holy Roman Empire comprised a multitude of small

THE FRANKFURT FAIR IN THE EARLY MODERN PERIOD 3

Buchgasse

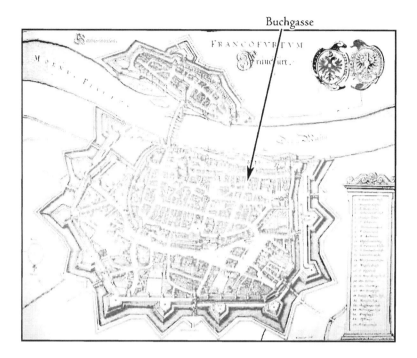

Fig. 1. Map of Frankfurt by Matthaeus Merian (1646?), showing the location of the Buchgasse. From *Topographia Hassiae et regionum vicinarum ...*, 2nd edn, Frankfurt am Main, 1655

states: merely travelling from Bamberg to Frankfurt involved passing through nine separate territories, and on the stretch from Miltenberg to Frankfurt it was obligatory to use Miltenberg boats.[6] On the Rhine, tolls were exacted at 31 points between Basle and Cologne.[7] Going overland from Nuremberg to Frankfurt, a couple of hours by train today, took six days, involved passing through six separate territories, required four changes of escort,[8] while tolls and levies were exacted at every border, the amount charged often being set arbitrarily. On average it seems that the cost of transporting goods from Nuremberg to Frankfurt added a quarter to the price of the goods themselves.

4 FAIRS, MARKETS AND THE ITINERANT BOOK TRADE

The Frankfurt fair was only one of many. Towns large and small throughout Europe held fairs on a regular basis.[9] They would develop at places where trade routes intersected, where goods had to be loaded on to or off ships, and at places where rivers were crossed by bridges.[10] Leipzig, where the fair can be traced back to 1268, lay on the intersection of two major trade routes, the so-called *Via Regia* from Frankfurt via Erfurt to Leipzig and on to Breslau and Poland, and the *Via Imperii*, leading from Venice, Verona, across the Brenner to Innsbruck, Augsburg, Nuremberg, Leipzig, Wittenberg, and on to the Hanseatic cities of Lübeck and Hamburg and beyond to Scandinavia. The Leipzig fair became even more important as German expansion eastwards continued in the later Middle Ages. Although itinerant traders could theoretically turn up anywhere at any time, it was in the interests of purveyors of bulky or heavy goods to go where people congregated. We need to remember that places we think of as major European cities today were, by our standards, very small in the early modern period: even Vienna's population was only about 20,000 in 1500. Merchants' travel plans were largely dictated by the dates of the fairs. At Vienna there were two major fairs: at Ascensiontide and around St Katharine's Day (25 November), each lasting for two weeks before and two weeks after the religious festival itself. At Krems they had the St James's Fair on 25 July and the Sts Simon and Jude Fair on 28 October.[11] At Linz, where the fairs can be traced back to the thirteenth century, there was the Easter Fair, lasting two weeks, and the St Bartholomew's Fair which lasted for four weeks around 24 August.[12] At Leipzig the Spring Fair started on the third Sunday after Easter (*Jubilate* Sunday) and ran for a week until *Cantate* Sunday, while the Michaelmas Fair began on the Sunday after Michaelmas (29 September) and ended the following Sunday.[13] At Friedberg in Hessen (20 miles north of Frankfurt) there were two fairs, each lasting a fortnight, one starting on St Walpurgis' Day, 1 May, and the Michaelmas fair beginning on 29 September. As for Frankfurt itself, the dates of the Lenten (Easter, Spring) Fair varied considerably over time, and precise details are now hard to determine. From 1366 it lasted two weeks, from *Oculi* (the fourth Sunday before Easter) until *Judica* (Passion Sunday, the second Sunday before Easter); the fair proved such a success that from 1384 to 1394 it was extended to almost four weeks, from *Oculi* until the end of Holy Week, much to the wrath of the ecclesiastical authorities; in 1399 it was agreed that, as from 1400, it should run from *Oculi* to the Friday before Palm Sunday, thus lasting just under three weeks. However,

THE FRANKFURT FAIR IN THE EARLY MODERN PERIOD 5

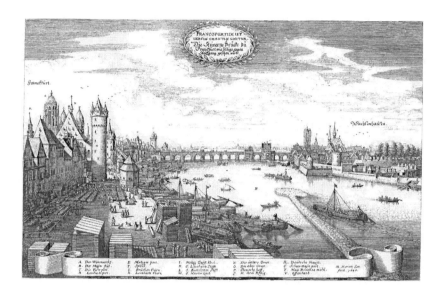

Fig. 2. The Main Quay (Mainkai), Frankfurt am Main, drawn by Matthaeus Merian the Elder in 1646, from *Topographia Hassiae et regionum vicinarum* ..., 2nd edn, Frankfurt am Main, 1655. The legend implies that the barrels in the foreground are wine barrels.

in practice merchants often did not, or could not, adhere to the official dates: much depended on whether Easter was early or late and on what travel conditions were like — ice on the rivers and flooding often affected transport arrangements, and much confusion resulted. In 1502, for example, the fair began in Holy Week (when it should have ended) and ran for two weeks after Easter. In the seventeenth century it generally ran from *Judica* (Passion Sunday) to Easter Tuesday.[14] From 1710 it commenced on the first Sunday after Easter, not least because the weather was generally better then, but this had the consequence of forcing traders to choose between Frankfurt and Leipzig; Frankfurt soon realized its mistake, and in 1726 an imperial edict decreed that the Frankfurt fair should begin on Easter Tuesday — but it was too late: the fairs still overlapped and Leipzig had already gained the upper hand.[15] The Frankfurt Autumn Fair was originally held around the time of the feast of the Assumption (15 August), then was moved to the period 24 August–8 September, but in

6 FAIRS, MARKETS AND THE ITINERANT BOOK TRADE

1349 it was decreed that it should run from 15 August to 8 September, then from 15 August to 22 September, but from 1394 it was determined that it should end a week after the Nativity of the Virgin (8 September), thus on 15 September. In the late sixteenth century the Autumn fair, lasting three weeks, always began on a Monday between 6 and 12 September; the precise date depending on what day of the week the Nativity of the Virgin was celebrated: if this fell on Monday, Tuesday or Wednesday, the fair began on the Monday falling between 6 and 8 September; if it fell on Thursday, Friday, Saturday or Sunday, it would begin on the Monday falling between 9 and 12 September.[16]

The fairs were obviously hectic places, and seeing that they tended to follow one another in different places in quick succession there were inevitably sometimes mishaps. The inexorable calendar of events meant that printers would be under pressure to have a book ready for a certain deadline. After all, the fairs provided almost the only possibility for publishers to sell books in large quantities, particularly to other book dealers. To cite one example: the Zurich publisher Christoph Froschauer took 2,000 copies of his folio and octavo editions of Joachim von Watt's *Epitome trium terrae partium* to the Frankfurt fair in 1534 and managed to sell half of them.[17] Obviously, therefore, it was vital to have one's books ready in time. If you missed one Frankfurt fair you had to wait six months for the next. A good instance of the importance of keeping to the schedule is furnished by Johann Schönsperger the Younger, who entered into an agreement with the Augsburg parchment-maker, paper merchant and publisher Peter Aprell to bring out an edition of 1,000 New Testaments on paper with six copies on vellum for Frederick the Wise, Elector of Saxony. However, according to Schönsperger, Aprell let him down badly: not only was he not able to supply sufficient vellum of a suitable quality, which meant that he incurred the wrath of the Elector, but the printing of the thousand copies on paper was delayed, too, so that he missed the deadline for the Frankfurt fair and lost money thereby.[18] Many contemporary books show evidence of the pressure under which printers and publishers were working. For instance, the corrector of Jacob Wimpheling's *Epitome rerum Germanicarum*, Strasbourg: J. Prüss, 11 March 1505, apologises for any errors by saying that they had been forced to print the work quickly because of the imminent Frankfurt fair: *Coacti sumus ob imminentes nundinas Francofurdenses intra brevissimum tempus id opus formis excudere.*[19] And we know that when Luther's New Testament translation was being printed in the summer of 1522, extreme measures had to be taken by the printer Melchior Lotter at Wittenberg to ensure it was ready for the Leipzig Michaelmas fair. Another rush job is reported by Euricius Cordus, Professor of Medicine at Marburg, who compiled a treatise on the English Sweating Sickness, a terrible epidemic ravaging Germany in the summer of 1529: writing on Thursday, 2 September that year, he says his Marburg printer was anxious to get his book to Frankfurt, about 100 km away, for the fair that began on 6 September; the book was printed on Saturday, 4 September.[20] In 1557 we find a Leipzig bookseller having to defend himself before the authorities for selling an objectionable political pamphlet, offering the plausible excuse that he and his colleagues had not actually read the book while they were in Frankfurt because the fair was so hectic; they had merely glanced at the title, purchased a few copies and packed them up and sent them to Leipzig for resale, not realizing what the contents of the books were until they unpacked them again.[21] Another kind of pressure resulting from the fair is exemplified by the Augsburg book-seller Georg Willer. In October 1559 he was in prison because of his involvement with sectarian printers. His wife pressed for his release on the grounds that the books he had bought in Frankfurt were expected immi-nently and, if they were impounded, not only would Willer himself suffer because he would be unable to supply his customers, who were already waiting for them, but the books themselves would be useless because, being calendars, practical handbooks and the like, they had a short shelf-life and would soon be obsolete.[22]

Given the difficulties and hazards of travel it was not possible for every merchant to attend every fair in person. Some might make a point of attending a particular fair, at Frankfurt, for example, on a regular basis, or at least ensure that they were represented — Plantin, for instance, would send his son-in-law Moretus. Or they might concentrate on the fairs in a particular area — booksellers from southern Germany in particular regularly visited fairs at the towns on the Danube, with Linz proving an important venue for booksellers from Poland, Germany and Italy.[23] Another Austrian venue was Hall in Tirol, on the north/south trade route, where a fair was established in 1356 and which in the sixteenth century became an important outlet for south German booksellers.[24] This doubtless explains why this area was targeted for an inquiry into what kind of books were owned by the local population by the commission instituted by Arch-duke Ferdinand of Tyrol in 1569, as they were suspected of possessing

8 FAIRS, MARKETS AND THE ITINERANT BOOK TRADE

many Protestant books.[25] As an alternative to visiting the fairs in person a merchant might employ the services of an agent living locally or indeed he might choose to have himself represented at the fair by an agent not himself resident in the fair town. The Lyon printer Sebastian Gryphius, for instance, marketed his books at Frankfurt through the Basle printer Andreas Cratander: nearly all of Gryphius's books of scholarly interest, more than 140 titles, are listed in Cratander's 1539 catalogue of the books available through his Frankfurt depot.[26] Later, Plantin, too, would represent other publishers on a commission basis, their goods being held on sale or return.

There was rivalry between the fairs, and regulation became necessary, for the establishment of a fair in one place could have a serious impact elsewhere. Thus the development of the Leipzig fairs resulted in the banning of smaller fairs in the bishoprics of Magdeburg, Halberstadt, Meissen, Merseburg and Naumburg, as confirmed by Pope Leo X in 1514. As early as 1469 Emperor Frederick III banned the New Year's Fair at Halle since it rivalled the New Year's Fair at Leipzig whose charter he had confirmed in 1466.[27] And in 1488 the Leipzig Council stripped Leipzig merchants of their citizenship who maintained outlying branches at Halle and Naumburg.[28] In 1497 Emperor Maximilian I granted the Leipzig fairs the status of imperial fairs, which meant that towns within a radius of fifteen German miles (about 70 English miles) were forbidden to hold rival markets. At a later date, in 1675, Duke Rudolf August of Lüneburg and Braunschweig petitioned Emperor Leopold I to allow Braunschweig to hold two fairs like Frankfurt and Leipzig; both these cities protested vehemently.[29]

*

Over time the Frankfurt fair's European importance grew to such an extent that Henri Estienne II (1528/31–1598) eulogized it in his *Francofordiense emporium* (1574) as 'Omnium totius orbis emporiorum compendium', 'the sum of all the fairs of the whole world'.[30] His account tells how all kinds of goods were traded there. Augsburg sent cloth, Ulm linen, Nuremberg's craftsmen their metal-ware. Wine and clothing came from the Rhine area, dried fish, horses, hops and furs came from the north, glass from Bohemia, ironware from Styria, silver and pewter from Saxony, copper from Thuringia. Estienne describes it as 'a veritable workshop of war', so many and varied were the weapons on display. Then there were vast numbers of fine horses for sale, and he enthuses about the succulent

THE FRANKFURT FAIR IN THE EARLY MODERN PERIOD   9

Fig. 3. The fair in the late seventeenth century, from *Warhaffter und eigentlicher Schau-Platz der weitberühmten Franckfurter Mess*, n.pl., 1696. The picture shows the area in front of the Römer, the fourteenth-century city hall.

10   FAIRS, MARKETS AND THE ITINERANT BOOK TRADE

Westphalian hams, sufficient to feed an army on. Then there were luxury goods: spices, clothing, items of gold, silver and bronze, iron kitchen equipment, *objets d'art*, Dutch paintings, pottery, fine vases and painted earthenware. Only then does he come to what he calls the second fair, the book fair, which he calls an 'Academy of the Muses', for the Muses assemble their printers and booksellers there and order them to bring with them the books of the poets, the orators, the historians and the philosophers, not only of Greece and Italy, but of every land the Muses have touched. For Estienne Frankfurt had become what Athens had once been, and this idea is reflected in a German poem published in 1596 in which the author, Konrad Lautenbach, marvels at the wide range of scholars of all lands and disciplines who patronized the fair:

> Hie findst Geistliche und Juristen,
> Medicos und Alchymisten:
> Berümbte gewaltige Doctores
> Vornehmer Schulen Professores;
> Von Marpurg, Leipzig, Wittemberg,
> Tübing, Basel, Heidelberg.
> Wie auch von Löwen in Holland
> Ochsenfurt in Engelland
> Padua in Italien,
> Und von Cantabrigien.
> Also auch von Geneve, deßgleich
> Von Parise auss Franckreich.[31]

Here you'll find clerics and lawyers, medics and alchemists, famous authoritative doctors, the professors of distinguished academies, at Marburg, Leipzig, Wittenberg, Tübingen, Basle, Heidelberg, as well as Louvain in Flanders, Oxford in England, Padua in Italy, and Cambridge, from Geneva, too, and Paris in France.

The book fair had developed out of a general trade fair. Evidently manuscripts were sold there in the fourteenth century, for Gerhard Groote (1340–84), founder of the Brothers of the Common Life, is already reported to have preferred to buy his books at Frankfurt.[32] Printed books were being sold at the Frankfurt fair certainly by 1462. Indeed, it is worth recalling that the earliest reference we have to Gutenberg's 42-line Bible relates to Frankfurt around the time of the autumn fair 1454. In a letter of 12 March 1455 to the Spanish Cardinal Juan de Carvajal, the humanist Enea Silvio Piccolomini, the later Pope Pius II but at the time secretary to the Holy Roman Emperor Frederick III, reported that while he had been attending the Imperial Diet at Frankfurt in October 1454 — he is known to have been there from 5 to 31 October — he had seen samples of a printed Bible 'that could be read without glasses', produced for inspection by 'a marvellous man'. Whether this was Gutenberg himself or, perhaps more likely, his associate Peter Schöffer, we do not know, and although these samples were more probably displayed in the context of the Imperial Diet rather than at the trade fair, it is intriguing, even significant, that they were exhibited at Frankfurt during or very close to the period of the fair.[33]

The fair seems quickly to have established itself as something members of the book trade from near and far should attend. Thus we know that the Basle printers Johann Amerbach and Michael Wenssler were at the fair in 1478.[34] It attracted not only booksellers, but paper merchants, type-founders, bookbinders, and printers hoping to dispose of some of their products through an agent. Also there would be many scholars wanting to relieve themselves of their stock of complimentary copies of their own works in exchange for other books, and authors touting manuscripts, promising potential publishers large sales and profits in this life and a heavenly reward in the next. A measure of the growing trade is that already on 24 March 1485 Berthold von Henneberg, Archbishop of Mainz, demanded of the Frankfurt council that it should examine the books offered for sale at the Lenten fair.[35] Already in 1488 printer-publishers accounted for one-twelfth of the rental income for stalls at the fair.[36] Perhaps the earliest reference we have to the Frankfurt fair and the trade with England is in a letter written in London on 8 August 1495 by Andreas Ruwe, probably a Cologne merchant who describes himself as a German bookdealer, to Johann Amerbach (from Basle) at Frankfurt at St Leonhard's at the sign of the swan. He asked Amerbach to supply 50 copies each of Augustine, *Super Johannem*,[37] *De civitate Dei*[38] and *De Trinitate*,[39] Robert Holkot's *Super librum sapientiae*,[40] the works of St Ambrose,[41] and St Bernard's *Liber meditationum*,[42] plus various other books.[43] But it seems to have been the presence of Italian humanist pub-lishers from the late fifteenth century onwards that made the German scholarly world aware of the fair.[44] The first Venetian printers appeared at the fair in 1497.[45]

Frankfurt provided the necessary conditions for the development of trade. The city authorities supported the development of commerce. They controlled prices charged for food and lodging, tolls on the movement of

12   FAIRS, MARKETS AND THE ITINERANT BOOK TRADE

goods were light, and trading was generally relatively free of restrictions, while safety was, if not guaranteed, then at least reasonably assured, merchants coming to and leaving the city being provided with armed escorts. Robbers and highwaymen were generally not particularly interested in books,[46] though this did not mean that consignments of books were safe. Thus Anton Koberger reported to Johann Amerbach on 9 July 1506:

I am sorry to say that when the carrier came via Wimpfen, he was waylaid. The robbers led the carrier together with the wagon off the road into a wood where they broke into the barrels and looked for money. Later it rained and half the books in the three barrels were drenched and damaged. There went my profit.[47]

The opening of the fair was announced by the ringing of the church bells, the imperial flag was flown from the towers, and shields bearing the city arms were hung from the gates for the duration of the fair. A particular feature was that there was a special court to deal expeditiously with disputes between merchants; Henri Estienne was effusive in his praise for the court's impartiality.[48] The second week of the Frankfurt fair was the week when merchants settled up (in so far as they did in cash[49]) with one another, not only finalizing business concluded at Frankfurt itself but settling their accounts for transactions agreed elsewhere. Merchants from Italy, Basle, Augsburg and Nuremberg would meet here with merchants from the Hanseatic cities in the north. The custom developed for them to give credit from fair to fair, that is, on a six-monthly basis, accounts being reckoned in Rhenish Goldgulden (gold florins), but customers with large accounts and in good standing would sometimes be given a year's credit. Late medieval merchants were not usually in a position to pay cash on the spot, so credit and trust were important. The use of letters of credit, promissory notes and bills of exchange enabled them to operate without openly transgressing religious sanctions against usury, and payments would be made through a network of business contacts, friends and mutual acquaintances. Sellers and buyers would agree a time when payment would be made. Indeed Frankfurt was the principal place for completing financial transactions.[50] Only later did the fair at Lyon become another alternative.[51] But there were still many uncertainties and difficulties, as is evident from a letter written by Anton Koberger to Johann Amerbach on 1 March 1500:

There is no need to write much except that I'm afraid that I cannot come to Frankfurt for I do not want to put myself in such danger and I am also sure that no reliable and trustworthy person from here [Nuremberg] will come through with whom I can make arrangements or payment to you at Frankfurt. Therefore I am sending you this special messenger to inform you in good faith that you should not come to this Lenten fair at Frankfurt for my sake, for I cannot make payment to you; but I will arrange for the 1000 Rhenish florins due you and Master Hans to be paid at the Lyons Easter fair that takes place a little after the Frankfurt fair through my cousin Hans Koberger, and I hope and trust that you are not annoyed about it for I assume that it will not cause you or Master Hans any loss. You may bring the money more safely from Lyons to Basle than from Frankfurt to Basle [...].[52]

On 20 July 1504 Koberger wrote to Amerbach expressing the fear that, because of military conflicts in the area, the Frankfurt Autumn fair might even be cancelled and that a large sum of money he had expected to receive after the Easter fair at Lyon would have to remain there until the August fair since no one was willing to transport the money to Nuremberg because of the war.[53] Paying money at a distance was a complex and hazardous affair. Thus Andreas Ruwe, writing from London to Johann Amerbach on 8 August 1495, said,

I have already sent you three letters to inform you that you would receive the money you lent me via two merchants of Cologne. As I understand it, they have cheated both of us. Now I am appointing yet a third merchant from Cologne, Hermann Blitterswich. If I am not mistaken, he or one of his agents will pay you in my name and I will no longer be in arrears.[54]

Booksellers could take only part of their stock with them, so often they would leave supplies in the hands of agents or in storage from one fair to the next.[55] Anton Koberger of Nuremberg in 1506 established a warehouse at Frankfurt at which he could leave his stock, and later Christopher Plantin similarly had a warehouse there, where after the Lenten fair 1579, for instance, he held 11,617 books, representing some 240 different titles.[56] Although the focus of the book trade in Frankfurt was around the Buchgasse and St Leonhard's church very few precise addresses seem to be known. Johann Amerbach, from Basle, had his Frankfurt depot at the sign of the swan, and Jorg Aschenburger, attested from 1500 to 1513, had his at the house Alte Burg near St Leonhard's.[57] Hans Scherpf, a Frankfurt resident, was the official representative of the Venetian printer Bernardinus Stagninus (Stanquino) from 1505 to 1508; Stagninus often came to the fair in person and stored his books at the house Rustenberg (Rüstenberg).[58] In 1518 Thomas Anshelm from Haguenau (near Strasbourg) had his store in 'Her Brünnen Hauß bey sant Lienhart'.[59] In the mid-1520s Hans Moreller had a house in the Gelnhäuser Gasse where he represented the

14 FAIRS, MARKETS AND THE ITINERANT BOOK TRADE

interests of his father-in-law, the Strasbourg printer Hans Knobloch.[60] These storage depots are described as vaults. We can imagine that the title-pages of the latest publications and poster-style catalogues were affixed to the outer doors and windows to attract customers to come inside to examine the wares. Books which might be suspect to the authorities would probably be hidden in dark corners or on high shelves, away from prying eyes. Only the merchants themselves would know what books they had in their stores at any one time.

These depots might sometimes develop into outlying branches of a major firm. Thus the Augsburg printer Johann Schönsperger the Younger not only established a branch of his business at Zwickau in 1523 but also had depots in Nuremberg, Frankfurt, Linz, Vienna and Speyer. The bookseller and publisher Paul Brachfeld, originally from Antwerp, who maintained branches of his business at Frankfurt am Main, Leipzig and Frankfurt an der Oder, mentions in the prefaces to his own catalogues (produced from 1595 to 1598) that in Frankfurt am Main he had a shop that was open throughout the year, not just at fair times.[61] The Strasbourg bookseller Lazarus Zetzner (*fl.* 1585–1616) also had shops in Cologne and Frankfurt: Frankfurt was a Lutheran city, Cologne was Catholic, so Zetzner was clearly trying to have the best of both worlds (a safe Cologne imprint could help facilitate sales in Italy). A catalogue of the books he offered in his Frankfurt shop in 1606 survives in the form of a broadside poster, headed *Catalogus Librorum Francofurti in Taberna Lazari Zetzneri Bibliopolae Argentinensis publice prostantium, anno millesimo sexcentesimo sexto.*[62] It lists some 122 books, arranged alphabetically, with formats but no dates or prices.

*

This brings us to the question of the fair catalogues. The book trade was centuries ahead of any other trade in issuing catalogues of its wares. Lists of books issued by individual printer-publishers are known from the late 1460s, and by the early sixteenth century it became increasingly necessary for publishers to issue catalogues of their stock. These would be distributed by the publishers or agents at the fairs, much as happens today, but in due course a general catalogue listing the new books on sale at the fairs became desirable. These comprehensive fair catalogues were in effect the forerunners of national bibliographies; indeed, as recently as 1931 the *Deutsche Nationalbibliographie* superseded what had originally been the Leipzig fair catalogues.

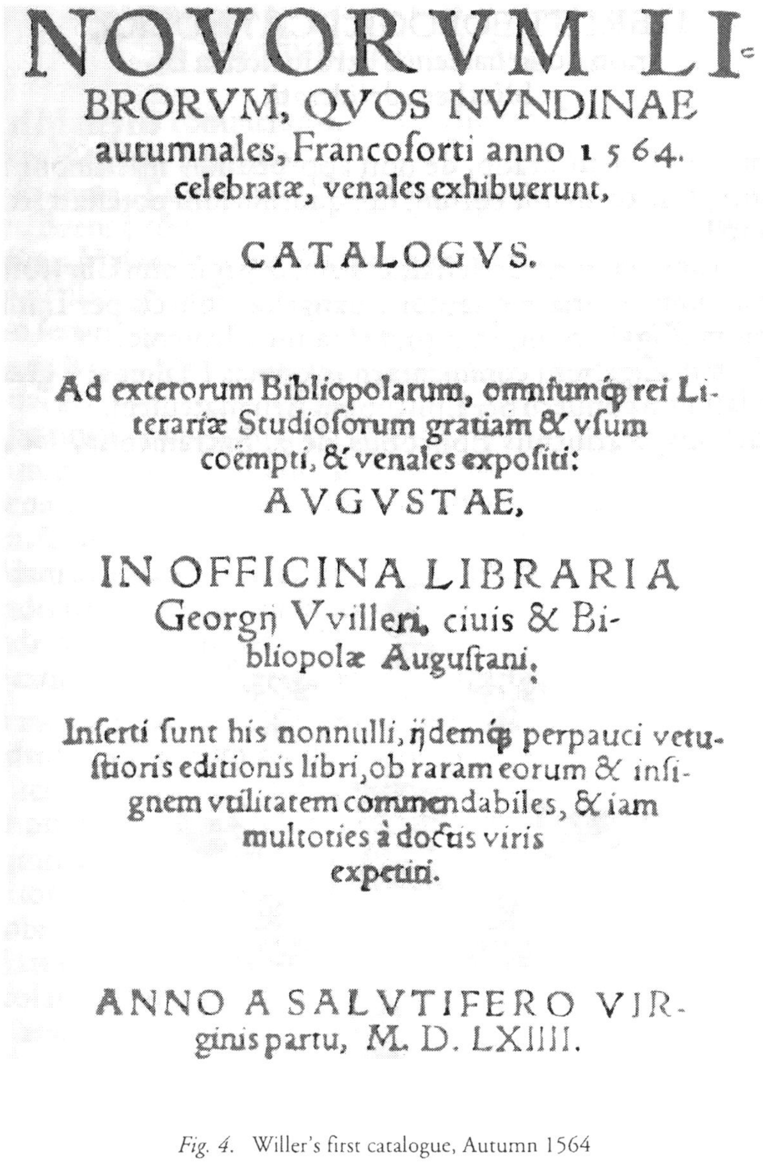

THE FRANKFURT FAIR IN THE EARLY MODERN PERIOD   15

NOVORVM LI=
BRORVM, QVOS NVNDINAE
autumnales, Francoforti anno 1 5 64.
celebratæ, venales exhibuerunt,

CATALOGVS.

Ad exterorum Bibliopolarum, omniumꝗ rei Li-
terariæ Studioforum gratiam & vfum
coëmpti, & venales expofiti:
AVGVSTAE,

IN OFFICINA LIBRARIA
Georgꝯ Vvilleri, ciuis & Bibliopolæ Auguftani,

Inferti funt his nonnulli, ꝗdemꝗ perpauci vetu-
ftioris editionis libri, ob raram eorum & infi-
gnem vtilitatem commendabiles, & iam
multoties à doctis viris
expetiti.

ANNO A SALVTIFERO VIR-
ginis partu, M. D. LXIIII.

Fig. 4. Willer's first catalogue, Autumn 1564

16 FAIRS, MARKETS AND THE ITINERANT BOOK TRADE

The initiative for bringing out a general listing came from the Augsburg bookseller Georg Willer (active from 1548 to 1593) who produced the first such catalogue in the autumn of 1564; thereafter it appeared twice yearly. Surviving copies have been reproduced in facsimile by Bernhard Fabian.[63] Willer's first catalogue, *Novorum librorum, quos nundinae autumnales Francofurti anno 1564 celebratae venales exhiberunt, catalogus* (Fig. 4), was a small quarto of 22 pages listing 252 books classified by subject (basically following the order of precedence of university faculties: theology, law, medicine, the liberal arts), as follows:

Catholic theology 'not new but hitherto in demand in our bookshop'[64]
Protestant theology in Latin
Catholic theology in Latin
Civil and canon law [in Latin]
Medicine in Latin and Greek
Sacred and secular history in Latin
Philosophy [including dialectic, rhetoric, grammar]
Poetry [in Latin]
Astrology and mathematics [in Latin]
German books on the Scriptures and Protestant theologians
German books on Catholic theology
German books on the law and on writing [i.e. drawing up legal documents]
German books on medicine
German books on history
Miscellaneous German books [these include titles such as *Reynicke Fuchs* and Brant's *Narrenschiff*, a book of pictures from the Bible, and books on mathematics and geometry]

With only minor modifications such as the addition of a section on music books already in the Spring 1565 catalogue and a separate section for Calvinist and Zwinglian theology in 1576, this arrangement continued throughout the sixteenth century and beyond.[65] Another section of interest is the long list of maps from Venice in the Autumn 1573 catalogue. With regard to law books, the remarks of a contemporary are worth noting. When in 1580 the Frankfurt patrician Nikolaus Rucker edited a volume of legal opinions by the Italian lawyer Johannes Baptista Zilettus, he observed in the preface that such books, especially from Italy, were in such demand that at recent Frankfurt fairs nearly 200 publications of this type had been on offer.[66]

CATALOGVS NOVVS,

EX NVNDINIS

QVADRAGESIMALIBVS FRANCO.
FVRTI AD MOENVM ANNO M. D. LXXIII.
celebratis. Eorum nempe librorum, qui poft nundinas Autumnales
proximè elapfas ad has vfque partim omnino noui, partim de-
nuo vel forma, vel loco à prioribus editionibus diuerfi,
vel accefsione aliqua locupleriores in lu-
cem prodierunt.

QVIBVS ADIECTI SVNT PAVCI
QVIDAM VETVSTIORES, QVOS TAMEN
Bibliotheca VVilleriana hactenus non vidit. Annum
imprefsionis numerus fingulis præpofitus
demonftrat.

Veneunt Augustæ in ædibus Georgij VVilleri, ciuis
& Bibliopolæ Augustani.

Verzeichnus der Newen Bücher / welche
feidher der nechftuerfchienen Herbftmeß/fo viel mir
bewußt/in offentlichen Truck außgangen/ vnd zu
Franckfurt diefe Faftenmeß mehrer theils
feil gehabt worden findt.

Getruckt zu Franckfurt am Main / bey
Peter Schmidt.

Anno M. D. LXXIII.

Fig. 5. Willer's Easter 1573 catalogue

18   FAIRS, MARKETS AND THE ITINERANT BOOK TRADE

Willer stressed the fact that most of the books he listed were available in his shop at Augsburg. Initially he listed only the titles of German and foreign books which he had bought in Frankfurt for reselling, but from 1573 (Fig. 5) he included books that he knew only from information supplied by publishers or dealers. To ensure that the catalogues were as up-to-date as possible, from 1567 he had them printed at Frankfurt,[67] apparently so that he could sell copies at the fair itself and thus attract customers who would be unlikely to order books from him at Augsburg afterwards. His earliest catalogues did not include publishers' names, but from Autumn 1568 just over half the entries include this detail, fairly regularly but by no means consistently. Otherwise, however, no information is given — no date, no pagination, no price. Only from Autumn 1567 was the date of publication helpfully given in the margin so that one could see at a glance which were the latest books.[68] Figure 6 shows a page from Willer's 1592 catalogue with the year and place of publication,[69] publisher and format all clearly set out, with Latin titles in roman and German ones in gothic.[70] No prices were given because a fixed book price did not yet exist. Amongst themselves booksellers would agree special rates, the so-called Frankfurt *Tax* ('Frankfurt rate'), whereby in the case of books smaller than folio the price would be set according to the number of sheets involved. As booksellers would have to explain to their customers, these prices were not retail prices but a kind of net price to which transport, packing, customs and other charges had to be added; costs could depend on the number of copies purchased, the distance they had to be transported, and even the state and safety of the trade route along which they had to pass.[71]

That catalogues such as Willer's really were needed is shown by the fact that he soon had his rivals. In 1577 a similar catalogue was issued by another Augsburg firm, Johann Georg Portenbach and Thibaus (Tobias) Lutz, and continued by them and their successors until 1616.[72] By the 1590s there were others, too.[73] This situation prompted the Frankfurt Council on 10 August 1598 to ban the publication of private fair catalogues and to institute its own official one,[74] a sensible precaution given the existence of the Catholic-orientated Imperial Book Commission (established in 1569 to prevent the circulation of seditious and defamatory material). Frankfurt had been officially Lutheran since 1535.[75] The institution of an official catalogue enabled the Council not only to demonstrate to the Emperor that it was being vigilant but helped it to enforce stricter control of the trade, keep a check on the observance of printers' privileges

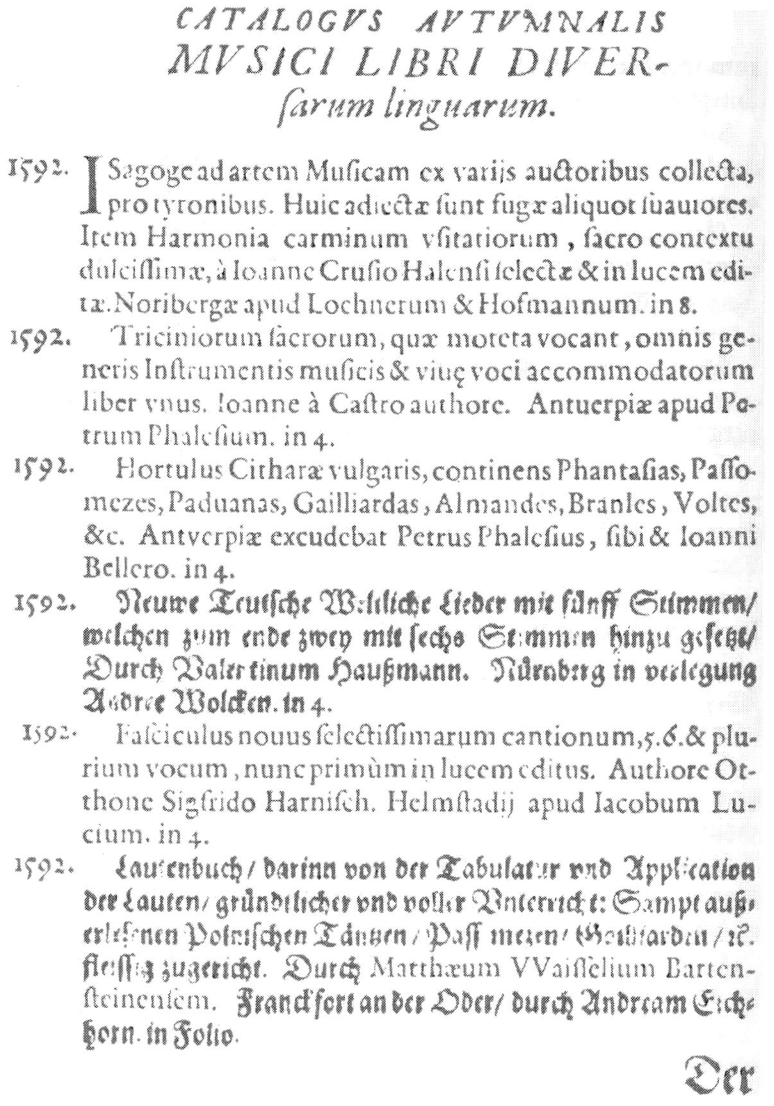

CATALOGVS AVTVMNALIS
MVSICI LIBRI DIVER-
sarum linguarum.

1592.   Isagoge ad artem Muficam ex varijs auctoribus collecta, pro tyronibus. Huic adiectæ funt fugæ aliquot fuauiores. Item Harmonia carminum vfitatiorum , facro contextu dulciffimæ, à Ioanne Crufio Halenfi felectæ & in lucem editæ. Noribergæ apud Lochnerum & Hofmannum. in 8.

1592.   Triciniorum facrorum, quæ moteta vocant, omnis generis Inftrumentis muficis & viuç voci accommodatorum liber vnus. Ioanne à Caftro authore. Antuerpiæ apud Petrum Phalefium. in 4.

1592.   Hortulus Citharæ vulgaris, continens Phantafias, Paffomezes, Paduanas, Gailliardas, Almandes, Branles, Voltes, &c. Antuerpiæ excudebat Petrus Phalefius, fibi & Ioanni Bellero. in 4.

1592.   Neuwe Teutfche Weltliche Lieder mit fünff Stimmen/ welchen zum ende zwey mit fechs Stimmen hinzu gefetzt/ Durch Valentinum Haußmann. Nürnberg in verlegung Andree Wolcken. in 4.

1592.   Fafciculus nouus felectiffimarum cantionum, 5. 6. & plurium vocum, nunc primùm in lucem editus. Authore Otthone Sigfrido Harnifch. Helmftadij apud Iacobum Lucium. in 4.

1592.   Lautenbuch/ darinn von der Tabulatur vnd Application der Lauten/ gründtlicher vnd voller Vnterricht: Sampt außerlefenen Polnifchen Tänzen/ Paff metzen/ Galliarden/ zc. fleffig zugericht. Durch Matthæum VVaiffelium Bartenfteinenfem. Franckfort an der Oder/ durch Andream Eichhorn. in Folio.

Der

Fig. 6. A page from Willer's Autumn 1592 catalogue

and ensure that the required copies of books were deposited.[76] The Council was concerned not least to ensure confessional objectivity; nevertheless, even the official catalogue was soon the cause of complaint to Emperor Rudolph II: already in 1602 Nikolaus Stein (Stain), a Catholic printer at Frankfurt, sought an imperial privilege to produce a Catholic catalogue because the official one was allegedly biased against Catholicism.[77] The booksellers and publishers were required to register their wares with the authorities:[78] in 1686 (presumably confirming previous practice) it was specified that details had to be submitted between Monday and Wednesday of the first week of the fair, so that the catalogue could be available at the latest on the Monday of the second week. This catalogue appeared — latterly somewhat fitfully — until about 1750. By the mid-seventeenth century the Frankfurt catalogue alone had a print-run of 1,200 copies, costing 1 Gulden for five copies.[79]

At Leipzig, too, a fair catalogue was produced, but whereas Frankfurt would have its official catalogue, in Leipzig it always stayed in private hands.[80] The first Leipzig catalogue was issued by Henning Grosse in 1594 and it remained in the hands of his successors until 1759.[81] From 1598 to 1619 a second catalogue was produced by Abraham Lamberg, and from 1620 Grosse and Lamberg issued the catalogue jointly. Because the Leipzig fairs followed those held at Frankfurt the Leipzig catalogues largely contained the same books as in the Frankfurt ones, though they often included a (sometimes substantial) section of 'books not shown at Frankfurt'. In 1637 the spring books from Frankfurt arrived late in Leipzig, with the result that only one catalogue was produced in Leipzig that year, claiming to cover the spring and autumn books from both centres.[82]

Over time the catalogues changed in character. In the earliest Willer listed the books he could supply *from* the fair; later they listed all the books available *at* the fair. The earlier catalogues included not just new publications but older books too. In the seventeenth and eighteenth centuries, on the other hand, they often included books that had not yet appeared, some of which indeed never appeared. Sometimes titles would change, one instance being that of Joachim von Sandrart, 'the German Vasari's', *Teutsche Academie* (Nuremberg, 1675) which was first announced in the Michaelmas 1672 Leipzig catalogue under the title *Academia Universale della Pittura, Scultura & Architectura: Oder: Gründliche Beschreibung der edlen Mahlerey/Bildhauerey und Baukunst ...*, while in the Frankfurt Autumn 1675 catalogue the same book, now at last available, appears under the title *Teutsche Academie der Edlen Bau- Bild und Mahlerey Künste*.[83] Overall it has to be said that the catalogues have their limitations as reliable sources of information inasmuch as they record only a proportion of the books produced at the time — it is reckoned that only about 20–25 per cent of the books available were actually listed in the catalogues.[84] Primarily they focus on books of scholarly interest, especially in Latin, with a potential for wide geographical dissemination. Hence small works, books of sermons, prayer-books, university theses, calendars and the like scarcely feature. Nevertheless, as long as we remember that the catalogues' purpose was to advertise and to generate interest, not to serve as comprehensive bibliographical aids, they must be considered invaluable and indispensable sources, giving a reasonable picture of the German and international book trade of the early modern period.

As the first regularly appearing current awareness bulletins, these catalogues long remained essential reading for scholars and bibliomanes. Already in 1611 Georg Draud, a Lutheran pastor, attempted comprehensive compilations based on the individual catalogues.[85] The catalogues' importance as sources of bibliographical information is shown by the fact that in July 1615 the curators of the Bodleian Library agreed to meet within a week of the arrival of the Frankfurt fair catalogues to select books, and from 1617 they seem to have used the London bookseller John Bill's own English version of the Frankfurt catalogue which appeared from 1617 to 1628 (STC 11328–11331.2);[86] Bill's lists contained only selections from the latest issue of the Frankfurt catalogue, omitted all books in German, and added some older titles still available in London. In 1685 Jean-Paul de La Roque, editor of the *Journal des savants* in Paris, in welcoming the founding of the German periodical *Acta eruditorum* in 1682, specifically remarks that until then German books had been known in France only through the Frankfurt fair catalogues.[87]

One indication of the centrality of the book fairs in the marketing strategy of German publishers is the fact that many books, irrespective of where they were actually produced, bore the words 'Frankfurt und Leipzig' on their titlepages, a phenomenon which has caused bibliographers and cataloguers much confusion; 'Frankfurt und Leipzig' often meant nothing more than that these were the places where the books were traded, or else was intended to imply something about the quality of the book (rather like our own claim that a particular work is 'available from all good bookshops'); it is possible also that it was intended circumspectly to conceal the true place of printing.[88] As the importance of the Frankfurt fair grew, the more the local book trade benefited. Frankfurt printer-publishers waited for the world to come to them, though doubtless they, too, would arrange to be represented at Leipzig and elsewhere. It is likely that Frankfurt publishers brought out certain titles specifically to catch the biannual fair trade, though as far as I know this aspect has not yet been properly researched. A prime example is the *Historia von D. Johann Fausten*, the first Faust book, which seems to have been quite a sensation at Autumn fair in 1587. This anonymous Lutheran tract, which the printer, Johann Spies, referred to as 'this modest fair ware' (*geringer Meßkram*) in his preface dated Monday, 4 September,[89] was an instant success: at least four unauthorized reprints are known from the same year, Spies himself brought out an expanded version in 1588, and the total number of authorized and unauthorized reprints, adaptations (for instance, a Catholic version and a verse version) and translations the work experienced from 1587 into the 1590s is impressive, to say the least.[90] The English translation, *The Historie of the Damnable Life and Deserved Death of Doctor Iohn Faustus*, made 'according to the true Copie printed at Franckfort' and published in 1592,[91] served as the basis for Christopher Marlowe's *Tragical History of Doctor Faustus*.

Even more interesting perhaps as products specifically brought out in connection with the fair are the so-called *Meßrelationen*. These newsbooks, generally quartos of about a hundred pages, gave a digest of current affairs, mostly political and military events and commercial news but sometimes also sensations, comets and the like. They have sometimes been seen as forerunners of newspapers, but in fact they were very different. Whereas early newspapers appeared weekly and later even more frequently, the *Meßrelationen* were published biannually in connection with the fairs. Nor can they be seen as direct forerunners of the periodical press because whereas the *Meßrelationen* were first issued in the 1580s, the first proper periodicals in Germany date from nearly a century later.[92] Several *Meßrelationen* appeared at Cologne in the 1580s and 90s, one was published at Strasbourg in connection with the fair there in the autumn of 1590, and the first Frankfurt *Historische Relation* appeared for the Lent fair 1591, with others at Magdeburg around 1600. At Leipzig the first came out for the Spring fair 1605 and the last appeared around 1730.[93]

For information as to who attended the Frankfurt fairs we are dependent on such correspondence, account books, and lists that have chanced to survive.[94] We know the names of a few publishers from such places as Mainz and Basle who attended in the fifteenth century, and the rich correspondence relating to Anton Koberger of Nuremberg shows that between autumn 1493 to spring 1509 he visited the fair in person on at least fifteen occasions and was represented by others at least five more times.[95] The prolific publisher Giovanni Battista Ciotti (1560–after 1625) of Venice regularly visited the Frankfurt fair from 1583 onwards. In 1587 he had a book printed there by Johann Wechel. Ciotti books are recorded at Frankfurt in 1594 (3 titles), 1599 (7), 1600 (45), 1601 (40), 1602 (26) and 1605 (3).[96] The London printer and bookseller John Bill, who was active from 1604 until his death in 1630, was a regular annual visitor to the fair. He was an agent for King James I, Sir Thomas Bodley, the 9th Earl of Northumberland and others. Another regular visitor to the Frankfurt fair in the third quarter of the seventeenth century was the Copenhagen bookseller Peter Haubold who also listed 56 titles in the catalogue between 1667 and 1682, missing out only 1679 while his colleague Daniel Paulli announced 117 titles over the same period, missing out only 1674.[97]

A good example of the rare surviving documentation records the Frankfurt publisher Sigmund Feyerabend's sales at the Spring fair 1565. He sold books to a total of 106 booksellers. Sixty-one of these, who accounted for 1403 books, came from southern Germany (i.e. from south of the Main); 36, buying 983 books, came from northern Germany. Three booksellers from Antwerp bought 83 volumes, three from Switzerland 23, two from Paris 17, and one from Venice 57. In addition he sold 69 books to unspecified individuals.[98] A list of all the booksellers and publishers who visited the Autumn fair in 1579 has survived.[99] This records 70 printers and publishers, 30 booksellers, and also names twenty men not actually present at that time but who normally came. Altogether 36 different towns are mentioned.[100] Among the people mentioned are several who did not produce books themselves but were exclusively booksellers. Between 10 and 16 September 1579 these traders were all questioned by three named officials, being required to produce, where applicable, their imperial privileges (the only form of copyright then in force), to show that the copies they were required to deposit with the authorities had in fact been supplied, and to provide lists or catalogues of their books.

That Frankfurt was very much a hub of the book trade is revealed by an analysis of Sigmund Feyerabend's customers in his records for the years 1590–97. There were approximately 350 customers from 110 different

24 FAIRS, MARKETS AND THE ITINERANT BOOK TRADE

places. Of these only 10–15% were individual readers; the overwhelming majority were trade customers. About two thirds of them were from major commercial centres or from university towns. Apart from Frankfurt itself, the towns most strongly represented were Nuremberg and Cologne, then Stuttgart, Strasbourg, Leipzig and Augsburg, followed by Wittenberg, Jena, Leiden, Antwerp, Venice, Magdeburg, Heidelberg, Tübingen, Ulm, Worms, Basle and Schwäbisch Hall; then came Zurich, Braunschweig and Hamburg. Dealers from some of these places will have sold their books on to customers further afield; thus a bookseller from Nuremberg may well have found customers in Bohemia and one from Leipzig customers in Poland. And Georg Willer in Augsburg is known to have covered fairs and markets all over southern Germany down to Lake Constance, Bavaria south of the Danube, Lower and Upper Austria, Styria, Carinthia as far as Lubljana, and the Tyrol down as far as Bozen (Bolzano).[101]

Business at Frankfurt was not necessarily always as lucrative as some might have hoped. Take the case of Casiodoro de Reyna, a Spaniard who in 1567 had advanced 400 Gulden to the famous Basle printer Johann Oporinus to print 1,100 copies of the first Bible in Spanish.[102] Oporinus died deep in debt in 1568, and his private library had to be sold off to satisfy his creditors. This took several years to arrange, but at last in 1574 the whole collection was knocked down for 800 Gulden to Casiodoro de Reyna. Casiodoro had the books sent to Frankfurt where he hoped to get better prices for them than in Basle. However, things were not as easy as he imagined: at the next Frankfurt fair he sold barely 60 Gulden worth, though in the long run things turned out well enough: he found favour as a supplier of books to the court libraries at Heidelberg and Kassel, and in 1575 he had a book published at his own expense in which he described himself as 'Genius Bibliothecae Oporinianae' ('genius of the Oporinian collection').[103]

The growth in importance of the Frankfurt fair was due in part to the general increase in the demand for books. German universities were increasing in number and size;[104] greater prestige and value was attaching to the possession of books; the educational book market was changing; and the cosmopolitan nature of the Latin book trade were all significant factors.[105] But already by the end of the sixteenth century the glory days were past, and a long decline set in. There was a downturn in the number of Latin books advertised after 1630, and the commercial attractiveness of Frankfurt declined after it was besieged by the Swedes under King

Gustavus Adolphus in 1631, when other publishing centres, notably Leipzig and Leiden, began to come to prominence. Commercial greed and sharp practice had their part to play also, but the factors were many.[106] Important firms such as those of Wechel and Zetzner were laid low because the supply of books exceeded demand. Another factor was the institution of the Imperial Book Commission in 1569. In principle the city authorities had been bound by the Archbishop and Elector of Mainz to censor the books on offer at the fair, but they showed themselves so tolerant in such matters that eventually Emperor Maximilian II instituted a commission with the duty during the fair of inspecting the booksellers' stands, examining the privileges and the catalogues, and seeking out objectionable books.[107] The Imperial Commission lay largely in the hands of the Jesuits who made of it a rigorous instrument for furtherance of the Counter-Reformation. Given that Frankfurt at this time had four times as many Protestants as Catholics, the Commission's partisan and arbitrary censorship inevitably led to the decline of the book trade. The difficulties were compounded in 1597 when Emperor Rudolph II appointed two commissioners whose task was to exercise *permanent* oversight over the book trade, not just at fair times. In 1605 this commission was also charged with inspecting books on behalf of papal authority too. The rigorous manner in which the commissioners performed their duties and especially their zeal in rejecting Protestant publications, not to mention their rapacious demand for free copies,[108] contributed not a little to the ruination of the Frankfurt fair, even though the city still retained a leading position in the production and marketing of types and the design and printing of illustrated books. Whereas in 1650 twice as many books were on offer at Frankfurt as at Leipzig, by 1670 the numbers were more or less equal, and by 1700 Frankfurt's share was less than half that of Leipzig.[109] The Venetians and the Dutch had stopped coming, and by 1720 the number of Leipzig firms coming to Frankfurt was down to five, falling later to two. The table on the next page illustrates the decline of the fair as an international event.[110]

Even though the absolute number of titles traded steadily increased between 1564 and the outbreak of the Thirty Years' War (1618) and, after a decline, recovered to some extent after the war, the proportion of foreign books as a percentage of all the books on offer declined inexorably from almost 40 per cent in the 1560s to less than 21 per cent in 1618, less than 12 per cent in 1660, and dwindled to virtually nothing by 1700. Indeed

26   FAIRS, MARKETS AND THE ITINERANT BOOK TRADE

Number of titles listed in the fair catalogues 1564–1709, by decade
(boxed figures relate to the Thirty Years' War period)

	1564–69	1570–79	1580–89	1590–99	1600–09	1610–19	1620–29	1630–39	1640–49	1650–59	1660–69	1670–79	1680–89	1690–99	1700–09
German-speaking countries	1225	2967	4196	5645	10228	12300	9480	5996	7581	7269	7068	7204	7460	9499	11494
France	152	438	464	394	564	918	562	252	75	128	81	40	57	13	2
Italy	381	614	492	536	1082	559	286	34	75	40	16	10	23	6	4
England	0	21	27	10	36	151	77	15	7	27	3	2	33	0	0
Antwerp and southern Low Countries	247	411	349	363	619	781	740	486	522	474	123	6	1	1	12
Amsterdam and northern Low Countries	2	4	48	226	384	798	416	665	826	865	727	326	336	247	22
TOTAL	2007	4455	5576	7174	12913	15507	11561	7448	9086	8803	8018	7588	7910	9766	11534
Foreign imports as percentage of total	*39.0*	*33.4*	*24.7*	*21.3*	*20.8*	*20.7*	*18.0*	*19.5*	*16.6*	*17.4*	*11.8*	*5.1*	*5.7*	*2.7*	*0.3*

THE FRANKFURT FAIR IN THE EARLY MODERN PERIOD   27

Italian books have almost disappeared by 1630 and French books by 1640, while English books barely have a toe-hold at any time, not least because of the high prices charged for them.[111] The only area of significant growth is in books from Amsterdam which increase steadily from about 1590 to 1660. The collapse of supply from the southern Low Countries is linked to the decision by Plantin's heirs and their Antwerp colleagues in 1660 not to attend the fairs, and even though books from Amsterdam and the northern Low Countries continued for a while longer, their numbers dwindled too, especially as Frankfurt declined and the importance of the less internationally oriented Leipzig fair increased around 1700.[112] The effect of the Thirty Years' War on the German book trade is illustrated also by Neddermeyer's statistics of books on history and classics published from 1600 to 1709. Taking the years 1610–19 as = 100, he arrives at the following percentage values.[113]

1600–09	1610–19	1620–29	1630–39	1640–49	1650–59	1660–69	1670–79	1680–89	1690–99	1700–09
86	100	78	40	47	77	95	73	55	97	123

The Thirty Years' War (1618–48) had terrible consequences for Germany. Although Frankfurt itself was at first less affected than some other towns, the fundamental changes that occurred in the social, political, cultural and economic life of Germany in the later seventeenth century had such serious effects on the traditional book trade that the fair inevitably suffered, though the situation at Leipzig seems to have been even worse.[114] The impact of the war is highlighted in the graph on the next page, contrasting the number of titles listed in the fair catalogues with book production in Britain.[115] Although, strictly speaking, we are not comparing like with like (a better comparison would be total book production in Germany rather than the number of titles in the catalogues, but these figures are not available), the graph shows rather dramatically how — decade by decade — the number of titles in the catalogues declined after 1620, reached its low point in the 1630s, and even after the end of the war stagnated for 40 years, whereas by contrast British book production consistently outstripped the fair catalogue figures from the 1630s onwards.

Many dealers, especially foreigners, did not bother to resume their activities in Frankfurt after the Treaty of Westphalia in 1648, the restrictions imposed by the Imperial Book Commission being a serious disincentive. Between 1680 and 1690 publishing at Frankfurt collapsed,

28 FAIRS, MARKETS AND THE ITINERANT BOOK TRADE

and thereafter the centres of book production in Germany were predominantly in the centre and north rather than as previously in the south. In
particular, north German Protestant presses flourished. Leipzig moved
quickly into the forefront of the German book world, and its book fair
outstripped Frankfurt's in importance. Leipzig was favoured by its
accessible position in central Europe, the privileges that the Saxon
government bestowed on the trade fairs and the liberality with which the
city council interpreted them, as well as by the importance of its university,
and above all the business acumen of members of the book trade there.[116] It
was a member of the Leipzig trade, Philipp Erasmus Reich (1717–87), a
partner of the firm of Weidmann (founded in 1682), who in effect put an
end to the Frankfurt fair by closing his Frankfurt warehouse in 1764 and
encouraging others to do the same.[117]

According to Paul Raabe, it was only in 1765 that the number of titles
published in Germany (1,517) reached the level of 1600 again.[118] In the
last quarter of the eighteenth century German book production increased
rapidly: from 1,800 titles a year in 1770 to 3,500 in 1790 and more than
4,000 in 1800.[119] During this period also the balance between Latin and
German books shifted significantly. The ratio of Latin to German books
listed in the Frankfurt and Leipzig catalogues was 71:29 in 1650, 38:62 in
1700, 28:72 in 1740, and 4:96 in 1800.[120]

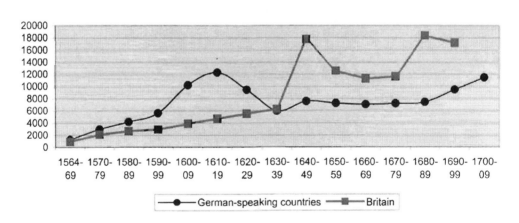

NUMBER OF TITLES LISTED IN THE FAIR CATALOGUES 1564–1709 COMPARED WITH
BRITISH BOOK PRODUCTION FIGURES (ten-year totals apart from 1564–69)

Frankfurt's loss was, then, Leipzig's gain. During the first decade of the eighteenth century four times as many publications were listed in the Leipzig catalogue as in that of Frankfurt. Details are naturally hard to come by, but in 1741 312 firms from 106 different towns were represented at the Leipzig fair. Of these 152 came from 60 towns in north Germany, 119 from 29 towns in southern Germany, while 41 firms came from 17 towns in other countries (several of them from Switzerland).[121] In contrast, at Frankfurt ever fewer books were exhibited from year to year, and the fair ceased entirely in 1749, ironically enough in the very year of the birth of Frankfurt's most famous son and Germany's greatest writer, Johann Wolfgang Goethe. A few years later, in 1765, Goethe went as a student to Leipzig. When he arrived at Michaelmas the fair was in full swing, and he records in his autobiography, *Dichtung und Wahrheit* (Part II, Book 6), with what interest he wandered amongst the stalls; he was particularly impressed by the exotic visitors from Poland, Russia and Greece. From a few years later, we have the reminiscences of Magnus Swederus (1748–1836), bookseller in Uppsala from 1775. In his autobiography he boasts of having been the first Swedish bookseller to visit the Leipzig fair, where his Swedish origin aroused such attention that he received about 150 visitors in four days; he sold 20 to 50 copies of some of his books to several firms and established accounts with more than 130 colleagues all over Europe. He notes that German booksellers granted six months' credit together with a 10 to 25 per cent trade discount, whereas he received a meagre 5 per cent discount 'for prompt payment' in London.[122] But Leipzig never attracted foreign booksellers and publishers on the scale that Frankfurt had done in its heyday: Leipzig was essentially a German, rather than an international, fair.

However, although the Leipzig fair attracted few booksellers from abroad, this does not mean that foreign books were not to be found there. Let us consider the case of English books. In the Frankfurt catalogues relatively few English books were listed: 36 in the first decade of the seventeenth century, 151 during the second, and 77 during the third, with virtually nothing in the English language thereafter.[123] (The significant increase during the second decade Blum attributes to growing interest in the fair by English booksellers following the marriage of James I's daughter to the Elector Palatine Frederick V in 1612.) It is only in the eighteenth century, in the Leipzig catalogues, that books by English authors begin to appear more regularly.[124] In 1733 Henning Grosse, bookseller and

30 FAIRS, MARKETS AND THE ITINERANT BOOK TRADE

publisher of the Leipzig fair catalogue, offered Isaac Newton, in a Latin edition produced in Amsterdam. But in the catalogue for Michaelmas 1737 Grosse advertised the availability of 26 works in English, including John Dart's *History and Antiquities of the Cathedral Church of Canterbury* (1726), Alexander Pope's *Literary Correspondence* (1735–7), and *The History of Poland under Augustus II* (1734), John Stacie's translation of the work by Jean Baptiste Desroches de Parthenay. In the Michaelmas 1755 catalogue, another Leipzig bookseller, Johann Wendler (1713–99), listed editions of a number of literary authors including Thomas Gray, Milton, Pope, Thomson, and Young, and moreover Wendler mentioned that he was issuing a special catalogue of English books free of charge — unfortunately no copy of this seems to have survived.

*

In conclusion, a word about the Frankfurt and Leipzig fairs today. Despite the retention of the traditional name, Frankfurter Buchmesse, the Frankfurt book fair cannot really be seen as continuing the old tradition. When after a break of 200 years it was established in 1949, after the Second World War and the sealing of the division of Germany, it was initially intended to be an internal German affair, rather than an international showcase. Accordingly just 200 German publishers and booksellers exhibited there that year. But already in 1950 publishers from other countries were attracted to it, and steady growth continued thereafter — in 2004 6,691 publishers from 110 countries exhibited 350,619 titles.

The Leipzig trade fairs were the international showcase of the former German Democratic Republic and as such were regularly celebrated on postage stamps. Today the Leipzig Book Fair continues to be held over four days in March each year, but it is a markedly smaller affair than its Frankfurt counterpart. In 2005 there were 2,142 exhibitors from 31 countries, and the event attracted only 108,000 visitors, almost 50 per cent of whom came from Leipzig and within a 100 km radius.

References

1. See Günter Richter, 'Christian Egenolffs Erben 1555–1667', *Archiv für Geschichte des Buchwesens*, 7 (1967), cols 449–1130.
2. For further information on these see, respectively, Herwarth von Schade, 'Peter Braubach in Frankfurt (1540–1567). Ein Werkverzeichnis', *Archiv für Geschichte des Buchwesens*, 21 (1980), 849–964; Imke Schmidt, *Die Bücher aus der Frankfurter Offizin Gülfferich – Han – Weigand Han-Erben. Eine literarhistorische und buchgeschichtliche Untersuchung zum Buchdruck in der zweiten Hälfte des 16. Jahrhunderts*

THE FRANKFURT FAIR IN THE EARLY MODERN PERIOD 31

(Wiesbaden: Harrassowitz, 1996); Heinrich Pallmann, *Siegmund Feyerabend, sein Leben und seine geschäftlichen Verbindungen,* Archiv für Frankfurts Geschichte und Kunst, n.F. 7 (Frankfurt am Main: Völcker, 1881); Ian Maclean, 'André Wechel at Frankfurt 1572–1581', *Gutenberg-Jahrbuch,* 63 (1988), 146–76.

3. Claus Nordmann, *Nürnberger Großhändler im spätmittelalterlichen Lübeck,* Nürnberger Beiträge zu den Wirtschafts- und Sozialwissenschaften, 37/38 (Nuremberg: Krische, 1933), p. 142.

4. For the Lent fair 1579 Plantin sent six barrels containing 5,212 copies of 67 different titles. Cited by Colin Clair, *A History of European Printing* (London: Academic Press, 1976), p. 223. Cholinus (d. 1588) was official printer to the city of Cologne and member of the city council. For full details of shipping and road transport routes to Frankfurt in the early modern period see Alexander Dietz, *Frankfurter Handelsgeschichte,* 5 vols (Frankfurt am Main, 1910–25), III, 287–360.

5. The 'Buchgaß' is mentioned several times by the Frankfurt poet Konrad Lautenbach in his *Marckschiff oder Marckschiffer Gespräch von der Franckfurter Meß* (1596). (On this see note 31 below.)

6. Nordmann [note 3], p. 137.

7. Pierre L. Van der Haegen, *Der frühe Basler Buchdruck,* Schriften der Universitätsbibliothek Basel, 5 (Basle: Schwabe, 2001), p. 75.

8. Gerald Strauss, *Nuremberg in the Sixteenth Century* (Bloomington: University of Indiana Press, 1976), p. 132. Nor could the escort be relied upon. As Anton Koberger explained to Johann Amerbach in a letter of 14 February 1502, he did not expect to attend the Lenten fair at Frankfurt because 'the princes will not ride escort, so it does not seem to me a good idea to put myself in danger and ride there without escort', cited from *The Correspondence of Johann Amerbach. Early Printing in its Social Context,* selected, translated, edited, with commentary by Barbara C. Halporn (Ann Arbor: University of Michigan Press, 2000), p. 241, after *Die Amerbachkorrespondenz,* ed. Alfred Hartmann and Beat R. Jenny, 10 vols (to date) (Basle: Verlag der Universitätsbibliothek, 1942–), I, no. 148.

9. For an early account of fairs and their role see Paul Jacob Marperger, *Beschreibung der Messen und Jahr-Märckte …* (1711, repr. Frankfurt/Main, 1968) (Klassiker der Betriebswirtschaftslehre, 2). (A slightly earlier edition, of 1710, is in Munich, Bayerische Staatsbibliothek: Res.Merc.141.)

10. The Danube provides a good example: bridges were built at Vienna in 1439, at Krems in 1463 and in 1497 at Linz.

11. Likewise there was a Simon and Jude fair at Basle (see Oscar von Hase, *Die Koberger* (Amsterdam and Wiesbaden, 1967), p. 306). Other important fairs were at Nördlingen where, even though this was principally a wool and cloth fair, we hear of a literary manuscript being bought in 1458, the Augsburg printers Johann Bämler and Jodocus Pflanzmann selling 20,000 indulgences (Hans-Jörg Künast, *'Getruckt zu Augspurg': Buchdruck und Buchhandel in Augsburg zwischen 1468 und 1555* (Tübingen: Niemeyer, 1997), p. 153) and the Strasbourg printer Adolf Rusch selling scholarly works in 1470 (von Hase, p. 307). Strasbourg itself had fairs at Shrovetide and St John's Day (von Hase, p. 307). In general, because of its fortunate location Strasbourg proved a very convenient place at which to transact business, especially for merchants from Basle,

32 FAIRS, MARKETS AND THE ITINERANT BOOK TRADE

Lyon, and Nuremberg (on Koberger's use of Strasbourg see von Hase, pp. 307–9).
Strasbourg also played a major role in shipping on the Rhine.

12. Norbert Bachleitner, Franz M. Eybl and Ernst Fischer, *Geschichte des Buchhandels in
Österreich*, Geschichte des Buchhandels, 6 (Wiesbaden: Harrassowitz, 2000), p. 11.

13. Elector Frederick II later established a New Year's fair at Leipzig, too. This was confirmed by Emperor Frederick III in 1466. On the Leipzig fairs see von Hase [note 11],
pp. 310–16.

14. The literature reveals much uncertainty over the dates of the Frankfurt Spring Fair.
The details given here are from Dietz [note 4], I, 37–8. See also Friedrich Kapp and
Johann Goldfriedrich, *Geschichte des Deutschen Buchhandels* (Leipzig, 1886–1913), II,
221, 225. Künast [note 11], p. 162, note 316, says it began on *Oculi* Sunday (the third
Sunday in Lent), and ended on the day before Palm Sunday.

15. Kapp/Goldfriedrich [note 14], II, 222, 225.

16. Dietz [note 4], I, 40. According to von Hase [note 11], p. 331, the Frankfurt Autumn
fair began on 20 September, the eve of St Matthew's Day.

17. Cited by Clair [note 4], p. 221. The British Library has copies of both the folio and the
octavo editions (pressmarks 566.i.26 and 793.b.2, respectively).

18. Hans-Jörg Künast, 'Johann Schönsperger d. J. und seine gescheiterten Unterneh-
mungen in Sachsen', *Leipziger Jahrbuch zur Buchgeschichte*, 8 (1998), 297–318, here
p. 300 and p. 317f. for the relevant documentation. The New Testament (VD16
B4323) did eventually appear, in 1523, presumably in time for the autumn fair.

19. Kapp/Goldfriedrich [note 14], I, 455.

20. See John L. Flood, '"Safer on the battlefield than in the city": England, the "Sweating
Sickness", and the Continent', *Renaissance Studies*, 17 (2003), 147–76.

21. They had 'solch buch zu Frangkfurt nicht gelesen, sondern wie es pflegt inn Messen in
gedreng und eil zuzugehen, nicht mehr dann den Titel gesehen, und ein anzahl
Exemplaria hingesetzt und alsbald eingeschlagen und aufladen lassen, und nicht eher
inn erfarung kommen seind, was inn gemeltem Buch stehet, bis das sie die Buecher
anher gebracht, und aus den Fassen genommen'. Cited by Reinhard Wittmann,
Geschichte des deutschen Buchhandels (Munich: Beck, 1991), p. 59, after Kapp/
Goldfriedrich [note 14], I, 470.

22. Künast [note 11], p. 162, esp. note 317.

23. Heinrich Grimm, 'Die Buchführer des deutschen Kulturbereichs und ihre Nieder-
lassungen in der Zeitspanne 1490 bis um 1550', *Archiv für Geschichte des Buchwesens*, 7
(1967), cols 1153–1772, here col. 1741; Bachleitner [note 12], p. 10.

24. Helga Noflatscher-Posch, *Die Jahrmärkte von Hall in Tirol. Ein Handelszentrum Tirols
in der frühen Neuzeit* (Hall/Tirol, 1992).

25. John L. Flood, 'Subversion in the Alps: Books and Readers in the Austrian Counter-
Reformation', *The Library*, VI, 12 (1990), 185–211.

26. Günter Richter, 'Buchhändlerische Kataloge vom 15. bis um die Mitte des 17.
Jahrhunderts', in Reinhard Wittmann (ed.), *Bücherkataloge als buchgeschichtliche
Quellen in der frühen Neuzeit*, Wolfenbütteler Schriften zur Geschichte des
Buchwesens, 10 (Wiesbaden: Harrassowitz, 1985), pp. 33–65, here pp. 54–5. The sole
surviving copy of Cratander's 1539 catalogue is in the Austrian National Library,

Vienna (Richter, p. 37, note 15). This arrangement serves to illustrate the important role played by Basle as a channel for cultural exchange.

27. Von Hase [note 11], p. 310.

28. Von Hase [note 11], p. 312–13.

29. Their protests are printed in Ernst Hasse, 'Notizen zur Geschichte des Verfalls der Frankfurter Büchermesse', *Archiv für Geschichte des Deutschen Buchhandels*, 4 (1879), 221–3.

30. Henricus Stephanus [= Henri Estienne], *Francofordiense emporium sive Francofordienses nundinae* (Geneva, 1574), p. 15. This text is also available in *The Frankfurt Book Fair: The Francofordiense Emporium of H. Estienne*, edited with historical introduction, original Latin text with English translation on opposite page and notes by J. W. Thompson (Chicago: Caxton Club, 1911; repr. Amsterdam, 1969). For the history of the book fairs generally see Kapp/Goldfriedrich [note 14], vols I and II, *passim*; Alexander Dietz, *Zur Geschichte der Frankfurter Büchermesse 1462–1792*, Schriften des Frankfurter Messamts, 5 (Frankfurt am Main, 1921); and especially Rainer Koch (ed.), *Brücke zwischen den Völkern. Zur Geschichte der Frankfurter Messe* (Frankfurt am Main, 1991), comprising three volumes: 1. *Frankfurt im Messenetz Europas – Erträge der Forschung*; 2. *Beiträge zur Geschichte der Frankfurter Messe* (pp. 195–203 deal with the book fair); 3. *Ausstellungskatalog zur Geschichte der Frankfurter Messe* (pp. 190–210 relate to the book trade). See also Michael Rothmann, *Die Frankfurter Messen im Mittelalter*, Frankfurter historische Abhandlungen, 40 (Stuttgart: Steiner, 1998), and Sabine Niemeier, *Funktionen der Frankfurter Buchmesse im Wandel — von den Anfängen bis heute*, Buchwissenschaftliche Beiträge aus dem Deutschen Bucharchiv München, 68 (Wiesbaden: Harrassowitz, 2001).

31. *Marckschiff oder Marckschiffer Gespräch von der Franckfurter Meß. Darinn alles, was in derselben Meß namhafftes und seltzames zusehen, beschrieben ist durch Marx Mangold* [= Konrad Lautenbach (1534–95)]. The complete text is printed in Julius Ziehen (ed.), *Der Frankfurter Markt oder die Frankfurter Messe von Heinrich Stephanus* (Frankfurt am Main: Diesterweg, 1919), pp. 45–78.

32. Kapp/Goldfriedrich [note 14], I, 449.

33. On the Gutenberg Bible at Frankfurt, see Martin Davies, 'Juan de Carvajal and Early Printing', *The Library*, VI, 18 (1996), 193–215.

34. Van der Haegen [note 7], p. 70. For other early visitors to the fair, see von Hase [note 11], pp. 316–32.

35. Kapp/Goldfriedrich [note 14], I, 453.

36. Von Hase [note 11], 1967, p. 318.

37. Amerbach's edition is unsigned but was probably published in 1490 (London BL: IB.37461).

38. Amerbach published editions in 1489 (London BL IB.37313) and 1490 (London BL: IB.37328).

39. Amerbach published editions in 1489 (London BL IB.37313(2)) and 1490 (London BL: IB.37328(2)).

40. Amerbach's edition appeared in 1489 (London BL: IB.37324).

41. Amerbach's edition appeared in 1492 (London BL: IB.37347).

42. Amerbach's edition appeared in 1492 (London BL: IA.37349).

34 FAIRS, MARKETS AND THE ITINERANT BOOK TRADE

43. Halporn [note 8], pp. 86–9; *Amerbachkorrespondenz*, I, no. 38.
44. Von Hase [note 11], p. 376.
45. Kapp/Goldfriedrich [note 14], I, 457. The Venetian printer Baptista de Tortis attended both Frankfurt fairs in 1498 (see *Archiv für Geschichte des Deutschen Buchhandels*, 4 (1879), 215–16).
46. 'Es tuen die Straßenplacker den Buchführern nichts, lassen sie ziehen, weil die Juden auf Bücher das allerwenigste Geld geben. Manche Reiter aber nehmen ein Büchel an, das man ihnen verehrt.' Cited by Grimm [note 23], col. 1171.
47. Halporn [note 8], p. 269, after *Amerbachkorrespondenz*, I, no. 306.
48. Estienne [note 30], pp. 9–10.
49. In the early period booksellers usually bartered books in sheets against equivalent sheets of other publications, so-called *Tauschhandel*. While this helped dealers with their cash-flow problems and ensured diversification of stock, it had the undesirable side-effect of encouraging unscrupulous publishers to produce sub-standard works which they exchanged for works of higher quality. This eventually led leading publishers, such as Philipp Erasmus Reich (1717–87), co-owner of Weidmann's at Leipzig, to demand cash payment or six-monthly settlement with a discount. Opponents such as Johann Thomas Edler von Trattner (1717–98) in Vienna resorted to ruthless piracy of Leipzig publications, which led to their exclusion from the Leipzig fair, to which they responded by selling their wares through itinerant booksellers and pedlars. See Richard Mummendey, *Von Büchern und Bibliotheken*, 2nd edn (Darmstadt: Wissenschaftliche Buchgesellschaft, 1964), p. 313.
50. On this particular role of Frankfurt see von Hase [note 11], p. 328, who observes that Koberger might sometimes have money collected at fairs in Lyon and Leipzig, but always took care to despatch money to the home addresses of individuals at Basle or Strasbourg if he could not meet them at Frankfurt.
51. The Lyon fair can be traced back to 1420. Initially there were three fairs a year, each lasting twenty days, but in 1463 Louis XI granted *lettres de franchise* for four fairs annually, each of two weeks. One was held in August, another at All Souls'. Merchants of all nationalities were admitted, apart from the English, 'noz ennemis anciens'. From 1484 until 1498 the fairs were suppressed, allegedly on account of the nearness of Lyon to the frontier which had resulted in the perpetration of frauds, but in 1498 Louis XII confirmed the four fairs with their privileges, and these were reconfirmed in 1514, 1547 and 1559. Among the firms that established branches of their business at Lyon were the Giunta family. For recent work on the book trade at Lyon see contributions in *Le Berceau du livre: autour des incunables. Etudes et essais offerts au professeur Pierre Aquilon par ses élèves, ses collègues et ses amis*, *Revue Française d'Histoire du Livre*, 118–21 (Geneva, 2004).
52. Halporn [note 8], p. 230, after *Amerbachkorrespondenz*, I, no. 110.
53. Halporn [note 8], p. 259, after *Amerbachkorrespondenz*, I, no. 231.
54. Halporn [note 8], p. 87, after *Amerbachkorrespondenz*, I, no. 38.
55. The larger firms would hold supplies of books in major towns all over Europe, and only the owner would know what he had in stock and where at any given time. Such stocks were valuable assets, though their worth would decline with age (diminished topicality) and physical condition (damage through damp, mice, worms). Books that

THE FRANKFURT FAIR IN THE EARLY MODERN PERIOD   35

were not selling might be reissued under a new titlepage, creating the impression of a new edition, but in reality such methods were but desperate attempts to dispose of dead stock.

56. Cited by Clair [note 4], p. 220.

57. Grimm [note 23], cols 1490–8, details bookdealers resident in Frankfurt itself.

58. Grimm [note 23], col. 1492.

59. Kapp/Goldfriedrich [note 14], I, p. 455.

60. Grimm [note 23], col. 1492.

61. Richter [note 26], p. 54. Rudolf Blum, 'Vor- und Frühgeschichte der nationalen Allgemeinbibliographie', *Archiv für Geschichte des Buchwesens*, 2 (1960), 233–303, here p. 237, states that this first permanent bookshop was established in 1597.

62. The only known copy, measuring 380 x 305 mm, is in Milan, Bibl. Ambrosiana (S.M.L.IV, 25/4). See Christian Coppens, 'Five unrecorded German bookseller's catalogues, end 16th–early 17th century', *Archiv für Geschichte des Buchwesens*, 54 (2001), 157–69. Zetzner's catalogue is reproduced on p. 162. On Zetzner see Ian Maclean, 'Mediations of Zabarella in Northern Germany, 1586–1623', in Gregorio Piaia (ed.), *La presenza dell'aristotelismo padovano nella filosofia della prima modernità* (Rome and Padua: Antenore, 2002), 173–98, here pp. 177–80.

63. Bernhard Fabian (ed.), *Die Meßkataloge des sechzehnten Jahrhunderts*, 5 vols (Hildesheim and New York: Olms, 1972–2001). Vol. I covers Autumn 1564 to Autumn 1573 (with the exception of Easter 1566 and Easter 1567, for which no catalogues seem to have been produced), vol. II Easter 1574 to Autumn 1580, vol. III Easter 1581 to Autumn 1587, vol. IV Easter 1588 to Autumn 1592, and vol. V Easter 1593 to Autumn 1600 but lacks Autumn 1598, for which no copy has been found. On this see David Paisey, 'German Book Fair Catalogues', *The Library*, VII, 4 (2003), 417–27. See also Bernhard Fabian (ed.), *Die Meßkataloge des sechzehnten, siebzehnten und achtzehnten Jahrhunderts. Microfiche-Edition* (Hildesheim and New York: Olms, 1977–86), covering the Leipzig catalogues from 1594 to 1860. A study covering the catalogues over a long period and attempting a statistical analysis is Gustav Schwetschke, *Codex Nvndinarivs Germaniae Literatae Bisecvlaris: Meß-Jahrbücher des Deutschen Buchhandels von dem Erscheinen des ersten Meß-Katalogs im Jahre 1564 bis zu der Gründung des ersten Buchhändler-Vereins im Jahre 1768* (Halle, 1850–77; repr. Nieuwkoop: de Graaf, 1963). Paisey, *op. cit*, p. 426, voices justifiable reservations about the reliability of Schwetschke's statistics, noting, for instance, that he offers no figure for pre-1601 publications from Cambridge even though STC 25363, 25368, 25367 (all listed in Willer) and 17121 (listed in Portenbach/Lutz) are known to have been available at Frankfurt. See further Wolfgang Borm, *Catalogi Nundinales 1571– 1852. Die Frankfurter und Leipziger Messkataloge der Herzog August Bibliothek Wolfenbüttel* (Wolfenbüttel, 1982). For the catalogues' importance as forerunners of a national bibliography see Blum [note 61].

64. 'Libri theologici catholici, non noui; hactenus verò in nostra Bibliotheca desiderati'. Four titles only.

65. For an analysis of the books on music see Albert Göhler, *Verzeichnis der in den Frankfurter und Leipziger Messkatalogen der Jahre 1564 bis 1759 angezeigten Musikalien* (Leipzig: Kahnt, 1902). See also Stephen Rose, 'The mechanisms of the music trade in

36 FAIRS, MARKETS AND THE ITINERANT BOOK TRADE

central Germany, 1600–40', *Journal of the Royal Musical Association*, 130 (2005), 1–37, esp. pp. 5–12 on 'Music at the Book Fairs'.

66. Karl Schottenloher, *Die Widmungsvorrede im Buch des 16. Jahrhunderts*, Reformationsgeschichtliche Studien und Texte, 76/77 (Münster, n.d.), pp. 153–4. The book in question is Rucker's edition of *Matrimonialium consiliorum tomi duo ... per Joannem Baptistam Zilettum ...*, Frankfurt am Main: M. Lechler for S. Feyerabend, 1580.

67. See Oliver Duntze, 'Die Frankfurter und Leipziger Meßkataloge als buchgeschichtliche Quellen', *Buchhandelsgeschichte*, 2002, no. 1, pp. 10–18, here p. 18, note 48, says they were printed by Martin Lechler, but as Fig. 5 shows, by 1573 they were being printed by Peter Schmidt.

68. Virtually all the books were very recent publications, though Paisey [note 63], p. 418, noticed one title dating from 1513.

69. Frankfurt does not dominate in any way. From outside the German-speaking area there are many books from Venice, Paris, Antwerp, Rome, Lyon, some from Prague, Vilna, Cracow, even Coimbra, and a handful from London, Oxford, Cambridge and Edinburgh.

70. On the use of gothic types by German printers as a Protestant manifesto see John L. Flood, 'Nationalistic currents in early German typography', *The Library*, VI, 15 (1993), 125-41.

71. The uncertainty of the transport also added to the cost. Thus Anton Koberger in Nuremberg complained to Johann Amerbach on 1 March 1500: '[...] Those barrels have still not all arrived and some of those that did arrive are completely soaked. Please have thick, strong barrels made and pay more for them so that the books are better protected' (Halporn [note 8], p. 229; *Amerbachkorrespondenz*, I, no. 110). Again, on 9 February 1503, he complained: '[...] five barrels arrived, all five wet and completely soaked. Please see to getting good barrels and especially when you are sending me the manuscript exemplars in them' (Halporn, p. 250; *Amerbachkorrespondenz*, I, no. 182). And yet again, on 17 June 1504, he complained that the barrels Amerbach used were 'very thin and weak' and 'completely unsuitable for long-distance shipping [from Basle to Frankfurt]' (Halporn, p. 258; *Amerbachkorrespondenz*, I, no. 229).

72. The British Library holds an incomplete set of these (pressmark C.107.bb.3), covering the years 1577–97, beginning with *Catalogus nouus nundinarum autumnalium Francofurti anno M.D.LXXVII. celebratarum*. For some notes comparing Portenbach/Lutz's catalogues with those of the same years by Willer see Paisey [note 63], pp. 423–4.

73. These included one by the Frankfurt publisher Sigmund Feyerabend for the Lenten fair 1584, one by Peter Schmidt in 1590, and several by Peter Brachfeld issued from Spring 1595 to Spring 1598. For a fuller account see Graham Pollard and Albert Ehrman, *The distribution of books by catalogue from the invention of printing to A.D. 1800* (Cambridge, 1965), pp. 79–84.

74. The decision is recorded in Bürgermeisterbuch 1598, fol. 84, in the Stadtarchiv, Frankfurt am Main. See Richter [note 26], p. 54, note 98. The titlepage of the Autumn 1598 catalogue is illustrated in *Lexikon des gesamten Buchwesens. LGB²*, ed. Severin Corsten *et al.* (Stuttgart: Hiersemann, 1987–), V, 156.

THE FRANKFURT FAIR IN THE EARLY MODERN PERIOD   37

75. For a sketch of the history of Frankfurt within the Empire and further literature on the city's history see Gerhard Köbler, *Historisches Lexikon der deutschen Länder*, 6th revised edn (Darmstadt: Wissenschaftliche Buchgesellschaft, 1999), pp. 175–6.

76. Examples of privileges are discussed by Ian Maclean, 'The market for scholarly books and conceptions of genre in Northern Europe, 1570–1630', in Georg Kauffmann (ed.), *Die Renaissance im Blick der Nationen Europas* (Wiesbaden: Harrassowitz, 1989), pp. 17–31, here pp. 22–3.

77. See Wolfgang Brückner, 'Eine Messbuchhändlerliste von 1579 und Beiträge zur Geschichte der Bücherkommission', *Archiv für Geschichte des Buchwesens*, 3 (1958), cols 1629–48, here col. 1641. For the subsequent history of these rival catalogues see cols 1642–8. The Catholic catalogues were published at Mainz from 1606 to 1614, then at Frankfurt until 1619, and from 1625 to 1627 in parallel at Munich and Frankfurt. See Pollard/Ehrman [note 73], pp. 80–2. Paisey [note 63], p. 423, also mentions short-lived catalogues from Heidelberg and Munich.

78. See Albrecht Kirchhoff, 'Beiträge zur Geschichte der Preßmaßregelungen und des Verkehrs auf den Büchermessen im 16. und 17. Jahrhundert, II: Zur Geschichte der Kais. Bücher-Commission in Frankfurt a. M.', *Archiv für Geschichte des Deutschen Buchhandels*, 4 (1879), 96–137, here pp. 129–30.

79. Dietz [note 4], III, 60–1. Richter [note 26], p. 51, note 81, gives the price as 1 Schilling a copy in 1590.

80. See Duntze [note 67], p. 11.

81. On the Leipzig catalogues see Albrecht Kirchhoff, 'Die Anfänge des Leipziger Meßkatalogs,' *Archiv für Geschichte des Buchhandels*, 7 (1882), 101–22; and 'Weiteres über die Anfänge des Leipziger Meßkatalogs,' ibid., 8 (1883), 22–7. See Gernot Gabel (ed.), *Der erste Leipziger Messekatalog aus dem Jahr 1595. Faksimileausgabe nach dem Exemplar der Universitäts- und Stadtbibliothek Köln* (Cologne, 1995). After the Leipzig catalogue was taken over by the Weidmann'sche Buchhandlung in the later eighteenth century, it was thoroughly reorganized by Philipp Erasmus Reich who gave up the traditional subject classification in favour of an alphabetical listing. In this form the catalogue continued until 1860 (see Duntze [note 67], p. 11). On Grosse see *Lexikon des gesamten Buchwesens* [note 74], III, 283–4.

82. Paisey [note 63], pp. 424–5.

83. See Susanne Meurer, 'The Composition and Context of Joachim von Sandrart's *Teutsche Academie*', Ph.D thesis, University of London (Warburg Instute), 2005, pp. 151 and 158.

84. On the problems presented by the fair catalogues see Peter Düsterdieck, 'Buchproduktion im 17. Jahrhundert. Eine Analyse der Meßkataloge für die Jahre 1637 und 1658', *Archiv für Geschichte des Buchwesens*, 14 (1974), cols. 163–220; David L. Paisey, 'Literatur, die nicht in den Meßkatalogen steht', in Paul Raabe (ed.), *Bücher und Bibliotheken im 17. Jahrhundert*, Wolfenbütteler Schriften zur Geschichte des Buchwesens, 6 (Hamburg: Hauswedell, 1980), pp. 115–25; and Duntze [note 67]. Further literature of relevance is cited by A. H. Laeven, 'The Frankfurt and Leipzig book fairs and the history of the Dutch book trade in the seventeenth and eighteenth centuries', in *Le Magasin de l'Univers. The Dutch Republic at the Centre of the European*

38 FAIRS, MARKETS AND THE ITINERANT BOOK TRADE

   Book trade, ed. C. Berkvens-Stevelinck, H. Bols *et al.* (Leiden, 1992), pp. 185–98, here, p. 189, note 10.

85. *Bibliotheca Classica, Siue Catalogus officinalis: In Qvo Singvli Singvlarvm Facvltatvm Ac Professionvm Libri, Qvi In Qvavis Fere Lingva Extant, Qviqve Intra Hominvm fere memoriam in publicum prodierunt, secundum artes & disciplinas, earumque titulos & locos communes, Authorumque Cognomina singulis classibus subnexa, ordine alphabetico recensentur* (Frankfurt am Main: N. Hoffmann for P. Kopff, 1611), and *Bibliotheca Librorvm Germanicorvm Classica. Das ist: Verzeichnuß aller vnd jeder Bücher, so fast bey dencklichen Jaren in Teutscher Spraach von allerhand Materien hin vnd wider in Truck außgangen, vnd noch den mehrertheil in Buchläden gefunden werden: Darinnen nicht allein Jedere Facultet in jhre besondere Classes der gestalt ist abgetheilet daß so wol die Materien, als auch die Autores ... sampt Anzeigung wann, wo, vnd in was Format oder Grösse ein jedes getruckt, ganz leichtlich vnd ohne besondere Mühe zu finden ...* (Frankfurt am Main: J. Saur for P. Kopff, 1611). British Library pressmarks: 820.e.24 and 820.e.25, respectively.

86. *The Cambridge History of the Book in Britain*, IV: *1557–1695*, ed. John Barnard and D. F. McKenzie (Cambridge: CUP, 2002), p. 160. On Oxford and Bill see also Maclean [note 76], p. 27, and particularly Julian Roberts, 'Importing books for Oxford, 1500–1640', in James P. Carley and Colin G. C. Tite (eds), *Books and Collectors 1200–1700. Essays presented to Andrew Watson* (London: British Library, 1997), pp. 317–33, especially pp. 328–9, where he notes the puzzling rarity of copies of the Frankfurt (not to mention the Leipzig) catalogues in Britain.

87. *Journal des savants*, Année 1685 (Amsterdam: G. P. and J. Blaeu, 1686), 'Au lecteur'.

88. On 'Frankfurt und Leipzig' see *Archiv für Geschichte des Deutschen Buchhandels*, 4 (1879), 223.

89. *Historia von D. Johann Fausten. Text des Druckes von 1587. Kritische Ausgabe*, ed. Stephan Füssel and Hans Joachim Kreutzer, Reclams Universalbibliothek, 1516 (Stuttgart: Reclam, 1988), p. 6. In one of the episodes Faust himself visits the Frankfurt Lenten fair (p. 100).

90. Fairly full details of all the early *Faust* editions may be found in Hans Henning, *Beiträge zur Druckgeschichte der Faust- und Wagnerbücher des 16. und 18. Jahrhunderts* (Weimar, 1963), and Füssel/Kreutzer [note 89]. For the expurgated Catholic version see Peter Amelung, 'Ein unbekanntes Faust-Buch von 1588', *Gutenberg-Jahrbuch*, 63 (1988), 177–82, and for the verse version, produced by Tübingen students, see *Der Tübinger Reim-Faust von 1587/88*, ed. Günther Mahal (Kirchheim/Teck: Schweier, 1977).

91. The edition printed by Thomas Orwin in 1592 (STC 10711; British Library C.27.b.43) was possibly not the *editio princeps*. See John Henry Jones (ed.), *The English Faust Book* (Cambridge: CUP, 1994), esp. p. 146.

92. The first periodical published in Germany was Otto Mencke's *Acta eruditorum* (1682), inspired by the *Journal des savants* and the *Philosophical Transactions* of the Royal Society in London.

93. On these see *Lexikon des gesamten Buchwesens* [note 74], V, 157–8. For a fuller account, with reference to much secondary literature, see Ulrich Rosseaux, 'Die

THE FRANKFURT FAIR IN THE EARLY MODERN PERIOD   39

Leipziger Meßrelationen 1605–1730. Ein Beitrag zur Medien- und Kommunikations-
geschichte der Frühen Neuzeit', *Leipziger Jahrbuch zur Buchgeschichte*, 12 (2003), 11–
31. An old but still valuable treatment of the subject generally is Felix Stieve, 'Ueber
die ältesten halbjährigen Zeitungen oder Messrelationen und insbesondere über deren
Begründer Freiherrn Michael von Aitzing', *Abhandlung der Historischen Classe der
Königlich Bayerischen Akademie der Wissenschaften*, 16, 1 (Munich, 1881), pp. 177–
265. For a checklist see Klaus Bender, *Relationes Historicae. Ein Bestandsverzeichnis der
deutschen Meßrelationen von 1583 bis 1648* (Berlin: de Gruyter, 1994).

94. Examples include the correspondence of Amerbach and Anton Koberger, the account
books of Froben and Episcopius (see Rudolf Wackernagel, *Rechnungsbuch der Froben &
Episcopius, Buchdrucker und Buchhändler zu Basel, 1557–1564* (Basle: Schwabe, 1881)),
the Frankfurt publisher Sigmund Feyerabend (see Pallmann [note 2] and also note 98
below), and Michael Harder (see Ernst Kelchner and Richard Wülcker (eds), *Mess-
Memorial des Frankfurter Buchhändlers Michael Harder, Fastenmesse 1569* (Frankfurt
am Main and Paris: Baer, 1873)), and the official lists of booksellers attending in 1569
(see Kapp/Goldfriedrich [note 14], I, 661ff. and 772ff.) and 1579 (Brückner [note
77]).

95. Von Hase [note 11], p. 320–1.

96. Dennis E. Rhodes, 'Some neglected aspects of the career of Giovanni Battista Ciotti',
The Library, VI, 9 (1987), 225–39, here p. 228. See also Maclean [note 62], p. 177.

97. See Ingrid Ilsøe, 'Bøger og boghandlere under Christian V.', *Fund og Forskning*, 25
(1981), 19–46, here pp. 30–1. Haubold and Paulli were the first to publish annual lists
of Danish books.

98. See Heinrich Pallmann, 'Ein Meßregister Sigmund Feyerabend's aus dem Jahre 1565',
Archiv für Geschichte des Deutschen Buchhandels, 9 (1884), 5–46.

99. Brückner [note 77].

100. These are: Cologne, Strasbourg, Augsburg, Nuremberg, Mainz, Frankfurt, Basle,
Zurich, Lausanne, Antwerp, Heidelberg, Wittenberg, Leipzig, Jena, Tübingen, Erfurt,
Magdeburg, Vienna, Bamberg, Speyer, Neustadt an der Haardt [now Neustadt an der
Weinstrasse], Hildesheim, Braunschweig, Helmstedt, Ursel, Paris, Venice, Lyon,
Turin, and Geneva. Towns mentioned as not being represented at the Autumn 1579
fair include Ingolstadt, Marburg, Trier, Prague, Dinkelsbühl and Würzburg.

101. Hilkert Weddige, *Die 'Historien vom Amadis auss Franckreich'. Dokumentarische
Grundlegung zur Entstehung und Rezeption* (Wiesbaden: Steiner, 1975), pp. 121–2.

102. Carlos Gilly, *Die Manuskripte in der Bibliothek des Johannes Oporinus*, Schriften der
Universitätsbibliothek Basel, 3 (Basle: Schwabe, 2001), pp. 18–19. Oporinus died
before printing could be put in hand.

103. Gilly [note 102], pp. 21–4. The book in question is Jean Boulaise, *Tabula chrono-
graphica* (Frankfurt am Main: N. Basseus, 1575), published 'impensis Genii Bibliothecae Oporinianae'.

104. Foundation dates of universities in the Holy Roman Empire: Prague 1348, Vienna
1365, Heidelberg 1386, Cologne 1388, Erfurt 1392, Würzburg 1402/1582, Leipzig
1409, Rostock 1419, Greifswald 1456, Freiburg 1457, Basle 1460, Ingolstadt 1472,
Tübingen 1477, Mainz 1477, Graz 1486, Wittenberg 1502, Breslau 1505, Frankfurt

40 FAIRS, MARKETS AND THE ITINERANT BOOK TRADE

an der Oder 1506, Marburg 1527, Königsberg 1544, Jena 1548, Strasbourg 1566/1621, Helmstedt 1576, Giessen 1605, Rinteln 1621, Altdorf 1622, Kiel 1665, Halle 1694, Göttingen 1737, Erlangen 1743. Frankfurt am Main itself did not have a university until 1914.

105. For an analysis of the changing market for scholarly books see Ian Maclean [note 76].

106. For an illuminating discussion, based on an analysis of posthumous editions of Melanchthon, see Ian Maclean, 'Melanchthon at the book fairs, 1560–1601: editors, markets and religious strife', in Günter Frank and Kees Meerhoff (eds), *Melanchthon und Europa, 2. Teilband: Westeuropa*, Melanchthon-Schriften der Stadt Bretten, 6 (Stuttgart: Thorbecke, 2002), pp. 211–32.

107. Maclean [note 2], pp. 155–6, reprints Wechel's own handwritten catalogue of 1579, preserved among the papers of the Imperial Book Commission at Vienna. On Wechel's catalogues see also Maclean [note 76], p. 24. On the Wechel business generally see R. J. W. Evans, *The Wechel Presses: Humanism and Calvinism in Central Europe, 1572–1627* (Oxford: Past and Pesent Society, 1975).

108. Originally two copies had to be deposited at Frankfurt, but this was increased to five in 1570, reduced to two in 1608, increased to three in 1621 and to five in 1650. In 1678 the commissioner Georg Friedrich Sperling demanded seven: five for the Emperor, one for the Elector of Mainz as Archchancellor of the Empire, and one for himself. See Hans Widmann, *Geschichte des Buchhandels vom Altertum bis zur Gegenwart*, revised edn (Wiesbaden: Harrassowitz, 1975), I, 89; Adalbert Brauer, 'Die kaiserliche Bücher-kommission und der Niedergang Frankfurts als Buchhandelsmetropole Deutschlands', *Genealogisches Jahrbuch*, 19 (1979), 185–99, here p. 194. Brauer's article traces in detail the relations between the city council and successive commissioners. On the Imperial Book Commission generally see Ulrich Eisenhardt, *Die kaiserliche Aufsicht über Buchdruck, Buchhandel und Presse im Heiligen Römischen Reich Deutscher Nation (1496–1806): ein Beitrag zur Geschichte der Bücher- und Pressezensur*, Studien und Quellen zur Geschichte des deutschen Verfassungsrechts, A, 3 (Karlsruhe: C. F. Müller, 1970). On its arbitrary workings and ultimate failure see Stephan Fitos, *Zensur als Mißerfolg. Die Verbreitung indizierter deutscher Druckschriften in der zweiten Hälfte des 16. Jahrhunderts* (Frankfurt am Main etc.: Lang, 2000).

109. These details from Laeven [note 84], p. 187.

110. These figures, somewhat simplified, are taken from Laeven [note 84], p. 191. Based on Schwetschke and Kapp/Goldfriedrich, they conflate the Frankfurt and Leipzig catalogues. The boxed figures relate to the war period.

111. On the high prices of English books see *The Cambridge History of the Book in Britain*, IV: *1557–1695* [note 86], p. 736. Paisey [note 63], pp. 419–23, makes a provisional listing of some 60 pre-1601 books from Britain in the Frankfurt catalogues. Among them are 3 books published by John Legat at Cambridge, 2 from Henry Charteris at Edinburgh, 2 from Joseph Barnes at Oxford, and the remainder from London (including 8 published by George Bishop, 3 by John Day, 9 by Thomas Vautrollier, and 13 by John Wolfe). Moreover, Paisey notes several items which appear not to be recorded in STC, as well as 22 recorded by Willer with dates between one and four years later than those listed in STC, possibly indicating reissues intended by the

original British publishers for supply to Frankfurt. See also Max Spirgatis, 'Englische Litteratur auf der Frankfurter Messe von 1561 bis 1620', *Beiträge zur Kenntnis des Schrift-, Buch- und Bibliothekswesens*, 7 (Sammlung bibliothekswissenschaftlicher Arbeiten, 15; Leipzig, 1902), pp. 37–89; Irene Wiem, *Das englische Schrifttum in Deutschland von 1518–1600*, Palaestra, 219 (Leipzig, 1940). There is no evidence of books in German by London printers in the sixteenth century, but some books in other languages, particularly Italian, were produced for the continental market and appear in the Frankfurt catalogues, e.g. books by John Wolfe with false imprints (STC 17161, 15414.6, 19911, 19913; see Paisey [note 63], p. 421).

112. Laeven [note 84], p. 192.

113. Uwe Neddermeyer, *Von der Handschrift zum gedruckten Buch*, 2 vols, Buchwissenschaftliche Beiträge aus dem Deutschen Bucharchiv München, 61 (Wiesbaden; Harrassowitz, 1998), I, 417, table 6 (a). The boxed figures relate to the war period.

114. Widmann [note 108], I, 88. On Frankfurt in the Thirty Years' War see Dietz [note 4], IV, 1–17.

115. The figures for Britain are derived from the statistical tables compiled by John Barnard and Maureen Bell, in *The Cambridge History of the Book in Britain*, IV: *1557–1695* [note 86], pp. 779–84.

116. For the workings of the book commission in Leipzig see Albrecht Kirchhoff, 'Die Kurf. sächsische Bücher-Commission in Leipzig', *Archiv für Geschichte des Deutschen Buchhandels*, 9 (1884), 47–176.

117. See S. H. Steinberg, *Five Hundred Years of Printing*, new edition, revised by John Trevitt (London: British Library, and New Castle DE: Oak Knoll, 1996), p. 94.

118. Paul Raabe, 'Der Buchhändler im achtzehnten Jahrhundert in Deutschland', in Giles Barber and Bernhard Fabian (eds), *Buch und Buchhandel in Europa im achtzehnten Jahrhundert: The Book and the Book Trade in Eighteenth-Century Europe*, Wolfenbütteler Schriften zur Geschichte des Buchwesens, 4 (Hamburg: Hauswedell, 1981), pp. 271–91, here p. 275.

119. Raabe [note 118], p. 282.

120. Figures from Steinberg [note 117], pp. 54–5. It is noted there that, naturally enough, Latin predominated longer in university towns such as Jena and Tübingen than in mercantile centres like Hamburg.

121. These statistics, cited by Thomas Bürger, 'Aufklärung in Zürich', *Archiv für Geschichte des Buchwesens*, 48 (1997), 1–278, here p. 143, are based on the *Verzeichniß der meistlebenden Herren Buchhändler, Welche Die Leipziger und Franckfurther Messen insgemein zu besuchen pflegen* (1741) (Deutsches Buch- und Schriftmuseum Leipzig: Bö C VIII, 28).

122. Sten G. Lindberg, 'The Scandinavian Book trade in the Eighteenth Century', in Barber/Fabian [note 118], pp. 225–48, here p. 232. The source is Magnus Swederus, *Biografiska Småsaker til minnes för efterlefwande, 2. stycket* (Uppsala: Bruzelius, 1832).

123. Blum [note 61], p. 256. Paisey [note 63], p. 424, reports that the earliest book in the English language he has found in the catalogues is Thomas Bilson's *The True Difference between Christian Subjection and Unchristian Rebellion* (Oxford, 1585) (STC 3071, in the Portenbach/Lutz catalogue for Autumn 1586).

42 FAIRS, MARKETS AND THE ITINERANT BOOK TRADE

124. The following details derive from Bernhard Fabian, 'Die Meßkataloge und der Import englischer Bücher nach Deutschland im achtzehnten Jahrhundert', in Reinhard Wittmann and Berthold Hack (eds), *Buchhandel und Literatur. Festschrift für Herbert G. Göpfert zum 75. Geburtstag am 22. September 1982*, Beiträge zum Buch- und Bibliothekswesen, 20 (Wiesbaden: Harrassowitz, 1982), pp. 154–68.

[13]

The market for scholarly books and conceptions of genre in Northern Europe, 1570 – 1630

IAN MACLEAN

It is traditional, if not commonplace, to look on the last decades of the sixteenth century and the early decades of the seventeenth as the 'autumn' of the Renaissance, a period marked at best by consolidation, at worst by decline[1]. It is alleged that political crises and confessional strife disrupt intellectual life both directly and indirectly, giving rise to a mentality often described as 'baroque', in which the optimism of the high Renaissance is succeeded by scepticism or even pessimism, serenity by violence and instability, conviction by doubt[2]. The respublica literaria is threatened by the gradual disintegration of the encyclopaedic aspirations of earlier generations of humanists, by increasing uncertainty as to whether learning and ethics, *studia* and *mores*, are as intimately linked as Erasmus claimed, by the manifest failure of scholars to agree on matters concerning religious truth[3]. The antagonism between established centres of learning, still dominated by scholasticism or neo-Aristotelianism, and radical movements associated with neoplatonism, with hermeticism, with alchemy, and with the observational and experimental sciences is reflected in the crisis faced by academic institutions, both long-established and of more recent foundation: a crisis exacerbated in German-speaking parts of Europe by the catastrophic events of the Thirty Years War[4]. While it has been shown that humanistic enquiry

---

1 See, for example, Jean Lafond and André Stegmann (eds.), *L'automne de la Renaissance, 1580 – 1630* (Actes du XXIIᵉ colloque international d'études humanistes, Tours), Paris, 1981.
2 For a general historical survey of this period in Northern Europe, see R. J. W. Evans, *The making of the Hapsburg monarchy, 1550 – 1700*, Oxford, 1979, pp. 41 – 116; for a recent study of baroque, see Claude-Gilbert Dubois, *Le baroque*, Paris, 1973.
3 W. J. Ong, S.J., *Ramus, method and the decay of dialogue*, New York, 1958, pp. 295 – 318; Anthony Grafton and Lisa Jardine, *From humanism to the humanities*, Cambridge, Mass., 1986; W. Schmidt-Biggemann, *Topica universalis: eine Modellgeschichte humanistischer und barocker Wissenschaft*, Hamburg, 1983.
4 R. J. W. Evans, "German universities after the Thirty Years War", *History of Universities*, i (1981), 169 – 90; F. Yates, *Giordano Bruno and the hermetic tradition*, London 1964; id., *The occult philosophy in the Elizabethan age*,

continues to yield impressive scholarly results – the names of Joseph
Scaliger, Denis Lambin, Marc-Antoine Muret, Justus Lipsius, Isaac
Casaubon, Friedrich Sylburg spring to mind – this is often interpreted as
yet another demonstration that the owl of Minerva flies at dusk[5].

Not all of these assertions are uncontroversial[6]; but they find *prima
facie* confirmation in the statistics of the trade in scholarly books.
Schwetschke's figures for the Frankfurt Book Fair show a marked and
lasting downturn in the number of Latin books advertised after 1630;
and the most recent authoritative account of publishing in France talks
also of a severe decline at the end of the sixteenth century, caused by the
passing away of a generation of humanist printer-publishers and the
saturation of available markets[7]. It would seem therefore unwise to
deny the existence of a crisis in Northern European humanism at this
time; but it is possible to ask whether this particular configuration of
historical events and conditions is a sufficient explanation of it. It is
traditional to assume that ideas emanating from scholars are freely
received and exchanged; but these ideas are communicated in the material form of books, by a process which involves money at all levels –
printing, advertising and distribution. I wish to investigate the economic
conditions which may have contributed to intellectual decline; and especially the dialectical relationship which exists between producer and
consumer not in terms of author and reader, as is traditional, but publisher and purchaser; and I hope to show that the material and legal
conditions governing publication promoted certain trends in the marketing and consumption of books which influenced conceptions of genre
and contributed to the collapse – perhaps more accurately described as
implosion – of the boom in scholarly books in the 1620s. To do this, it

London 1979; Brian Vickers (ed.), *Occult and scientific mentalities in the
Renaissance*, Cambridge, 1984; Charles B. Schmitt, *The Aristotelian tradition
and Renaissance universities*, London, 1984.

5 Anthony Grafton, *Joseph Scaliger: a study in the history of classical scholarship: i, textual criticism and exegesis*, Oxford 1983; Jean Jehasse, *La Renaissance de la critique: l'essor de l'humanisme érudit de 1560 à 1614*, Saint
Etienne, 1976.

6 For accounts of such controversy, see Brian Vickers, "Frances Yates and the
writing of history", *Journal of Modern History*, li (1979), 287 – 316; Charles
B. Schmitt, "Aristotelianism in the Veneto and the origins of modern science: some considerations on the problem of continuity", *Aristotelismo Veneto e scienza moderna*, Padua, 1983, pp. 104 – 123; id., 'La cultura scientifica
in Italia nel quattrocento: problemi d'interpretazione', *Studi filosofici*, iii
(1980), 55 – 70, esp. 68 – 69.

7 Lucien Febvre and Henri-Jean Martin, *L'apparition du livre*, Paris, 1958,
pp. 233 ff., 331 ff.; and the statistical evidence in Gustav Schwetschke,
Codex nundinarius Germaniae literatae bisecularis, Halle, 1850 – 77.

The market for scholarly books and conceptions of genre in Northern Europe   19

will be necessary to offer a general account of the Northern European book market, before focussing attention on publishers themselves and investigating their finances, their connections with the world of scholarship, and their influence on the way scholarly activity is categorised and described.

The market in scholarly books is international in that its lingua franca is Latin; it has broad geographical limits which may be established from various sources, notably the balance sheets of international publishers such as Sigmund Feyerabend of Frankfurt, who flourished between 1560 and 1590, Christophe Plantin of Paris and Antwerp who died in 1589, and of the Basle and Strasbourg printers of the late sixteenth century whose activities have been examined by Bietenhotz and Chrisman[8]. A glance at these half-yearly accounts – drawn up after the twice-yearly book fairs at Frankfurt – shows that their commercial activities extend throughout the German-speaking area of Europe and into France, Switzerland, the Low Countries, Northern Italy, and, later, England and Central Europe, mainly through agents and booksellers. The list of publishers cited in the general catalogue of the Frankfurt book fairs confirms this network of outlets for scholarly publication. Printers, publishers, booksellers, agents and scholars congregated there in remarkably favourable commercial and intellectual conditions, which the humanist publisher Henri Estienne describes in glowing terms in his famous eulogy of the Fair printed in 1574[9]. Andreas Wechel, the Paris-based publisher of classical texts, settles in Frankfurt in 1572, having been forced to flee from France after the St Bartholomew's Day Massacre in 1572, and his newly founded presses flourish there through three generations[10]. Eustache Vignon of Geneva, Jacques Dupuis of Paris, Etienne du Harsy of Lyon travel regularly to Frankfurt, whose attraction lies not only in its commercial possibilities and relative toler-

8 Heinrich Pallmann, *Sigmund Feyerabend: sein Leben und seine geschäftlichen Verbindungen nach archivalischen Quellen*, Frankfurt, 1881; Leon Voet, *The golden compasses*, 2 vols, Amsterdam, 1969 – 72; P. G. Bietenholz, *Basle and France in the sixteenth century. The Basle humanists and printers in their contacts with francophone culture*, Geneva, 1971; Miriam U. Chrisman, *Lay culture, learned culture: books and social change in Strasbourg, 1480 – 1599*, Yale, 1982.

9 *Der Frankfurter Markt oder die Frankfurter Messe von Henricus Stephanus*, ed. J. Ziehen, Frankfurt, 1919; also Hubert Languet, *Epistolae politicae et historicae scriptae quondam ad Philippum Sydnaeum*, Frankfurt, 1633, xciii, p. 339.

10 R. J. W. Evans, *The Wechel presses: humanism and Calvinism in Central Europe, 1572 – 1627*, Oxford, 1975; Ian Maclean, "L'Economie du livre érudit: le cas Wechel (1572 – 1627)", in *Le livre dans l'Europe de la Renaissance*, ed. H.-J. Martin and P. Aquilon, Paris, 1988, pp. 230 – 240.

20   Ian Maclean

ance, but also in its position on a number of trade routes between Italy and Northern France and Eastern and Western Europe[11]. This happy state of affairs ceases abruptly in 1631, at the time of the siege of the Imperial City by Gustavus Adolphus, after which other publishing centres gain prominence, notably Leipzig and Leyden[12].

The final decades of Frankfurt's success mark also its most extensive display of scholarly books – an annual average of 1000 new publications in Latin, a brute figure not to be equalled for more than a century in Germany, representing three times the number of books of a similar sort declared annually in the decade 1570 – 80[13]. It is of interest to ask by what means a threefold increase in production – which includes a high percentage of new editions of classical texts, or of new commentaries and expositions – was generated, and how it was sustained, especially as there is some evidence that books produced in Germany did not readily find French and Italian outlets[14]. Does this increase betoken an expanding class of purchasers – expanding either by geographical extension (to England and Central and Eastern Europe) or by the spread of Latinity and erudition to new categories of readers? Or a widespread demand for the latest and best edition of a given text? Or that print runs were smaller during these decades and that the expansion is illusory? How was this impressive commercial expansion (if such it was) financed? Such questions are not answered directly by contemporaries in their assessments of the market for books: these, on the whole, are restricted on the one hand to lamentations (by the publishers themselves) about the precariousness of their trade, and on the other by claims that is brought them vast profits (claims made for the most part by aspirant authors whose manuscripts had been rejected)[15]. An examination of the financial conditions of scholarly publication explains to some degree how these incompatible views come to be formulated.

Very few publishers in this sector of the book market were engaged solely in this activity. As well as taking the financial risks involved in printing, advertising and distributing a manuscripts, they also acted as printers for other publishers, as booksellers (a rôle forced upon them by

---

11 See note 9, above, and Friedrich Kapp, *Geschichte des deutschen Buchhandels*, Leipzig, 1886, pp. 448 – 521.

12 Johann Goldfriedrich, *Geschichte des deutschen Buchhandels, 1648 – 1740*, Leipzig, 1908, pp. 163 – 167; Henri-Jean Martin and Roger Chartier (eds.), *Histoire de l'édition française*, Paris, 1983, i. 398.

13 This estimate is based on Schwetschke's figures.

14 Pallmann, *Feyerabend* (see fn. 8 above), pp. 128 – 133; Maclean, "André Wechel at Frankfurt 1572 – 81", *Gutenberg-Jahrbuch*, 1988, pp. 146 – 176.

15 *Ibid.*, p. 153; M. Magnien, "Un humaniste face aux problèmes d'édition: J.-C. Scaliger et les imprimeurs", *Bibliothèaue d'humanisme et Renaissance*, xliv (1982), 307 – 329.

The market for scholarly books and conceptions of genre in Northern Europe   21

the practice of *Tauschhandel*, by which they exchanged their own books for those of competitors at the book fair), as hosts for visiting scholars and for scholar-proofreaders, as postal agents, as bankers and as money changers[16]. Even as publishers they often shared financial risks with colleagues and with other denizens of the book trade, notably paper manufacturers. Such interdependence often reveals itself in the form of mortgages: not only do they make over their stock and printing materials as surety to obtain loans from fellow publishers, but they even sacrifice their houses and real estate. Thus it is that Sigmund Feyerabend takes on the mortgage of his former colleague's, Simon Hüter's, house, collaborates with his paper manufacturer Heinrich Tack, employs Andreas Wechel to print books for him, but later sells his house at a moment of financial difficulty to Andreas's heirs, who at the same time had accepted from Christophe Plantin of Antwerp his valuable collection of Greek punches and dyes as surety for a loan[17]. It seems that a great deal of commercial activity in the book trade involves such paper transactions: the half-yearly accounts of Pallmann and others yield evidence of considerable movements of stock and exchange of goods, but few signs of satisfactory cash flow, causing frequent crises even in well-established publishing houses. The threefold increase in production between 1570 and 1630 seems even more extraordinary in the light of such financial conditions.

There were also important legal constraints on publishers. From the late 1560s, Imperial censorship in the form of a Bücherkommission operated fitfully in Frankfurt, designed to prevent the circulation of defamatory and seditious material. What successive Holy Roman Emperors did not envisage was that the commission would serve two masters – Empire and Roman Catholic Church – and that its activities would eventually concentrate on the question of the precedence of Catholic over Protestant books in the Fair Catalogues[18]. The religious bias of the commission has been cited as a cause for the decline of the Book Fair itself, in that it discouraged the presence of foreign protestant publishers, although it is not clear how far it was effective in imposing its

16 Goldfriedrich, *Geschichte* (see fn. 12 above), pp. 89 ff.; Evans, *The Wechel presses* (see fn. 10 above); Maclean, "André Wechel" (see fn. 14 above). The botanist Charles de l'Escluse [Clusius] even used booksellers and publishers to distribute daffodil bulbs to his friends throughout Europe (see F. W. T. Hunger, *Charles de L'Escluse 1529 – 1609*, The Hague, 1972 – 43, ii. 75).

17 Pallmann, *Feyerabend* (see fn. 8 above), pp. 37 – 39; Maclean "André Wechel" (see fn. 14 above), pp. 161 – 164; Voet, *The Golden Compasses* (see fn. 8 above), i. 120, ii. 91; Evans, *The Wechel presses* (see fn. 10 above), p. 4.

18 Kapp, *Geschichte* (see fn. 11 above), pp. 607 ff.; U. Eisenhardt, *Die kaiserliche Aufsicht über Buchdruck, Buchhandel und Presse im Heiligen Römischen Reich*, Karlsruhe, 1970, pp. 85 ff.

22   Ian Maclean

desired reforms[19]. This is not the only point where questions of law affect the book trade; these are much more in evidence in the licences (privilèges, impressoria) granted to authors or publishers to protect new editions from piracy in a given geographical ambit. Because the market in scholarly books written in Latin was particularly susceptible to piracy, it is common to find licences attached to them, sometimes from more than one jurisdiction, for it was possible for non-nationals and even petitioners of different confessional persuasions to obtain them. Judging by the Imperial impressoria preserved in the Haus-, Hof- und Staatsarchiv in Vienna, these were carefully drafted by several echelons of Chancery officials. The final text, complete with Imperial or royal seal, was an impressive and very expensive document[20].

In many cases the genre of the protected book is cited, thus giving generic categories a legal status. When the son-in-law of Melanchthon, Caspar Peucer, petitions the Emperor for a licence to print his father-in-law's *Opera* (including his *Opera theologica*), the licence grants permission under the surprising general rubric 'res literaria, militaris disciplina et literaria monumenta', presumably because of the embarrassment implicit in a Holy Roman Emperor sanctioning the publication of Lutheran theology. In other cases, petitioners' requests are attenuated, and the term 'Christian' preferred to 'Catholic', suggesting an irenic influence at work in the Chancery. Publishers can also be granted general licences: the French refugee Andreas Wechel receives one in 1574 which affords protection for all his books except those in the domain of theology and history[21]. The former exclusion is readily comprehensible, as Wechel was a protestant; the latter is more unusual, especially as Wechel declares his intention to specialise in the publication of ancient and medieval historical documents in 1575[22]. The category 'libri historici' in Frankfurt Book Fair Catalogues includes, however, tendentious accounts of very recent history; it may be for this reason that the category is denied imperial protection. If so, it suggests that the generic categories cited in licences are those of the Fair Catalogues themselves.

19 W. Brückner, "Der kaiserliche Bücherkommissar Valentin Leucht", *Archiv für Geschichte des Buchwesens*, iii (1961), cols. 97 – 178, and Evans, *The Wechel Presses* (see fn. 10 above), pp. 29 – 31.
20 The cost of privileges is attested by Erasmus in a letter to Willibald Pirckheimer (see *Opus epistolarum*, ed. P. S. Allen and H. M. Allen, Oxford 1924; 1341, pp. 201 – 202 and 1344 pp. 232 – 233). See also Albert Labarre, "Editions et privilèges des héritiers d'André Wechel à Francfort et à Hanau 1582 – 1627", *Gutenberg-Jahrbuch*, 1970, pp. 238 ff.
21 Haus-, Hof- und Staatsarchiv, Vienna, Impressoria, FZ 2, ff. 251 – 256; FZ 76, ff. 253 – 255, FZ 79, ff. 174 – 206.
22 Wechel's dedicatory letter in Albert Krantz, *Wandalia*, Frankfurt, 1575, Aa2[r].

The market for scholarly books and conceptions of genre in Northern Europe   23

It is also common to find references to the combined personal and public interest served by scholarly books: the publisher acts 'in the public interest' ('ad commodum rei[publicae] literariae': 'in bonum publicum') in promoting learning and scholarship, but desires 'fair recompense' ('speratum laborum suorum emolumentum') for his 'heavy outlay of money' ('gravissima impensa' 'magna sumpta'). This is one of the very rare occasions on which the commercial interests involved in intellectual life become explicit[23].

The most important feature of the licence for our purposes, however, is the fact that it can only be granted for a new or improved edition. Thus, in order to obtain protection for a book, publishers are obliged to claim that it is 'editio nova' or 'recognita', or 'locupletior'. As the licence was expensive, publishers must only have sought it when they were reasonably sure that a book would be profitable: this inference is confirmed by the readiness of publishers to reprint each other's scholarly productions outside the jurisdiction of the licence protecting them[24]. Such activity, which is very common in the period under discussion, suggests that the whole academic sector of the market was lucrative; but not all historians agree on this point. Robert Kingdon has argued that humanist publishers such as Christophe Plantin or Henri Estienne chose to subsidise the publication of grandiose scholarly projects from the profits to be made from the sales of liturgical books in the first (Catholic) case, and psalters in the second[25]. Dyroff's account of the activities of Gotthard Vögelin suggests that he subsidised scholarship by text book sales; this may be true also in the case of Andreas Wechel[26].

One might also argue – with equal, if not greater, plausibility from the available data – that publishers did not take risk on books which they thought would not make a profit. The point is of some importance and can be tested by using the evidence provided by contemporary publishers' catalogues. Are these no more than means for advertising all available stock? Or do they contain judgements as to the desirability of certain sorts of publication? Do they aspire to comprehensive coverage in certain specialised areas? In what ways do they reflect the publishers' conception of the market and its divisions?

23 Impressoria, FZ 2, F 251; FZ 65 s.v. Wechel; FZ 56 f. 25^r, 245^r; FZ 79, ff. 181 – 184.
24 On examples of this practice, and the disputes which arise from it, see Maclean, "André Wechel" (see fn. 10 above), pp. 150 – 152.
25 R. M. Kingdon, "The business activities of printers Henri and François Estienne", in *Aspects de la propagande religieuse*, ed. G. Berthoud, Geneva, 1957, pp. 258 – 275.
26 H. D. Dyroff, "Gotthard Vögelin – Verleger, Drucker, Buchhändler 1597 – 1631", *Archiv für Geschichte des Buchwesens*, iv (1963), cols. 1131 – 1423; Maclean, "André Wechel" (see fn. 10 above).

24   Ian Maclean

Such catalogues, which are distributed both as broadsheets and in the form of pamphlets, vary considerably, but the majority list more than just the most recently published volumes. Most are arranged not alphabetically but by genre, no doubt to assist the potential purchaser; it is extremely rare to find any reference either to the year of publication or the price. In many cases, they include a fairly complete back list including books inherited from previous owners of the presses; sometimes they record the results of *Tauschhandel* or speculative bookselling. Some follow the order of categories laid down in the Book Fair catalogues, that is, the precedence of subjects in universities: theology, law, medicine, liberal arts, followed by extra-curricular subjects. Most others give prominence to the specialities of the press in question: such is the case for Johannes Gymnich of Cologne and Zacharias Palthen of Frankfurt, both of whom concentrate on legal publications[27]. A well-documented set of examples of such lists is provided by the Wechel press: as well as the manuscript catalogue submitted by Andreas Wechel to the Bücherkommission in 1579, the printed lists of 1594, 1602 and 1618 survive[28]. The number of entries increases from 190 to 523 in this time: more or less all of the catalogue of 1594 is available in 1618, as well as some Wechel publications dating from the 1560s which were not declared in 1594. The order of entries changes in 1618 to conform to that of the Book Fair; in earlier catalogues the innovative textbooks of Greek grammar, logic and rhetoric, the prestigious editions of the classics, the collection of historical documents begun in 1575, and the writings of Ramus were given pride of place. It is possible to construct from these lists a number of academic preferences and objectives – an investment in Ramus's pedagogical texts, and his encyclopedic view of learning; an irenic version of Calvinism; a conviction that the classical heritage should be preserved and purified; but it is difficult to separate such

27 *Die Messkataloge des sechzehnten Jahrhunderts 1564 – 92*, ed. Bernhard Fabian, 4 vols., Hildesheim and New York, 1972 – 8; G. Pollard and A. Ehrman, *The distribution of books by catalogue from the invention of printing to A.D. 1800, based on material in the Broxbourne Library*, Cambridge, 1965; G. Richter, "Bibliographische Beiträge zur Geschichte buchhändlerischer Kataloge im 16. und 17. Jahrhundert", in *Beiträge zur Geschichte des Buches und seiner Funktion in der Gesellschaft, Festschrift für Hans Widman*, Stuttgart, 1974, pp. 183 – 229; R. Engelsing, "Deutsche Verlegerplakate des 17. Jahrhunderts", *Archiv für Geschichte des Buchwesens*, ix (1969), 217 – 338; Reinhart Wittmann (ed.), *Bücherkataloge als buchgeschichtliche Quellen in der frühen Neuzeit*, Wiesbaden, 1984.
28 The present location of these catalogues is respectively the Stadtbibliothek, Mainz, the Staatsbibliothek, Bamberg, and the Bodleian Library, Oxford.

The market for scholarly books and conceptions of genre in Northern Europe 25

objectives from notions of profit[29]. Kingdon's hypothesis that humanist publishers financed marginal scholarly publication from staples in the form of liturgical books or school books seems, even in this case, implausible; a more reasonable inference from the available data is that no risk was taken unless there was a good chance of uptake by the market. It is tempting to interpret the retention of all titles on the list as a sign of faith in the intrinsic value of their products; but it is more plausible to assume that nothing was to be lost by the continued advertisement of unsold stock.

The Wechel presses exemplify also the importance of insuring that books have known outlets. From the 1570s onwards, the Wechels are associated with an international set of scholars, court officials and schoolteachers who assisted with sales and supplied copy. This network, which extends from England to the Imperial court and beyond, has been skilfully uncovered by Robert Evans; a similar configuration has been shown to feature in the success of the Plantin press by Leon Voet[30]. Such networks, which are, in effect, a form of patronage, often represent fairly narrow confessional interests which publishers, as their clients, reflect. Thus their lists are influenced by a number of commercial and sectarian interests, at the same time as presenting to the broad public what purports to be timeless learning. But this is not all. As well as subscribing to the view that the truths of scholarship are eternal, publishers are obliged, by the system of licences and the nature of the market in which they operate – a market which requires that new and better editions are forever pressed on the potential purchasers of scholarly books – to accede to the view that there is continual improvement and expansion in the world of letters, and thereby to commit themselves both to an ideology of progress and, practically, to the view that publishing is an expanding economy.

These paradoxes reappear if we turn out attention to institutional and private purchasers at this time, and to the bibliographers through whom they accede to the market. We have already seen that the Frankfurt Book Fair Catalogues follow approximately the precedence of university faculties: theology, law, medicine, philosophy; when Georg Draut of Marburg publishes the second edition of his immense cumulative bib-

29 Evans, *The Wechel Presses* (see fn. 10 above); Maclean, "L'Economie du livre érudit" (see fn. 10 above), and "André Wechel" (see fn. 14 above).

30 Evans, *The Wechel Presses* (see fn. 10 above), pp. 6 – 37; Voet, *The Golden Compasses* (see fn. 8 above), i. 60 – 73; also Ursula Baumeister, "Gilles Beys, 1541/2 – 1595", in *Imprimeurs et libraires parisiens du XVIᵉ siècle: ouvrage publié d'après les manuscrits de Philippe Renouard*, Paris, 1979, iii. 312 – 373; Kingdon, "The business activities of printers Henri and François Estienne" (see fn. 25 above).

liography of these fairs (which he supplements from the catalogues of individual publishers) in 1625, he justifies this order in a portentous prefatory letter to his patrons, the teaching staff of the High School of Marburg. Knowledge is here portrayed as the colossus of Babylon, whose head is theology, arms and chest are law, stomach is medicine and legs are philosophy, that propedeutic discipline which leads to ('supports', in this metaphor) the higher faculties. The contents of theology and philosophy contain much which does not relate to those disciplines in themselves – either as propaganda or polemics, or as informal accounts of the mysteries of the universe; the category 'libri historici, geographici et politici' is intercalated between medicine and philosophy; and the categories 'libri poetici' and 'libri musici' come at the end, and contain humanistic schoolbooks such as Virgil and Ovid which one might have expected to be listed with the liberal arts. This general order has some sort of justification based on notions of disciplinary precedence[31]. It is recommended also by the French scholar and librarian Gabriel Naudé in his *Advis pour dresser une bibliothèque* of 1627 because, he avers, it is the traditional manner in which libraries are arranged and thus simplifies the task of those seeking given texts[32]; and it even is used as the general principle of organisation by the speculative bibliographer La Croix du Maine in his *Desseins ou projets pour dresser une bibliothèque parfaite* which were composed in the 1580s[33].

The sub-categories of bibliographical arrangement are, however, often less conservative, and reflect the intellectual trends of this period more clearly. In La Croix du Maine's ideal library, alchemy is placed between philosophy, mathematics and music; Naudé, a known habitué of scientific and libertin circles in Paris, recommends the purchase of many subversive modern thinkers under innocuous headings, and even goes so far as to suggest that books altogether beyond the disciplinary map on 'matières peu cognues' should be purchased[34]: suggestions which were put into effect by the important French patron of scholarship and book collector Nicolas-Claude Fabri de Peiresc[35]. Another practical example of the shifts in the disciplinary map is provided by

31 Draut, *Bibliotheca classica*, Frankfurt, 1625, esp. *2ʳ – 4ᵛ. The books about disciplinary precedence are listed in cols. 1451 – 2.
32 Guillaume Naudé. *Advis pour dresser une bibliothéque*, Leipzig, 1963, pp. 100 – 101.
33 *Les bibliothéques françoises de la Croix de Maine et de Du Verdier*, ed. M. de la Monnoye et al., Paris, 1772, ii.xxv – xxx.
34 *Advis* (see fn. 32 above), pp. 45 – 46.
35 The catalogue of the library of Peiresc is at present being prepared for publication at the Institut de Recherche et d'Histoire des Textes, C.N.R.S., in Paris under the direction of Mlle Edith Bayle, to whom I am indebted for having sent me photocopies of the section on philosophy.

The market for scholarly books and conceptions of genre in Northern Europe   27

Thomas James's subject catalogue of arts produced in 1624/5 to help Oxford graduates and possibly undergraduates consulting the holdings of the newly founded Bodleian Library[36]. The entries in this bibliography were all acquired between 1600 and the date of its composition; the majority were bought fresh from Book Fair Catalogues or through the bookseller Thomas Bill of London, who was dispatched abroad in 1603 in quest of specific books[37]. This catalogue represents therefore a selection made to be of use to scholars in Oxford and also to enhance the prestige of the newly-founded library. It lists in turn books on grammar, geometry, astronomy, architecture, arithmetic, optics, cosmography, geography, chronology, music, logic, Aristotle, metaphysics, military arts, moral philosophy, politics, natural philosophy, rhetoric and history: each subject has sub-divisions within which titles are arranged alphabetically by author. History is the largest category, but the proliferation of mathematical genres should be noted, as well as the low priority given to Aristotle. James's spread of subjects does not accord well with the arts curriculum at Oxford in his time; this would suggest that the Bodleian Library was seen to be somewhat distanced from the immediate pedagogical concerns of the University.

The emergence of finding lists such as that of Draut or that of Philibert Mareschal which appeared at Paris in 1598[38] may well have had its own effect on the world of letters. Draut's *Bibliotheca classica* is notable for its complex and exhaustive sub-categories and for its cross-referencing. Under each general rubric, there is an alphabetical series of topics by which it is possible to establish a crude bibliography for almost any subject from Hebrew grammar to sleepwalking, from anagrammology to the lives of famous Jesuits, from naval battles to exorcism. Under the names of classical authors, all known editions are listed according to date and editor, but no value judgements are made; this is also the case with topic headings. Indeed, Draut, a Lutheran pastor, even goes so far as to cite – and occasionally to intermingle – Catholic, Lutheran and other Protestant theological books under such inflammatory headings as justification by faith, the real presence, and predestination, perhaps in the hope that some super-theologian would emerge who would be capable, having read all the available material, of reaching a verdict on a

---

36 G. W. Wheeler, *The earliest catalogues of the Bodleian Library*, Oxford, 1928, pp. 104 – 114; the copy I have consulted of James's subject catalogue is that preserved in Queen's College, Oxford (MS 199).

37 W. D. Macray, *Annals of the Bodleian Library*, Oxford, 1890, p. 50, quoted by Pollard and Ehrman, *The distribution of books* (see fn. 27 above), p. 77; Thomas Hearne, *Reliquiae Bodleianeae*, Oxford, 1703, p. 66, quoted by Pollard and Ehrman, *ibid.*, p. 86.

38 Viz. *La guide des arts et sciences, et promptuaire de tous livres, tant composez que traduicts en françois*, Paris, 1598.

28   Ian Maclean

given issue. Draut's cross-references reflect a different feature of intellectual life of the late Renaissance: the interpenetration of disciplines. It
had of course long been the case that lawyers had invoked medicine and
theology, doctors law and theology, theologians medicine and law, and
philosophers all three. The scholastic reliance on the corpus and logical
method of Aristotle had ensured to some degree the communication
from one discipline to another[39]. But titles like *Idea morborum Her-
metico-Hippocratica methodo Rameâ adornata, Tractatus politico-
iuridicus de Nobilitate et mercatura* or *Physica Christiana, seu de rerum
creatarum creatione* suggest a more radical transgression of disciplinary
boundaries[40].

How do these finding lists and bibliographical aids relate to the purchasers of scholarly books at this time? Connections are sometimes hard
to establish. It seems, for example, that in spite of Draut's listing of all
available editions of a given classic, and Naudé's recommendation that
the most recent and best editions should be purchased together with all
available commentaries and expositions, most libraries did not possess
more than one copy of any given text, and, indeed, did not necessarily
substitute their edition for the latest one to appear. Such an inference
can be drawn from the extant catalogues of religious houses whose libraries were founded in the late Renaissance; it is also true of the Bodleian Library at Oxford, although there are counter-examples in a
number of Cambridge colleges[41]. This suggests that there must have
been an expanding market for humanistic texts at the end of the sixteenth century, presumably supplying the plethora of new educational
establishments of various confessional kinds throughout Europe. Non-
curricular subjects, especially history and philosophy, do not have such
an obvious outlet. There is ample evidence that a market existed not
only for topical historical books, but also texts relating to much earlier
periods. When Andreas Wechel sets up his printing presses anew in

39 See in general, Charles B. Schmitt, *Aristotle and the Renaissance*, Cam-
    bridge Mass., 1983; also Edward Grant, "Aristotelianism and the longevity
    of the medieval world view", *History of Science*, xvi (1978), 93 – 106.
40 These examples are taken from Draut, *Bibliotheca classica* (see fn. 31
    above), cols. 948, 790, 491.
41 See, for example, Dom Abrassart, "Catalogue alphabétique de la Bibliothè-
    que de Tours" (Bibliothèque municipale, Tours, MS 1482), an inventory of
    confiscated libraries prepared for the Comité d'Instruction in the early
    1790s, including many religious houses founded in the period 1580 – 1640;
    Wheeler, *Catalogues of the Bodleian Library* (see fn. 36 above), p. 17. Dr.
    Elizabeth Leedham-Green, the author of *Books in Cambridge Inventories:
    book lists from Vice-Chancellor's Court Probate Inventories in the Tudor and
    Stuart Periods*, Cambridge, 1986, has informed me of counter-examples in
    Cambridge colleges.

The market for scholarly books and conceptions of genre in Northern Europe   29

Frankfurt in 1574, he confides to his friend and protector Hubert Languet that he has decided to specialise in historical books and documents because these are attractive to 'many different kinds of reader' ('ad plurima genera lectorum'): he and his heirs produce a series of folio volumes of immense erudition, density and cost between 1575 and the 1620s which seem to have been collected as a series; their purchasers, such as Jan Rutgers, a court official of Gustavus Adolphus, may have read them for their intrinsic interest, but it is more likely that they looked upon them as investments or as prestigious possessions. Certainly, they were beyond the purse of University students[42].

A more accessible category of book is found under the rubric 'libri philosophici'. Texts explaining the wonders of nature, of human procreation and of the secrets of the universe proliferate between the middle of the sixteenth century and 1630; these were produced in small formats and frequently reprinted. One such book is the *De subtilitate* or Cardano, which first appeared in 1550; its author sets out to lay bare the principles by which the universe operates in a manner accessible to non-specialists[43]. Many other such works, often associated with magic and the occult, follow in its wake, written by such authors as Levinius Lemnius, Giambattista della Porta, John Dee, Pierre de la Primaudaye, Robert Fludd[44]. These books are classified by Draut as philosophy, although that category also contains textbooks on logic and other univerity subjects. His general rubric therefore, in this and other cases, conflated a number of different purchasing groups from which a tripartite division can be deduced: buyers of textbooks in schools and universities; specialists in a given profession; and general readers, the 'studiosi', on whose purchases much of the speculative part of the market depends[45].

The case of Cardano illustrates the relative profitability of different market sectors quite well. His book enjoyed a spasm of success in the 1550s and again in the 1580s, but is thereafter not reprinted in the period

42 Wechel's dedicatory letter in Albert Krantz, *Wandalia* (see fn. 22 above); Evans, *The Wechel Presses* (see fn. 10 above), pp. 11 – 14; *Catalogus Bibliothecae Jani Rutgersii Dordraceni . . . quorum auctio habebitur in aedibus Elzevierianis I. Martii Anno 1633*, Leyden, 1633.
43 See for this topic in general, *Occult and scientific mentalities in the Renaissance*, ed. Brian Vickers, Cambridge 1984.
44 *Ibid.*
45 Ian Maclean, "Philosophical books in European markets, 1570 – 1630: the case of Ramus", in *New perspectives in Renaissance thought*, ed. S. Hutton and J. Henry, London 1990, pp. 253 – 263: *Histoire de l'édition française*, i. 543 – 583; Chrisman, *Lay culture, learned culture* (see fn. 8 above), pp. 71 ff; Rudolf Hirsch, *Printing, selling and reading 1450 – 1550*, Wiesbaden, 1967, p. 31.

which concerns us. But the text of Julius Caesar Scaliger, the neo-Aristotelian who undertook to refute Cardano in a series of *Exercitationes* first published in 1557, was reprinted again in 1576 as a university textbook and thereafter reappeared at least once a decade for the next sixty years. Scaliger's refutation was taken to be a statement of orthodox Aristotelianism in German Universities, or was used to provide subjects for short theses[46]. Both Cardano and Scaliger are frequently cited by turn-of-the-century scholars[47]; but from the point of view of the publisher and bookseller, only Scaliger is worthy of mention. Cardano's book may have fallen victim to its own claim to have explicated natural phenomeny more completely, more clearly and with greater authority than ever before; such a claim could be repeated by subsequent popular authors in the same field, and was in any case open to refutation by the advances made in observational and experimental science.

This survey of the scholarly book market from the point of view of its material producers has been necessarily elementary and sketchy; but it seems worthwhile in conclusion to measure the distance we have travelled from the commonplace view of academic decline in the late sixteenth century, and from the ideals of the early humanists. For them a library was a locus amoenus in which all texts would be restored to their first and authoritative state by palingenesis, would be provided once and for all with wholly adequate critical apparatus, and be placed at the appropriate point, on the approriate shelf, under the appropriate rubric which itself formed part of the ideal encyclopaedia[48]. It was to this end that the praiseworthy and indefatigable efforts of late Renaissance scholars were directed, and I wish to stress that I have not set out in any way to vilify their work or impugn their motives. Seen in a commercial light, however, their texts and critical apparatus are not immaterial idealities, but the very life blood of the publishing industry,and are reproduced as much for financial as for scholarly ends. Palingenesis – the perfect restitution of texts – can never be allowed to come about, because it would make redundant new 'improved' editions with the protection they enjoyed by licence or *privilège* and bring an expanding market to a

46 Ian Maclean, "The interpretation of natural signs: Cardano's *De subtilitate* versus Scaliger's *Exercitationes*", in *Occult and scientific mentalities* (see fn. 43 above), pp. 231 – 252.

47 *Ibid.*, and Kristian Jensen, "Protestant rivalry, metaphysics and rhetoric in Germany, 1590 – 1620", *Journal of Ecclesiastical History*, xli (1990), 24 – 43.

48 *Histoire de l'édition française* (see fn. 12 above), i. 429 – 457; H. Fischer, "Conrad Gessner (1516 – 65) as bibliographer and encyclopaedist", *The Library*, v. 21 (1966), 269 – 281; R. McKeon, "The transformation of the liberal arts in the Renaissance", in *Developments in the early Renaissance*, ed. B. S. Levy, Albany, 1972, pp. 158 – 223.

The market for scholarly books and conceptions of genre in Northern Europe   31

premature end. Genre is no longer an ideal category belonging to a close and sufficient system of categories; rather it is, at best, a crude reflection of the contemporary state of knowledge in relation to existing academic institutions, at worst a means by which potential purchasers could be attracted to the parts of a sale catalogue most susceptible to be of interest to them: our humanist encyclopaedia has become open-ended and rough-and-ready. The cry is no longer 'abeant studia in mores', but rather 'abeant studia in libros', or even 'abeant libri in libros'[49]. The book becomes, furthermore, an object to be preserved and catalogued for itself, thus making the fact of publication culturally significant no matter through what means or in whose interest it first came about. The book becomes also an object to be collected as a potentially valuable possession, as a token of social or intellectual prestige, as an item of exchange, and not just the physical manifestation of a message to be consumed by an intellect[50]. Part of this development can be ascribed to the technology of printing, which facilitated the production and distribution of texts; part can be laid at the door of the laws governing publishing in Europe at this time; part can be seen as the logical extension of bibliographical activities which encourage the production of books on books. But whatever causes one ascribes to the publishing boom, and especially the boom in the interpretation and mediation of texts, between 1570 and 1630, it seems difficult to deny it a rôle in the decline and eventual demise of the world of humanism of which it was the material expression.

49 Cf. Montaigne, *Essais*, ed. A. Thibaudet and M. Rat, Paris, iii. 13, p. 1045: "Il y a plus affaire à interpreter les interpretations qu'à interpreter les choses, et plus de livres sur les livres que sur autre subject: nous ne faisons que nous entregloser."

50 Cf. the subtitle of Gessner's *Bibliotheca universalis* of 1545: "sive catalogus omnium scriptorum locupletissimus, in tribus linguis, latina, graeca et hebraica: extantium et non extantium, veterum et recentiorum in hunc usque diem, doctorum et indoctorum, publicatorum et in bibliothecis latentium." See also Roger Chartier, *Les usages de l'imprimé (XVᵉ – XIXᵉ siècle)*, Paris, 1987.

[14]

Bibliographical Note

THE SURVIVAL AND LOSS RATES OF PSALMS, ABCs, PSALTERS AND PRIMERS FROM THE STATIONERS' STOCK, 1660–1700

JOHN BARNARD

A COMPARISON OF TWO SOURCES, the record of psalms, ABCs, psalters and primers ordered by the Treasurer of the Stationers' Company for the warehouse between 1663 and 1700,[1] and Wing's record[2] of extant copies of the same, allows a tentative sense of the survival and loss rates of these works. The two sets of figures are not directly comparable. Wing records editions (reissues and variant title-pages, a difficulty elsewhere in using Wing for statistical purposes, are not a problem in these categories of book). The Treasurer, of course, recorded not editions but the quantities ordered.

In the table given below for psalms, the Wing figures are based on the years 1660 to 1700, while the Treasurer's totals are based on four selected three-year periods (1663/4–65/6, 1673/4–75/6, 1683/4–85/6, and 1693/4–95/6). Because the Company gave permission, at a price, to the King's Printers, and later to Oxford University's printers, to print their own impressions, particularly in small formats, these figures are lower than the number of books actually in circulation. But the point here is to compare those editions published between the years 1660 and 1700 which Wing identifies as printed for the Stationers' Company with those recorded as passing through the Treasurer's hands. The significant point of comparison is therefore the overall proportions of psalms in different formats when set against those of extant editions recorded in Wing.

TABLE 1

Format	Treasurer's Orders	Percentage of Total	Wing Editions	Percentage of Total
2°	3,200	1%	11	9%
4°	5,408	2%	7	6%
8°	27,244	11%	39	32%
12°	163,497	69%	60	49%
24°	45,452	19%	6[3]	5%
Totals	244,801		123	

[1] The figures for the Treasurer's orders are taken from John Barnard, 'The Stationers' Stock 1663/4 to 1705/6: Psalms, Psalters, Primers and ABCs', forthcoming in *The Library*.

[2] Donald Wing, *Short-Title Catalogue of Books Printed in England, Scotland, Ireland, Wales and British America, and of English Books Printed in Other Countries, 1641–1700*, revised 2nd edn., 3 vols (New York, 1982–94).

[3] This total excludes two further 24mo psalms printed in 1692 at Oxford and Cambridge (B2581–81aA); neither mentions the Company in its imprint.

Bibliographical Note   149

As is to be expected, folio, quarto and octavo psalms are proportionately over-represented in Wing (47% as against 14%), while the two smallest formats are under-represented (54% as against 88%). Where the Treasurer ordered six times as many duodecimos as octavos, Wing has a ratio of 1:1.5, and where the Treasurer ordered almost twice the number of 24mo psalms as octavo, Wing's octavo psalms outnumber 24mo by 5:1.[4]

However, when compared with the very high loss rates for the other three stocks-in-trade for the Company, ABCs, psalters, and primers (see below), the figures for surviving editions of small-format psalms look suspiciously high, even though they are clearly under-represented in the Wing record. The probable explanation, impossible to prove without examining every single instance of copies of psalms located by Wing, is that many, if not most, of the entries for small formats are of psalms bound in as part of the London patentees' Bibles or with Books of Common Prayer.[5] Psalms may therefore be a protected species since many were preserved as part of larger works.

The evidence for the loss rate of ABCs, psalters and primers will be given in ascending order of magnitude. ABCs regularly ordered in large numbers by the Treasurer throughout the four three-year periods, always in octavo, are represented in Wing by at most five entries.[6] They brought in relatively little for the Company in terms of income. Psalters, however, which in 1676/7 amounted to 5.7% in quantity (14,600) but 17.4% of value (nearly £250 out of £4643) of the whole stock including almanacs,[7] and which in the same selected three-year periods from 1663/4 to 1695/6 average some 14,000 annually, are represented in Wing by only four entries, one of which, B2478A dated 1662, is, very unusually, in folio.

The example provided by primers is even more extreme. In 1676/7, 84,000 passed through the Treasurer's hands and were worth 12% of the total value. These are represented in Wing by a single 16mo black-letter copy in the British Library, dated c. 1670 (P3463).[8]

This evidence of the loss-rates for ABCs, psalters and primers reinforces the point made earlier: the profile of the Stationers' Company's psalms taken from the Treasurer's records and that taken from the Wing record, as in Table 1 above, is typical not of the survival rate of short books in small formats, but of substantial books sufficiently in demand, of which there must have been relatively few, published in the full range of formats

[4] The proportional relationships change relatively little if the numbers of copies of each edition are used rather than the number of editions alone.

[5] For an example of the variety of combinations of formats and of other titles bound with psalms, see John Barnard and Maureen Bell, *The Early Seventeenth-Century York Book Trade and John Foster's Inventory of 1616* (Leeds, 1994), pp. 58–62.

[6] A36A (1677), A38 (1683), A38A (1687), and A38B (1698), with A37 (1680) being a possible addition.

[7] John Barnard, 'Some Features of the Stationers' Company and its Stock in 1676/7', *Publishing History*, 36 (1994), 5–38 (pp. 22–26).

[8] Strikingly, Wing records no fewer than eleven Catholic primers, all printed on the Continent.

150   *Bibliographical Note*

from folio to 24mo. The most forcible way to emphasize the high loss rates among short, small-format publications is that the primer, printed in tens of thousands year by year from 1660 to 1700, is now represented by only a single copy in a single library.

Leeds   JOHN BARNARD

Part V
Reading

[15]

The Impact of the Early Printed Page on the History of Reading *

Paul Saenger, Chicago

The invention of the printing press has long been seen by both scholars and by the general public as an event of paramount importance. In 1962, Marshall Mcluhan's *Gutenberg Galaxy*[1] and more recently, Elizabeth Eisenstein's *The Printing Press as an Agent of Change*[2] as well as Walter Ong's *Orality and Literacy*[3] have contributed to popularizing the notion that the invention of printing wrought revolutionary change in all aspects of European intellectual life in the fifteenth and sixteenth century.[4] Elizabeth Eisenstein, in particular, has contrasted a medieval manuscript culture marked by imprecision, textual confusion, and orality with a sixteenth-century culture, which by virtue of printing came to be characterized by scientific rigor, textual integrity and silent visual study. To be sure, such global characterizations contain elements of truth. However, when baldly stated, they lift the history of printing out of its proper context, the history of the late medieval book. To enhance claims for an immediate revolutionary impact of the new mechanical method of producing codices, all manner of assertions have been made that violate the experience of codicologists and analytical bibliographers, scholars who have focused their attention on books as discrete artifacts regardless of their mode of production. Modern fiction

* Earlier versions of this article were delivered as public lectures at Reed College and the University of Notre Dame.

1. Herbert Marshall McLuhan, *The Gutenberg Galaxy: The Making of Typographic Man*, Toronto, 1962.

2. *The Printing Press as an Agent of Change: Communications and Cultural Transformations in Early Modern Europe*, Cambridge, 1979; revised in one volume as *The Printing Revolution in Early Modern Europe*, New York, 1983.

3. Walter J. Ong, *Orality and Literacy: The Technologizing of the Word*, London, 1982, pp. 117-38.

4. These ideas have been given currency in general textbooks such as John Bossy's *Christianity in the West 1400-1700*, Oxford, 1985, pp. 97-104.

Bulletin du bibliophile

writers have remarked that to populate a novel with genuine types, an author must begin with the description of real individuals and the novelist who begins by writing about types will create only stereotypes. Similarly, a historian seeking to narrate the impact of printing on the book ought properly to begin with describing actual books lest he or she postulate seductive generalizations that fail to correspond to bibliographic reality.

Fifteenth-century libraries did not generally distinguish between manuscript and printed volumes.[1] In monasteries and universities throughout Western and Central Europe, librarians shelved manuscript and printed codices adjacent to each other, usually horizontally, within the same rough schemes of subject classification. Both kinds of books were often held in place by chains, and both manuscript and printed texts were identified with similar handwritten titles placed on either of their covers. The *ex libris*, formulaic inscriptions that identified ownership, were also identical. The same craftsmen bound manuscript volumes and incunables (as well as volumes containing both varieties of text), using the same blind stamps to decorate their leather exteriors. In many early bound printed volumes, manuscript portions are so prevalent as to constitute truly hybrid volumes. A Newberry Library incunable codex containing the earliest extant printed missal, is in fact an example of a cooperative product of printers and scribes (fig. 1). Its calendar was entirely written in manuscript in both red and black ink. In contrast, the text of the missal proper was partly printed and partly written in manuscript.[2]

Late fifteenth-century booksellers sold both manuscripts and printed books in the same shops.[3] Indeed, in the fifteenth century it was very unusual to segregate printed books from manuscripts.[4] The custom of

1. See the remarks of Pieter F. J. Obbema, "The Rooklooster Register Evaluated," *Quaerendo*, 7 (1987), 333n and 339 and Dominique Coq, "L'Incunable, un bâtard du manuscrit ?", *Gazette du livre médiéval*, no. 1 (1982), 10-11.

2. Inc f7428.5*. In the printed portion, all of the red text, excluding the canon of the Mass, was manuscript; the decoration and illumination were also manuscript. For the term incunable codex, see Paul Saenger and Michael Heinlen, "Incunable Description and Its Implications for the Analysis of Fifteenth-Century Reading Habits," in Sandra L. Hindman, ed., *Printing the Written Word*, Ithaca, 1991, pp. 225-258.

3. Eleanor P. Spencer, "Antoine Vérard's Illuminated Vellum Incunables," and Mary Beth Winn, "Antoine Vérard Presentation Copies and Printed Books," in J. B. Trapp, ed., *Manuscripts in the Fifty Years After the Invention of Printing: Some Papers Read at the Colloquium at the Warburg Institute on 12-13 March 1982*, London, 1983, respectively, pp. 62-65 and 66-74.

4. The library of Saint Emmeram in Regensburg offers a rare example where, in 1500, manuscript books on vellum, manuscript books on paper and printed books on paper were systematically separated from each other. See Christine Elizabeth Ineichen-Eder, *Bayerische Akademie der Wissenschaften: Mittelalterliche Bibliothekskataloge Deutschlands und der Schweiz*, 4, pt. 1 (1977), 99-388; Hans Lüfling, "Die Fortdauer der handschriftlichen Bücherstellung nach der Erfindung des Buchdrucks - ein buchgeschichtliches Problem," in L. Hellinga and H. Härtel, eds., *Buch und Text in 15. Jahrhundert*, Hamburg, 1981, pp. 17-26.

1. The earliest printed Roman Missal, Central Italy (Newberry Library, Inc. f. 7428.5*, ff. 6v-7).

separating printed from handwritten volumes in corporate and private libraries evolved only gradually in the course of the sixteenth century as the latter type of codex gradually fell from use in deference to the former. [1] Only in the eighteenth century did scholars in Paris and Florence take initial steps toward developing separate catalogues with discrete bibliographical norms for printed and manuscript volumes, and only in the early twentieth century, after the pioneering studies of Henry Bradshaw, did codicology evolve into an autonomous academic discipline distinct from analytical bibliography, the science of printed book description. [2] Throughout most of the twentieth century the two disciplines have remained entirely separate from each other.

In contrast, fifteenth-century printers and scribes knew no firm distinctions between script and print. Especially in the early period, printers consistently anticipated that professional scribes would complement their work. In so doing they maintained the patterns of division of labor that characterized the late medieval scriptorium where one scribe or group of scribes prepared the textual substratum and others, in a discrete stage, added rubrics, punctuation, *prosodiae* (the Latin term for the signs we generally term diacritical marks), finding notes, headings, and schematic diagrams, all designed to elucidate visually the meaning of the text. [3] This fifteenth-century collective confecting of the book should be distinguished from the modern reader's private individualistic annotations, for medieval readers in general and especially the confreres of religious orders viewed

1. For examples see Barbara Halporn, "The Carthusian Library of Basle," *The Library Quarterly,* 54 (1984), pp. 226 and 234; Elisabeth Pellegrin, "La Bibliothèque de l'ancien collège de Dormans-Beauvais à Paris," *Bulletin philologique et historique,* 1944-45, pp. 157-59. In inventories prepared after decease, printed books were still intermingled, Roger Doucet, *Les Bibliothèques parisiennes au XVIe siècle,* Paris, 1956, p. 25.

2. Bradshaw recognized no distinction between the principles for describing manuscript and printed volumes, see his *The Early Collection of Canons Known as the Hibernensis: Two Unfinished Papers,* Cambridge, 1893, pp. 43-44 and Paul Needham, *The Bradshaw Method: Henry Bradshaw's Contribution to Bibliography,* The Seventh Haines Lecture; Chapel Hill, North Carolina, 1988.

3. The first errata lists that emerged among humanist printers in Italy (probably at Venice) in the incunable period are to be interpreted in this light, for they explicitly instructed the reader to write in emendations. See for example the two leaves of errata that accompany some copies of Aldus Manutius' edition of Urbano Valeriani's *Institutiones graecae grammaticae* printed in Venice in 1498, Antoine Auguste Renouard, *Annales de l'imprimerie des Alde,* 3rd edition; Paris, 1834, pp. 11-12. That the reader should write in the corrections was implicit in the instructions to the very early errata list found in Antonio di Bartolomeo da Miscomini's 1482 edition of Horace (Goff H-447). In the Newberry copy, Inc f6142, a contemporary emendator actually wrote in the corrections, e.g. ff. 11, 16 and 49 verso. Although this volume was printed in Florence, Bartolomeo began his career in Venice. The practice of writing in corrections had its origins in the emendations inserted by printers themselves, see Curt F. Bühler, "Stop-Press and Manuscript Corrections in the Aldine Edition of Benedetti's *De bello Carolino,*" "Aldus Manutius and his First Edition of the Greek Musaeus," and "Manuscript Corrections in the Aldine Edition of Bembo's *De Aetna,*" in his *Early Books and Manuscripts: Forty Years of Research,* New York, 1973, pp. 138-144, 162-169, and 170-175.

The Impact of the Early Printed Page on the History of Reading

textual emendation as part of a continuing process of book making and as such a permanent benefit for the community.

Late medieval scribes were at ease with printed books and readily used them as exemplars. The copying of a manuscript from a printed book, which seems bizarre to the average reader of the late twentieth century, is now recognized to have been common practice in the third quarter of the fifteenth century.[1] At the Newberry Library in a collection that now numbers about two hundred and fifty pre-1500 manuscript books, at least a half-dozen manuscripts dating from the last third of the fifteenth century were copied from printed exemplars, and in several cases the manuscripts are every bit as legible as their printed antecedents.

If we restrict our perusal to high quality calligraphic manuscript books and to volumes like the Newberry copy of the first missal and another Newberry incunable codex composed of devotional texts printed in Cologne augmented with manuscript additions from Saint Mary's of Königstein in Taunus (Hesse Nassau),[2] we might easily draw the conclusion that printing *per se* had no influence on visible language and therefore no real impact on the evolution of rapid private reading. To be sure, the introduction of printing was not a critical turning point in the history of medieval legibility. Ameliorations in text format that had transpired between the seventh and twelfth century had far more important implications for altering reading habits from the oral recitation of written text, the dominant mode of reading in late antiquity, to the silent scanning of text that typified private reading in the late Middle Ages. The distinction between lower and upper case letters, the introduction of word separation, and the perfection of signs for syntactic punctuation in written Latin that first transpired in the British Isles and then spread to the European Continent all antedate the introduction of printing

---

1. See Curt F. Bühler, *The Fifteenth-century Book*, Philadelphia, 1960, pp. 34-39; M. D. Reeve, "Manuscripts Copied from Printed Books," in Trapp, *Manuscripts in the Fifty Years After Printing*, pp. 12-20. For some Yale Beinecke Library examples, consult Cora E. Lutz, "Manuscripts copied from Printed Books," in her *Essays on Manuscripts and Rare Books*, Hamden, Conn., 1975, pp. 129-38.

2. Newberry Library Inc 886-958.5 is an example of an incunable codex that combines closely related manuscript and printed devotional texts. The works were bound together in the same monastery of Saint Mary's of Königstein in Taunus (Hesse Nassau) where the manuscript portions were apparently copied and the entire codex (manuscript and printed text alike) was enhanced by emendations in both black and red ink, not far from Cologne where the volume's printed elements were produced. The manuscript emendations included *traits d'union* or hyphens to link the parts of words divided at line endings and marginal letters of the alphabet that indicated points for cross references. Red Arabic opening numbers (see below note 5 p. 262) were added by the rubricator throughout the codex. In addition, the principal scribe of the manuscript portion emulated the decorative terminal marks that typify Cologne printed books, and it is not impossible that the manuscript was a line by line copy of a printed text not readily available when the codex was assembled.

by at least half a millenium.[1] Nor should we think that printing necessarily had an immediate impact on the level of literacy by augmenting the availability of books. Deluxe books often printed on parchment, such as the Gutenberg Bible and the French vernacular impressions of Colard Mansion, were intended in so far as it was possible to be indistinguishable from manuscripts, and although they may have been produced with greater rapidity, these printed volumes were not necessarily produced in numbers greater than the luxurious manuscript editions of the mid-fifteenth century. For example, Pietro Delfino, the Venetian Camaldolite reformer and prior general of his order, produced only forty copies (all on vellum) of his Camaldolite Breviary printed in Florence in 1484,[2] a quantity roughly similar to that of the ponderous vernacular didactic summae that were disseminated in highly standardized manuscripts to members of the Burgundian Order of the Toison d'Or under Philip the Good and Charles the Bold.[3] Particularly for liturgical and didactic works intended for religious orders and lay confraternities, the advantage of printing lay more in establishing textual uniformity between copies, and consequently uniformity in liturgical practice and in scholastic doctrine, than in augmenting the quantity of copies produced.[4]

However the conclusion that the first fifty years of printing had no impact on the mode of reading would be injudicious. There were specific but limited ways in which printing altered Western European reading habits at a time when the ability to read fluently was still restricted to a growing but

---

1. Paul Saenger, "Silent Reading: Its Impact on Late Medieval Script and Society," *Viator,* 13 (1982), 366-414; *Space Between Words: The Origins of Silent Reading* (forthcoming, Stanford University Press); Malcolm Parkes, *Pause and Effect: An Introduction to the History of Punctuation*, Berkeley, 1993.

2. *GW* 5191 (Goff B-1132); Edmond Martène and Ursin Durand, *Veterum scriptorum et monumentorum historicorum... amplissima collectio*, Paris, 1724-1733, III, 1129 (Ep. 178). On Delfino, see *Nouvelle biographie générale* 13 (1855), 459-60; *Dictionnaire d'histoire et de géographie ecclésiastique*, 14 (1960), 179-80.

3. Paul Saenger, "Colard Mansion and the Evolution of the Printed Book," *The Library Quarterly*, 45 (1975), 405-18. Mary Beth Winn's excellent forthcoming study provides comparable data for the circle of Antoine Vérard. For Greek manuscripts and printed books in Italy, see also Nicolas Barker, *Aldus Manutius and the Development of Greek Script and Type in the Fifteenth Century*, second edition, New York, 1992, pp. 11-20, 35 and 100.

4. The relatively low numbers of surviving breviaries other than for the Use of Rome as recorded in *GW* volume 5 tends to confirm that the audience for and consequently the production of these books was limited. In contrast relatively large numbers of copies survived, almost all printed on paper, of the titles printed at Subiaco and Rome by Sweynheym and Pannartz, see E. Gordon Duff, "Sweynheim and Pannartz: Notes and Collations," *Publications of the Edinburgh Bibliographical Society*, 9 (1904-1913), 28 and 35-36, Konrad Burger, *Buchhändleranzeigen des 15. Jahrhunderts*, Leipzig, 1907, pl. 10; cf. the appropriate *GW* entries.

The Impact of the Early Printed Page on the History of Reading

relatively small elite. [1] These largely ignored links between printing, legibility and rapid reading are worthy of attention. The limited but none the less important effects of printing on the visual presentation of text are the subject of this study.

To begin, economic factors inherent in the printing process dictated rationalizations in production that in certain instances inadvertently resulted in incremental increases in legibility. One of these innovations was the gradual elimination of ligatures, the connecting strokes that frequently linked handwritten letters together in late medieval scripts. [2] In cheaply produced late medieval manuscript books copied in low grade, Gothic cursive script, the use of ligatures reduced the cost of production, for any scribe could write faster when not required to lift his pen from the support. In contrast, printing was most economical when the number of *sorts*, i.e. characters in the printer's font, was limited. This economic incentive for using discrete letters eventually resulted in greater visible integrity for many words. Nevertheless, it must be remembered that early printers were eager to replicate the appearance of the manuscript page, and therefore, despite the additional effort and cost, they continued for many years to mold additional typographic characters to represent frequently employed ligatures. In manuscripts some of these combinations, such as the *ct* and *st* ligatures in humanistic scripts, may actually have facilitated reading by enhancing the global image of words (in the parlance of modern psychology, their Bouma shape [3]). Other combinations, such as the ligatured minim strokes that formed the letters *u*, *m*, and *n* as well as the double *ii* and various combinations of these letters in Gothic scripts inhibited legibility and were a frequent source of the textual corruptions that marred scholastic books copied by university stationers and the books of hours mass-produced in the mid-fifteenth century. [4] Early printers in Germany, the Low Countries and England used specific multi-letter sorts for various combinations such as *ii*,

1. Raymond Irwin, "General Introduction," to Francis Wormald and C. E. Wright, *The English Library Before 1700*, London, 1958, p. 5.

2. Barker, *Aldus Manutius*, pp.109-112.

3. See Insup and Martin Taylor, *The Psychology of Reading*, New York, 1983. The name comes from Herman Bouma, the noted Dutch cognitive psychologist.

4. Cf. Louis Havet, *Manuel de critique verbale appliquée aux textes latins*, Paris, 1911; reprinted, Rome, 1967, pp. 162, 165 and 191 (arts. 628, 631, 654-55, 813); James Willis, *Latin Textual Criticism*, Urbana, 1972, pp. 63-64. Even in incunables, the apposite font lacking, printers would occasionally invert the letter *n* to represent an *ii*, capitalizing on the fact that fifteenth century readers were accustomed to ambiguous minims.

Bulletin du bibliophile

iu, ni, in, mi, and *im.*[1] Even these printed ligatures advanced legibility over manuscripts in so far as that within them the letter *i* was invariably pointed or accented, which was very frequently not the case in manuscript.[2] In the last decade of the fifteenth century, printers increasingly eliminated the use of these multi-letter sorts, relying instead on a discrete pointed or accented character for all instances of the letter *i.*

Another area in which the technology of print reduced ambiguity was that of abbreviations. The Middle Ages had produced a bewildering array of abbreviations. At the end of the last century, these were reproduced by Adriano Cappelli in his *Lexicon abbreviaturarum.*[3] Although many of the abbreviations Cappelli enumerated represent only scribal variants of basic forms, in their actual use they varied sufficiently for numerous common words to be written by a perplexing variety of shapes. Since modern psychology tells us that experienced readers often recognize words by their global image or Bouma shape rather than by the synthetic combination of letters, it is important to note that the medieval reader of manuscript books regularly encountered alternative visual representations of the same word with far greater frequency than a modern reader of printed text regardless of type font. The traditional abbreviations employed by specific disciplines, regions and religious orders divided Europe's largely university-trained literate elite into subcommunities, each accustomed to its own variant form of visible Latin. Inconsistencies were even prevalent among short words, notably the conjunctions, relative pronouns and other common function words that constituted the essential building blocks of scholastic Latin syntax.[4]

Even before printing, certain scribal practices had encouraged a propensity towards greater similitude in textual format and consequently in abbreviated forms among copies of the same text. From the eighth century onwards, scribes, first in Britain and subsequently in France and Germany

---

1. See for early German examples *Veröffentlichengen der Gesellschaft für Typenkunde des XV Jahrhunderts,* Halle, 1902-1914 and the plates of Hellmut Lehmann-Haupt, *Peter Schoeffer of Gernsheim and Mainz with a List of his Surviving Books and Broadsides,* New York, 1950, pp. 26-34; cf. Paul Needham, "Mainz and Eltville: The True Tale of Three Compositors," *Bulletin du Bibliophile,* 1992, pp. 257-304; for the Netherlands and Belgium, Wytze and Lotte Hellinga, *The Fifteenth-Century Printing Types of the Low Countries,* Amsterdam, 1966; for England, Lotte Hellinga, *Caxton in Focus: The Beginning of Printing in England,* London, 1982, p. 3.

2. In certain incunables only the letter *i* in proximity to letters formed from minim strokes was denoted, while the character when used separately went unmarked, see for example Guillaume Tardif's *Grammatica,* below note 5 p. 250. On the origin of the pointed *i,* see Jules Desnoyers, "Note sur l'origine des i pointés," *Bibliothèque de l'École des chartes,* 13 (1852), 563-64.

3. *Lexicon abbreviaturarum: Dizionario di abbreviature latine ed italiane,* first edition, Milan, 1899.

4. See the perceptive comments of Henri-Jean Martin, *Histoire et pouvoirs de l'écrit,* Paris, 1988, p. 154.

The Impact of the Early Printed Page on the History of Reading

copied their exemplars not from dictation, whether external or internal, but visually. This practice tended to produce copies that replicated the same space patterns with the same abbreviations and forms of punctuation marks occurring in the same places in the text.[1] For example, within the corpus of fifteenth-century manuscript copies of Thomas à Kempis' *De imitatione Christi* produced in the Low Countries and Northern Germany, certain frequently employed words like *presbyter, commemoratio, Ihesus,* and *ergo* were regularly represented in the same position within the text in different copies by the same or related abbreviated forms.[2] The phenomenon of visually representing graphic word forms can be closely documented when fifteenth-century scribes copied word by word using an incunable as an exemplar.[3] Once a work had been printed, type setters of subsequent incunable editions exhibited precisely the same mentality, and thus fifteenth-century reprintings tended to adhere to the established pattern of text format in regard to word representation, form and position of abbreviation, capitalization, and punctuation.[4] Printing thus accelerated and broadened an already on-going evolution towards the visual uniformity among copies of the same texts.

Concomitant with the increase in graphic textual uniformity, the economic burden of casting and maintaining sorts was an important impetus to the elimination of functionless redundancy in graphic language.[5] Complex abbreviations came to be represented by a fixed combination of a few characters alleviating the obligation of the printer to design and cast relatively seldom used sorts. By disseminating a single standard set of visible abbreviated word forms in Germany, the Low Countries and France, printed glossaries such as the *Modus legendi abbreviaturas* doubtlessly reinforced this phenomenon.[6] Inexorably, the visible images of words in texts printed

1. Paul Saenger, "Word Separation and Its Implications for Manuscript Production," in Pieter Rück, ed., *Die Rationalisierung der Buchherstellung im Mittelalter und in der frühen Neuzeit,* Elementa diplomatica, 2; Marburg/Lahn, 1994, pp. 41-50, cf. Linda Nix, "Manuscript Layout and Re-Production of the Text in Anglo-Saxon England: A Preliminary Examination," *Gazette du livre médiéval,* 25 (1994), 17-23.

2. Compare for example the text of the fourth book in the diplomatic edition of L. M. J. Delaissé, *Le manuscrit autographe de Thomas à Kempis et l'imitation de Jésus-Christ: Examen archéologique et édition diplomatique du Bruxellensis 5055-6,* Paris, 1956, and the manuscript copy of the same text contained in Newberry Library Inc 886-958.5.

3. Bühler, *The Fifteenth-century Book,* p. 34.

4. See for examples, Needham, "Mainz and Eltville: The True Tale of Three Compositors," and Margaret Bingham Stillwell, "The *Fasciculus Temporum*: A Genealogical Survey of Editions before 1480," in *Bibliographical Essays: A Tribute to Wilberforce Eames,* Cambridge, Mass., 1924, p. 415.

5. Ernst Crous, "Die Abkürzungzeichen in den Wiegendrucken," *Gutenberg Festschrift zur Feier des 25 jaehrigen Bestehens des Gutenbergmuseums in Mainz,* Mainz, 1925, pp. 288-94.

6. Goff M-741-760.

between 1470 and 1500 became increasingly more consistent, regardless of the specific scholastic genre of the text in which they occurred. The standardization and simplification of abbreviations in print broke down the distinctions between the varieties of visible Latin employed by the subcommunities of the late medieval university scholars. The German emigrés who spread printing throughout Europe in the second half of the fifteenth century consolidated a corpus of simplified abbreviated forms, many of which were borrowed from the manuscript tradition of Western Germany. Before 1450, mastery of the art of reading abbreviations implied a lengthy apprenticeship in one of the traditional university-defined disciplines: liberal arts, theology, law, or medicine. In the second half of the century, as the same printers increasingly used identical sorts to publish diverse works of grammar, philosophy, theology, canon and civil law as well as classical and medieval texts, a broad reading public emerged that found its visual language freed from the encumbrance of unfamiliar and hence ambiguous abbreviations. Instead of maintaining an extensive mental thesaurus of alternative scribal forms, the reader simply relied on memorizing a fixed number of discrete and readily discernible permutations of a limited number of typographic signs. Thus, the much vaunted interdisciplinary quality of Renaissance culture, which had already begun to emerge in the mid-fifteenth century in the Low Countries in the manuscripts that contained the far ranging *opera* of Denys the Carthusian, was materially encouraged by the new mode of mechanically producing books. [1]

The technology of print also increasingly standardized visible Latin by first marginalizing and then eliminating the lower and more current grades of Gothic cursive from the hierarchy of scripts characteristic of late medieval manuscript book production. While many of the carefully copied formal parchment manuscripts in Oxford, Paris and Bologna in the thirteenth and fourteenth centuries were just as legible as early printed volumes, the former were time consuming and therefore expensive to produce. The increasing use of paper for book production in the first half of the fifteenth century had encouraged scholars to use non-calligraphic, hastily scrawled, cursive scripts to produce their own cheap copies of entire texts and even to compile highly personal collections of extracts. The latter were used chiefly for pedagogic and mnemonic purposes, for abbreviating a complex scholastic text was recognized as a highly effective way of mastering and retaining the essence of

---

1. For the interdisciplinary character of Denys' works, see Kent Emery, "Denys the Carthusian and the Invention of Preaching Materials," *Viator*, 25 (1994), 377-409.

The Impact of the Early Printed Page on the History of Reading

its contents. In Central Europe where the use of low grades of Gothic cursive was particularly prevalent, the pages of texts copied in it were visually dissimilar even if their textual content was the same.[1] Unlike their formal counterparts, such inexpensive manuscript books often presented grave problems of legibility. Librarians of German abbeys who were obliged to catalogue them complained that they could not read them.[2] At the Abbey of Saint Emmeram near Munich, the Benedictine librarians regarded them as a separate genre to be segregated both from manuscripts written on parchment and printed volumes.[3] Despite their inconvenience, the dearth of legible text manuscripts was such that paper books copied in current cursive script were reused by subsequent late medieval readers who relied on their familiarity with the subject of the text and its particular vocabulary to overcome inherent graphic ambiguity. In order to aid readers, German scribes frequently provided headings and incipits in a highly legible formal script while employing current cursive for the remainder. These cues aided the reader to find his place and to orient himself psychologically by bringing to mind any prior knowledge of the text's probable content.

By eliminating low-grade forms of Gothic cursive, printing, which had little effect on the legibility of missals, breviaries, or Bibles (late medieval copies of which texts were almost always written on vellum in formal grades of script), had a remarkable impact on the legibility of the ordinary books that constituted the usual private reading matter of scholars.[4] By virtue of moveable type, these cheap books rapidly came to be elevated to a standard of legibility set by the most deluxe products of the best scriptoria. As a consequence, the intensity of the impact of printing on the legibility of scholastic books varied greatly across Europe. In Paris where a rich accumulation of formal parchment books produced by university stationers in the thirteenth and early fourteenth century largely met the needs of a fifteenth-century university depopulated by the Black Death and the Hundred Years War, the immediate impact of printing on legibility was slight.[5] In Germany, the Low Countries and Eastern France where rapidly

---

1. Consult on these books Gerhardt Powitz, "*Modus scolipetarum et reporistarum: Pronuntiatio* and Fifteenth-century University Hands," *Scrittura e civiltà*, 12 (1988), 203-07.

2. See for an example, Paul Saenger, *A Catalogue of the Pre-1500 Manuscript Books at the Newberry Library*, Chicago, 1989, pp. 127-130.

3. See p. 238 note 4.

4. An example is the Newberry Library's copy of Fredericus Sunzel's *Collecta et exercita in VIII libros Physicorum Aritotelis*, Hagenau, 11 May 1499 (Goff S-869, Inc 3198).

5. See Carla Bozzolo and Ezio Ornato, *Pour une histoire du livre manuscrit au Moyen Âge*, Paris, 1983, pp. 13-121.

growing newly established universities, such as those of Basel, Cologne, Louvain, and Valence had recourse only to very limited stocks from prior centuries, the impact was very significant. In these universities, the *pecia* system run by professional stationers and scribes scarcely existed, and consequently prior to 1460 the "ecological" niche of the *pecia* produced books of Oxford, Paris and Bologna, was largely filled by difficult-to-read, privately-made books copied on paper in Gothic cursive. These volumes were often produced orally in special dictation sessions that complemented the regular lecture courses of the univerity.[1] Group dictation permitted even the very poorest students to bring to class copies of the required text. After 1460, the need for classroom texts was increasingly met by far more legible books produced in printing shops.[2]

The profound impact that printing had on the legibility of inexpensive books in Central Europe is readily perceptible in the distinction between the printed text and the script deemed appropriate for the handwritten elements that normally complemented the printed substratum of the incunables used in universities. Whereas in deluxe printed missals, manuscript and print might merge to form a seamless web, in the inexpensive printed books intended for ordinary private study, there was typically a discontinuity in legibility between the very easily read printed text and the difficult to decipher handwritten headings and marginal finding notes, for the emendator scribes who annotated such volumes usually employed the same low grade current Gothic cursive script that had been characteristic of the privately produced, marginally legible, paper manuscripts that had been abundant a generation earlier. By 1485, printing had spread and the class of cheaply produced paper manuscript books had largely disappeared. From the vantage point of legibility, hand-annotated printed books constituted the exact converse of the earlier German paper manuscripts written in Gothic cursive of which the headings and incipits had been written in formal *textualis*.[3] In time, this gap in legibility between manuscript emendations and printed text disappeared as part of the general

---

1. Karl Christ, "Ein Kapital mittelalterlicher Buchgeschichte," *Zentralblatt für Bibliothekswesen,* 55 (1938), 1-44; A. Van Hove, "La bibliothèque de la faculté des arts de l'Université de Louvain," in *Mélanges d'histoire offerts à Charles Moeller à l'occasion de son jubilé de 50 années de professorat à l'Université de Louvain 1863-1913,* Louvain, 1914, I, 616; Powitz, "*Modus scolipetarum et reporistarum,*" pp. 203-04.

2. For England, see James J. Murphy, "The Double Revolution of the First Rhetorical Textbook Published in England: The *Margarita eloquentiae* of Gulielmus Traversagnus (1479)," *Texte: Revue de critique et de théorie littéraire,* 1989, pp. 367-76.

3. Newberry Library Inc f905.5.

The Impact of the Early Printed Page on the History of Reading

"blackening of the incunable page" that transpired during the final two decades of the fifteenth century when printers supplanted scribal annotators and rapidly assumed the task of providing the book's textual substratum with fully printed headings, initials, marginal finding notes, punctuation, paragraph marks, and schematic diagrams. [1]

A third contribution of printing to visible language was to enhance metalinguistic consciousness. Scribes in *scriptoria* were not given to introspection about what they did or why they did it and least of all did they articulate alternative methods for improving the legibility or the convenience of their product. No more striking example of the force of tradition and the apparent lack of the awareness of visible language can be found than in late medieval accounts of punctuation and *prosodiae*. Although Continental scribes in the early eleventh century had dramatically altered the contours of the written page, notably by introducing word separation and the *trait d'union* (the modern hyphen) to facilitate rapid reading, the standard medieval monastic and scholastic nomenclature for punctuation — apart from a few Carthusian and Cistercian instructions relating to the performance of public liturgy — remained substantially mere repetitions of terms that had been used by late Roman grammarians in the context of different signs, scripts and supports. [2] For the ancients, punctuation and *prosodiae* had been signs generally added to texts when schoolboys copied them onto wax tablets as an aid to the classroom recitation of texts written in *scriptura continua*. The signs invented in the Middle Ages, such as the *trait d'union* marking words divided at line ending, the *punctus flexus* and *punctus elevatus* to denote phrases and dependent clauses, the colored paragraph mark, and capitalization (both to denote proper names and sentence beginnings) went unmentioned in grammatical texts composed prior to 1400.

In the late fourteenth and the first half of the fifteenth century, a few manuscript sources for the first time specifically enumerated new and entirely post-classical encoded signs that included the *trait d'union* and the parenthesis. Among the earliest of these grammatical texts were the *Ars punctandi* of Jacopo Alpoleio († 1431) and the *De arte punctandi* of the Paduan humanist Gasparino Barzizza († 1445). Although the *trait d'union* had been invented in England in the eighth century and came into common

---

1. Saenger and Heinlen, "Incunable Description and Its Implications for the Analysis of Fifteenth-Century Reading Habits," pp. 252-54, cf. Lehmann-Haupt, *Peter Schoeffer*, p. 54.

2. N. R. Ker, *English Manuscripts in the Century After the Norman Conquest*, Oxford, 1960, pp. 49 and 58-59.

use throughout Northern Europe by the mid-eleventh century, Alpoleio's treatise was the first to refer to it by name and to define its use. He termed it the *semipunctus*.[1] Barzizza designated the *trait d'union* by the same term.[2] His treatise, not widely circulated in manuscript, was recast into dialogue form by Johannis de Lapide, the German-born professor at the University of Paris who was co-patron with Guillaume Fichet of the first Paris printing press. Lapide's frequently reprinted *Dialogus de arte punctandi*[3] specifically stated that the *trait d'union* (*semipunctus*) was intended to enhance the rapidity of reading.[4] Niccolò Perotti of Fano (1429-1480), in his popular *Rudimenta grammatices*, also used the term *semipunctus*.[5] Although many early printers still left it to scribal emendators to add *traits d'union* as part of a printed tome's final confection, already in Mainz in the mid-1450's Johannes Gutenberg and Peter Schoeffer were casting and regularly employing special sorts to represent this sign, and Lapide himself used a similar character for the *trait d'union* in his Sorbonne print shop.

The marking of capitals denoting the beginning of sentences with red strokes was one of the standard functions of scribes who added rubrication and emendations to incunables. The significance of capitalization for delimiting sentences, virtually unmentioned in grammatical treatises dating from before the mid-fifteenth century, became a source of conscious concern for printers who had to calculate the relative need of lower and upper case letters in order to have on hand a sufficient provision of sorts for a given

1. Francesco Novati, "Di un' *Ars punctandi* erroneamente attribuita a Francesco Petrarca," *Rendiconti del Reale Istituto lombardo di scienze e lettere*, ser. 2, vol. 42 (1909). In 1484, this text was printed and erroneously attributed to Petrarch (Goff P-366).

2. For a partial edition, see Aurelio Roncaglia, "Note sulla puntegiatura medievale e il segno di parentesi," *Lingua nostra*, 3 (1941), 6-9; cf. Charles Thurot, "Notices et extraits de divers manuscrits latins pour servir à l'histoire des doctrines grammaticales au Moyen Âge," in *Notices et extraits des manuscrits de la Bibliothèque nationale*, 22, pt. 2 (1868), 416 (Paris, BNF lat. 10922, f. 58v); reprinted M. Hubert, *Corpus stymologicum minus* in *Bulletin du Cange*, 37 (1970), 168. R. G. G., Mercer, *The Teaching of Gasparino Barzizza with Special Reference to his Place in Paduan Humanism*, London, 1979, pp. 60-61; Guido Martellotti, *Dizionario biographico degli italiani*, 7 (1965), 37.

3. Christiane Marchello-Nizia, "Ponctuation et unités de lecture dans les manuscrits médiévaux ou je ponctue, tu lis, il théorise," *Langue française*, 40 (1978), p. 34; Anatole Claudin, *The First Paris Press*, London, 1898, p. 50; Jeanne Veyrin-Forrer, "Aux origines de l'imprimerie française: L'atelier de la Sorbonne et ses mécènes," in *L'Art du livre à l'Imprimerie nationale*, Paris, 1973, pp. 38-39.

4. "Alterum semipunctum nominant quad recto fieri solet per transversum ad dextram partem protactum, cui in fine alieius linee dictio scinditur in altera mox linea suscipiens complementus sic - vel sic =." I cite from Goff R-170.

5. See below p. 252, note 2. The term *semipunctus* also occurs in Paris, BNF lat. 10922, 58v dating from the end of the fifteenth century, Thurot, "Notices et extraits de divers manuscrits latins," p. 416; reprinted by M. Hubert, *Corpus stymologicum minus*, p. 168. Guillaume Tardif in his *Grammatica* (Paris, c. 1476; BNF Rés X 1570) used the term *virgula*.

The Impact of the Early Printed Page on the History of Reading

impression. The earliest description of the grammatical function of capitalization that I have found occurs in an anonymous commentary on Alexandre de Villedieu contained in Paris, BNF lat.17882 (olim Notre-Dame 175), a French manuscript copied in 1468 under Louis XI just two years before the establishment of the first Paris press. [1]

The parenthesis, however, was the single sign most closely linked to printing. Although Alpoleio's famous contemporary Coluccio Salutati had employed a variant bracket sign for the parenthesis in the books and letters he copied, he did not mention it in his only brief discussion of punctuation. [2] The bracket form for the parenthesis is extremely rare in fifteenth-century manuscripts (I know of no example apart from those in Salutati's own hand), and to date I have encountered only a scattering of instances of its occurrence in incunables. [3] It was the modern, semi-circular form of parenthesis that achieved success, and it did so solely because German printers adopted it at an early date. Although the semi-circular parenthesis was first described by Gasparino Barzizza half a century before the first printed books were produced, I know of no example of the round parenthesis occurring in a manuscript predating printing containing any text other than Barzizza's own treatise on punctuation. [4] It apparently was not used frequently by major humanistic scribes until the 1490's. [5] In contrast, early printers in Mainz were among the few who read Barzizza's work, and almost from the very beginning they employed a semi-circular parenthesis sort. Peter Schoeffer and Johannes Fust's *fere* humanistic type font included

1. Thurot, "Notices et extraits de divers manuscrits latins," pp. 55 and 416; cf. Léopold Delisle, *Inventaire des manuscrits latins conservés à la Bibliothèque Nationale sous les numéros 8823-18613*, Paris, 1863-71, V, 72; Charles Samaran, *Catalogue des manuscrits en écriture latine portant des indications de date, de lieu ou de copiste*, 3, 1974, 597 and pl. 184.

2. Francesco Novati, ed., *Epistolario di Coluccio Salutati*, III, Rome, 1896, pp. 176-78.

3. The bracket form of parenthesis is present in the Strasbourg, c. 1481 edition of Guillermus Parisiensis' *Postilla super Epistolas et Evangelia*, Strasbourg, Printer of the 1481 *Legenda Aurea* (Goff G-656), Simon de Cassia's *Expositio super totum corpus Evangeliorum*, Strasbourg, c. 1482-84 (Goff S-522) and in the Low German Bibles printed by Heinrich Quentell in c. 1478 (*GW* 4307 and 4308). It is also present in the *Stella clericorum* printed for Denis Roce c. 1494 (Goff S-781; I am indebted to Eric Reiter for this reference).

4. Newberry Library MS 96, f.2 constitutes a relatively early example; Saenger, *A Catalogue of the Pre-1500 Manuscript Books at the Newberry Library*, pp.184-85. For one of Barzizza's manuscripts (Paris BNF lat. 8731, ff. 35-40, see Gilbert Ouy, "Orthographie et ponctuation dans les manuscrits autographes des humanistes français des XIVe et XVe siècles", in A. Maierù R-17, *Grafia e interpunzione del latino nel medioevo*, Rome, 1987, pp. 182-87. See also Paris, BNF lat. 10922, f. 58v.

5. The first instance recorded by James Wardrop, *The Scripts of Humanism: Aspects of Humanistic Script 1460-1560*, Oxford, 1963, plate 28 is Bartolomeo Sanvito's copy of Cicero's *De officiis*, London, British Library Harley 6051, copied in 1494. By 1494 printed editions of the *De officiis* had existed for three decades. Albina de la Mare, *Handwriting of Italian Humanists*, Oxford, 1973 reproduces no post-Salutati examples in the influential handwritings of Niccolò Niccoli and Poggio.

it, and it appears in the first edition of Cicero's *De officiis*.[1] Co-workers disseminated it in Basel and Paris; Italians, however, were not early users of the round parenthesis. Niccolò Perotti, in his *Rudimenta grammatices*, enumerated and defined the parenthesis as a sign of punctuation, but in the early editions of his work the parentheses were represented typographically as a pair of colon-like marks (:) standing at either end of the designated phrase.[2] A 1472 Venetian printed edition of the *De officiis* used round parentheses only sparsely.[3] Contemporary emendators added round parentheses in manuscript over a simple *punctus* and other printed signs in Newberry Library copies of Wendelin of Speyer's c. 1470 Venice edition of Juvenal's *Saturae*.[4] In 1477 Erhard Ratdolt in Venice was still in the process of adding round parentheses to his type font.[5]

Northern European printers freely used a round form of the parenthesis as a visible sign of any irregularities in what medieval grammarians termed the natural word order, i.e. the subject-verb-object order. Schoeffer and Fust in their *De officiis* notably employed them for setting off embedded *ut* clauses. In general, the round parenthesis was used instead of other typographic signs when a cluster of syntactically related words forming a complete sentence or dependent clause was inserted either between a larger sentence's subject and verb or verb and object.[6] In particular, they denoted the syntactical element *ut ait* when introducing indirect discourse. Only rarely did typographic round parentheses isolate the aside or inserted change of subject that constituted the rhetorical *parenthesis* described by Quintilian.[7]

---

1. *GW* 6921 (Goff C-575); Lehmann-Haupt, *Peter Schoeffer*, pp. 20-25 and 33, fig. 16b. Parentheses occur also in Schoeffer's prospectus to lovers of canon law printed in 1472, Lehmann-Haupt, *Peter Schoeffer*, p. 94, fig. 25.

2. See Goff P-309 and P-318. The *editio princeps* of Perotti's translation of Polybius' *Historiae* printed in Rome by Sweynheym and Pannartz in December 1473 (Goff P-107) employed pairs of colon-like marks rather than the round parenthesis character.

3. See *GW* 6927 (Goff C-581).

4. Goff J-363, Newberry Library Inc 4059, f. 35.

5. It was absent from the first volume of his Appianus, *Historia Romana de bellis civilibus*, *GW* 2290 (Goff A-928), but he used it frequently in the second volume, both dated Venice, 1477.

6. "Parenthesim vero quam ab incepta clausula sed nondum perfecta clauditur duabus semicirculis (sic enim plerique eam ut hoc uides, notare solent) poterit intercludere," Johannes de Lapide, *Dialogus de arte punctandi*. "Parenthesis que est uni sentencie alterius interposicio ipsam quidem interpositam sentenciam dimidiis dictis circulis includit," Guillaume Tardif, *Grammatica*, see above note 5 p. 250. "Parentesis ( )... parentesis denique quando sentencie inchoate et non perfecte adiungitur in media alia sententia," Paris, BNF lat. 10932, f. 58v, Thurot, "Notices et extraits de divers manuscrits latins," p. 416.

7. For Quintilian's definition and a modern example of the use of the sign, see the Loeb Classical Library edition of *The Institutio Oratoria of Quintilian*, ed. H. E. Butler, III, London, 1921, pp. 458-62 (IX, lii, 23-26).

The Impact of the Early Printed Page on the History of Reading

The typographical use of printed parentheses was rather consonant with the definition of *parenthesis* as a deviation from natural word order that the thirteenth-century Dominican friar and grammarian Johannes de Balbis of Genoa in his *Catholicon* had extrapolated from Donatus' *Ars maior*.[1] However, neither in manuscript nor in print did the textual tradition of the *Catholicon* evince the semicircular parenthesis sign. For while grounded in medieval Latin grammar, the printed semicircular parenthesis sign was in fact a peculiar innovation of Renaissance graphic culture, a unique variety of visible construction note that was intended to augment reading speed. In addition, printers employed round parentheses for other purposes. In a Mainz edition of Biblical commentaries, parentheses were employed lavishly as a typographic means of aiding the reader to rapidly distinguish the text of the Bible from its commentary.[2] In marginal side notes, tables of contents and notably in the prayers of vernacular books of hours, parentheses were used as a sign to set off line continuations placed in blank space at the end of the previous line.[3]

The round parenthesis spread within editions of Latin humanistic texts and scholastic disputations in a trajectory that epitomized the manner in which the new technology of printing was breaking down barriers between late medieval textual communities. In the vernacular, however, where typographic construction notes eliminating ambiguity from irregularities in word order were not generally required, the semicircular parenthesis was seldom used.[4]

1. Parenthesis est interpositio ratiocinatio diverse sententie, ut "Eneas, neque enim patrius consistere mentem passus amor rapidum ad naves premittit Achaten [*Aeneid* I, 643]." Secundum Donatum [*Ars maior*, III, 6], quotiens sententia inchoatur, eique interponitur quelibet rationatio parenthesis est, ut in predicto exemplo. Debuit enim dicerere, "Eneas rapidum Achaten premittit ad naves," et sic demum subiungere "Neque enim patrius amor passus est consistere mentem." Item Apostolus ad Galathas, "Cum vidissent gratiam que data est mihi qui enim operatus est Petro in apostolatu operatus est et mihi inter gentes Iacobus, Cephos et Iohannes dextras dederunt mihi et Barnabe societatis [cf. Galatians 2, 8-9]," Johannes de Balbis, *Catholicon*, GW 3195 (Goff B-30), quire g. leaf 2; cf. Donatus, *Ars maior*, ed L. Holtz, *Donat et la tradition de l'enseignement grammatical*, Paris, 1981, pp. 670-71. The *Catholicon* was first printed in Mainz by Gutenberg in 1460. There were numerous incunable reprintings, Goff B-21-34.

2. See Peter Schoeffer's edition of Johannes de Turrecremata's *Expositio super toto Psalterio* printed in Mainz in March of 1476, Goff T-522, Lehmann-Haupt, *Peter Schoeffer*, p. 54 and plate 13. Erasmus used parentheses for this purpose in the *annotationes* that formed the second volume of his New Testament (Basle: Johannes Froeben, 1516).

3. See the second volume of Appianus' *Historia Romana* (above note 5 p. 252) and the first edition of Niccolò Perotti's *Rudimenta grammatices* (Goff P-307; Treviso, 1476). An example of this usage in a vernacular book of hours is Goff H-350, see below p. 274 at note 2.

4. See Paul Saenger, "The Order of Words and the Separation of Words: The Genesis of Medieval Reading," *Scrittura e Civiltà*, 14 (1990), 49-74. For example, in the Paris c. 1500 bilingual edition of Ps. Jerome's *Regula monacharum* (Goff H-189; Copinger 2975*), the printer used parentheses freely within the Latin text but rarely in its French translation.

Printing also stimulated an enhanced consciousness of the physical divisions of text, and consequently typography had a profound impact on the *notae* that indicated physical location on the page. Originating in late antiquity, the codex had created new possibilities for establishing arbitrarily fixed points within a text that could be used for locating information. Numerous ancient Greek papyri leaves contain leaf numbers (i.e. numbers on the recto of the leaf) or page numbers (i.e. numbers on each side, recto and verso).[1] These practices, however, seem never to have penetrated into ancient Latin books despite the pervasive Roman emulation of Greek literate culture. Indeed, the Greeks themselves exploited neither leaf numbers nor pagination for reference purposes; they compiled no tables referring to either foliation or pagination, and in literary or historical sources there are no references to the foliation of a book. Leaf numbers in ancient times apparently served only to guarantee that the leaves of a codex were correctly ordered prior to binding.

In the eighth and ninth centuries, partial numbering of leaves in order to insure correct sequencing within the quire was introduced into Latin texts copied in the British Isles, perhaps in emulation of Byzantine models.[2] In the eleventh century, when Continental scribes began to separate words with regularity, a few scribes began to number consistently the leaves of the codices that they produced. In so doing, they may have been inspired by contemporary Oriental models, for some Greek scribes continued to foliate some books throughout the Middle Ages, and medieval Coptic scribes perpetuated the ancient Greek practice of pagination.[3] The earliest examples of foliation used for reference purposes occurred in Latin books from the monastery of Farfa near Rome. One of Farfa's series of massive, specialized cartularies, the *Liber largitorius* compiled by Gregorio di Catino († 1132), was prefaced by an alphabetical table of subjects indicating the folio number and a letter of the alphabet placed in the margin at the apposite point of the designated leaf.[4] The reader could thus first locate in

1. Eric G. Turner, *The Typology of the Early Codex*, Philadelphia, 1977, pp. 75-76.

2. Paul Lehmann, "Blätter, Seiten, Spalten, Zeilen" in *Erforschung des Mittelalters*, Leipzig, 1941-62, III, 16-17; R. I. Best, *The Commentary on the Psalms with Glosses in Old Irish*, Dublin, 1936, p.12. While in some incunables, leaf signatures still seem to have served this purpose, it is clear that they also served as an aid to reference consultation.

3. See Lehmann, "Blätter," pp. 8-10; Bentley Layton, *Catalogue of Coptic Literary Manuscripts in the British Library Acquired Since the Year 1906*, London, 1987 includes numerous reference to medieval Coptic pagination. I am grateful to Robert Babcock for this reference.

4. Giuseppi Zucchetti, *Liber largitorius vel notarius monasterii Pharphenis*, Rome, 1913-32; *Archivio paleografico italiano*, 6 (1924, reprinted s.d.), pl. 100; *Italy: Catalogo dei manoscritti datati e databili*, 1 (1971), no. 2 and pls. 22-23.

The Impact of the Early Printed Page on the History of Reading

the table a reference to a given priory or tract of land and then rapidly turn to the indicated leaf to find the passage containing the information. In the mid and late twelfth century, scriptoria in certain French Cistercian abbeys frequently numbered their leaves. Pierre de Limoges, the late thirteenth-century Sorbonne scholar, numbered the folios of some of the volumes of his library and prepared tables referring to these numbers as points for cross reference.[1] Other scholars including the Cistercian Pierre de Ceffons, the Franciscan Alexander Langeley, Gérard of Abbeville and Godefroy of Fontaines did the same,[2] and in Florence in the fourteenth century, chant books were regularly produced with mid-leaf foliation.[3] While thirteenth and fourteenth century leaf numberings were generally highly accurate and hence useful, they remained an exceptional practice. No literary works contained tables with folio references as an integral part of a text, i.e. an element forming part of the author's exemplar intended for scribal replication.

It is reasonable to estimate that in 1450 less than 10 percent of manuscript books then existing contained either original or subsequently added leaf numbering.[4] Although university books constituted the class of codices most likely to be foliated, the great majority of them even at this late date still did not bear leaf numbers.[5] The neo-Latin terms *pagina* and *pagella* referred to a leaf with two sides, that is, a folio, and the pagination of manuscripts — the numbering of both sides of a leaf termed *facies*, *latus* or *semipagina* — while not unknown, was very rare.[6] Thus, if one were to peruse the stacks of a large

1. Madeleine Mabille, "Pierre de Limoges et ses méthodes de travail," in Guy Cambier, ed., *Hommages à André Boutemy*, Collection Latomus, 145; Brussels, 1976, pp. 244-251.

2. William J. Couteney, "Alexander Langeley, O. F. M.," *Manuscripta*, 18 (1974), 101-103; Richard H. Rouse and Mary A. Rouse, *Preachers, Florilegia and Sermons: Studies on the Manipulus Florum of Thomas of Ireland*, Toronto, 1979, pp. 22-23.

3. Newberry Library MS + 74 has these numbers. For other examples, see Laurence B. Kanter et al., *Painting and Illumination in Early Renaissance Florence 1300-1450*, exhibition catalogue, The Metropolitan Museum of Art, New York, 1994, pp. 206-216.

4. The comments of Konrad Haebler, *The Study of Incunabula*, trans. L. E. Osborne, New York, 1933, p. 69 are misleading on this point.

5. Based on data recorded by R. Macken, *Bibliotheca Manuscripta Henrici de Gandavo*, Louvain, 1979, 23.3% of medieval manuscripts containing texts of Henry of Ghent were foliated at any time during the Middle Ages. Of those that were, most appear to have been foliated in the fifteenth century. In about 1400, the manuscripts containing the scholastic questions of Thomas of Cracow were unfoliated, but the folio was used as a reference point for discussing topics within each question, see Zenon Kaluza, *Thomas de Cracovie: Contribution à l'histoire du collège de la Sorbonne*, Wroclaw, 1978, pp. 66, 74 and 75.

6. On the meaning of *pagina*, see Silvia Rizzo, *Il lessico filologico degli umanisti*, Sussidi eruditi, 26; Rome, 1973, pp. 35-40. For rare examples of pagination see A. G. Little and F. Pelster, *Oxford Theology and Theologians c. A.D. 1282-1302*, Oxford, 1934, pp. 61-62; Lehmann, "Blätter," pp. 45-51. In incunables, *pagina* was always used as a synonym for folio, e.g. the table of Anton Koburger's Virgil of 1492 meant reference to the folio and not the page in the modern sense; Goff V-188.

manuscript collection, such as those of the Bibliothèque Nationale and the British Library, in the overwhelming majority of those volumes bearing medieval leaf numbering the numbering would date from after 1450, the period generally contemporary with printing. In contrast, if one were to browse incunable volumes in the same institutions, a far higher percentage of the leaves would be foliated, either by the printer or by a fifteenth century emendator. Of those incunables that appear to have remained unfoliated in the year 1500, many contain printed tables that explicitly or implicitly indicate the printer's expectation that foliation would be added by an emendator. However, in the event the scribal work force was unequal to the task, and the anticipated foliation in these volumes was never actually done. [1]

The nexus between printing and leaf numbering can be documented as early as 1465. [2] In addition many incunables, especially large and cumbersome ones such as sermon collections, had other arbitrary systems of denoting place, principally by means of printed alphabets that served as alternatives to foliation in affording the reader more rapid access to specific points in the text (see below). The principal advantage of foliation and the other arbitrary systems of denoting locus within the text was that the reader who used tables keyed to them did not require a prolonged apprenticeship in the arcane and often highly complex principles of textual division peculiar to each of scholasticism's varied genres of text, particularly philosophy, theology and law.

Although theoretically foliation in printed volumes created reference points that readers could employ in widely separated copies of the same edition, fifteenth-century sources suggest that such concerns did not play a role in foliation's emerging popularity. In their formal compositions and letters, fifteenth-century authors when citing works never referred to a folio number in a particular edition. Indeed, medieval inter-volume folio cross references were extremely rare and then usually between volumes within a scholar's private library or within a series of familial or institutional registers. The earliest unambiguous references to folio numbers in generally consultable copies are to manuscript registers alluded to in the records of judicial proceedings. [3] A rubric in a manuscript prayer book copied for Anne

1. In a few instances, foliation was obliterated by subsequent trimming and rebinding, but most rebindings leave at least traces of prior manuscript numeration.

2. See below p. 263, note 2.

3. See the example of Ugolino di Giovanni accused of falsifying a specific folio of his account book in a deposition of 12 May 1473, Archivio storico del comune di Cortura, ser. A: Atti criminali, pezzo 1: 1473, ff. 7-9 and 50v-52v; I am grateful to Daniel Bornstein for this reference. William J. Couteney has suggested that a few rare references to foliation in scholastic texts may be to books located in specific libraries that were open for scholarly consultation, see his "Alexander Langeley, O. F. M.," pp. 100-103.

The Impact of the Early Printed Page on the History of Reading

of Brittany in Florence c. 1500 refers to an indulgence recorded in a papal register. [1] The earliest reference to the specific printed leaf number of a printed book of which I am aware occurs in a contemporary manuscript note added to the title page of the Newberry Library's copy of Ps. Gerson's *Alphabetum divini amoris* printed in Basle not after 1491. [2] Here the emendator refers to a *folium* in Jean Mombaer's *Rosetum,* a text that had been issued in at least two foliated editions in the fifteenth century. Only in the second decade of the sixteenth century, when the shift to pagination was already beginning to transpire, did scholars begin to refer to folio numbers of specific editions to designate loci within printed texts. [3]

The preoccupation with defined locations within texts that came to be characteristic of printed books is revealed in the prefatory notices to the tables that accompanied incunables. These instructions reflect a new concern with precision and the elimination of ambiguity in denoting arbitrary place references. [4] In certain books, the printer included instructions on where the manuscript numbering should begin, i.e. on the first leaf of text after the initial blank or title page, in order to eliminate confusion. [5] Some tables even elucidated the ambiguities of the additive and subtractive principles governing fifteenth-century Roman numerals. [6] In incunables with printed foliation, the numbers on the leaves were frequently denoted with the specific designation *folium* or its synonyms *carta* and *pagina,* and these terms also frequently occur in the sequential, methodical, or alphabetical tables that accompanied these works. [7] The verbal reiteration of foliation is of special importance in printed books precisely because in manuscripts through the mid-fifteenth century it remained ambiguous as to

1. Newberry Library MS 83, see Saenger, *A Catalogue of Pre-1500 Manuscript Books at the Newberry Library,* p. 156.

2. Newberry Library Inc 7637 (Goff A-528). I am indebted to Eric Reiter who discovered this note in October 1995 while working under the auspices of a Newberry Short Term Fellowship.

3. See Guillaume Budé's letter to Erasmus of 7 July 1516, Marie-Madeleine de la Garanderie, *La correspondance d'Érasme et de Guillaume Budé,* Paris, 1967, pp. 65-66; P. S. Allen, *Opus epistolarum Des. Erasmi Roterodami,* Oxford, 1906-58, II, no. 435. Allen spells out the numbers verbally. In the early printed editions they are in Roman numerals, which have been restored in the translation of M. M. de la Garanderie.

4. Examples include the instructions to the table of Bernardus Nerlius' edition of Virgil's *Opera,* Florence, 1487 (Goff V-183) and the reformatted Aldine edition of Perotti's *Cornucopiae,* Venice, 1499.

5. See the introduction to the table accompanying the Newberry copy of Duns Scotus' *Super secundum librum Sententiarum* (*GW* 9073, Goff D-379, ii; Venice: Johannes of Cologne and Johannes Manthen, 1478), f4327.5* see below p. 273, note 9.

6. For example, see the table accompanying Werner Rolewinck's *Fasciculus temporum,* see below.

7. In Goff H-16 (below p. 267, note 4) the term *folium* was placed uniquely on the first five leaves so as to indicate to the reader the significance of these numbers.

whether the numbers on the leaves of a codex designated the *folium* (i.e. recto and verso of a single leaf) or the opening, the two pages visible in an open book. In most manuscripts, the numbers as they appear on the leaves do not make this clear, although the scribe of one Ghent liturgical manuscript copied in about 1470 placed folio numbers on both the recto and verso so as to eliminate any possibility that his numbers might indicate openings.[1] Such indications on the leaves or in the tables of manuscripts that permit the reader readily to distinguish the numbering of folios from the numbering of openings are extremely rare and always postdate the introduction of printing.[2] Generally in manuscript books, only the verification of references given in the tables of contents or of internal cross references allowed the reader to be certain as to which unit was being denumbered.

From the first emergence of medieval leaf numbering in the early twelfth century until the dawn of printing, the denotation of folios predominated over the denotation of openings. Some thirteenth-century scribes, however, designated openings rather than folios. An example is Newberry Library MS 128, a recently acquired late thirteenth-century Italian copy of the Dominican friar Bartholomeo da Trento's *Liber epilogorum in gesta sanctorum* (a precursor of the *Legenda aurea*). In it a table prepared by the original scribe directs the reader to Arabically numbered openings. In the thirteenth and fourteenth centuries, the peculiarly English system of numbered columns and lines was implicitly oriented towards the opening,[3] and in England and on the Continent the *cavillae* or rotary book marks of the late Middle Ages were constructed so as to indicate position within the four columns of each opening.[4] Openings were also important units for medieval book artists. A preference for the opening was particularly evident in certain fifteenth-century Flemish scriptoria that produced books of hours into which illuminated leaves devoid of text and blank on one side were regularly inserted in order to form decorative openings at the beginnings of the

---

1. MS 59.1; Saenger, *A Catalogue of the Pre-1500 Manuscript Books at the Newberry Library*, pp. 110-114.

2. See for comparison the ultimate numbered half openings (verso only) in Jerome's *Epistolae* (see below p. 261, note 2) and the manuscript numbering of the Newberry copy of Franciscus Mayrones' *Super primum Sententiarum*, Inc f6468 (see below p. 262, note 1).

3. A. G. Little and Pelster, *Oxford Theology and Theologians c. A. D. 1282-1302*, Oxford, 1934, pp. 61-62; Pelster, *Zeitschrift für kathol. Theologie*, 54 (1930), pp. 522, 526, 527; *Zeitschrift Scholastik*, I p. 61ff.; Lehmann, "Blätter," pp. 57-59.

4. Graham Pollard, "The Construction of English Twelfth-Century Bindings," *The Library*, ser. 5, vol. 17, p. 16, n. 1; Mirella Ferrari, "Segnalibri del secolo XV in codici bobbiesi," *Italia medioevale e umanistica*, 12 (1969), 324.

258

The Impact of the Early Printed Page on the History of Reading

principal liturgical sections.[1] Some medieval devotional texts incorporated the opening as an integral aspect of their text format. The intricate iconography and page lay-out of both the Latin and French vernacular manuscripts of Ps. Ludolph of Saxony's *Speculum humanae salvationis* presupposed the use of openings as the basic unit of book organization, and scribes copying this work regularly began on the verso of the first leaf and ended on the recto of the last leaf (fig. 2).[2] Similarly, in certain unillustrated textual manuscripts, some dating from as early as the twelfth century, the initial rubric announcing the title of a work was placed on a blank verso preceding the beginning of a text.[3]

Nevertheless, the majority of medieval manuscript books including the majority of illuminated books of hours were conceived as compilations of gatherings each beginning with a recto and ending with a verso. The principal advantage of this bibliographic conception was that it was more conducive to the efficient formation of composite volumes. At Oxford, Paris and Bologna, the folio and not the opening was the unity respected by university stationers who produced books by means of the *pecia* system.[4] In Paris, Pierre de Limoges in his marginalia referred to folios.[5] In Italy, the authorial codex of the sermons of Robert d'Anjou prepared for use in a lay aristocratic court contained a table using both Roman and Arabic numbers to refer to the scribe's foliation.[6] While in both Northern Europe and in Italy

1. See for example, Newberry Library MS 41. These leaves have confused some manuscript cataloguers who, thinking in terms of pages, have been uncertain as to where to denote the beginning of the text. For examples of different approaches, see Saenger, *A Catalogue of the Pre-1500 Manuscript Books at the Newberry Library* and Barbara Shailor, *Catalogue of Medieval and Renaissance Manuscripts in the Beinecke Rare Book and Manuscript Library, Yale University* I, Binghamton, 1984.

2. Duke Philip the Good of Burgundy's spectacular copy of the *Speculum humanae salvationis*, Newberry Library f.40, as well as its twin, Chantilly, 139 document this orientation; see Saenger, *A Catalogue of the Pre-1500 Manuscript Books at the Newberry Library*, pp. 70-71. Cf. J. Lutz and P. Perdrizet, *Speculum humanae salvationis: Texte critique*, Leipzig, 1907. The same orientation is to be found in incunable editions of the *Speculum*; J. Ph. Berjeau, ed., *Speculum humanae salvationis: Le plus ancien monument de la xylographie et la typographie réunies reproduit en fac-similé*, London, 1861 = the Pembroke Huntington copy, W. L. Schreiber, *Manuel de l'amateur de la gravure sur bois et sur métal au XVᵉ siècle*, 4, Leipzig, 1902, 118; and the first typographic edition, Augsburg, Günther Zainer, not after 1473, see *Incunabula from the Court Library at Donaueschingen* (sales catalogue, Sotheby's 1 July 1994), frontispiece and pp. 237-38.

3. See for example Newberry Library MS 8; Saenger, *A Catalogue of the Pre-1500 Manuscript Books at the Newberry Library*, p.18.

4. Newberry Library MS 121.

5. Mabille, "Pierre de Limoges et ses méthodes de travail," pp. 245-46.

6. Rome, Bibl. Angelica 150 and 151. I am grateful to Darleen Pryds for bringing this manuscript to my attention and sharing her microfilm of it with me. For descriptions, see Marc Dykmans, *Robert d'Anjou: La vision bienheureuse, traité envoyé au pape Jean XXII*, Miscellanea historiae pontificae, 30; Rome, 1970, pp. 54*-55*.

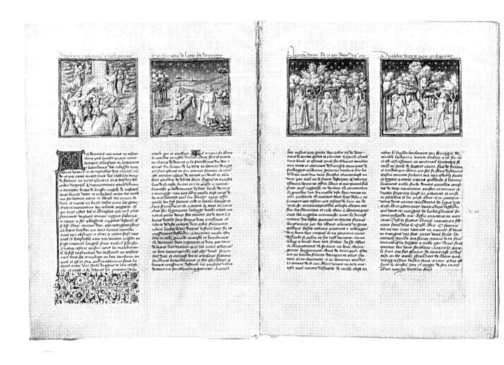

2. The *Speculum humanae salvationis* (in french), Flanders, c. 1455 (Newberry Library, MS. f.40, ff. 1v-2).

The Impact of the Early Printed Page on the History of Reading

reference to the folio was more usual, the situation remained fraught with ambiguity, and in the manuscript period it was ultimately the reader using a volume's table who had to verify the principle of place location that governed a particular codex, introductory notes to explain the use governing a particular table being unknown.

The latent ambiguity between *folium* and opening had not been resolved by the mid-fifteenth century as tables in mid-fifteenth-century codices with leaf numbering confirm. In the Newberry Library, five manuscripts have fifteenth-century tables referring to some form of leaf numbers, and two of these, including one written in Liège by a humanist scribe of Italian training and another by an Italian scribe, designated openings and not folios.[1] A preliminary examination of the Newberry's collection of approximately two thousand incunables has revealed five additional codices with added manuscript leaf numbering that also refer to the openings rather than to folios, a far lower incidence than for manuscripts. The earliest of these is the Newberry copy of the Strasbourg printer Johannes Mentelin's 1469 edition of Jerome's *Epistolae*, a collection that already in manuscripts dating from the mid-fifteenth century had developed into a highly complex bibliographical entity that was difficult for readers to consult.[2] In the Newberry copy of the incunable, the text was preceded by a manuscript table prepared by the same hand that numbered the leaves. This table referred to openings and within each opening to the four columns and to eight imaginary alphabetical subdistinctions, *a* through *h*.[3] A second example of numbered openings occurs in the Newberry's copy of Sixtus Riessinger's not later than 1470, Rome edition of Jerome's *Epistolae*.[4] Here, the printed table refers to folios but includes a blank space for folio numbers; the leaves bear no printed foliation. Riessinger clearly intended that a scribe emendator would add the requisite numbers both in the table and on the leaves. In the event, the fifteenth-century Italian emendator of the second volume of the Newberry copy added Arabic numbers to the table and on the leaves that refer the reader to openings and not folios. In Newberry Inc f6468, Franciscus Mayronnes' *Super primum Sententiarum* (Treviso, 1476), another Italian

---

1. MS f57 was written c.1462-64; Saenger, *A Catalogue of the Pre-1500 Manuscript Books at the Newberry Library*, pp. 106-09. The second is MS 152, a recent acquistion written in humanistic script dated in 1471.

2. Inc 258.5-203*, Goff H-162. In its use of imaginary distinctions, this table resembled the *tabula magistralis* that Peter Schoeffer described in the prologue to his 1470 edition of Jerome's *Epistolae* (Goff H-165) as a tool that readers might compile as an aid for rapid reference consultation. Schoeffer's table, however, explicitly related to folios and not openings.

3. On imaginary alphabetical distinctions, see below pp. 279-80.

4. Inc f6747; Goff H-163.

emendator, writing in humanistic script, annotated the volume's printed table of *distinctiones* with Arabic numbers denoting the openings that he also denumbered on the leaves.[1]

Additional examples of manuscript opening numbering in the Newberry's incunable collection occur in volumes containing texts printed in Cologne in the early 1470's. In Newberry Inc 831-834-957.9, a volume that originally contained four discrete printed elements dating from 1470-1472, the Roman numerals in the manuscript table refer to openings.[2] In Newberry Inc 856-863, containing two Cologne printed elements that were once in the medieval library of the Austin priory of Rooklooster near Brussels, the leaves of the second text within the first printed element (a short work of Ps. Cyprian) were numbered with red Roman numerals with the first specifically identified as "Folium I."[3] However, on close examination, it is clear that the numbers were intended to refer to the openings, for the page layout of the text was such that when these numbers are construed as opening numbers, they simultaneously guide the reader to each of the twelve *gradus* or paragraph-long *distinctiones* into which the printed text was divided.[4] In the incunable codex from Saint Mary's of Königstein in Taunus formed from elements printed in Cologne in about 1472-1475, the scribe who confected the entire book numbered both printed and manuscript leaves in red ink and prepared a table that confirms, when the references are verified, that his indications are to openings.[5] Consistent with prior manuscript practice, the scribe placed the heading of the first manuscript text on the verso of the last printed text that preceded it.[6] Within tables of contents, the ambiguity between indications to folio and opening was on occasion clarified in the

1. Goff M-90; BMC VI 887 (IB28345).

2. The three elements present are Jean Gerson's *De cognitione castitatis, De pollutionibus diurnis, Forma absolutionis sacramentalis* [Ulrich Zel, 1470, Goff G-195]; Egidius of Assisi, O.F.M., *Aurea verbi* [Ulrich Zel, c.1470, Goff A-62, *GW* 265]; Pierre d'Ailly, *Circa Septem psalmos penitentiales* [Arnoldus Ther Hoernen, c.1470, Goff A-479]. The numbering of openings is confirmed by the manuscript table written by the same hand that numbered the leaves.

3. The first printed element of this text (Goff I-856) included Isidore's *De Summo bono* and Ps. Cyprian, *De duodecim abusivis saeculi* [=Ps. Augustine, *De duodecim abusionum gradibus*] Printed by Ulrich Zel not after 1472. In the Newberry copy, the same rubricator who denoted the openings of Ps. Cyprian also denoted the books of Isidore. The second element (Goff A-1353) containing Augustine's *De vita beata* and *De vita mulierum*, and Bernard of Clairvaux's *Speculum de honestate vitae* was printed in Cologne in about 1470.

4. In the first text of the same element the same rubricator identified the books and chapters of Isidore's *De summo bono*.

5. Inc 886-958.5, see above p. 241, note 2.

6. Although beginning a text with an opening and the numbering of openings are clearly related, there are incunables like Martin Shott's c. 1483 Strasbourg edition of Leonardus Matthaei de Utino's *Sermones de sanctis* which begin with an opening but of which the tables are referring to folios. See below p. 274, note 1.

The Impact of the Early Printed Page on the History of Reading

post-1465 period in both manuscripts and incunables. In Newberry manuscripts f57 and 152 and in incunables 831-834-957.9, 886-958.5 and f6468, tables referring to openings evince bracket-like marks added by the scribe which graphically suggest that the numerical references were to the extended breadth of an opening rather than to the two sides of a leaf (fig. 3).[1]

In printed volumes in which printed tables contain printed reference to leaf numeration but in which the leaves bear no printed numbers and where therefore an emendator or rubricator was expected to write the actual leaf numbers, the printed numbers mostly refer to folios. The first printed book with such a table of which the numerical indications are verifiably foliation was Conradus Sweynheym and Arnoldus Pannartz's edition of Lactantius' *Opera*, dated 29 October 1465.[2] Although Sweynheym and Pannartz worked in Italy, they came from the Rhineland, and similar tables can be found in the early Cologne editions of Arnold Ther Hoernen, Ulrich Zel and the anonymous "printer of the *Flores sancti Augustini*."[3] They occur as well among the editions of the first Paris press that printers of German origin established in the Sorbonne.[4] Thus from its inception, printing, like its technical precursor the *pecia* system, tended to privilege the folio and by consequence the quire beginning with a recto and ending with a verso as the basic physically defined textual unit. The orientation towards the quire facilitated

1. For Newberry Library MS f57, see Saenger, *A Catalogue of the Pre-1500 Manuscript Books at the Newberry Library*, pp.106-08. In Newberry Library Inc f6468 these bracket-shaped marks were added to the volumes printed table of *distinctiones*.

2. *GW* 9807 (Goff L-1). The Newberry Library copy of this book was emendated with manuscript Arabic numbers that correspond entirely to the indications inserted into the table after the printed word *folio*. The printed table also provided concordant references to book, chapter number and chapter incipit. The same scribe also added three leaves of additional texts at the end including a list of errata attributed to the Franciscan theologian Antonio de Ro that referred to book and chapter in the medieval manner, but not to folio. In subsequent reprintings in Rome and Venice, the material here added in manuscript was printed, but the printed word *folio* was deleted. Space, however, was left for folio references to be added, and, indeed, such emendations were made in some copies containing similar tables. An example is Newberry Library Inc f4423, Andreas de Paltasichis' reprinting of Sweynheym and Pannartz's edition of Aulus Gellius' *Noctes Atticae* (*GW* 10596). In the fifth volume of Sweynheym and Pannartz's *editio princeps* of De Lyra (1472), the word folio was again printed in the table.

3. See for example Walter Burley, *De vita et moribus philosophorum* [Ulrich Zel, c.1470], Goff B-750; Thomas Aquinas, *Quaestiones de duodecim quodlibet* (Arnold Ther Hoernen, 1471), Goff T-183; and Boccacio, *De genealogia deorum* [Printer of the *Flores sancti Augustini*, c. 1473], Goff B-750.

4. The Newberry's copy of Jacques Legrand's *Sophologium*, printed by the Sorbonne Press in 1477, Inc 7848.5, is an example.

263

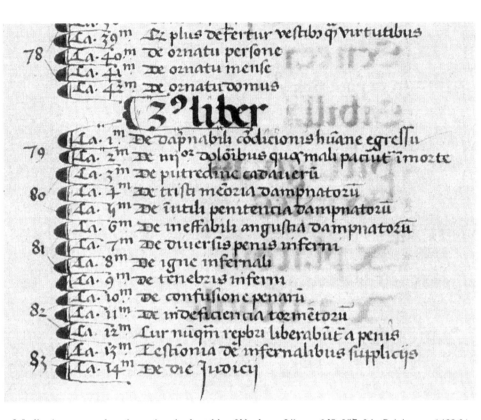

3. Indications to numbered openings in the table of Newberry Library, MS. f.57, f. iv, Belgium, c. 1462-64.

The Impact of the Early Printed Page on the History of Reading

the easy compilation of printed *opuscula* into the thematic composite tomes that are so characteristic of incunables preserved in their original bindings.[1] However, printers more than scribes strove to make their leaf numbers unambiguous. Günther Zainer in preparing the first edition of Peter Comestor's *Historia scholastica* (Augsburg, 1473) placed Roman numbers indicating folios on both the recto and verso of each leaf in order to eliminate any doubt that the numbering indicated the folios and not openings.[2] The same recto and verso numbering occurred again in the first edition of Johannes de Garlandia's *Cornatus* printed by Heinrich Gran in Hagenau in 1489.[3]

In the late 1480's, such double numeration of folios was not a needless redundancy, for even in printed volumes the folio had not yet established itself as the exclusive unit for printed leaf reference. Ulrich Zel, whose Ps. Cyprian had been formatted specifically for the manuscript addition of opening numbers, on 19 May 1482 printed an edition of the *Legenda aurea* with typographically denumbered openings.[4] The text of this edition was prefaced by a table referring to its openings, and Zel also placed Roman numbers *I* through *IV* preceded by the term *folium* on the opposing pages of each of the book's first four openings of text (fig. 4). Zel subsequently followed the same pattern of explicitly designating openings in a series of four editions that appeared between 1482 and 1483.[5] A handful of other examples of numbered openings and references to them, mostly Venetian, date from the 1490's.[6] In 1498, Aldus Manutius in explicating the use of his earliest recorded errata sheet instructed the reader to count line numbers beginning at the upper left of an opening that ran across two leaves.[7] One

---

1. See Halporn, "The Carthusian Library at Basle," p. 235. Newberry Library incunable codex 978.5-979-861* is an example of a composite volume of Augustine's works formed from three discrete printed elements produced in Cologne c. 1470.

2. Goff P-458. My observation is based on the examination of the copy in the Library of the University of Iowa.

3. Goff G-82. I am grateful to the Pierpont Morgan Library for providing me with a microfilm of their copy.

4. Goff J-102.

5. The *Gesta Romanorum* (c. 1482), Guillermus Parisiensis' *Postilla super Epistolas evangelia* (16 July 1482), Bartholomaeus de Pisa's *Summa de casibus de conscientia* (21 February 1483), and a 1483 re-edition of the *Legenda aurea*; *BMC* I 196-99, IB 2027, IB 3030, IB 3033, IB 3036 and IB 3068.

6. Margaret Smith, "Printed Foliation: Forerunner to Printed Page Numbers," *Gutenberg Jahrbuch*, 1988, p. 57.

7. "Tu vero lector scito accepisse hic nos chartas, ambas, quas vides paginas, aperto libro, et numerum post chartarum numerum, versus significare; numerarique versus a primo primae paginae usque ad ultimum secundae, id est a primo usque ad quartum et quinquagesimum...," Urbano Valeriani's *Institutiones graecae grammaticae* printed in Venice in 1498, see above p. 240, note 3.

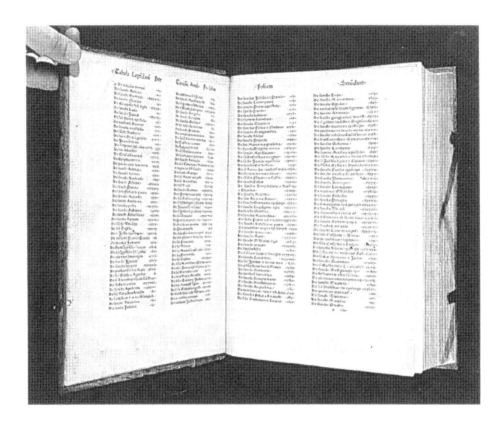

4. Jacobus de Voragine, *Legenda aurea*, Cologne, Ulrich Zel, 1482, ff. 1v-2 (Newberry Library).

The Impact of the Early Printed Page on the History of Reading

Venetian volume contains two entirely distinct texts with two discrete tables, the table for the first text refers to openings while the table of the second text directs the reader to folios.[1] Despite such lingering instances of profound ambiguity, indications to the folio became the standard after the early 1470's, reflecting a mentality surrounding the printed book that was increasingly uniform.

Scholars who have relied entirely on the bibliographical descriptions of the *Gesamtkatalog der Wiegendrucke* have seriously underestimated the nexus between printing and leaf numbering.[2] In fact, printing was the bibliographic milieu in which leaf numbering — manuscript as well as printed — first flourished. This is clear when it is understood that printed books with printed foliation on the leaves constitute only a portion of the phenomena that link leaf numbering to print. Often, as has been noted, printers produced books with references to foliation in their tables, and emendator scribes added the actual leaf numbers. Sometimes scribes added folio references and foliation to books without printed tables or with simple printed tables of *capitula* or other *distinctiones*. Printers on occasion implied that emendators should make such additions by suppressing typographical reference in the table to a work's numbered or numberable textual subdivisions or by leaving ample spaces where leaf numbers might be inserted.[3] In still other instances, a scribe or owner prepared manuscript tables referring to a foliation that was added to the leaves by the same hand. Particularly for errata, references in printed tables were often to print leaf signatures, an indication that these numbers, usually assumed to have been used only by binders, were exploited as locus points by readers.[4] Although, as we have seen, such numbering within the quire had a long history in manuscripts, tables referring to them do not occur in manuscript books and

---

1. *GW* 3104. No special instructions distinguished the two tables.

2. See the study of M. Smith cited in note 6 p. 265.

3. See for example the tables of Sixtus Glockengiesser's edition of Augustinus de Ancona's *De laudibus virginis Mariae*, Lyon, 1485 (Goff A-1362), Guillaume Tardif's *Grammatica* (see above p. 250, note 5), Antoine Vérard's book of hours for the use of Orléans (below note 2 p. 274) and the reprintings of Lactantius' *Opera* (above p. 263, note 2).

4. For examples of reader tables referring to signatures, see Felix Hemmerlin's *Opuscula* printed by an unidentified press apparently in Strasbourg after 13 August 1497 (Goff H-17). In a subsequent Strasbourg printing (Goff H-16) the table was replaced by one referring to printed Roman foliation on the leaves. Johannes Otmar's first edition of Gabriel Biel's *Epitoma expositionis sacri canonis*, Tübingen, 1499 (*GW* 4334, Goff B-654) also has a table referring to printed signatures. Franz Renner's 1482-1483 edition of Nicolaus of Lyra's *Postilla* included a table that referred to *carta* identified by quire letter and leaf number. A similar table is to be found in the *Abbreviamentum statutorum* printed in London c. 1482, Goff A-3.

267

their presence in printed volumes confirms both the heightened consciousness of physically defined textual units that printing generated and the priority that printing gave to quires and consequently to leaves as the principal arbitrarily defined locus points within a codex. [1]

While the relationship between printing and leaf number was a profound one, it should be remembered that the link between changing mentalities and new technology was still somewhat loose. Indeed, the earliest works composed with authorial folio tables as an integral part of their content were manuscripts that apparently were never intended for publication in print, although they do postdate the production of the first printed books. David Aubert's *Histoire de Charles Martel et ses successeurs*, (Brussels, Bibliothèque Royale MSS 6-9) was copied by its author at Brussels between 1463 and 1465 with tables giving references to the manuscript's folio numbers. [2] Aubert intended these four volumes, which antedate by a decade the introduction of printing into the Netherlands, for the library of Philip the Good of Burgundy whose court was a center for the production of leaf-numbered vernacular manuscripts. Guillaume Fillastre's *Histoire de la thoison d'or*, composed at Philip's court and copied in Bruges in the years immediately following 1468, was distributed in manuscript in a series of deluxe, highly standardized, illuminated codices prepared for knights of the Order of the Golden Fleece. [3] Fillastre prefaced his work with a detailed table of contents with reference to folios that was essential for its consultation and was present in each manuscript copy, for while the *Histoire de la thoison d'or* was a thoroughly scholastic work, it lacked all traces of the structure of numbered parts (questions, chapters, or paragraphs) that had typified scholastic texts. It and copies of comparable works by Burgundian authors, including Jean Mansel, Jean Germain, Raoul Lefevre, Jean du Chesne and Vasco of Lucena, indicate that foliation was emerging as an integral element in the texts disseminated by the active scriptoria of Brabant and Flanders just prior to printing's penetration into the Low Countries. [4] At the Burgundian court,

---

1. Of course this was not true in every case, cf. above p. 262, note 5.

2. L. M. J. Delaissé, *Le Siècle d'or de la miniature flamande*, Exhibition catalogue, Brussels, Bibliothèque Royale, 1959, pp. 124-26; Georges Doutrepont, *La littérature française à la cour des ducs de Bourgogne*, Paris, 1909, pp. 30-35.

3. Doutrepont, *La littérature française à la cour des ducs de Bourgogne*, pp. 161-167. The *Histoire de la thoison d'or* was printed for the first time only in 1514.

4. See for example, the following MSS: Paris, BNF fr. 139, 140, 432, 721, 981, 20067; Brussels, BR 9263, 9000-07, 11703; London, BL Roy. 17 E V; Copenhagen, KB Thott 463, 464, 465, 544. For additional examples, see Delaissé, *Le Siècle d'or*.

The Impact of the Early Printed Page on the History of Reading

emendators systematically added leaf numbers to old vernacular codices,[1] and vernacular texts of the previous century were recopied in the new leaf-numbered format.[2] In the 1460's, leaf numbers were also present in the Latin books copied for Burgundy's urban elite whose vernacular tongue was Netherlandish.[3]

The Burgundian scriptoria strove to produce standardized manuscript copies with standardized text format, illustration and foliation. However, scribes found it impossible to realize this ideal, for despite efforts in Bruges, Hesdin, Valenciennes, and Ghent to replicate exemplars exactly, various copies of the same texts differed in length, and consequently the folio references in the table of each copy also varied. In addition, although the tables in these volumes regularly referred to the *fueillet, foeullet,* or *feullet,* the numbers in approximately fifteen percent of these vernacular leaf-numbered manuscripts referred to openings rather than to folios,[4] and in the table of one such book, Brussels BR 9263, the scribe actually became confused as to which unit he was supposed to be denumbering.

In Northern Europe in the 1460's and 1470's, the popularity of manuscript books with numbered folios or openings was a distinctly regional phenomenon. In Bruges and Brussels, the usage was probably popular in the vernacular books copied for Philip the Good, Charles the Bold and Louis of Bruges because laymen found foliated books easier to manipulate. However, while vernacular and some Latin codices in the Burgundian Low Countries were being copied with numbered leaves, the leaves of similar manuscripts produced in Paris and the Loire Valley for the French royal court of Charles VII, Louis XI, and Charles VIII were uniformly unnumbered.

In contrast, in the Rhine Valley, the leaf numbering of manuscripts was relatively popular, and Cologne was a particularly important center for manuscript leaf numbering at a time when bonds of patronage linked the University and the city to the court of Burgundy.[5] At the Carthusian

---

1. See Brussels, BR 9024, Georges Dogaer and Marguerite Debae, *La Librairie de Philippe le Bon,* exhibition catalogue, Bibliothèque Royale; Brussels, 1967, pl. 24.

2. See for example, Louis of Bruges' copy of Pierre Bersuire's translation of Livy, Paris, BNF fr. 34.

3. Brussels, BR 168-94 and 708-19 from Rooklooster are examples. For other Rooklooster books with foliation see P. J. H. Vermeeren, "Op zoek naar de librije van Rooklooster," *Het Boek,* ser. 3, 35 (1962), 134-73 and above at p. 262, note 3. Newberry Library MS f57 copied in Liège is another example of a book with leaf numbers originating in a Netherlandish milieu.

4. Copenhagen, KB Thott 544, 463 and 465 are examples.

5. Richard Vaughn, *Philip the Good: The Apogee of Burgundy,* London, 1970, p.295 and *passim; Ibid, Charles the Bold: The Last Valois Duke of Burgundy,* London, 1973, pp. 313-20 and *passim;* Léon Baudry, *La querelle des futurs contingents, Louvain 1465-1475: Textes inédits,* Études de philosophie médiévale, 38; Paris, 1950.

monastery of Saint Barbara's in Cologne, the author-scribe Heinrich Dissen of Osnabrück regularly prepared codices with tables and leaf numbers placed midway in the outer margin of the leaf, [1] the same place used for foliation in fourteenth-century Florentine chant books, and it was surely not merely coincidental that in Cologne in the early 1470's, similarly placed numbers characterized the first printed books with typographic foliation produced by Arnold Ther Hoernen. [2] Indeed in his colophons, Ther Hoernen boasted of his fidelity to the author's autograph exemplar. [3] His first foliated book was the *editio princeps* of the *Sermo in festo presentationis beatissimae Mariae Virginis* composed by Werner Rolewinck (1425-1502), a monk from Saint Barbara's. This slim volume appeared in 1470 with printed Arabic foliation in the middle of the outer margins. The concluding clause of the title page, "... si placet videre poterit in folii latere sequenti,» implies a printer conscious of physical format. [4] Because the *Sermo* was a work consisting of a single quire, it is at least conceivable that leaf numbers may have been merely intended to aid assemblage. [5] However, at about the same time another Cologne printer, Ulrich Zel, printed the first edition of Walter Burley's lengthy *De vita et moribus philosophorum* with a prefatory table containing Arabic folio numbers that an emendator or owner was clearly expected to add to the volume beginning on the first leaf of text. [6] In 1474 Ther Hoernen printed the first edition of Werner Rolewinck's *Fasciculus temporum*, a historical reference work based on chronological tables, aimed at a general audience, that achieved great popularity. The *Fasciculus temporum* constituted the first printed work in which foliation constituted an intrinsic aspect of the text. [7] The very title of Rolewinck's *opus* was a conscious advertisement of the codex format of a work that belonged to a genre that

1. Richard Bruce Marks, *The Medieval Manuscript Library of the Charterhouse of Saint Barbara in Cologne*, Analecta Cartusiana, 22; Salzburg, 1974, I, 52-54. These numbers were placed on the verso of the leaves, and thus they may have indicated openings rather than folios.

2. *BMC* I 201-10.

3. *BMC* I nos. IB 3127, IB 3135, and IB 3257.

4. A facsimile of the title page has been published by Alfred W. Pollard, *Last Words on the History of the Title-Page with Notes on some Colophons and Twenty-Seven Facsimiles*, London, 1891, pp. 14-15.

5. Bernardus Nerlius' edition of Virgil's *Opera* (see above p. 257, note 4) is a rare instance where a combination of printed leaf numbers and leaf signatures were intended to assure correct ordering in binding. The Roman folio numbers in the table were intended to correspond to numbers added in handwriting.

6. *GW* 5781 (Goff B-1315). Such foliation was in fact added to the copy in the British Library, IA 2883, *BMC* I 188; cf. above p. 263, note 3.

7. Stillwell, "The *Fasciculus Temporum*," (above p. 245, note 4), p. 417.

The Impact of the Early Printed Page on the History of Reading

had frequently been disseminated in roll format during the late Middle Ages.[1] In Ther Hoernen's first edition, the alphabetical table that preceded the chronology proper referred to Arabic numbers that an emendator was expected to add in manuscript on the leaves, and these numbers were in fact added by a contemporary emendator to both the rectos and versos of the leaves in the copy now at the Pierpont Morgan Library.[2] According to the explicit introductory notes characteristic of printed tables, if a point preceded the folio number, the reference was to the recto; if the point followed the number, the reference was to the verso (fig. 5).[3] The lack of chapter or other numerical divisons in the work confirms that Rolewinck, like manuscript-authors Aubert and Fillastre, considered leaf numbering to be an integral element of his *opus*, and it is logical to suppose that a table with folio references had existed in the author's autograph, now lost, that served as Ther Hoernen's exemplar.[4] Rolewinck's work, never systematically disseminated in manuscript was composed for the printing press, and the numerous reprintings of the work in its original Latin retained the table and modified the first edition significantly only by adding typographic foliation to the leaves. Apparently because exact locus reference points were more important to readers of Latin as a second language than of the vernacular, both the French and Dutch translations of the *Fasciculus* suppressed the references to recto and verso.[5]

As the text history of the *Fasciculus temporum* suggests, Cologne played a crucial role in introducing the reformatting texts with foliation into printed books. The practice can already be documented in about 1470 by Zel's

---

1. An example is a genealogical chronicle of the kings of France, copied in Paris, c. 1450, recently acquired by the Newberry Library (MS 132).

2. They have also been added in manuscript, in the mid-folio position, in the British Library copy, IB 3127, *BMC* I 204.

3. "Tabula brevis et utilis super libello quodam que dicitur fasciculus temporum et ubi inuenitur punctus ante numerum est in primo latere ubi uero post in secundo latere." See Stillwell, "The *Fasciculus Temporum*," p. 417.

4. Ther Hoernen in his colophon stated that he had printed the work "sicut ab autore suo quondam devoto Carthusiensi Colonie edita est ac secundum primum exemplar quod ipse venerabilis autor propriis conscripsit manibus," cited by A. G. W. Murray, "The Edition of the *Fasciculus Temporum* Printed by Arnold ther Hoernen in 1474," *The Library*, ser. 3, vol. 4 (1913), p. 58.

5. The numbers in the tables of these incunable editions refer to either folios or openings. In the first edition of the French translation (Geneva, 1495; Goff R-279), the numbers are the same as in the Latin original, but reference to the points is suppressed, although the printer following a Latin model actually failed to omit a few of the points when he set the type of the table. All the points were omitted in the Paris, 1513 edition prepared for Jean Petit and Michel Lenoir. In the Dutch version (Utrecht: Johannes Veldener, 1480; Goff R-278) the numbers were altered and adjusted so as to refer to openings.

5. Werner Rolewinck, *Fasciculus temporum,* Strasbourg, Johann Prüss, s.d., f. 2 (Newberry Library).

The Impact of the Early Printed Page on the History of Reading

edition of Burley's *De vita et moribus*.[1] In 1471, Ther Hoernen published the second recorded edition of Thomas Aquinas' *Quaestiones de quodlibet*.[2] The preceding Roman edition had followed in the tradition of university manuscripts and provided a table referring to the *distinctiones* of the text.[3] However, Ther Hoernen, in the course of setting the type for his table began to introduce folio references in Arabic numbers to complement the table's references to the text's numbered questions and articles.[4] In 1481, the tables of Thomas Aquinas' *Commentum super secundo libro Sententiarum* were similarly reformatted in Cologne.[5] A similar evolution marked other medieval texts printed in Germany. The earliest printed editions of Durandus' *Rationale divinorum officiorum* contained neither references to foliation in their tables nor printed foliation on their leaves, and folio references were still absent in Ulrich Gallus' Roman edition of 1473.[6] However, Johannes Zainer in his Ulm edition of 3 December 1473 added a table with reference to its typographical Roman numeral leaf numbers.[7] The same pattern of an early unfoliated edition followed by a reformatted foliated one is to be found in the text tradition of the *Manipulus curatorum* of Guy de Monterochier (fl. c. 1333) and the *Gesta Romanorum*.[8] Johannes of Cologne and Johannes Manthen reworked Duns Scotus' *Super libris Sententiarum* as they introduced this lengthy and prestigious work into print. For example, they initially printed the *Liber secundus* with a conventional table of distinctions but subsequently supplemented it with a sophisticated table referring to foliation, column and position in the column.[9]

1. See above p. 263, note 3 and p. 270, note 6.

2. Goff T-183; *BMC* I 203 (IB 3112).

3. Goff T-182; *BMC* IV 36 (IB 17449).

4. References to folio numbers are omitted on the first recto and second recto of the table in the Newberry Library copy.

5. Cf. Goff T-163 T-170. The Venetian edition of Johannes Herbort de Seligenstadt, Goff T-171, was also reformatted.

6. *GW* 9104 (Goff D-406).

7. *GW* 9105 (Goff D-407).

8. The Esslingen c. 1476-78 edition of the *Manipulus curatorum* (Goff G-573) and Ulrich Gering's Paris 4 June 1478 (Goff G-577) edition were printed with neither foliation nor tables. However, the leaves of Leonardus Pachel's and Uldericus Scinzenzeler's Milan edition of 31 January 1481 (Goff G-582) bore printed Arabic foliation and included two tables referring to that foliation. For the *Gesta Romanorum*, the Koberger 1494 edition (Goff G-294) had a table indicating chapter numbers whereas the Strasbourg edition of January 1499 (Goff G-296) added references to folios to the chapter references. A brief note at the head of the table elucidated the meaning of the sets of numbers.

9. *GW* 9073 (Goff D-379, ii), see above note 5 p. 257. The revised table, unrecorded in the *GW*, is present in Newberry Inc f4327.5*.

Texts pertaining to medicine and law, editions of the Church Fathers and ancient classics were transformed in like manner. Authors whose life spans overlapped the spread of printing were from the 1470's onward increasingly likely to have their works printed with foliation. For example, the sermon collections of the Dominican friar Leonardus Matthaei de Utino († 1469) were printed within the decade following his death in editions that were foliated. [1]

Printers also introduced foliation to books of hours, breviaries, sermon collections and Bibles. In manuscript, these books had virtually never been foliated because scribes could rely on a clerical reader's familiarity either with iconographical conventions (books of hours) or with textual sequencing based on the liturgical calendars (breviaries and sermon collections) or a set order of books and chapters that was instilled by extensive rote memorization (the Bible). On 14 August 1500, Félix Baligault printed for Antoine Vérard a book of hours for the use of Orléans with a table of contents, virtually without precedent in manuscript *horae*, that anticipated with generous space the addition of folio numbers. [2] In 1483, Nicolaus de Frankfurt reprinted the Dominican Breviary and added a table containing folio numbers. [3] Because the sequence of elements within medieval breviaries was not entirely fixed by convention, the new table was followed by a second table designed to ensure that the binder would correctly order the quires so that when an emendator subsequently added leaf numbers, the manuscript numbers would correspond to those of the printed table. Johannes Grüninger also included a table referring to the foliation in his Premonstratenian Breviary (Strasbourg, 1490), but in addition he printed folio numbers on the leaves. [4] A few thirteenth-century manuscript Bibles were foliated in the mid-fifteenth century, and Anton Koberger and Konrad Winter introduced printed foliation to the Bible in Cologne in 1478-1479. [5] By the year 1501, the triumph of the folio was virtually complete. Although the heirs of Heinrich Quentell still felt it necessary in 1508 to mark consecutive folio numbers on the verso and recto of the first opening of the

1. Thomas Kaeppeli, *Scriptores ordinis praedicatorum medii aevi*, 3 (1980) nos. 2873, 2874, and 2875. Cf. above p. 262, note 6.

2. Goff H-350.

3. *GW* 5218 (Goff B-1141).

4. *GW* 5231 (Goff B-1144).

5. Newberry Library MS -18 is a rare instance where an emendator in the fifteenth century added Arabic foliation and a table referring to that foliation to a thirteenth-century Bible; Saenger, *A Catalogue of the Pre-1500 Manuscript Books at the Newberry Library*, pp. 34-35.

The Impact of the Early Printed Page on the History of Reading

Cologne professor Arnoldus von Tongern's *Directorium concubinariorum saluberrimum,* they probably did so because the text in his printing began on the first verso, a practice which in the previous century had often been characteristic of some books in which the numbers on the leaves connoted openings. [1] Henceforth it was the opening that had to be explicitly designated when it was used for an exceptional effect. Thus when in 1511, the Giunta Press in Venice printed a Bible with numbered openings, the typesetters felt obliged to place the numbers both in the upper left verso and the upper right recto of each opening throughout the volume in order to eliminate all possible ambiguity. [2] In 1516, Guillaume Budé in a letter to Erasmus clearly regarded both foliation and his alphabetical subject table referring to that foliation as integral elements of his *De Asse.* [3]

In summary, the practice of foliating printed books was invented by Germans, and generally speaking, like printed parentheses, it occurred first in German cities, such as Cologne, Augsburg, Ulm and Speyer and spread west and south to Strasbourg, Paris and Italy. This progression constitutes a geographic pattern of cultural diffusion of culture running contrary to the general south to north movement of the Italian Renaissance. [4] Nevertheless, Italian scribes, and subsequently Italian printers, were precocious in two aspects of foliation. One was in their far more consistent use of Arabic numbers. In manuscripts that were foliated prior to printing, denumbering leaves with Arabic numbers began in the thirteenth-century in Italy, and in the fifteenth century Arabic numbers for foliation were more consistently evident in Italian manuscripts than in those of Northern Europe. While printers at Cologne and Strasbourg used Arabic numbers for foliation at an early date, in general Roman numerals predominated in Northern incunables. In contrast, printed Arabic foliation flourished in Italy, particularly in Venice in the 1480's and 1490's.

The second important Italian innovation came at the very end of the fifteenth century when in 1499 the Venetian printer Aldus Manutius modified foliation into pagination. He did so as an exceptional feature to aid

---

1. Adams, D-680.

2. Newberry Library, Wing ZP 535 .G431 and ZP 435 .G431a.

3. De la Garanderie, *La correspondance d'Érasme,* pp. 65-66; Allen, no. 435 (7 July 1516).

4. See Sweynheym and Pannartz's edition of Lactantius' *Opera,* dated 29 October 1465, above note 2 p. 263. Wendelin of Speyer's Duns Scotus, *Quaestiones in primum librum Sententiarum,* (*GW* 9079, Goff D-374; Venice, 5 November 1472) is another early example of an Italian imprint by a German emigré with a table containing Arabic numbers referring to a foliation that an emendator was expected to provide.

the reader in his specially reformatted edition of Niccolò Perotti's *Cornucopiae linguae latinae,* a large, densely printed and difficult to manipulate grammatical reference tool prefaced by the author's extensive table of Latin terms that was advertised on the title page. [1] Because the leaves of the *Cornucopiae* contained so many characters, using the numbered *semipaginae* (Aldus's term) and lines as reference points had evident utility. The succeeding Venetian edition of 1501, however, was not paginated. [2] While a very few isolated examples of manuscript pagination had occurred in Western manuscript books from the twelfth to the fifteenth century, pagination as a normal aspect of the page was a contribution to visible language made by early sixteenth-century humanism. [3] Either because of a putative knowledge of ancient precedent or, more probably, because a precise definition of page locus was most useful to the reader of a foreign tongue far more difficult than Latin, Aldus's precocious use of pagination was closely tied to Greek. In the years prior to 1515, he used pagination particularly for Greek editions containing tables and lists of variant readings. [4] After Perotti's *Cornucopiae* in 1499, only three of Aldus's Latin books were paginated. [5]

Erasmus (who worked for Aldus for seven months in 1508) and Johannes Froeben, the favorite printer of Erasmus' later years were responsible for bringing pagination from Venice to the North and spreading it in Latin texts. [6] Unlike Aldus for whom *pagina* had been a synonym for folio, [7]

---

1. Goff P-296. "Index copiossimus et novo ordine, quo facillime, quodcunque quaeritur vocabulum inveniri potest. Notatae enim sunt totius operis singulae semipaginae ac singuli semipaginarum omnium versus arithmeticis numeris." Renouard, *Annales de l'imprimerie des Alde,* p. 19.

2. Johannes Tacuinus' edition replaced pagination with numbered columns and lines combined with marginal alphabets.

3. Lehmann, "Blätter," pp. 45-51; François Avril, "Trois manuscrits napolitains des collections de Charles V et de Jean de Berry," *Bibliothèque de l'École des chartes,* 127 (1969), 294, n.1 and plate facing 296.

4. See his Johannes Grammaticus (1504), Lucian (1508) and Isocrates' *Orationes* (1513).

5. Pliny's *Epistolae* (1508), Horace's *Poemata* (1509) and Sallust's *De coniuratione Catalinae* (1509). The prefatory leaves of the Horace conclude with a list of errata (*emendationes*) referring to page and verse number. In Aldus's 1500 edition of the *Epistles* of Catherine of Siena (which bore printed Roman folio numbers), the numbers *CI* and *CII* actually refer to pages (Goff C-281).

6. The notion that Erasmus introduced pagination to Aldus has no historical foundation, cf. P. S. Allen, *Erasmus: Lectures and Wayfaring Sketches* (Oxford, 1934), p. 56. Similarly false is K. Froelich's report that the *Biblia latina cum glossa ordinaria* which Froeben, Petri and Amerbach printed in Basel in 1502 contained printed pagination, see the introduction of the reprint edition of the *Glossa ordinaria,* K. Froelich and Margaret T. Gibson, eds., Turnhout, 1992, p. xix, col. 2.

7. See the title page of the *Cornucopiae,* above note 1, and the introductory notes to the errata leaves of Aldus's edition of Urbano Valeriani's *Institutiones graecae grammaticae,* above p. 240, note 3 and p. 265, note 7. The first volume of Aldus's *Poetae Christiani veteres* (1501) also contained a list of errata that referred to quire letter and *pagina, pagina* meaning folio and not page.

The Impact of the Early Printed Page on the History of Reading

Erasmus in his correspondence regularly employed *pagina* in the modern sense of meaning one side of the leaf.[1] Froeben incorporated pagination into his edition of Erasmus' Seneca (1515) and New Testament (1516), and in the former volume, Froeben took credit for preparing an alphabetical table referring to *paginae*. The second volume of Erasmus' New Testament, the *Annotationes*, contained two pages of errata referring to *pagina* and *versus* to indicate page and line number.[2] Medieval lists of theological errors had referred to the scholastic subdivisions of a text, and the first humanistic printed errata had been to folio, or far more commonly, to signature and leaf. After Erasmus, errata lists referring to pagination came to be characteristic of humanist culture.

Johannes Froeben also printed a paginated index volume as a final part of Erasmus' eight volume 1516 edition of Jerome's *Opera omnia*. In 1518, Froeben printed Erasmus, *Epigrammata* with pagination, and in the same year he began to paginate regularly his editions of works of other authors including Thomas More's *Utopia*.[3] In 1520, Froeben produced a new, greatly augmented, paginated edition of the *Adagia* to which Erasmus, who admired the indices of Budé that gave reference to folios, personally added two alphabetical tables referring to *paginae*.[4] In 1528, Erasmus reformatted this table adding letters (*p, m* and *f*) after the page numbers to indicate position on the page, beginning, middle and end. In the errata list for this tome, Erasmus, ever fastidious, referred to line numbers in the modern fashion counting both from the top and bottom of the page.

A glance at the evolving text format of the *Adagia* gives one indication of why Erasmus preferred pagination. The incunable editions of the *Adagia* had been slim volumes with a number of characters per page that were roughly equivalent to a late medieval manuscript. Later editions of the *Adagia* contained densely printed quarto-size pages, reflecting the desire of printers to reduce production costs.[5] For pages containing much larger quantities of words, pagination was far more useful than foliation. Also, for Erasmus, who continuously revised and expanded his works, page numbering provided a

---

1. De la Garanderie, *La correspondance d'Érasme*, pp. 166, 181. The table of Erasmus' edition of Pliny the Elder's *Historia naturalis* printed by Froeben in 1525 employed *facies* as an alternative to *pagina*.

2. Volume II, pp. 628-29.

3. He introduced pagination to the text tradition of More's work. The prior Paris 1516 printing included a list of errata referring to *pagina* (*i* or *ii* for recto and verso respectively) and line number. The first edition of the *Utopia*, like Erasmus' first edition of the *Adagia*, was neither foliated nor paginated.

4. De la Garanderie, *La correspondance d'Érasme*, p. 78 and n. 26.

5. See Allen, *Opus epistolarum* III, no. 630, V, no. 1349 and XI, no. 3093.

convenient device for adding manuscript revisions and insertions to a personal copy of his published text.[1] The secretaries who aided Erasmus in preparing new editions cited the pagination of variant printed versions and even paginated their own informal working notes.[2] Erasmus, the premier Northern humanist, was also the father of the modern paginated Latin book.

From Basle, pagination spread to Cologne where Peter Quentell, Eucharius Cervicornus (who pirated Froeben's edition of Jerome's *Epistolae*), Gottfried Hittorp and Hieronymus Alopecius issued paginated editions of theological tracts and the classics (Aulus Gellius, Herodotus and Thucydides) as early as 1525-1527.[3] From Switzerland and Germany, pagination spread via humanist printers in France. Robert Estienne I used pagination in his edition of Valeriano Bolzani's *Castigationes et varietates Virgilianae lectionis* (Paris, 1529), and in subsequent years he paginated numerous volumes.[4] In Lyon, Sébastien Gryphe paginated some books as early as 1532-1534.[5] In Italy, where printed pagination was born, it won general acceptance slowly. In Venice, it became current in Latin titles only in the second half of the sixteenth century.[6] In contrast to foliation for which scribes and printers used both Arabic and Roman numbers, printers in both Northern and Southern Europe used Arabic numbers almost exclusively for page numbers.[7]

1. See the autograph notes referring to page numbers in Erasmus' own copy of the Basle, Johannes Froeben 1523 edition of the *Adagia* sold at Sotheby's on November 20, 1990, lot no. 397, sales catalogue, p. 397 (2 plates).

2. See Margaret Mann Phillips, *The Adages of Erasmus*, Cambridge, 1964, pp. 149 and 151.

3. The earliest of these appears to be Peter Quentell's 1525 edition of Johannes Cochlaeus' *De Petro et Roma adversus Valenum Lutheranum libri quatuor* printed by Quentell in 1525. Cologne printers favored the term *facies* for the modern page, and Cochlaeus' work referred to pages as *facies* (*fa.*) in the list of errata. The errata list of Eucharius Cervicornus' 1527 edition of John Fisher's *De veritate corporis et sanguinis Christi* similarly referred to pages as *facies*. However in the errata list for his 1526 Latin Herodotus, Cervicornus referred to pages as folios.

4. Fred Schreiber, *The Estiennes: An Annotated Catologue of 300 Highlights of their Various Presses*, New York, 1982, no. 40 and pp. 55-104.

5. See his editions of Nicolaus Leonicus Thomaus' *De varia historiae* (1532) and the *Novae Academicae Florentinae opuscula* (1534).

6. In Paris in the first half of the sixteenth century and in Venice in the second half of the sixteenth-century printers placed a or b after the Arabic numbers in tables in order to distinguish references to recto and verso, thus providing an alternate mode of designating the page. See for example Michael Vascosanus' 1533 edition of Rodolphus Agricola's *De inventione dialectica* and Iuntas' 1553 edition of Virgil's *Opera*.

7. Galliot Du Pré's edition of Francesco Patrizi's *Enneas de regno et regis institutione*, Paris, 1531 is a very rare example of a volume paginated with printed Roman numerals.

The Impact of the Early Printed Page on the History of Reading

Foliation and pagination were not the only medieval modes of identifying locus within the book that printers exploited and popularized. In the tenth and eleventh centuries at various monasteries in Northern France, scribes had placed letters of the alphabet in the margin of manuscripts as a means of identifying specific loci within the codex. In the same period, sequential alphabetical tie notes (akin to modern footnotes) had been used to connect marginal glosses to the text. [1] Initially, these signs were used for texts of classical authors, but in the thirteenth century they were introduced into the corpus of civil law in manuscripts produced at Bologna and elsewhere in central Italy, and early printers in Germany and Italy knew them principally from Italian university juristic manuscripts produced by the *pecia* system in the fourteenth century.

In the early twelfth century at the abbey of Farfa, Gregorio di Catino's *Liber largitorius* combined letters of the alphabet with foliation as a means of locating specific references. However, cartularies like the *Liber largitorius* were useful only at a single abbey and therefore normally existed in but a single copy. In the thirteenth century, Thomas of Ireland made use of marginal letters similar to those in the *Liber largitorius* in his *Manipulus florum*, a compilation of *exempla* intended as a reference aid for preachers. Although widely disseminated in personal copies and in manuscripts produced by the *pecia* system, its marginal-letter text format was emulated by only a very few other works, all apparently Dominican. One of these was the *Opus trivium* composed by friar Johannes de Bromyard († a. 1352). [2] Another was friar Martinus Polonus' († 1426) *Sermones de sanctis*. [3] Apart from this mendicant tradition, marginal letters occurred only in conjunction with the indices that scholars like Pierre de Limoges prepared for the books of their own libraries. [4]

The Dominicans in the early thirteenth century also developed a more generally used alphabetical system for locating information on the page. For their Biblical concordance, the friars of the convent of Saint-Jacques at the University of Paris were obliged to invent a technique for identifying specific passages (for in the thirteenth century Biblical verses had not yet been numbered). Capitalizing on the standard chapter divisions for the Old and

---

1. Paul Saenger, *Spaces Between Words: The Origins of Silent Reading* (above page 242, note 1).

2. Kaeppeli, *Scriptores ordinis praedicatorum medii aevi*, 2 (1975), no. 2235.

3. See Newberry Library MS 138 (acquired 1994); unrecorded by Kaeppeli, *Scriptores ordinis praedicatorum medii aevi*, 3 (1990), 123-24.

4. See Rouse and Rouse, *Preachers, Florilegia and Sermons*, p. 23.

New Testaments that had been created in Paris in the late twelfth century, the friars of Saint-Jacques perfected a system by which the reader mentally divided these chapters, short and long, into four or seven subdistinctions of equal length, *a* through *d* or *a* through *g* respectively.[1] This system was also used in certain liturgical indices appended to thirteenth-century Bibles,[2] and it was used as well, at least in England, for the writings of the Church Fathers.[3] We have already encountered a variation of it in the manuscript table of the Newberry copy of the Strasbourg, 1469 edition of Jerome's *Epistolae.*[4] However, because its reference points were mental and not graphic, this system inevitably was approximative and therefore time-consuming to employ.

The first small quarto printed Bibles were intended to replicate mechanically the page format of the portable manuscript Bibles that had been mass produced at Paris and Oxford in the thirteenth century, the Bibles with which the Dominican concordances had been regularly employed.[5] Unlike fifteenth-century France where an inherited supply of portable manuscript Bibles was ample for a university population that had been greatly reduced by plague and war, the Italian Peninsula had an unsatisfied need of portable Bibles, which prior to printing had to be imported from beyond the Alps. The printed Bibles produced by German emigrés to Venice met this demand. While Cologne printers in 1478-79 had introduced foliation into large-format folio Bibles, books usually intended for liturgical purposes, this innovation was not emulated by the printers of small portable Bibles. Instead in 1477 in a revolutionary departure, Bernhard Richel used marginal *B* through *D* and *B* through *G* in the New Testament portion of his Bible, the letter *A* remaining mental. In 1482, two Germans residing in Lyon, Marcus Reinhard of Strasbourg (an associate of the Strasbourg innovator of printed text format, Johannes Grüninger) and Nicolaus Philippi of Bensheim, placed equally spaced marginal typographic

1. A few thirteenth-century manuscript Bibles, like Newberry Library MS 22, have letters written in their margins, but these additions, although they likely served a finding function, seem to be unrelated to the Dominican system of chapter subdivision. Similar letters were added in the margins of Newberry inc f4456 (*GW* 4233, Goff B-558), a Bible printed in Venice in 1478.

2. Newberry Library MS -19, a Franciscan Bible makes use of this system, Saenger, *A Catalogue of Pre-1500 Manuscript Books at the Newberry Library*, p. 35.

3. In the thirteenth and fourteenth century, see Rouse and Rouse, *Preachers, Florilegia and Sermons*, pp. 19-20. The fourteenth-century Italian Franciscan friar Astesanus de Ast also used this system in the tables he himself composed for his *Summa Astensis.*

4. See above p. 261, note 2.

5. See for example *GW* 4222 (Goff B-547).

The Impact of the Early Printed Page on the History of Reading

capital letters *A* through *D* and *A* through *G* (for longer chapters) in the New Testament of their portable Bible (fig. 6). [1] The letters constituted locus points for a marginal concordance that conveniently offered cross references to book, chapter, and alphabet for the New Testament. [2] In Venice in 1484, in Basle in 1486 and in Speyer in 1486, Johannes Herbort de Seligenstadt, Johannes Amerbach and Peter Drach adopted the same system. [3] In manuscript, similar letters had existed only in Wycliffite English vernacular New Testaments dating from c. 1400, some of which were very small and portable. [4] Here again a German printer discovered a graphic device employed in manuscript within a closely defined textual community and appropriated it for far more general use.

Subsequent German printers extended the marginal locus letters and marginal concordance to the Old Testament. In effect, they converted the Dominican mental system of place reference into a visual one that was easier for an inexperienced reader to manipulate. In June 1491, Johannes Froeben, having placed marginal letters in both the Old and New Testament, announced on the title page that his octavo Bible was a *Biblia integra, summata, distincta, superemendata, utriusque testamenti concordantia illustrata*. [5] In the same year, the conventual Franciscan friar Gabriel Bruni published an alphabetical table that referred to Biblical book and chapter as a prefatory text to a portable Bible printed in Basel. [6] No later than 1495, his table was

1. The Basle Bible is *GW* 4228 (Goff B-553); the Lyon Bible is *GW* 4249 (Goff B-574). In autumn 1995, the firm of H. P. Kraus presented a copy of this important and very rare volume to the Newberry Library. On the type-font and familial relationships between Reinhard and Johannes Grüninger, see Robert Proctor, "Marcus Reinhard and Johannes Grüninger," in his *Bibliographical Essays*, London, 1905, pp. 19-38. The description in the *BMC* suggests that the full complement of letters may have already occurred in the Amerbach Bibles of 1479, 1481, and 1482, *GW* 4236, 4246 and 4248, but I have not been able to examine this book.

2. Marginal references in the New Testament to the Old Testament were to book and chapter only. There were no marginal concordance references in the Old Testament of this volume.

3. *GW* 4255 (Goff B-580); *GW* 4258 (Goff B-581), *GW* 4264 (Goff B-587). I am most grateful to Tim Graham for bringing the 1486 Amerbach Bible, of which a copy now is in the collection of The Scriptorium Center for Christian Antiquities in Grand Haven, Michigan, to my attention. See M. H. Black, "The Printed Bible," in *The Cambridge History of the Bible: III The West from the Reformation to the Present Day*, Cambridge, 1963, p. 419; E. J. Kenney, *The Classical Text: Aspects of Editing in the Age of the Printed Book*, Berkeley, 1974, p. 152. I am indebted to Paolo Trovato for these references.

4. Four of these very small vernacular New Testament manuscripts with marginal letters in the Gospels and the Epistles and a vernacular lectionary that refers to marginal letters in the Gospels are in the collection of The Scriptorium Center for Christian Antiquities in Grand Haven, Michigan. I am indebted to Kimberly Molinari for bringing these books to my attention.

5. *GW* 4269 (Goff B-592). The Bible began with a concise prose summary of its contents. Similar supplementary aids had frequently been appended to portable manuscript Bibles.

6. A. van den Wyngaert, *Dictionnaire d'histoire et de géographie ecclésiastique*, 10 (1938), 943-44.

Lucas

6. Latin Bible, Lyon, Marcus Reinhard and Nicolaus Philippi, 1482, f. 386 (P₃) (Newberry Library).

The Impact of the Early Printed Page on the History of Reading

reprinted with references to typographic marginal letters added. Between 1485 and 1496 the Dominican *Concordance*, which could be used with far greater convenience in conjunction with the new Bibles that contained typographic marginal letters, was reprinted in large press runs in Nuremberg, Speyer and Basel.[1]

Inspired by the reformatting of portable Bibles, Venetian printers went on to place evenly spaced, marginal letters in the large format folio Bibles that contained either the *Postilla* of Nicolaus of Lyra or the *Postilla* of Hugh of Saint-Cher, the standard medieval guides to the historical exposition of Scripture[2]. These letters provided the reference points for the Cologne Franciscan friar Peter Mollenbecke's *Tabula directoria in libros Veteris et Novi Testamenti Nicolai de Lyra*, a self-contained index to Lyra's *Postilla* that functioned just as well as a detailed subject index to any small portable Bible containing printed marginal letters.[3]

Printers also applied the system of marginal letters to other texts. The earliest editions of Peter Lombard's *Sententiae* replicated the medieval manuscript text format with tables keyed to numbered books and *distinctiones*.[4] Nicolas Kesler's Basel edition contained new tables referring to an alphabetical denumbering of the questions within each *distinctio*. The letters were not printed in the text and were presumably either imaginary or to be added by an emendator. In subsequent editions produced in September 1488 and in 1489, Kesler added marginal alphabets, as in a Bible, next to each *quaestio*.[5] A modified system of marginal alphabets keyed to specific reference points (as in the *Liber largitorius* and the *Manipulus florum*) occurred in the first edition of Robert Holcot's commentary on Lombard's *Sententiae* (Lyon, Johannes Trechsel, 1497).[6]

1. *GW* 7420-7422, erroneously placed under the name of Conradus de Halberstadt; see Rouse and Rouse, *Preachers, Florilegia and Sermons*, pp. 9-11; Richard H. and Mary A. Rouse, "The Verbal Concordance to the Scripture," *Fratrum archivum praedicatorum*, 44 (1974), 5-30.

2. Johannes Froeben and Johannes Petri used them in their 1498 edition of the Bible accompanied by the *Postilla* of the Franciscan friar Nicolaus of Lyra *GW* 4284 (Goff B-609). They occur again in Johannes Amerbach's edition of Hugh of Saint-Cher, Basel, 1498-1502 (*GW* 4285).

3. Cologne; not before 1480; Goff M-807.

4. Goff P-480. The table of the Newberry Library copy, Inc f4413 was emendated with references to Arabic numbers of the *quaestiones* that were also added, by the same hand, to the leaves. The table could just as easily have been adapted to foliation.

5. Goff P-491 and P-492.

6. Goff H-487.

Fifteenth-century printers were also well aware of another medieval alphabetical system, the alphabetical tie notes common in the fourteenth-century Italian juristic codices mentioned above. Such signs were difficult to replicate in print, and in his 1468 *Institutiones*, Peter Schoeffer had instead used *lemmata* to attach commentary to text.[1] However, Schoeffer in his 5 April 1473 *Liber sextus decretalium*[2] and in his 23 November 1473 edition of the *Decretales*[3] began the process of introducing printed alphabetical tie notes to supplement the *lemmata* to provide a more rapid access. Although these editions constituted a clear effort to reproduce the page format of the fourteenth-century juristic manuscripts produced by Italian university stationers employing the *pecia* system, Schoeffer and subsequent early printers at Nuremberg and Venice in the 1470's and early 1480's were only capable of producing tie notes in juxtaposition to the marginal gloss; their technique was not yet sufficient to reproduce mechanically the superscript letters within the text.[4] Since the letters designating locus in the text were not present, the responsibility of providing them as a redundant cue to the printed *lemmata* devolved to emendator scribes (fig. 7).[5] Only when the entire tie note apparatus was printed, did printed juristic books truly equal the legibility of a handwritten copy produced by the pecia system in the fourteenth century.

In the medium of print, alphabetical tie note systems flourished and migrated from juristic to other genres of text and other regions of Europe as they spread across the academic communities that characterized scholasticism. Johannes Zainer used a crude form of intratextual tie note (characters identical to those he used to divide texts into distinctions, see below) to link marginal concordance references to the apposite point in the text in a folio-sized Bible printed in Ulm in 1480.[6] Soon thereafter other

1. *GW* 7580 (Goff J-506), Lehmann-Haupt, *Peter Schoeffer*, p. 112, no. 29 and plate 8.

2. Lehmann-Haupt, *Peter Schoeffer*, p. 113, no. 45, *GW* 4853.

3. Goff G-447; Lehmann-Haupt, *Peter Schoeffer*, p. 113, no. 47.

4. Cf. Lehmann-Haupt, *Peter Schoeffer*, pp. 48-49 and pls. 9 and 10; Jean Destrez, *La pecia dans les manuscrits universitaires du XIIIe et du XIVe siècle*, Paris, 1935, pls. 22-25.

5. See Newberry Inc f2026, the *Digestum vetus*, Nuremberg, Anton Koberger, 22 November 1482 (Goff-J549) ff. 4 and 30 where tie notes have been added in black and humanistic magenta script. By contrast, printed letters in the text were present in Koberger's 20 June 1486 edition of the *Liber sextus decretalium* and his 15 March 1486 printing of the *Constitutiones Clementis* (Goff B-1001 and C-727), as well as in the *Decretales* printed by Bernardinus Stagninus de Tridino in Venice in 1486; Goff G-462. As late as 1489, Baptista de Tortis in his *Novellae post Codicem*, Venice (Goff J-596) was still printing tie notes in the margins only.

6. *GW* 4242 (Goff B-567). I am indebted to Simon Finch for providing me with photocopies of a copy in his possession; cf. below p. 295, note 3.

7. Tie notes added in manuscript in the *Digestum vetus,* Nuremberg, Anton Koberger, 1482 (Newberry Library, Inc. f. 2026, f. 4).

German printers introduced perfected superscript forms of the new notes into Nicolaus of Lyra's *Postilla literalis* on the Old and New Testaments, the most widely read commentary on the Bible during the late Middle Ages.[1] In the late medieval manuscript tradition, Lyra's *Postilla* had generally been transcribed in volumes separate from the Bible to which it was related by the usual system of *lemmata* or headings.[2] The 1471 first editions of Lyra's *Postilla* used the *lemmata* system,[3] and Adolph Rusch employed it in his folio-sized Strasbourg, pre-1481 edition of the Bible to link the *Glossa ordinaria* to the Vulgate text.[4] However, Johannes Herbort (the same German printer who had reformatted portable Bibles in Venice) in July of 1481 in a volume printed for Nicolas Jenson and Johannes of Cologne complemented the *lemmata* with alphabetical tie notes identical to those used in juristic texts.[5] The entire apparatus, including both the tie notes in the gloss and the superscript characters in the Vulgate text, was typographic. These notes were replicated in many later editions of Lyra.[6] In effect, tie notes marking locus within the text served as precise indications for Biblical verses at a time when these verses were not yet numbered (fig. 8).[7] Editions of Nicolaus of Lyra and Hugh of Saint-Cher that had equally spaced marginal alphabets (located in the outer margin adjacent to the *Postilla*) used lower case letters in the margin of the Biblical text to link the *Postilla* to the text.[8]

Other Biblical commentaries were similarly reformatted during the incunable period. When in about 1485 Georg Reyser in Würzburg printed Bruno of Würzburg's *Commentary on the Psalms*, Reyser linked Bruno's

---

1. John Moorman, *A History of the Franciscan Order from its Origins to the Year 1517*, Oxford, 1968, pp. 395-96.

2. See for examples Koert van der Horst, *Illuminated and Decorated Medieval Manuscripts in the University Library, Utrecht: An Illustrated Catalogue*, Cambridge, 1989, figs 124, 129, 130, 133, and 674.

3. Rome, Conradus Sweynheym and Arnoldus Pannartz, 1471-1472; Goff N-131.

4. *GW* 4242 (Goff B-607).

5. The book is dated 31 July 1481; *GW* 4286 (Goff B-611). It is illustrated in *Valuable English and Continental Books from the Bute Library* (Christie's sales catalogue of 15 March 1995), lot 251. Herbort also printed on 10 September 1481 an edition of the *Decretales cum Glossa* (Goff G-453; *BMC* V, 302) that may also have had a completely typographic apparatus, but I have not been able to examine a copy of this volume.

6. These included Franciscus Renner's 1482-1483 edition (Goff B-612), Anton Koberger's Nuremberg edition of 1487 (*GW* 4289; Goff B-614) as well as Johannes Grüninger's Strasbourg edition of 1492 (*GW* 4293; Goff B-617; reprinted Frankfurt am Main: Minerva, 1971).

7. *GW* 4287 (Goff B-612), *GW* 4289 (Goff B-614), *GW* 4291 (Goff B-616).

8. See for example Froeben and Petri's Basel 1499 edition of Lyra's *Postilla*; *GW* 4284 (Goff B-609). Johannes Amerbach used the same format for the *Postilla* of Hugh of Saint-Cher, Basel, 1498-1502 (*GW* 4285; Goff B-610).

in bibliam

Quia vero pharao derelictus: surgit in scandalū: contra omnes tentatiões dat salubre remediū vicēs. Facile cōtēnit oia zc. Et sic pz diuisio z cōtinentia epistole pñtis: nūc ad expositiōez īre accedamus. a Frater Ambrosius zc. Istam literam inueni in eplis Hieronymi. cōstrue sic. Frater q̃daz noie Ambrosi: perferens mihi munuscula tua, a te missa. retulit: z.i. simul. suauissimas lras q̃ præferebāt. id est prætēdebant. fidē.i. certitudinē vel veritatem. fidei. i. fidelitatis. probate. p operuz exhibitionem a pricipio amiciciaru inter nos cōtractarū z pfere bāt fide. i. certitudinē siue vera citarē. veteri amicitie. quasi di.be se apparebat in literis tuis q̃ fisti tu mihi fidelis erq̃ nos mutuo diserimus z q̃ vere dilexisti me: i modernis bibliis scribitur, sic. Que in principio amiciciaru fidē iā probate fidei: cōstructio nō mutat. Et sequik. z veteris amicitie noua pserebāt.i. ptendebāt noua amicitie veteris.i. q̃ vetus

Incipit epla sancti Hieronymi ad Paulinū psby-terū: de oiłb diuine historie libris. Capitulū. j.

Rat Ambrosius tua mihi munuscula p ferens retulit sił z suauissimas lras q̃ a principio amicicias

d'ciaz fidē: pbate iā fidei: z veteris amicitie noua psere bāt. Vera eñ illa necessitatū e z rpi glutino copulata quā nō vtilitas rei familiaris nō psentia tm corporū nō subdola et palpans adulatio: sz rei timor z diuinarū scripturarū studia cōciliāt. Legimus in veteribus historijs: quosdā lustrasse prouincias nouos adijsse ppłos: maria transisse: vt eos quos ex libris no uerant coram quoq̃ viderent sic Pythagoras memphiticos vates: sic Plato egyptum z architam tarentinum eāq̃ oram Italie q̃

sequitur. Iste interrogatus quid profiteret philosophum se esse respondit. id est studiosus vel amatorem sapientie quoniam sapientem profiteri arrogantissimū videbatur

annoz. Hec oia melius inuenies in pdicto opusculo. l Nouos.i. ignotos m Adijsse populos. ssume sup ple legimus. n Corā quoq̃ viderent.i. vt psentialiter viderent eos quoz famā p scripta nouerāt. u Corā.i. psentialiter. aduerbum est.

o Sic pythagoras memphiticos vates. scz adijt vel pagrauit. Nota q̃ pythagoras philosophus fuit de Samos insula oriūd' vñ Isi. etymo. xiiij Samos insula est in mari. Egeo vbi nata e imo: ex qua fuit Sibylla Samia z pythagoras Sami'a q̃ phie no men inuentum est Itē Aug. de ciuitate dei libro. viij. ca. ñ. duo philosophorū genera tradun tur Unum ytalicū ex ea parte Italie que quondam magna grecia nuncupata est. Alterum ionicum in eis terris: vbi z nūc Grecia nominat. Italicuz genus aucto rem habuit pythagorā Samiū zc. et

8. Volume I of the Latin Bible with the *Postilla* of Nicolaus of Lyra, Nuremberg, Anton Koberger, s. d., f. a iii (Newberry Library).

Bulletin du bibliophile

Commentum by *lemmata* or simply juxtaposed it to the text.[1] In contrast, Anton Koberger in his 1494 and 1497 Nuremberg editions employed alphabetical tie notes.[2] In 1494 in Augsburg, Erhardt Ratdolt used alphabetical tie notes to link a line by line German translation of the Psalms (printed in the margins) to the Latin Vulgate.[3]

As noted above, classical texts had employed the alphabetical tie notes used in the tenth and eleventh centuries, but they were supplanted by the system of *lemmata* in the twelfth century. Petrarch returned to this former tradition when he commissioned a copy of Virgil for his own library, and he himself used alpabetical tie notes, along with other symbols, to annotate his personal copy of Horace.[4] Before printing, Petrarch's example seems not to have been emulated. However, a century later Angelo Poliziano used alphabetical tie notes to annotate a copy of Virgil's *Opera* printed in Rome in 1479.[5] Nevertheless, it was the traditional *lemmata* that occurred in the earliest printed editions of Terence's *Comoediae*, produced at Milan and Venice between 1475 and 1479.[6] *Lemmata* were also employed in Paulo de Ferraria's edition of the *Comoediae* dated July 5, 1481. In most copies of these editions, rubricating scribes underscored the *lemmata* with red to aid the reader. However, in the Newberry Library's copy of the 1481 printing a rubricator, perhaps inspired by contemporary emendators of juristic printed books, added manuscript tie notes in typically humanistic magenta ink to complement the printed *lemmata*.[7] In the Paris edition of Terence that Georg Wolf printed on October 20, 1492, the *lemmata* system was still present.[8] In contrast, Johannes Grüninger in his Strasbourg printed editions of November 1496 and February 1499 substituted alphabetical tie notes and

---

1. Goff P-1046.

2. Goff P-1050 and P-1057.

3. Goff P-1067.

4. In the copy of Virgil's *Opera* the scribe clearly emulated the text format of a juristic codex when he used alphabetical tie notes to link the gloss of Servius to the text. I am indebted to Armando Petrucci for this reference, see his *La scrittura di Francesco Petrarca*, Studi e testi, 248; Vatican City, 1967, p. 120 and pl. XII; Franz Steffins, *Lateinische Paläographie*, Trier, 1909, pl. 101; De la Mare, *The Handwriting of Italian Humanists*, p. 11, no. 4, and a facsimile edition edited by G. Galbiati, Milan, 1930. For the Horace that Petrarch annotated, Florence, Biblioteca Laurenziana Plut 34.1, see Wardrop, *The Script of Humanism*, plate 1.

5. Paris, BNF Rés g. Yc 236 (5), described by Ida Maïer, *Les Manuscrits d'Ange Politien*, Geneva, 1965, frontispiece and p. 353.

6. Goff T-72 and T-74.

7. Inc f6501; Goff T-79. See f. 74. Cf. above p. 284, note 5.

8. Goff T-89a.

The Impact of the Early Printed Page on the History of Reading

added new methodical tables referring to the tie notes as precise loci within the book's numbered *folia*, a system that built on the typographical achievement of Lyra's 1481 *Postilla* (fig. 9). [1] In his 1503 Terence, Grüninger refined these tables even further by distinguishing with a lower case Roman number between the two or even three different alphabetical sequences that sometimes occurred within the recto and verso of a single leaf. [2]

Editions of Horace evinced an evolution similar to those of Terence. The Florence 1482 edition printed by Antonio di Bartolommeo contained a roughly ordered alphabetical table referring to the volume's printed Roman foliation and had no tie notes. [3] A more refined alphabetical index with folio references occurs in two Venetian editions of 1498. [4] Johannes Grüninger of Strasbourg, who had introduced alphabetical tie notes and tables referring to them in conjunction with foliation and tie notes to the typographical tradition of Terence, did the same for Horace in 1498. [5]

Alphabetical tie notes and tables referring to them were also introduced into standard scholastic texts, notably the first editions of Bonaventure's *Commentum super librum Sententiarum Petri Lombardi* printed at Nuremberg by Anton Koberger in 1491 and reprinted at Freiburg-im-Breisgau roughly two years later. [6] In manuscript, Bonaventure's commentary, like Lyra's *Postilla*, had usually been copied separately from the text it elucidated, but here the *Sententiae* and its *Commentum* were combined in one volume just as German printers after 1481 had juxtaposed Lyra's *Postilla* with the Vulgate. In addition to the alphabetical notes, the earliest editions of Bonaventure had marginal Arabic subsection numbers, probably modeled on the case numbers used in fifteenth-century manuscripts and printed editions of the summae of cases of conscience composed by friars such as Bartholomew of San Concordio and Angelo Carletti of Chivasso. [7] The alphabetical tie notes

---

1. Goff T-94 and T-101.

2. Newberry Library, Wing folio ZP 547. G912.

3. Goff H-447. In the Venetian reprinting of this volume in 1483 (Goff H-448), printed folio numbers were omitted in both the table and on the leaves, the task of adding them in both places being left to an emendator.

4. Goff H-459 and H-460.

5. Goff H-461.

6. Goff P-486 and P-487.

7. The history of the evolution of these numbers from the thirteenth to the fifteenth century has yet to be written, cf. L. E. Boyle, "The *Summa confessorum* of John of Fribourg," in *St. Thomas Aquinas 1274-1947: Commemorative Studies*, Toronto, 1974, II, 249-50 and Destrez, *La Pecia dans les manuscrits universitaires*, pl. 21 of Arras, Bibliothèque Municipale 525 (829) copied in 1316. Cf. *New Palaeographical Society*, series II, pl. 21.

Adelphorum   CXII

9. Terence, *Comodiae*, Strasbourg, Johannes Grüninger, 1499, f. 112 (Newberry Library).

The Impact of the Early Printed Page on the History of Reading

and Arabic place numbers enabled a scholar to read and cite Bonaventure's commentary to Peter Lombard's text with far greater rapidity than had been possible within the text format of manuscripts produced by the *pecia* system. [1]

Over the course of the last century many misleading assertions have been made regarding the origin of printed verse numbers that since the mid-sixteenth century have come to be accepted as the standard Biblical reference points. In classical antiquity, occasional mention was made of verse numbers in regard to poetry and the orations of Cicero, but there is no evidence that ancient scribes ever actually wrote verse numbers on scrolls or leaves for reference purposes. Actual verse numbering first appeared during the Middle Ages, but only in a few thirteenth-century scholastic manuscripts of English origin. Like foliation and printing, verse numbers did not flourish until the time of printing, when they appeared for the first time in the Mainz, 1468 edition of Johannes Brunner's *Grammatica rhythmica*. [2] Johannes Herbort prefaced each book of his 1484 New Testament with Arabic numbered titles for the *capitula*, producing a page format that visually resembled numbered verses. [3] Then in 1496, also in Venice in the *editio princeps* of the Vulgate Psalter accompanied by the *Postilla* of Hugh of Saint-Cher, Johannes and Gregorius de Gregoriis used marginal Arabic numbers, as in modern editions, to denote Biblical verses (fig. 10). [4] This incunable edition constituted the first use of Biblical verse numbering, a practice unknown in medieval manuscripts. In 1509 and 1513, Henri Estienne emulated these numbers in his *Psalterium quincuplex*. [5] The new format was again emulated by the converted Jew and Austin friar Felice da Prato, who used verse numbers for his new Latin translation of the Psalms, a volume that

1. Destrez, *La Pecia dans les manuscrits universitaires*, pl. 7, cf. Steffins, *Lateinische Paläographie*, pl. 98. The complex process of maintaining separate *peciae* for text and commentary that was employed in the production of juristic manuscripts at Italian universities was never applied to theological texts.

2. *GW* 5592 (Goff B-1223); Konrad Haebler, *Handbuch der Inkunabelkunde*, Leipzig, 1925, p. 58; Lehmann, "Blätter," p. 59; Lehmann-Haupt, *Peter Schoeffer*, p. 112 no. 28. Later examples of numbered lines include Aldus Manutius' reformatted edition of Perotti's *Cornucopiae linguae latinae*, see above note 1 p. 276.

3. These numbers, however, served an entirely different function.

4. Goff H-530; Hain 8972*. In ancient Hebrew manuscripts, numbers were used to denote the verses of the Book of Lamentations for liturgical purposes, and traces of this practice survive in the form of transliterations of Hebrew alpha-numerical characters in early medieval Latin Bibles. For examples see Robert Babcock, "Beinecke Studies in Early Manuscripts," *The Yale Library Gazette*, 66, supl. (1991), pp. 106-07. These transliterations are preserved in the standard text of the Vulgate.

5. Martin, *Histoire et pouvoirs de l'écrit*, p. 296; Antoine Auguste Renouard, *Annales de l'Imprimerie des Estienne*, second ed., Paris, 1843, pp. 5-6 and 43-44; Schreiber, *The Estiennes*, no. 8.

10. Hugh de Saint-Cher, *Postilla super Psalterium*, Venice,
Johannes and Gregorius de Gregoriis, 1496, f. 113v (Newberrry Library).

The Impact of the Early Printed Page on the History of Reading

Pope Leo X commissioned and Daniel Bomberg printed in Venice in 1515. In 1528 the Dominican friar and Hebraist Santes Pagnini extended the system of verse numbers to the entire text of his new Latin translation of the Bible from the original Greek and Hebrew, thereby creating the modern system for Biblical reference; in 1551 Robert Estienne employed printed verse numbers in his Latin and Greek New Testament. [1] Estienne's bilingual Latin/French editions of *Le Nouveau Testament, Les Psaumes de David,* and *Les Proverbes de Salomon* were all printed in 1552 with verse numbers announced on their title pages. [2] In 1555, Estienne printed a Latin Bible with verse numbers in both the Old and New Testament and vaunted the advantages of using it in conjunction with the new Biblical concordance that he had produced earlier the same year where he had added verse numbers to complement the traditional alphabetical references. [3] The insertion of intratextual verse numbers in Estienne's Bibles was clearly modeled on the alphabetical tie notes incorporated into the text format of the Venetian and Basel incunable editions of Nicolaus of Lyra, the medieval commentator most important for the development of Protestant Biblical exegesis. [4]

Alpha-numerical systems consisting of a numbered alphabet, usually noted in headings at the top of the page, and letters printed in the text or margin resembled leaf and verse numbering in that they established easily retrievable, specific fixed reference points within texts. Like the others, this system originated in manuscript but first flourished in printed books, particularly the sermon collections that served as reference works for fifteenth-century preachers, volumes that were among the bulkiest and most

1. F. Vigouroux, *Dictionnaire de la Bible,* 4 (1912), cols. 1949-50; Renouard, *Annales de l'Imprimerie des Estienne,* pp. 78-79; Nicolas Barker in his preface to Schreiber, *The Estiennes,* p. 3 and p. 101, no.112.

2. Elizabeth Armstrong, *Robert Estienne Royal Printer,* Cambridge, 1954, p. 228; Renouard, *Annales de l'Imprimerie des Estienne,* p. 81. The title page of the Psalms reads: "Les Psaumes de David tant en latin qu'en francois, les deux traductions de l'hebrieu, respondantes l'une à l'autre, verset à verset, notez par nombres."

3. "Biblia R. Stephanus lectori. En tibi Bibliorum Vulgata editio in qua iuxta Hebraicorum versuum rationem singula capita versibus distincta sunt, numeris praefixis, qui versuum numeris, quos in concordantiis nostris novis et integris, post literas marginales A B C D E F G adidimus respondent, ut quaerandi molestia leveris, quum tibi tanquam digito, quod quaeris demonstrabunt." Renouard, *Annales de l'Imprimerie des Estienne,* p. 86; Schreiber, *The Estiennes,* p. 101; "Concordances de la Bible," *Dictionnaire de la Bible,* 2 (1910), col. 807.

4. Moorman, *History of the Franciscan Order,* p. 396; Paul Saenger, "The Earliest French Resistance Theories: The Role of the Burgundian Court," *The Journal of Modern History,* Supplement to vol. 51, no. 4 (1979), pp. 1225-1249.

difficult to manipulate tomes in fifteenth-century libraries.[1] Some of these compilations, such as the *Speculum aureum decem preceptorum* of the Dutch reformed Franciscan Henry of Herpf († 1477), were clearly intended solely for private reference consultation. The general mode of identifying particular sermons in collections before 1400 had been by their sequential position in the calendar of the Roman Church, a principle that could be employed by any cleric trained in the use of a breviary. Normally this was the only point of access offered by the usually unfoliated sermon manuscripts produced in England, France, and Italy. The principal reason that the authorial manuscript of the sermons of Robert of Anjou, a layman, was foliated was that it — the work of a layman — was not organized according to the liturgical calendar.[2]

Alpha-numerical systems — or the simple printed numbering of the sermons — provided a simple to use, mechanical substitute for reliance on the liturgical calendar and an alternative to foliation. A form of alpha-numerical verse finding system was used in the late 1460's by the Strasbourg printer Johannes Mentelin who appended a detailed alphabetical subject table keyed to a printed marginal alphabet *A* through *CL* to denumber the paragraphs in his edition of Book IV of Augustine's *De doctrina christiana*, titled *De arte praedicandi*.[3] This text format was replicated in Mainz by Johannes Fust and Peter Schoeffer before March 1467.[4] In Germany, the Franciscan Johannes Grütsch's collection of sermons for Lent, the *Quadragesimale*, was initially disseminated in manuscripts copied in Basel and Strasbourg on the eve of the introduction of printing with an alpha-numerical system present as an intrinsic textual element. The calendrically organized collection was divided into 48 discretely numbered distinctions that in turn were subdivided into 23 alphabetical subdistinctions *A-Z* (there being no character for *W* and no distinction between *I* and *J* and *U* and *V*). The alphabetical table of subjects that preceded the text referred to the 1,104 arbitrary *distinctiones* thus created. This late medieval system of subject access was peculiarly Teutonic and almost unknown before printing in the older centers of manuscript production in France, Italy and England.[5]

---

1. The only description of these systems has been by Adolf Schmidt, «Zeilenzählung in Druckwerken: Inhaltsverzeichnisse und alphabetische Register in Inkunabelen,» *Zentralblatt für Bibliothekswesen*, 13 (1896), 13-30.

2. See above note 2 p. 261.

3. *GW* 2871 (Goff A-1226).

4. *GW* 2872 (Goff A-1227), Lehmann-Haupt, *Peter Schoeffer*, p. 112 no. 250.

5. An early reference to marginal alphabets occurs in the writings of John Hiltalinger of Basle, see D. Trapp, «Hiltalinger's Augustinian Quotations,» *Augustiniana*, 4 (1954), 416-417.

The Impact of the Early Printed Page on the History of Reading

Johannes Zainer's Ulm 1475 *editio princeps* (H 8063) of Grütsch reproduced the alpha-numerical text format and tables of the manuscripts, and the work with its special form of rapid access became a "bestseller".[1] Early German printers, particularly in Strasbourg, disseminated this new system of retrieving specific places in texts. A closely related text format and tables occurred again in the *Sermones de tempore et de sanctis* of the Dominican friar Johannes Nider (c.1380-1438).[2] Nider's *Praeceptorium divinae legis* was printed with a typographically variant version in which the letters were inserted within the text.[3] The printers expected emendating rubricators subsequently to highlight these reference letters with red strokes in order to aid the reader to find them rapidly.[4]

As with foliation, authors writing after the introduction of printing, notably Germans, composed texts with marginal alphabets as an intrinsic text element. The Alsatian musician Conradus of Saverne, who died between 1476 and 1481, incorporated marginal letters denoting paragraphs into his treatise on the monochord, and these were reproduced in Peter Schoeffer's Mainz edition of about 1475.[5] A different kind of alphabetical index system formed an intrinsic textual element of Denys the Carthusian's *Monopanton*.[6] The alphabetical system actually rivaled foliation in some text traditions. In the Strasbourg 1488 second edition of Jean Gerson's *Opera* (a very popular set of four volumes), Johannes Grüninger replaced the printed foliation used in the first edition with numbered alphabetic arbitrary distinctions with the Arabic number of each alphabet placed on the upper right recto of the appropriate leaves.[7] When alpha-numerical distinctions were not present in a printed text, emendators sometimes added them as, for example, in the Newberry Library's copy of Anton Sorg's printing of Giacomo Filippo

1. André Murith, *Jean et Conrad Grütsch de Bâle: Contribution à l'histoire de la prédication franciscaine au XVe siècle*, Fribourg, Switz., 1940, pp. 54-55.

2. Goff N-216 and N-219.

3. Goff N-199, N-213, N-216.

4. Printers of later editions of the *Praeceptorium*, moved the alphabetical place markers into the margins to enhance their visibility.

5. *GW* 7430 (Goff C-859), Lehmann-Haupt, *Peter Schoeffer*, p. 205, no. 209. See the critical edition of Werner Gümpel, *Die Musiktraktate Conrads von Zabern*, Akademie der Wissenschaften und der Literatur, Abhandlungen der Geistes- und Sozialwissenschaften Klasse, Mainz, 1956, no. 4.

6. See Kent Emery, *Dionysii Cartusiensis Opera selecti Prolegomena*, Corpus Christianorum, 121; Turnhout, 1991, p. 48.

7. *GW* 10714 (Goff G-186).

Foresta's (1434-1520) *Postilla Catonis seu Speculum regiminis* (Augsburg, 1475) [1] and in the Newberry codex containing Augustine's *Opuscula* (Strasbourg, 1485) and Hugh of Saint Victor's *De sacramentis Christianae fidei* (Strasbourg, 1485). [2] Marginal letters as locus markers also occurred on the manuscript leaves of incunable codices. [3]

In 1484, an anonymous printer in Strasbourg applied a modified version of the alpha-numerical system to Ps. Pierre de Palud's *Sermones thesauri novi de tempore*. [4] Here, each leaf bearing printed foliation was divided into alphabetical loci designated by marginal letters; a table referred to folio and the alphabetical location *A-H* on the folio. In the same year, the printer reformatted Ps. Jerome's *Vitae patrum* in a similar manner. [5] The *Vitae patrum* also included a table referring to both the folio and alphabetical distinctions. This modified version was often in effect an efficient mode of distinguishing recto from verso. Like Rolewinck's point system, it effectively indicated pagination before the fact. Texts such as Augustine's *Sermones* and Jacobus de Voragine's *Legenda aurea* were reformatted along these lines by printers in Ulm, Strasbourg, and Basel to facilitate reference consultation. [6] Specially placed marginal letters (similar to those in the first edition of Robert Holcot) were used in conjunction with foliation to provide easy reference points in Petrus de Plasii's Venetian edition of Petrarch's *Triumphi* (1490) and Dante's *Commedia* (1491) as well as Albrecht van Eyb's *Margarita poetica* printed in Venice in January 1493 by Johannes Rubeus. [7]

As early as the 1470's, it became evident that for sermon collections, German printers preferred alpha-numerical systems while French and Italians preferred foliation, especially for the editions of contemporary authors. The *Speculum aureum decem praeceptorum* was printed in Mainz, Nuremberg, and Speyer with extensive printed marginal alphabets. [8] In contrast, editions of the three sermon collections of the Florentine Dominican Leonardo Matthaei de Utino, when printed in Italy and France, were generally foliated or intended for foliation, as for example, Franz

1. Inc f1643; *GW* 6277 (Goff C-292). Unfortunately I have not had the opportunity of examining the manuscripts, see R. Aubert, *Dictionnaire d'histoire et de géographie ecclésiastique* 17 (1971), 1040-41.

2. Inc f691a-597, Goff A-1221, Strasbourg, Martin Flach, 1491 and Goff H-535, Strasbourg, [Printer of the 1483 Jordanus de Quedlinburg], 30 July 1485.

3. Inc 886-958.5; see above p. 241, note 2.

4. Goff P 520.

5. Goff H-207.

6. Goff J-91, Goff J-92; *GW* 2920 (Goff A-1308).

7. Goff P-386, D-33, and E-177.

8. Goff H-38; Goff H-39; Goff H-40.

The Impact of the Early Printed Page on the History of Reading

Renner's Venice 1471 edition that contained a table of contents suited for the addition of folio references.[1] The Sorbonne press edition of *Sermones quadragesimales de legibus dicti,* printed in 1477 contained printed foliation and two tables: one alphabetical table of topics indicating the number of the sermon and the rough position within it (not alphabetically designated as in the German manner) and the other a table of the sermons' calendrical sequence with indication of folio.[2] However, the following year Johannes Zainer's Ulm edition of the very same collection followed the Teutonic model with an alphabetical table referring to sermon number and alphabetical distinction.[3] The printed text tradition of the Florentine Franciscan friar of the strict observance Michael of Carcano († 1484) also evinces a preference for foliation. His *Sermonarium de peccatis per Adventum et per duas Quadragesimes* was printed by Franz Renner and Nicolaus of Frankfurt in Venice in 1476 with a table referring to Arabic folio numbers,[4] and Gregorius and Michael de Gregoriis printed Carcano's *Sermonarium de decem praeceptis per quadragesimam* in 1493 with a table referring to the printed Arabic foliation of the *cartae.*[5] Antonio of Vercelli's († 1483) *Sermones quadragesimales* printed in 1492 by the same press contained a similar table usable in conjunction with similar printed foliation.

Finally, the changes in textual presentation that I have enumerated above were accompanied by two important changes relating to bindings. The first was the evolution of finding tabs. Primitive finding tabs created by placing a piece of folded parchment at a specific section of text had originated in the thirteenth century, the earliest example occurring in Southern Italy in a Cistercian milieu.[6] Two more examples come from the Cistercian abbey of Cadouin south of Périgueux in the fourteenth century.[7] In the mid-fifteenth century, parchment tabs were placed on the leaves of a pocket Psalter copied for the Carthusian monastery of Saint Barbara.[8] Although finding tabs

1. Goff L-140.

2. Goff L-145.

3. Goff L-146.

4. The table also referred to the sermons by sequential Arabic numbers. Neither set of numbers was printed on the leaves; *GW* 6131 (Goff C-194). Nicolaus de Francfort's 1487 edition of the *Sermonarium de poenitentia, GW* 6130 (Goff C-196) was foliated.

5. *GW* 6133 (Goff C-193).

6. See F. Troncarelli and E. B. Di Gioia, "Scrittura, testo, immagine in un Manoscritto Gioachimita," *Scrittura e civiltà,* 5 (1981), 151. I am indebted to Professor Armando Petrucci for this reference.

7. Périgueux, Archives départmentales de la Dordogne, MSS 160 and 163.

8. Newberry Library MS 142.

clearly antedate printing, they, like many of the typographic aspects of text format discussed above, proliferated to an unprecedented degree in the age of the printed book. In incunables, the finding tabs were usually formed from leather strips often stained magenta. These were especially evident in composite volumes, sermon books and other large compilations where rapid and efficient access was desired. In Newberry Inc 534, the first volume of the the 1488 second edition of Jean Gerson's *Opera*, finding tabs enabled the reader to retrieve swiftly each of the twenty-three numbered alphabets into which the text had been divided (fig. 11). In Bibles, tabs marked each book and each letter within the glossary of Hebrew names. [1] In the first half of the sixteenth century, printers began to produce books with printed thumb tabs similar to those found in modern dictionaries. [2] The finding tab abetted a growing practice of reference consultation.

A second important change linking bindings to reference consultation in the final decades of the fifteenth century was a dramatic shift towards the vertical shelving of books. Before 1450 libraries in which books were shelved vertically were extremely rare. [3] In the late fifteenth century the practice became more common. [4] Precisely in the circle of Erasmus where pagination

1. See Newberry Library Inc f4431 (Goff B-556).

2. See Giovanni Mariani's tables of currency conversions printed in Vinegia by Francesco Bindoni and Mapheo Pasini in 1531 and G.A. and P. fratelli of Nicolini da Sabio in 1543, also printed in Vinegia. See Nicolas Rauch, Catalogue no. 2 [1949], no. 148 with plate.

3. For what appears to be a twelfth-century example, see Pollard, "The Construction of Twelfth-Century Bindings," pp. 17-18 and plates 1 and 2.

4. Léon Gilissen, *La Reliure occidentale antérieure à 1400 d'après les manuscrits de la Bibliothèque royale Albert-1ᵉʳ à Bruxelles*, Turnhout, 1983, p. 27. See Marks, *The Medieval Manuscript Library of the Charterhouse of Saint Barbara*, I, 26-27 and Halporn, "The Carthusian Library at Basel," pp. 232 and 236. Titles that read across the spine, such as those at Cologne, are a sure indication of vertical shelving; those that read up or down the spine, as at Basel, may well indicate vertical shelving since titles reading in this manner are more common than those reading across the spine on contemporary volumes. (I am grateful to Martin Steinmann for providing me with details concerning the disposition of the Basel spine labels.) The titles written across their fore edges indicate that volumes at the Carthusian monastery of Buxheim were shelved vertically in the early sixteenth century. Newberry Library Inc f739, a copy of Johannes Grütsch's *Sermones quadragesimales* (Strasbourg, 31 December 1493) has an apparently contemporary title that reads across the fore edge that also indicates vertical shelving. Similar early titles occur on Newberry Library Inc 4766.5, an edition of the *Decretales* printed in Venice on December 15, 1489 and Newberry Library Inc 7766, a *Decretales*, printed in Basel by Johannes Froeben and Johannes Amerbach in 1500. A woodcut in this last incunable depicts a study in which some volumes are shelved vertically. In a woodcut illustrating editions of Sebastian Brant's *Stultifera navis* (Goff B-1086 and 1093), a volume on frontal display in a scholar's study is askew so that the fore edge is visible to the reader, a scene which may be compared to typical fifteenth-century scenes depicting the frontal display of vertically positioned bindings in Paris, BNF fr. 995, copied c. 1500, Ann Tukey Harrison and Sandra L. Hindman, *The Dance Macabre of Women*, Kent, Ohio, 1994, pp. 51 and 125. A circa 1500 woodcut illustrating the Carthusian Gregor Reisch's *Margarita philosophica* (Strasbourg, 1512) depicts a bookcase with numerous volumes shelved vertically; Eva-Maria Hannebutt-Benz, *Die Kunst des Lesens: Lesemöbel und Leserverhalten vom Mittelalter bis zur Gegenwart*, Frankfurt am Main, s.d, p. 50.

11. The first volume of Jean Gerson, *Opera*, 1488 (Newberry Library, Inc. f.534).

Bulletin du bibliophile

began to supplant foliation, woodcuts depicting private studies reflect a growing preference for vertical shelving.[1] The practice of vertical shelving, which facilitated rapid consultation, is confirmed by the position of spine and fore edge title in the early bindings of Erasmus' works, such as his nine-volume 1516-21 edition of Jerome's *Opera* that belonged to Jacobus Marquardus, one of his contemporaries.[2] A similar early binding without metallic bosses on the Newberry Library's copies of Froeben's printings of Erasmus' edition of Terence confirms the growing preference among Northern humanists for vertical shelving.[3]

In conclusion, printing had three far reaching effects on certain aspects of page format. First, by eliminating Gothic cursive script, it dramatically enhanced the legibility of the cheapest grade of book thereby removing the last vestiges of orality in private book production and reading. Second, printing increased metalinguistic awareness and stimulated the wider use of selected forms of punctuation, most notably the parenthesis, the *trait d'union*, and the pointed i. Third, by rendering copies more similar, printing stimulated the proliferation of foliation, alpha-numerical locus designation, and pagination and encouraged authors to regard these systems as intrinsic aspects of their texts. Printing introduced little that was new to the reading process, but it made highly legible and easily consultable volumes available to far greater numbers of readers. By virtue of printing, unprecedented numbers of individuals could participate in the rapid silent reading and reference consultation, unknown in antiquity, that medieval monks and scholars had invented.

1. See the image of Jerome in his study on the last verso of John Fisher's *De veritate corporis et sanguinis Christi* (Cologne, Eucherius Cervicornus, 1527) and the woodcut of Erasmus dictating to his secretary, reproduced by Johan Huizinga, *Erasmus and the Age of Reformation*, New York, 1957, facing p. 191. See also the depiction of Denys the Carthusian in his study, *De perfecto mundi contemplatione*, Cologne, Apud Melchiorem Novesiensem, 1530.

2. Now in the collection of the Newberry Library, fC 507.394.

3. Case f PA 6390.A2. The binding is dated 1534 and bears the initials *V. S.* on the cover.

The Impact of the Early Printed Page on the History of Reading

Résumé

Les conséquences de l'apparition de la page imprimée sur l'histoire de la lecture

Les conséquences de l'apparition de l'imprimerie sur l'histoire de la lecture ont souvent été exagérées. Alors que les changements paléographiques firent évoluer profondément la page des manuscrits latins au haut Moyen Âge, l'imprimerie ne modifia pas beaucoup la physiologie du processus de lecture. L'imprimerie amena cependant un certain nombre de lentes évolutions dans la mise en page du texte qui améliorèrent la lisibilité et encouragèrent la lecture rapide et silencieuse. L'imprimerie fit disparaître les ligatures, amena la standardisation et la diminution des abréviations. Elle entraîna la marginalisation et finalement la disparition de l'usage, pour la réalisation de livres entiers, de la gothique cursive difficile à lire.

En uniformisant la présentation visuelle du latin, l'imprimerie abolit les barrières entre les communautés textuelles et elle développa la conscience métalinguistique en assurant une large diffusion de nouveaux signes de ponctuation et du vocabulaire qui sert à les décrire. Elle encouragea le recours aux divisions matérielles du texte qui, créées arbitrairement, servent de points de repère et favorisa une large diffusion des systèmes alphanumériques, foliotation et pagination, dans l'entourage d'Érasme. Les index de livres imprimés développèrent une attention nouvelle portée à la précision de la citation, ce qui favorisa la consultation d'ouvrages de référence.

[16]

"STUDIED FOR ACTION": HOW GABRIEL HARVEY READ HIS LIVY

Lisa Jardine
Anthony Grafton

I

PROLOGUE: "THE ACTIVITY OF READING"

This essay forms part of a larger, book-length project, which is intended to contribute to the historical understanding of the ways in which humanistically trained readers assimilated and responded to the classical heritage.[1] But it seeks to go beyond the traditional, textual definition of this field to reconstruct the social, professional and personal contexts in which reading took place.[2] Although the present study deals with a topic historians tend to label as "high culture", it will be clear that we also intend it to be in dialogue with a body of recent publications on the history of reading and of the book. That work, although by no means homogeneous, broadly concerns itself with the production and circulation of printed texts, and with setting the activity of reading in its historical and cultural contexts, as well as with some of the social implications that result from a particular locating of reading in history.

All historians of early modern culture now acknowledge that early modern readers did not passively receive but rather actively reinterpreted their texts, and so do we. But we intend to take that notion of *activity* in a strong sense: not just the energy which must be acknowledged as accompanying the intervention of the scholar/reader with his text, nor the cerebral effort involved in making the text the reader's own, but reading as intended to *give rise to something else*. We argue that scholarly reading (the kind of reading we are concerned with here) was always goal-orientated — an active, rather than a passive pursuit. It was conducted under conditions of strenuous attentiveness; it employed job-related equipment (both machinery

[1] A. Grafton, L. Jardine and W. Sherman, *Reading in the Renaissance* (provisional title).

[2] Although the project is a significantly new one, treating Renaissance texts as the basis for transactions among designated groups of readers, we recognize that individual studies of humanistic influence provide important precedents for our own work. See, for example, M. Lowry, "The Arrival and Use of Continental Printed Books in Yorkist England", in P. Aquilon and H.-J. Martin (eds.), *Le livre dans l'Europe de la Renaissance: actes du XXVIIIe colloque international d'études humanistes de Tours* (Paris, 1988), pp. 447-59, at pp. 456-7. We are grateful to Warren Boutcher of Trinity Hall, Cambridge, for this reference.

and techniques) designed for efficient absorption and processing of the matter read; it was normally carried out in the company of a colleague or student; and was a public performance, rather than a private meditation, in its aims and character.[3]

Above all, as we shall see, this "activity of reading" characteristically envisaged some other outcome of reading beyond accumulation of information; and that envisaged outcome then shaped the relationship between reader and text. In consequence, a single text could give rise to a variety of goal-directed readings, depending on the initial brief.[4] Inevitably this has consequences for specific readings of given texts by a reader briefed (by himself or others) in particular ways, which mean that the modern historian cannot afford to prejudge what will constitute its focus or central theme. Indeed, we would argue that, if we use our own understanding of the salient features of the text of Livy (say) to identify the points of crucial importance to an Elizabethan reader, we are very likely to miss or to confuse the methods and objects at which reading was directed.

We believe that our study will significantly enrich what has recently come to be called "the history of reading". Students of this burgeon-

---

[3] See, for example, a suggestive passage in Henry Wotton's commonplace-book: "In reading of history, a soldier should draw the platform of battles he meets with, plant the squadrons and order the whole frame as he finds it written, so he shall print it firmly in his mind and apt his mind for actions. A politique should find the characters of personages and apply them to some of the Court he lives in, which will likewise confirm his memory and give scope and matter for conjecture and invention. A friend to confer readings together most necessary": L. P. Smith, *The Life and Letters of Sir Henry Wotton*, 2 vols. (Oxford, 1907), ii, p. 494.

[4] A fine example of this is the reading which John Dee offered Sir Edward Dyer, in 1597, of Dee's own *General and Rare Memorials Pertayning to the Perfect Arte of Navigation* of twenty years earlier (1577). Dyer had written requesting Dee's advice on "Her Maties Title Royall and Sea Soveraigntie in St Georges Chanell; and in all the Brytish Ocean; any man[er] of way next envyroninge, or next adioyning vnto, England, Ireland and Scotland, or any of the lesser Iles to them apperteyning": British Lib., London (hereafter Brit. Lib.), Harleian MS. 249, fos. 95-105, at fo. 95. What Dee gives Dyer is a route through *General and Rare Memorials* which will yield a "reading" which answers his question, and he does this with great textual precision: "In the 20th page of that boke, (against the figure, 9 in the margent) begynneth matter, inducing the consideration of her Maties Royall Sealimits, and her peculiar Iurisdiction, in all the Seas, next, vnto her Maties kingdomes, dominions and Territories. {Note this worde, NEXT for it will haue diuerse vses in the Consideration, De Confinio in Mari statuendo, vt in Terra} And here vppon, in the 21 page, both in the Text, and allso in the Margent, is pregnant matter conteyned: and the same confirmed by the lawes Ciuile: and the great Ciuilien doctors Iudgm[en]t, there alledged" etc. (*ibid.*). William Sherman is currently working in the Cambridge University English Faculty on this and other of Dee's manuscript writings, in the context of Dee's own role as a political facilitator (or "intelligencer", as Sherman prefers to term him). This work will form part of our collaborative book, *Reading in the Renaissance*.

ing discipline, above all Robert Darnton and Roger Chartier, have done much to focus scholars' attention on the process of reading and the ways in which this has changed over time. They have shown that factors as diverse as the typographical layout of a text, the physical circumstances under which it is read and the process by which the reader obtains it have a powerful effect on the reader's experience of the text itself. They have turned up rich information about authors' and readers' expectations within early modern novels and treatises. They have sometimes been able to discover readers in the process of response, explaining to booksellers or authors themselves exactly how they were struck by a given text.[5] But this new historiography has yet to show an interest in the kind of material we tackle here.

One reason for this may be that the transactional model of reading which we use assumes that a single text may give rise to a plurality of possible responses, not a tidily univocal interpretation. Historians of reading have been inclined to settle for rather simple models for the reading practices of definable social groups and to locate sharp moments of transition when one set of practices yields to another: when reading passes from speech to silence, from public to private settings, from intensive to extensive or passive to active. But, even in the realm of popular culture, a variety of kinds of reading were understood to take place, and such readings were not sealed off from more "serious" and "educated" encounters with the written word.[6] Aspects of the leisured reading of the élite and of the urban consumption of *bibliothèque bleue* volumes undoubtedly also shape the reading which takes place in the scholarly study or the university classroom.[7]

What we attempt here is to show one kind of purposeful reading in process. We have chosen to focus on directed reading conducted in the circle (and under the auspices) of prominent Elizabethan political figures, because we ourselves find the interaction between

[5] See, for example, R. C. Darnton, "Readers Respond to Rousseau", in his *The Great Cat Massacre and Other Episodes in French Cultural History* (New York, 1984); R. Chartier, *The Cultural Uses of Print in Early Modern Europe*, trans. L. G. Cochrane (Princeton, 1987). A classic study of reading by someone not primarily identified as a student of this field is C. Ginzburg, *The Cheese and the Worms*, trans. J. and A. Tedeschi (Baltimore, 1980).

[6] As symptoms of the plurality of possibilities for the use of texts at a specified historical moment, see the preface to John Lyly, *Euphues* (London, 1578); introductory epistle to Thomas Nashe, *The Unfortunate Traveller* (London, 1594); preface to Ben Jonson, *Bartholomew Fair* (London, 1631).

[7] Chartier, *Cultural Uses of Print*, ch. 5, "Publishing Strategies and What the People Read, 1530-1660", ch. 7, "The *Bibliothèque bleue* and Popular Reading"; R. Chartier, "Texts, Printing, Readings", in L. Hunt (ed.), *The New Cultural History* (Berkeley, 1989), pp. 154-75.

politics and scholarship here particularly exciting for the light it can cast *both* on political affiliation (who shared what political beliefs) *and* on the activity of the scholars these figures retained more or less formally in their service. At one level, of course, the discovery of close connections between political theory as contained in classical texts and Tudor political practice is not unexpected; it is the *nature* of the connection which is surprising (its methodical character, its persistence as an emphasis in scholarly reading, the seriousness with which "reading" was treated by those active in the political arena). Elsewhere, in work we are currently engaged in on other readings in other contexts (medical, astronomical, philosophical and dialectical), where the modern reader is less prepared for it, we are finding equally unexpected, related conjunctions of reading practice and application to specified goals.

II

"A WORD WILL SUFFICE FOR THE WISE": SCHOLARS AND
MARTIALISTS

On 18 February 1601 Sir Thomas Arundel wrote a letter to Sir Robert Cecil, defending himself against any implication in the Essex rising, and urging clemency for the earl of Southampton.[8] With this letter was enclosed an unsigned paper in the same hand, which contains the following passage:

> I can not but wrighte what I think may avayle you so dothe my love manyfest my follye. Theare is one Cuff a certayne purytane skoller one of the whottest heades of my lo: of Essex his followers. This Cuff was sente by my lo: of Essex to reade to my lo: of Southampton in Paris where hee redd Aristotles polyticks to hym wth sutch exposytions as, I doubt, did hym but lyttle good: afterwards hee redd to my lo: of Rutlande. I protest I owe hym no mallyce, but yf hee showd [?] faultye heerein, wch I greatelye doubte, I can not but wish his punishment. [In Latin] A word will suffice for the wise (*verbum sapienti*).[9]

Henry Cuffe, one-time professor of Greek at Oxford, and secretary to the earl of Essex, had as one of his duties (according to Arundel)

---

[8] Bodleian Lib., Oxford, Ashmolean MS. 1729, fo. 189, Sir Thomas Arundel to Sir Robert Cecil, 18 Feb. 1601. We are extremely grateful to Paul Hammer for bringing this letter and its enclosure to our attention, and for his unerring ability, in the course of his own work, to pick up from the political correspondence of the 1590s items which confirm our intuitions about the relationship in that period between "arms and letters".

[9] *Ibid.*, fo. 190. In a personal communication, 21 July 1989, Paul Hammer comments: "In enclosing this note on a separate piece of paper and unsigned, it seems very probable Arundel was following a common procedure for dealing with sensitive information".

that of professional reader: "to reade to my lo: of Southampton", and to provide his own expositions of the text (Aristotle's *Politics*).[10] The note suggests that there was a specific category of employee in a noble household such as Essex's: the scholar, retained to "read" with his employer and his employer's associates. And there is a strong suggestion that this reading is politically aware, that it serves a political purpose, of which the scholar/secretary is apprised, and in which he is actively involved ("hee redd Aristotles polyticks to hym wth sutch exposytions as, I doubt, did hym [Southampton] but lyttle good"). This might lead us to reassess the accusation levelled at Cuffe by Essex after his arrest (according to Camden; proof, according to Mervyn James, of Essex's violation of "all the canons of honour"): "you were the principal man that moved me to this perfidiousness".[11] Was it to Cuffe's line in "exposytions" that Essex was attributing blame, on the grounds that these had led him to believe that his political activities were sanctioned by the authority of classical political texts?[12]

A second letter from the Essex circle further supports the idea of scholar-secretaries employed for "reading" — providing interpretations of textual material on pragmatic political themes. An undated letter to Fulke Greville, attributed to Essex, advises Greville as follows:

[10] Henry Cuffe was in the end hanged for his part in the abortive rebellion (Southampton got life imprisonment). Here, however, we set on one side the emotive "conspiracy" testimonies of the state papers and Camden's *Annales*, and concentrate on Cuffe's *profession*. The state papers (but not Camden) contain a version of Cuffe's scaffold speech which is entirely appropriate to the profession of scholar in service to the man of arms: "Schollars and Martiallists (thoughe learning and vallour should have the p[re]hemynence yet) in England must dye like dogges and be hanged: To mislike this, were but folly; to dispute of it, but tyme lost; to alter it impossible; but to endure it manlye, and to scorne it magnanimitye": Public Record Office, London (hereafter P.R.O.), SP12/279, no. 26. See also the document containing Cuffe's final confession, in which he tried to maintain a distinction between the guidance he gave on policy (which he admitted) and the use to which that advice was put (for which, he tried to maintain, he could not be held responsible). The document records, "My Lord Graye saide, this is no time for Logicke": P.R.O., SP12/279, no. 25.

[11] William Camden, *Historie of Elizabeth Queene of England* (London, 1630), p. 187; cited in Mervyn James, *Society, Politics and Culture: Studies in Early Modern England* (Cambridge, 1986), p. 458: "Particularly discreditable was his betrayal of a dependant, his secretary Henry Cuffe, and his ascription to him of such a high politic act as his revolt, which his status required him to take upon himself. When the earl taxed Cuffe that 'you were the principal man that moved me to this perfidiousness', the latter in his turn 'taxed briefly and sharply the earl's inconstancy, in that he betrayed those most devoted to him' ".

[12] See also Henry Wotton, *Of Robert Devereux, Earl of Essex: And George Villiers, Duke of Buckingham: Some Observations by Way of Parallel, in the Time of their Estates of Favour*, ed. Sir Egerton Brydges (priv. pr., Lee Priory, Kent, 1816), pp. 32-4.

HOW GABRIEL HARVEY READ HIS LIVY   35

Cosin Foulke: you tell me you are going to Cambridge and that the Ends of yor going are, to get a Scholar to yor liking, to liue wth you, and some 2, or 3 others to remain in the Uniuersitie, and gather for you; and you require my Opinion, what Instruction, you shall giue those Gatherers. to wch I will, more out of Affection for yor Satisfaction, to do what I can, then out of Confidence that I can doo any thing: and though you get nothing ells by this idle discourse; yet you shall learn this, that, if you will haue yor Friend pe[r]form what you require, you must require nothing aboue his Strength. Hee that shall out of his own Reading gather for the use of another, must (as I think) do it by Epitome, or Abridgment, or under Heads, and common places.[13]

In our earlier work on humanist education we noted, tentatively, that some humanist teachers suggested that a nobleman or prince might employ a poor but gifted young man to read and excerpt the classics for him. Here we suggest that some Elizabethan great houses supported a recognizable class of scholar who performed exactly this function, acting less as advisers in the modern sense than as facilitators easing the difficult negotiations between modern needs and ancient texts. Such readers read, either alone or in company, on their employers' rather than on their own behalf, for purposes and with methods that varied dramatically from occasion to occasion. We propose to show how one such individual actually used his skills to derive counsel from the texts. Our facilitator is Gabriel Harvey; his employment was in the household of the earl of Leicester.[14]

III

READING "IN THE TRADE OF OUR LIVES": THE PHILIP SIDNEY READING

Gabriel Harvey was born in 1550 of a prominent Saffron Walden burgher family, and died there a highly respected local public figure in 1630. He took his B.A. at Christ's College, Cambridge, in 1569-70, was a fellow of first Pembroke Hall (where he took his M.A., against some internal college opposition), and then Trinity Hall (of which he made an unsuccessful attempt to become master). He occupied a number of university posts, including university praelector of rhetoric (1573-5) and university proctor (1583). He obtained his LL.B. in 1584, and was incepted Doctor of Civil Law at Oxford in 1585. In the late 1580s he practised in the Court of Arches in London.

---

[13] Bodleian Lib., Tanner MS. 79, fos. 29^r-30^v. We are grateful to Paul Hammer for this reference also, and to William Sherman for making a preliminary transcription for us. The remainder of the letter details methods for making epitomes and commonplace collections, and the kinds of work usefully to be epitomized.

[14] We owe the term "facilitator" here to Rachel Weil of the University of Georgia.

He held a secretarial post with the earl of Leicester briefly in 1580, and appears to have had other official connections with members of the court circle (in particular members of the so-called "war party" — Low Church opponents of Elizabeth's policy of political appeasement in Europe). He published both "high" educational works, and popular works (including several exchanges of letters with his friend Edmund Spenser, and some "low" pamphlet material). His publishing career was terminated after a rancorous series of pamphlet exchanges with Thomas Nashe, at the end of which, in 1599, both men's works were banned from publication.[15]

Harvey's Livy is a grand and heavy folio in sixes, printed in Basle in 1555.[16] In this edition, the text of Livy appears flanked by both critics and supporters. Two elaborate commentaries, one by Ioannes Velcurio and one by Henricus Glareanus, follow the text and explicate it, often phrase by phrase. Instructions for reading history, by Simon Grynaeus, precede it. Lorenzo Valla's iconoclastic demonstration that Livy had committed a genealogical error also appears, lest the reader feel more reverence than a Roman classic properly demands. The entire book is densely annotated by Harvey, indicating successive readings over a period of more than twenty years.[17]

At the end of book three of the first decade of Harvey's Livy there is the following note:

> The courtier Philip Sidney and I had privately discussed these three books of Livy, scrutinizing them so far as we could from all points of view, applying a political analysis, just before his embassy to the emperor Rudolf II. He went to offer him congratulations in the queen's name just after he had been made emperor. Our consideration was chiefly directed at the forms of states, the conditions of persons, and the qualities of actions. We paid little attention to the annotations of Glareanus and others.[18]

[15] This summary is based on V. F. Stern, *Gabriel Harvey: His Life, Marginalia and Library* (Oxford, 1979); G. C. Moore Smith, *Gabriel Harvey's Marginalia* (Stratford-upon-Avon, 1913). For some recent remarks on Harvey's relationship with Andrew Perne at Cambridge, see Patrick Collinson, "Andrew Perne and his Times" (unpublished paper).

[16] Princeton University Lib., Deposit of Lucius Wilmerding Jr., *T. Livii Patavini, Romanae historiae principis, decades tres, cum dimidia* (Basle, 1555) (hereafter Harvey's Livy). The volume is inscribed "ex dono D^ns Henrici Harveij. A. 1568", and contains notes made during the period 1568-90. We are extremely grateful to the owner and to Princeton University Library for allowing us access to this volume.

[17] On Harvey's habits of annotating, see Moore Smith, *Gabriel Harvey's Marginalia*; C. Brown Bourland, "Gabriel Harvey and the Modern Languages", *Huntington Lib. Quart.*, iv (1940-1), pp. 85-106; H. S. Wilson, "Gabriel Harvey's Method of Annotating his Books", *Huntington Lib. Bull.*, ii (1948), pp. 344-61; J.-C. Margolin, "Gabriel Harvey, lecteur d'Erasme", *Arquivos do Centro Cultural Portugues*, iv (1972), pp. 37-92; Stern, *Gabriel Harvey* (and her bibliography, *ibid.*, pp. 272-3).

[18] Harvey's Livy, p. 93. In all instances where excerpts from Harvey's marginalia are given in modern English this indicates that the original annotation was in Latin.

HOW GABRIEL HARVEY READ HIS LIVY   37

Here is an extremely precise reference. Just these three books, read through by Harvey and Sidney, *tête-à-tête*, with an eye to political analysis, and "shortly before his embassy to Emperor Rudolph II". They were particularly interested in types of republic, in the protagonists' character and circumstances, and in the types of action. They deliberately ignored — as men of action perhaps should — the humanist commentaries.

In October 1576 Sidney returned from Ireland, probably escorting the body of the earl of Essex, who had died there on 22 September.[19] While in Ireland he had accompanied his father, Sir Henry Sidney (governor-general in Ireland), with the task of dealing (apparently pretty unsuccessfully) with bands of rebels.

This was Sidney's first active service. He set out on his embassy to Rudolph in February 1577. Between Ireland and this first diplomatic service Sidney was in England; he visited John Dee on 16 January 1577 and sent a letter from Leicester House on 8 February.[20] It seems reasonable to infer that he and Harvey read Livy at Leicester House between October 1576 and February 1577.[21]

In book one of the third decade Harvey once again links a "reading" of Livy with members of Sidney's circle or associates:[22]

[19] See H. Hore, "Sir Henry Sidney's Memoir of his Government", *Ulster Jl. Archaeol.*, v (1857), pp. 299-323: "Here [Galway] heard we first of the extreame and hopelesse sickness of the earl of Essex, by whom Sir Philip being often most lovingly and earnestly wished and written for, he with all the speed he could make went to him, but found him dead before his coming, in the castle at Dublin" (p. 314). We are grateful to William Maley for this reference.

[20] The Dee visit included Leicester, Philip Sidney and "the latter's close friend, Edward Dyer": J. M. Osborn, *Young Philip Sidney, 1572-1577* (New Haven and London, 1972), pp. 449, 451.

[21] An additional clue is that on sig. Fii[r] of Gabriel Harvey, *Gratulationes Valdinenses* (London, 1578), "a poem is described as having been presented to Leicester in 1576": Stern, *Gabriel Harvey*, p. 39. There is one further piece of tantalizing circumstantial evidence suggesting that Harvey may have been in some way associated with Sidney even earlier. In Osborn, *Young Philip Sidney*, pp. 402-3, there is a series of three letters from the biographer of Ramus, Théophile de Banos, concerning his edition of Ramus's *Commentaries*, preceded by a biography of Ramus, which the printer Wechel (also a friend of Sidney's) had just produced. The first letter promises that: "if I cannot find a friend to take them [Ramus's *Commentaries*], I will send a man specially to Master Harvey in Antwerp, so that you will safely receive them". "Master Harvey" must have been returning to England, thus a carrier for the book. In the event, de Banos sends two further anxious letters, because the book has apparently not arrived, and in March he receives word from Sidney that he has still not received it: *ibid.*, pp. 408-9, 416-17. From January until the beginning of the Cambridge Easter term (April?), Harvey was inexplicably out of Cambridge, and nothing is known of his whereabouts: Stern, *Gabriel Harvey*, pp. 30-1. Harvey was a dedicated Ramist, and in any case the Sidney/Ramus/Wechel connection — Sidney exchanges letters with Wechel authorizing him to buy him the latest books at the Frankfurt book fair, for which he will reimburse him — is intriguing.

[22] On fo. 53[r] of Brit. Lib., Sloane MS. 93 (the so-called Harvey letter-book),

(cont. on p. 38)

Each decade is fine, but this one should be studied by the best actors. The quality of the content, and its great power; where the virtue of the Romans suffers so much. Certainly some light can be shed by Louis le Roy's Commentaries on Aristotle's Politics; Bodin's Republic and Methodus; du Poncet's Turkish Secrets in the Gallic Court; Sansovino's Political Maxims; the recent works on politics by Althusius and Lipsius; a few others. And it is fitting for prudent men to make strenuous efforts to use whatever sheds light on politics: and to increase it as much as they can. Two outstanding courtiers thanked me for this political and historical inquiry: Sir Edward Dyer and Sir Edward Denny. But let the project itself — once fully tried — be my reward. All I want is a lively and effective political analysis of the chief histories: especially when Hannibal and Scipio, Marius and Sylla, Pompey and Caesar flourished.[23]

Other evidence complements these notes, enabling us to reconstruct Harvey's role in full. In Harvey's Sacrobosco (now in the British Library), which carries the inscription "Arte, et virtute, 1580" on its title-page,[24] a note on sig. aii^r reads: "Sacrobosco & Valerius, Sir Philip Sidneis two bookes for the Spheare. Bie him specially commended to the Earl of Essex, Sir Edward Dennie, & divers gentlemen of the Court. To be read with diligent studie, but sportingly, as he termed it".[25]

So Sidney, by 1580, apparently had his own views on "reading" for those in the political arena. Or did he? Osborn prints a letter from Sidney to Edward Denny which came to light in a "near-contemporary transcript" in 1971. It is dated 22 May 1580, on the eve of Denny's departure (like Spenser) in the train of Lord Grey, the new governor of Ireland, appointed to put down Irish disturbances more single-mindedly than had Henry Sidney.[26] It apparently answers an inquiry from Denny as to what he should read to improve his mind (and presumably his prospects), and is something of a set piece. It also makes clear, as Sidney does elsewhere in his letters, that in the face of Elizabeth's determined resistance to military engagement

---

(n. 22 cont.)

somewhat cryptically inserted in the narrative, is a fragment of a letter from "Immerito" (Spenser) at court which reads: "The twoe worthy gentlemen, Mr. Sidney and Mr. Dyer, have me, I thanke them, in sum vse of familiaritye; of whom and to whome what speache passith for your creddite and estimation, I leave yourselfe to conceyve, havinge allwayes so well conceyvid of my vnfainid affection and good will towardes yow. And nowe they have proclaymid in there αρειωπαγω". Stern mistakenly makes this a letter *from* Harvey: Stern, *Gabriel Harvey*, p. 39.

[23] *Harvey's Livy*, p. 277.

[24] Stern, *Gabriel Harvey*, pp. 233-4.

[25] Transcribed *ibid.*, p. 79.

[26] See L. Jardine, "'Mastering the Uncouth': Gabriel Harvey, Edmund Spenser and the English Experience in Ireland", in J. Henry and S. Hutton (eds.), *New Perspectives on Renaissance Thought: Essays in the History of Science, Education and Philosophy in Memory of C. B. Schmitt* (London, 1990), pp. 68-82.

aspiring men of action like himself and Denny have a good deal of time
on their hands, and that "reading" and "study" are the approved,
character-forming way of relieving boredom:

> You will me to tell you my minde of the directinge your studyes. I will
> doe it as well as the hast of your boy [the waiting messenger], and my little
> judgement will hable me. But first let me reioyse with you, th' since the
> vnnoble constitution of our tyme, doth keepe vs from fitte imployments,
> you doe yet keepe your selfe awake, w' the delight of knowledge.[27]

For the foundation of study Sidney naturally prescribes scriptural
reading. But when he comes to "the trade of our lives", he specifies
reading which is (we would argue) quite clearly based on that "reading" with Gabriel Harvey three years earlier:

> The second parte consists as it were in the trade of our lives. For a physician
> must studdy one thinge, and a Lawyer an other, but to you th' with good
> reason bend your selfe to souldiery, what bookes can deliver, stands in the
> books th' profess the arte, & in historyes. The first shewes what should be
> done, and the other what hath bene done. Of the first sorte is Langeai in
> french, and Machiavell in Italian, and many other wherof I will not take
> vpon me to iudge, but this I thinke if you will studdy them, it shall be
> necessary for you to exercise your hande in setting downe what you reed,
> as in descriptions of battaillons, camps, and marches, with some practise
> of Arithmetike, which sportingly you may exercise. Of them I will say noe
> further, for I am witness of myne owne ignoraunce. For historicall maters,
> I woold wish you before you began to reed a little of Sacroboscus Sphaere, &
> the Geography of some moderne writer, wherof there are many & is a very
> easy and delightful studdy. You have allready very good iudgement of the
> Sea mappes, which will make the other much easier; and provide your
> selfe of an Ortelius, th' when you reed of any place, you may finde it out, &
> have it, as it were before your eyes.[28]

"Some practise of Arithmetike, which sportingly you may exercise" — echoed in Harvey's "To be read with diligent studie, but
sportingly, as [Sidney] termed it" in his copy of Sacrobosco —
indicates that Harvey saw this letter (it is even possible he wrote it).[29]
It seems clear to us that we do indeed have here an agreed "reading"
of history, for the "trade of our lives" — politics and "souldiery".
And the source of that reading, since, as we shall see, the copiousness
and consistency of Harvey's annotations must establish him as its
originating influence, is that "armchair" politician (as he used to be
characterized) Gabriel Harvey.

We begin here because the Denny letter/Harvey marginalia connection establishes at the outset some real-life events and outcomes for

---

[27] Osborn, *Young Philip Sidney*, appendix 5, pp. 535-40, at p. 537.

[28] *Ibid.*, p. 539.

[29] Or Spenser, with Denny in Ireland, saw it. At any rate, there is a direct connection
between Harvey and the letter.

Harvey's reading of Livy. It will be an important part of our argument to maintain that Renaissance readers (and annotators) persistently envisage action as the *outcome* of reading — not simply reading as active, but reading as trigger for action. Here we may note how the chance opportunity to collate the marginal notes of an individual known only as a reader (and thus labelled politically non-participant by later scholars) with a "letter of advice" from an individual known to be politically and diplomatically active seems to sharpen up "reading" into potential "advice", and provide a link between the absorption of information (as we would tend to judge reading) and public practice.

IV

"I RAN OVER THIS DECADE ON HANNIBAL IN A WEEK": THE COLONEL THOMAS SMITH READING

At the bottom of page 428 of the Livy Harvey records a debate he participated in at Hill House, Theydon Mount, home of his patron Sir Thomas Smith, in which Livy's historical commentary stimulated a lively topical discussion of Elizabethan military strategy:

> Thomas Smith junior and Sir Humphrey Gilbert [debated] for Marcellus, Thomas Smith senior and Doctor Walter Haddon for Fabius Maximus, before an audience at Hill Hall consisting at that very time of myself, John Wood, and several others of gentle birth. At length the son and Sir Humphrey yielded to the distinguished secretary: perhaps Marcellus yielded to Fabius. Both of them worthy men, and judicious. Marcellus the more powerful; Fabius the more cunning. Neither was the latter unprepared [weak], nor the former imprudent: each as indispensible as the other in his place. There are times when I would rather be Marcellus, times when Fabius.

We can date the event to which this note refers with some accuracy. Between 1566 and 1570 Sir Humphrey Gilbert was on active service in Ireland.[30] He was knighted for his services on 1 January 1570, and returned to England at the end of that month, remaining there until July 1572, when he was sent to the Netherlands against the Spanish.[31] From summer 1571 he was certainly involved with Sir Thomas Smith in a speculative project to obtain a monopoly on a supposed procedure for transmuting iron into copper.[32] Sir Thomas Smith was in France

[30] D. B. Quinn, *The Voyages and Colonising Enterprises of Sir Humphrey Gilbert*, 2 vols. (London, 1940), i, p. 12.

[31] *Ibid.*, i, pp. 17-18, 22-3.

[32] M. Dewar, *Sir Thomas Smith: A Tudor Intellectual in Office* (London, 1964), pp. 149-55; Quinn, *Voyages and Colonising Enterprises of Sir Humphrey Gilbert*, i, pp. 20-1.

from December 1571.[33] Harvey knew John Wood in 1569, when he noted in his copy of Smith's *De recta et emendata linguae anglicae scriptione dialogus* (London, 1567), that the book was a gift from Smith's nephew, his "special friend".[34] The Hill House debate, then, took place some time in 1570, or early 1571.

In 1571 three of the four participants in the debate were actively involved in military and diplomatic affairs. Specifically, Sir Thomas Smith, his son and Sir Humphrey Gilbert were all actively engaged in the Elizabethan conquest and settlement of Ireland. Gilbert (the ruthless suppressor by force of the Fitzmaurice rebellion) and Smith junior (shortly to head the military campaign for the Smith family settlement venture in the Ards) argue the case for Marcellus, whose unscrupulousness and ruthlessness Livy contrasts with Fabius' measured strategy. Sir Thomas Smith and the elderly diplomat Haddon win the debate with their case for the rule of law and policy.[35] These distinguished Elizabethans used Livy — and Harvey — to work out anew in debate the Roman relationship between morals and action — law and military engagement.

At the bottom of page 518 Harvey writes in the margin:

I ran over this decade on Hannibal in a week, no less speedily than eagerly and sharply, with Thomas Smith, son of Thomas Smith the royal secretary, who was [Smith junior] shortly afterwards royal deputy in the Irish Ards — a young man as prudent as spirited and vigorous. We were freer and sometimes sharper critics of the Carthaginians and the Romans than was fitting for men of our fortune, virtue or even learning, and at least we learnt not to trust any of the ancients or the moderns sycophantically, and to examine the deeds of others, if not with solid judgement, at least with our whole attention. We put much trust in Aristotle's and Xenophon's politics, in Vegetius' book *Of Military Affairs* and Frontinus' Stratagems. And we chose not always to agree with either Hannibal, or Marcellus, or Fabius Maximus; nor even with Scipio himself.

Evidently the Hill House debate emerged from or accompanied a full-scale reading of the text. This can be dated: the letters patent

---

[33] See below, p. 42.

[34] Stern, *Gabriel Harvey*, pp. 14-15. The book is now in the Wilmerding deposit, Princeton; another inscription identifies it as "John Wood's book, a gift from the author himself" (Johannis Woddi liber ex ipso Authoris dono).

[35] Haddon (1516-72) wrote Elizabeth's answer to Osorius in 1563, published in Paris "through the agency of Sir Thomas Smith, the English ambassador": *s.v.* Walter Haddon, *Dictionary of National Biography* (hereafter *D.N.B.*). In 1567 Thomas Hatcher published a collection of Haddon's works, *Lucubrationes passim collectae et editae: studio et labore Thomae Hatcheri Cantabrigiensis*; Hatcher also published *In Commendation of Carr and Wilson's Demonsthenes* (*s.v.* Hatcher, *D.N.B.*). Hatcher and Harvey were apparently friends, and Harvey's copy of Demonsthenes' *Gnomologiae* had previously belonged to Hatcher; Harvey acquired it in 1570.

authorizing the Smiths to embark on a private venture to colonize the Ards region of Ireland were issued on 16 November 1571; Sir Thomas Smith was appointed principal secretary in July 1572, but "long before that" (any time after spring 1571) Burghley and others were referring to him as "secretary"; he left for France on an ambassadorial assignment on 15 December 1571.[36] Thomas Smith junior, Sir Thomas's natural and only son, was recruiting volunteers in Liverpool early in 1572, and was killed in Ireland, during the unsuccessful first attempt to establish the Smith venture, in October 1573.[37] So the reading referred to also took place some time early in 1571. This date is corroborated by a remark in Harvey's *Foure Letters* (London, 1592), in which he records that the earl of Oxford "bestowed Angels upon mee in Christes Colledge in Cambridge, and otherwise voutsafed me many gratious favours at the affectionate commendation of my Cosen, M. Thomas Smith, the sonne of Sir Thomas, shortly after Colonel of the Ards in Ireland".[38] Harvey was elected to a fellowship at Pembroke Hall at the end of 1570, and presumably left Christ's (the college at which he took his B.A.) shortly thereafter — that is, early in 1571.

So while Thomas Smith prepared himself for his crucial military expedition to Ireland (the expedition which was supposed to make his career politically, as well as his own and his father's fortunes), he read Livy with his intellectual companion and close friend ("cosen") Gabriel Harvey. We shall see later what form that reading took (using the copious notes to book three and their repeated references to Thomas Smith's opinions as our guide).

V

"OWR SPECIAL NOTES & PARTICULAR OBSERVATIONS WEE COMMITTED TO WRITING": THE THOMAS PRESTON READING

In 1584 (probably), Harvey read the first decade intensively again, with apparently more academic intent. This time he read with Thomas Preston, newly appointed master of Trinity Hall (a post which Harvey had hoped to win himself).[39] That this reading was a "theoretical"

---

[36] Dewar, *Sir Thomas Smith*, pp. 123, 131.

[37] D. B. Quinn, "Sir Thomas Smith (1513-1577) and the Beginnings of English Colonial Theory", *Proc. Amer. Philos. Soc.*, lxxxix (1945), pp. 543-60, at pp. 548-9.

[38] Cited in Stern, *Gabriel Harvey*, pp. 65-6.

[39] But, as throughout this piece, the marginal notes contradict the conventional account of this failure to achieve office leaving Harvey a broken and disappointed man (based largely on Nashe).

one is made explicit by the fact that its key text was Machiavelli's commentary/discourse on the same decade:

> I had reason to take the greater paines in reading the first decad of Liuie, bie meanes of mie dailie & almost howerlie conference with M. Thomas Preston a fine discourser, & the Queenes onlie pensionar scholler:[40] when in owre chambers in Trinitie hall with mutch delight, & more profit wee read togither in Italian, which the Florentine secretarie writeth with an elegant & sweet grace: Discorsi di Niccolo Machiauelli, sopra la prima deca di Tito Liuio. Which politique discourses wee thorowghly redd-ouer: with diligent & curious obseruations of the notable actions of the Romans, accomplished at home, & abrode, bie publique, & priuate counsell: at home in the first booke: abrode in the 2; both bie publique counsell: at home & abrode bie priuate counsell, in the 3. Which Method in Machiauels discourses wee soone discouered: & the more easely distinguished his politique positions. Supposing his Councels of state, very fitt to be annexed to owr principall councels, & souerain decisions in Lawe. Wee then had studied Hotomans Lawe-booke Quaestionum illustrium. And were in hand with Marantas ten disputations Quaestionum legalium.[41]

Harvey makes this note at the end of the first decade. At the top of the same page, he writes "Prestons, and Harueys familiar conference concerning the first decad of Liuie: & of Machiauels politique discourses upon this decad. Owre cheife autours for direction and resolution, were not manie, but essentiall, & for the most part iudicious". To which he had added, at some other time:

> Especially Aristotle & Bodine for groundes of pollicie: Sansauino & Danaeus for aphorismes: Patritius & Plutarch for discourse: Hotoman & Maranta for lawe: sumtime Vigelius & excellent Hopperus. Thowgh otherwhiles wee had the Censures of Danaeus & Hotoman in suspicion: the one for sum irregular rules, rather Ephorismes, then Aphorismes: the other for his peramptorie & almost seditious Francogallia. Dangerous [the note continues down the right margin] panflets in a monarchie or politique kingdom; & flat opposite to the imperiall ciuil lawe of the prudent, valorous, & reputed iust Romans. Such were owr resolutions vpon Liuie, & Machiauel. Owr special notes & particular obseruations, both moral, politique, militarie, stratagematical, & other of anie worth or importance, wee committed to writing.

At the close of the text of the first decade, on the page facing the one on which the above remarks are inscribed, Harvey adds a further note on his and Preston's reading of Danaeus:

> We have come this far with Daneau's Aphorisms and Machiavelli's Discourses on Livy. But one should note that: "The aphorisms that could be drawn from the third decade were more or less copied from Polybius and

---

[40] The *Dictionary of National Biography* tells us that in 1564, in Cambridge, Preston "addressed the queen in a Latin oration on her departure, when she invited him to kiss her hand, and gave him a pension of 20l. a year, with the title of 'her scholar' ": *s.v.* Preston.

[41] Harvey's Livy, p. 266.

44   PAST AND PRESENT   NUMBER 129

can be found there too: those that could have been selected from the fourth decade clearly agree with the earlier ones". Therefore Daneau thought he had satisfied his readers fully when he finished his aphorism collection with the first decade. Machiavelli uses much the same method, save in a few details.[42]

We shall return to these comments on Livy/Danaeus/Machiavelli. For now the point to note is that these remarks specify a close and informed reading, with a diplomatic or political end in mind, evidently with the appropriate books open on the table before them (as was the case when Harvey worked on his dialectic books in this intellectually probing way).[43]

VI

AUGUSTINE ON LIVY: WHAT IS EXEMPLARY READING?

Around 1590 Harvey left Cambridge permanently in order to practice as a lawyer in the London (ecclesiastical) Court of Arches.[44] And in 1590 Harvey read Livy from still another point of view — one which for the first time heavily focused on the morality of the Livy. "I haue seene", he wrote,

few, or none fitter obseruations, or pithier discoursers upon diuers notable particulars in Liuie, then sum special chapters in Augustines excellent bookes De Ciuitate Dei. Where he examines, & resolues manie famous actions of the Romans, with as sharp witt, deep iudgment, & pregnant application, as anie of those politicians, discoursers, or other notaries, which I haue read vpon Liuie.[45]

As this quotation continues, it is evident that Harvey now has in mind the forensic pleading of cases, and the problem of grafting theology and morality on to the patently pagan heroism of his text — a task for which Augustine's comments on Livy are peculiarly helpful: "Therefore I still saye: [In Latin] Hand me Augustine in those cases which Augustine discusses and settles perceptively and reliably. I know no theologian or dialectician or philosopher or politician, nor even scholar, philologian or critic who is more acute than he". Here, finally, Harvey's engagement with Livy ends, with a rejection of pagan values, and the pagan exemplary figures who go with them, in favour of the Christian ethic:

Certainly here for observations on Livy I prefer Augustine to any other

[42] *Ibid.*, p. 267.
[43] See L. Jardine, "Gabriel Harvey: Exemplary Ramist and Pragmatic Humanist", *Revue des sciences philosophiques et théologiques*, lxx (1986), pp. 36-48.
[44] Stern, *Gabriel Harvey*, pp. 80-1.
[45] Harvey's Livy, sig. Z5ʳ, after "finis indicis".

HOW GABRIEL HARVEY READ HIS LIVY   45

theologian of the highest quality. This is one reader's opinion, that there is hardly a competent judge of Roman history who did not previously have knowledge of Augustine's wise doctrine on the City of God. I am delighted that I have added this at last to the political philosophy of Aristotle and Plato. And I confess that the ideal state of philosophers or heroes is as a shadow by comparison with the City of God.

Gabriel Harvey. 1590.

Harvey did not read *The City of God* on its own, but together with its almost equally vast Renaissance companion, the commentary by Juan Luis Vives, famous for its learning, penetrating inquiries into Augustine's lost sources, and exuberant excursuses. In the course of this reading Harvey often found that subjects touched on by Augustine had been studied "a little more precisely" by the modern scholar.[46] At the end of twenty or more years of political reading, here at last we find a kind of reading which the modern student of humanism would recognize: the personal, moralized, ruminative reading to be adduced tellingly to defend a course of action, or to enhance a specifically Anglican point of view.

VII

THE SETTING FOR READING

Harvey's marginal annotations enable us to build up a picture of consecutive, detailed readings of Livy, given point and direction by a specified occasion for reading and (sometimes) companion with whom to read. At this point, as part of our historical reconstruction, we need a digression on equipment. For it should be apparent from the examples of "readings" of Livy cited, that Harvey did not give his attention to one book at a time, even when reading in company. Even from among the comparatively small number of his annotated books which survive (or have been traced) his marginal notes make it clear that he annotated groups of books together on any one occasion, always in the same regular hand, with an even pen-pressure which does not suggest any awkwardness in writing or reading (he rarely blots or erases a single word). In the case of the Livy, there is at least the sense that the Livy text is, so to speak, *central* — that it sits at the centre of the reading. In other cases, such as the annotations of groups of dialectic books, and associated classical works (Cicero's *Topica*, Quintilian's *Institutiones oratoriae*, Demosthenes' *Gnomolog-*

---

[46] *Ibid.*, p. 310; see below, pp. 53-4, for a fuller treatment.

iae), it is by no means clear which text sits at the centre of the reader's field of vision and attention.[47]

How did Harvey read a large number of volumes systematically? The sheer practical problems of keeping from five to fifteen parallel texts and reference works constantly at hand seem daunting. So does that of entering notes in all of them, as Harvey did, in a handwriting more elaborate than that of "many a copyholder or magistral scribe that holds all his living by setting schoolboys copies" (as Nashe, his enemy, described it).[48] How did he muster the vast amount of uncluttered flat surface that this exercise in close reading and fine penmanship required?

Roger Chartier has recently called attention to the many changes that our devices for storing books have undergone. He illustrates one of the most strikingly alien of these to be produced in early modern Europe: the book-wheel. (See Plate.) This splendid combination of cabinetry and cog-wheels was new in the sixteenth century. As Ramelli's illustration shows, it enabled its user to lay out on flat surfaces as many books as he might choose, to move them as he needed them without losing his places, and to stop at any selected text — thanks to the cog-wheels.[49] Jacopo Corbinelli saw such a wheel in the library of the great jurist Cujas at Valence. It could hold

> 60 or 70 portions out of large volumes, open, not counting the tiny ones. You sit and with your hand you bring portions of these large volumes before you three at a time. To put it in a nutshell, you can make a whole study revolve, and so easily that it is a delightful exercise.[50]

Harvey's method of reading requires something like the book-wheel to be physically feasible. And the book-wheel, when seen in the new light cast on it by Harvey's practices, is more than a

[47] It was Robert Darnton who first asked us why we believed that in a reading of a group of texts any single text *necessarily* had to be at the centre of the reading. We express our gratitude to him for launching us on a train of thought which led us eventually, after a certain amount of detective work, to the book-wheel.

[48] T. Nashe, *Selected Writings*, ed. S. Wells (Cambridge, Mass., 1965), p. 285.

[49] Bill Saslaw has brought to our attention a modern version of the rotating desk, in which the outer and central sections of a circular desk rotated independently, horizontally: it was owned by Harlow Shapley, director of the Harvard College Observatory in the 1930s, and remained in the office he had occupied until the 1960s. For a photograph, see H. Shapley, *Ad astra per aspera: Through Rugged Ways to the Stars* (New York, 1969).

[50] R. Calderini de Marchi, *Jacopo Corbinelli et les érudits français d'après la correspondance inédite Corbinelli-Pinelli (1566-1587)* (Milan, 1914), p. 176. Ramelli's plate had already been reproduced, together with a photograph of a surviving book-wheel in Wolfenbüttel and useful remarks, in A. Hobson, *Great Libraries* (London, 1970), pp. 206-7. Another working example is to be found in the Bibliotheca Thysiana, Leiden.

The book-wheel from *The Various and Ingenious Machines of Agostino Ramelli,* ed. M.
Teach Gnudi and E. S. Ferguson (New York and Aldershot, 1987), p. 509.

Photo: by permission of Dover Publications

device for neat storage of momentarily interesting texts. It belongs to Harvey's cultural moment, in which collation and parallel citation were an essential, constructive part of a particular kind of reading; it allowed the imbedding of text in context, after the fashion that Harvey and (we would argue) many of his professional academic contemporaries practised. The book-wheel and the centrifugal mode of reading it made possible amounted to an effective form of information retrieval — and that in a society where books were seen as offering powerful knowledge, and the reader who could focus the largest number of books on a problem or an opportunity would therefore appear to have the advantage.[51]

We suggest that it was people who did accumulate volumes who conceived of themselves as "readers" in the sense in which we are excavating the term and provided themselves with the modern machinery for making such reading possible. In other words, the book-wheel suggests a social perception of certain individuals as skilled readers, as other men might be skilled woodworkers or leatherworkers.[52] We imagine Harvey using the book-wheel — or a rival device — in London, during the periods in which we know he was employed *for* his reading skills, in some kind of advisory, secretarial position (notably 1577-8, 1580 and 1590; dated readings in surviving volumes cluster closely round these dates).

The reader at the book-wheel is an unfamiliar *type*: the reader as facilitator. The reader, himself immobile and attentive to his books, is the agent to another's action, employed in the activity of reading in such a way that his own selfhood as a reader is not at issue. Ramelli, describing his "artful machine", suggests that it might well serve a man with gout — who found movement difficult and painful — and this captures the intermediary quality of the book-wheel reading. It is not the scholar-reader who acts, but it is he who facilitates action.[53]

We propose the book-wheel as a kind of emblem — it (or something like it, allowing consultation and annotation of multiple volumes simultaneously) represents the professional reader or facilitator's "tools of his trade". And we suggest that in spite of the fact that

---

[51] We suggest that this adds point to Chartier's evidence that remarkably few readers owned quantities of books (rather than one or two culturally key texts like the Bible and the Golden Legend): Chartier, *Cultural Uses of Print.*

[52] Categories of persons who Chartier shows to have been familiar with print, but who were not "expert" readers.

[53] See, for instance, Roger Ascham's 1541 letter to Archbishop Edward Lee, offering him his services as just such a reader, in *The Whole Works of Roger Ascham*, ed. J. A. Giles, 3 vols. (London, 1865), i, pp. 17-19, at p. 19.

history has apparently left little trace of this activity outside the as yet under-explored marginal notes in contemporary volumes, Harvey's was not an unusual activity for a sixteenth-century intellectual, but was consistent with the kind of professional service that Henry Cuffe performed for the earl of Essex, and John Dee for Edward Dyer.[54] As Harvey wrote to Leicester in 1579: "I speake it without vanity that a poore litle schollar would do your Lordshippe more honour in his speciall respects then sum of your gallants and courtlyest servants".[55]

VIII
SOME BOOKS ON THE WHEEL IN 1580

In August 1580 Edmund Spenser, secretary in Leicester's service, left for Ireland with Lord Grey, and Gabriel Harvey entered Leicester's employment in his place.[56] A striking group of historical and political texts belonging to Harvey are inscribed with the date "1580", either on their title-page, or somewhere in the marginalia. We may take these as a sample of what was "on the wheel" during Harvey's first known period of public service. The works are as follows:

T. Livii Patavini, Romanae historiae principis, decades tres, cum dimidia . . . (Basle, 1555);[57]
The Arte of Warre: Written in Italian by Nicholas Machiuel: And Set Foorth in English by Peter Withorne . . . (London, 1573);[58]
Florio his First Fruites: A Perfect Induction to the Italian and English Tongues (London, 1578);[59]

[54] See above, pp. 31, 33-4. As Nicholas Clulee suggests, Dee's involvement in the various projects of the Sidney/Dyer group was not that of an initiator, but a seeker of documentary precedents for policy — in our terms a facilitator. See N. H. Clulee, *John Dee's Natural Philosophy: Between Science and Religion* (London, 1988), p. 188: "In summary, Dee's major role in these projects for exploration was in the definition of the ideological context of ideas of a British Empire in which they took place and not that of a technical advisor let alone that of a leader in the movement". Linda Levy Peck gives an account of Sir Robert Cotton's work as an advisor to the earl of Northampton between 1603 and 1614 which closely matches our model of reading for policy-making: L. Levy Peck, *Northampton: Patronage and Policy at the Court of James I* (London, 1982), pp. 103-4.
[55] Historical Manuscripts Commission, *Marquess of Bath MSS.*, 5 vols. (London, 1904-80), v, *Talbot, Dudley and Devereux Papers, 1533-1659*, p. 199. We owe this reference to Paul Hammer.
[56] Stern, *Gabriel Harvey*, p. 68.
[57] "G.H. 1580" at end of first long note.
[58] "1580. ♂" on the title-page. Now in Princeton Univ. Lib., Lucius Wilmerding Jr. deposit. For location of the other volumes in this list, see Stern, *Gabriel Harvey*.
[59] Dated 1580 at end of text, just above "finis". At end of text, above "finis", at top of fo. Eei^v, Harvey writes: "Florio, & Eliot mie new London Companions for Italian, & French[e?]. Two of the best for both". And lower down the page (later): "Now to the

(cont. on p. 50)

William Thomas, *The Historie of Italie* (London, 1561);[60]

The Strategemes, Sleyghtes, and Policies of Warre, Gathered Togyther, by S. Julius Frontinus, and Translated into Englyshe, by Richard Morysine (London, 1539);[61]

Paulus Jovius, *Libellus de legatione Basilii magni principis Moschoviae ad Clementem VII: pontificem max. in quo situs regionis antiquis incognitus, religio gentis, mores, & causae legationis fidelissime referuntur . . .* (Basle, 1527);[62]

T. Livii Patavini conciones, cum argumentis et annotationibus Ioachimi Perionij . . . (Paris, 1532);[63]

Politique Discourses, Treating of the Differences and Inequalities of Vocations, as well Publique, as Priuate: With the Scopes or Endes Wherevnto They are Directed: Translated out of French by Aegremont Ratcliffe Esquire (London, 1578);[64]

Ioannes de Sacrobosco, *Textus de sphaera . . . introductoria additione . . . commentarioque, ad utilitatem studentium philosophiae Parisiensis Academiae illustratus . . .* (Paris, 1527);[65]

P. Du Ploiche, *A Treatise in Englishe and Frenche, Right Necessarie and Profitable for all Young Children . . .* (London, 1578);[66]

Detti et fatti piacevoli, et gravi: di diversi principi, filosofi, et cortigiani: raccolti dal Guicciardini: et ridotti a moralita (Venice, 1571);[67]

Lucae Gaurici geophonensis, episcopi civitatensis, tractatus astrologicus (Venice, 1552);[68]

(n. 59 cont.)
4. books of Guazzo [1581], the sweetest & daintiest of Italian Dialogues. Then to Eliots French Dialogues: as fine, as those Italian, & more pleasant . . .". Harvey's copy of John Eliot, *Ortho-epia Gallica: Eliots First Fruits for the French* (London, 1593), survives: Stern, *Gabriel Harvey*, p. 211.
   [60] Title-page missing, no date. But marginal annotations contemporary with other 1580 volumes, for example (cited in Stern, *Gabriel Harvey*, p. 237): "Excellent Histories, & notable Discourses for everie politician, pragmatician, negotiatour, or anie skillfull man. A necessarie Introduction to Machiavel, Guicciardin, Jovius". And complete passages of Thomas are transcribed in the margins of Harvey's Florio.
   [61] (Hereafter Harvey's Frontinus). Dated 1580 on first blank page.
   [62] Title-page missing, but annotations contemporary with 1580 volumes.
   [63] Dated 1578 on title-page and last page, but contains marginal notes contemporary with Harvey's Livy. In assembling this list we noted that a good number of these works (and some others) were acquired and/or read thoroughly for the first time in 1578. Another large set of books can be identified for 1590.
   [64] "Gabriel Harvey, et amicorum". Not dated, but notes contemporary with 1580 volumes.
   [65] Not yet seen. "gabrielis harvejus", "Plus in recessu, quam in fronte", "Arte et virtute. 1580" on title-page: Stern, *Gabriel Harvey*, pp. 233-4.
   [66] Not seen. *Ibid.*, p. 210.
   [67] Not seen. *Ibid.*, p. 218: "gabriel harvejo. Ratione, et diligentia. 1580".
   [68] Not seen. "gabriel harvejus. 1580" on title-page; "gabrielis harveij, et amicorum. 1580" at end. Discussion of Harvey's use of astrology must wait for another time and place. We have omitted a couple more "1580" volumes whose topics are not relevant to the discussion as currently framed: Pindar (see *ibid.*, p. 230), Rowlands, *The Post of the World* (see *ibid.*, p. 233), and Tusser, *Five Hundred Pointes of Good Husbandrie* (see *ibid.*, pp. 237-8).

HOW GABRIEL HARVEY READ HIS LIVY   51

Ioachim Hopperus, *In veram iurisprudentiam Isagoges ad filium libri octo* ... (Cologne, 1580);[69]

Iuris civilis totius absolutissima methodus: in qua, bone lector, non solum omnes totius iuris ciuilis titulos, sed & singulas singulorum titulorum leges, singulos singularum legum paragraphos, miro ordine ad suos locos habes redactos & dispositos: opus multis retro annis, a multis doctissimis uiris exoptatum, a multis tentatum, tandem autoris sumptibus perfectum: autore Nicolao Vigelio iurisconsulto (Basle, J. Oporinus, 1561).[70]

These volumes and their annotations give a vivid, concrete sense of what it meant to engage in the activity of reading as Harvey did, in 1580 (in preparing this paper we have had the annotations for the first eight volumes on this list before us, and six volumes before us simultaneously, either physically — the first two on the list — or in photographic reproduction — the next four). In addition to the richness and density of annotation throughout them, there is persistent echoing of sentiments from one book to another; cross-referencing of one of these authors in the margins of another; recognizable continuity of handwriting, to the extent that we can sometimes hazard a guess as to which book succeeded which other in the circulating process of reading and annotation; narrative notes about contemporary or near contemporary affairs continued from the margins of one volume to another (notably, from the back of the Frontinus to the margins of the Florio; and from the Thomas to the margins of Florio). Cumulatively, the effect is one of unexpected *cohesiveness* — a sense of the grouped volumes as cohering around a project which Harvey (the reader) keeps constantly before him.[71]

IX

POSITIONING THE READING: CHOOSING YOUR OCCASION

The Sidney, Smith junior, Preston and "Arches" readings by Harvey of his Livy (to which we can assign fairly precise dates) give us distinctive contexts for reading (and therefore, we shall argue, distinctive "ways of reading", which need have little in common with one another). The first (chronologically, with Smith junior) we, like Harvey, might term "pragmatic" — or "militarie, stratagematical". This reading is addressed by the prior agreement of the readers to a

---

[69] "Gabrielis Harveij, 1580" on title-page: Moore Smith, *Gabriel Harvey's Marginalia*, pp. 175-87; Stern, *Gabriel Harvey*, p. 221.

[70] Gonville and Caius College, Cambridge, H.6.12. Title-page: "GabrielisHarueij. 1580. Mense Aprile.", "Arte, et Virtute". (Not in Stern).

[71] Unexpected, because a twentieth-century reader would not anticipate volumes with this range of topics and subject-matter converging on anything.

specific Elizabethan political context, and in particular, to the demands of impending military campaigns. The version of strategy which it yielded turned out in the event to be of limited relevance to the task in hand, and we might want to argue that this is intrinsic to the sources: Livy was never very strong on campaigns.[72] This was also, one might add, Harvey's earliest engagement with "politics" via history, and therefore arguably the most ambitious in terms of the pay-off he hoped for.

The second reading (with Sidney) we might term "moral, politique". This, we would argue, is a careerist reading — one designed to promote the career of a courtier, and at the same time to bring the hopeful facilitator to the notice of a court circle. This side of Harvey (and of his reading) has been repeatedly invoked by those who have encountered his marginalia, but needs to be looked at again, as we shall do here. The appropriate context is provided by the closing passages of a familiar letter from Harvey to John Wood.[73]

The salient point is that Harvey treats the relationship between university political theory and court political practice as reciprocal: "you must needes acknowledge us your Masters in all generall poyntes of Gouernment, and ye greate Archepollycyes of all aoulde, and newe Commo[n] welthes". "Particular matters of counsell, and pollicye, besides daylye freshe newes, and A thousande both ordinary, and extraordinary occurrents, and accidents in ye worlde" are provided by those actively engaged in law and politics: but these nevertheless must be assessed against the general theory that only university men can provide.[74]

The third reading with Preston is the one which historians of political thought might want to take most seriously. It solidly exemplifies the aspiration generally stated in the letter to Wood: that university men should be able to provide political theory to match

---

[72] See Jardine, "Mastering the Uncouth".

[73] We have used Walter Colman's transcription, which we gratefully acknowledge.

[74] One might want to observe that the somewhat insistent note in Harvey's remarks about the usefulness of university men to the court has less to do with pushiness than with the need to earn a living. There are a number of points in Harvey's biography, starting with the Pembroke quarrel with Neville, where it is obvious that Harvey's career is suffering from his not being a man of means, and therefore financially self-sufficient *before* any earnings from the various posts he sought. See, for example, the letter to the master of Pembroke, John Young, on the disputed Greek lectureship in 1574: "For the bestowing of the lecture, do in it as you shal think best for the behoof of the Collidg. For mi part I am the more desirus of it, I must needs confes, bicaus of the stipend, which notwithstanding is not great": Brit. Lib., Sloane MS. 93, fos. 27^r-34^v, cited in Stern, *Gabriel Harvey*, pp. 26-7. Contrast Sir Thomas Smith's earnings, as itemized in the *Dictionary of National Biography*.

contemporary political requirements.[75] It is a reading which the marginal notes "position" rather carefully. As we have seen, Harvey and Preston took care to note that while Hotman's *Francogallia* was relevant to their discussion, its Tacitean argument that the king's right to rule depended upon the favour of the people rather than on right of inheritance was seditious.[76]

Harvey's reading of Livy with Augustine, though perhaps solitary in execution, had at least two distinct purposes. On the one hand, Augustine was himself a rich source for the early history of Rome. As Vives pointed out, he had read the lost books of Livy and the lost works of the great Roman scholar Varro; accordingly, even in his opposition to Roman values, he filled in many details tantalizingly omitted or left vague in Livy. Read with Vives's commentary — which tried to use all available information to dot every i of fact, date or place-name that Augustine had left incomplete — *The City of God* made a splendid reference book. And it was thus that Harvey used it when, for example, he referred to Augustine's "extremely important chapter" (*caput valdè notabile* — v.22) on the duration of Rome's wars with the Carthaginians, Mithridates and the pirates, and remarked "see also Vives's commentary" (*observandis etiam L. Vivis animadversionibus*). Augustine's chapter lists the durations of these wars to show that they depend on God's decision; Vives's commentary emphasizes historical details, locations of battles and alternate values for the durations found in other classical sources.[77]

On the other hand, Harvey also makes many references, direct and implicit, to Augustine's historical doctrines. Unlike Augustine's contemporary, Orosius, and many of his own contemporaries, he grasped Augustine's view of Roman virtue and the moral use of

---

[75] The letter to Fulke Greville which we cited earlier takes an almost identical position (even down to the "tags" used): "The . . . hardest point is y[e] Choice of the Notes themselues: w[ch] must be naturall, morall, Politick, or Military. Of the 2 first your Gatherers may haue good Iudgment; but you shall haue little use: of the 2 later, yo[r] use is greatest, and their Iudgement least. I doubt not, but in the Universitie you shall find Choice of many excellent Witts, and in things, wherein they haue waded, manie of good Understanding. But they that haue the best Eyes, are not alwaies the best Lapidaries and according to the Proverb, The greatest Clarks are not euer the wisest men. A meer Scholar in State, or Military Matters will no more satisfie you, then Phormio did Han[n]ibal": Bodleian Lib., Tanner MS. 79, fos. 29[r]-30[v], at fos. 30[r-v].

[76] On Hotman's "red Tacitism", see P. Burke, "Tacitism", in T. A. Dorey (ed.), *Tacitus* (London, 1969).

[77] Harvey's Livy, p. 268; Augustine, *De civitate Dei libri XXII*, ed. L. Vives (Lyons, 1580), pp. 325-6; on Augustine's use of lost sources, see *ibid.*, pp. 208-9, where Vives comments on iv.1.

examples from Roman history. He picked out key chapters — like i.15, the long treatment of the Roman hero Regulus — for recording in his margins. And he made clear that he understood Augustine's fundamental insistence, in this and similar passages, that even in shared virtues — like those that animated Regulus to sacrifice his life for Rome — the Christians outdid the pagans.[78] This reading was genuinely Augustinian in tone and content — and we are currently undecided as to how Harvey reconciled it with his other readings.[79]

At the end of the Livy are two Harvey notes which we may take as our own "positioning". Both relate the reading of history to Harvey's own mentors and patrons, and thus to the immediate social and political context of his study of Livy. The first (after the "Finis") relates to Sir Thomas Smith, Harvey's hero on at least three grounds: for his personal support of Harvey's own university studies and encouragement of his political career aspirations; for his own exemplary progress via political theory and university office to the diplomatic service and high government office; and for his uncompromising intellectual and publishing career:

> Sir Thomas Smyth, the Queenes principal secretarie; in his trauails in Fraunce, Italie, Spaine, & Germanie; but especially in his ambassages in Scotland, Fraunce, & Netherlande; found no sutch use of anie autours, as I heard himself say, as of Liuie, Plutarch, & Iustinian. He mutch commended Sallust, Suetonius, Tacitus, & sum other of the best: but his classical and statarie historians were Liuie, Plutarch, Halicarnasseus; & verie fewe other. Of the new, Cominaeus, Guicciardine, Jouius, Paulus AEmilius, Egnatius, & but fewe other. Not the most, but the Best; was his rule. And I am for Geometrical, not Arithmetical Proportion. An other of owre cunningest, & shrewdest ambassadours in Fraunce, Sir Nicholas Throgmarton, was altogither for Cesar, & Liuie; Liuie & Cesar. Not a more resolute man in Ingland: & few deeper heds: as Mie Lord Burgley will still saye.[80]

The second note, at the end of the *elenchus* of Glareanus, sets up the relationship between the various reading contexts just described, and the Livy:

---

[78] Harvey's Livy, p. 268.

[79] Harvey manages to reconcile Livy and Augustine at least once, in an interesting note on the beginning of book thirty-one (*ibid.*, p. 519), where he has Livy and Augustine agree unproblematically about the forces that propelled Rome to world empire. But we still cannot reconcile these remarks with the others quoted in our exposition. Our thanks to Jill Kraye for comment on this and other points.

[80] *Ibid.*, p. 829. This seems to be the only reference to Throckmorton in the marginalia. Throckmorton and Smith were ambassadors together in France in 1562-4: according to the *Dictionary of National Biography* (*s.v.* Sir Thomas Smith), Smith junior — aged fifteen — was in France with his father on this embassy. Throckmorton died in February 1571.

HOW GABRIEL HARVEY READ HIS LIVY   55

The notablest men, that first commended the often & aduised reading of Liuie vnto mee, were theise fiue, Doctor Henrie Haruey, M. Roger Ascham, Sir Thomas Smyth, Sir Walter Mildmay, Sir Philip Sidney: all learned, expert, & verie iudicious in the greatest matters of priuate, or publique qualitie. Once I heard M. Secretarie Wilson, & Doctor Binge preferr the Romane historie before the Greek, or other: and Liuie before anie other Romane historie. But of all other Sir Philip Sidney, Colonel Smyth [i.e. Smith junior], and Monsieur Bodin wunne mie hart to Liuie. Sir Philip Sidney esteemes no general Historie, like Iustines abridgment of Trogus: nor anie special Roman historie like Liuie: nor anie particular historie, Roman, or other, like the singular life, & actions of Cesar: Whome he values aboue all other, & reputes the greatest actour, that euer the World did afforde. And therefore makes exceeding account of Sallust, Velleius, Suetonius in Latin; Plutarch, Dion, Iulian in Greek: Who as effectually, as briefly display him in his liuelie colours. But of none makes so high reckoning as of Cesars owne Commentaries, peerles & inualuable works. Where his frends, & enimies beholde a most worthie man; modest in profession; pithie in discourse; discreet in iudgment; sound in resolution; quiet in expedition; constant in industrie; most uigorous in most daunger; surmounting the wisest in pollicie, the brauest in valour, the terriblest in execution, the cunningest in huge artificial works; allwaies inuincible, often incomparable, sumtime admirable in the accomplishment of the weightiest affaires, dowtiest exploits, & finest designes, that could be plotted bie himself in the profunditie of his surprising conceit. The onlie Mirrour of most excellent valour, & more excellent Witt: to this day vnmatchable, in so manie reuolutions of high, & deepe spirits; aspiring to the greatest things vpon Earth; & leauing no possibilitie vnextended. Yet amongst so manie valorous minds, & euen amongst so many puissant Cesars, still but one Cesar. He, that brauely gaue it owt for his resolute word, Aut Caesar, aut nihil: howsoeuer exceedingly beholden to Machiauel, was indeed nihil in comparison of Cesar.[81]

On the one hand we have Henry Harvey, Roger Ascham, Sir Thomas Smith and Sir Walter Mildmay, "all learned, expert, & verie iudicious in the greatest matters of priuate, or publique qualitie" — significant men with one foot in the university world, the other in diplomacy. On the other we have Smith junior and Bodin (of whom more shortly), distinctively in the world of politics, strategy and opportunity. In the middle we have Sir Philip Sidney, symbol, even before his death, of both camps — the man of cultivation and learning, court figure and literary darling, but whose achievements were cemented by his exemplary performances in active military engagement (and in the first place, in Ireland).[82]

[81] Harvey's Livy, sig. P 1ʳ. This note can be dated before 1586, since Sidney's views are recorded in the present tense.

[82] See the verses written by Harvey for the Cambridge volume *Academiae Cantabrigiensis lachrymae tumulo nobilissimi equitis: d. Philippi Sidneij* (1587). The second poem is headed, "De subito & praematuro interitu nobilis viri, Philippi Sydneij, utriusque militiae, tam armatae, quam togatae, clarissimi equitis" (Concerning the sudden and premature death of that noble man, Philip Sidney, the most celebrated knight of both kinds of office, as much of arms as of civil affairs).

X

IF THIS IS READING, WHAT WAS POLITICAL THOUGHT?

There seems no reason not to take seriously Harvey's aspiration to read Roman history in a way directly applicable to contemporary affairs of state. We take Bodin, Machiavelli, Daneau and Hotman seriously because they published (thus demonstrating a persisting academic preference for the treatise as "authentic" intellectual history). It might, however, be argued that Harvey is a better source for understanding of Elizabethan political thought, precisely because his observations are juxtaposed with the text of Livy itself, and because, as he indicates, contemporary politicians valued the readings he gave. As to whether Harvey's claims to have the ear of the politically influential are genuine: the claims of individuals are often, in intellectual history, our only guide to contact and influence. And although the pamphleteering Nashe has seen to it that posterity disparages Gabriel Harvey's achievements, it is interesting to note how often Nashe's jibes may equally be read as *confirming* Harvey's own claims.[83]

Harvey's methods and concerns were clearly shared with those members of the political élite with whom he claimed connections. Thomas Smith, his patron — and an eminently respectable figure in modern histories of political thought — lived in a world as steeped in classical texts and modern technical writers as Harvey's own. Smith's friend Walter Haddon once wrote to ask his opinion of a recent dinner-table conversation where the French ambassador had denied that Cicero was a competent lawyer (an argument that "became so heated that it was very hard to find a way to end it"). Smith replied

[83] See, for example, Nashe's remarks about Harvey's legal practice in the Court of Arches, cited by Stern, *Gabriel Harvey*, pp. 81-2. Or we may choose to accept Harvey's own word (as set out in a 1598 letter to Sir Robert Cecil) that given the opportunity, in the form of reliable financial support and secure employment, he would have published: "manie other mie Traicts & Discourses, sum in Latin, sum in Inglish, sum in verse according to the circumstance of the occasion, but much more in prose; sum in Humanitie, Historie, Pollicy, Lawe, & the sowle of the whole Boddie of Law, Reason; sum in Mathematiques, in Cosmographie, in the Art of Navigation, in the Art of Warr, in the tru Chymique without imposture (which I learned of your most learned predecessour, Sir Thomas Smith, not to contemne) & other effectual practible knowlage, in part hetherto unrevealed, in part unskilfully handeled for the matter, or obscurely for the forme; with more speculative conceit, then industrious practis, or Method, the two discovering eies of this age". For, says Harvey: "I had ever an earnest & curious care of sound knowledg, & esteemed no reading, or writing without matter of effectual use in esse: as I hope shoold soone appeare, if I were setled in a place of competent maintenance, or had but a foundation to build upon": *ibid.*, p. 125.

HOW GABRIEL HARVEY READ HIS LIVY   57

at length from Paris, where he was serving as English ambassador,
with appropriate diplomatic tact, that Cicero had been a splendid
lawyer, *given the condition of the law of his day*. The scholar-diplomat's
mature grasp on such issues, which enabled him to reply so deftly to
a difficult question, came from the circle of "facilitators" he fre-
quented in Paris. He had been discussing such issues — though less
frequently than he would have liked — with Petrus Ramus and Louis
le Roy, as he had discussed them years before with their predecessor
at the Collège Royal, Jean Strazel.[84] And he would soon produce a
spectacularly successful adaptation of his own of an ancient model
for political writing: a brilliant account of England's institutions,
modelled on his "conjectural reconstruction of the form used by
Aristotle in his lost books on many of the Greek states".[85] Very likely
it was Smith who introduced Harvey to the thought of Bodin —
whose innovative ideas on inflation Smith accepted.[86]

In at least one case we can watch Harvey and the Smiths, father
and son, responding to a single supplementary reading of a sharply
"political" kind. Harvey remarks on his reading of the third decade
that:

> M. Thomas Smith, & I reading this decade of Liuie togither, found verie
> good vse of M. Antonie Copes Inglish historie of the two most noble
> Captaines of the World, Annibal, & Scipio. Which sumtime giues a notable
> light to Liuie; & was worthie to be dedicated to King Henrie the VIII. in
> the opinion of Sir Thomas Smith, who much commended it to his sonne.
> [In Latin] However, it is sweeter to drink the waters from the very source.
> And I am one of those who will never have had their fill of Livy's wise and
> lively style.[87]

The introduction to Cope's *Historye of the Two Most Noble Captaynes of the World, Anniball and Scipio* (London, 1548), specifies in
an introductory letter (to which Harvey here refers) that Cope writes
as a scholar (he was chamberlain to Queen Katherine Parr), to make
his own scholarly contribution to knowledge useful for warfare and
conquest. Among the military achievements which Cope maintains
contribute to Henry VIII's international political standing he includes
"the wyse and woorthy conquest of the realme of Irelande, wher of
at this present your maiestee weareth the Diademe".[88] An appropriate

---

[84] W. Haddon, *Lucubrationes* (London, 1567), pp. 280-1, 284-7. See also above, p.
42.

[85] Haddon, *Lucubrationes*, p. 306.

[86] See Thomas Smith, *A Discourse of the Commonweal of this Realm of England*, ed.
M. Dewar (Charlottesville, 1969), pp. xv n. 14, xxvi.

[87] Harvey's Livy, p. 269.

[88] A. Cope, *Historye of the Two Most Noble Captaynes of the World, Anniball and
Scipio* (London, 1548), sig. aiv.

volume for Sir Thomas Smith to draw to the attention of his son as part of his "political" preparation for the Ards campaign. Harvey's racily pragmatic annotations in English to this decade do indeed appear to take their tone from the Cope. For example, at the top of the page following the inscription above: "Annibal, a laborious & hardie; a valiant & a terrible Youth. A ventrous & redowted Captain in the Prime of his age. [In Latin] He acted accordingly".[89] And at the top of the next: "The Romanes neuer so matched & tamed, as bie Annibal a long time. And therefore his Historie the more notable in manie weightie respects".[90] In his copy of Frontinus — which we have on our book-wheel; and which elsewhere in the Livy Harvey notes he and Smith included in their reading — Harvey heads the discussion of Hannibal's tactics "in Aphrike agaynste Scipio": "Yᵉ order of Annibal, & Scipio, in that most famous battel betwene them. These orders, more particularly analyzed in yᵉ Inglish History of Annibal, & Scipio: owt of Liuy, &c".[91]

Observations such as these (which in Harvey's Livy form a series of running heads to the third decade) represent Hannibal as a freebooting buccaneer. They culminate in a marginal note to the speech of Hannibal's which closes the decade. In this speech Hannibal, who has been recalled to Carthage after sixteen years' sustained combat against the Romans, philosophically comes to terms with his situation, sues for peace as instructed, and warns Scipio not to trust in fortune, but only in reason. At the top of the page Harvey records Thomas Smith's enthusiasm for such lofty thoughts from the great captain of the world:

M. Smith, Colonel of the Ardes in Ireland, did maruell at nothing more in all Liuie, then at this discreete, & respectiue oration of Annibal, after so manie braue resolutions, impetuous aduentures, & maine battels.
[In Latin] A wise oration of Hannibal's.
Full of sagacity, tried and tested, and maturely reflected upon.[92]

These last two sentences are from an earlier reading, possibly actually contemporary with the Smith reading, as opposed to retrospective (the first note). At the bottom of the page Harvey writes:

Here at last we see Hannibal as more a cautious counsellor than a fierce general. It is not surprising that Hannibal made Fabius a politician and a

[89] Harvey's Livy, p. 270.
[90] *Ibid.*, p. 271.
[91] Harvey's Frontinus, sig. E ivᵛ-E vʳ. See above, p. 50.
[92] Harvey's Livy, p. 511.

pragmatic:[93] for Scipio makes Hannibal himself orator and philosopher. The spirit of youthful courage is one thing; that of mature prudence, another; that of old age's temperance, yet another. Each has its own diction, its own style, more or less temperate and, as it were, bridled.[94]

XI

AFFECTIVE STYLE: AN EFFECTIVE FORCE FOR ACTION

There seems to be an interesting tension here, between the *aspiration* to find advice on tactics and strategems in such episodes, and Harvey's very evident attraction to the stylistic and affective in such a speech. Once again, this contributes to our sense of the reader, Harvey, as intermediary between text and its effect in practice: style and affectiveness are textual catalysts; the occasions for their recall may be those on which oratory does indeed provoke, and alters the course of events. There is clearly a strong sense in which Harvey sees the cut and thrust of political debate — particularly in the pointed exchange between military adversaries — as a serious and important part of "gaining the upper hand" in political and military affairs. Near the beginning of the Livy he has a long note on Livy's style and its importance:

> Livy's style, especially in the speeches. No Latin or Greek speeches deserve more careful reading or meticulous selection than Livy's; Périon assembled them into a sort of technical order. Hence, when I have time to read, or to imitate, or even to emulate speeches, I prefer no others to these, or others of Livy's, which are both sharp in sense and polished in expression. Nothing, in general, is either more toughly concise, or more vividly expressed. Atticism itself seems to be outdone here. [Later] The style is meticulously polished here: now splendidly ample, now brilliantly concise, now expertly modulated, often adamantine. It is always budding or flowering. Had he not known Caesar, Sallust, Virgil intimately, I would find his method of composition amazing. It is at once so brilliant and so solid; no more brilliant than grave, no less subtle than ornate. [Later] Certain well-rounded and clever sayings — like Spartan apophthegms — are also most delightful. His variety almost never fails, and his strength almost never flags. This judgement is still mine; nor could I be easily induced or desperately coerced to adopt another view.[95]

---

[93] We translate Harvey's "*pragmaticus*" as "pragmatic" throughout, for want of a more appropriate word. Harvey takes the term directly from Cicero, *De oratore*, where Antonius advises the orator not to fill his head with legal detail, but to employ someone to get it up for him: "This is why, in the lawcourts, those who are the most accomplished practitioners retain advisors who are expert in the law (even though they are very expert themselves), and who are called 'pragmatics'" (Itaque illi disertissimi homines ministros habent in causis iuris peritos, cum ipsi sint peritissimi, et qui . . . pragmatici vocantur). See also Quintilian, *Institutiones oratoriae*, xii.3.4.

[94] Harvey's Livy, p. 511.

[95] *Ibid.*, leaf facing p. 1, recto.

When we turn to Harvey's copy of Livy's *Conciones* we do indeed find them annotated confidently as politically effective (not simply exercises in speech-making):

> Anyone must be delighted by that vividly varied style. Relevant here are the political letters of Mehmet II to popes, emperors, kings, princes, states, with the answers. Also some very prudent and sharp opinions in the letters of the rulers of the world. What is more spirited, more skilful, more concise, more penetrating than either of these? What is more appropriate to a judicious orator, especially an ambassador or a royal counsellor? Every excellent pragmatic must become thoroughly conversant with them.[96]

These notes give a vivid sense of how Harvey treats virtuoso oratory as an integral part of strategy, comparable with military tactics in its ability to influence the outcome of political confrontation (even though elsewhere, as we shall see, he made serious efforts to master Roman writings on warfare tactics and battle formation). We should not find this surprising. Livy and Machiavelli had both stressed the vital importance of effective rhetoric to generals as well as to statesmen; and Harvey had given much of his career to the study of oratory.

Between these two extremes, Harvey appears ultimately to settle for *aphoristic* history, as crucially policy-forming for the politician; and this is consistent with his commitment to Bodin, Daneau, Hotman and others, associated with contemporary moves to reform the legal systems and political structures of modern states using ancient models. It is in a book of aphoristic sayings from Demosthenes that Harvey quotes Bodin on history; and it is at the end of that work that he cross-refers (evidently for something like the first time) to "Daneau's very new aphorisms", as appropriate reading at this point.[97] Annotating the introductory letter (addressed to Henry VIII) in his copy of Morysine's translation of Frontinus' *Stratagems*, Harvey writes: "Aphorisms and examples will speedily make you great and admirable. Of longer discourses and histories there is no end. They tire the body and confuse the intellect and the memory".[98] The passage against which this is written is also marked with Harvey's

[96] Transcription by Walter Colman. Copy in Worcester College, Oxford. See also Sir Thomas Smith's library list, Queen's College, Cambridge: R. Simpson, *Sir Thomas Smith's Booklists, 1566 and 1576* (Warburg Institute Surveys and Texts, xv, forthcoming). This copy of Livy's *Conciones* has Thomas Smith's signature on its title-page ("Thomas Smyth"), that is, Smith junior. Which suggests that the two might well have had the two Livy texts together (on the book-wheel!) during their reading.

[97] Transcription by Walter Colman; Harvey's copy of Demosthenes, *Gnomologiae*, sig. o3ʳ (now in Brit. Lib.).

[98] Harvey's Frontinus, at present in the Houghton Lib., Harvard, sig. a viʳ. Another marginal note here refers the reader to Aphthonius' *Progymnasmata* for similar aphorisms.

HOW GABRIEL HARVEY READ HIS LIVY   61

"martial" sign (♂), and the "aphorisms" in question are pointedly triggering to action (and peculiarly appropriate as usual to the "war party" among whom Harvey sought his patrons):

> Whan tyme byddeth spende, sparynge is great waste. Loue is lewdenesse, whan tyme biddeth hate. Peace is to be refused, wha[n] tyme forceth men to warre. Wherefore, I haue besides this my tra[n]slation [of Frontinus], in an other tryfle of myn, exhorted al my contrey me[n], peace laid aside, to prepare for warre.

At the bottom of page 271 of the Livy, on a page which Harvey heads in his "military" vein, "The Romanes neuer so matched & tamed, as bie Annibal a long time", we find a marginal note in his diplomatic mode: "No repose or delay here. No notes can equal the author himself, not even the sharpest discourses or aphorisms. He is still sharper himself, and deeper". Over the page this allusion to Daneau and Machiavelli is filled out as follows:

> One who wants political axioms here should read Daneau's political axioms from Polybius, or rather should himself collect more prudent ones, and more appropriate to civil and military discipline, from political principles. For example: Justinian's rules of law, Vegetius' rules of war, Isocrates' rules of civilized life. Or like the political principles of Aristotle, which come from Herodotus, Thucydides, Xenophon, Homer and others. There is no specialist in political, or economic, or ethical axioms drawn from histories and poems to match Aristotle in his Politics, Oeconomics, Ethics. But how much greater would he have been had he known histories that were so much greater — especially Roman history? Machiavelli certainly outdid Aristotle in observation of this above all, though he had a weaker foundation in technical rules and philosophical principles. Hence I generally prefer Aristotle's rules, Machiavelli's examples.[99]

Harvey's search for first principles of politics — at once derived from the Aristotelian belief that the highest form of science consists in the provision of such principles, and connected with the effort of so many of his contemporaries to crystallize the most powerful ideas they had about law, morality and politics into adages, emblems and *regulae iuris* — is not surprising.[100] What may surprise us, though — and here the need to study the habits of actual readers emerges — is the nature of the source where he looks for them. Harvey boasts of his knowledge of Aristotle and Machiavelli. But he finds actual guidance in formulating aphorisms in the much humbler little collection of political axioms by the Calvinist pastor and theologian Lambert Daneau.

The political aphorisms in Daneau appropriate to this episode in Livy (the fall of Saguntum and the subsequent Roman embassy to

[99] Harvey's Livy, p. 273.
[100] See P. Stein, *Regulae iuris* (Edinburgh, 1966).

Carthage) are indeed to be found among those drawn from Polybius (since we recall that Daneau only collects aphorisms from Livy's first decade). There we find aphorisms like the following, succinctly drawing the lessons from the events:

> Those who must wage a great war at a long distance must leave no hostile position that threatens them to the rear (that is why Hannibal took Saguntum)
>
> Those who break public treaties first are starting wars in a hateful way (that is why Polybius condemns the Carthaginians)
>
> In an empire consisting of several diverse peoples and provinces it is wisest to entrust the defence of one province to soldiers from another province, and vice versa. Thus they may be linked to one another by the performance of these reciprocal duties (thus Hannibal sent Spaniards to Africa, and moved Africans across to Spain).[101]

The focus of Harvey's (and presumably Preston's) interest in this episode, however, is the conduct of the legation sent by the Romans to Carthage after the fall of Saguntum, ostensibly to ask "whether Hannibal had attacked Saguntum with the authority of the government", but actually authorized formally to declare war on the Carthaginians. At the top and bottom of the page in which the Roman ambassadors and their Carthaginian hosts exchange speeches, Harvey writes:

> The first bloom and vigour of Roman history, in the opinion of a couple of readers. Virtue regains strength after being wounded; it is the adamantine basis for generous rivalry and excellence. Had Carthage not been Rome's bitter enemy, Rome would never have become the powerful mistress of the world. The harsher the ill fortune, the greater the favourable fortune in the end, where unvanquished virtue, the splendid contestant for victory, serves.
>
> [Bottom of page] I want a politician who fixes the adamantine basis on deeper foundations, and illustrates the best precepts with the best examples — and thus outdoes Aristotle himself in weight of principles, Machiavelli in choice of histories. I would like to begin where Machiavelli and Daneau leave off, and use the later counsels, laws, arms, judgements, magistracies, enterprises, industries and public directives of the Romans to correct the earlier ones skilfully and enlarge them diligently. Also to add the most supremely excellent ones from the other successful empires, kingdoms, republics of the world. Then to leave nothing unexamined or unexplained in the subtlest school doctors or deepest worldly pragmatics, which could improve or enlarge the principles.[102]

In the middle of this page appears a virtuoso exchange between Quintus Fabius and the Carthaginians. The Carthaginian speaker elegantly finds Roman precedent for Carthage's and Hannibal's ac-

---

[101] Lambert Daneau, *Politicorum aphorismorum silua, ex optimis . . . scriptoribus . . . collecta* (Leiden, 1620; first pubd. 1591), pp. 132-3.

[102] Harvey's Livy, p. 275.

tions. Fabius' reply is blunt. He gathers his toga into a pouch and says, "Here we have for you either war or peace; take whichever you wish".

> To this the senate shouted angrily that he might give them whichever he wished. Dropping the pouch of his toga as if to pour out its contents, he said that he gave them war. To this they answered that they accepted, and would wage it with the same courage as they had accepted it.
> This straightforward declaration of war seemed more befitting the dignity of the Roman people than wrangling about the validity of the two treaties.[103]

In the margin Harvey has written: "The extraordinarily honourable embassies of the Romans: to the Carthaginians, Spaniards, Gauls. No historian plays the ambassador or jurisconsult so vividly as Livy, here, above, below. It is most useful to a pragmatic to examine all these legations thoroughly".[104] And on the following page: "Roman ambassadors are grave and decisive; also more ready or prepared than the Spartans".[105]

This emphasis on ambassadorial virtuosity is supported by another group of notes, which link performances by protagonists in the Livy with real-life stories of Elizabethan ambassadors "winning the day" with their feats of words.[106] By juxtaposing the vivid recent example with his printed text, Harvey stresses the "relevance" of the Livy reading to court diplomacy. The most vivid example comes in two marginal notes concerning "Doctor Dale".[107] On page 813 we find the story of Popilius' legation to Antiochus:

> When Antiochus was four miles from Alexandria he was met by the Roman commissioners. He saluted them and held his hand out to Popilius. Popilius asked him first to read a document which he handed him. He did so, and said he would call and consult his ministers, whereupon Popilius with customary directness drew a circle around the king with the staff in his hand and said: "Give me your answer to the senate before you step out of this circle". The king was stunned by this peremptory order, but after hesitating a moment replied, "I will do as the senate bids". Popilius then deigned to give him his right hand, as a friend and ally.
> Antiochus evacuated Egypt by the prescribed date, and the Romans sailed to Cyprus. From this base they expelled Antiochus' fleet, which already had conquered the Egyptian ships in battle. This embassy became renowned throughout the world. For it was obviously responsible for Antiochus' withdrawal from Egypt after the country already was in his power.

[103] Livy, xxi.

[104] Harvey's Livy, p. 275.

[105] *Ibid.*, p. 276.

[106] The reference to Harvey's discussions of diplomatic and political issues with the courtiers Edward Dyer and Edward Denny (quoted above, p. 38) comes on the page following this discussion of Roman diplomacy.

[107] See *D.N.B.*

This story has all the right ingredients: a crucial point in the war and a vital legation. Events turn on "customary directness" incisively mastering the situation and gaining the required response. It even has an unlikely outcome in military terms — gaining the verbal upper hand when in fact your adversary had the upper hand in terms of the battle, and *thus* beating him. In the right margin Harvey writes: "Popilius was an earnest and effective ambassador: having comparable authority even with the ruling house. [Later in English] One of doctor Dales great Examples: when he was Lord Ambassadour in Fraunce, & in Netherland".[108] At the bottom of the page Harvey relates Dale's preference for this story to his own success as an ambassador (also dealing with an adversary with "customary directness"):

> Doctor Dale, Lord Ambassadour in Fraunce, & the Lowe Countries, was as resolute after his fashion, as Popilius himself: and stood upon as peremptorie termes with the French Kinge, the duke of Parma, & other mightie Princes, as the stowtest Romane euer did in the like cases. When the Earle of Darbie, & other Ambassadours respectiuely quailed, he was allwaies in harte, absolute, & inuincible. The Prince of Parma was neuer so berded to his face, bie anie Ambassadour.[109]

At the very end of the Livy (after "finis indicis") we find out more about this bearding of the prince of Parma on the eve of the Armada:

> Doctor Dale — the great pragmatic, and the most judicious ambassador I have known — used to say "Give me no. 1" when he wanted Justinian; "Give me no. 2" when he wanted his Speculum iuris;[110] "Give me no. 3" when he wanted Livy. For he made more of these three authors than of all the rest, and he supplied himself with a manuscript notebook of secrets. William Spite [Speight?], procurator of the Court of Arches, and Dr. Dale's secretary in the Belgian legation to the duke of Parma, often told me this among other memorable doings of his. When the well-equipped Spanish fleet, commanded by the duke of Medina, was preparing to invade England in the near future, Dale was the only ambassador who dared to claim precedence over the duke of Parma when out walking, as the representative of a higher prince, his mistress; and wanted to precede, or refused to follow. When the duke of Parma fiercely uttered terrible threats, as though already thinking of the invasion of England, he laughed, and contemptuously replied with a non-verbal noise, as of lips smacking[!]. No other legate ventured anything like this against the brave Parma, in the midst of his fierce army. But the fearless doctor never showed dismay. In fact he showed open contempt for the vast army, mindful both of Livy's examples and of his kingdom, his fatherland, his rank. I have known few such readers of Livy, but the rarer, the more remarkable. Doctor Haddon and Doctor Wilson preferred Cicero and Caesar. But as ambassadors they were more elegant than effective; they were stiff in carrying out orders,

---

[108] Harvey's Livy, p. 813.

[109] *Ibid.*

[110] See Stern, *Gabriel Harvey*, pp. 266-7.

and flaccid in grave transactions involving the queen's interest — compared with those two sharp pragmatics, Doctor Smith, the knight, and Doctor Wotton, the queen's counsellor. They applied themselves to Livy and Tacitus.

Here indeed is Livy's lesson of the highly wrought speech as crux and fulcrum on which events turn, in action.

Harvey's view of Livy's style — and his belief in its peculiar transparency as narrative — emerges most clearly from his note on the commentator Velcurio's effort to define the historical style. Velcurio writes for students learning to imitate. He explains Livy's style as "copious" and "grave", and emphasizes Livy's trick of weaving a special form of "period" "from several clauses or members, in such a way that it both expresses a given matter copiously and embraces and connects several matters in the same sentence".[111] This quality sets Livy off from other historians like Sallust and Caesar. Velcurio advises the student to cut Livy's "periods into their constituent parts" to see the historical style in detail, and gives rules for producing it in one's own prose (for example, "Very often in the historical period several nominatives and other cases are referred to a single verb, as if predicated"). And he makes clear that Livy's periodic prose makes him second only to Cicero as a teacher and model of eloquent Latin.[112]

Harvey disagrees. His comment reads:

> Second to Cicero. Yet he is often ahead of him in the force of his aphorisms. Often, too, he describes persons, places, actions and things of great beauty more vividly. I have often found Quintilian a sort of composite of Cicero and Livy. Nor did any later Roman have a more florid style, more splendid aphorisms, or a more profound intellect, or a freer judgment, or finally more faith in his own intellect. Had there been no Livy there would have been no Fabius [Quintilian]; and had there been no Fabius, there would have been no Lorenzo Valla, whom I have felt to be the leader of so many modern critics.[113]

Harvey sees Livy as a master in a different sense than Velcurio does. Livy's prose presents people and events concretely, in three dimensions, offering an experience more cinematic than literary in our terms. Yet at the same time he offers exactly the sort of tuition one would expect to find in a master of rhetoric: invention, judgement and elocution, the basic parts of rhetoric, appear in the less explicit categories Harvey applies.[114] Livy offers both explicit and implicit

---

[111] Harvey's Livy, sig. H 6ᵛ.

[112] *Ibid.*, sig. Iʳ.

[113] *Ibid.*

[114] See Harvey's annotations in his copy of Livy, *Conciones*.

lessons: both the immediate vision of war *in actu* and the considered formulations needed by the statesman *in potentia*.

XII

"NO ONE DEPICTS SO GRAPHICALLY": SHARPENING THE IMAGES BY REPEATED READINGS

The best way to enhance our sense of how Harvey made Livy meaningful is to proceed from principles to applications. As Harvey notes approvingly: "Livy is certainly the best in Roman history. Each book is outstanding, in its kind. The variety of appealing facts is amazing. No historian either observes more seriously or depicts so graphically".[115] But the graphic description requires insistent excavation: for how are the lessons of the ancient Roman Republic to be made applicable to a sixteenth-century monarchy?

> In histories, the sayings and deeds of those considered wisest, strongest, most just by their fellows are praised. But what sort of politician speaks and acts, and to what end, and in what sort of state, and in what specific circumstances — these are vital too. Each acts in accordance with his estate, public or private, and no one binds his own hands. Many things were said and done with the greatest prudence in the Roman Republic, which it would be absurd to do in a kingdom and nowadays. Nothing is good that lacks the salt of judgement. Whatever is praiseworthy should also be appropriate.[116]

How did Livy's early Rome change contours, shadows and colours as Harvey inspected its crucially vivid narrative on successive occasions? Tackling the dense body of notes, with their persistent challenging of and intervention into the text presents a daunting and unmanageable task. But two selective analyses of his ways of reading will give some idea of how the reading altered according to the type of analysis he was using.

Towards the middle of book one Livy tells the story of the Horatii and the Curiatii. Romans and Albans, both descendants of the Trojans, have both stolen one another's cattle, refused restitution, and levelled ultimatums. They confront one another in order of battle but decide, given the danger posed by the Etruscans to both parties, to avoid a full-scale combat and arrange a trial by battle in its place. Each army has a set of triplets, the Roman Horatii and the Alban

---

[115] Harvey's Livy, sig. a3ʳ (at end of preface).

[116] This is part of a long note on the first blank page of the volume. The note ends (immediately after the passage quoted): "G.H. 1580". We may therefore take this to be the sentiment behind the "reading" of Livy which Harvey undertook at the beginning of his period of serious political employment (when he was publicly appointed to serve Leicester, whatever his status thereafter).

Curiatii, that can represent it. A treaty is made and solemnized with elaborate ritual. The brothers fight. Two Romans fall, but the third, unhurt, runs away, separates the three Albans and kills them one by one. Horatius, returning in triumph to the city, meets his sister, who had been engaged to one of the Curiatii. She cries out with sorrow on learning of her lover's death. Horatius promptly kills her, is found guilty of treason — and is then freed because of his popularity and his sister's lack of patriotism. Peace is made; but it does not last long.

The story has everything. Livy gives the details of disagreements among ancient scholars (over which set of triplets, the Roman or the Alban, had which family name). He lovingly describes Roman institutions, showing the *"fetial"* (priest) pluck and use the holy herb needed for making treaties and describing how the king and duumvirs declared and staged a trial for treason. Horatius provides an example of courage, patriotism and athletic prowess — but also of the errors to which too much zeal and courage can lead. Mettius the Alban provides an example of statesmanlike prudence and eloquent oratory. And Horatius' nameless sister makes a fine subject for a cautionary tale about the eternal female conflict between love and duty.

Harvey had ample exegetical resources on hand as he attacked this passage. The commentators in his Livy, Glareanus and Velcurio, both discussed book one, and though Glareanus left the Horatii alone, Velcurio treated them at length. He paraphrased every phrase or sentence that could possibly pose a difficulty. After the first two Horatii die, Livy describes the situation of the third: *"Forte is integer fuit, ut universis solus nequaquam par, sic adversus singulos ferox"* (The young man, though alone, was unhurt. No match for his three opponents together, he was yet confident of his ability to face them singly).[117] Velcurio found a surprising amount of grist for his mill here, and ground it slow and small: *"Is)* that is Horace. *Integer)* that is, not wounded. *Vniversis)* that is, by the three together".[118] And he went into technical detail of a more refined sort as well when it came to the legal aspects of Horatius' murder case, explaining at length why the taking of private revenge amounted to treason as well as parricide: "He punished his sister by private vengeance, when she should have been punished by the magistrate".

Harvey's notes on the passage show no interest whatever either in elementary problems of construing or in deeper ones of law and antiquities. Instead, he draws a political lesson:

[117] Livy, i.25.7.
[118] Harvey's Livy, sig. K 1ʳ.

A splendid example of single combat. But this was a rash rather than a politically prudent way to reach a decision. It is in fact not politically prudent to entrust the general welfare to the virtue or fortune of so few. But this custom derived from the heroic virtue of a few of the ancients, by which, it seemed, all great questions should be decided.[119]

Harvey was hardly eccentric to suggest that this trial by combat had been imprudent and was not an example to emulate. Daneau also derived a similar axiom from the same passage: "It is always danger-ous and often useless to entrust the general welfare (*summa rerum*) to a duel of two or more in a war. For the vanquished do not keep faith, and they do not suffer a great loss because of it".[120] And Machiavelli — who no doubt lurks, here as elsewhere, behind Daneau — had devoted three chapters of his *Discorsi sopra la prima deca di Tito Livio* to the story. He made it the pretext for a long and general argument that "one must never risk one's entire fortune with part of one's forces" (i.22). He drew from it the specific recommendation that one should not try to stop an enemy at one's border by confronting him with a small force (i.23). And he found in it food for reflection on the corruption of republics, arguing that while good citizens must be rewarded, it had been wrong simply to let Horatius go free after he had been fairly condemned for killing his sister (i.24).

Harvey begins from the prudential, "political" reading of Daneau and Machiavelli. Like them — and like his contemporary Justus Lipsius, whom he much admired — he wanted to extract and shrink to durable, concise, axiomatic form the pragmatic lessons of the text. But unlike them, he wanted to speculate about other matters as well. What captivated his imagination was less the imprudence of the custom Livy described than the reasons why it had been practised. He locates these in the ancients' belief in individual heroism, which made them think single combat an appropriate way to solve such problems. He may deplore the early Romans' heedlessness, but he applauds their chivalry. And his other notes show that what he — and Sidney — most appreciated in Livy was less the pragmatic maxims he could inspire than the heroic feats of arms that he so vividly described. Harvey's further notes on the passage include a Mars symbol; the exclamation "Vnicus Horatius" (Peerless Hora-tius); and, most revealing of all, a reflection on the feigned flight by which Horatius tricked his opponents into separating: "A strategic

[119] *Ibid.*, p. 13.
[120] Daneau, *Politicorum aphorismorum silua*, p. 234.

flight. Not even Hercules could handle three, or even two of the most outstanding opponents in a fight".[121]

Here we see Harvey making clear what Livy meant to him: a treasury of military devices to be imitated and heroic battles to be savoured. This was what Harvey found in Roman history as he read about it elsewhere as well: for example, in his copy of Machiavelli's *Arte of Warre* (also now in Princeton) where one battle scene more than a page long is decorated with a Mars symbol at the end of every line. Harvey read not simply to reflect, boil down and imitate, but also to savour, speculate and admire. No wonder that the pleasures of the naked text outweighed the more refined rewards of learned commentary when he and Sidney did their reading. And they were not alone in their desire to view the Roman past as highly coloured and in three dimensions.[122]

A further note on the slaying of Horatius' sister, however, takes quite a different tack:

> See Augustine, City of God, iii.14, on the impiety of the war that the Romans waged against the Albans, and the victory that resulted from desire to rule; there he skilfully treats the Horatii and the Curiatii. [In darker ink] Cf. the biblical duel of David and Goliath. Also the heroic ones of Hercules and Cygnus in Hesiod, Achilles and Hector in Homer, Aeneas and Turnus in Virgil.[123]

Here Harvey, reading by himself and later in life, refers to the eloquent chapter (iii.14) of *The City of God* in which Augustine ponders the Horatii and the Curiatii, condemns the murder of Horatius' sister and insists that the war itself deserved not honour but condemnation, like a gladiatorial combat. Harvey knew that Augustine's account amounted to an attack on the whole Roman heroic scheme of values: "See how, and how often, the divine wisdom of Augustine refutes the human prudence of Livy", he wrote early in book one.[124] He concluded that while each city had its virtues, the

---

[121] Harvey's Livy, p. 13.

[122] George Gascoyne, in the fourth dumb show of his *Iocasta* — a play performed at the Inner Temple — gives a re-enactment of the episode. In his version, Horatius is a "politique" of his own day; and by treating his retreat as tactical, Gascoyne produces a vivid and convincing version of the scene as a whole: "The third perceiuing, that he only remayned to withstand the force of iii. enimies, did politiquely runne aside: wherewith immediatly one of the iii. followed after him, and when he had drawen his enimie thus from his companie, hee turned against and slewe him" (We are grateful to Mac Pigman for this reference). Harvey owned a copy of *Iocasta*, now in the Bodleian Library; he does not comment on the interlude.

[123] Harvey's Livy, p. 13.

[124] *Ibid.*, p. 6: "Ecce quoties et quomodo humanam Livij prudentiam, divina redarguit Augustini Sapientia".

divine one was both "more securely built" and "more fortunate". The application of Augustine in the 1590s seems to undermine the "heroic" reading of Livy with Sidney in the mid-1570s, as if the older and wiser Harvey — his career expectations curtailed by the deaths of first Sidney and then Leicester, and the downfall of the aggressive Protestantism Sidney symbolized — had repented. Yet this simple (and sentimental) account does violence to the form and content of Harvey's note. He does not stop with Augustine. His final lines on the passage list heroic duels from Hesiod, Homer, Virgil — and the Old Testament — offering David and Goliath, perhaps, as an example of a vivid heroism that even Augustine could not condemn.

A second specific form of reading is exemplified in the third decade. When Velcurio tries to explain the use of history as the student should study it in Livy, he emphasizes the traditional virtue of providing worked examples of ethical and unethical conduct:

> Examples of virtue and probity to be imitated, and of vices to be avoided, can easily be derived from Livy and from other historians. Thus hypotheses — that is, good, or bad, or intermediate examples of individuals — can properly be drawn from history; these are then considered and assigned to theses, that is, to their commonplaces (*loci communes*), and to the general principles of morality and other things.[125]

Harvey, by contrast, annotating this passage, sticks to practicalities. Livy offers laws being made and institutions being created, not moral principles being tested:

> No historian is as appropriate to a jurisconsult, or pragmatic, or legate, or royal counsellor, or finally a politician, as Livy, especially when accompanied by Tacitus, Suetonius, Frontinus; not to mention Valerius Maximus . . . When reading Livy, I often feel that I am reading the jurisconsults themselves — especially the Scaevolas, Sulpitii, Trebatii, Papiniani, that sort of very prudent ones.[126]

Harvey's summary references through the third decade to Hannibal and the Romans consistently reveal these interests. They are single-minded in their concentration on leadership:

> Fabius Max[imus] bie Warie, & cautelous proceding, sumwhat cooled his [Hannibal's] heate: but liker slie Saturne, then gallant Jupiter, or braue Mars. Onlie Marcellus, & Scipio beat him at handstrokes the One in Italie, the other in Afrique.[127]
> Braue & redowted young Scipio: full of mightie courage, & valour.[128]
> [In Latin] Flavius, a shrewd pragmatic.[129]

[125] *Ibid.*, sig. I 1^r.
[126] *Ibid.*
[127] *Ibid.*, p. 294; Livy, xxii *ad int.*
[128] Harvey's Livy, p. 318; Livy, xxii.53.
[129] Harvey's Livy, p. 379; Livy, xxv.16.

Martius, a most braue & terrible knight, at a pinch. Which of the Heroical Worthyes cowld haue dun more in the time?[130]

[In Latin] Fabius, more adept in war; Martius in combat; Martius in action; Nero in forced marches; Scipio the most outstanding in all glorious military enterprises.[131]

[Scipio] As peerles fine, as matchles braue: a Mirrour of sweetest courtesie, & terriblest valour.[132]

The purpose of these check-lists of heroic virtue is plain. Harvey saw — and no doubt took part in — debates about Carthaginian and Roman leaders. These lists of deeds and adjectives were the substantive preparation for such debate. Much as Erasmus compiled as his distinctive aid to eloquence a matchless list of two hundred and fifty ways to say "Thank you for the letter" in classical Latin, Harvey and Smith junior devoted much of their private effort to assembling material to be used in public.

But the third decade has a strong narrative line as well as individual stories of heroism. At the outset Hannibal's march on Rome seems irresistible, his victory inevitable. By the end his army is in disarray and Hannibal himself in despair, while Scipio returns to Rome in triumph. Harvey's marginal notes show how eagerly he followed Hannibal's progress and appreciated the Carthaginian general's "industry, and appalling vigilance".[133] Hannibal stalks onward, apparently implacable and unbeatable. But Harvey found more than virtue in Hannibal's feats of arms. He saw the seeds of Hannibal's eventual failure planted early in his campaign. In book twenty-two he fails to take the opportunity afforded by Cannae and attack Rome at once; in book twenty-three Hannibal winters in Capua, letting his army lose cohesion and morale; in book thirty he has become pitiable. Harvey remorselessly tracks each error of judgement. At book thirty he reflects: "Hannibal was beaten first in spirit; it is no surprise, then, that he was immediately beaten in the flesh as well. One's fortune corresponds to one's strength of mind and body".[134]

Harvey finds a simple explanation for Hannibal's many related failures. He lacked the indomitable will needed to make the most of each opportunity as it occurred. "Occasion is only a point: now or never". "The sole essential for a great man is to seize the instant with great possibilities forcefully, with shocking power, and to play the

---

[130] Harvey's Livy, p. 391; Livy, xxv.37-9.
[131] Harvey's Livy, p. 404; Livy, xxvi.20.
[132] Harvey's Livy, p. 460; Livy, xxviii.18.
[133] Harvey's Livy, p. 296.
[134] *Ibid.*, p. 510.

powerful leader, when it is important to do so, with terrifying power".[135] Indecision, Machiavelli had long ago shown, was the most destructive of all errors in a ruler. Now Harvey read indecision into Livy's Hannibal.

The motives for this reading are not far to seek. In a sense it was over-determined, since it was inspired at least in part by Livy's own clues as well as by Harvey's immediate needs. But Harvey read the Carthaginian and Roman past above all in the terms of the English present. A rising member of the rising war party, he ached for action, like his patrons. In his copy of Withorne's translation of Machiavelli's *The Arte of Warre* (also annotated in 1580), against a passage in which Machiavelli advises the military leader not to make war in winter because

> All the industrie that is vsed in the discipline of warre, is vsed for to bee prepared to fighte a fielde with thy enemie, because this is the ende, whereunto a Capitayne oughte to go or endeuour him selfe: For that the foughten field, geueth thee the warre wonne or loste.[136]

Harvey has marked the word "ende", and writes exasperatedly in the margin: "This Ende, allmost at an ende, now a dais". By finding the reason for Hannibal's failure not in want of resources but in failure of will, he taught exactly the historical lesson that Walsingham and Leicester would have most liked Elizabeth — anxious always to avoid "the foughten field", and "the warre" (whether won or lost) — to learn. The alchemy of present needs turned Hannibal from a determined Fortinbras into a wavering Hamlet, in the margins if not in the text.

Harvey's transformation of Hannibal involved not only the explanation of a failure, but the development of sympathy for it. Harvey seems, as the third decade proceeds, to feel increasingly sorry for the fact that Hannibal did not carry out his aims. If he had only acted when he should have . . . "Maharbal's excellent advice [to march on Rome immediately after Cannae] could have made Hannibal as great as Alexander. But Hannibal, intent on lesser goods, lost his one chance for the greatest success. Now or never".[137] To find the moral he needed in the third decade, Harvey had to feel sympathy for the devil; to find in Livy's glorification of Rome the possibility of a

---

[135] *Ibid.*, p. 317. On Harvey's obsession with action, see N. Orsini, *Studii sul Rinascimento italiano in Inghilterra* (Florence, 1937), pp. 101-20; M. Praz, *The Flaming Heart* (New York, 1958), pp. 101-2.

[136] Harvey's copy of Machiavelli, *Arte of Warre*, fo. xciij^r. Underlinings Harvey's.

[137] Harvey's Livy, p. 317.

counter-history that glorified Carthage. This he did with an ease and
dexterity that one might not expect from a humanist.

XIII

HOW WELL DID HARVEY READ?

Harvey's reading of Livy would not earn the admiration of most
modern classicists. He accepts Livy's accounts even when they are
certainly erroneous — as in the case of Hannibal's disastrous delay
at Capua, which the parallel account in Polybius shows to be Livy's
own moralizing invention. But he also read Livy as Livy meant to be
read — as a master rhetorician offering the history Cicero had called
for in *De oratore*, a "work for orators" — and in doing so he praised
exactly those qualities in Livy that had impressed his own classical
model of the good rhetorician, Quintilian. Often he did pick up and
work with small but important clues in Livy's text, clues that reveal
Livy's own ambivalent assumptions. At one point, for example,
reading Velcurio's comment on Romulus' and Numa's efforts to
establish a religion at Rome, Harvey remarks that "There are many
things that I think in passing as I read, which I hardly dare to write
down".[138] Surely he referred here to Livy's own sense that the ancient
Roman religion was literally false but socially useful, a tool to create
social discipline — a sense that conflicts clearly, most modern readers
would think, with Livy's efforts to proclaim his piety. Here and
elsewhere Harvey's sheer skill and penetration are impressive.[139]

Was Harvey deluded to think that flexible reading could take him
to the top? Not necessarily. Another surviving piece of political
"ephemera" suggests how much a part of a contemporary agenda his
aspirations to annotate the margins of contemporary political practice
may have been. A memorandum prepared by Robert Beale in 1592
for the private use of Edward Wotton, it explains in severely practical
terms "The Office of a Councellor and Principall Secretarie to Her
Majestie". It offers sage advice about how to define the privy council's
agenda, avoid cabinet council "which does but cause iealousie and
envie", and abbreviate the letters submitted to the council so that its
members will at least have read a summary of the matters they
must decide on. It also offers readings of many ancient historians:
"Remember what Arrian saith in the life of Alexander . . . So likewise

---

[138] *Ibid.*, sig. I 3ʳ.
[139] For Livy's intentions and reception in antiquity, see P. Walsh, *Livy* (Cambridge,
1970).

towards your fellow councellors behave yourself as Maecenas counsel-
led Augustus . . . Be diligent. Remember the saying of Salust". Beale
is quite unapologetic in his provision of these humanist axioms.
Indeed he stresses in his conclusion that a good principal secretary
must be a good reader of the classics: "By the readinge of histories you
may observe the examples of times past, judging of their successe".[140]

In his copy of *The Arte of Warre* Harvey summarizes the authors
he would wish to have to hand in designing his own spurs to action
in the field of war, including contemporary advisers after the manner
of Beale's to Wotton:

> Mie principal Autors for Warr, after much reading, & long consideration:
> Caesar, & Vegetius: Machiauel, & Gandino: Ranzouius, & Tetti: with owr
> Sutcliff, Sir Roger Williams, & Digges Stratioticos: all sharp, & sound
> masters of Warr. For ye Art, Vegetius, Machiauel, & Sutcliff: for Strat-
> agems, Gandino, & Ranzouius: for Fortification, Pyrotechnie, & engins,
> Tetti, & Digges: for ye old Roman most worthie Discipline & Action,
> Caesar: for ye new Spanish, & Inglish excellent Discipline & Action, Sir
> Ro: Williams. Autors enowgh; with ye most cunning, & valorous practis
> in Esse. [Another time] Owr Inglish militar Discipline, vnder General
> Norris, in ye Dialogue, intitulid, The Castle of Pollicy: Vnder ye Earle of
> Leicester, In his owne Lawes, & Ordinances. The Spanish Discipline,
> vnder ye Duke d'Alua, & ye Prince of Parma, ye best Discipline now in
> Esse, newly discoouerid by Sir Roger Williams.[141]

We suggest that Harvey hoped his skills could win him a position
exactly like Beale's, as a valued political adviser who combined
practical experience and legal expertise with detailed study of the
ancients. Harvey's mode of reading, in fact, was precisely the sort
of serious political discourse that his authoritative contemporaries
esteemed (and employed university men for). And we suggest that
though Harvey did not succeed as completely as he hoped, his
humanism was not at fault.[142] Harvey's ability to read was perhaps

---

[140] Conyers Read, *Mr Secretary Walsingham and the Policy of Queen Elizabeth*, 3 vols.
(Cambridge, Mass. and Oxford, 1925), i, appendix, pp. 423-43. Wotton also failed to
achieve the office he expected, either in 1592 or three years later, when the matter was
broached again: *ibid.*, i, p. 423.

[141] Harvey's *Arte of Warre*, fo. Cix^r. The "newly discoouerid by Sir Roger Williams"
dates this to 1590-1.

[142] In spite of Nashe's exuberant fantasies about Harvey's being chased back to
Cambridge after an ignominiously brief employment with Leicester, these marginalia
suggest a much more continuous toing-and-froing on Harvey's part between Cambridge and London, and constant contact with the political circle he claimed to advise
in London. Spenser praises Harvey as a "looker-on" who "Ne fawnest for the fauour
of the great . . . But freely doest", in a 1586 sonnet, written from his own minor-
official post in Dublin: Moore Smith, *Gabriel Harvey's Marginalia*, p. 57, which
confirms that Harvey held no official post, but nevertheless suggests that Harvey is
intellectually active, in a desirably unconstrained fashion, in the circles of "onlookers"
outside the immediate court circle.

his one uncontested asset; it took him far and yielded fascinating and contradictory visions of the Roman past.[143]

If Harvey was ultimately proved wrong, and the fashion for employing this type of erudite facilitator in policy-making was short-lived, this may have more to do with political events than with the individual practitioners. Isaac Casaubon came to England in 1610. Although he shared Harvey's intense interest in reading history, and even his belief that the lessons of history could be reduced usefully to succinct axioms, he had no patience with learned advisors in the political arena.

> Note [he wrote in one miscellany] that just as the "book-trained doctor" whom we read about in Galen and Aristotle and the "book-trained ship's pilot" are very dangerous, so absolutely is the "book-trained politician" (*politicus e libro*). The count of Essex's case is a tragic example of this. When this man, noble in other respects, was at a loss, a scholar who was later hanged gave him advice in Lucan's words. The tag was to this effect: you who have found no friends as a private individual will find many once you take arms. That verse doomed Essex.[144]

So much for Henry Cuffe, one of the learned readers with whom we began. To Casaubon — who translated and commented on Polybius, but nourished no personal hope of advancement in court and political circles — the world of the late Elizabethan facilitator already belonged to a lost past which seemed alien and a little absurd, as well as tragic.

XIV
"READ WHAT YOU CAN THEN RIGHTLY CALL YOUR OWN": HARVEY'S PROGRAMME

Harvey's Livy and its companions on the wheel seem to show, when considered together, a coherent programme to master the whole world of learning and make it readily usable in political action. This is no coincidence or aberration; Harvey's intellectual ambitions in fact embraced the mapping of the whole intellectual landscape of his

---

[143] Possibly by 1590 the more "topical" works on the technology of war and military tactics were making Harvey's humanistic approach appear a little dated. See G. Parker's citation of Sir Roger Williams, also writing in 1590, saying that Alexander, Caesar, Scipio and Hannibal were doubtless "the worthiest and famoust warriors that ever were", but that their example had little relevance to the modern age: G. Parker, *The Military Revolution: Military Innovation and the Rise of the West, 1500-1800* (Cambridge, 1988).

[144] Bodleian Lib., MS. Casaubon 28, fo. 127[r]. For Casaubon's instructions on deriving axioms from classical historians (specifically Tacitus), see MS. Casaubon 24, fo. 125[r-v]. For Casaubon and Polybius, see A. Momigliano, "Polybius' Reappearance in Western Europe", in his *Essays in Ancient and Modern Historiography* (Oxford, 1977), pp. 79-98.

time. No single book offered more data between two covers than that great information-retrieval tool of the sixteenth century, Simler's epitome of Conrad Gesner's *Bibliotheca*. This vast, alphabetically ordered compendium gave brief notices, bibliographies and judgements of the writings of all serious authors, ancient and modern alike, from Aaron Batalaeus to Zyzymus. Harvey read it with care, marking the margins continuously with *signes de renvoi* and occasionally calling attention to his special favourites among the authors listed: notably Rudolph Agricola and Lorenzo Valla. After the preface he entered a programmatic note that reveals as explicitly as anything he ever wrote the contours of his intellectual enterprise as a whole:

> One needs Gesner's great Bibliotheca, especially for summaries and critiques of different authors. These are most important in reading classic and many other authors thoroughly and with the proper attentiveness and utility. Certainly any philologist must find it helpful to have at hand succinct summaries and intelligent critiques of all outstanding writers, and especially those who are classics or of outstanding importance in their field. This is the most important skill of modern criticism, and the highest vocation of the knowledgeable discourser. This is how important it is to be a suggestive summarizer and a sharp critic. But note, I use Hesiod's distinction: "half is more than the whole". One must select the best material from the best writers; the most appropriate material from individuals; the most active, from the best and most appropriate writers . . . Read what you can then rightly call your own. The sum of Socrates's wisdom is this: "Think and act". "Experience outdoes inexperience". Everything rests on art and virtue.
>
> Gabriel Harvey. 1584.[145]

Thus critical reading, skilful annotation and active appropriation emerge as the central skills, not just of the student of history, but of the intellectual *tout court*. Reading always leads to action — but only proper reading, methodical reading — reading in the manner of a Gabriel Harvey.

And here we must emphasize again that Harvey's ideals and methods were not idiosyncratic or whimsical. No text by Philip Sidney has provoked more debate than his letter to his brother of 15 October 1580 on the reading of history. Some have seen this as a manifesto of Sidney's commitment to the modern, continental style of reading history — a reasonable inference given his praise of Tacitus and emphasis on the technical study of chronology. Others have taken it as a criticism of contemporary over-emphasis on the theory of historiography — also a reasonable inference given his remark that "For the method of writing Historie, Bodin hath written at large,

[145] Moore Smith, *Gabriel Harvey's Marginalia*, pp. 125-6; our thanks to the Houghton Library, Harvard, for letting us inspect the Gesner (now in that collection).

HOW GABRIEL HARVEY READ HIS LIVY   77

yow may reade him and gather out of many wordes some matter".
In fact, however, a comparison between this document and Harvey's
Livy makes clear that Sidney was purveying, not his own wit, but
Harvey's method, to his brother. As Harvey had insisted in practice,
Sidney insisted in theory on the variety of roles each historian plays —
and in which he must be appreciated by the competent reader: "An
Orator in making excellent orations *out of the substance of the matter*
[e re nata] which are to be marked, but marked with the note of
rhetoricall remembrances; a Poet in painting forth the effects, the
motions, the whisperings of the people". Like Harvey, Sidney saw
the chief task of the intellectual, ancient or modern, as serving as "a
Discourser, which name I give to who soever speakes *not just concerning what happened, but about the qualities and circumstances of what
happened* [non simpliciter de facto, sed de qualitatibus et circumstan-
tiis facti]"[146] — a definition that embraces both what Harvey saw in
Livy and what he hoped himself to become. And even in taking an
independent attitude towards Bodin, Sidney did not deviate from,
but continued, Harvey's brand of humanist scholarship. Harvey's
tactics as a reader, in short, yield us a general insight into the ways
in which some late sixteenth-century intellectuals tried to cope with
the flood of information that the presses poured over them.

Just occasionally, the carefully-weighed political inferences in
which Harvey took such pride are interrupted by a more emotional
response of the kind we tend to like now — though even then the
emotion was directed not at the book he read, but at the act of reading
it. "Why am I delaying so?" he exclaims at the beginning of book
six, where he thought that Livy's detailed account of antiquities left
off and a more strictly political narrative began. He urged himself
simply to read, and not to write anything down:

> This vulgar bad habit of writing often makes readers dilatory and usually
> makes actors cowardly. The followers of Socrates were wiser: they preferred
> teachings that were unwritten, spoken, preserved by memorization. "Take
> your hand from the picture", runs the old saying. "Take the pen from
> your hand", so runs my saying now.[147]

Here, for once, Harvey, as reader, offers a response of the intensity
the modern reader hopes for. Our challenge in the present exploration

---

[146] See above, p. 36, for Harvey's record of precisely such a concern on Sidney's
part when reading Livy's third decade: "[In reading,] our consideration was chiefly
directed at the forms of states, the conditions of persons, and the qualities of actions".
On Sidney's letter, see E. Story Donno, "Old Mouse-Eaten Records: History in
Sidney's *Apology*", *Studies in Philology*, lxxii (1975), pp. 275-98.
[147] Harvey's Livy, p. 149.

of Renaissance reading has been to find a position which will allow us not to prefer such occasional exclamations to Harvey's self-consciously measured aphorisms, but to make both together a part of the reconstruction of an entirely unfamiliar brand of engagement with experience and intellectual history.[148]

Queen Mary and Westfield College,   *Lisa Jardine*
London
Princeton University   *Anthony Grafton*

---

[148] Here as in other areas the methods used by early modern historians are more primitive than those that have long been used by students of earlier periods. The need to study literature, reading, the making of books and the interpretation of texts in conjunction was understood by biblical and classical scholars of the eighteenth century; see F. A. Wolf, *Prolegomena to Homer [1795]*, trans. A. Grafton *et al.* (Princeton, 1985). Medievalists have assimilated the same lesson without undue difficulty or resistance; see, for example, B. Stock, *The Implications of Literacy* (Princeton, 1983), with its significant subtitle: *Written Language and Models of Interpretation in the Eleventh and Twelfth Centuries*. Even the best-informed historians of the book in the early modern period have taken a narrower view of their task; see R. Chartier, "Intellectual History or Sociocultural History? The French Trajectories", in D. LaCapra and S. L. Kaplan (eds.), *Modern European Intellectual History: Reappraisals and New Perspectives* (Ithaca and London, 1982), pp. 38-9, for a programmatic statement exemplary in both its strengths and its limitations.

[17]

Books as Totems in Seventeenth-Century England and New England

David Cressy

Books in seventeenth-century England and New England enjoyed a cultural significance that extended beyond their textual content. The Bible in particular was employed as a magical talisman, as an aid to divination, as medicine, and as a device for social display. In New England in 1642 contesting Puritans carried a Bible atop a pole during a community affray. Understanding this episode requires examination of other occasions when people made unorthodox, nonliterary, or symbolic use of books.

When John Osgood of Andover, Massachusetts, made his will on 12 April 1650, he assigned eighteen shillings to the meeting house of Newbury "to buy a cushion for the minister to lay his book upon."[1] This provision of a luxurious material, a soft padding for the heavy word of God, reminds us of the extraordinary reverence with which the Bible was treated in the seventeenth century. Valued for its content, as Holy Scripture, the book was also venerated as a sacred artefact, as a Puritan totem, and as the touchstone of the Protestant Reformation. Even in austere New England, in a religious culture set firm against superstition, the physical bound volume possessed some of the attributes of a religious icon or talisman. John Osgood's will, providing an eighteen-shilling cushion for a five-shilling book, reminds us that the Bible was worthy of unusual handling, devout care, and special public presentation. The Bible cushion was, perhaps, the Puritan successor to the elaborately embellished lectern of Old World religion.

Books, of course, have always had a cultural significance that extends beyond their mere textual content. Intellectual historians in particular may need to be reminded that a book is a physical object with weight, bulk, and dimensions. Regardless of the quality of its content, a book has basic properties in common with other books—type printed on paper, squared edges, sewn fascicles, and usually some kind of binding. It can

David Cressy *is associate professor of history, California State University, Long Beach.*

93

be held in the hand, clasped to the breast, stuffed in a pocket, stacked
on a shelf, laid on a table, or tossed in the air; it can be purchased, lent,
stolen, given away, or burned.[2] While librarians and physical bibliographers are familiar with this notion, historians, whose interest in books
is largely confined to the *ideas* they contain, may find it arresting.

My concern here is the deployment of books as magical talismans, as
aids to divination, as devices for social display, and for other nonliterary purposes, in England and New England in the seventeenth century. I shall also be citing some examples from earlier and later periods.
In a culture that venerates the book, where religious ideology is shaped
by the book, it should not be surprising to find irregular and nonliterary
uses of the books alongside more orthodox applications. By studying
what people did with books, especially Bibles, and how they *handled* them
in ritually sensitive settings, we may gain insight into some of the lesser-
known workings of early modern culture. Behavior, in some contexts,
may prove to be more informative than text, just as folk wisdom knows
that actions speak louder than words.

Seventeenth-century almanacs, chapbooks, pamphlets, periodicals, and
other ephemeral publications were pressed into service for a variety of
uses after their primary textual purpose had expired. Indeed, their ver-
satile serviceability may partly explain why so few of them have survived. We find printed paper being used as draught excluders, for stuff-
ing cracks in chimneys and windows, as lining for boxes, and as spills to
light a fire or a pipe. Old books were useful in the kitchen, where their
pages could serve as foundations for a pie or as wrapping for spice.
Countless sheets of printed paper must have gone into privies, employed
as toilet paper.[3] Cheap secular books, it seems, had no more residual
value than scraps of paper, too soiled to write on but serviceable for
menial household tasks. No reverence was attached to the chapbook
text, and there was none of the Chinese reverence for written characters
that deserved a solemn cremation. The English displayed, rather, an un-
sentimental, utilitarian attitude toward ordinary books. We find this
attitude revealed in such seventeenth-century probate inventory nota-
tions as "his books and other trash."[4]

The Bible, by contrast, was normally exempt from these destructive
and practical applications. As a sacred text, the Bible would not usually
be found in the privy, or as a fireside commodity in the kitchen. As the
word of God, as the fundamental text of Protestant Christendom, the
Bible enjoyed a special reverence that no other book could claim. It was
the most commonly owned book in the seventeenth century, in England
and New England, and could even be found in households where nobody could read.[5]

But because of its special religious significance, the Bible, more than

any other book, was subject to a multitude of irregular uses. It was
sometimes deployed in circumstances other than those for which it was
intended and for purposes quite alien to its scriptural content. For example, the Bible served for swearing oaths, registering births, curing the
sick, making decisions, predicting the future, and warding off devils. It
could be imagined as a shield or a weapon, or used as a talisman or
totem.[6] In seventeenth-century New England we even find townsmen
carrying a Bible on a pole, like a legionary standard, when they went to
dispute with their reprobate neighbors. The Bible, held aloft, served as
an inspirational emblem and as a weapon, even without the necessity of
being opened. This episode deserves close attention.

Early in 1642 Thomas Lechford, a lawyer, resettled in London after
four unhappy years in America and wrote a critical account of conditions in New England. His work was published in 1642 as *Plain Dealing,
or News from New England* and was revised and reissued two years later as
New Englands Advice to Old England. The book set out to warn against the
"anarchy and confusion" that followed when congregational indepen-
dency was adopted in place of orderly episcopal government. Lechford
tells the following story, which climaxes with the martial display of a
book on a pole, like a military standard carried into battle:

> At Northam, alias Piscataqua, is master Larkham pastor. One
> master H.K. was also lately minister there, with master Larkham.
> They two fell out about baptising children, receiving of members,
> burial of the dead; and the contention was so sharp that master K.
> and his party rose up and excommunicated master Larkham and
> some that held with him. And further, master Larkham flying to
> the magistrates, master K. and a captain raised arms, and expected
> help from the Bay; master K. *going before the troop with a Bible upon
> a pole's top*, and he or some of his party giving out that their side
> were the Scots, and the other English.[7]

What was going on? We have two issues to untangle; first, the background to this extraordinary story, and second, the significance of dis-
playing the Bible as a battle standard, brandished on a pole. As is often
the case with such anecdotes, a brief remark in an historical source
points to a telling episode, but what it "tells" is likely to be hidden beneath the surface.

The Piscataqua River cuts Maine from New Hampshire, some eighteen
miles northeast of the Massachusetts border. Outside of the strict jurisdiction of the Bay Colony, and neglected by the proprietary government
at Strawberry Bank, places like Northam (later renamed Dover, New

95

Hampshire) became rowdy frontier settlements, notorious for their drunkenness, ill discipline, and irreligion. The early 1630s saw a violent clash along the Piscataqua between a trading party from Plymouth Colony and Lord Seye's men, which left several people dead. Religious dissidents from Massachusetts migrated to this area of lax ecclesiastical administration. Piscataqua received religious incendiaries like John Wheelwright, the antinomian, and crypto-Laudians and sensualists like George Burdet. By 1639 Dover (also known as Northam and Piscataqua) was "a scene of confusion and trouble, both civil and ecclesiastical," and its religious community was rent with "factions and strange confusions."

Into this troubled town came Hanserd Knollys, the "master H.K." of Lechford's narrative, soon to be joined by his nemesis Thomas Larkham. Knollys, an English cleric, arrived in New England in 1636 already tainted with suspicions of religious unorthodoxy. The Bay Colony refused him permission to settle, on account of his sympathy for Wheelwright and the antinomians, so Knollys moved north to New Hampshire. By 1639 he was installed as minister at Dover, trying to achieve a godly reformation, criticizing and then ingratiating himself with the colonial leadership at Boston, and at the same time conspiring with Captain John Underhill of Dover to bring the Piscataqua township under the jurisdiction of Massachusetts.

Thomas Larkham joined the Dover church in 1640 and became Knollys's pastoral assistant. Being himself "a preacher of good talents," Larkham soon eclipsed Knollys, "raised a party" of his own, and had Knollys excommunicated. The Dover Christians split into factions. Driven by a narrow and idiosyncratic interpretation of Scripture, closer to Wheelwright and the antinomians than to the Massachusetts Puritans, Knollys restricted baptism, burial, and church membership to a tested elect. Larkham, by contrast, "baptized all the children of the town, making no distinction between a parish and a gathered church." Here, on the northern frontier, the protagonists were battling over one of the central theological controversies of the seventeenth century.

From the beginning Knollys appears to have been impetuous and unstable, the kind of man who was likely to enter a religious affray with a Bible on a pole. An extravagant letter he wrote to friends in England "greatly scandalized the church and civil state." Apologizing to John Winthrop, he turned the blame on "the Devil," who had "caused my wretched heart to conceive, nourish and bring forth such a monstrous imp so like himself, to wit, an accusation of the brethren." In his dispute with Larkham, Knollys produced a twenty-two point testimony of disagreement, based on points from the Bible, and led his followers in violent disruptions of church meetings. In his own account of events,

Larkham cast doubt on Knollys's sanity, citing "his wild and weak and pope-like carriage in this church, and odd phrases in sermons, unwarrantable and unpatterned expositions of Scripture, and other absurd yet impudent practices." Both preachers accused the other of moral misconduct, and evidence surfaced to prove each of them right. "The revelation of Larkham's scandalous private life led to Knollys' reinstatement, but the night after Larkham had been excommunicated for moral misconduct (he had made a widow big with child) Knollys himself was discovered in the bed of his maid."

The affair came to a climax in the scene described by Thomas Lechford. Knollys had publicly assaulted Larkham, who in turn sought assistance from the local magistrates. In a state of righteous agitation, the Knollys faction gathered their forces "and so marched out to meet Mr. Larkham, one carrying a Bible on a halberd for an ensign, Mr. Knollys being armed with a pistol." Perhaps awed by their opponents' firepower, perhaps taking account of the political as well as the physical risks of combat, and no doubt awed by the mighty biblical standard, the Larkham forces withdrew. The tables were soon turned, however, when the governor sent reinforcements from Strawberry Bank (Portsmouth, N.H.). Knollys's house was besieged (nobody mentions whether the halberded Bible was still on display), and he and his supporters were punished. Both ministers soon returned to England, Knollys in 1641, Larkham in 1642. (Both became chaplains in the Parliamentary army, serving with neither happiness nor distinction.)

The affair reveals an unstable community polarized and shaken by religious dispute. Closely associated was the constitutional and jurisdictional issue of whether Dover should submit to New Hampshire or Massachusetts. And, if the records were adequate, we would probably see a social and economic division involving migration patterns, livelihoods, and landownership too. The aborted battle of Northam may have been a forerunner of the kind of intense community dispute that later did so much damage at Salem.[8]

But for present purposes, we must return to the book. Knollys, or one of his supporters, brandished the Bible above the heads of the mob, "mounted on an halberd, for an ensign." Like a legionary standard, like regimental colors, the book provided a visual focus for the disputants as well as talismanic protection. Who could prevail against the Book of God? And lo, their enemies scattered! Held aloft, the Bible served as an inspirational emblem and as a weapon, even without being opened. Knollys's dispute with Larkham hinged on biblical exegesis—hence his twenty-two articles—and the physical bound volume symbolized this textual and theological contest. Knollys's pole-top Bible was almost certainly a Geneva Bible, loaded (larded?) with Calvinist commentary,

97

which waged symbolic battle against the Authorized (King James) version used by Larkham.[9] It was probably a quarto volume, in black-letter rather than roman type, and it would be interesting to learn how it was attached to the pole. Finally, we learn from Lechford that as the Knollys forces paraded into Dover, led by the Bible, they represented themselves as "Scots" and their opponents as "English." This can only refer to recent events in England, when the Scottish armies invaded to protest the imposition of the Anglican prayer book. It is worth remembering that the Scots revolt in 1638 began with the tossing of a book, the hated English *Book of Common Prayer*, across the aisles of Edinburgh Cathedral. By identifying with the Scots, who drew their inspiration from one book (the Geneva Bible) in defiance of another book (the English *Book of Common Prayer*), the dissidents at Dover cast their opponents as Laudians and as enemies of True Scripture. The Bible was an appropriate physical symbol for this contest, as well as for control of the Piscataqua congregation.[10]

To further understand this episode we must place it in the context of other symbolic or unorthodox uses of the Bible in early-modern England. The potency of the book on the pole makes more sense when we understand how people deployed the Bible in other circumstances. I shall describe two totemic uses: one in which the book was treated as a sacred object, and did not have to be opened to have its effect, and another in which some reading was required, although not of the sort that the church fathers intended.

An incident from the sixteenth century provides a convenient point of reference. In 1559, while Queen Elizabeth was in procession through the streets of London on her way to her coronation, she passed beneath an allegorical tableau on which a Bible was displayed. "A Bible in English, richly covered, was let down to her by a silk lace from a child that represented Truth. She kissed both her hands, with both her hands she received it, then she kissed it, afterwards applied it to her breast, and lastly held it up, thanking the City especially for that gift, and promising to be a diligent reader thereof."[11]

A full explication of this episode would require comment on Elizabeth's birth as a precipitant of the English Reformation, on her accession as a deliverance from Marian Catholicism, and on the earlier history of the English Bible, which Elizabeth's father had introduced into every parish. The silk thread from on high might be connected to the breath of God or the workings of a *deus ex machina*, while the Truth-child could be associated with Renaissance putti. More significant is Elizabeth's reaction, a ritual performance in several stages. First she kissed her hands (a purifying gesture?), then reverently took the book (as one might take the body of Christ at communion?), formally kissed it (an intimate transaction involving her own breath?), embraced it to her breast (more intimacy?), then held it high for all to see (as the priest might elevate the host?). When the book was proffered, the queen evidently knew exactly what to do, and the crowd and chronicler knew just what to observe. This episode only makes sense if we understand the ''richly covered'' volume as a sacred *object*, something like a totem or fetish fraught with ancestral, religious, and communal meaning.

Kissing the book was an important part of seventeenth-century court proceedings. A defendant not only swore to speak truth, ''his hand upon the book,'' but also ''must kiss the book, in testimony that he sweareth.'' Witnesses had to ''lay their hands upon a Bible or Testament,'' then, having taken the oath, they ''are to kiss the said book.''[12] (One wonders, parenthetically, whether these books ever wore out from the repeated pressure of lips, or whether the constant kissing was a means of transmitting disease.) Swearing on a book was, in fact, in direct descent from the medieval practice of swearing on holy relics. The procedure did not require *opening* the book, and certainly needed no literacy. What was important was the public acknowledgment of the power of the volume to amplify and sanctify an oath.

Nor were courts of law unique in this regard. Dozens of incidents are known in which individuals made use of the Bible for magical, talismanic, or curative purposes. The holy book was credited with medicinal powers, as a universal specific, a remedy for ailments of all sorts. Some people believed that the holy pages had healing properties, quite apart from the text that was printed on them. The Bible might, for example, be invaluable in child-bearing, or be laid on the head of a restless patient in order to induce sleep. Seventeenth-century reformers attacked this practice— ''surely God's word should rather awake men than cast them into a sleep,'' challenged the Puritan Barten Holyday—but it was not one they could easily eradicate. In other applications the Bible might be made a pillow, placed under the head, as a restorative, or simply be brought into the sickroom as an aid to health.[13]

On the eve of the English civil war the Royalist rector of Finningham, Suffolk, Edmund Taylor, told his parishioners that ''a Bible in a house would keep the devil out.'' The mere presence of the book would ward off evil spirits. Since many diseases were thought to have spiritual or diabolic dimensions, such a device could be especially useful. It may be significant that in probate inventories that show the location of possessions room by room, the Bible was often found in the bedchamber, where it was available for use by the sick or dying.[14]

In 1703 an English traveler described primitive biblio-medicine as practiced in Scotland, ''My landlord having one of his family sick of a fever, asked my book as a singular favour for a few moments: I was not

99

a little surprised at the honest man's request, *he being illiterate*, and when he told me the reason of it I was no less amazed, for it was to fan the patient's face with the leaves of the Book; and this he did at night. He sought the book again next morning, and again in the evening, and then he thanked me for so great a favour, and told me the sick person was much better for it; and thus I understood that they had an ancient custom of fanning the face of the sick with the leaves of the Bible.'' Martin Martin, the Augustan Englishman who tells this story, cites it as an example of ''heathenism and pagan superstition'' found in the Western Isles. But he could have found similar instances closer to home.[15]

He could also have read in St. Augustine how the Gospel of St. John was laid on the heads of those suffering with fever, or recalled the ancient ceremony for consecrating a bishop, in which a Bible was laid on his head, ''as the means of communicating the Spirit and Christ's indwelling.'' And he would surely have been aware of those stories from the English civil war involving ''the marvellous preservation of soldiers by Bibles in their pockets which have received the bullets.''[16] The implication in all these cases is that the power of the Bible lay not simply in its text, to be unlocked by rigorous exegesis, but rather in its ineffable holiness, its sacred magic. The Bible as an object, symbolizing and encapsulating the word of God, was believed to do duty comparable to or superior to the Scripture as text.

Nor were such beliefs confined to remote areas or to the pre-industrial epoch. They are not unknown in modern Britain and modern America and may well have had credence in colonial New England. From old Hampshire, England, at the end of the nineteenth century, comes the extraordinary story of the woman who ''ate a New Testament, day by day and leaf by leaf, between two sides of bread and butter, as a remedy for fits.''[17] This may have provided excellent roughage, good for the digestion, but the physiological benefits were surely secondary to the psychological. Ingesting the word of God, and systematically destroying a book in the process, swept aside the need for conventional, and literary, religious practices. It places this Victorian countrywoman in the same tradition as those in the fifteenth century who employed communion bread as a poultice for boils or who wore scraps of paper with holy phrases as amulets to cure disease or as security for good health.

Literate and sophisticated people also found multifarious uses for the Bible. For many centuries men of letters had resorted to the *Iliad* or the *Aeneid* to help them resolve a crisis. Random opening of the text would display a phrase or passage that could then be interpreted as a guide to immediate action. This ancient practice, the *sortes Virgilianae*, survived into the modern era, with the printed Bible substituting for the pagan epic. In each case the primary book of the age, the most venerable writings of the culture, were brought to bear as implements for making decisions. Bibliomancy of this sort was widely used in seventeenth-century England, despite the misgivings of some Puritan divines. Some preachers disapproved of this undisciplined use of the Bible, quoting Deuteronomy 18 to the effect that divination is an abomination to the Lord. And since ''to foreknow man's purpose or lot is God's prerogative,'' not ours, any attempt to guess the future is tainted with blasphemy.[18] Yet devout Christians, Puritans included, fell back on the *sortes Biblicae* when otherwise frustrated or lost.

Young John Dane, for example, was ''utterly forlorn in . . . spirit and knew not what to do,'' before it occurred to him to go to New England in the early 1630s. The Bible, randomly opened, not only confirmed Dane's decision to emigrate but turned his parents from opponents to supporters of the venture. This is John Dane's story from ''A declaration of remarkable providences in the course of my life.'' ''I sat close by a table where there lay a Bible. I hastily took up the Bible, and told my father if where I opened the Bible there I met with any thing either to encourage or discourage, that should settle me. I opening of it, not knowing no more than the child in the womb, the first I cast my eyes on was: 'come out from among them, touch no unclean thing, and I will be your god and you shall be my people.' '' That clinched the matter. ''My father and mother never more opposed me, but furthered me in the thing, and hastened after me as soon as they could.'' By 1636 the Danes were settled at Roxbury, Massachusetts.[19]

It could be objected, of course, that Dane had fixed the book, or had so often studied the passage in question that it naturally fell open, or even that he made up the whole story to embellish his autobiography. But that would be beside the point. Dane and many of his contemporaries evidently believed in the power of the randomly opened book and sought meaning and guidance from phrases and verses culled quite separately from their scriptural context. A guiding message sprang out from the book on the table, like a voice from heaven or a *deus ex machina*. A few more examples will illustrate this practice of bibliomancy.

Arise Evans, a visionary preacher of the 1630s and 1640s, was launched on his career by a voice that told him, ''Go to thy book.'' The voice alone, good enough for the likes of Joan of Arc, directed Evans to a superior source of wisdom, the holy text. ''I suddenly started up,'' he relates, ''and to the table went where my Bible lay open, immediately fastening mine eyes upon Ephesians 5.14, being these words . . . 'Awake thou that sleepest . . . and Christ shall give thee light.' '' It might be argued that this was not strictly a *sortes Biblicae* since the book already lay open, perhaps where Evans had left off reading. But at other times, Arise Evans made deliberate and explicit use of the Bible as a source

101

of random instruction and inspiration. In a state of religious frenzy, coupled with paralyzing indecision, "I opened the book three times suddenly, not caring where, and fastened mine eyes upon the place that first presented itself to me." This time the Bible gave him passages from Isaiah and from Joel, to the effect of "Awake ye drunkards" and "I have called him." Taken out of context, as personal messages, these stray verses gave Arise Evans the confidence and inspiration for his mission. Believing that God had called him to deliver a personal message of prophecy and warning to the king, Evans steeled himself for this task by once again employing a *sortes Biblicae*. "With much fear I opened the Book the fourth time, and the place was in Exodus . . . 'Behold I send an angel before thee.'" That was enough! Evans was on his way.[20]

The king himself, the target of Arise Evans's prophecies, is said to have employed books for predictive or divinatory purposes. One writer claims that Charles I resorted to a *sortes Biblicae* to help him decide whether to support or abandon the Earl of Strafford, and that another time he tried his fate with a copy of Virgil in the Bodleian Library. These stories are probably apocryphal, since Charles was the least superstitious of monarchs, but their circulation attests to the presumed power and efficacy of the book-opening process.[2]

In 1660 we find Lord George Berkeley, "being sick, and under some dejection of spirit, opening my Bible to see what place I could first light upon which might administer comfort." Berkeley's finger fell on the line in Hosea, "come, let us return unto the Lord," and at once he commenced a spiritual as well as medical recovery. Berkeley, a moralist of refinement and scholarship, felt sheepish in using such an unsophisticated practice, and so offers this apology: "I am willing to decline superstition upon all occasions, yet think myself obliged to make this use of such a providential place of scripture"[22] Providence supplied the key. The book had power, which could be released and focused through blind stabbing at a randomly opened page. God would so work it that an appropriate message would come to the fore.

Practices of this sort continued on both sides of the Atlantic long after the seventeenth century, testifying to the security people found in the book, as well as to their unschooled and irregular use of the text. An oracular fragment, randomly discovered, might be more serviceable than the underlying message of the Scriptures, and, of course, reading it took much less time and effort. As the most commonly available book in most households, and as the book invested with the most sacred power, the Bible was uniquely suited to this purpose. The Bible, the good book, contains hundreds of thousands of verses, which, like fortune cookies or readings from the *I Ching*, could be taken as counsels of comfort, incitements to action, or guides to the future. In America a widespread custom was to make a wish, and if the Bible opened at the words "it came to pass" the wish would come true.[23]

In Victorian Oxfordshire "it was customary to dip into the Bible before twelve o'clock on New Year's Day, and the first verse that meets the eye indicates the good or bad fortune of the enquirers through the ensuing year." We hear, for example, of the distress of a woman who remembered that she had not yet "dipped" in the Bible. "Last year," she reported, "I opened on *Job*; and sure enough, I have had nought but trouble since."[24]

As late as 1900 English folklorists could report that Bible "dipping" on New Year's Day "is a superstitious practice observed in some parts of the country, and much credit is attached to it. It is usually set about with some little ceremony on the morning, before breakfast, as it must be done fasting. The Bible is laid on the table unopened, and the parties who wish to consult it are then to open it at random. Wherever this may happen to be, the inquirer is to place his finger on the chapter contained in the two pages, but without any previous perusal or examination. It is believed that the good or ill fortune, the happiness or misery of the consulting party, during the ensuing year, will be in some way or other described and foreshown by the contents of the chapter."[25]

The *sortes Biblicae* involved reading, if only a single verse, but another popular practice made use of the Bible without any immediate connection to its text. The ritual of the book and key, as a sure guide to thief detection, was widely known in England from the Middle Ages to the modern period. Examples survive from before the Reformation; a writer in Lancashire in 1907 acknowledged that the practice "may not be even now entirely obsolete."[26]

William Newport, vicar of St. Owens, Gloucester, in 1551, used his Bible in the following manner. First he "inserted the key and tied the book up with string. He then invoked the Father, the Son and Holy Ghost, bidding the key to turn when he reached the name of the guilty party. It turned when he pronounced the name of Margaret Greenhill; and the participants left the chancel of the church, where the ritual had been carried out, to search the suspect's straw bed for the missing objects."[27] William Barckseale of Fareham, Hampshire, employed the book and key ceremony with similar success in the seventeenth century to identify some robbers. Examined in 1632 about "what art or meanes he used to discover those parties, saith he used no magical art or communication but only a key and a Bible."[28] In an eighteenth-century account, "a Bible having a key fastened in the middle, and being held between the two forefingers of two persons, will turn round after some words said, as, if one wishes to find a thief, a certain verse taken out of

103

a Psalm is to be repeated, and those who are suspected nominated, and if they are guilty the Book and key will turn, else not."[29]

Divination by book and key was reportedly "very prevalent" in Victorian England, especially in country areas. Nineteenth-century villagers in Surrey made use of the Bible for detecting a thief, in the ancient manner. With a key placed in the book of Ruth, chapter 1, verse 16, and the book tight shut with a string, "the Bible falls to the ground" when the name of the guilty party is pronounced. The same "ordeal of the key and Bible" was used to ensnare a thief on the Welsh borderlands in 1871. By then, however, the ancient practice had lost its power, so a supplementary test was made to find the criminal. In this case the thief-finders boiled a live toad inside a ball of clay, expecting the toad to scratch the name of the guilty party in the clay before it died.[30]

A variant of the ritual was in use in Victorian Lancashire, where the book and key were used to divine the name of a future lover rather than the name of a thief. A girl tied up the key in the Bible, again inserting the key at the book of Ruth. The key verse read "whither thou goest I will go," and taken out of context it could be used in either courtship or thief detection rituals. "Holding the Bible suspended by joining the ends of her little fingers inserted under the handle of the key," the girl recited the names of prospective suitors. When the right name was mentioned the book miraculously turned and the identification was made.[31]

The Lancashire girls had evidently mixed up two quite separate traditions regarding the nonliterary employment of the Bible. Besides the technique for identifying criminals, the Bible was also used, with naive irreverence, for forecasting the names of future lovers. " 'Tis a custom among Country Girls to put the Bible under their pillows at night, with sixpence clapt in the Book of Ruth, in order to dream of the men destined to be their husbands," explains the eighteenth-century antiquarian John Brand.[32]

Reports of such practices provide valuable illumination of the darkest areas of social and cultural history. They indicate ways in which people made use of the tools at their disposal, Bibles in particular, to gain control over uncertainty or to rally to a common symbol. They also serve as a corrective to the view that books were simply conveyors of ideas and information, and that analysis of their text is enough.

Notes

1. *The Probate Records of Essex County, Massachusetts, vol. I, 1635–1664* (Salem, 1916), p. 141.

2. Natalie Zemon Davis, "Beyond the Market: Books as Gifts in Sixteenth-Century France," *Transactions of the Royal Historical Society*, 5th ser., 33 (1983):

69–88. For examples of charitable distribution of books, see Richard Baxter, *Reliquiae Baxterianae* (London, 1696), p. 89; and "Diary of Cotton Mather," *Massachusetts Historical Society Collections*, ser. 7, 7 (1911): 54, 65. For theft of Bibles, possibly for superstitious purposes, see John Cordy Jeaffreson (ed.), *Middlesex County Records* (Clerkenwell, 1888), III: 24, 36. Professor D. W. Krummel reminds me of Sir Walter Greg's insistence that bibliography is "the study of books as physical objects, irrespective of their contents."

3. Joseph Addison, *The Spectator* 367 (1 May 1712); Holbrook Jackson, *The Anatomy of Bibliomania* (London: Soncino Press, 1930–1931), pp. 156–157; Margaret Spufford, *Small Books and Pleasant Histories: Popular Fiction and Its Readership in Seventeenth-Century England* (Athens: University of Georgia Press, 1982), pp. 48–50.

4. See, for example, Francis Steer (ed.), *Farm and Cottage Inventories of Mid-Essex 1635–1749*, 2nd ed. (London: Phillimore, 1969); Margaret Spufford, *Contrasting Communities: English Villagers in the Sixteenth and Seventeenth Centuries* (London: Cambridge University Press, 1974), p. 211.

5. For Bible ownership in England, see Peter Clark, "The Ownership of Books in England, 1560–1640: The Example of Some Kentish Townsfolk," in Lawrence Stone (ed.), *Schooling and Society* (Baltimore: Johns Hopkins University Press 1976), pp. 95–111; Norwich Survey Unit, University of East Anglia, files on "Probate Inventories and Book Ownership." For Bibles in New England probate inventories, see William B. Traske (ed.), *Suffolk County Wills* (Baltimore: Genealogical Publishing, 1984), and *Probate Records of Essex County* (Salem: Essex Institute, 1916).

6. See, for example, the striking depiction of Protestant Bibles as a battering ram, a shield, and a projectile against Papism, in Natalie Zemon Davis, "The Sacred and the Body Social in Sixteenth-Century Lyon," *Past and Present* 90 (1901): facing p. 57. The great Dr. Johnson is said to have used an Elizabethan folio edition of the Greek Bible to strike down a bookseller (Jackson, *Anatomy of Bibliomania*, p. 167).

7. Thomas Lechford, *New Englands Advice to Old England* (London, 1644), Sig. A3v, 44, my emphasis. Other versions of the story appear in James Kendall Hosmer (ed.), *Winthrop's Journal, "History of New England" 1630–1649* (New York: C. Scribner's Sons, 1908), II: 27–28; Jeremy Belknap, *The History of New Hampshire* (Boston, 1792), I: 34–51; Nathaniel Bouton (ed.), *Provincial Papers: Documents and Records Relating to the Province of New Hampshire* (Concord, N.H., 1867), I: 120–123. Modern commentators include Charles E. Clark, *The Eastern Frontier: The Settlement of Northern New England 1610–1763* (New York: Knopf, 1970), pp. 39–41; and Francis J. Bremer, *The Puritan Experiment* (New York: St. Martin's Press, 1976), p. 87. The account that follows is based on these sources, supplemented by Massachusetts Historical Society, *Winthrop Papers, Vol. 4, 1638–1644* (Boston: Massachusetts Historical Society, 1944), pp. 143–144, 176–179, 317–319; Everett Emerson (ed.), *Letters from New England* (Amherst: University of Massachusetts Press, 1976), pp. 229*n*, 180; David D. Hall, *The Faithful Shepherd: A History of the New England Ministry in the Seventeenth Century* (New York: Norton, 1974), p. 97; "Hansard Knollys," *New England Historical and Genealogical Register* 19 (1865): 131–132; William L. Sachse, *The Colonial American in Britain* (Madison: University of Wisconsin Press, 1956), pp. 135, 139; *Dictionary of National Biography*, sub. "Knollys," "Larkham."

8. Paul Boyer and Stephen Nissenbaum, *Salem Possessed: The Social Origins of Witchcraft* (Cambridge, Mass.: Harvard University Press, 1974).

105

9. Harry S. Stout, "Word and Order in Colonial New England," in Nathan O. Hatch and Mark A. Noll (eds.), *The Bible in America: Essays in Cultural History* (New York: Oxford University Press, 1982), pp. 31, 38.

10. For modern accounts of the English background, see Kevin Sharpe, "The Personal Rule of Charles I," in Howard Tomlinson (ed.), *Before the English Civil War* (London: Macmillan, 1983), pp. 53–78; and J. Sears McGee, "William Laud and the Outward Face of Religion," in Richard L. DeMolen (ed.), *Leaders of the Reformation* (London: Susquehanna University Press, 1984), pp. 318–344.

11. John Hayward, *Annals of the First Four Years of the Reign of Queen Elizabeth* (Camden Society, London, 1841), p. 17. For the context of this Elizabethan entry, see Sydney Anglo, *Spectacle, Pageantry and Early Tudor Policy* (Oxford: Clarendon Press, 1969), pp. 350–351.

12. H. Conset, *Practice of the Spiritual or Ecclesiastical Courts* (London, 1685), pp. 99, 100, 113.

13. Keith Thomas, *Religion and the Decline of Magic* (New York: Scribner, 1971), p. 45; Barten Holyday, *Motives to a Good Life* (Oxford, 1657), pp. 129–130; Jackson, *Anatomy of Bibliomania*, p. 170.

14. A. G. Matthews, *Walker Revised* (Oxford: Clarendon Press, 1948), p. 339.

15. Martin Martin, *A Description of the Western Islands of Scotland* (London, 1703), p. 248.

16. James Hastings (ed.), *Encyclopaedia of Religion and Ethics* (New York: Charles Scribner's Sons, 1926), II: 611; Baxter, *Reliquiae*, p. 46; W. H. D. Longstaffe (ed.), *Memoirs of Mr. Ambrose Barnes* (Durham: Surtees Society, 1867), p. 107; Jackson, *Anatomy of Bibliomania*, p. 166.

17. *Notes and Queries*, 9th ser., 8 (1901): 103. Ritual use of the Bible to cure nose bleeds, warts, and ganglions is recorded in modern America, in Wayland D. Hand, Anna Casetta, and Sondra B. Thiederman (eds.), *Popular Beliefs and Superstitions: A Compendium of American Folklore from the Ohio Collection of Newbell Niles Puckett* (Boston: G. K. Hall, 1981), pp. 1638–1639. I am grateful to Roger Abrahams for introducing me to American Bible folklore.

18. Thomas, *Religion and the Decline of Magic*, p. 118; Holyday, *Motives to a Good Life*, p. 128.

19. John Dane, "A Declaration of Remarkabell Provedenses in the Corse of my Lyfe," *New England Historical and Genealogical Register* 8 (1854): 152–154.

20. Arise (Rhys) Evans, *An Eccho to the Book Called a Voyce from Heaven* (London, 1653), pp. 10–15.

21. William E. A. Axon, "Divination by Books," *Manchester Quarterly* 26 (1907): 27; James Welwood, *Memoirs of the Most Material Transactions in England*, 3rd ed. (London, 1700), p. 106; Jackson, *Anatomy of Bibliomania*, pp. 179–181.

22. George Berkeley, *Historical Applications and Occasional Meditations* (London, 1670), p. 90.

23. See, for example, Vance Randolph, *Ozark Superstitions* (New York: Columbia University Press, 1947), p. 336; and J. D. Clark, "North Carolina Superstitions," *North Carolina Folklore* 14 (1966): 18.

24. *Notes and Queries*, 2nd ser., 12 (1861): 303.

25. T. F. Thiselton Dyer, *British Popular Customs* (London, 1876), p. 5.

26. Thomas, *Religion and the Decline of Magic*, p. 214; Axon, "Divination by Books," pp. 31, 32.

27. *Transactions of the Bristol and Gloucestershire Archaeological Society* 60 (1938): 120–121.

106   JLH/*Books as Totems*

28. R. C. Anderson (ed.), *The Book of Examinations and Depositions, 1622–1644* (Southampton: Cox and Sharlands, 1931), II: 108.

29. John Brand, *Observations on Popular Antiquities* (London, 1813), II: 641.

30. *Notes and Queries*, 1st ser. (1850): 413; William Plover (ed.), *Kilvert's Diary 1870–71* (London: J. Cape, 1938), p. 301.

31. *Notes and Queries*, 1st ser. (1850): 5.

32. Brand, *Observations on Popular Antiquities*, II: 469, quoting from "Poems by Nobody" (1770).

Name Index